D1277864

ELEVENTH EDITION

The Little, Brown Handbook

High School Version

H. Ramsey Fowler
St. Edward's University

Jane E. Aaron

Longman

Boston   Columbus   Indianapolis   New York   San Francisco
Upper Saddle River   Amsterdam   Cape Town   Dubai   London   Madrid
Milan   Munich   Paris   Montreal   Toronto   Delhi   Mexico City
São Paulo   Sydney   Hong Kong   Seoul   Singapore   Taipei   Tokyo

Executive Editor: Suzanne Phelps Chambers
Associate Development Editor: Erin Reilly
Senior Supplements Editor: Donna Campion
Senior Media Producer: Stefanie Liebman
Marketing Manager: Alicia Orlando
Production Manager: Jacqueline A. Martin
Project Coordination, Text Design, and Electronic Page Makeup:
Nesbitt Graphics, Inc.
Cover Designer/Manager: John Callahan
Cover Photos: (clockwise from top): David Fischer/Digital Vision/Getty Images,
Inc.; Stone/Getty; Yuri Arcurs/shutterstock.com; Trista Weibell/
istockphoto.com; Image Source/Getty
Senior Manufacturing Buyer: Roy L. Pickering, Jr.
Printer and Binder: RR Donnelley & Sons Company, Crawfordsville
Cover Printer: Phoenix Color Corporation, Hagerstown

For permission to use copyrighted material, grateful acknowledgment is made to the copyright holders on pp. 889–890, which are hereby made part of this copyright page.

Library of Congress Cataloging-in-Publication Data

Fowler, H. Ramsey (Henry Ramsey)
The Little, Brown handbook : high school version / H. Ramsey Fowler, Jane
E. Aaron. -- 11th ed.
p. cm.
Includes bibliographical references and index.
ISBN-13: 978-0-13-211692-3 (high school binding)
ISBN-10: 0-13-211692-8 (high school binding)
1. English language--Grammar--Handbooks, manuals, etc. 2. English
language--Rhetoric--Handbooks, manuals, etc. 3. Report writing--Handbooks,
manuals, etc. I. Aaron, Jane E. II. Title.
PE1112.F64 2010
808'.042--dc22
                                      2010029708

Copyright © 2011, 2007 by Pearson Education, Inc.

All rights reserved. No part of this publication may be reproduced, stored in a retrieval system, or transmitted, in any form or by any means, electronic, mechanical, photocopying, recording, or otherwise, without the prior written permission of the publisher. Printed in the United States. To obtain permission to use material from this work, please submit a written request to Pearson Education, Inc., Permissions Department, 1900 E. Lake Ave., Glenview, IL 60025 or fax to (847) 486-3938 or e-mail glenview.permissions@pearsoned.com. For information regarding permissions, call (847) 486-2635.

www.PearsonSchool.com/Advanced

Longman
is an imprint of

2 3 4 5 6 7 8 9 10—DOC—13

ISBN-13: 978-0-13-211692-3 (High School Binding)
ISBN-10:   0-13-211692-8 (High School Binding)

Preface for Students: Using This Book

The high school version of *The Little, Brown Handbook* is an essential resource that will answer almost any question you have about writing. Here you can find how to get ideas, develop paragraphs, punctuate quotations, search the Internet, cite sources, or write a college-application essay. The handbook can help you build the writing skills you will need to prepare for college-level coursework in many disciplines.

Don't let the size of the handbook put you off. You need not read the whole book to get something out of it, and no one expects you to know everything included. Primarily a reference tool, the handbook is written and arranged to help you find the answers you need when you need them, quickly and easily.

Using this book will not by itself make you a good writer; for that, you need to care about your work at every level, from finding a subject to spelling words. But learning how to use the handbook and its information can give you the means to write *what* you want in the *way* you want.

Reference aids

You have many ways to find what you need in the handbook:

- **Use the table of contents.** A list of the book's entire contents follows the preface (pp. xii–xxii).
- **Use a glossary.** "Glossary of Usage" (pp. 845–61) clarifies more than 275 words that are commonly confused and misused. "Glossary of Terms" (pp. 862–88) defines more than 350 words used in discussing writing.
- **Use the index.** Beginning on page 891, the extensive index includes every term, concept, and problem word or expression mentioned in the book.
- **Use a list.** Three helpful aids fall at the back of the book: (1) " CULTURE LANGUAGE Guide" pulls together all the book's material for ESL and ELL students and for students using standard English as a second dialect. (2) "Editing Symbols" explains abbreviations often used to comment on papers. And (3) "Useful Lists and Summaries" indexes topics that students frequently ask about.
- **Use the elements of the page.** As shown in the illustration on the next page, the handbook constantly tells you where you are and what you can find there.

The handbook's page elements

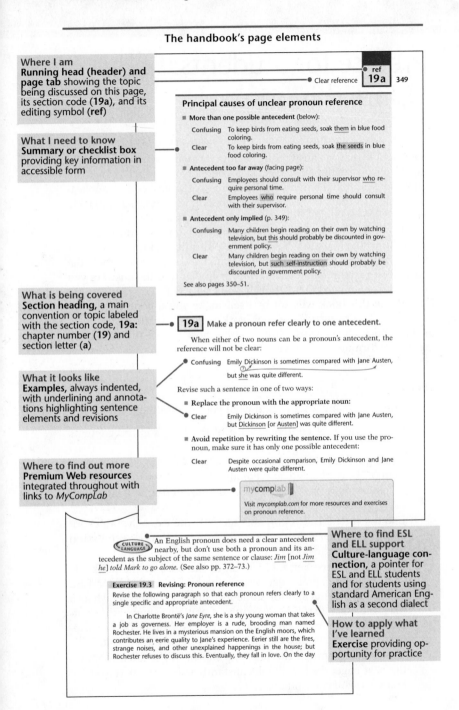

Where I am
Running head (header) and page tab showing the topic being discussed on this page, its section code (**19a**), and its editing symbol (**ref**)

Clear reference | ref **19a** | 349

Principal causes of unclear pronoun reference

■ **More than one possible antecedent** (below):

Confusing   To keep birds from eating seeds, soak <u>them</u> in blue food coloring.

Clear   To keep birds from eating seeds, soak <u>the seeds</u> in blue food coloring.

■ **Antecedent too far away** (facing page):

Confusing   Employees should consult with their supervisor <u>who</u> require personal time.

Clear   Employees <u>who</u> require personal time should consult with their supervisor.

■ **Antecedent only implied** (p. 349):

Confusing   Many children begin reading on their own by watching television, but <u>this</u> should probably be discounted in government policy.

Clear   Many children begin reading on their own by watching television, but <u>such self-instruction</u> should probably be discounted in government policy.

See also pages 350–51.

What I need to know
Summary or checklist box providing key information in accessible form

What is being covered
Section heading, a main convention or topic labeled with the section code, **19a**: chapter number (**19**) and section letter (**a**)

19a Make a pronoun refer clearly to one antecedent.

When either of two nouns can be a pronoun's antecedent, the reference will not be clear:

Confusing   Emily Dickinson is sometimes compared with Jane Austen, but <u>she</u> was quite different.

Revise such a sentence in one of two ways:

■ **Replace the pronoun with the appropriate noun:**

Clear   Emily Dickinson is sometimes compared with Jane Austen, but <u>Dickinson</u> [or <u>Austen</u>] was quite different.

■ **Avoid repetition by rewriting the sentence.** If you use the pronoun, make sure it has only one possible antecedent:

Clear   Despite occasional comparison, Emily Dickinson and Jane Austen were quite different.

What it looks like
Examples, always indented, with underlining and annotations highlighting sentence elements and revisions

Where to find out more
Premium Web resources integrated throughout with links to *MyCompLab*

mycomplab
Visit *mycomplab.com* for more resources and exercises on pronoun reference.

(CULTURE LANGUAGE) An English pronoun does need a clear antecedent nearby, but don't use both a pronoun and its antecedent as the subject of the same sentence or clause: <u>Jim</u> [not <u>Jim he</u>] told Mark to go alone. (See also pp. 372–73.)

Where to find ESL and ELL support
Culture-language connection, a pointer for ESL and ELL students and for students using standard American English as a second dialect

Exercise 19.3 Revising: Pronoun reference

Revise the following paragraph so that each pronoun refers clearly to a single specific and appropriate antecedent.

In Charlotte Brontë's *Jane Eyre*, she is a shy young woman that takes a job as governess. Her employer is a rude, brooding man named Rochester. He lives in a mysterious mansion on the English moors, which contributes an eerie quality to Jane's experience. Eerier still are the fires, strange noises, and other unexplained happenings in the house; but Rochester refuses to discuss this. Eventually, they fall in love. On the day

How to apply what I've learned
Exercise providing opportunity for practice

Content and organization

Briefly, the book divides into the following sections:

- **Chapters 1–5:** The big picture, including the writing process, paragraphs, and document design.
- **Chapters 6–11:** Reading and writing in school, with chapters on academic skills; critical reading, listening, and writing; academic writing; reading arguments; writing arguments; and reading and using visual arguments.
- **Chapters 12–26:** Sentence basics, including the conventions of English grammar, errors that affect clarity, and techniques of effective sentences.
- **Chapters 27–36:** Punctuation and mechanics (capital letters, italics, and the like).
- **Chapters 37–40:** Words—how to use them appropriately and precisely, how to edit them for conciseness, how to spell them.
- **Chapters 41–47:** Research writing, from planning through revising, including detailed help on finding and evaluating electronic sources and avoiding plagiarism, a complete guide to citing sources, and two sample papers.
- **Chapters 48–52:** Writing in the academic disciplines, including concepts, tools, and source citations in literature, other humanities, the social sciences, and the natural and applied sciences.
- **Chapters 53–57:** Practical information about essay exams, online writing, business and other public writing, oral presentations, and applying to college.

Recommended usage

The conventions described and illustrated in this handbook are those of standard American English—the label given the dialect used in higher education, business, and the professions. (See also pp. 170–72.) The handbook stresses written standard English, which is more conservative than the spoken dialect in matters of grammar and usage. A great many words and constructions that are widely spoken remain unaccepted in careful writing.

When clear distinctions exist between the language of conversation and that of careful writing, the handbook provides examples of each and labels them *spoken* and *written*. When usage in writing itself varies with the level of formality intended, the handbook labels examples *formal* and *informal*. When usage is mixed or currently changing, the handbook recommends that you choose the more conservative usage because it will be accepted by all readers.

Preface for Teachers

The Little, Brown Handbook always aims to address both the current and the recurrent needs of writing students and teachers. This eleventh edition is no exception. Writing and its teaching change continuously, and the handbook has changed in response. At the same time, much about writing does not change, and the handbook remains a comprehensive, clear, and accessible guide that prepares students for the rigors of college-level writing and beyond.

The Little, Brown Handbook is actually many books in one, and each is stronger in this edition. The revisions—highlighted below with New—affect most pages.

A comprehensive guide to academic writing in high school

The handbook gives students a solid foundation in the goals and requirements of writing in academic situations.

- **New** A reorganized Part 2 ("Reading and Writing in High School") proceeds through a chapter each on academic skills in general, critical thinking and reading, and academic writing. The part concludes with three chapters on arguments—reading them, writing them, and using visual arguments.
- **New** The chapter on academic skills emphasizes time management, reading for comprehension, and preparing for exams.
- **New** The chapter on developing critical skills includes a new discussion of critical listening.
- **New** The chapter on academic writing shows students how to write in response to texts. The chapter concludes with two sample critiques—a response to a text and a new paper analyzing an advertisement.
- **New** Synthesis receives special emphasis wherever students might need help balancing their own and others' views, such as in responding to texts.
- **New** Expanded advice on avoiding plagiarism shows students at every turn how to acknowledge borrowed material.
- Parts 9 and 10 give students a solid foundation in research writing, writing about literature, and writing in other humanities, the social sciences, and the natural and applied sciences. Extensive, specially highlighted sections on documentation and format cover the most recent updates of MLA, Chicago, APA, and CSE styles.
- Chapter 57 on applying to college provides tips for taking the SAT, ACT, and AP English exams and for writing an effective college-application essay.

A step-by-step guide to research writing

With detailed advice and two sample MLA papers, the handbook always attends closely to research writing. The discussion stresses using the library as Web gateway, evaluating and synthesizing sources, integrating source material, and avoiding plagiarism.

■ **New** A research-paper-in-progress on green consumerism follows a student through the research process and culminates in an annotated paper documented in the most current MLA style.

■ **New** An expanded discussion of evaluating sources shows the application of critical criteria to sample articles, sample Web documents, and a sample blog.

■ **New** Many kinds of electronic sources—blogs, wikis, and multimedia as well as Web documents—are discussed as possible sources that require careful evaluation and documentation.

■ **New** The advice for generating primary sources now covers conducting observations and surveys as well as interviews.

■ **New** Paired examples of summaries, paraphrases, and quotations compare plagiarized and unplagiarized versions.

■ **New** Updated source lists in Part 10 provide reliable starting points for research in every discipline.

A reliable guide to documenting sources

The extensive coverage of documentation in four styles—MLA, Chicago, APA, and CSE—reflects each style's latest version and includes many examples of electronic sources.

■ **New** MLA style is expanded and completely updated to reflect the 2009 *MLA Handbook for Writers of Research Papers*, Seventh Edition.

■ **New** Chicago style is updated to reflect the 2010 *Chicago Manual of Style*, Sixteenth Edition.

■ **New** APA style is updated to reflect the 2010 *Publication Manual*, Sixth Edition.

■ **New** CSE style is updated to reflect the 2006 *Scientific Style and Format: The CSE Manual for Authors, Editors, and Publishers*, Seventh Edition.

■ **New** Annotated samples of key source types illustrate MLA and APA documentation, showing students how to find the bibliographical information needed to cite each type.

■ **New** For all styles, color highlighting makes authors, titles, dates, and other citation elements easy to grasp.

An illustrative guide to the writing process

The handbook takes a practical approach to assessing the writing situation, generating ideas, developing the thesis statement, revising, and other elements of the writing process.

- **New** A first-year college student's work-in-progress on globalization and outsourcing illustrates the stages of the writing process.
- **New** Diagrams visually reinforce the recursiveness of the writing process.
- **New** A discussion of voice helps students inject themselves into their academic writing.
- **New** Expanded coverage of thesis development now includes examples of explanatory and argumentative thesis questions and statements.
- An extensive chapter on paragraphs provides nearly fifty annotated examples.
- An extensive chapter on document design includes help with using illustrations and a section on designing for readers with vision loss.

An accessible guide to usage, grammar, and punctuation

The handbook's core reference material reliably and concisely explains basic concepts and common errors, provides hundreds of annotated examples from across the curriculum, and offers frequent exercises in connected discourse (including end-of-part exercises that combine several kinds of problems).

- **New** Seven added boxes cover helping verbs, sentence fragments, comma splices and fused sentences, misplaced modifiers, appropriate language, word choice, and spelling.
- **New** Color highlighting in boxes stresses and distinguishes sentence elements for quick reference.
- **New** Advice on avoiding the informalities common to online communication targets nonstandard grammar, punctuation, abbreviations, and spelling.

A guide for ESL, ELL, and linguistically and culturally diverse writers

At notes and sections labeled ⟨CULTURE LANGUAGE⟩, the handbook provides extensive rhetorical and grammatical help for writers whose first language or dialect is not standard American English.

- Fully integrated coverage, instead of a separate section, means that students can find what they need without having to know which problems they do and don't share with native SAE speakers.
- "⟨CULTURE LANGUAGE⟩ Guide," on pages 952–53 orients students with advice on mastering SAE and pulls all the integrated coverage together in one place.

A relevant guide to visual literacy

The handbook helps students process visual information and use it effectively in their writing.

- **New** The discussion of viewing images critically uses fresh and diverse examples to demonstrate identifying and analyzing visual elements.
- **New** A student work-in-progress illustrates the process of analyzing an advertisement and culminates in a sample critique.
- **New** The chapter on reading and using visual arguments includes new graphs and advertisements and a new photograph for analysis.
- Detailed help with preparing or finding illustrations appears in the discussions of document design, research writing, and Web composition.
- Illustrations in many of the handbook's student papers show various ways to support written ideas with visual information.

An accessible reference guide

The handbook is designed to be easy to use.

- **New** A clean, uncluttered page design uses color and type clearly to distinguish parts of the book and elements of the pages.
- **New** Color highlighting in boxes and on documentation models distinguishes important elements.
- Annotations on both visual and verbal examples connect principles and illustrations.
- Dictionary-style headers in the index make it easy to find entries.
- More than 160 boxes provide summaries and checklists of key information.
- A preface just for students outlines the book's contents, details reference aids, and explains the page layout.

Flexible digital solutions for many learning environments

The handbook's digital solutions are designed to meet the needs and comfort levels of teachers and students. Teachers have the flexibility to integrate any or all of the online resources to better manage and enhance instruction. The digital solutions include the handbook's companion Web site, *MyCompLab* (see p. x), and a Pearson e-text version of *The Little, Brown Handbook*.

Supplements

Pearson offers a variety of support materials to help teachers save time and students improve as writers. For a more detailed list of supplements, visit *pearsonschool.com/advanced* or contact your local Pearson sales representative.

For teachers

- *MyCompLab* (*www.mycomplab.com*) with e-text is provided upon textbook adoption. *MyCompLab* offers teachers many time-saving features. The "To Do" feature enables teachers to create and deliver assignments online and helps them keep students on track by listing due dates and assignment details in one place. The flexible "Gradebook" feature captures students' grades from the self-grading exercises on the site as well as those on teacher assignments. *MyCompLab* can be used as an independent, self-directed instructional and assessment student resource or be fully integrated into classroom instruction. Teachers can obtain preview or adoption access to *MyCompLab* in one of the following ways: (1) Register at *www.PearsonSchool.com/Access_Request* and select "Premium Media Solutions." After following the registration prompts, you will receive an e-mail with access information. (2) Ask your sales representative for a Preview Access Code Card (ISBN 978-0-131-11589-7). (3) Ask your sales representative for an Adoption Access Code Card (ISBN 978-0-130-34391-8). Teachers will receive access codes for distribution to their students. Each year, teachers will receive renewal information via e-mail.

The following supplements are available in print and electronically. Downloads are available through the Instuctor Resource Center (IRC). Register at *www.PearsonSchool.com/Access_Request* and select "Instructor Resource Center." After following the registration prompts, you will receive an e-mail with access information. Use the component ISBN to locate your resource.

- *Teacher's Resource Manual* (ISBN 978-0-132-49217-1) is a freestanding, two-color paperback that includes answers to the handbook's exercises, essays on teaching, ideas for class discussion and activities, tips for SAT and ACT preparation, and a correlation to the AP standards.
- *Diagnostic and Editing Tests and Exercises* (ISBN 978-0-205-69276-7) are cross-referenced to *The Little, Brown Handbook*.

For students

- *MyCompLab* (*www.mycomplab.com*) with e-text is provided upon textbook adoption. *MyCompLab* empowers student writers and facilitates writing instruction by uniquely integrating a composing space and e-portfolio with resources and tools. Students have writing, grammar, and research help at their fingertips as they draft and revise, and they receive feedback, through peer and teacher reviews, within the context of their own writing. This seamless and flexible environment, developed in partnership with writing teachers across the country, helps students accomplish everyday composition tasks more easily and effectively.

■ The companion Web site (*www.pearsonhighered.com/fowler*) provides video tutorials, exercises, checklists, sample student papers, and links to additional resources on the Web for self-directed learning and assessment opportunities.

Acknowledgments

For this edition of the high school version of *The Little, Brown Handbook*, we are grateful to the teachers and educators whose helpful reviews guided us in addressing the needs of today's students: Charles F. Gill, Jr., Arroyo Grande High School, California; Rita Keogh, Montini Catholic High School, Illinois; James D. Lester, Jr., Clarksville High School, Tennessee; and Barbara Williams, Clarksville High School, Tennessee.

We are also grateful to the many college instructors who offered suggestions for the handbook's improvement: Paula Berggren, Baruch College, City University of New York; Sandra Cooper, Central Florida Community College; Lori Rios Doddy, Texas Woman's University; Hilary Englert, New Jersey City University; Holly French, Bossier Parish Community College; Richard F. Gaspar, Hillsborough Community College; Diana Gatz, St. Petersburg College; Mickey Hall, Volunteer State Community College; Barbara Hanna, East Mississippi Community College; Daryl Y. Holmes, Nicholls State University; Melissa Joarder, Delaware County Community College; Kathleen Keating, Greensboro College; Joselle LaGuerre, Miami Dade College, Homestead; Jaquelyn S. Lyman, Anne Arundel Community College; Gladys Jane McClain, University of West Georgia; John Schaffer, Blinn College; Nancy M. Staub, Lamar University; and Mary Wright, Christopher Newport University.

In responding to the ideas of these thoughtful critics, we had the help of several creative people. Caroline Crouse, George Washington University, guided us through the labyrinth of the contemporary library. Nanette Tamer, Villa Julie College, provided helpful suggestions to improve many exercises. Sylvan Barnet, Tufts University, continued to lend his expertise in the chapter "Reading and Writing About Literature," which is adapted from his *Short Guide to Writing About Literature* and *Introduction to Literature* (with William Burto and William E. Cain). Ellen Kuhl provided creative and meticulous help with the material on research writing. And Carol Hollar-Zwick served as originator, critic, coordinator, researcher, and friend.

A superb publishing team helped us make this book. At Pearson, our editors, Suzanne Phelps Chambers, Erin Reilly, and Anne Brunell Ehrenworth offered perceptive insights into teachers' and students' needs, while the production editor, Jackie Martin, guided the manuscript through production. At Nesbitt Graphics, Jerilyn Bockorick created the striking new design, and Susan McIntyre performed her usual calm (and calming) miracles of scheduling and management to produce the book. We are grateful to all these collaborators.

Contents

Preface for Students: Using This Book iii
Preface for Teachers vi

The Writing Process

PART 1

1
Assessing the Writing Situation

"Writing is easy," snarled the late sportswriter Red Smith. "All you do is sit down at the typewriter and open a vein." Most writers would smile in agreement, and so might you. Like anything worthwhile, writing well takes hard work. This chapter and the next two will show you some techniques that successful writers use to ease the discomfort of writing and produce effective compositions.

1a Understanding how writing happens

Every time you sit down to write, you embark on a **writing process**—the term for all the activities, mental and physical, that go into creating what eventually becomes a finished piece of work. Even for experienced writers the process is usually messy, which is one reason that it is sometimes difficult. Though we may get a sense of ease and orderliness from a published magazine article, we can safely assume that the writer had to work hard to achieve those qualities, struggling to express half-formed thoughts, shaping and reshaping paragraphs to make a point convincingly.

There is no *one* writing process; no two writers proceed in the same way, and even an individual writer adapts his or her process to the task at hand. Still, most writers experience writing as a **recursive** process in which the following stages overlap and influence one another:

- **Analyzing the writing situation:** considering subject, purpose, audience, and other elements of the project (pp. 4–17).
- **Developing or planning:** gathering information, focusing on a central theme, and organizing material (pp. 18–46).
- **Drafting:** expressing and connecting ideas (pp. 48–52).
- **Revising and editing:** rethinking and improving structure, content, style, and presentation (pp. 52–69).

mycomplab

Visit *mycomplab.com* for more resources and exercises on the writing situation and the writing process.

The writing process

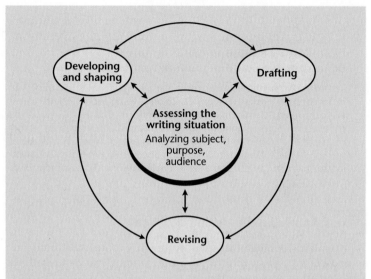

Writing is usually a recursive process: at each stage your work can affect and be affected by every other stage. Assessing the writing situation generally starts the process and then continues in the other stages.

With experience, as you complete varied assignments and try the varied techniques described in this book, you will develop your own basic writing process.

Note Like many others, you may believe that writing is only, or even mainly, a matter of correctness. True, any written message will find a more receptive audience if it is correct in grammar, spelling, and similar matters. But these concerns should come late in the writing process, after you've allowed yourself to discover what you want to say, freeing yourself to make mistakes along the way. As one writer put it, you need to get the clay on the potter's wheel before you can shape it into a bowl, and you need to shape the bowl before you can perfect it. So get your clay on the wheel, and work with it until it looks like a bowl. Then worry about correctness.

Exercise 1.1 Starting a writing journal

Recall several writing experiences that you have had—a letter you had difficulty composing, an essay you enjoyed writing, hours spent happily or miserably on a research paper, a posting to a blog that received a surprising response. What do these experiences reveal to you about writing, particularly your successes and problems with it? Consider the following questions:

Do you like to experiment with language?
Are some kinds of writing easier than others?
Do you have trouble getting ideas or expressing them?
Do you worry about grammar and spelling?
Do your readers usually understand what you mean?

Record your thoughts as part of continuing journal entries that track your experiences as a writer. (See pp. 21–23 on keeping a journal, and see the exercises titled "Considering your past work" in Chapters 1–4.) As you complete writing assignments for your composition course and other courses, keep adding to the journal, noting especially which procedures seem most helpful to you. Your aim is to discover your feelings about writing so that you can develop a dependable writing process of your own.

1b Analyzing the writing situation

Any writing you do for others occurs in a context that both limits and clarifies your choices. You are communicating something about a particular subject to a particular audience of readers for a specific reason. You are establishing yourself as a writer with something to say. You may need to conduct research. You'll be up against a length requirement and a deadline. And you may be expected to present your work in a certain format.

These are the elements of the **writing situation,** and analyzing them at the very start of a project can tell you much about how to proceed. (For more information about these elements, refer to the page numbers given in parentheses.)

Context
- **What is your writing for?** A class in school? The student newspaper? Something else? What do you know of the requirements for writing in this context?
- **Will you present your writing on paper, online, or orally?** What does the presentation method require in preparation time, special skills, and use of technology?
- **How much leeway do you have for this writing?** What does the stated or implied assignment tell you?

Subject (pp. 7–9)
- **What does your writing assignment require you to write about?** If you don't have a specific assignment, what subjects might be appropriate for this situation?
- **What interests you about the subject?** What do you already know about it? What questions do you have about it?

The rhetorical triangle

The elements of the writing situation listed on these pages contribute to **rhetoric**, a term from the work of the ancient Greek philosopher Aristotle (384–22 BCE). Rhetoric describes how writers and speakers use ideas and language to inform or persuade an audience.

Rhetoric is often drawn as a triangle that represents the three basic elements to be considered in any writing situation:

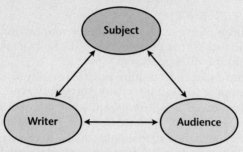

The arrows on the triangle show the interdependence of the three points:

- The **subject** and the evidence the writer uses to address it;
- The **audience** and the ideas, knowledge, beliefs, and attitudes that the writer must take into account;
- The **writer**, who adapts his or her voice to meet the expectations of the audience and the requirements of the subject.

- What does the assignment require you to do with the subject?

Purpose (pp. 10–12)
- What aim does your assignment specify? For instance, does it ask you to explain something or argue a point?
- Why are you writing?
- What do you want your work to accomplish? What effect do you intend it to have on readers?
- How can you best achieve your purpose?

Audience (pp. 12–16)
- Who will read your writing?
- What do your readers already know and think about your subject? What characteristics—such as education or political views—might influence their response?
- How should you project yourself in your writing? What role should you play in relation to your readers—friend, colleague, expert, or something else? What information should you provide?

- What do you want readers to do or think after they read your writing?

Voice (pp. 16–17)

- How formal or informal should your writing be, considering your audience and your purpose?
- What tone should you use to convey your attitude—for instance, concerned, forceful, alarmed, pleased, confident?

Research (pp. 550–615)

- What kinds of evidence will best suit your subject, purpose, and audience? What combination of facts, examples, and expert opinions will support your ideas?
- Does your assignment require research? Will you need to consult sources or conduct interviews, surveys, or experiments?
- Even if research is not required, what information do you need to develop your subject? How will you obtain it?
- What documentation style should you use to cite your sources? (See pp. 614–15 on source documentation in the academic disciplines.)

Deadline and length

- When is the assignment due? How will you apportion the work you have to do in the time available?
- How long should your writing be? If no length is assigned, what seems appropriate for your subject, purpose, and audience?

Document design

- What organization and format does the assignment require? (See pp. 113–14 on format in the academic disciplines and pp. 802–12 on format in public writing.)
- How might you use margins, headings, and other elements to achieve your purpose? (See pp. 118–22.)
- How might you use graphs, photographs, or other images to support ideas and engage readers? (See pp. 122–26, 226–29.)

Exercise 1.2 Analyzing a writing situation

The following assignment was given in an American history course. What does the assignment specify about the elements of the writing situation? What does it imply? Given this assignment, how would you answer the questions above and on the previous page?

Explore the causes of the colonists' victory in the Revolutionary War. First briefly explain the combination of factors that worked in the colonists' favor, and then explain one cause in detail. Quote from contemporary accounts of both colonists and the British to support your claims, and document your sources. Papers should be 3–5 pages, typed.

1c | Discovering and limiting a subject

For most writing you do in high school, you will respond to an assignment. The assignment may specify your subject, or it may leave the choice to you. (If you're stuck, you can use the discovery techniques on pp. 18–28 to think of subjects.) Whether the subject is assigned or not, it will probably need some thought if it is to achieve these aims:

- The subject should be suitable for the assignment.
- It should be neither too general nor too limited for the length of the project and the deadline assigned.
- It should be something you are willing to learn more about, even something you care about.

1 | Responding to a specific assignment

Many assignments will set boundaries for your subject. For instance, you might be asked to discuss what makes psychotherapy effective, to prepare a lab report on a physics experiment, or to analyze a character in a short story.

Such assignments may seem to leave little room for you to move around, but in fact you'll have several questions to answer:

- **What's wanted from you?** Writing assignments often contain words such as *discuss, describe, analyze, report, interpret, explain, define, argue,* and *evaluate.* These words specify the way you are to approach your subject, what kind of thinking is expected of you, and what your general purpose is. (See pp. 10–12 for more on purpose.)
- **For whom are you writing?** Many assignments will specify or imply your readers, but sometimes you will have to figure out for yourself who your audience is and what it expects from you. (For more on analyzing audience, see pp. 12–16.)
- **What kind of research is required?** Sometimes an assignment specifies the kinds of sources you are expected to consult, and you can use such information to choose your subject. (If you are unsure whether research is required, check with your instructor.)
- **How can you narrow the assigned subject to do it justice in the length and time required?** (See below.)

2 | Responding to a general assignment

Many assignments specify features such as length and amount of research, but they leave the choice of subject fairly open—for instance, *Analyze the conflict in one of the short stories we read in this unit* or *Investigate a problem you see in school policy.* When the topic or the approach is more open, consider the following:

- **What subject do you already know something about or have you been wondering about?** College athletic scholarships? A proposed dress code at your school?
- **Have you recently disagreed with someone over a substantial issue?** The change in relations between boys and girls? The methods being used to fight terrorism?
- **What have you read or seen lately?** A shocking book? A violent or funny movie? An effective television commercial?
- **What topic in the reading or class discussion for a course has intrigued you?** A psychological problem such as depression? A literary topic such as plot twists in an author's work?
- **What makes you especially happy or especially angry?** A hobby? The behavior of your friends?
- **Which of your own or others' dislikes and preferences would you like to understand better?** The demand for hybrid cars? The decision to become a vegetarian?

Once you have a subject, you'll also need to answer the questions in the bulleted list opposite.

3 | Narrowing a subject to a question

Whether you arrive at a subject through an assignment or on your own, you will need to narrow it in order to provide the specific details that make writing significant and interesting—all within the assigned length and deadline.

One helpful technique for narrowing a subject is to ask focused questions about it, seeking one that seems appropriate for your assignment and that promises to sustain your interest through the writing process. The following examples illustrate how questioning can scale down broad subjects to specific subjects that are limited and manageable:

Broad subjects	Specific subjects
Social-networking sites	What draws people to these sites?
	How do the sites alter the ways people interact?
	What privacy protections should the sites provide for users?
Mrs. Mallard in Kate Chopin's "The Story of an Hour"	What changes does Mrs. Mallard undergo?
	Why does Mrs. Mallard respond as she does to news of her husband's death?
	What does the story's irony contribute to the character of Mrs. Mallard?

Broad subjects	Specific subjects
Lincoln's weaknesses as President	What was Lincoln's most significant error as commander-in-chief of the Union army?
	Why did Lincoln delay emancipating the slaves?
	Why did Lincoln have difficulties controlling his cabinet?
Federal aid to poor districts	What kinds of school districts should be entitled to federal aid?
	How adequate is federal aid to meet the needs of poor districts?
	Why should the federal government aid poor schools more than other districts?

As these examples illustrate, your questions should not lend themselves to yes-or-no answers but should require further thinking.

Here are some guidelines for posing questions:

- **Reread the assignment.** Consider what it tells you about purpose, audience, sources, length, and deadline.
- **Pursue your interests.** If questions don't come easily, try freewriting or brainstorming (pp. 23–25) or use a tree diagram (p. 38).
- **Ask as many questions as you can think of.**
- **Test the question that seems most interesting and appropriate by roughly sketching out the main ideas.** Consider how many paragraphs or pages of specific facts, examples, and other details you would need to pin those ideas down. This thinking should give you at least a vague idea of how much work you'd have to do and how long the resulting paper might be.
- **Break a too-broad question down further, and repeat the previous step.**

The Internet can also help you limit a general subject. On the Web, browse a directory such as *BUBL LINK* (*bubl.ac.uk*). As you pursue increasingly narrow categories, you may find a suitably limited topic.

Don't be discouraged if the perfect question does not come easily or early. You may find that you need to do some planning and writing, exploring different facets of the general subject and pursuing your specific interests, before you hit on the best question. And the question you select may require further narrowing or may shift subtly or even dramatically as you move through the writing process.

Exercise 1.3 Narrowing subjects

Following are some general writing assignments. Use the given information and your own interests to pose specific questions for three of these assignments.

1. For a composition class, consider how Web sites such as *YouTube* are altering the experience of popular culture. Length: three pages. Deadline: one week.
2. For a biology class, explain the life cycle of a particular animal or plant species. Deadline: two weeks.
3. For a literature class, respond to a novel or short story you are reading. Length: three pages. Deadline: one week.
4. For a government class, consider possible restrictions on legislators. Length: five pages. Deadline: two weeks.
5. For a journalism class, write a feature story for the town newspaper in which you describe the effects of immigration on your community. Length: two pages. Deadline: unspecified.

Exercise 1.4   Considering your past work: Discovering and limiting a subject

Think of something you've recently written—perhaps an application essay, a critical essay, or a research paper. How did your subject evolve from beginning to end? In retrospect, was it appropriate for your writing situation? How, if at all, might it have been modified?

Exercise 1.5   Finding and narrowing a subject for your essay

As the first step in developing a three- to four-page essay for the teacher and the other students in your writing class, choose a subject and narrow it. Use the guidelines in the previous section to come up with a question that is suitably interesting, appropriate, and specific.

1d   Defining a purpose

When you write, your **purpose** is your chief reason for communicating something about a topic to a particular audience. Purpose thus links both the specific situation in which you are working and the goal you hope to achieve. It is your answer to a potential reader's question, "So what?"

The general purposes for writing

Purpose for writing	Kinds of writing
To explain or to inform (exposition)	Reports, research papers, essay exams, application letters
To persuade (argument)	Editorials, speeches, opinion papers, proposals
To express feelings or ideas	Journals or diaries, personal narratives, poetry
To entertain	Stories, dialogs, parodies

1 | Defining a general purpose

Your purpose may fall into one of four general categories: explanation, persuasion, self-expression, or entertainment. These purposes may overlap in a single piece of writing, but usually one predominates. And the dominant purpose will influence your particular slant on your topic, the supporting details you choose, and the language you use.

In high school and public writing, by far the most common purposes are explanation and persuasion:

- **Writing that is mainly explanatory is often called** *exposition* (from a Latin word meaning "to explain or set forth"). Using examples, facts, and other evidence, you present an idea about your subject so that readers understand it as you do. Almost any subject is suitable for exposition: how to pitch a knuckleball, why you want to attend college, the implications of a new discovery in computer science, the interpretation of a short story, the causes of an economic slump. Exposition is the kind of writing encountered most often in newspapers, magazines, and textbooks.

- **Writing that is primarily persuasive is often called** *argument.* Using examples, facts, and other evidence, you support your position on a debatable subject so that readers will at least consider your view and perhaps agree with it or act on it. A newspaper editorial favoring city council reform, a proposal for a new recycling program at your school, a student paper recommending more math and science classes or defending a theory about human psychological development—all these are arguments. (Chapters 9–11 discuss argument in some detail and provide examples.)

2 | Defining a specific purpose

Purpose can be conceived more specifically, too, in a way that incorporates your particular subject and the outcome you intend—what you want readers to do or think as a result of reading your writing. Here are some examples of specific purposes:

To explain how Annie Dillard's "Total Eclipse" builds to its climax so that readers appreciate the author's skill

To explain the methods and results of a science experiment so that readers understand and accept your conclusions

To explain why the county has been unable to attract new businesses so that readers better understand the local economic slump

To persuade readers to support the school administration's plan for a dress code

To argue against laws that ban cell phone use while driving

To argue for additional gun-control laws so that readers agree on their necessity

Often, a writing assignment will specify or imply both a general and a specific purpose. Say, for instance, that an English teacher assigns a paper on the use of language in three poems by Emily Dickinson. You know that the purpose is generally to explain, more specifically to show similarities in vocabulary, word order, and tone in the poems. You want readers to come away understanding how Emily Dickinson used language for certain effects in her poems. In addition, you want your teacher to see that you can competently read poetry and write about it. (See p. 167 for more on purpose in academic writing.)

With any writing assignment, try to define your specific purpose as soon as you have formed a question about your subject. Don't worry, though, if you feel uncertain of your purpose at the start. Sometimes you may not discover your purpose until you begin drafting, or you may find that your initial sense of purpose changes as you move through the writing process.

Exercise 1.6 Finding purpose in assignments

For each of your questions from Exercise 1.3 (p. 9), suggest a likely general purpose (explanation, persuasion, self-expression, entertainment) and try to define a specific purpose as well.

Exercise 1.7 Considering your past work: Defining a purpose

Look over two or three things you've written in the past year or so. What was your specific purpose in each one? How did the purpose influence your writing? Did you achieve your purpose?

Exercise 1.8 Defining a purpose for your essay

For your essay-in-progress, use your thinking so far about your subject (Exercise 1.5, p. 10) to define a general and specific purpose for your writing.

1e Considering the audience

- **Who are my readers:** teachers, classmates, school population, or a general and unspecified audience?
- **Why will the audience read my writing:** to evaluate or to be informed, entertained, or persuaded?

- **What will readers need from me:** data, experts' views, examples, anecdotes, connections to their interests?
- **What do I want readers to think or do after they read my writing:** change their minds, agree, give credit, laugh, engage in action?
- **How do I want to be perceived by the audience:** as a reporter, an expert, an advocate, or something else?

These questions are central to any writing project, and they will crop up again and again. Except in writing meant only for yourself, you are always trying to communicate with readers—something about a particular subject, for a particular purpose.

Your audience will often be specified or implied in a writing assignment. When you write a story for the student newspaper, your audience consists of students at your school. When you write a report on a physics experiment, your audience consists of your physics teacher and perhaps your classmates. (See p. 168 for more on audience in academic writing.) Whatever the audience, considering its needs and expectations can help you form or focus a question about your subject, gather answers to the question, and ultimately decide what to say and how to say it.

1 | Knowing what readers need

As a reader yourself, you know what readers need:

- **Context:** a link between what they read and their own knowledge and experiences.
- **Predictability:** an understanding of the writer's purpose and how it is being achieved.
- **Information:** the specific facts, examples, and other details that make the subject clear, interesting, and convincing.
- **Respect:** a sense that the writer respects their values and beliefs, their backgrounds, and their intelligence.
- **Voice:** a sense that the writer is a real person whose mind and values are expressed in the writing (see p. 16).
- **Clarity and correctness:** writing free of unnecessary stumbling blocks and mistakes.

For much academic and public writing, readers have definite needs and expectations. Thus Chapter 8 discusses academic writing in general, Chapters 48–52 discuss writing in various disciplines, and Chapter 55 discusses public writing. Even in these areas, you must make many choices based on audience. In other areas where the conventions of structure and presentation are vaguer, the choices are even more numerous. The box on the next page contains questions that can help you define and make these choices.

Questions about audience

Identity and expectations

- **Who *are* my readers?**
- **What are my readers' expectations for the kind of writing I'm doing?** Do readers expect features such as a particular organization and format, distinctive kinds of evidence, or a certain style of documenting sources?
- **What do I want readers to know or do after reading my work?** How should I make that clear to them?
- **How should I project myself to readers?** How formal or informal will they expect me to be? What role and tone should I assume?

Characteristics, knowledge, and attitudes

- **What characteristics of readers are relevant for my subject and purpose?** For instance:

  Age and sex
  Occupation: students, coworkers, etc.
  Social or economic role: subject-matter experts, voters, car buyers, potential employers, etc.
  Economic or educational background
  Ethnic background
  Political, religious, or moral beliefs and values
  Hobbies or activities

- **How will the characteristics of readers influence their attitudes toward my subject?**
- **What do readers already know and *not* know about my subject?** How much do I have to tell them?
- **How should I handle any specialized terms?** Will readers know them? If not, should I define them or avoid them?
- **What ideas, arguments, or information might surprise, excite, or offend readers?** How should I handle these points?
- **What misconceptions might readers have of my subject and/or my approach to it?** How can I dispel these misconceptions?

Uses and format

- **What will readers do with my writing?** Should I expect them to read every word from the top, to scan for information, to look for conclusions? Can I help by providing a summary, headings, illustrations, or other aids? (See pp. 113–27 on document design.)

2 Appealing to your audience

Your sense of your audience will influence three key elements of what and how you write to appeal to your readers:

- **The reasoning you use in making general claims and supporting them with evidence.** Your claims should be supportable,

Rhetorical appeals

Rhetoric defines three primary methods of appealing to an audience:

- **Logical appeal,** or **logos:** Appealing to readers' reason by supporting claims with examples, facts, details, and other evidence.
- **Emotional appeal,** or **pathos:** Appealing to readers' emotions by calling on feelings of empathy, sympathy, anger, fear, and so on.
- **Ethical appeal,** or **ethos:** Appealing to readers by establishing yourself as a trustworthy and credible writer.

and that support should be clearly provided as concrete details, facts, examples, or other evidence that also suits your readers' backgrounds, biases, and special interests. When you reason with readers by providing specific information to support your ideas, you are using a **logical appeal:**

The school parking lot is too small to accommodate the students who drive to school. A recent survey of juniors and seniors found that thirty percent drive every day, bringing more cars to campus than the lot can hold and forcing many students to park on surrounding streets. [The first sentence makes a claim, and the second sentence provides evidence for the claim.]

- **The emotions you try to evoke in your readers.** Depending on your purpose, you may want to use language as well as facts, examples, or other evidence to lead readers to sympathy, anger, fear, or some other emotion. When you appeal to readers in this way, you are using an **emotional appeal:**

Yesterday I saw a student sitting in her car in the middle of the parking lot crying because the lot was full and she knew she would once again be marked tardy. [Readers are likely to feel the student's frustration and fear of punishment.]

- **The role you choose to play in relation to your readers.** The possible roles are many and varied—for instance, scholar, storyteller, guide, reporter, advocate, inspirer—and will depend on your purpose and your attitude toward your topic. In addition, you will want readers to perceive you as reasonable, competent, and trustworthy. When you establish yourself as a believable writer, you are using an **ethical appeal:**

Everybody who must be at the school and begin the day at the same time—staff, faculty, and students—needs and deserves space to park. [Establishes the writer as concerned about equality and fairness.]

For more on appeals, see pages 208–09 and 228–29.

3 Considering your writer's voice

Often you adapt your **writer's voice** to your writing situation. Voice consists in part of the role you choose to play in relation to your readers (see the previous page), but it also consists of the level of formality and the tone of your writing. Tone in writing is like tone of voice in speaking: words and sentence structures on the page convey some of the same information as pitch and volume in the voice. Depending on your writing situation and what you think readers will expect and respond to, your writing may be formal or informal, and your tone may be serious or light, forceful or calm, irritated or cheerful.

Even when you're writing on the same subject, the information you provide, the feelings you tap into, and the role and tone you assume may change substantially for different audiences. Both memos below were written by a student who worked part-time in a small company and wanted to get the company to recycle paper. But the two memos address different readers.

To coworkers

Ever notice how much paper collects in your trash basket every day? Well, most of it can be recycled with little effort, I promise. Basically, all you need to do is set a bag or box near your desk and deposit wastepaper in it. I know, space is cramped in these little cubicles. But can't we all accept a little more crowding when the earth's at stake? . . .

Voice: a peer who is thoughtful, cheerful, and sympathetic

Information: how employees could handle recycling; no mention of costs

Role: colleague

Tone: informal, personal (*Ever notice; Well; you; I know, space is cramped*)

To management

In my four months here, I have observed that all of us throw out baskets of potentially recyclable paper every day. Considering the drain on our forest resources and the pressure on landfills that paper causes, we could make a valuable contribution to the environmental movement by helping to recycle the paper we use. At the company where I worked before, employees separate clean wastepaper from other trash at their desks. The maintenance staff collects trash in two receptacles, and the trash hauler (the same one we use here) makes separate pickups. I do not know what the hauler charges for handling recyclable material. . . .

Voice: a subordinate who is thoughtful, responsible, and serious

Information: specific reasons; view of company as a whole; reference to another company; problem of cost

Role: employee

Tone: formal, serious (*Considering the drain; forest resources; valuable contribution;* no *you*)

Typically for business writing, the voice grows more professional as the readers increase in rank.

Projecting your writing voice can be challenging when you are responding to another's work or drawing on multiple sources for evidence. Especially if you feel unconfident about your subject, you may be tempted to let the other writers do the talking for you. You can find advice on pages 164–67 and 593–94 for maintaining your voice by using synthesis.

Exercise 1.9 Considering audience

Choose one of the following subjects and, for each audience specified, ask the questions on page 14. Decide on four points you would make, the role you would assume, and the tone you would adopt for each audience. Then write a paragraph for each based on your decisions.

1. The effects of smoking: for elementary school students and for adult smokers
2. Your opposition to a proposed law requiring all bicyclists to wear helmets: for cyclists who oppose the law and for people who favor it
3. Why your school should have a dress code: for your classmates and for the school administrators

Exercise 1.10 Considering your past work: Writing for a specific audience

How did audience figure in a piece of writing you've done in the recent past—perhaps an essay for an application or a paper for a class? How did you decide who your readers were? How and when did your awareness of readers influence your choices as a writer? Consider the evidence you used, the way you presented yourself, and whether you appealed to readers' emotions.

Exercise 1.11 Analyzing the audience for your essay

Use the questions on page 14 to determine as much as you can about the probable readers of your essay-in-progress (see Exercises 1.5 and 1.8). What might be an appropriate voice for your writing? What specific information will your readers need? What role do you want to assume? What tone will best convey your attitude toward your topic?

2

Developing and Shaping Ideas

Once you have assessed your writing situation, or even while you're assessing it, you'll begin answering the question you posed about your subject (pp. 7–8). As you generate ideas and information, they in turn may cause you to rephrase your lead question, which will open up new areas to explore. Throughout this discovery process, you'll also be bringing order to your thoughts, eventually focusing and organizing them so that readers will respond as you intend.

2a Discovering ideas

For some writing projects, you may have little difficulty finding what you have to say about your subject: possible answers to your starting question will tumble forth as ideas on paper or screen. But when you're stuck for what to say, you'll have to coax answers out. Instead of waiting around for inspiration to strike, use a technique to get your mind working. Anything is appropriate: if you like to make drawings or take pictures, for instance, then try that.

The following pages describe techniques for discovering ideas. These techniques are to be selected from, not followed in sequence: some may help you during early stages of the writing process, even before you're sure of your topic; others may help you later on; and one or two may not help at all. Give yourself ample time with the techniques, experimenting to discover which ones work best for you.

Note Whatever techniques you use, **do your work in writing, not just in your head.** Your work will be retrievable, and the act of writing will help you concentrate and lead you to fresh, sometimes surprising, insights.

mycomplab

Visit *mycomplab.com* for more resources and exercises on discovering and shaping ideas.

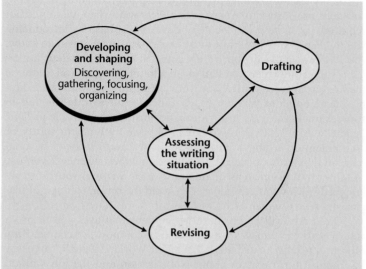

Developing and shaping ideas

Developing ideas and shaping them may occur at any point in the writing process, from the initial choice of subject through drafting and revision.

CULTURE LANGUAGE The discovery process encouraged here rewards rapid writing without a lot of thinking beforehand about what you will write or how. If your first language is not standard American English, you may find it helpful initially to do this exploratory writing in your native language or dialect and then to translate the worthwhile material for use in your drafts. This process can be productive, but it is extra work. You may want to try it at first and gradually move to composing in standard American English.

Techniques for developing a subject

- Read (p. 20).
- Keep a journal (p. 21).
- Observe your surroundings (p. 23).
- Freewrite (p. 23).
- Brainstorm (p. 24).
- Cluster and map ideas (p. 25).
- Use the journalist's questions (p. 26).
- Use rhetorical strategies (p. 27).

1 Reading

Many assignments require you to respond to reading or to consult texts as sources for your writing. But even when reading is not required, it can help you locate or develop a subject by introducing you to ideas you didn't know or by expanding on what you do know. For example, say you were writing in favor of amateur athletics, a subject to which you had given a lot of thought. You might be inclined to proceed entirely on your own, drawing on facts, examples, and opinions already in your head. But a little digging in sources might open up more ideas. For instance, an article in *Time* magazine could introduce you to an old rule for amateur status, or a comment on a blog could suggest an argument in favor of amateurism that hadn't occurred to you. Remember: whenever you use the information or ideas of others in your writing, you must acknowledge your sources in order to avoid the serious offense of plagiarism. (See Chapter 44.)

Often you will be given an assignment that asks you to use a text or texts in your writing. In a college composition course, Katy Moreno's teacher distributed "It's a Flat World, After All," an essay by Thomas L. Friedman about globalization and the job market. The instructor then gave the following assignment, calling for a response to reading:

> In "It's a Flat World, After All," Thomas L. Friedman describes today's global job market, focusing not on manufacturing jobs that have been "outsourced" to overseas workers but on jobs that require a college degree and are no longer immune to outsourcing. Friedman argues that keeping jobs in the United States requires that US students, parents, and educators improve math and science education. As a college student, how do you respond to this analysis of the global market for jobs? Does anything Friedman says cause you to rethink how you will spend your college years or what your major will be?

To respond to Friedman's essay, Moreno had to digest its argument. On first reading the essay, she had found it convincing because Friedman's description of the job market matched her family's experience: her mother had lost her job when it was outsourced to India. After rereading the essay, however, Moreno was not persuaded that more math and science would necessarily improve students' opportunities and preserve their future jobs. She compared Friedman's advice with details she recalled from her mother's experience, and she began to develop a response by writing in her journal:

> Friedman is certainly right that more jobs than we realize are going overseas— that's what happened to Mom's job and we were shocked! But he gives only one way for students like me to compete—take more math and science. At first I thought he's totally right. But then I thought that what he said didn't

really explain what happened to Mom—she had lots of math + science + tons of experience, but it was her salary, not better training, that caused her job to be outsourced. An overseas worker would do her job for less money. So she lost her job because of money + because she wasn't a manager. Caught in the middle. I want to major in computer science, but I don't think it's smart to try for the kind of job Mom had—at least not as long as it's so much cheaper for companies to hire workers overseas.

When you read for ideas, you need to be active, probing the text and illustrations with your mind, nurturing any sparks they set off. Always write while you read, taking notes on content and—just as important—on what the content makes you *think*. If you read passively, absorbing content like a sponge and not interacting with it, you won't have much to say about it. (See pp. 133–36 for specific tips on active reading.)

2 | Keeping a journal

A journal is a place to record your responses, thoughts, and observations about what you read, see, hear, or experience. It can also be a good source of ideas for writing. It is a kind of diary, but one more concerned with ideas than with day-to-day events. *Journal* comes from the Latin for "daily," and many journal keepers do write faithfully every day; others make entries less regularly, when the mood strikes or an insight occurs or they have a problem to work out.

Advantages of a journal

Writing in a journal, you are writing to yourself. That means you don't have to worry about main ideas, organization, correct grammar and spelling, or any of the other requirements of writing for others. You can work out your ideas and feelings without the pressure of an audience "out there" who will evaluate your thinking and expression. The freedom and flexibility of a journal can be liberating. Like many others, you may find writing easier, more fun, and more rewarding than you thought possible.

You can keep a journal either on paper (such as a notebook) or on a computer. If you write in the journal every day, or almost, even just for a few minutes, the routine will loosen up your writing muscles and improve your confidence. Indeed, journal keepers often become dependent on the process for the writing practice it gives them, the concentrated thought it encourages, and the connection it fosters between personal, private experience and public information and events.

Usually for the same reasons, teachers sometimes require students to keep journals. The teachers may even collect students' journals to monitor progress, but they read the journals with an understanding of purpose (in other words, they do not evaluate work that was not written to be evaluated), and they usually just credit rather than grade the work.

CULTURE LANGUAGE A journal can be especially helpful if your first language is not standard American English. You can practice writing to improve your fluency, try out sentence patterns, and experiment with vocabulary words. Equally important, you can experiment with applying what you know from experience to what you read and observe.

Uses of a journal

Two uses of a journal are discussed elsewhere in this book: a reading journal, in which you think critically (in writing) about what you read (pp. 142, 693); and a research journal, in which you record your activities and ideas while you pursue a research project (p. 551). But you can use a journal for other purposes as well. Here are just a few:

- **Prepare for or respond to a class you're taking** by puzzling over a reading or a class discussion.
- **Build ideas for specific writing assignments.**
- **Sketch possible designs for a Web composition.**
- **Explore your reactions to events, trends, or the media.**
- **Confide your hopes.**
- **Write about your own history:** an event in your family's past, a troubling incident in your life, a change you've seen.
- **Analyze a relationship that disturbs you.**
- **Explore your writer's voice by practicing various forms or styles of writing**—for instance, poems or songs, reviews of movies, or reports for TV news.

The writing you produce in your journal will help you learn and grow, and even the personal and seemingly nonacademic entries can supply ideas when you are seeking a subject to write about or are developing an essay. A thought you recorded months ago about a chemistry lab may provide direction for a research paper on the history of science. Two entries about arguments with your brother may suggest what you need to anchor a psychology paper on sibling relations. If you keep your journal on a computer, you can even copy passages from it directly into your drafts.

On pages 20–21 we saw Katy Moreno's journal response to an essay she read. The next two student samples give a taste of journal writing for different purposes. In the first, Evan Michaels tries to work out a personal problem with a friend:

Nathan's sarcastic moods are happening more frequently—and becoming less predictable and more nasty. Sometimes it's hard to be his friend, even though he's been my best friend for so many years—he's like a brother. But lately I've been avoiding him, because when we're together I get really stressed, trying too hard to keep things light. What can we do to change the way we interact?

In the second example, Megan Polanyis ponders something she learned from her biology textbook:

Ecology and *economics* have the same root—Greek word for house. Economy = managing the house. Ecology = studying the house. In ecology the house is all of nature, ourselves, the other animals, the plants, the earth, the air, the whole environment. Ecology has a lot to do with economy: study the house in order to manage it.

3 Observing your surroundings

Sometimes you can find a good subject or good ideas by looking around you, not in the half-conscious way most of us move from place to place in our daily lives but deliberately, all senses alert. On a bus, for instance, are there certain types of passengers? What seems to be on the driver's mind? At school, what are students eating for lunch? Do students moving from class to class look relaxed or stressed?

To get the most from observation, you should have a handheld computer or a notepad and pen handy for taking notes and making sketches. If you have a camera, you may find that the lens sees things your unaided eyes do not notice. (When observing or photographing people, though, keep some distance, take photographs quickly, and avoid staring. Otherwise your subjects will feel uneasy.) Back at your desk, study your notes, sketches, or photographs for oddities or patterns that you'd like to explore further.

In some academic writing, you'll be expected to formalize observation with surveys, interviews, or experiments. See pages 576–78.

4 Freewriting

Writing into a subject

Many writers find subjects or discover ideas by **freewriting**: writing without stopping for a certain amount of time (say, ten minutes) or to a certain length (say, one page). The goal of freewriting is to generate ideas and information from *within* yourself by going around the part of your mind that doesn't want to write or can't think of anything to write. You let words themselves suggest other words. *What* you write is not important; that you *keep* writing is. Don't stop, even if that means repeating the same words until new words come. Don't go back to reread, don't censor ideas that seem dumb or repetitious, and above all don't stop to edit: grammar, punctuation, vocabulary, spelling, and the like are irrelevant at this stage.

The physical act of freewriting may give you access to ideas you were unaware of. For example, the following freewriting by a student, Robert Benday, drew him into the subject of writing as a disguise:

> Write to write. Seems pretty obvious, also weird. What to gain by writing? never anything before. Writing seems always—always—Getting corrected for trying too hard to please the teacher, getting corrected for not trying hard enuf. Frustration, nail biting, sometimes getting carried away making sentences to tell stories, not even true stories, *esp.* not true stories, *that* feels like creating something. Writing just pulls the story out of me. The story lets me be someone else, gives me a disguise.

(A later phase of Benday's writing appears on p. 26.)

If you write on a computer, try this technique for moving forward while freewriting: turn off your computer's monitor, or turn its brightness control all the way down so that the screen is dark. The computer will record what you type but keep it from you and thus prevent you from tinkering with your prose. This **invisible writing** may feel uncomfortable at first, but it can free the mind for very creative results. When you've finished freewriting, simply turn the monitor on or turn up the brightness control to read what you've written, and then save or revise it as appropriate. Later you may be able to transfer some of your freewriting directly into your draft.

(CULTURE LANGUAGE) Invisible writing can be especially helpful if you are uneasy writing in standard American English and you tend to worry about errors while writing. The blank computer screen leaves you no choice but to explore ideas without giving attention to the way you are expressing them. If you choose to write with the monitor on, concentrate on *what* you want to say, not *how* you are saying it.

Focused freewriting

Focused freewriting is more concentrated: you start with your question about your subject and answer it without stopping for, say, fifteen minutes or one full page. As in all freewriting, you push to bypass mental blocks and self-consciousness, not debating what to say or editing what you've written. With focused freewriting, though, you let the physical act of writing take you into and around your subject.

An example of focused freewriting can be found in Katy Moreno's journal response to Thomas L. Friedman's "It's a Flat World, After All" (pp. 20–21). Since she already had an idea about Friedman's essay, Moreno was able to start there and expand on the idea.

5 Brainstorming

In **brainstorming**, you focus intently on your subject for a fixed amount of time (say, fifteen minutes), pushing yourself to list every idea and detail that comes to mind. Like freewriting, brainstorming requires turning off your internal editor so that you keep moving ahead instead of looping back over what you have already written to correct it. It makes no difference whether the ideas and details are expressed in phrases or complete sentences. It makes no difference if they seem silly or irrelevant. Just keep pushing. If you are working on a computer, the technique of invisible writing, described opposite, can help you move forward.

Here is an example of brainstorming by a student, Johanna Abrams, responding to the question *What can a summer job teach?*

summer work teaches—

> how to look busy while doing nothing
> how to avoid the sun in summer
> seriously: discipline, budgeting money, value of money

which job? Burger King cashier? baby-sitter? mail-room clerk?
mail room: how to sort mail into boxes: this is learning??
how to survive getting fired—humiliation, outrage
Mrs. King! the mail-room queen as learning experience
the shock of getting fired: what to tell parents, friends?
Mrs. K was so rigid—dumb procedures
Mrs. K's anger, resentment: the disadvantages of being smarter than your boss
The odd thing about working in an office: a world with its own rules for how to act
what Mr. D said about the pecking order—big chick (Mrs. K) pecks on little chick (me)
probably lots of Mrs. Ks in offices all over—offices are all barnyards
Mrs. K a sad person, really—just trying to hold on to her job, preserve her self-esteem
a job can beat you down—destroy self-esteem, make you desperate enough to be mean to other people
how to preserve/gain self-esteem from work??
if I'd known about the pecking order, I would have been less show-offy, not so arrogant

(A later phase of Abrams's writing appears on p. 38.)

When you think you've exhausted the ideas on your topic, you can edit and shape the list into a preliminary outline of your paper (see p. 37). Working on a computer makes this step fairly easy: you can delete weak ideas, expand strong ones, and rearrange items with a few keystrokes. You can also freewrite from the list if you think some items are especially promising and deserve more exploration.

6 Clustering and idea mapping

Many writers find ideas by using **clustering** or **idea mapping**. Like freewriting and list making, these techniques draw on free association and rapid, unedited work. But they also emphasize the *relations* between ideas by combining writing and nonlinear drawing. When clustering, for example, you radiate outward from a center point—your topic. When an idea occurs, you pursue related ideas in a branching structure until they seem exhausted. Then you do the same with other ideas, staying open to connections, continuously branching out or drawing arrows.

The example of clustering below shows how Robert Benday used the technique for ten minutes to expand on the topic of creative writing as a means of disguise, an idea he arrived at through freewriting (see p. 24). Though he ventured into one dead end, Benday also circled into the interesting possibility (at the bottom) that the fiction writer is like a god who forgives himself by creating characters that represent his good and bad qualities.

Clustering

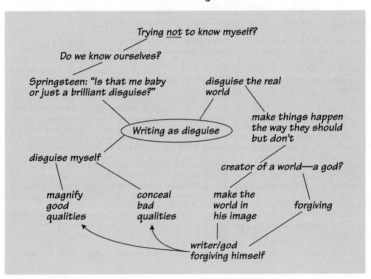

7 Using the journalist's questions

Asking yourself a set of questions about your subject—and writing out the answers—can help you look at the subject objectively and see fresh possibilities in it. Asking questions can also provide some structure to the development of ideas.

One such set of questions is that posed by a journalist with a story to report:

- Who was involved?
- What happened and what were the results?
- When did it happen?
- Where did it happen?
- Why did it happen?
- How did it happen?

These questions can also be useful in probing an essay subject, especially if you are telling a story or examining causes and effects. (See also the next page.)

8 Using rhetorical strategies

Rhetorical strategies—also called **patterns of development**—include narration, definition, comparison and contrast, and classification. They are ways we think about and understand a vast range of subjects, from our own daily experiences to the most complex scientific theories. They also serve as strategies and patterns for writing about these subjects, as illustrated by the discussions and paragraph-length examples on pages 94–102. You may want to refer to those pages for more information about each strategy.

To see your subject from many angles and open up ideas about it, you can ask the following questions based on the rhetorical strategies. Not all these questions will be productive, but at least a few should open up new possibilities.

How did it happen?

In narration you develop the subject as a story, with important events usually arranged chronologically (as they occurred in time): for instance, an exciting basketball game or the steps leading to a war.

How does it look, sound, feel, smell, taste?

In description you use sensory details to give a clear impression of a person, place, thing, or feeling, such as a species of animal, a machine, a friend, a building, or an experience.

What are examples of it or reasons for it?

The pattern of **illustration** or **support** suggests development with one or more examples of the subject (one couple's efforts to adopt a child, say, or three states that outlaw Internet gambling) or with the reasons for believing or doing something (three reasons for running for student council, four reasons for increasing federal aid to poor school districts).

What is it? What does it encompass, and what does it exclude?

These questions lead to **definition:** specifying what the subject is and is not to give a precise sense of its meaning. Abstract terms—such as *justice, friendship,* and *art*—especially need defining (see p. 183).

What are its parts or characteristics?

Using the pattern of **division** or **analysis,** you separate a subject such as a bicycle or a short story into its elements and examine the relations between elements. The first step in critical thinking, analysis is also discussed on pages 148–49.

What groups or categories can it be sorted into?

Classification involves separating a large group (such as cars) into smaller groups (subcompact, compact, and so on) based on the characteristics of the individual items (the sizes of the cars). Another example: academic, business, personal, literary, and other types of writing.

How is it like, or different from, other things?

With **comparison and contrast** you point out the similarities and differences between ideas, objects, people, places, and so on: the differences between two similar musical instruments, for instance, or the similarities between two opposing political candidates.

Is it comparable to something that is in a different class but more familiar to readers?

This question leads to **analogy**, an extended comparison of unlike subjects. Analogy is often used to explain a topic that may be unfamiliar to readers (for instance, the relation of atoms in a molecule) by reference to a familiar topic (two people dancing close together).

Why did it happen, or what results did it have?

With **cause-and-effect analysis,** you explain why something happened or what its consequences were or will be, or both: the causes of cerebral palsy, the effects of a Supreme Court decision, the causes and effects of a gradual change in the climate.

How do you do it, or how does it work?

In **process analysis** you explain how the subject happens (how a plant grows, how a robot works) or how to accomplish it (how to write an essay).

Exercise 2.1   Considering your past work: Developing a topic

In the past how have you generated the ideas for writing? Have you used any of the techniques described on the preceding pages? Have you found the process especially enjoyable or difficult? If some writing tasks were easier than others, what do you think made the difference?

Exercise 2.2   Keeping a journal

If you haven't already started a journal on your own or in response to Exercise 1.1 (pp. 3–4), try to do so now. Every day for at least a week, write for at least fifteen minutes about anything on your mind—or consult the list on page 22 for ideas of what to write about. At the end of the week, write about your experience. What did you like about journal writing? What didn't you like? What did you learn about yourself or the world from the writing? How can you use this knowledge?

Exercise 2.3   Using freewriting, brainstorming, or clustering

Experiment with freewriting, brainstorming, or clustering. Continue with the subject you selected in Exercise 1.5 (p. 10), or begin with a new subject. Write or draw for at least ten minutes without stopping to reread and edit.

(Try using invisible writing as described on p. 24 if you're freewriting or brainstorming on a computer.) When you finish your experiment, examine what you have written for ideas and relationships that could help you develop the subject. What do you think of the technique you tried? Did you have any difficulties with it? Did it help you loosen up and generate ideas?

Exercise 2.4 Sending an online query

When you have spent some time developing your subject, consider any doubts you may have or any information you still need. Send an online message to your classmates posing your questions and asking for their advice and insights.

Exercise 2.5 Developing your subject

Use at least two of the discovery techniques discussed on the preceding pages to develop the subject you selected in Exercise 1.5 (p. 10). (If you completed Exercise 2.3 above, then use one additional technique.) Later exercises for your essay-in-progress will be based on the ideas you generate in this exercise.

2b Developing a thesis

Your readers will expect an essay you write to be focused on a central idea, or **thesis,** to which all the essay's paragraphs, all its general statements and specific information, relate. The thesis is the controlling idea, the main point, the conclusion you have drawn about the evidence you have accumulated. It is the answer to the question you have been posing about your subject, shaped to convey your purpose and your role as a writer.

CULTURE LANGUAGE In some cultures it is considered rude or unnecessary for a writer to state his or her main idea outright or to state it near the beginning. When writing in American schools or workplaces, you can assume that your readers expect a clear and early idea of what you think.

1 Conceiving a thesis statement

A thesis is an idea. Spelling out the idea in a **thesis statement** gives you something concrete to work with. Such a statement, or even the thesis idea itself, probably will not leap fully formed into your head. You may begin with an idea you want to communicate, but you will need to refine that idea to fit the realities of the paper you write. Often you will have to write and rewrite before you come to a conclusion about what you have. For this reason, you may prefer to delay conceiving a thesis statement until you are well into drafting. Instead, you can proceed with a **thesis question** that begins when you try to narrow your subject (pp. 8–9) and sharpens as you discover ideas and information. Either a tentative thesis statement or a thesis question can help you organize your ideas, start drafting, and stay focused when changes inevitably occur during drafting and revision.

As an expression of the thesis, the thesis statement serves five crucial functions and one optional one.

Functions of the thesis statement

- The thesis statement **narrows your subject** to a single, central idea that you want readers to gain from your essay.
- It **claims something specific and significant** about your subject, a claim that requires support.
- It **conveys your purpose for writing**—often explanation or argument.
- It **previews your approach to your audience**, how you will appeal to your readers.
- It **establishes your writer's voice** in the minds of your readers.
- It often concisely **previews the arrangement of ideas**, in which case it can also help you organize your essay.

Here are some examples of thesis questions and answering thesis statements. As assertions, the thesis statements each consist of a topic (usually naming the general subject) and a claim about the topic. Notice how each statement also expresses purpose. Statements 1–3 are **explanatory**: the writers mainly want to explain something to readers, such as the conflicts among fictional characters. Statements 4–6 are **argumentative**: the authors mainly want to convince readers of something, such as that drivers' use of cell phones should be outlawed.

Thesis question	Explanatory thesis statement
1. What are the key conflicts in *The Scarlet Letter*?	Although the conflicts among the three major characters in *The Scarlet Letter* appear dominant, the real conflict each character faces is the internal struggle between doing good and doing evil. [**Topic:** the real conflict each character faces. **Claim:** is the internal struggle between doing good and doing evil.]
2. Why did Abraham Lincoln delay in emancipating the slaves?	Lincoln delayed emancipating any slaves until 1863 because his primary goal was to restore and preserve the Union, with or without slavery. [**Topic:** Lincoln's delay. **Claim:** was caused by his goal of preserving the Union.]
3. What steps can prevent juvenile crime?	Juveniles can be diverted from crime by active learning programs, full-time sports, and intervention by mentors and role models. [**Topic:** juveniles. **Claim:** can be diverted from crime in three ways.]

Thesis question	Argumentative thesis statement
4. Why should drivers' use of cell phones be banned?	Drivers' use of cell phones should be outlawed because people who talk or text and drive at the same time cause accidents. [**Topic**: drivers' use of cell phones. **Claim**: should be outlawed because it causes accidents.]
5. Which school districts should be entitled to federal aid?	As an investment in its own economy, the United States should provide grants to school districts in impoverished areas. [**Topic**: US school aid. **Claim**: should go to school districts in impoverished areas.]
6. Why should strip-mining be controlled?	Strip-mining should be tightly controlled in this region to reduce its pollution of water resources, its destruction of the land, and its devastating effects on people's lives. [**Topic**: strip-mining. **Claim**: should be tightly controlled for three reasons.]

Often the thesis statement predicts the organization of the essay that will follow, as statements 3 and 6 do. For example, the essay that followed from statement 3 had three main points: active learning programs, full-time sports, and mentors and role models. Many students prefer this type of thesis statement because it helps them organize their writing and keep on track during drafting.

2 Drafting and revising a thesis statement

To draft a thesis statement, read over your notes and mark words, phrases, or sentences that stand out as central. Consider your question about your subject. If you have sharpened the question as you generated ideas and information, answering it can get you started.

Question Why did Lincoln delay in emancipating the slaves?

Answer Lincoln's goal was primarily to restore and preserve the Union.

Question To what extent do I agree or disagree with Friedman's argument that students today need better technical training to compete in the global job market?

Answer Based on my mother's experience of having her job outsourced, I disagree with Friedman that better technical training will necessarily give students the skills they need to compete in today's global job market.

Question What can be done to relieve students' frustration over parking at our school?

Answer The school must provide adequate parking for students who drive to school.

The next step is to spell out the answer in a sentence that names the topic and makes a claim about it. Creating this sentence may require several drafts.

Katy Moreno went through a common process in developing her thesis statement on the global job market. She first answered her starting question, as shown in the second pair of examples on the previous page. Then she tried a statement derived from her answer:

> The outsourcing of my mother's job proves that Thomas L. Friedman's advice to improve students' technical training is too narrow.

This statement gave Moreno a sense of direction, and she used it in her first draft (p. 51). At that point, however, she saw that the statement put too little emphasis on her starting topic (*technical training*) and overstated her disagreement with Friedman (*proves . . . is too narrow*). In addition, a reader's comment showed Moreno that her claim wasn't specific: too narrow for what? In her first revision, Moreno tried to emphasize her intended subject:

> Technical training by itself . . .

Then she worked on her claim:

> . . . can be too narrow to produce the communicators and problem solvers needed by contemporary businesses.

This statement clarified the claim (*can be too narrow to produce . . .*) and said why the subject was significant (*. . . communicators and problem solvers needed by contemporary businesses*). However, Moreno had dropped her mother's experience of losing her job to outsourcing, which was a key point in her response to Friedman's essay. Moreno tried again, adding her mother's experience:

> My mother's experience of having her job outsourced showed that technical training by itself can be too narrow to produce the communicators and problem solvers needed by contemporary businesses.

For her final revision, Moreno responded to another reader's suggestion that she state her point of disagreement with Friedman more clearly:

> My mother's experience of having her job outsourced taught a lesson that Thomas L. Friedman overlooks: technical training by itself can be too narrow to produce the communicators and problem solvers needed by contemporary businesses.

Often you must deliberately consider your audience as you draft the thesis statement. One student, Ben Nelson, worked on a thesis based on the answer to the question on the previous page about the lack of student parking at his school. He arrived fairly easily at his claim that the school needed to provide more parking space for students. However, to persuade the school administrators to take action, he needed to focus on them as his audience and revise his thesis statement accordingly. In one revision, he addressed the school administrators using a logical appeal:

> Many students who participate in extracurricular activities and hold after-school jobs must drive to school, and they need places to park.

In his second revision, below, Nelson brought in an emotional appeal as well, and he strengthened his writer's voice:

> The school must provide enough parking spaces to accommodate the many students who must drive to school and to protect all students from otherwise dangerous traffic congestion.

As you draft and revise your thesis statement, keep in mind the following:

- Naming the subject and making a claim about it.
- Clearly communicating your subject and claim to your audience.
- Establishing your writer's voice.

Then check your statement against the following questions:

Checklist for revising the thesis statement

- How well does the **subject** of your statement capture the subject of your paper? What **claim** does your statement make about your subject?
- What is the **significance** of the claim? How does it answer "So what?" and convey your purpose?
- How can the claim be **limited** or made more **specific**? Does it state a single idea and clarify the boundaries of the idea?
- How **unified** is the statement? How does each word and phrase contribute to a single idea about the subject?
- What does the thesis statement suggest about your **appeals** to your audience?
- How well does the statement convey your **writer's voice**?

Here are other examples of thesis statements revised to meet the requirements in the box above:

Original	Revised
Seat belts can save lives, but now carmakers install air bags. [Not unified: how do the two parts of the sentence relate?]	If drivers had used lifesaving seat belts more often, carmakers might not have needed to install air bags.

Original	Revised
Toni Morrison won the Nobel Prize in Literature in 1993. [A statement of fact, not a claim about Morrison's work: what is significant about her winning the prize?]	Toni Morrison's 1993 Nobel Prize in Literature, the first awarded to an African American woman, affirms both the strength of her vivid prose style and the importance of her subject matter.
People should not go on fad diets. [A vague statement that needs limiting with one or more reasons: what's wrong with fad diets?]	Fad diets can be dangerous when they deprive the body of essential nutrients or rely excessively on potentially harmful foods.
Televised sports are different from live sports. [A general statement: how are they different, and why is the difference significant?]	Although television cannot transmit all the excitement of a live game, its close-ups and slow-motion replays reveal much about the players and the strategy of the game.
Television viewing can reduce loneliness, cause laughter, and teach children. [Lacks voice: what is the writer's attitude toward the subject?]	Despite its many faults, television has at least one strong virtue: it provides replacement voices that can ease loneliness, spark healthful laughter, and even educate young children.

Note You may sometimes need more than one sentence for your thesis statement, particularly if it requires some buildup:

> Modern English, especially written English, is full of bad habits that interfere with clear thinking. Getting rid of these habits is a first step to political regeneration. —Adapted from George Orwell, "Politics and the English Language"

However, don't use this leeway to produce a wordy, general, or disunified statement. The two (or more) sentences must build on each other, and the final sentence must present the key assertion of your paper.

Exercise 2.6 Evaluating thesis statements

Evaluate the following thesis statements, considering whether each one is sufficiently significant, specific, and unified. Also consider whether each conveys the writer's voice. Rewrite the statements as necessary to meet these goals.

1. Aggression usually leads to violence, injury, and even death, and we should use it constructively.
2. The religion of Islam is widely misunderstood in the United States.
3. Manners are a kind of social glue.
4. One episode of a radio talk show amply illustrates both the appeal of such shows and their silliness.

5. The poem is about motherhood.

Exercise 2.7 Considering your past work: Developing a thesis

Have you been aware in the past of focusing your essays on a central idea, or thesis? Have you found it more efficient to try to pin down your idea early or to let it evolve during drafting? To what extent has a thesis helped or hindered you in shaping your draft?

Exercise 2.8 Drafting and revising your own thesis statement

Continuing from Exercise 2.5 (p. 29), write a thesis statement for your essay-in-progress. As much as possible at this point, your statement should be significant, specific, and unified, and it should convey your attitude toward your subject.

2c Organizing ideas

An effective essay has a recognizable shape—an arrangement of parts that guides readers, helping them see how ideas and details relate to each other and contribute to the whole. You may sometimes let an effective organization emerge over one or more drafts. But many writers find that organizing ideas to some extent before drafting can provide a helpful sense of direction, as a map can help a driver negotiate a half-familiar system of roads. If you feel uncertain about the course your essay should follow or have a complicated topic with many parts, devising a shape for your material can clarify your options.

Before you begin organizing your material, look over all the writing you've done so far—freewriting, clustering, notes from reading, whatever. Either on paper or on a computer, pull together a master list of all the ideas and details you think you might want to include. You can add to or subtract from the list as you think about shape.

1 Distinguishing the general and the specific

To organize material for an essay, you need to distinguish general and specific ideas and see the relations between ideas. **General** and **specific** refer to the number of instances or objects included in a group signified by a word. The "ladder" below illustrates a general-to-specific hierarchy.

Most general

↑ life form
plant
flowering plant
rose
American Beauty rose
↓ Uncle Dan's prize-winning American Beauty rose

Most specific

Here are some tips for arranging the ideas in your preliminary writing:

- **Underline, boldface, or circle the most general ideas.** These are the ideas that offer the main support for your thesis statement. They will be more general than the evidence that in turn supports them.

- **Make connections between each general idea and the more specific details that support it.** On paper, start with a fresh sheet, write each general idea down with space beneath it, and add specific information in the appropriate spaces. On a computer, rearrange supporting information under more general points. Your word processor may include a Comment function that allows you to add notes about connections.

- **Respect the meanings of ideas.** Think through the implications of ideas as you sort them. Otherwise, your hierarchies could become jumbled, with *rose,* for instance, illogically subordinated to *animal,* or *life form* somehow subordinated to *rose.*

- **Remove information that doesn't fit.** If you worry about losing deleted information, transfer the notes to a separate sheet of paper or computer file.

- **Fill holes where support seems skimpy.** If you recognize a hole but don't know what to fill it with, try using a discovery technique such as freewriting or clustering, or go back to your research sources.

- **Experiment with various arrangements of general ideas and supporting information.** Seek an order that presents your material clearly and logically. On paper, you can cut the master list apart and paste or tape each general idea and its support on a separate piece of paper. Then try different orders for the pages. On a computer, first save the master list and duplicate it. To move material around, select a block of text and either copy and then paste it where you want it or (a little quicker) drag the selected text to where you want it.

2 Choosing an organizing tool

Some writers view outlines as chores and straitjackets, but they need not be dull or confining. There are different kinds of outlines, some more flexible than others. All of them can enlarge and clarify your thinking, showing you patterns of general and specific, suggesting proportions, and highlighting gaps or overlaps in coverage.

Many writers use outlines not only before but also after drafting—to check the underlying structure of the draft when revising it (see p. 54). No matter when it's made, though, an outline can be changed to reflect changes in your thinking. View any outline you make as a tentative sketch, not as a fixed paint-by-numbers diagram.

A scratch or informal outline

For many essays, especially those with a fairly straightforward structure, a simple listing of ideas and perhaps their support may provide adequate direction for your writing.

A **scratch outline** lists the key points of the paper in the order they will be covered. Here is Katy Moreno's scratch outline for her essay on the global job market:

Thesis statement

My mother's experience of having her job outsourced taught a lesson that Thomas L. Friedman overlooks: technical training by itself can be too narrow to produce the communicators and problem solvers needed by contemporary businesses.

Scratch outline

Mom's outsourcing experience
    Excellent tech skills
    Salary too high compared to overseas tech workers
    Lack of planning + communication skills, unlike managers who kept jobs
Well-rounded education to protect vs. outsourcing
    Tech training, as Friedman says
    Also, experience in communication, problem solving, other management skills

Moreno put more into this outline than its simplicity might imply, not only working out an order for her ideas but also sketching their implications.

An **informal outline** is usually more detailed than a scratch outline, including key general points and the specific evidence for them. A student's informal outline appears below.

Thesis statement

After Home Inc.'s hiring practices were exposed in the media, the company avoided a scandal with policy changes and a well-publicized outreach to employees and consumers.

Informal outline

Background on scandal
    Previous hiring practices
    Media exposure and public response (brief)
Policy changes
    Application forms
    Interviewing procedures
    Training of personnel
Outreach to employees
    Signs and letters
    Meetings and workshops
Outreach to consumers
    Press conference
    Store signs
    Advertising—print and radio

A tree diagram

In a **tree diagram,** ideas and details branch out in increasing specificity. Like any outline, the diagram can warn of gaps, overlaps, and digressions. But unlike more linear outlines, it can be supplemented and extended indefinitely, so it is easy to alter for new ideas and arrangements discovered during drafting and revision.

Below is a tree diagram by Johanna Abrams, based on her earlier brainstorming about a summer job (p. 25) and the following thesis statement:

Thesis statement

Two months working in a large government agency taught me that an office's pecking order should be respected.

Tree diagram

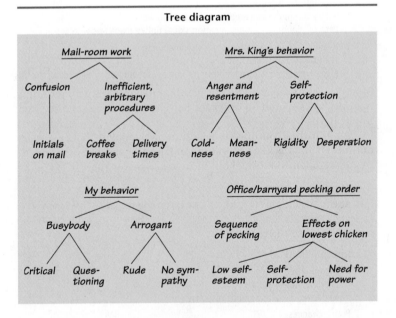

Each main part of the four-part diagram represents a different general idea about the summer-job experience. Within each part, information grows more specific as it branches downward.

A tree diagram or other visual map can be especially useful for planning a project for the Web. The diagram can help you lay out the organization of your project and its links and later can serve as a site map for your readers. (For more on composing for the Web, see pp. 796–802.)

A formal outline

For complex topics requiring complex arrangements of ideas and support, you may want or be required to construct a **formal outline.** More rigidly arranged and more detailed than other outlines, a formal outline not only lays out main ideas and their support but also shows the relative importance of all the essay's elements and how they connect with one another.

Note Because of its structure, a formal outline can be an excellent tool for planning a revision. For instance, you might use an outline to check that your organization is logical or to see how a new section might fit in. Katy Moreno created the following formal outline to plan expansions and other changes that were suggested by readers of her first draft.

Thesis statement

My mother's experience of having her job outsourced taught a lesson that Thomas L. Friedman overlooks: technical training by itself can be too narrow to produce the communicators and problem solvers needed by contemporary businesses.

Formal outline

I. Summary of Friedman's article
   A. Reasons for outsourcing
      1. Improved technology and access
      2. Well-educated workers
      3. Productive workers
      4. Lower wages
   B. Need for improved technical training in US
II. Mother's experience
   A. Outsourcing of job
      1. Mother's education, experience, performance
      2. Employer's cost savings
   B. Retention of managers' jobs
      1. Planning skills
      2. Communication skills
III. Conclusions about ideal education
   A. Needs of US businesses
      1. Technical skills
      2. Management skills
         a. Communication
         b. Problem solving
         c. Versatility
   B. Personal goals
      1. Technical training
      2. English and history courses for management skills

Moreno's outline illustrates several principles of outlining that can help to ensure completeness, balance, and clear relationships.

Principles of the formal outline

- Labels and indentions indicate order and relative importance.
- Sections and subsections reflect logical relationships.
- Topics of equal generality appear in parallel headings.
- Each subdivision has at least two parts.
- Headings are expressed in parallel grammatical form.
- The introduction and conclusion may be omitted (though not, of course, from the essay).

These principles largely depend on distinguishing between the general and the specific. (See pp. 35–36.)

- **All the outline's parts are systematically indented and labeled.** Roman numerals (I, II) label primary divisions of the essay, followed by capital letters (A, B) for secondary divisions, Arabic numerals (1, 2) for principal supporting points, and small letters (a, b) for details. Each succeeding level contains more specific information than the one before it.
- **The outline divides the material into several groups.** A list like the one following needs tighter, more logical groups to show the relationships between A and B and between C and D. (Compare this example with part III of Moreno's actual outline.)

    III. Conclusions about ideal education
    - A. Business needs for technical skills
    - B. Needs for management skills such as communication and problem solving
    - C. Personal goal of technical training
    - D. Additional courses for management skills

- **Within each part of the outline, distinct topics of equal generality appear in parallel headings,** with the same indention and numbering or lettering. In the following example, points 3, 4, and 5 are more specific than point 2, not equally general, so they should appear as subheadings a, b, and c under it. (See section III.A of Moreno's outline.)

    - A. Needs of US businesses
        1. Technical skills
        2. Management skills
        3. Communication
        4. Problem solving
        5. Versatility

- **All subdivided headings in the outline break into at least two parts** because a topic cannot logically be divided into only one part. The following example violates this principle:

    B. Personal goals
       1. Technical training along with other courses for management skills

Any single subdivision should be matched with another subdivision (as in section III.B of Moreno's actual outline), combined with the heading above it, or rechecked for its relevance to the heading above it.

■ **All headings are expressed in parallel grammatical form** (see pp. 400–04 on parallelism). Moreno's is a **topic outline,** in which the headings consist of a noun (*summary, reasons,* and the like) with modifiers (*of Friedman's essay, improved,* and the like). In a **sentence outline** headings are expressed as sentences, as in the following rewrite of part III.A of Moreno's outline.

III. Friedman's article and my mother's experience lead me to conclusions about the ideal education.
    A. US businesses have dual needs for the jobs they keep here.
       1. They need employees with technical training.
       2. They need employees with management skills.

See pages 669–70 for a complete sentence outline.

■ **The outline covers only the body of the essay, omitting the introduction and the conclusion.** The beginning and the ending are important in the essay itself, but you need not include them in the outline unless you are required to do so or you anticipate special problems with their organization.

3 Choosing a structure

Introduction, body, and conclusion

Most essays share a basic shape:

■ **The *introduction,* usually a paragraph or two, draws readers into the world of the essay.** At a minimum, it announces and clarifies the topic. Often it ends with the thesis statement, making a commitment that the rest of the essay delivers on. (See pp. 105–08 for more on introductions.)

■ **The *body* of the essay develops the thesis and thus fulfills the commitment of the introduction.** The paragraphs in the body develop the general points that support the thesis—the items that would be labeled with Roman numerals and capital letters in a formal outline like the one on page 39. These general points are like the legs of a table supporting the top, the thesis. Each general point may take a paragraph or more, with the bulk of the content providing the details, examples, and reasons (the wood of the table) to support the general point and thus the thesis.

■ **The *conclusion* gives readers something to take away from the essay**—a summary of ideas, for instance, or a suggested course of action. (See pp. 108–10 for more on conclusions.)

This basic shape applies mainly to traditional essays. A composition for the Web probably will have a more flexible structure and will lack a formal conclusion. See pages 796–802 for more on composing for the Web.

CULTURE LANGUAGE If you are not used to reading and writing American academic prose, its pattern of introduction-body-conclusion and the particular schemes discussed below may seem unfamiliar. For instance, instead of introductions that focus quickly on the topic and thesis, you may be used to openings that establish personal connections with readers or that approach the thesis indirectly. And instead of body paragraphs that first emphasize general points and then support those points with specific evidence, you may be used to general statements without support (because writers can assume that readers will supply the evidence themselves) or to evidence without explanation (because writers can assume that readers will infer the general points themselves). When writing American academic prose, you need to take into account readers' expectations for directness and for the statement and support of general points.

Organizing the body by space or time

Two organizational schemes—spatial and chronological—grow naturally out of the topic. A **spatial organization** is especially appropriate for essays that describe a place, an object, or a person. Following the way people normally survey something, you move through space from a chosen starting point to other features of the subject. Describing a building, for instance, you might begin with an impression of the whole, then scan exterior details from top to bottom, and then describe interior spaces.

A **chronological organization** reports events as they occurred in time, usually from first to last. This pattern, like spatial organization, corresponds to readers' own experiences and expectations. It suits an essay in which you do one of the following:

- **Recount a sequence of events,** such as a championship baseball game or the Battle of Gettysburg.
- **Explain a process from beginning to end**—for instance, how to run a marathon or how a tree converts carbon dioxide to oxygen.
- **Explain the causes that led to an effect,** such as the lobbying that helped to push a bill through the legislature. Alternatively, explain how a cause, such as a flood or a book, had multiple effects.
- **Tell a story about yourself or someone else.**
- **Provide background**—for instance, the making of a film you are analyzing or the procedure used in an experiment you are reporting.

Schemes for organizing ideas in an essay

- Space
- Time
- Emphasis

General to specific	Increasing importance (climax)
Specific to general	Decreasing familiarity
Problem-solution	Increasing complexity

Organizing the body for emphasis

Some organizational schemes must be imposed on ideas and information to aid readers' understanding and achieve a desired emphasis.

General to specific

Two ways of organizing essays depend on the distinction between the general and the specific, discussed on pages 35–36. The **general-to-specific scheme** is common in expository and argumentative essays that start with a general discussion of the main points and then proceed to specific examples, facts, or other evidence. The following thesis statement forecasts a general-to-specific organization:

> As an investment in its own economy, the United States should provide tuition grants to school districts in impoverished areas.

The body of the essay might first elaborate on the basic argument and then provide the supporting data.

Specific to general

Sometimes you may anticipate that readers will not appreciate or agree with your general ideas before they see the support for them—for instance, in an expository essay that presents a unique way of looking at common experience, or in an argumentative essay that takes an unpopular view. In these cases a **specific-to-general scheme** can arouse readers' interest in specific examples or other evidence, letting the evidence build to statements of more general ideas. The following thesis statement could be developed in this way:

> Although most of us are unaware of the public relations campaigns directed at us, they can significantly affect the way we think and live.

The writer might devote most of the essay to a single specific example of a public relations campaign and then explain more generally how the example typifies public relations campaigns.

Problem-solution

Many arguments use a **problem-solution scheme:** first outline a problem that needs solving; then propose a solution. (If the solution involves steps toward a goal, it may be arranged chronologically.) The following thesis statement announces a problem-solution paper:

> To improve the tutoring services, the department should train tutors to work more effectively with groups of students.

Climax

A common scheme in both explanations and arguments is the **climactic organization,** in which ideas unfold in order of increasing drama or importance to a climax. For example, the following thesis statement lists three effects of strip-mining in order of their increasing severity, and the essay would cover them in the same order:

> Strip-mining should be tightly controlled in this region to reduce its pollution of water resources, its destruction of the land, and its devastating effects on people's lives.

As this example suggests, the climactic organization works well in arguments because it leaves readers with the most important point freshest in their minds. In exposition such an arrangement can create suspense and thus hold readers' attention.

Familiarity or complexity

Expository essays can also be arranged to take account of readers' knowledge of the subject. An essay on the effects of air pollution might proceed from **most familiar to least familiar**—from effects readers are likely to know to ones they may not know. Similarly, an explanation of animals' nervous systems might proceed from **simplest to most complex,** so that the explanation of each nervous system provides a basis for readers to understand the more difficult one following.

4 | Checking for unity and coherence

In conceiving your organization and writing your essay, you should be aware of two qualities of effective writing that relate to organization: unity and coherence. When you perceive that someone's writing "flows well," you are probably appreciating these two qualities. An essay has **unity** if all its parts relate to and support the thesis statement. Check for unity with these questions:

■ Is each main section relevant to the main idea (thesis) of the essay?

■ Within main sections, does each example or detail support the principal idea of that section?

An essay has **coherence** if readers can see the relations among parts and move easily from one thought to the next. Check for coherence with these questions:

■ Do the ideas follow in a clear sequence?
■ Are the parts of the essay logically connected?
■ Are the connections clear and smooth?

A unified and coherent outline will not necessarily guide you to a unified and coherent essay because so much can change during drafting. Thus you shouldn't be too hard on your outline, in case a seemingly wayward idea proves useful. But do cut obvious digressions and rearrange material that clearly needs moving.

Sample essay

The following essay illustrates some ways of achieving unity and coherence (highlighted in the annotations).

A Picture of Hyperactivity

Hyperactive salespeople improve profits. Hyperactive committee members can run things efficiently. But when children are hyperactive, there are no benefits. A collage of those who must cope with hyperactivity in children—doctors, families, and the children themselves—is a picture of frustration, anger, and loss.

Introduction establishing subject of essay

Thesis statement

The first part of the collage is the doctors. In their terminology, the word *hyperactivity* has been replaced by *ADHD*, attention-deficit hyperactivity disorder, to describe children who are abnormally or excessively busy. But doctors do not fully understand the problem, and so they differ over how to treat it. Some recommend a special diet, others recommend behavior-modifying drugs, and still others, who do not consider ADHD a medical problem, recommend psychotherapy. The result is a merry-go-round of tests, often inconclusive, that frustrate doctors and confuse children and their families.

Paragraph idea, linked to thesis statement

Paragraph developed with evidence supporting its idea

For families, the second part of the collage, a diagnosis of ADHD means worry and disruption. Parents are often anxious about doing what's best for their ADHD child, and they are frustrated when the child doesn't improve. They may feel anger that spills over to the child or to the whole family. Siblings can feel jealous of the attention the ADHD child receives, embarrassed by the child's erratic behavior in public, guilty about the jealousy and embarrassment, and above all helpless. As the sister of a child with ADHD, I have felt all of these emotions.

Paragraph idea, linked to thesis statement

Paragraph developed with evidence supporting its idea

Transition	The weight of ADHD, however, does not rest on the doctors and
Paragraph idea, linked to thesis statement	families. The darkest part of the collage belongs to the children. From early childhood they may be dragged from doctor to doctor, medicated until they're numb, and constantly discussed by physicians, teachers, neighbors,
Paragraph developed with evidence supporting its idea	and even strangers on the street. They may be highly intelligent, but they do poorly in school because of their short attention spans. Their peers dislike them because of their temper and their unwillingness to follow rules. Even their pets mistrust them because of their erratic behavior. They feel isolated and unconfident.
Conclusion echoing thesis statement, summarizing, and looking ahead	Taken as a whole, the collage is dark and somber. *ADHD* is a term with uncertain, unattractive, and bitter associations. But living with my brother, I have also seen a bright spot in the picture. Inside every ADHD child is a loving, trusting, and calm person waiting to be recognized.

—Tara Devereaux (student)

Unity and coherence within paragraphs

The unity and coherence of writing begin in its paragraphs, so the two concepts are treated in greater detail in Chapter 4. You may want to consult several sections in particular before you begin drafting:

- **The topic sentence and unity** (pp. 75–78)
- **Transitions and coherence** (pp. 80–91, 110–11)
- **Linking paragraphs in the essay** (p. 112)

Unity and coherence on the Web

Unity and coherence may seem unimportant in compositions for the Web, in which entire documents are linked to each other so that it's easy to move among them. However, precisely because the Web is such a fluid medium, you risk losing or confusing your readers if you don't consider unity and coherence. Your project should have a clear purpose and clear ideas relating to that purpose, and the connections between ideas should be spelled out to orient readers. (For more on composing for the Web, see pp. 796–802.)

Exercise 2.9   Organizing ideas

The following list of ideas was extracted by a student from freewriting he did for a brief paper on soccer in the United States. Using his thesis statement as a guide, pick out the general ideas and arrange the relevant specific points under them. In some cases you may have to infer general ideas to cover specific points in the list.

Thesis statement

Although its growth in the United States has been slow and halting, professional soccer may finally be poised to become a major American sport.

List of ideas

In countries of South and Latin America, soccer is the favorite sport.

In the United States the success of a sport depends largely on its ability to attract huge TV audiences.

Soccer was not often presented on US television.

In 2007 and 2010, the World Cup final was broadcast on ABC and on Spanish-language Univision.

In the past, professional soccer could not get a foothold in the United States because of poor TV coverage and lack of financial backing.

The growing Hispanic population in the United States could help soccer grow as well.

Investors have poured hundreds of millions of dollars into the top US professional league.

Potential fans did not have a chance to see soccer games.

Failures of early start-up leagues made potential backers wary of new ventures.

Recently, the outlook for professional soccer has changed dramatically.

In 2010, the US television audience for the World Cup US-Ghana match was larger than the audience for baseball's World Series.

Exercise 2.10 Creating a formal outline

Use your arrangement of general ideas and specific points from Exercise 2.9 as the basis for a formal topic or sentence outline. Follow the principles given on pages 39–41.

Exercise 2.11 Considering your past work: Organizing ideas

What has been your experience with organizing your writing? Many writers find it difficult. If you do, too, can you say why? What kinds of outlines or other organizing tools have you used? Which have been helpful and which have not?

Exercise 2.12 Organizing your own essay

Continuing from Exercise 2.8 (p. 35), choose an appropriate organization for your essay-in-progress. Then experiment with organizing tools by preparing a tree diagram or other visual map or a scratch, informal, or formal outline.

3

Drafting and Revising

The separation of drafting and revising from the planning and development discussed in Chapters 1 and 2 is somewhat artificial because the stages almost always overlap during the writing process. Indeed, if you compose on a computer, you may not experience any boundaries between stages at all. Still, your primary goal during the writing process will usually shift from gathering and shaping information to forming connected sentences and paragraphs in a draft and then restructuring and rewriting the draft.

3a | Writing the first draft

The only correct drafting style is the one that works for you. Generally, though, the freer and more fluid you are, the better. Some writers draft and revise at the same time, but most let themselves go during drafting and *especially* do not worry about errors. Drafting is the occasion to find and convey meaning through the act of writing. If you fear making mistakes while drafting, that fear will choke your ideas. You draft only for yourself, so errors do not matter. Write freely until you have worked out what you want to say; *then* focus on any mistakes you may have made.

Starting to draft sometimes takes courage, even for seasoned professionals. Students and pros alike find easy ways to procrastinate—checking e-mail, talking with friends, napping. Such procrastination may actually help you if you let ideas for writing simmer at the same time. At some point, though, enough is enough: the deadline looms; you've got to get started. If the blankness still stares back at you, then try one of the following techniques for unblocking.

Ways to start drafting

- **Read over what you've already written**—notes, outlines, and so on. Immediately start your draft with whatever comes to mind.

Visit *www.mycomplab.com* for more resources and exercises on drafting, revising, editing, and

collaborating.

- **Freewrite** (see p. 23).
- **Write scribbles or type nonsense** until words you can use start coming.
- **Pretend you're writing to a friend about your subject.**
- **Describe an image that represents your subject**—a physical object, a facial expression, two people arguing over something, a giant machine gouging the earth for a mine, whatever.
- **Write a paragraph.** Explain what you think your essay will be about when you finish it.
- **Skip the opening and start in the middle.** Or write the conclusion.
- **Start writing the part that you understand best or feel most strongly about.** Using your outline, divide your essay into chunks—say, one for the introduction, another for the first point, and so on. One of these chunks may call out to be written.

Drafting

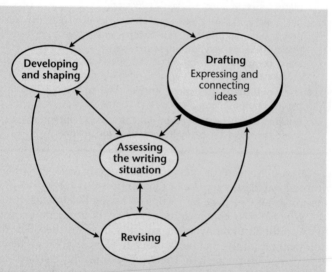

When you draft an essay, you work toward expressing and connecting the ideas you've developed. If you change direction or run out of ideas during drafting, you can always circle back to renew your purpose, discover new ideas, or rethink your thesis.

You should find some momentum once you've started writing. If not, however, or if your energy flags, try one or more of the following techniques to keep moving ahead.

Ways to *keep* drafting

- **Set aside enough time for yourself.** For a brief essay, a first draft is likely to take at least an hour or two.
- **Work in a quiet place.**
- **Make yourself comfortable.**
- **If you must stop working, write down what you expect to do next.** Then you can pick up where you stopped with minimal disruption.
- **Be as fluid as possible, and don't worry about mistakes.** Spontaneity will allow your attitudes toward your subject to surface naturally in your sentences, and it will also make you receptive to ideas and relations you haven't seen before. Mistakes will be easier to find and correct later, when you're not also trying to create.
- **Keep going.** Skip over sticky spots; leave a blank if you can't find the right word; put alternative ideas or phrasings in brackets so that you can consider them later. If an idea pops out of nowhere but doesn't seem to fit in, quickly write it into the draft and bracket or boldface it for later attention. Use an asterisk (*) or some other symbol to mark places where you feel blocked or uncertain.
- **Resist self-criticism.** Don't worry about your style, grammar, spelling, punctuation, and the like. Don't worry about what your readers will think. These are very important matters, but save them for revision. On a computer, turn off automatic spelling- or grammar-checking functions if they distract you, or try invisible writing (p. 24).
- **Use your thesis statement and outline** to remind you of your planned purpose, organization, and content.
- **But don't feel constrained by your thesis and outline.** If your writing leads you in a more interesting direction, follow.

If you write on a computer, frequently save the text you're drafting—at least every five or ten minutes and every time you leave the computer. See page 57 for tips on saving documents.

Whether you compose on paper or on a computer, you may find it difficult to tell whether a first draft is finished. The distinction between drafts can be significant because creating text is different from rethinking it and because your teacher may ask you and your classmates to submit your drafts, either on paper or over a computer network, so that others can give you feedback on them. For your own revision or others' feedback, you might consider a draft finished for any number of reasons: perhaps you've reached the assigned length and have run out of ideas; perhaps you find yourself writing the conclusion; perhaps you've stopped adding content and are just tinkering with words.

Sample first draft

Following is Katy Moreno's first-draft response to Thomas L. Friedman's "It's a Flat World, After All." As part of her assignment,

Moreno showed the draft to four classmates, whose suggestions for revision appear in the margin of this draft. They used the Comment function of *Microsoft Word*, which allows users to add comments without inserting words into the document's text. (Notice that the classmates ignore errors in grammar and punctuation, concentrating instead on larger issues such as thesis, clarity of ideas, and unity.)

Title?

In "It's a Flat World, After All," Thomas L. Friedman argues that, most US students are not preparing themselves as well as they should to compete in today's economy. Not like students in India, China, and other countries are. The outsourcing of my mother's job proves that Thomas L. Friedman's advice to improve students' technical training is too narrow.

Comment [Jared]: Your mother's job being outsourced is interesting, but your introduction seems rushed.

Comment [Rabia]: The end of your thesis statement is a little unclear—too narrow for what?

Friedman describes a "flat" world where recent technology like the Internet and wireless communication make it possible for college graduates all over the globe, in particular in India and China, to get jobs that once were gotten by graduates of US colleges and universities. He argues that US students need more math and science in order to compete.

Comment [Erin]: Can you include the reasons Friedman gives for overseas students' success?

I came to college with first-hand knowledge of globalization and outsourcing. My mother, who worked for sixteen years in the field of information technology (IT), was laid off six months ago when the company she worked for decided to outsource much of its IT work to a company based in India. My mother majored in computer science, had sixteen years of experience, and her bosses always gave her good reviews. She never expected to be laid off and was surprised when she was. She wasn't laid off because of her background and performance. In fact, my mother had a very strong background in math and science and years of training and job experience. The reason was because her salary and benefits cost the company more than outsourcing her job did. Which hurt my family financially, as you can imagine.

Comment [Nathaniel]: Tighten this paragraph to avoid repetition? Also, how does your mother's experience relate to Friedman and your thesis?

A number of well-paid people in the IT department where my mother worked, namely IT managers, were not laid off. As my mother explained at the time, they kept their jobs because they were better at planning and they communicated better, they were better writers and speakers than my mother.

Comment [Erin]: What were the managers better at planning for?

Like my mother, I am more comfortable in front of a computer than I am in front of a group of people. I planned to major in computer science. Since my mother lost her job, though, I have decided to take courses in English and history too, where the classes will require me to do different kinds of work. When I enter the job market, my well-rounded education will make me a more attractive job candidate, and, will help me to be a versatile, productive employee.

> **Comment [Nathaniel]:** Can you be more specific about the kinds of work you'll need to do?

> **Comment [Rabia]:** Can you work this point into your thesis?

We know from our history that Americans have been innovative, hard-working people. We students have educational opportunities to compete in the global economy, but we must use our time in college wisely. As Thomas L. Friedman says, my classmates and I need to be ready for a rapidly changing future. We will have to work hard each day, which means being prepared for class, getting the best grades we can, and making the most of each class. Our futures depend on the decisions we make today.

> **Comment [Jared]:** Conclusion seems to go off in a new direction. Friedman mentions hard work, but it hasn't been your focus before.

> **Comment [Rabia]:** Don't forget your works cited.

Exercise 3.1 Analyzing a first draft

Compare Moreno's draft with the previous step in her planning (her scratch outline) on page 37. List the places in the draft where the act of drafting led Moreno to rearrange her information, add or delete material, or explore new ideas. Mark Moreno's thesis statement and each key idea developing the thesis. Note places where you think the ideas could be clearer or better supported.

Exercise 3.2 Considering your past work: Drafting

Think back over a recent writing experience. At what point in the writing process did you begin drafting? How did drafting go—smoothly, haltingly, painfully, painlessly? If you had difficulties, what were they? If you didn't, why do you think not?

Exercise 3.3 Drafting your essay

Prepare a draft of the essay you began in Chapters 1 and 2. Use your thesis statement and your outline as guides, but don't be unduly constrained by them. Concentrate on opening up options, not on closing them down. Do not, above all, worry about mistakes.

3b Revising the first draft

Revision literally means "re-seeing"—looking anew at ideas and details, their relationships and arrangement, the degree to which they work or don't work for the thesis. While drafting, you focus inwardly, concentrating on pulling your topic out of yourself. In revising, you

Revising

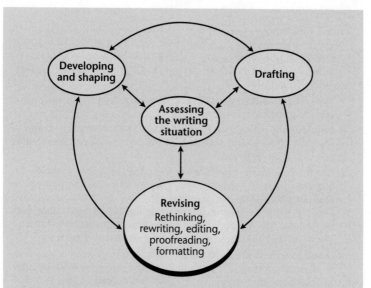

Often the process of revising requires you to rethink your purpose, clarify your thesis statement, develop more ideas, or reorganize. Save editing and proofreading until you are satisfied with the overall focus, development, and shape of your draft.

look out to your readers, trying to anticipate how they will see your work. You adopt a critical perspective toward your work, examining it as a pole-vaulter or dancer would examine a video of his or her performance. (Writing teachers often ask students to read each other's drafts partly to develop this critical perspective. See p. 69 for more on such collaboration.)

1 Gaining distance from your work

Reading your own work critically can be difficult. Changing or even deleting material that you've worked hard to express can be still more difficult. The key is to gain some objectivity toward your writing. The following techniques may help.

Ways to gain distance from your work

■ **Take a break after finishing the draft.** A few hours may be enough; a whole night or day is preferable. The break will clear your mind, relax you, and give you some objectivity.

(continued)

Ways to gain distance from your work
(continued)

- **Ask someone to read and react to your draft.** Many writing teachers ask their students to submit their first drafts so that the teacher and, often, the other members of the class can serve as an audience to help guide revision. (See also pp. 71–72 on receiving and benefiting from comments.)
- **Type a handwritten draft.** The act of transcription can reveal gaps in content or problems in structure.
- **Print out a word-processed draft.** You'll be able to view all pages of the draft at once, and the different medium can reveal weaknesses you didn't see on screen.
- **Outline your draft.** Highlight the main points supporting the thesis, and write these sentences down separately in outline form. (If you're working on a computer, you can copy and paste the sentences.) Then examine the outline you've made for logical order, gaps, and digressions. A formal outline can be especially illuminating because of its careful structure. (See pp. 37–41 for a discussion of outlining.)
- **Listen to your draft.** Read the draft out loud to yourself or a relative or classmate, record and listen to it, or have someone read the draft to you. Experiencing your words with ears instead of eyes can alter your perceptions.
- **Ease the pressure.** Don't try to re-see everything in your draft at once. Use a checklist like the one on p. 56, making a separate pass through the draft for each item.

2 Revising, then editing

Strictly speaking, revision includes editing—refining the manner of expression to improve clarity or style or to correct errors. In this chapter, though, revision and editing are treated separately to stress their differences: in revision you deal with the underlying meaning and structure of your essay; in editing you deal with its surface. By making separate drafts beyond the first—a revised one and then an edited one—you'll be less likely to waste time tinkering with sentences that you end up cutting, and you'll avoid the temptation to substitute editing for more substantial revision.

The temptation to edit while revising can be especially attractive on a computer because it's easy to alter copy. Indeed, writers sometimes find themselves editing compulsively, spinning their wheels with changes that cease to have any marked effect on meaning or clarity and that may in fact sap the writing of energy. Planning to revise and then to edit encourages you to look beyond the confines of the screen so that deeper issues of meaning and structure aren't lost to surface matters such as word choice and sentence arrangement.

3 Titling your essay

The revision stage is a good time to consider a title. After drafting, you have a clearer sense of your direction, and the attempt to sum up your essay in a title phrase can help you focus sharply on your topic, purpose, and audience.

Here are suggestions for titling an essay:

- *A descriptive title* **is almost always appropriate and is often expected for academic writing.** It announces the topic clearly, accurately, and as briefly as possible. The final title of Katy Moreno's essay is an example: "Can We Compete? College Education for the Global Economy." Other examples include "Images of Lost Identity in *North by Northwest*," "An Experiment in Small-Group Dynamics," "Why Lincoln Delayed Emancipating the Slaves," and "Structure in 'A Rose for Emily.'"

- *A suggestive title* —**the kind often found in popular magazines— may be appropriate for more informal writing.** Examples include "Making Peace" (for an essay on the Peace Corps) and Thomas L. Friedman's "It's a Flat World, After All" (on the global job market). For a more suggestive title, Moreno might have chosen "Training for the New World" or "Education for a Flat World" (echoing Friedman's title). A suggestive title conveys the writer's attitude and main concerns but not the precise topic, thereby pulling readers into the essay to learn more. A source for such a title may be a familiar phrase, a fresh image, or a significant expression from the essay itself.

- **A title tells readers how big the topic is.** For Moreno's essay, the title "Globalization and Jobs" or "Competing in Today's Job Market" would have been too broad, whereas "Outsourcing Our Jobs" or "The Importance of a Broad Education" would have been too narrow because each deals with only part of the paper's content.

- **A title should not restate the assignment or the thesis statement,** as in "The Trouble with Thomas L. Friedman's View of the Global Job Market" or "What I Think About Technical Training and Today's Job Market."

For more information on essay titles, see pages 351–52 (avoiding reference to the title in the opening of the paper), 485 (capitalizing words in a title), and 665 (formatting a title in the final paper).

4 Using a revision checklist

Set aside at least as much time to revise your essay as you took to draft it. Plan on going through the draft several times to answer the questions in the checklist on the next page and to resolve any problems. (If you need additional information on any of the topics in the checklist, refer to the page numbers given in parentheses.) Note that the checklist can also help you if you have been asked to comment on another writer's draft (see pp. 70–71).

Checklist for revision

See also specific revision checklists for arguments (p. 213), research papers (p. 618), and literary analyses (p. 709).

Purpose
What is the essay's purpose? Does that purpose conform to the assignment? Is it consistent throughout the paper? (See pp. 10–12.)

Thesis
What is the thesis of the essay? Where does it become clear? How well do thesis and paper match: Does the paper stray from the thesis? Does it fulfill the commitment of the thesis? (See pp. 29–34.)

Structure
What are the main points of the paper? (List them.) How well does each support the thesis? How effective is their arrangement for the paper's purpose? (See pp. 35–36, 41–45.)

Development
How well do details, examples, and other evidence support each main point? Where, if at all, might readers find support skimpy or have trouble understanding the content? (See pp. 18–28, 93–94.)

Voice
How clearly can readers hear your writer's voice? What role will they see you as playing? What tone will they hear? How appropriate is your voice for your subject, purpose, and audience? (See pp. 16–17.)

Unity
What does each sentence and paragraph contribute to the thesis? Where, if at all, do digressions occur? Should they be cut, or can they be rewritten to support the thesis? (See pp. 44–46, 75–78.)

Coherence
How clearly and smoothly does the paper flow? Where does it seem rough or awkward? Can any transitions be improved? (See pp. 44–46, 80–82.)

Title, introduction, conclusion
How accurately and interestingly does the title reflect the essay's content? (See p. 55.)
How well does the introduction engage and focus readers' attention? (See pp. 105–08.)
How effective is the conclusion in providing a sense of completion? (See pp. 108–10.)

5 | Revising on a computer

Word processors have removed the mechanical drudgery of revising by hand or on a typewriter, but they have also complicated the process: you must conscientiously save your changes and manage the files you create, both discussed below. At the same time, like the more cumbersome revision methods, word processors allow you to display changes as you make them.

Saving changes

Computers malfunction frequently. You can avoid losing your work by taking two precautions:

- **Save your work every five to ten minutes.** Most word processors have an Auto Save function that will save your work automatically as you type, at the interval you specify. Still, get in the habit of saving manually whenever you make major changes.
- **After doing any major work on a project, create a backup version of the file.** Use a second hard drive, a removable disk, or a removable flash drive.

Displaying changes

You can keep track of the revisions you make in a document with an option often called Track Changes and usually found under the Tools or File menu. The function highlights additions and deletions so they're easy to spot (see Katy Moreno's revised draft on the next page). Tracking changes may encourage you to revise more freely because you can always revert to your original text. You can weigh the original and revised versions as you view them side by side. You can also evaluate the kinds of changes you are making. For instance, if during revision you see only minor surface alterations (word substitutions, added punctuation, and the like), then you might consider whether and where to read more deeply for more fundamental changes.

3c | Examining a sample revision

Katy Moreno was satisfied with her first draft: she had her ideas down, and the arrangement seemed logical. Still, from the revision checklist she knew the draft needed work, and her classmates' comments (pp. 51–52) highlighted what she needed to focus on. The following revised draft shows Moreno's changes in response to these comments. Moreno used the Track Changes function on her word processor, so that deletions are crossed out and additions are in blue.

<table>
<tr>
<td>

Descriptive title names topic and forecasts approach.

</td>
<td>

Can We Compete?

College Education for the Global Economy

~~Title?~~

</td>
</tr>
</table>

Today's students cannot miss news stories about globalization of the economy and outsourcing of jobs, but are students aware of how these trends are affecting the job market? In "It's a Flat World, After All," Thomas L. Friedman argues that most US students are not preparing themselves as well as ~~they should to compete in today's economy. Not like~~ students in India, China, and other countries ~~are.~~ to compete in today's economy, which requires hard-working, productive scientists and engineers. Friedman's argument speaks to me because my mother recently lost her job when it was outsourced to India. But her experience taught a lesson that Friedman overlooks: technical training by itself can be too narrow to produce the communicators and problem solvers needed by contemporary businesses. ~~The outsourcing of my mother's job proves that Thomas L. Friedman's advice to improve students' technical training is too narrow.~~

Friedman describes a "flat" world where recent technology like the Internet and wireless communication makes it possible for college graduates all over the globe, ~~in particular~~ to compete for high paying jobs that once belonged to graduates of US colleges and universities. He focuses on workers in India and China, who graduate from college with excellent educations in math and science, who are eager for new opportunities, and who are willing to work exceptionally hard, often harder than their American counterparts and, for less money. ~~to get jobs that once were gotten by graduates of US colleges and universities. He~~ Friedman argues that US students must be better prepared academically, especially in ~~need more~~ math and science, so that they can get and keep jobs that will otherwise go overseas. ~~in order to compete.~~

~~I came to college with first hand knowledge of globalization and outsourcing. My mother, who worked for sixteen years in the field of information technology (IT), was laid off six months ago when the company she worked for decided to outsource much of its IT work to a company based in India. My mother~~ At first glance, my mother's experience of losing her job might seem to support the argument of Friedman that better training in math and science is the key to competing in the global job market. Her experience, however, adds dimensions to the globalization story, which Friedman misses. First my mother had the kind of strong background in math and science that Friedman says, today's workers need. She majored in

Expanded introduction draws readers into Moreno's topic, clarifies her point of agreement with Friedman, and states her revised thesis.

Expanded summary of Friedman's article specifies qualities of overseas workers.

New opening sentences connect to introduction and thesis statement, restating points of agreement and disagreement with Friedman.

computer science, rose within the information technology (IT) department of a large company, ~~had sixteen years of experience,~~ and her bosses always gave her good performance reviews. Still, when her employer decided to outsource most of its IT work, my mother lost her job. ~~She never expected to be laid off and was surprised when she was. She wasn't laid off because of her background and performance. In fact, my mother had a very strong background in math and science and years of training and job experience.~~ The reason wasn't because her technical skills were inadequate. Instead, her salary and benefits cost the company more than outsourcing her job did. Until wages rise around the globe, jobs like my mother's will be vulnerable. No matter how well you are trained. ~~Which hurt my family financially, as you can imagine.~~

Revisions condense long example of mother's experience.

Concluding sentences reinforce the point of the paragraph and connect to thesis statement.

    The second dimension that Friedman misses is that ~~A~~a number of well-paid people in ~~the~~ my mother's IT department ~~where my mother worked~~, namely IT managers, were not laid off. As my mother explained at the time, they kept their jobs because they were experienced at figuring out the company's IT needs, planning for changes and, researching and proposing solutions. They also communicated better and were better at writing and speaking than my mother was. ~~were better at planning and, they communicated better, they were better writers and speakers than my mother.~~ Friedman misses these skills by focusing only on technical training. Without the ability to solve problems creatively and to communicate, people with technical expertise alone may not have enough to save their jobs. It wasn't enough to save my mother's.

Numbered point (second) connects this paragraph to the previous one.

New examples support general point.

Concluding sentences connect paragraph to thesis.

    Like my mother, I am more comfortable in front of a computer than I am in front of a group of people, and I had planned to major in computer science. Since my mother lost her job, ~~though~~ however, I have decided to take courses in English and history too, where the classes will require me to ~~do different kinds of work~~ read broadly, think critically, research, and communicate ideas in writing—skills that make managers. When I enter the job market, my well-rounded education will make me a more attractive job candidate, and, will help me ~~be a versatile, productive employee~~ become the kind of forward-thinking manager that US companies will always need to employ here in the US.

New examples add specificity.

Expanded sentence connects to thesis statement.

    ~~We know from our history that Americans have been innovative, hard working people. We students have educational opportunities to compete in the global economy, but we must use our time in college wisely. As Thomas L. Friedman says,~~ Many jobs that require a college degree are indeed going

New conclusion recaps Friedman's points and Moreno's thesis and points to the future.

overseas, as Thomas L. Friedman says, and **my classmates and I need to be ready for a rapidly changing future.** But rather than focus only on math and science, we need to broaden our academic experiences so that the skills we develop make us not only employable, but also indispensable. ~~We will have to work hard each day, which means being prepared for class, getting the best grades we can, and making the most of each class. Our futures depend on the decisions we make today.~~

Work Cited

New work-cited entry. (See p. 628 on MLA style.)

Friedman, Thomas L. "It's a Flat World, After All." *New York Times Magazine* 3 Apr. 2005: 32-37. Print.

Exercise 3.4 Analyzing a revised draft

Can you see the reasons for most of the changes Moreno made in her revised draft? Where would you suggest further revisions, and why?

Exercise 3.5 Considering your past work: Revising

In the past, have you usually revised your drafts extensively? Do you think your writing would benefit from more revision of the sort described in this chapter? Why or why not? Many students who don't revise much explain that they lack the time. Is time a problem for you? Can you think of ways to resolve the problem?

Exercise 3.6 Revising your own draft

Revise your own first draft from Exercise 3.3 (p. 52). Use the checklist for revision on page 56 as a guide. Concentrate on purpose, content, and organization, leaving smaller problems such as sentence structure, word choice, and grammar for the next draft.

3d Editing the revised draft

Editing for style, clarity, and correctness may come second to more fundamental revision, but it is still very important. A carefully developed essay will fall flat with readers if you overlook awkwardness and errors.

1 Discovering what needs editing

After you've read and reread a draft to revise it, finding awkwardness and errors can be difficult. Try the following approaches to spot possible flaws in your revised draft:

Ways to find what needs editing

- **Take a break,** even fifteen or twenty minutes, to clear your head.
- **Read the draft** *slowly,* **and read what you** *actually see.* Otherwise, you're likely to read what you intended to write but didn't. (If you have trouble slowing down, try reading your draft from back to front, sentence by sentence.)
- **Read as if you are encountering the draft for the first time.** Put yourself in the reader's place.
- **Have a classmate, friend, or relative read your work.** Make sure you understand and consider the reader's suggestions, even if eventually you decide not to take them.
- **Read the draft aloud or, even better, record it.** Listen for awkward rhythms, repetitive sentence patterns, and missing or clumsy transitions.
- **Learn from your own experience.** Keep a record of the problems that others have pointed out in your writing. (See p. 63 for a suggested format.) When editing, check your work against this record.

In your editing, work first for clear and effective sentences that flow smoothly from one to the next. Then check your sentences for correctness. Use the questions in the following checklist to guide your editing, referring to the page numbers in parentheses as needed.

Checklist for editing

Are my sentences clear?

Do my words and sentences mean what I intend them to mean? Is anything confusing? Check especially for these:

Exact language (pp. 513–25)

Parallelism (pp. 400–06)

Clear modifiers (pp. 361–69)

Clear reference of pronouns (pp. 347–53)

Complete sentences (pp. 332–39)

Sentences separated correctly (pp. 340–46)

Are my sentences effective?

How well do words and sentences engage and hold readers' attention? How appropriate and effective is the voice created by words and sentences? Where does the writing seem wordy, choppy, or dull? Check especially for these:

Expression of voice (pp. 16–17)

Emphasis of main ideas (pp. 380–88)

(continued)

Checklist for editing
(continued)

Smooth and informative transitions (pp. 88–90, 110–11)
Variety in sentence length and structure (pp. 407–14)
Appropriate language (pp. 504–12)
Concise sentences (pp. 525–32)

Do my sentences contain errors?
Where do surface errors interfere with the clarity and effectiveness of my sentences? Check especially for these:

- **Spelling errors** (pp. 533–36)
- **Sentence fragments** (pp. 332–39)
- **Comma splices** (pp. 340–45)
- **Verb errors**

  Verb forms, especially -*s* and -*ed* endings, correct forms of irregular verbs, and appropriate helping verbs (pp. 274–90)

  Verb tenses, especially consistency (pp. 291–97, 357)

  Agreement between subjects and verbs, especially when words come between them or the subject is *each, everyone,* or a similar word (pp. 303–10)

- **Pronoun errors**

  Pronoun forms, especially subjective (*he, she, they, who*) vs. objective (*him, her, them, whom*) (pp. 266–73)

  Agreement between pronouns and antecedents, especially when the antecedent contains *or* or the antecedent is *each, everyone, person,* or a similar word (pp. 311–15)

- **Punctuation errors**

  Commas, especially with comma splices (pp. 340–45), with *and* or *but* (424–26), with introductory elements (427–28), with nonessential elements (429–31), and with series (445)

  Apostrophes in possessives but not plural nouns (*Dave's/witches*) and in contractions but not possessive personal pronouns (*it's/its*) (pp. 454–59)

The third paragraph of Katy Moreno's edited draft appears below. Among other changes, she tightened wording, improved parallelism (with *consistently received*), corrected several comma errors, and repaired the final sentence fragment.

> At first glance, my mother's experience of losing her job might seem to support ~~the~~ Friedman's argument ~~of Friedman~~ that better training in math and science is the key to competing in the global job market. However, ~~H~~her experience~~, however,~~ adds dimensions to the globalization story~~, which~~ that Friedman misses. First, my mother had the kind of strong

background in math and science that Friedman says~~,~~ today's workers need. She majored in computer science, rose within the information technology (IT) department of a large company, and consistently received ~~her bosses always gave her~~ good performance reviews. Still, when her employer decided to outsource most of its IT work, my mother lost her job. The reason wasn't ~~because~~ that her technical skills were inadequate. Instead, her salary and benefits cost the company more than outsourcing her job did. Until wages rise around the globe, jobs like my mother's will be vulnerable~~,~~ ~~N~~no matter how well ~~you are~~ a person is trained.

2 | Tracking your errors

You won't make all the errors described in this book; instead, you may make the same three or four kinds of errors in each essay you write. The key to correcting such errors is recognizing them, keeping track of them, and checking for them each time you edit your writing.

To track your errors, try making a chart like the one below, with a vertical column for each assignment (or draft) and a horizontal row for each error or weakness that you or others have noted in your writing. Check marks indicate how often the problem occurs in every essay. The chart also provides a convenient place to keep track of words you misspell so that you can master their spellings. When you edit, check your work against the list so that you learn to see—and correct—the errors that you typically make.

Record of errors

Weaknesses	Assignment		
	1	2	3
not enough details for readers	✓	✓	✓
unity—wanders away from thesis	✓		
subject-verb agreement	✓		✓
comma splice	✓✓	✓	✓
misspellings	among deceive	rebel seize	omission cruelty

3 | Editing on a computer

When you write on a word processor, consider these additional approaches to editing:

- **Don't rely on a spelling or grammar/style checker to find what needs editing.** See the discussion of these checkers below.
- **If possible, work on a double-spaced paper copy.** Most people find it much harder to spot errors on a computer screen than on paper.
- **Use the Find command to locate and correct your common problems**—certain misspellings, wordy phrases such as *the fact that,* overuse of *there is,* and so on.
- **Resist overediting.** The ease of editing on a computer can lead to rewriting sentences over and over, stealing the life from your prose. If your grammar/style checker contributes to the temptation, consider turning it off.
- **Take special care with additions and omissions.** Make sure you haven't omitted needed words or left in unneeded words.

4 | Working with spelling and grammar/style checkers

A spelling checker and a grammar/style checker can be helpful *if* you work within their limitations. The programs miss many problems and may even flag items that are actually correct. Further, they know nothing of your purpose and your audience, so they cannot make important decisions about your writing. Always use these tools critically:

- **Read your work yourself to ensure that it's clear and error-free.**
- **Consider a checker's suggestions carefully, weighing each one against your intentions,** If you aren't sure whether to accept a checker's suggestion, consult a dictionary, writing handbook, or other source. Your version may be fine.

Using a spelling checker

Your word processor's spelling checker can be a great ally: it will flag words that are spelled incorrectly and will usually suggest alternative spellings that resemble what you've typed. However, this ally also has the potential to undermine you because of its limitations:

- **The checker may flag a word that you've spelled correctly** just because the word does not appear in its dictionary.
- **The checker may suggest incorrect alternatives.** In providing a list of alternative spellings for your word, the checker may highlight the one it considers most likely to be correct. For example,

if you misspell *definitely* by typing *definately,* your checker may highlight *defiantly* as the correct option. You need to verify that the alternative suggested by the checker is actually what you intend before selecting it. Consult an online or printed dictionary when you aren't sure about the checker's recommendations.

- **Most important, a spelling checker will not flag words that appear in its dictionary but you have misused.** The jingle in the following screen shot has circulated widely as a warning about spelling checkers (we found it in the *Bulletin of the Missouri Council of Teachers of Mathematics*).

Spelling checker

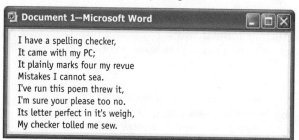

Document 1—Microsoft Word

I have a spelling checker,
It came with my PC;
It plainly marks four my revue
Mistakes I cannot sea.
I've run this poem threw it,
I'm sure your please too no.
Its letter perfect in it's weigh,
My checker tolled me sew.

A spelling checker failed to catch any of the thirteen errors in this jingle. Can you spot them?

Using a grammar/style checker

Grammar/style checkers can flag incorrect grammar or punctuation and wordy or awkward sentences. However, these programs can call your attention only to passages that *may* be faulty. They miss many errors because they are not capable of analyzing language in all its complexity. (For instance, they can't accurately distinguish a word's part of speech when there are different possibilities, as *light* can be a noun, a verb, or an adjective.) The checkers can't detect problems involving relationships between ideas, so they usually miss errors such as faulty parallelism, inconsistent verb tenses, and problems with adjectives or adverbs. And they often question passages that don't need editing, such as an appropriate passive verb or a deliberate and emphatic use of repetition. The screen shot on the next page illustrates the limitations.

You can customize a grammar and style checker to suit your needs and habits as a writer. (Select Options under the Tools menu.) Most checkers allow you to specify whether to check grammar only or grammar and style. Some style checkers can be set to the level of writing you intend, such as formal, standard, and informal. (For academic writing choose formal.) You can also instruct the checker to flag specific grammar and style problems that tend to occur in

Grammar/style checker

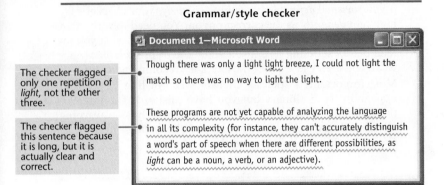

The checker flagged only one repetition of *light*, not the other three.

The checker flagged this sentence because it is long, but it is actually clear and correct.

Document 1—Microsoft Word

Though there was only a light light breeze, I could not light the match so there was no way to light the light.

These programs are not yet capable of analyzing the language in all its complexity (for instance, they can't accurately distinguish a word's part of speech when there are different possibilities, as *light* can be a noun, a verb, or an adjective).

your writing, such as mismatched subjects and verbs, apostrophes in plural nouns, overused passive voice, or a confusion between *its* and *it's*.

Exercise 3.7 Considering your past work: Editing

How do you find what needs editing in your drafts? What kinds of changes do you make most often? Have you tried focusing on particular kinds of changes, such as correcting mistakes you made in previous writing? If your readers often comment on editing concerns in your work, what can you do to reduce such comments?

Exercise 3.8 Editing your own draft

Use the checklist for editing (pp. 61–62) and your own sense of your essay's needs to edit the revised draft of your essay-in-progress.

3e Preparing and proofreading the final draft

After editing your essay, retype or print it once more for submission to your teacher. You may be required to use one of the formats covered in this book: MLA (pp. 664–66) or APA (pp. 761–64). If no format is specified, consult the document-design guidelines in Chapter 5. If you've composed on a computer, use the Print Preview function under the File menu to check for formatting problems that may not otherwise show up on your screen.

Be sure to proofread the final essay several times to spot and correct errors. To increase the accuracy of your proofreading, you may need to find ways to keep yourself from relaxing into the rhythm and the content of your prose. The following box gives a few tricks, including some used by professional proofreaders:

Techniques for proofreading

- **Read printed copy,** even if you will eventually submit the paper electronically. Most people proofread more accurately when reading type on paper than when reading it on a computer screen. (At the same time, don't view the printed copy as necessarily error-free just because it's clean. Clean-looking copy may still harbor errors.)
- **Read the paper aloud.** Slowly and distinctly pronounce exactly what you see.
- **Place a ruler under each line as you read it.**
- **Read "against copy."** Compare your final draft one sentence at a time against the edited draft you copied it from.
- **Ignore content.** To keep the content of your writing from distracting you while you proofread, read the essay backward, end to beginning, examining each sentence as a separate unit. Or, taking advantage of a computer, isolate each paragraph from its context by printing it on a separate page. (Of course, reassemble the paragraphs before submitting the paper.)

3f Examining a final draft

Katy Moreno's final essay begins below, typed in MLA format except for page breaks and numbers. Comments in the margins point out key features of the essay's content.

Katy Moreno
Professor Lacourse
English 110
14 November 2008

Can We Compete?

College Education for the Global Economy

Today's students cannot miss news stories about globalization of the economy and outsourcing of jobs, but are students aware of how these trends are affecting the job market? In "It's a Flat World, After All," Thomas L. Friedman argues that most US students are not preparing themselves as well as students in India, China, and other countries to compete in today's economy, which requires hard-working, productive scientists and engineers. Friedman's argument speaks to me because my mother lost her job when it was outsourced to India. But her experience taught a lesson that Friedman overlooks: technical training by itself can be too narrow to produce the communicators and problem solvers needed by contemporary businesses.

Descriptive title

Introduction

Thesis statement: basic disagreement with Friedman

Summary of Friedman's article

No source citation for Friedman because paragraph summarizes entire article and mentions Friedman's name

Transition to disagreements with Friedman

First disagreement with Friedman

Examples to support first disagreement

Example to qualify first disagreement

Clarification of first disagreement

Second disagreement with Friedman

Explanation of second disagreement

Conclusion summarizing both disagreements with Friedman

Final point: business needs and author's personal goals

Friedman describes a "flat" world where recent technology like the Internet and wireless communication makes it possible for college graduates all over the globe to compete for high-paying jobs that once belonged to graduates of US colleges and universities. He focuses on workers in India and China who graduate from college with excellent educations in math and science, who are eager for new opportunities, and who are willing to work exceptionally hard, often harder than their American counterparts, and for less money. Friedman argues that US students must be better prepared academically, especially in math and science, so that they can get and keep jobs that will otherwise go overseas.

At first glance, my mother's experience of losing her job might seem to support Friedman's argument that better training in math and science is the key to competing in the global job market. However, her experience adds dimensions to the globalization story that Friedman misses. First, my mother had the kind of strong background in math and science that Friedman says today's workers need. She majored in computer science, rose within the information technology (IT) department of a large company, and consistently received good performance reviews. Still, when her employer decided to outsource most of its IT work, my mother lost her job. The reason wasn't that her technical skills were inadequate; instead, her salary and benefits cost the company more than outsourcing her job did. Until wages rise around the globe, jobs like my mother's will be vulnerable, no matter how well a person is trained.

The second dimension that Friedman misses is that a number of well-paid people in my mother's IT department, namely IT managers, were not laid off. As my mother explained at the time, they kept their jobs because they were experienced at figuring out the company's IT needs, planning for changes, researching and proposing solutions, and communicating in writing and speech—skills that her more narrow training and experience had missed. Friedman misses these skills by focusing only on technical training. Without the ability to solve problems creatively and to communicate, people with technical expertise alone may not have enough to save their jobs, as my mother learned.

Like my mother, I am more comfortable in front of a computer than I am in front of a group of people, and I had planned to major in computer science. Since my mother lost her job, however, I have decided to take courses in English and history as well. Classes in these subjects will require me to read broadly, think critically, research, and communicate ideas in writing—in short, to develop skills that make managers. When I enter the job market, my well-rounded education will make me a more attractive job candidate and will help me to become the kind of forward-thinking manager that US companies will always need to employ here in the US.

Many jobs that require a college degree are indeed going overseas, as Thomas L. Friedman says, and my classmates and I need to be ready for a rapidly changing future. But rather than focus only on math and science, we need to broaden our academic experiences so that the skills we develop make us not only employable but also indispensable.

Work Cited

Friedman, Thomas L. "It's a Flat World, After All." *New York Times Magazine* 3 Apr. 2005: 32-37. Print.

Explanation of final point

Conclusion recapping points of agreement and disagreement with Friedman and summarizing essay

Work cited in MLA style (see p. 628)

Exercise 3.9 Proofreading

Proofread the following passage, using any of the techniques listed on page 67 to bring errors into the foreground. There are thirteen errors in the passage: missing and misspelled words, typographical errors, and the like. If you are in doubt about any spellings, consult a dictionary.

An envirnmental group, Natural Resources Defense Council, has estimated that 5500 to 6200 children who are preschool today may contract cancer durng there lives becuase of the pesticides they consume in there food In addition, these children will be at greater risk for kidney damage, problems with immunity, and other serious imparments. The government bases it's pesticide-safety standards on adults, but childen consume many more the fruits and fruit products likely too contain pestcides.

Exercise 3.10 Preparing your final draft

Prepare the final draft of the essay you have been working on throughout Chapters 1–3. Proofread carefully and correct all errors before submitting your essay for review.

3g Giving and receiving comments

1 Working collaboratively

Almost all the writing you do in high school will generate responses from a teacher. In classes that stress writing, you may submit early drafts as well as your final paper, and your readers may include your classmates as well as your teacher. Like Katy Moreno's, such classes may feature **collaborative learning**, in which students work together on writing, from completing exercises to commenting on each other's work to producing whole papers. (At more and more schools this group work occurs over a computer network. See pp. 793–96.)

Whether you participate as a writer or as a writing "coach," collaboration can give you experience in reading written work and in reaching readers through writing. You may at first be anxious about criticizing others' work or sharing your own rough drafts, but you'll soon grow to appreciate the interaction and the confidence it gives you in your own reading and writing.

CULTURE LANGUAGE In some cultures writers do not expect criticism from readers, or readers do not expect to think critically about what they read. If critical responses are uncommon in your native culture, collaboration may at first be uncomfortable for you. As a writer, consider that readers are responding to your draft or even your final paper more as an exploration of ideas than as the last word on your subject; then you may be more receptive to readers' suggestions. As a reader, allow yourself to approach a text skeptically, and know that your tactful questions and suggestions will usually be considered appropriate.

2 Responding to the writing of others

When you are the reader of someone else's writing, keep the following principles in mind:

Commenting on others' writing

- **Be sure you know what the writer is saying.** If necessary, summarize the paper to understand its content. (See pp. 136–37.)
- **Address only your most significant concerns with the work.** Use the revision checklist on p. 56 as a guide to what is significant. Unless you have other instructions, ignore mistakes in grammar, punctuation, spelling, and the like. (The temptation to focus on such errors may be especially strong if the writer is less experienced than you are with standard American English.) Emphasizing mistakes will contribute little to the writer's revision.
- **Remember that you are the reader, not the writer.** Don't edit sentences, add details, or otherwise assume responsibility for the paper.
- **Phrase your comments carefully.** Avoid misunderstandings by making sure comments are both clear and respectful. If you are responding on paper or online, not face to face with the writer, remember that the writer has nothing but your written words to go on. He or she can't ask you for immediate clarification and can't infer your attitudes from gestures, facial expressions, and tone of voice.
- **Be specific.** If something confuses you, say *why*. If you disagree with a conclusion, say *why*.

- **Be supportive as well as honest.** Tell the writer what you like about the paper. Word comments positively: instead of *This paragraph doesn't interest me,* say *You have an interesting detail here that I almost missed.* Comment in a way that emphasizes the effect of the work on you, the reader: *This paragraph confuses me because. . . .* And avoid measuring the work against a set of external standards: *This essay is poorly organized. Your thesis statement is inadequate.*
- **While reading, make your comments in writing.** Even if you will be delivering your comments in person later on, the written record will help you recall what you thought.
- **Link comments to specific parts of a paper.** Especially if you are reading the paper on a computer, be clear about what part of the paper each comment relates to. You can embed your comments directly into the paper, distinguishing them with highlighting or color. Or you can use the Comment function of a word processor (see below).

If you are reviewing others' drafts on a word processor, its Comment function will allow you to add comments without inserting words into the document's text. Usually found on the Insert menu, the function creates marginal annotations (such as those on Katy Moreno's first draft, pp. 51–52) or creates pop-ups that appear when readers move their cursors across words you have highlighted.

3 Responding to comments on your own writing

When you *receive* comments from others, whether your classmates or your teacher, you will get more out of the process if you follow the guidelines below.

Benefiting from comments on your writing

- **Think of your readers as counselors or coaches.** They can help you see the virtues and flaws in your work and sharpen your awareness of readers' needs.
- **Read or listen to comments closely.**
- **Know what the critic is saying.** If you need more information, ask for it, or consult the appropriate section of this handbook.
- **Don't become defensive.** Letting comments offend you will only erect a barrier to improvement in your writing. As one writing teacher advises, "Leave your ego at the door."

(continued)

Benefiting from comments on your writing
(continued)

- **Revise your work in response to appropriate comments.** Whether or not you are required to act on comments, you will learn more from actually revising than from just thinking about it.
- **Remember that you are the final authority on your work.** You should be open to suggestions, but you are free to decline advice when you think it is inappropriate.
- **Keep track of both the strengths and the weaknesses others identify.** Then in later assignments you can build on your successes and give special attention to problem areas.

As the last item in the preceding box indicates, you'll gain the most from collaboration if you carry your learning from one assignment into the next. To keep track of things to work on, try a chart like the one on page 63.

3h Preparing a writing portfolio

Your composition teacher may ask you to assemble samples of your writing into a portfolio, or folder, once or more during the year. Such a portfolio gives you a chance to consider all your writing over a period and to showcase your best work. In some school systems, students keep portfolios of their work throughout high school as a record of their development and achievement as writers.

Teachers' requirements for portfolios vary. For instance, some teachers ask students to choose their five or so best papers and to submit final drafts only. Others ask for final papers illustrating certain kinds of writing—say, one narrative, one critique, one argument, one research paper, and so on. Still others ask for notes and drafts along with selected papers in order to see students' writing processes. If your class is using online writing tools, your work may be archived as part of the course site and you may be asked to submit your portfolio electronically.

Just as teachers' requirements differ, so do their purposes. But most are looking for a range of writing that demonstrates your progress and strengths as a writer. You, in turn, see how you have advanced from one assignment to the next, as you've had time for new knowledge to sink in and time for practice. Teachers often allow students to revise papers before placing them in the portfolio, even if the papers were submitted earlier. In that case, every paper in the portfolio can benefit from all your learning.

An assignment to assemble a writing portfolio will probably also provide guidelines for what to include, how the portfolio will be evaluated, and how (or whether) it will be weighted for a grade. Be sure you understand the purpose of the portfolio and who will read it. For instance, if your composition teacher will be the only reader and her guidelines urge you to show evidence of progress, you might include a paper that took big risks but never entirely succeeded. In contrast, if you don't know all the teachers who will read your work and the guidelines urge you to demonstrate your competence as a writer, you might include only papers that did succeed.

Unless the guidelines specify otherwise, provide error-free copies of your final drafts, label all your samples with your name, and assemble them all in a folder. Add a cover letter or memo that lists the samples, explains why you've included each one, and evaluates your progress as a writer. The self-evaluation involved should be a learning experience for you and will help your teacher assess your development as a writer.

4

Writing and Revising Paragraphs

A **paragraph** is a group of related sentences set off by a beginning indention or, sometimes, by extra space. For you and your readers, paragraphs provide breathers from long stretches of text and indicate key changes in the development of your thesis. They help to organize and clarify ideas.

In the body of an essay, you may use paragraphs for any of these purposes:

- **To introduce and give evidence for a main point supporting your essay's central idea (its thesis).** See pages 29–34 for a discussion of an essay's thesis.
- **Within a group of paragraphs centering on one main point, to develop a key example or other important evidence.**

mycomplab

Visit *mycomplab.com* for more resources and exercises on paragraphs.

- **To shift approach**—for instance, from pros to cons, from problem to solution, from questions to answers.
- **To mark movement in a sequence,** such as from one reason or step to another.

In addition, you will use paragraphs for special purposes:

- **To introduce or to conclude an essay.** See pages 105 and 108.
- **To emphasize an important point or to mark a significant transition between points.** See pages 110–11.
- **In dialog, to indicate that a new person has begun speaking.** See page 111.

The following paragraph illustrates simply how an effective body paragraph works to help both writer and reader. The thesis of the essay in which this paragraph appears is that a Texas chili championship gives undue attention to an unpleasant food.

> Some people really like chili, apparently, but nobody can agree how the stuff should be made. C. V. Wood, twice winner at Terlingua, uses flank steak, pork chops, chicken, and green chilis. My friend Hughes Rudd of CBS News, who imported five hundred pounds of chili powder into Russia as a condition of accepting employment as Moscow correspondent, favors coarse-ground beef. Isadore Bleckman, the cameraman I must live with on the road, insists upon one-inch cubes of stew beef and puts garlic in his chili, an Illinois affectation. An Indian of my acquaintance, Mr. Fulton Batisse, who eats chili for breakfast when he can, uses buffalo meat and plays an Indian drum while it's cooking. I ask you.
>
> —Charles Kuralt, *Dateline America*

General statement relating to thesis: announces topic of paragraph

Four specific examples, all providing evidence for general statement

While you are drafting, conscious attention to the requirements of the paragraph may sometimes help pull ideas out of you or help you forge relationships. But don't expect effective paragraphs like Kuralt's to flow from your fingertips while you are grappling with what you want to say. Instead, use the checklist on the next page to guide your revision of paragraphs so that they work to your and your readers' advantage.

Note On the Web the paragraphing conventions described here do not always apply. Web readers sometimes skim text instead of reading word for word, and they are accustomed to embedded links that may take them from the paragraph to another page. Writing for the Web, you may want to write shorter paragraphs than you would in printed documents, and save embedded links for the ends

---

Checklist for revising paragraphs

- **Is the paragraph unified?** Does it adhere to one general idea that is either stated in a topic sentence or otherwise apparent? (See below.)
- **Is the paragraph coherent?** Do the sentences follow a clear sequence? Are the sentences linked as needed by parallelism, repetition or restatement, pronouns, consistency, and transitional expressions? (See p. 80.)
- **Is the paragraph developed?** Is the general idea of the paragraph well supported with specific evidence such as details, facts, examples, and reasons? (See p. 93.)

---

of paragraphs lest readers miss important information. (For more on composing for the Web, see pp. 796–802.)

CULTURE LANGUAGE Not all cultures share the paragraphing conventions of American academic writing. The conventions are not universal even among users of standard American English: for instance, US newspaper writers compose very short paragraphs that will break up text in narrow columns. In some other languages, writing moves differently from English—not from left to right, but from right to left or down rows from top to bottom. Even in languages that move as English does, writers may not use paragraphs at all. Or they may use paragraphs but not state the central ideas or provide transitional expressions to show readers how sentences relate. If your native language is not English and you have difficulty with paragraphs, don't worry about paragraphing during drafting. Instead, during a separate step of revision, divide your text into parts that develop your main points. Mark those parts with indentions.

4a Maintaining paragraph unity

Readers generally expect a paragraph to explore a single idea. They will be alert for that idea and will patiently follow its development. In other words, they will seek and appreciate paragraph **unity**: clear identification and clear elaboration of one idea and of that idea only.

In an essay the thesis statement often asserts the main idea as a commitment to readers (see p. 29). In a paragraph a **topic sentence** often alerts readers to the essence of the paragraph by asserting the central idea and expressing the writer's attitude toward it. In a brief essay each body paragraph will likely treat one main point supporting the essay's thesis statement; the topic sentences simply elaborate on parts of the thesis. In longer essays paragraphs tend to work in groups, each group treating one main point. Then the topic sentences will tie into that main point, and all the points together will support the thesis.

1 Focusing on the central idea

Like the thesis sentence, the topic sentence is a commitment to readers, and the rest of the paragraph delivers on that commitment. Look again at Kuralt's paragraph on chili on page 74: the opening statement conveys the author's promise that he will describe various ways to make chili, and the following sentences keep the promise. But what if Kuralt had written this paragraph instead?

> Some people really like chili, apparently, but nobody can agree how the stuff should be made. — Topic sentence: general statement
>
> C. V. Wood, twice winner at Terlingua, uses flank steak, pork chops, chicken, and green chilis. My friend Hughes Rudd, who imported five hundred pounds of chili powder into Russia as a condition of accepting employment as Moscow correspondent, favors coarse-ground beef. — Two examples supporting statement
>
> He had some trouble finding the beef in Moscow, though. He sometimes had to scour all the markets and wait in long lines. For any American used to over-stocked supermarkets and department stores, Russia can be quite a shock. — Digression

By wandering off from chili ingredients to consumer deprivation in Russia, the paragraph fails to deliver on the commitment of its topic sentence.

You should expect digressions while you are drafting: if you allow yourself to explore ideas, as you should, then of course every paragraph will not be tightly woven, perfectly unified. But spare your readers the challenge and frustration of repeatedly shifting focus to follow your rough explorations: revise each paragraph so that it develops a single idea.

While revising your paragraphs for unity, you may want to highlight the central idea of each paragraph to be sure it's stated and then focus on it. On paper you can bracket or circle the idea. On a computer you can format the idea in color or highlight it with a color background. Just be sure to remove the color or highlighting before printing the final draft.

2 Placing the topic sentence

The topic sentence of a paragraph and its supporting details may be arranged variously, depending on how you want to direct readers' attention and how complex your central idea is. In the most common arrangements, the topic sentence comes at the beginning of the paragraph, comes at the end, or is not stated at all but is nonetheless apparent. The advantages of each approach are described on these two pages. If you write on a computer, you can easily experiment with the position of the topic sentence by moving the sentence around (or deleting it) to see the effect. (The sentence will probably take some editing to work smoothly into various positions.)

Topic sentence at the beginning

When you place the topic sentence first in a paragraph, it can help you select the details that follow. For readers, the topic-first model establishes an initial context in which all the supporting details can be understood. Reading Kuralt's paragraph on page 74, we easily relate each detail or example back to the point made in the first sentence.

The topic-first model is common not only in expository paragraphs, such as Kuralt's, but also in argument paragraphs, such as the one following:

> It is a misunderstanding of the American retail store to think we go there necessarily to buy. Some of us shop. There's a difference. Shopping has many purposes, the least interesting of which is to acquire new articles. We shop to cheer ourselves up. We shop to practice decision-making. We shop to be useful and productive members of our class and society. We shop to remind ourselves how much is available to us. We shop to remind ourselves how much is to be striven for. We shop to assert our superiority to the material objects that spread themselves before us.
>
> —Phyllis Rose, "Shopping and Other Spiritual Adventures"

Topic sentence: statement of misconception

Correction of misconception

Topic sentence at the end

In some paragraphs the central idea may be stated at the end, after supporting sentences have made a case for the general statement. Since this model leads the reader to a conclusion by presenting all the evidence first, it can prove effective in argument. And because the point of the paragraph is withheld until the end, this model can be dramatic in exposition, too, as illustrated by the following example from an essay about William Tecumseh Sherman, a Union general during the US Civil War:

> Sherman is considered by some to be the inventor of "total war": the first general in human history to carry the logic of war to its ultimate extreme, the first to scorch the earth, the first to consciously demoralize the hostile civilian population in order to subdue its army, the first to wreck an economy in order to starve its soldiers. He has been called our first "merchant of terror" and seen as the spiritual father of our Vietnam War concepts of "search and destroy," "pacification," "strategic hamlets," and "free-fire zones." As such, he remains a cardboard figure of our history: a monstrous arch-villain to unreconstructed Southerners, and an embarrassment to Northerners.
>
> —Adapted from James Reston, Jr., "You Cannot Refine It"

Information supporting and building to topic sentence

Topic sentence

Expressing the central idea at the end of the paragraph does not eliminate the need to unify the paragraph. The idea in the topic sentence must still govern the selection of all the preceding details.

Central idea not stated

Occasionally, a paragraph's central idea will be stated in the previous paragraph or will be so obvious that it need not be stated at all. The following is from an essay on the actor Humphrey Bogart:

> Usually he wore the trench coat unbuttoned, just tied with the belt, and a slouch hat, rarely tilted. Sometimes it was a captain's cap and a yachting jacket. Almost always his trousers were held up by a cowboy belt. You know the kind: one an Easterner waiting for a plane out of Phoenix buys just as a joke and then takes a liking to. Occasionally, he'd hitch up his slacks with it, and he often jabbed his thumbs behind it, his hands ready for a fight or a dame.
>
> —Peter Bogdanovich, "Bogie in Excelsis"

Details adding up to the unstated idea that Bogart's character could be seen in his clothing

Paragraphs in descriptive writing (like the one above) and in narrative writing (relating a sequence of events) often lack stated topic sentences. But a paragraph without a topic sentence still should have a central idea, and its details should develop that idea.

Exercise 4.1 Finding the central idea

What is the central idea of each of the following paragraphs? In what sentence or sentences is it expressed?

1.   Today many black Americans enjoy a measure of economic security [1] beyond any we have known in the history of black America. But if they [2] remain in a nasty blue funk, it's because their very existence seems an affront to the swelling ranks of the poor. Nor have black intellectuals ever [3] quite made peace with the concept of the black bourgeoisie, a group that is typically seen as devoid of cultural authenticity, doomed to mimicry and pallid assimilation. I once gave a talk before an audience of [4] black academics and educators, in the course of which I referred to black middle-class culture. Afterward, one of the academics in the audience, [5] deeply affronted, had a question for me. "Professor Gates," he asked [6] rhetorically, his voice dripping with sarcasm, "what *is* black middle-class [7] culture?" I suggested that if he really wanted to know, he need only look around the room. But perhaps I should just have handed him a mirror: [8] for just as nothing is more American than anti-Americanism, nothing is more characteristic of the black bourgeoisie than the sense of shame and denial that the identity inspires.

—Henry Louis Gates, Jr., "Two Nations . . . Both Black"

2.   Though they do not know why the humpback whale sings, scien- [1] tists do know something about the song itself. They have measured the [2] length of a whale's song: from a few minutes to over half an hour. They [3] have recorded and studied the variety and complex arrangements of low moans, high squeaks, and sliding squeals that make up the song. And [4] they have learned that each whale sings in its own unique pattern.

—Janet Lieber (student), "Whales' Songs"

Exercise 4.2   Revising a paragraph for unity

The following paragraph contains ideas or details that do not support its central idea. Identify the topic sentence in the paragraph and delete the unrelated material.

In the southern part of the state, some people still live much as they did a century ago. They use coal- or wood-burning stoves for heating and cooking. Their homes do not have electricity or indoor bathrooms or running water. The towns they live in don't receive adequate funding from the state and federal governments, so the schools are poor and in bad shape. Beside most homes there is a garden where fresh vegetables are gathered for canning. Small pastures nearby support livestock, including cattle, pigs, horses, and chickens. Most of the people have cars or trucks, but the vehicles are old and beat-up from traveling on unpaved roads.

Exercise 4.3   Considering your past work: Paragraph unity

For a continuing exercise in this chapter, choose a paper you've written in the past year. Examine the body paragraphs for unity. Do they have clear topic sentences? If not, are the paragraphs' central ideas still clear? Are the paragraphs unified around their central ideas? Should any details be deleted for unity? Should other, more relevant details be added in their stead?

Exercise 4.4 Writing a unified paragraph

Develop the following topic sentence into a unified paragraph by using the relevant information in the supporting statements. Delete each statement that does not relate directly to the topic, and then rewrite and combine sentences as appropriate. Place the topic sentence in the position that seems most effective to you.

Topic sentence
Mozart's accomplishments in music seem remarkable even today.

Supporting information
Wolfgang Amadeus Mozart was born in 1756 in Salzburg, Austria.
He began composing music at the age of five.
He lived most of his life in Salzburg and Vienna.
His first concert tour of Europe was at the age of six.
On his first tour he played harpsichord, organ, and violin.
He published numerous compositions before reaching adolescence.
He married in 1782.
Mozart and his wife were both poor managers of money.
They were plagued by debts.
Mozart composed over six hundred musical compositions.
His most notable works are his operas, symphonies, quartets, and piano concertos.
He died at the age of thirty-five.

Exercise 4.5 Turning topic sentences into unified paragraphs

Develop three of the following topic sentences into detailed and unified paragraphs.

1. Men and women are different in at least one important respect.
2. The best Web search engine is [name].
3. Fans of _____ music [country, classical, rock, rap, jazz, or another kind] come in [number] varieties.
4. Professional sports have [or have not] been helped by extending the regular season with championship play-offs.
5. Working for good grades can interfere with learning.

4b Achieving paragraph coherence

A paragraph is unified if it holds together—if all its details and examples support the central idea. A paragraph is **coherent** if readers can see *how* the paragraph holds together—how the sentences relate to each other—without having to stop and reread.

Incoherence gives readers the feeling of being yanked around, as the following example shows.

Ways to achieve paragraph coherence

- Organize effectively (p. 82).
- Repeat or restate key words and word groups (p. 86).
- Use parallel structures (p. 86).
- Use pronouns (p. 87).
- Be consistent in nouns, pronouns, and verbs (p. 87).
- Use transitional expressions (p. 88).

The ancient Egyptians were masters of preserving dead people's bodies by making mummies of them. — **Topic sentence**

Mummies several thousand years old have been discovered nearly intact. The skin, hair, teeth, finger- and toenails, and facial features of the mummies were evident. One can diagnose the diseases they suffered in life, such as smallpox, arthritis, and nutritional deficiencies. The process was remarkably effective. Sometimes apparent were the fatal afflictions of the dead people: a middle-aged king died from a blow on the head, and polio killed a child king. Mummification consisted of removing the internal organs, applying natural preservatives inside and out, and then wrapping the body in layers of bandages. — **Sentences related to topic sentence but disconnected from each other**

The paragraph as it was actually written appears below. It is much clearer because the writer arranged information differently and also built links into his sentences so that they would flow smoothly:

- After stating the central idea in a topic sentence, the writer moves to two more specific explanations and illustrates the second with four sentences of examples.
- Circled words repeat or restate key terms or concepts.
- Boxed words link sentences and clarify relationships.
- Underlined phrases are in parallel grammatical form to reflect their parallel content.

The ancient Egyptians were masters of preserving dead people's bodies by making mummies of them. — **Topic sentence**

Basically, mummification consisted of removing the internal organs, applying natural preservatives inside and out, and then wrapping the body in layers of bandages. — **Explanation 1: What mummification is**

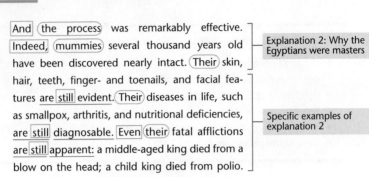

And (the process) was remarkably effective.
Indeed, (mummies) several thousand years old
have been discovered nearly intact. (Their) skin, — Explanation 2: Why the Egyptians were masters

hair, teeth, finger- and toenails, and facial features are still evident. (Their) diseases in life, such
as smallpox, arthritis, and nutritional deficiencies,
are still diagnosable. (Even) (their) fatal afflictions — Specific examples of explanation 2
are still apparent: a middle-aged king died from a
blow on the head; a child king died from polio.

—Mitchell Rosenbaum (student),
"Lost Arts of the Egyptians"

Though some of the connections in this paragraph were added in revision, the writer attended to them while drafting as well. Not only superficial coherence but also an underlying clarity of relationships can be achieved by tying each sentence to the one before—generalizing from it, clarifying it, qualifying it, adding to it, illustrating it. Each sentence in a paragraph creates an expectation of some sort in the mind of the reader, a question such as "How was a mummy made?" or "How intact are the mummies?" or "What's another example?" When you recognize these expectations and try to fulfill them, readers are likely to understand relationships without struggle.

1 Organizing the paragraph

The paragraphs on mummies illustrate an essential element of coherence: information must be arranged in an order that readers can follow easily and that corresponds to their expectations. The common organizations for paragraphs correspond to those for entire essays: by space, by time, and for emphasis. (In addition, the rhetorical strategies also suggest certain arrangements. See pp. 94–102.)

Note On a computer you can experiment with different paragraph organizations and emphases. Copy a paragraph, paste the copy into your document, and then try moving sentences around. To evaluate the versions, you'll need to edit each one so that sentences flow smoothly, attending to repetition, parallelism, transitions, and the other techniques for achieving coherence.

Organizing by space or time

A paragraph organized **spatially** focuses readers' attention on one point and scans a person, object, or scene from that point. The movement usually parallels the way people actually look at things, from top to bottom, from side to side, from near to far. Virginia Woolf follows the last pattern in the following paragraph:

Spatial organization

The sun struck straight upon the house, making the white walls glare between the dark windows. Their panes, woven thickly with green branches, held circles of impenetrable darkness. Sharp-edged wedges of light lay upon the window-sill and showed inside the room plates with blue rings, cups with curved handles, the bulge of a great bowl, the criss-cross pattern in the rug, and the formidable corners and lines of cabinets and bookcases. Behind their conglomeration hung a zone of shadow in which might be a further shape to be disencumbered of shadow or still denser depths of darkness.

—Virginia Woolf, *The Waves*

> Description moving from outside (closer) to inside (farther)

> Unstated central idea: Sunlight barely penetrated the house's secrets.

Another familiar way of organizing the elements of a paragraph is **chronologically**—that is, in order of their occurrence in time. In a chronological paragraph, as in experience, the earliest events come first, followed by more recent ones.

Chronological organization

In early spring, millions of monarch butterflies that have spent the winter months in Mexico begin an annual migration north to the monarch's summer habitats. After covering about fifty miles a day, most make their first stop in Texas, where they lay their eggs on milkweed and die soon after. Their offspring continue the flight to the northern United States and Canada, laying the eggs of the next generation of monarchs along the way. By late spring, these offspring or their offspring reach their summer homes. In August, the third or fourth generation of the original monarchs begins the long return migration south. They do not reproduce in the north but return to where their ancestors wintered and hibernate there. The following spring they start the cycle over by flying north to Texas.

—Ben Kampe (student), "The Monarch Trail"

> Topic sentence

> Details in order of their occurrence

Organizing for emphasis

Some organizational schemes are imposed on paragraphs to achieve a certain emphasis. The most common is the **general-to-specific** scheme, in which the topic sentence often comes first and then the following sentences become increasingly specific. The paragraph on mummies (pp. 81–82) illustrates this organization: each sentence is either more specific than the one before it or at the same level of generality. Here is another illustration:

General-to-specific organization

Perhaps the simplest fact about sleep is that individual needs for it vary widely. Most adults sleep between seven and nine hours, but occasionally people turn up who need twelve hours or so, while some rare types can get by on three or four. Rarest of all are those legendary types who require almost no sleep at all; respected researchers have recently studied three such people. One of them—a healthy, happy woman in her seventies—sleeps about an hour every two or three days. The other two are men in early middle age, who get by on a few minutes a night. One of them complains about the daily fifteen minutes or so he's forced to "waste" in sleeping.

—Lawrence A. Mayer,
"The Confounding Enemy of Sleep"

Topic sentence

Supporting examples, increasingly specific

In the less common **specific-to-general** organization, the elements of the paragraph contribute to a general conclusion. The following example illustrates the pattern. Its unusual punctuation is due to its nineteenth-century origins.

Specific-to-general organization

What would we really know the meaning of? The meal in the firkin [covered container]; the milk in the pan; the ballad in the street; the news of the boat; the glance of the eye; the form and the gait of the body—show me the ultimate reason of these matters; show me the sublime presence of the highest spiritual cause lurking, as always it does lurk, in these suburbs and extremities of nature; let me see every trifle bristling with the polarity that ranges it instantly on an eternal law, and the shop, the plough, and the ledger referred to the like cause by which light undulates and poets sing;—and the world lies no longer a dull miscellany and lumber-room, but has form and order; there is no trifle, there is no puzzle, but one design unites and animates the farthest pinnacle and the lowest trench.

—Ralph Waldo Emerson,
"The American Scholar"

Specific examples in response to opening question

General conclusion

As its name implies, the **problem-solution** arrangement introduces a problem and then proposes or explains a solution. The next paragraph explains how to gain from Internet newsgroups despite their limitations:

Problem-solution organization

Even when you do find a newsgroup with apparently useful material, you have no assurance of a correspondent's authority because of e-mail's inherent anonymity. Many people don't cite their credentials. Besides, anyone can pose as an expert. *[Topic sentence and clarification: statement of the problem]*

The best information you can get initially is apt to be a reference to something of which you were not aware but can then investigate for yourself. Internet newsgroups can be valuable for that alone. I have been directed to software-problem solutions, owners of out-of-print books, and important people who know nothing about communicating through electronic communities. It is best to start with the assumption that you are conversing with peers, people who know things that you don't, while you probably know things that they don't. Gradually, by trading information, you develop some virtual relationships and can assess the relative validity of your sources. Meanwhile, you will probably have learned a few things along the way. *[Solution to the problem]*

—Adapted from John A. Butler,
Cybersearch

When your details vary in significance, you can arrange them in a **climactic** order, from least to most important or dramatic:

Climactic organization

Nature has put many strange tongues into the heads of her creatures. *[Topic sentence]* There is the frog's tongue, rooted at the front of the mouth so it can be protruded an extra distance for nabbing prey. *[Least dramatic example]* There is the gecko lizard's tongue, so long and agile that the lizard uses it to wash its eyes. But the ultimate lingual whopper has been achieved in the anteater. The anteater's head, long as it is, is not long enough to contain the tremendous tongue which licks deep into ant-hills. Its tongue is not rooted in the mouth or throat: it is fastened to the breastbone. *[Most dramatic example]*

—Alan Devoe, "Nature's Utmost"

In other paragraph organizations, you can arrange details according to how you think readers are likely to understand them. In discussing the virtues of public television, for instance, you might proceed from **most familiar to least familiar,** from a well-known program your readers have probably seen to less well-known programs they may not have seen. Or in defending the right of government employees to strike, you might arrange your reasons from **simplest to most complex,** from the employees' need to be able to redress grievances to the more subtle consequences for relations between employers and employees.

2 | Repeating or restating key words

Repeating or restating the important words in a paragraph binds the sentences together and keeps the paragraph's topic uppermost in readers' minds. In the next example, notice how the circled words relate the sentences and stress the important ideas of the paragraph:

> Having listened to both (Chinese) and (English,) I also tend to be suspicious of any (comparisons) between the two (languages.) Typically, one (language)—that of the person doing the (comparing)—is often used as the standard, the benchmark for a logical form of expression. And so the (language) being (compared) is always in danger of being judged deficient or superfluous, simplistic or unnecessarily complex, melodious or cacophonous. (English) speakers point out that (Chinese) is (extremely difficult) because it relies on variations in tone barely discernible to the human ear. By the same token, (Chinese) speakers (tell me) English is (extremely difficult) because it is inconsistent, a language of too many broken rules, of Mickey Mice and Donald Ducks.
>
> —Amy Tan, "The Language of Discretion"

This paragraph links sentences through their structure, too, because the subject of each one picks up on key words used earlier:

Sentence 1: Having listened to both (Chinese) and (English,) I tend to be suspicious of any comparisons between the two (languages.)

Sentence 2: Typically, one (language). . .

Sentence 3: And so the (language). . .

Sentence 4: (English speakers). . .

Sentence 5: (Chinese speakers). . .

In many incoherent paragraphs, such as the one on mummification on page 81, each sentence subject introduces a topic new to the paragraph so that readers have trouble following the thread. (See pp. 382–84 for more on linking sentences through their subjects.)

3 | Using parallel structures

Another way to achieve coherence is through **parallelism,** the use of similar grammatical structures for similar elements of meaning within a sentence or among sentences. (See Chapter 25 for a detailed discussion of parallelism.) Parallel structures help tie together the last three sentences in the paragraph on mummies (p. 82). In the following paragraph, underlining highlights the parallel structures linking sentences. Aphra Behn (lived 1640–89) was the first English-woman to write professionally.

> In addition to her busy career as a writer, Aphra Behn also <u>found time</u> to briefly marry and spend a little while in debtor's prison. <u>She found time</u> to take up a career as a spy for the English in their war against the Dutch. <u>She made</u> the long and difficult voyage to Suri-name [in South America] and became involved in a slave rebellion there. <u>She plunged</u> into political debate at Will's Coffee House and defended her position from the stage of the Drury Lane Theater. <u>She actively argued</u> for women's rights to be educated and to marry whom they pleased, or not at all. <u>She defied</u> the seventeenth-century dictum that ladies must be "modest" and wrote freely about sex.
> —Angeline Goreau, "Aphra Behn"

Note Though planned repetition can be effective, careless or excessive repetition weakens prose (see pp. 529–30).

4 Using pronouns

Pronouns such as *she, he, it, they,* and *who* refer to and func-tion as nouns (see p. 237). Thus pronouns naturally help relate sen-tences to one another. In the following paragraph the pronouns and the nouns they refer to are circled:

> After dark, on the warrenlike streets of Brooklyn where (I) live, (I) often see (women) who fear the worst from (me.)(They) seem to have set (their) faces on neutral, and with (their) purse straps strung across (their) chests bandolier-style, (they) forge ahead as though bracing (themselves) against being tackled. (I) understand, of course, that the danger (they) per-ceive is not a hallucination. (Women) are particularly vulnerable to street violence, and young black males are drastically overrepresented among the perpetrators of that violence. Yet these truths are no solace against the kind of alienation that comes of being ever the (suspect,) a fearsome entity with (whom) pedestrians avoid making eye contact.
> —Brent Staples, "Black Men and Public Space"

5 Being consistent

Being consistent is the most subtle way to achieve paragraph coherence because readers are aware of consistency only when it is absent. Consistency (or the lack of it) occurs primarily in the tense of verbs and in the number and person of nouns and pronouns (see Chapter 20). Although some shifts will be necessary to reflect your meaning, inappropriate shifts, as in the following passages, will interfere with a reader's ability to follow the development of ideas.

Shifts in tense

In the Hopi religion, water is the driving force. Since the Hopi lived in the Arizona desert, they needed water urgently for drinking, cooking, and irrigating crops. Their complex beliefs are focused in part on gaining the assistance of supernatural forces in obtaining water. Many of the Hopi kachinas, or spirit essences, were directly concerned with clouds, rain, and snow.

Shifts in number

Kachinas represent the things and events of the real world, such as clouds, mischief, cornmeal, and even death. A kachina is not worshiped as a god but regarded as an interested friend. They visit the Hopi from December through July in the form of men who dress in kachina costumes and perform dances and other rituals.

Shifts in person

Unlike the man, the Hopi woman does not keep contact with kachinas through costumes and dancing. Instead, one receives a small likeness of a kachina, called a *tihu*, from the man impersonating the kachina. You are more likely to receive a tihu as a girl approaching marriage, though a child or older woman sometimes receives one, too.

Grammar checkers Grammar checkers cannot help you locate shifts in tense, number, or person among sentences. Shifts are sometimes necessary (as when tenses change to reflect actual differences in time). Furthermore, a passage with needless shifts may still consist of sentences that are grammatically correct, as all the sentences are in the preceding examples. The only way to achieve consistency in your writing is to review it yourself.

6 | Using transitional expressions

Specific words and word groups, called **transitional expressions,** can connect sentences whose relationships may not be instantly clear to readers. Notice the difference in the following two versions of the same paragraph:

Medical science has succeeded in identifying the hundreds of viruses that can cause the common cold. It has discovered the most effective means of prevention. One person transmits the cold viruses to another most often by hand. An infected person covers his mouth to cough. He picks up the telephone. His daughter picks up the telephone. She rubs her eyes. She has a cold.

Paragraph is choppy and hard to follow

It spreads. To avoid colds, people should wash their hands often and keep their hands away from their faces.

Medical science has thus succeeded in identifying the hundreds of viruses that can cause the common cold. It has also discovered the most effective means of prevention. One person transmits the cold viruses to another most often by hand. For instance, an infected person covers his mouth to cough. Then he picks up the telephone. Half an hour later, his daughter picks up the same telephone. Immediately afterward, she rubs her eyes. Within a few days, she, too, has a cold. And thus it spreads. To avoid colds, therefore, people should wash their hands often and keep their hands away from their faces.

—Kathleen LaFrank (student),
"Colds: Myth and Science"

Transitional expressions (boxed) remove choppiness and spell out relationships

There are scores of transitional expressions on which to draw. The box below shows many common ones, arranged according to the relationships they convey.

Transitional expressions

To add or show sequence
again, also, and, and then, besides, equally important, finally, first, further, furthermore, in addition, in the first place, last, moreover, next, second, still, too

To compare
also, in the same way, likewise, similarly

To contrast
although, and yet, but, but at the same time, despite, even so, even though, for all that, however, in contrast, in spite of, nevertheless, notwithstanding, on the contrary, on the other hand, regardless, still, though, yet

To give examples or intensify
after all, an illustration of, even, for example, for instance, indeed, in fact, it is true, of course, specifically, that is, to illustrate, truly

(continued)

Transitional expressions
(continued)

To indicate place
above, adjacent to, below, elsewhere, farther on, here, near, nearby, on the other side, opposite to, there, to the east, to the left

To indicate time
after a while, afterward, as long as, as soon as, at last, at length, at that time, before, earlier, formerly, immediately, in the meantime, in the past, lately, later, meanwhile, now, presently, shortly, simultaneously, since, so far, soon, subsequently, then, thereafter, until, when

To repeat, summarize, or conclude
all in all, altogether, as has been said, in brief, in conclusion, in other words, in particular, in short, in simpler terms, in summary, on the whole, that is, therefore, to put it differently, to summarize

To show cause or effect
accordingly, as a result, because, consequently, for this purpose, hence, otherwise, since, then, therefore, thereupon, thus, to this end, with this object

Note Draw carefully on the preceding list of transitional expressions because the ones in each group are not interchangeable. For instance, *besides, finally,* and *second* may all be used to add information, but each has its own distinct meaning.

To see where transitional expressions might be needed in your paragraphs, examine the movement from each sentence to the next. (On a computer or on paper, you can highlight the transitional expressions already present and then review the sentences that lack them.) Abrupt changes are most likely to need a transition: a shift from cause to effect, a contradiction, a contrast. You can smooth and clarify transitions *between* paragraphs, too. See pages 110 and 112.

(CULTURE LANGUAGE) If transitional expressions are not common in your native language, you may be tempted to compensate when writing in English by adding them to the beginnings of most sentences. But such explicit transitions aren't needed everywhere, and in fact too many can be intrusive and awkward. When inserting transitional expressions, consider the reader's need for a signal: often the connection from sentence to sentence is already clear from the context, or it can be made clear by relating the content of sentences more closely (see pp. 86–87). When you do need transitional expressions, try varying their positions in your sentences, as shown in the sample paragraph on the previous page.

Punctuating transitional expressions

A transitional expression is usually set off by a comma or commas from the rest of the sentence:

Immediately afterward, she rubs her eyes. Within a few days, she, too, has a cold.

See page 432 for more on this convention and its exceptions.

7 | Combining devices to achieve coherence

The devices for achieving coherence rarely appear in isolation in effective paragraphs. As any example in this chapter shows, writers usually combine sensible organization, parallelism, repetition, pronouns, consistency, and transitional expressions to help readers follow the development of ideas.

Exercise 4.6 Analyzing paragraphs for coherence

Study the paragraphs by Janet Lieber (p. 79), Hillary Begas (p. 94), and Freeman Dyson (p. 96) for the authors' use of various devices to achieve coherence. Look especially for organization, parallel structures and ideas, repetition and restatement, pronouns, and transitional expressions.

Exercise 4.7 Arranging sentences coherently

After the topic sentence (sentence 1), the sentences in the student paragraph below have been deliberately scrambled to make the paragraph incoherent. Using the topic sentence and other clues as guides, rearrange the sentences in the paragraph to form a well-organized, coherent unit.

We hear complaints about the Postal Service all the time, but we should not forget what it does *right*. The total volume of mail delivered by the Postal Service each year makes up almost half the total delivered in all the world. Its 70,000 employees handle 140,000,000,000 pieces of mail each year. And when was the last time they failed to deliver yours? In fact, on any given day the Postal Service delivers almost as much mail as the rest of the world combined. That huge number means over 2,000,000 pieces per employee and over 560 pieces per man, woman, and child in the country.

1
2
3
4
5
6

Exercise 4.8 Eliminating inconsistencies

The following paragraph is incoherent because of inconsistencies in person, number, or tense. Identify the inconsistencies and revise the paragraph to give it coherence. For further exercises in eliminating inconsistencies, see pages 356, 358–59, and 360.

The Hopi tihu, or kachina likeness, is often called a "doll," but its owner, usually a girl or woman, does not regard them as a plaything. Instead, you treated them as a valued possession and hung them out of the way on a wall. For its owner the tihu represents a connection with the kachina's spirit. They are considered part of the kachina, carrying a portion of the kachina's power.

Exercise 4.9   Using transitional expressions

Transitional expressions have been removed from the following paragraph at the numbered blanks. Fill in each blank with an appropriate transitional expression (1) to contrast, (2) to intensify, and (3) to show effect. Consult the list on pages 89–90 if necessary.

All over the country, people are swimming, jogging, weightlifting, dancing, walking, playing tennis—doing anything to keep fit. ___(1)___ this school has consistently refused to construct and equip a fitness center. The school has ___(2)___ refused to open existing athletic facilities to all students, not just those playing organized sports. ___(3)___ students have no place to exercise except in their rooms and on dangerous public roads.

Exercise 4.10   Considering your past work: Paragraph coherence

Continuing from Exercise 4.3 (p. 79), examine the body paragraphs of your essay to see how coherent they are and how their coherence could be improved. Do the paragraphs have a clear organization? Do you use repetition and restatement, parallelism, pronouns, and transitional expressions to signal relationships? Are the paragraphs consistent in person, number, and tense? Revise two or three paragraphs in ways you think will improve their coherence.

Exercise 4.11   Writing a coherent paragraph

Write a coherent paragraph from the following information, combining and rewriting sentences as necessary. First, begin the paragraph with the topic sentence given and arrange the supporting sentences in a climactic order. Then combine and rewrite the supporting sentences, helping the reader see connections by introducing repetition and restatement, parallelism, pronouns, consistency, and transitional expressions.

Topic sentence

Hypnosis is far superior to drugs for relieving tension.

Supporting information

Hypnosis has none of the dangerous side effects of the drugs that relieve tension.
Tension-relieving drugs can cause weight loss or gain, illness, or even death.
Hypnosis is nonaddicting.
Most of the drugs that relieve tension do foster addiction.
Tension-relieving drugs are expensive.
Hypnosis is inexpensive even for people who have not mastered self-hypnosis.

Exercise 4.12 Turning topic sentences into coherent paragraphs

Develop three of the following topic sentences into coherent paragraphs. Organize your information by space, by time, or for emphasis, as seems most appropriate. Use repetition and restatement, parallelism, pronouns, consistency, and transitional expressions to link sentences.

1. The most interesting character in the book [or movie] was _____.
2. Of all my classes, _____ is the one that I think will serve me best throughout life.
3. Although we in the United States face many problems, the one we should concentrate on solving first is _____.
4. The most dramatic building in town is the _____.
5. Children should not have to worry about the future.

4c | Developing the paragraph

In an essay that's understandable and interesting to readers, you will provide plenty of solid information to support your general statements. You work that information into the essay through the paragraph, as you build up each point relating to the thesis.

A paragraph may be unified and coherent but still be inadequate if you skimp on details. Take this example:

> Untruths can serve as a kind of social oil when they smooth connections between people. In preventing confrontation and injured feelings, they allow everyone to go on as before.

General statements needing examples to be clear and convincing

This paragraph lacks **development,** completeness. It does not provide enough information for us to evaluate or even care about the writer's assertions.

1 | Using specific information

If they are sound, the general statements you make in any writing will be based on what you have experienced, observed, read, and thought. Readers will assume as much and will expect you to provide the evidence for your statements—sensory details, facts, statistics, examples, quotations, reasons. Whatever helps you form your views you need, in turn, to share with readers.

Here is the actual version of the preceding sample paragraph. With examples, the paragraph is more interesting and convincing.

> Untruths can serve as a kind of social oil when they smooth connections between people. Assuring a worried friend that his haircut is flattering, claiming an appointment to avoid an

aunt's dinner invitation, pretending interest in an acquaintance's children—these lies may protect the liar, but they also protect the person lied to. In preventing confrontation and injured feelings, the lies allow everyone to go on as before.

> Examples specifying kinds of lies and consequences

—Joan Lar (student), "The Truth of Lies"

If your readers often comment that your writing needs more specifics, you should focus on that improvement in your revisions. Try listing the general statements of each paragraph on lines by themselves with space underneath. Then use one of the discovery techniques discussed on pages 18–28 (freewriting, brainstorming, and so on) to find the details to support each sentence. Write these into your draft. If you write on a computer, you can do this revision directly on your draft. First create a duplicate of your draft, and then, working on the copy, separate the sentences and explore their support. Rewrite the supporting details into sentences, reassemble the paragraph, and edit it for coherence.

2 Using rhetorical strategies

If you have difficulty developing an idea or shaping your information, try asking yourself questions derived from rhetorical strategies, also called patterns of development. (The same patterns can help with essay development, too. See pp. 27–28.)

How did it happen? (Narration)

Narration retells a significant sequence of events, usually in the order of their occurrence (that is, chronologically):

> Jill's story is typical for "recruits" to religious cults. She was very lonely in college and appreciated the attention of the nice young men and women who lived in a house near campus. They persuaded her to share their meals and then to move in with them. Between intense bombardments of "love," they deprived her of sleep and sometimes threatened to throw her out. Jill became increasingly confused and dependent, losing touch with any reality besides the one in the group. She dropped out of school and refused to see or communicate with her family. Before long she, too, was preying on lonely college students.

> Important events in chronological order

—Hillary Begas (student), "The Love Bombers"

As this paragraph illustrates, a narrator is concerned not just with the sequence of events but also with their consequence, their importance to the whole. Thus a narrative rarely corresponds to real time; instead, it collapses transitional or background events and focuses on events of particular interest. In addition, writers sometimes rearrange events, as when they simulate the workings of memory by flashing back to an earlier time.

How does it look, sound, feel, smell, taste? (Description)

Description details the sensory qualities of a person, place, thing, or feeling. You use concrete and specific words to convey a dominant mood, to illustrate an idea, or to achieve some other purpose. Some description is **subjective**: the writer filters the subject through his or her biases and emotions. In the subjective description by Virginia Woolf on page 83, the *glare* of the walls, the *impenetrable darkness*, the *bulge of a great bowl*, and the *formidable corners and lines* all indicate the feelings of the author about what she describes.

In contrast to subjective description, journalists, scientists, and other academic writers usually strive for description that is **objective**, conveying the subject without bias or emotion:

> Vanessa works in a trendy salon but also cuts hair in her apartment—for a few friends and friends of friends. Her client Lynn sits in a small barber's chair by the window, the place where you'd imagine a breakfast table, a mirror leaning against the wall in front of her. On the floor by the mirror there are a small bowl for Vanessa's dog and a vase with three yellow flowers. Vanessa stands behind Lynn, asking her questions about her hair, chitchatting a little. She keeps her eyes on Lynn's hair as she moves her fingers through it, lifting up, then pulling down one section, then another, then gesturing with her hands around the hair, indicating shape and movement. "How did you like the last haircut?" she asks. "How did it handle? Was it easy to manage? What's bugging you now? Does it feel heavy up front?" Lynn answers these questions, describing what she wants, relying on adjectives that have more to do with feeling than shape. She wants the cut "freshened," wants it "sassy."
> —Mike Rose, *The Mind at Work*

Objective description: specific record of sensory data without interpretation

What are examples of it or reasons for it? (Illustration or support)

Some ideas can be developed simply by **illustration or support**—supplying detailed examples or reasons. The writer of the paragraph on lying (pp. 93–94) developed her idea with several specific examples of her general statements. You can also supply a single extended example:

> The language problem that I was attacking loomed larger and larger as I began to learn more. When I would describe in English certain ⌉

concepts and objects enmeshed in Korean emotion and imagination, I became slowly aware of nuances, of differences between two languages even in simple expression. The remark "Kim entered the house" seems to be simple enough, yet, unless a reader has a clear visual image of a Korean house, his understanding of the sentence is not complete. When a Korean says he is "in the house," he may be in his courtyard, or on his porch, or in his small room! If I wanted to give a specific picture of entering the house in the Western sense, I had to say "room" instead of house— sometimes. I say "sometimes" because many Koreans entertain their guests on their porches and still are considered to be hospitable, and in the Korean sense, going into the "room" may be a more intimate act than it would be in the English sense. Such problems!

— Kim Yong Ik, "A Book-Writing Venture"

Topic sentence (assertion to be illustrated)

Single detailed example

Sometimes you can develop a paragraph by providing your reasons for stating a general idea:

There are three reasons, quite apart from scientific considerations, that mankind needs to travel in space. The first reason is the need for garbage disposal: we need to transfer industrial processes into space, so that the earth may remain a green and pleasant place for our grandchildren to live in. The second reason is the need to escape material impoverishment: the resources of this planet are finite, and we shall not forgo forever the abundant solar energy and minerals and living space that are spread out all around us. The third reason is our spiritual need for an open frontier: the ultimate purpose of space travel is to bring to humanity not only scientific discoveries and an occasional spectacular show on television but a real expansion of our spirit.

— Freeman Dyson, "Disturbing the Universe"

Topic sentence

Three reasons arranged in order of increasing drama and importance

What is it? What does it encompass, and what does it exclude? (Definition)

A **definition** says what something is and is not, specifying the characteristics that distinguish the subject from the other members of its class. You can easily define concrete, noncontroversial terms in a single sentence: *A knife is a cutting instrument* (its class) *with a sharp blade set in a handle* (the characteristics that set it off from, say, scissors or a razor blade). But defining a complicated or controversial topic often requires extended explanation, and you may need to devote a whole paragraph or even an essay to it. Such a definition may provide examples to identify the subject's characteristics. It may also involve other methods of development discussed here, such as classification or comparison and contrast.

The following definition of the word *quality* comes from an essay asserting that "quality in product and effort has become a vanishing element of current civilization":

> In the hope of possibly reducing the hail of censure which is certain to greet this essay (I am thinking of going to Alaska or possibly Patagonia in the week it is published), let me say that quality, as I understand it, means investment of the best skill and effort possible to produce the finest and most admirable result possible. **— General definition**
>
> Its presence or absence in some degree characterizes every man-made object, service, skilled or unskilled labor—laying bricks, painting a picture, ironing shirts, practicing medicine, shoemaking, scholarship, writing a book. **— Activities in which quality may figure**
>
> You do it well or you do it half-well. Materials are sound and durable or they are sleazy; method is painstaking or whatever is easiest. Quality is achieving or reaching for the highest standard as against being satisfied with the sloppy or fraudulent. It is honesty of purpose as against catering to cheap or sensational sentiment. It does not allow compromise with the second-rate. **— Contrast between quality and nonquality**
>
> —Barbara Tuchman, "The Decline of Quality"

What are its parts or characteristics? (Division or analysis)

Division and **analysis** both involve separating something into its elements, the better to understand it. Here is a simple example:

> A typical daily newspaper compresses considerable information into the top of the first page, above the headlines. **— The subject being divided**
>
> The most prominent feature of this space, the newspaper's name, is called the *logo* or *nameplate*. Under the logo and set off by rules is a line of small type called the *folio line*, which contains the date of the issue, the volume and issue numbers, copyright information, and the price. To the right of the logo is a block of small type called a *weather ear*, a summary of the day's forecast. And above the logo is a *skyline*, a kind of advertisement in which the paper's editors highlight a special feature of the issue. **— Elements of the subject, arranged spatially**
>
> —Kansha Stone (student),
> "Anatomy of a Paper"

Generally, analysis goes beyond simply identifying elements. Often used as a synonym for *critical thinking,* analysis also involves interpreting the elements' meaning, significance, and relationships. You identify and interpret elements according to your particular interest in the subject. (See pp. 147–53 for more on critical thinking and analysis.)

The following paragraph comes from an essay about soap operas. The analytical focus of the whole essay is the way soap operas provide viewers with a sense of community missing from their own lives. The paragraph itself has a narrower focus related to the broader one.

> The surface realism of the soap opera conjures up an illusion of "liveness." The domestic settings and easygoing rhythms encourage the viewer to believe that the drama, however ridiculous, is simply an extension of daily life. The conversation is so slow that some have called it "radio with pictures." (Advertisers have always assumed that busy housewives would listen, rather than watch.) Conversation is casual and colloquial, as though one were eavesdropping on neighbors. There is plenty of time to "read" the character's face; close-ups establish intimacy. The sets are comfortably familiar: well-lit interiors of living rooms, restaurants, offices, and hospitals. Daytime soaps have little of the glamour of their prime-time relations. The viewer easily imagines that the conversation is taking place in real time.
>   —Ruth Rosen, "Search for Yesterday"

Topic and focus: how "liveness" seems an extension of daily life

Elements:
Slow conversation

Casual conversation

Intimate close-ups

Familiar sets

Absence of glamour
Appearance of real time

What groups or categories can it be sorted into? (Classification)

Classification involves sorting many things into groups based on their similarities. Using the pattern, we scan a large group composed of many members that share at least one characteristic—workers, say—and we assign the members to smaller groups on the basis of some principle—salary, perhaps, or dependence on computers. Here is an example:

> In my experience, the parents who hire afternoon sitters for their school-age children tend to fall into one of three groups. The first group includes parents who work and want someone to be at home with their children after school. These parents are looking for an extension of themselves, someone who will give the care they would give if they were at home. The second group includes parents who may be home all day themselves but are too disorganized or too frazzled by their children's demands to handle child care alone. They are looking for an organizer and helpmate. The third and final group includes parents who do not want to be bothered by their children, whether they are home all day or not.

Topic sentence

Three groups:
Alike in one way
(all hire sitters)
No overlap in groups
(each has a different attitude)

Classes arranged in order of increasing drama

Unlike the parents in the first two groups, who
care for their children whenever and however they
can, these parents are looking for a permanent
substitute for themselves.
—Nancy Whittle (student),
"Modern Parenting"

How is it like, or different from, other things? (Comparison and contrast)

Asking about similarities and differences leads to **comparison and contrast:** comparison focuses on similarities, whereas contrast focuses on differences. The two may be used separately or together to develop an idea or to relate two or more things. Commonly, comparisons are organized in one of two ways. In the first, **subject by subject,** the two subjects are discussed separately, one at a time:

Consider the differences also in the behavior of rock and classical music audiences. At a rock concert, the audience members yell, whistle, sing along, and stamp their feet. They may even stand during the entire performance. The better the music, the more active they'll be. At a classical concert, in contrast, the better the performance, the more *still* the audience is. Members of the classical audience are so highly disciplined that they refrain from even clearing their throats or coughing. No matter what effect the powerful music has on their intellects and feelings, they sit on their hands.
—Tony Nahm (student),
"Rock and Roll Is Here to Stay"

> Subjects: rock and classical audiences
> Rock audience
> Classical audience

In the second comparative organization, **point by point,** the two subjects are discussed side by side and matched feature for feature:

Arguing is often equated with fighting, but there are key differences between the two. Participants in an argument approach the subject to find common ground, or points on which both sides agree, while people engaged in a fight usually approach the subject with an "us-versus-them" attitude. Participants in an argument are careful to use respectful, polite language, in contrast to the insults and worse that people in a fight use to get the better of their opponents. Finally, participants in an argument commonly have the goal of reaching a new understanding or larger truth about the subject they're debating, while those in a fight have winning as their only goal.
—Erica Ito (student),
"Is an Argument Always a Fight?"

> Subjects: arguing and fighting
> Approach to subject: argument, fight
> Language: argument, fight
> Goal: argument, fight

The following examples show the two organizing schemes in outline form. The one on the left corresponds to the point-by-point paragraph about the differences between arguing and fighting. The one on the right uses the same information but reorganizes it to cover the two subjects separately: first one, then the other.

Point by Point	Subject by Subject
I. Approach to subject	I. Argument
A. Argument	A. Approach to subject
B. Fight	B. Language
II. Language	C. Goal
A. Argument	II. Fight
B. Fight	A. Approach to subject
III. Goal	B. Language
A. Argument	C. Goal
B. Fight	

Is it comparable to something that is in a different class but more familiar to readers? (Analogy)

Whereas we draw comparisons and contrasts between elements in the same general class (audiences, disputes), we link elements in different classes with a special kind of comparison called **analogy**. Most often in analogy we illuminate or explain an unfamiliar, abstract class of things with a familiar and concrete class of things:

> We might eventually obtain some sort of bedrock understanding of cosmic structure, but we will never understand the universe in detail; it is just too big and varied for that. If we possessed an atlas of our galaxy that devoted but a single page to each star system in the Milky Way (so that the sun and all its planets were crammed on one page), that atlas would run to more than ten million volumes of ten thousand pages each. It would take a library the size of Harvard's to house the atlas, and merely to flip through it, at the rate of a page per second, would require over ten thousand years.
>
> —Timothy Ferris,
> *Coming of Age in the Milky Way*

Abstract subject: the universe, specifically the Milky Way

Concrete subject: an atlas

Why did it happen, or what results did it have? (Cause-and-effect analysis)

When you use analysis to explain why something happened or what is likely to happen, then you are determining causes and effects. **Cause-and-effect analysis** is especially useful in writing about social, economic, or political events or problems. In the next paragraph the author looks at the causes of Japanese collectivism, which he elsewhere contrasts with American individualism:

The *shinkansen* or "bullet train" speeds across the rural areas of Japan giving a quick view of cluster after cluster of farmhouses surrounded by rice paddies. This particular pattern did not

— Effect: pattern of Japanese farming

develop purely by chance, but as a consequence of the technology peculiar to the growing of rice, the staple of the Japanese diet. The growing of rice requires the construction and maintenance of an irrigation system, something that takes many hands to build. More importantly, the planting and the harvesting of rice can only be done efficiently with the cooperation of twenty or more people. The "bottom line" is that a single family working alone cannot produce enough rice to survive, but a dozen families working together can produce a surplus. Thus the Japanese

— Causes: Japanese dependence on rice, which requires collective effort

have had to develop the capacity to work together in harmony, no matter what the forces of disagreement or social disintegration, in order to survive.
—William Ouchi, *Theory Z*

— Effect: working in harmony

Cause-and-effect paragraphs tend to focus either on causes, as Ouchi's does, or on effects, as this paragraph does:

At each step, with every graduation from one level of education to the next, the refrain from bystanders was strangely the same: "Your parents must be so proud of you." I suppose that

— Cause: education

my parents were proud, although I suspect, too, that they felt more than pride alone as they watched me advance through my education. They seemed to know that my education was separating us from one another, making it difficult to resume familiar intimacies. Mixed with the instincts of parental pride, a certain hurt also communicated itself—too private ever to be adequately expressed in words, but real nonetheless.
—Richard Rodriguez, "Going Home Again"

Effects:
Pride

Separation
Loss of intimacies
Hurt

How does one do it, or how does it work? (Process analysis)

When you analyze how to do something or how something works, you explain the steps in a **process**. Paragraphs developed by process analysis are usually organized chronologically, as the steps in the process occur. Some process analyses tell the reader how to do a task:

As a car owner, you waste money when you pay a mechanic to change the engine oil. The job is not difficult, even if you know little about cars. All you need is a wrench to remove the drain

— Process: changing oil

plug, a large, flat pan to collect the draining oil, plastic bottles to dispose of the used oil, and fresh oil. First, warm up the car's engine so that the oil will flow more easily. When the engine is warm, shut it off and remove its oil-filler cap (the owner's manual shows where this cap is). Then locate the drain plug under the engine (again consulting the owner's manual for its location) and place the flat pan under the plug. Remove the plug with the wrench, letting the oil flow into the pan. When the oil stops flowing, replace the plug and, at the engine's filler hole, add the amount and kind of fresh oil specified by the owner's manual. Pour the used oil into the plastic bottles and take it to a waste-oil collector, which any garage mechanic can recommend.

Equipment needed

Steps in process

— Anthony Andreas (student),
"Do-It-Yourself Car Care"

Other process analyses explain how processes are done or how they work in nature. The paragraph on monarch butterflies (p. 83) is one example. Here is another:

What used to be called "laying on of hands" is now practiced seriously by nurses and doctors. Studies have shown that therapeutic touch, as it is now known, can aid relaxation and ease pain, two effects that may in turn cause healing. A "healer" must first concentrate on helping the patient. Then, hands held a few inches from the patient's body, the healer moves from head to foot. Healers claim that they can detect energy disturbances in the patient that indicate tension, pain, or sickness. With further hand movements, the healer tries to redirect the energy. Patients report feeling heat from the healer's hands, perhaps indicating an energy transfer between healer and patient.

Process: therapeutic touch

Benefits

Steps in process

How process works

— Lisa Kuklinski (student),
"Old Ways to Noninvasive Medicine"

Diagrams, photographs, and other figures can do much to clarify process analyses. See pages 122–26 for guidelines on creating and clearly labeling figures.

Combining rhetorical strategies

Whatever strategy you choose as the basis for developing a paragraph, others may also prove helpful. Combined strategies have appeared often in this section: Dyson analyzes causes and effects in presenting reasons (p. 96); Tuchman uses contrast to define *quality* (p. 97); Nahm uses description to compare (p. 99); Ouchi uses process analysis to explain causes (p. 101).

3 | Checking length

The average paragraph contains between 100 and 150 words, or between four and eight sentences. The actual length of a paragraph depends on the complexity of its topic, the role it plays in developing the thesis of the essay, and its position in the essay. Nevertheless, very short paragraphs are often inadequately developed; they may leave readers with a sense of incompleteness. And very long paragraphs often contain irrelevant details or develop two or more topics; readers may have difficulty following, sorting out, or remembering ideas.

When you are revising your essay, reread the paragraphs that seem very long or very short, checking them especially for unity and adequate development. If the paragraph wanders, cut everything from it that does not support your main idea (such as sentences that you might begin with *By the way*). If it is underdeveloped, supply the specific details, examples, or reasons needed, or try one of the methods of development we have discussed here.

Exercise 4.13 Analyzing paragraph development

Examine the paragraph by Henry Louis Gates, Jr. (p. 79) to discover how the author achieves paragraph development. What rhetorical strategy or strategies does the author use? Where does he support general statements with specific evidence?

Exercise 4.14 Analyzing and revising skimpy paragraphs

The following paragraphs are not well developed. Analyze them, looking especially for general statements that lack support or leave questions in your mind. Then rewrite one into a well-developed paragraph, supplying your own concrete details or examples.

1. One big difference between successful and unsuccessful teachers is the quality of communication. A successful teacher is sensitive to students' needs and excited by the subject of the class. In contrast, an unsuccessful teacher seems uninterested in students and bored by the subject.

2. Gestures are one of our most important means of communication. We use them instead of speech. We use them to supplement the words we speak. And we use them to communicate some feelings or meanings that words cannot adequately express.

3. I've discovered that a computer can do much—but not everything—to help me improve my writing. I can easily make changes and try out different versions of a paper. But I still must do the hard work of revising.

Exercise 4.15 Considering your past work: Paragraph development

Continuing from Exercises 4.3 (p. 79) and 4.10 (p. 92), examine the development of the body paragraphs in your writing. Where does specific information seem adequate to support your general statements? Where does support seem skimpy? Revise the paragraphs as necessary to make your ideas clearer and more interesting. It may help you to pose the questions on pages 94–101.

Exercise 4.16 Writing with rhetorical strategies

Write at least three unified, coherent, and well-developed paragraphs, each one developed with a different pattern. Draw on the topics provided here, or choose your own topics.

1. **Narration**
   An experience of public speaking
   A disappointment
   Leaving home
   Waking up
2. **Description (objective or subjective)**
   Your room
   A crowded or deserted place
   A food
   An intimidating person
3. **Illustration or support**
   Why study
   Having a headache
   The best sports event
   Usefulness or uselessness of a self-help book
4. **Definition**
   Humor
   An adult
   Fear
   Authority
5. **Division or analysis**
   A television news show
   A barn
   A Web site
   A piece of music
6. **Classification**
   Factions in a dispute
   Styles of playing poker
   Types of Web sites
   Kinds of teachers

7. **Comparison and contrast**
   Surfing the Web and watching TV
   AM and FM radio DJs
   High school and college football
   Movies on TV and in a theater
8. **Analogy**
   Taking a test and running a race
   The US Constitution and a building's foundation
   Graduating from high school and being released from prison
9. **Cause-and-effect analysis**
   Connection between tension and anger
   Causes of failing or acing a course
   Connection between credit cards and debt
   Causes of a serious accident
10. **Process analysis**
    Preparing for a job interview
    Setting up a blog
    Learning to play a musical instrument
    Making a jump shot

4d Writing special kinds of paragraphs

Several kinds of paragraphs do not always follow the guidelines for unity, coherence, development, and length because they serve special functions. These are the essay introduction, the essay conclusion, the transitional or emphatic paragraph, and the paragraph of spoken dialog.

1 Opening an essay

Most of your essays will open with a paragraph that draws readers from their world into your world. A good opening paragraph usually satisfies several requirements:

- It focuses readers' attention on your subject and arouses their curiosity about what you have to say.
- It specifies what your topic is and implies your attitude.
- Often it provides your thesis statement.
- It is concise and sincere.

The box on the next page gives options for achieving these goals.

Note If you are composing on the Web, you'll want to consider the expectations of Web readers. Your opening page may take the place of a conventional introduction, providing concise text indicating your site's subject and purpose, a menu of its contents, and links to other pages. (See pp. 796–802 for more on composing for the Web.)

CULTURE LANGUAGE The requirements and options for essay introductions may not be what you are used to if your native language is not English. In other cultures, readers may seek familiarity or reassurance from an author's introduction, or they may prefer an indirect approach to the subject. In academic and business English, however, writers and readers prefer concise, direct expression.

The funnel introduction

One reliably effective introduction forms a kind of funnel:

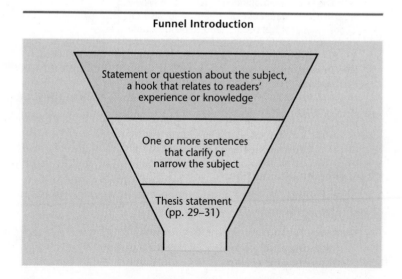

Funnel Introduction

Statement or question about the subject, a hook that relates to readers' experience or knowledge

One or more sentences that clarify or narrow the subject

Thesis statement (pp. 29–31)

Some strategies for opening paragraphs

- Ask a question.
- Relate an incident.
- Use a vivid quotation.
- Offer a surprising statistic or other fact.
- State an opinion related to your thesis.
- Outline the argument your thesis refutes.
- Provide background.

- Create a visual image that represents your subject.
- Make a historical comparison or contrast.
- Outline a problem or dilemma.
- Define a word central to your subject.
- In some business or technical writing, summarize your paper.

Here are two examples of the funnel introduction:

Can your home or office computer make you sterile? Can it strike you blind or dumb? The — *Questions about subject*

answer is: probably not. Nevertheless, reports of side effects relating to computer use should be examined, especially in the area of birth defects, eye complaints, and postural difficulties. Although — *Clarification of subject: bridge to thesis statement*

little conclusive evidence exists to establish a causal link between computer use and problems of this sort, the circumstantial evidence can be disturbing. — *Thesis statement*

—Thomas Hartmann,
"How Dangerous Is Your Computer?"

The Declaration of Independence is so widely regarded as a statement of American ideals that its origins in practical politics tend to be forgotten. — *Statement about subject*

Thomas Jefferson's draft was intensely debated and then revised in the Continental Congress. Jefferson was disappointed with the result. How- — *Clarification of subject: bridge to thesis statement*

ever, a close reading of both the historical con- text and the revisions themselves indicates that the Congress improved the document for its intended purpose. — *Thesis statement*

—Ann Weiss (student), "The Editing of the Declaration of Independence"

Other effective introductions

Several other types of introduction can be equally effective, though they are sometimes harder to invent and control.

Quotation leading into the thesis statement

"It is difficult to speak adequately or justly of London," wrote Henry James in 1881. "It is not a pleasant place; it is not agreeable, or cheerful, or easy, or exempt from reproach. It is only magnificent." | Quotation

Were he alive today, James, a connoisseur of cities, might easily say the same thing about New York or Paris or Tokyo, for the great city is one of the paradoxes of history. | Bridge to thesis statement

In countless different ways, it has almost always been an unpleasant, disagreeable, cheerless, uneasy and reproachful place; in the end, it can only be described as magnificent. | Thesis statement

—*Time*

Incident or image setting up the thesis statement

Canada is pink. I knew that from the map I owned when I was six. On it, New York was green and brown, which was true as far as I could see, so there was no reason to distrust the map maker's portrayal of Canada. When my parents took me across the border and we entered the immigration booth, I looked excitedly for the pink earth. Slowly it dawned on me: this foreign, "different" place was not so different. | Incident from writer's experience

I discovered that the world in my head and the world at my feet were not the same. | Thesis statement

—Robert Ornstein, *Human Nature*

Startling opinion or question

Caesar was right. Thin people need watching. I've been watching them for most of my adult life, and I don't like what I see. When these narrow fellows spring at me, I quiver to my toes. Thin people come in all personalities, most of them menacing. You've got your "together" thin person, your mechanical thin person, your condescending thin person, your tsk-tsk thin person. | Opinion

All of them are dangerous. | Thesis statement

—Suzanne Britt,
"That Lean and Hungry Look"

Background, such as a historical comparison

Throughout the first half of this century, the American Medical Association, the largest and most powerful medical organization in the world, battled relentlessly to rid the country of quack potions and cure-alls; and it is the AMA that is generally credited with being the single most powerful force behind the enactment of the early pure food and drug laws. | Historical background

Today, however, medicine's guardian seems to have done a complete about-face and become one of the pharmaceutical | Thesis statement

industry's staunchest allies—often at the public's
peril and expense.
—Mac Jeffery, "Does Rx Spell Rip-off?"

An effective introductory paragraph need not be long, as the following opener shows:

I've often wondered what goes into a hot dog. Now I know and I wish I didn't.
—William Zinsser, *The Lunacy Boom*

Ineffective introductions

When writing and revising an introductory paragraph, avoid the following approaches that are likely to bore readers or make them question your sincerity or control:

Openings to avoid

- **A vague generality or truth.** Don't extend your reach too wide with a line such as *Throughout human history . . .* or *In today's world. . . .* Readers can do without the warm-up.
- **A flat announcement.** Don't start with *The purpose of this essay is . . . , In this essay I will . . . ,* or any similar presentation of your intention or topic.
- **A reference to the essay's title.** Don't refer to the title of the essay in the first sentence—for example, *This is a big problem* or *This book is about the history of the guitar.*
- *According to Webster. . . .* Don't start by citing a dictionary definition. A definition can be an effective springboard to an essay, but this kind of lead-in has become dull with overuse.
- **An apology.** Don't fault your opinion or your knowledge with *I'm not sure if I'm right, but . . . ; I don't know much about this, but . . . ;* or a similar line.

2 Closing an essay

Most of your compositions will end with a closing statement or conclusion, a signal to readers that you have not simply stopped writing but have actually finished. The conclusion completes an essay, bringing it to a climax while assuring readers that they have understood your intention.

Note Compositions for the Web usually do not provide the kind of closure featured in essays. In fact, you'll need to ensure that your Web pages don't dead-end, leaving the reader stranded without options for moving backward or forward through your material. (For more on Web composition, see pp. 796–802.)

Effective conclusions

An essay conclusion may consist of a single sentence or a group of sentences, usually set off in a separate paragraph. The conclusion may take one or more of the following approaches:

> ## Some strategies for closing paragraphs
>
> - Recommend a course of action.
> - Summarize the paper.
> - Echo the approach of the introduction.
> - Restate your thesis and reflect on its implications.
> - Strike a note of hope or despair.
> - Give a symbolic or powerful fact or other detail.
> - Give an especially compelling example.
> - Create an image that represents your subject.
> - Use a quotation.

The following paragraph concludes the essay on the Declaration of Independence (the introduction appears on p. 106):

> The Declaration of Independence has come to be a statement of this nation's political philosophy, but that was not its purpose in 1776. Jefferson's | Echo of introduction: contrast between past and present
>
> passionate expression had to bow to the goals of the Congress as a whole to forge unity among the colonies and to win the support of foreign nations. | Restatement and elaboration of thesis
>
> —Ann Weiss (student), "The Editing of the Declaration of Independence"

Maxine Hong Kingston uses a different technique—a vivid image—to conclude an essay about an aunt who committed suicide by drowning:

> My aunt haunts me—her ghost drawn to me because now, after fifty years of neglect, I alone devote pages of paper to her, though not origamied into houses and clothes. I do not think she always means me well. I am telling on her, and she was a spite suicide, drowning | Summary
>
> herself in the drinking water. The Chinese are always very frightened of the drowned one, whose weeping ghost, wet hair hanging and skin bloated, waits silently by the water to pull down a substitute. | Image
>
> —Maxine Hong Kingston, "No Name Woman"

In the next paragraph the author concludes an essay on environmental protection with a call for action:

Until we get the answers, I think we had better keep on building power plants and growing food with the help of fertilizers and such insect-controlling chemicals as we now have. The risks are well known, thanks to the environmentalists. If they had not created a widespread public awareness of the ecological crisis, we wouldn't stand a chance. But such awareness by itself is not enough. — Summary and opinion

Flaming manifestos and prophecies of doom are no longer much help, and a search for scapegoats can only make matters worse. The time for sensations and manifestos is about over. Now we need rigorous analysis, united effort and very hard work. — Call for action

—Peter F. Drucker, "How Best to
Protect the Environment"

Ineffective conclusions

The preceding examples illustrate ways of avoiding several pitfalls of conclusions:

Closings to avoid

- **A repeat of the introduction.** Don't simply replay your introduction. The conclusion should capture what the paragraphs of the body have added to the introduction.
- **A new direction.** Don't introduce a subject different from the one your essay has been about. If you arrive at a new idea, this may be a signal to start fresh with that idea as your thesis.
- **A sweeping generalization.** Don't conclude more than you reasonably can from the evidence you have given. If your essay is about your frustrating experience trying to clear a parking ticket, you cannot reasonably conclude that *all* local police forces are tied up in red tape.
- **An apology.** Don't cast doubt on your essay. Don't say, *Even though I'm no expert* or *This may not be convincing, but I believe it's true* or anything similar. Rather, to win your readers' confidence, display confidence.

3 Using short emphatic or transitional paragraphs

A short emphatic paragraph can give unusual stress to an important idea, in effect asking the reader to pause and consider before moving on.

In short, all those who might have taken responsibility ducked it, and catastrophe was inevitable.

A transitional paragraph, because it is longer than a word or phrase and is set off by itself, moves a discussion from one point to another more slowly or more completely than does a single transitional expression or even a transitional sentence attached to a larger paragraph.

> These, then, are the causes of the current contraction in hospital facilities. But how does this contraction affect the medical costs of the government, private insurers, and individuals?

> So the debates were noisy and emotion-packed. But what did they accomplish? Historians have identified at least three direct results.

Use transitional paragraphs only to shift readers' attention when your essay makes a significant turn. A paragraph like the following one betrays a writer who is stalling:

> Now that we have examined these facts, we can look at some others that are equally central to an examination of this important issue.

4 Writing dialog

When recording a conversation between two or more people, start a new paragraph for each person's speech. The paragraphing establishes for the reader the point at which one speaker stops talking and another begins.

> The dark shape was indistinguishable. But once I'd flooded him with light, there he stood, blinking.
> "Well," he said eventually, "you're a sight for sore eyes. Should I stand here or are you going to let me in?"
> "Come in," I said. And in he came.
> —Louise Erdrich, *The Beet Queen*

Though dialog appears most often in fiction writing (the source of the preceding example), it may occasionally freshen or enliven narrative or expository essays. (For guidance in using quotation marks and other punctuation in passages of dialog, see pp. 438–40 and 464.)

Exercise 4.17 Analyzing an introduction and conclusion
Analyze the introductory and concluding paragraphs in the first and final drafts of the student essay in Chapter 3, pages 51–52 and 67–69. What is wrong with the first-draft paragraphs? Why are the final-draft paragraphs better? Could they be improved still further?

Exercise 4.18 Considering your past work: Introductions and conclusions
Examine the opening and closing paragraphs of the essay you've been analyzing in Exercises 4.3, 4.10, and 4.15. Do the paragraphs fulfill the requirements and avoid the pitfalls outlined on pages 105–10? Revise them as needed for clarity, conciseness, focus, and interest.

4e Linking paragraphs in the essay

Your paragraphs do not stand alone: each one is a key unit of a larger piece of writing. Though you may draft paragraphs or groups of paragraphs almost as mini-essays, you will eventually need to stitch them together into a unified, coherent, well-developed whole. The techniques parallel those for linking sentences in paragraphs:

- **Make sure each paragraph contributes to your thesis.**
- **Arrange the paragraphs in a clear, logical order.** See pages 35–46 for advice on essay organization.
- **Create links between paragraphs.** Use repetition and restatement to stress and connect key terms, and use transitional expressions and transitional sentences to indicate sequence, direction, contrast, and other relationships.

The essay "A Picture of Hyperactivity" on pages 45–46 illustrates the first two of these techniques. The following passages from the essay illustrate the third technique, with circled repetitions and restatements, boxed transitional expressions, and transitional sentences noted in annotations.

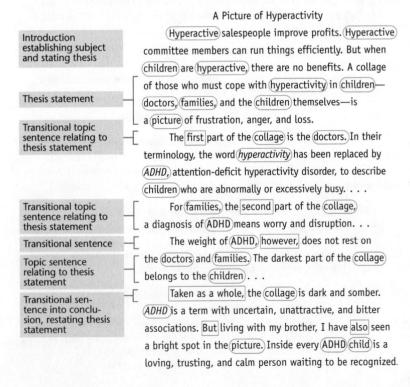

A Picture of Hyperactivity

Introduction establishing subject and stating thesis

Hyperactive salespeople improve profits. Hyperactive committee members can run things efficiently. But when children are hyperactive, there are no benefits. A collage of those who must cope with hyperactivity in children—

Thesis statement

doctors, families, and the children themselves—is a picture of frustration, anger, and loss.

Transitional topic sentence relating to thesis statement

The first part of the collage is the doctors. In their terminology, the word hyperactivity has been replaced by ADHD, attention-deficit hyperactivity disorder, to describe children who are abnormally or excessively busy. . . .

Transitional topic sentence relating to thesis statement

For families, the second part of the collage, a diagnosis of ADHD means worry and disruption. . . .

Transitional sentence

The weight of ADHD, however, does not rest on

Topic sentence relating to thesis statement

the doctors and families. The darkest part of the collage belongs to the children. . . .

Transitional sentence into conclusion, restating thesis statement

Taken as a whole, the collage is dark and somber. ADHD is a term with uncertain, unattractive, and bitter associations. But living with my brother, I have also seen a bright spot in the picture. Inside every ADHD child is a loving, trusting, and calm person waiting to be recognized.

Exercise 4.19 Analyzing paragraphs in an essay

Analyze the ways in which paragraphs combine in the student essay in Chapter 3, pages 67–69. What techniques does the writer use to link paragraphs to the thesis statement and to each other? Where, if at all, does the writer seem to stray from the thesis or fail to show how paragraphs relate to it? How would you revise the essay to solve any problems it exhibits?

Exercise 4.20 Considering your past work: Paragraphs in the essay

Examine the overall effect of the essay you've been analyzing in Exercises 4.3, 4.10, 4.15, and 4.18. Do all the paragraphs relate to your thesis? Are they arranged clearly and logically? How do repetition and restatement, transitional expressions, or transitional sentences connect the paragraphs? Can you see ways to improve the essay's unity, coherence, and development?

5

Designing Documents

Imaginehowharditwouldbetoreadandwriteiftextlookedlikethis. To make reading and writing easier, we place a space between words. This convention and many others—such as page margins, page numbers, and paragraph breaks—have evolved over time to help writers communicate clearly with readers.

5a Designing academic papers and other documents

The design guidelines offered in this chapter apply to all types of documents, including academic papers, Web sites, business reports, flyers, and newsletters. Each type has specific requirements as well, covered elsewhere in this book.

mycomplab

Visit *mycomplab.com* for more resources and exercises on document design.

1 Designing academic papers

Many academic disciplines prefer specific formats for students' papers. This book details two such formats:

- **MLA,** used in English, foreign languages, and some other humanities (pp. 664–66).
- **APA,** used in the social sciences (pp. 761–64).

Other academic formats can be found in the style guides listed on pages 724, 741–42, and 773.

The design guidelines in this chapter extend the range of elements and options covered by most academic styles. Your instructors may want you to adhere strictly to a particular style or may allow some latitude in design. Ask them for their preferences.

2 Writing online

In and out of school, you are likely to do a lot of online writing—certainly e-mail and possibly blogs and other Web sites. The purposes and audiences for online writing vary widely, and so do readers' expectations for its design. Chapter 54 details the approaches you can take in different online writing situations.

3 Designing business documents and other public writing

When you write outside your high school classes, your audience will have certain expectations for how your documents should look and read. Guidelines for such writing appear in the following chapters:

- **Chapter 55 on public writing:** letters, job applications, reports, proposals, flyers, newsletters, brochures.
- **Chapter 56 on oral presentations:** *PowerPoint* slides and other visual aids.

5b Considering principles of design

Most of the principles of design respond to the ways we read. White space, for instance, relieves our eyes and helps to lead us through a document. Groupings or lists help to show relationships. Type sizes, images, and color add variety and help to emphasize important elements.

The sample documents on pages 116–17 illustrate quite different ways one student designed a report for a college marketing course. Even at a glance, the revised document is easier to scan and read. It makes better use of white space, groups similar elements, uses

Principles of document design

- **Create flow** to conduct the reader through the document.
- **Space elements** to give the reader's eye a rest and to focus the reader's attention.
- **Group related elements** in lists or under similar headings.
- **Standardize elements** to match appearance with content and to minimize variations.
- **Emphasize important elements.**

bullets and fonts for emphasis, and successfully integrates and explains the chart.

As you design your own documents, think about your purpose, the expectations of your readers, and how readers will move through your document. Also consider the following general principles of design, noting how they overlap and support each other.

1 Creating flow

Many of the other design principles work in concert with the larger goal of conducting the reader through a document by establishing flow, a pattern for the eye to follow. In text-heavy documents like that on page 117, flow may be achieved mainly with headings, lists, and illustrations. In more visual documents, flow will come as well from the arrangement and spacing of information.

2 Spacing

The white space on a page eases crowding and focuses readers' attention. On an otherwise full page, just the space indicating paragraphs (an indention or a line of extra space) gives readers a break and reassures them that ideas are divided into manageable chunks.

In papers, reports, and other formal documents, spacing appears mainly in paragraph breaks, in margins, and around headings and lists. In publicity documents such as flyers and brochures, spacing is usually more generous between elements and helps boxes, headings, and the like pop off the page.

3 Grouping

Grouping information shows relationships visually, reinforcing the sense of the text itself. Here in this discussion, we group the various principles of design under visually identical headings to emphasize them and their similar importance. In the revised design

Original design

Runs title and subtitle together. Does not distinguish title from text.

Crowds the page with minimal margins.

Downplays paragraph breaks with small indentions.

Buries statistics in a paragraph. Obscures relationships with non-parallel wording.

Does not introduce the figure, leaving readers to infer its meaning and purpose.

Overemphasizes the figure with large size and excessive white space.

Presents the figure undynamically, flat on.

Does not caption the figure to explain what it shows, offering only a figure number and a partial text explanation.

Generation Online: College Students and the Internet

College life once meant classrooms of students listening to teachers or groups of students talking over lunch in the union. But the reality today is more complex: students interact with their peers and professors by computer as much as face to face. As these students graduate and enter the workforce, all of society will be affected by their experience.

According to the Pew Internet Research Center (2008), today's college students are practiced computer and Internet users. The Pew Center reports that 24 percent of students in college today started using computers between ages five and eight. By age eighteen all students were using computers. Almost all college students, 92 percent, rely on the Internet, with 66 percent of students using more than one e-mail address. Computer ownership among this group is also very high: 85 percent have purchased or have been given at least one computer.

Students are eager to tap into the Internet's benefits and convenience.

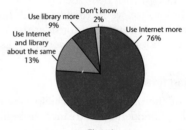

Figure 1

The Internet has eclipsed the library as the site of college students' research, as shown in Figure 1 from the Pew Report. In fact, a mere 9 percent of students

on the facing page, the bulleted list details statistics about students' computer use. The list uses similar wording for each item to reinforce the similarities in the data. Thinking of likely groups as you write can help you organize your material so that it makes sense to you and your readers.

4   Standardizing

As we read a document, the design of its elements quickly creates expectations in us. We assume, for instance, that headings in the same size and color signal information of the same importance or that a list contains items of parallel content. Just as the design creates expectations, so it should fulfill them, treating similar elements similarly. Anticipating design standards as you write a document can help you treat its elements consistently and emphasize the elements you want to draw attention to.

Revised design

**Generation Online:
College Students and the Internet**

College life once meant classrooms of students listening to teachers or groups of students talking over lunch in the union. But the reality today is more complex: students interact with their peers and professors by computer as much as face to face. As these students graduate and enter the workforce, all of society will be affected by their experience.

According to the Pew Internet Research Center (2008), today's college students are practiced computer users and Internet users.

- They started young: 24 percent were using computers between ages five and eight, and all were using them by age eighteen.
- They rely on the Internet: 92 percent have used the network, and 66 percent use more than one e-mail address.
- They own computers: 85 percent have purchased or have been given at least one computer.

Students are eager to tap into the Internet's benefits and convenience. Figure 1, from the Pew Report, shows that the Internet has eclipsed the library as the site of college students' research. In fact, a mere 9 percent of students reported using the library more than the Internet as a starting point for research.

- ■9% □2% ■76%
- ■13%
- ■ Use Internet more
- ■ Use Internet and library about the same
- ■ Use library more
- □ Don't know

Figure 1. College students' use of the Internet and the library for research

Distinguishes title from subtitle and both from text.

Provides adequate margins.

Emphasizes paragraph breaks with white space.

Groups statistics in a bulleted list set off with white space. Uses parallel wording for parallel information.

Introduces the figure to indicate its meaning and purpose.

Reduces white space around the figure.

Presents the figure to emphasize the most significant segment.

Captions the figure so that it can be read independently from the text.

Standardizing also creates clear, uncluttered documents. Even if they are used consistently, too many variations in type fonts and sizes, colors, indentions, and the like overwhelm readers as they try to determine the significance of the parts. Most formal documents, such as papers and reports, need no more than a single type font for text and headings, with type size and highlighting (such as CAPITAL LETTERS, **boldface,** or *italics*) distinguishing the levels of headings. Publicity documents, such as flyers and brochures, generally employ more variation to attract readers' attention.

5 Emphasizing

Part of a critical reader's task is to analyze and interpret the meaning of a document, and design helps the reader by stressing what's important. Type fonts and sizes, headings, indentions, color, boxes, white space—all of these elements establish hierarchies of information, so that the reader almost instinctively grasps what is crucial, what is less so, and what is merely supplementary. In this book, for example, the importance of headings is clear from their size and from the use of decorative elements, such as the box around 5c below; and boxes like the one on page 115 clearly mark summaries and other key information. As you design a document, considering where and how to emphasize elements can help you determine your document's priorities.

5c Using the elements of design

Applying the preceding principles involves margins, text, lists, headings, color, and illustrations. You won't use all these elements for every project, and in many writing situations you will be required to follow a prescribed format (see pp. 113–14). If you are addressing readers who have vision loss, consider as well the points discussed on page 127.

Note Your word processor may provide wizards or templates for many kinds of documents, such as letters, memos, reports, agendas, résumés, and brochures. **Wizards** guide you through setting up and writing complicated documents. **Templates** are preset forms to which you add your own text, headings, and other elements. Wizards and templates can be helpful, but not if they lead you to create cookie-cutter documents no matter what the writing situation. Always keep in mind that a document should be appropriate for your subject, audience, and purpose.

1 Setting margins

Margins at the top, bottom, and sides of a page help to prevent pages from overwhelming readers with unpleasant crowding. Most academic and business documents use a minimum one-inch margin on all sides. Publicity documents, such as flyers and brochures, often use narrower margins, compensating with white space between elements.

2 Creating readable text

A document must be readable. You can make text readable by choosing appropriate line spacing, type fonts and sizes, highlighting, word spacing, and line breaks.

Line spacing

Most academic documents are double-spaced, with an initial indention for paragraphs, while most business documents are single-spaced, with an extra line of space between paragraphs. Double or triple spacing sets off headings in both. Web sites and publicity documents, such as flyers and brochures, tend to use more line spacing to separate and group distinct parts of the content.

Type fonts and sizes

The readability of text also derives from the type fonts (or faces) and their sizes. For academic and business documents, generally choose a type size of 10 or 12 points, as in these samples:

```
10-point Courier        10-point Times New Roman
12-point Courier        12-point Times New Roman
```

Fonts like these and the one you're reading have **serifs**—the small lines finishing the letters, such as the downward strokes on the top of this T. Serif fonts are appropriate for formal writing and are easier for most people to read on paper. **Sans serif** fonts (*sans* means "without" in French) include this one found on many word processors:

10-point Arial   **12-point Arial**

Sans serif fonts are usually easier to read on a computer screen and are clearer on paper for readers with some vision loss (see p. 127).

Your word processor probably offers many decorative fonts as well:

10-point Bodega Sans   10-point Tekton
10-POINT STENCIL   10-point Ruzicka Freehand
10-point Lucida Sans   10-point Park Avenue

Decorative fonts are generally inappropriate in academic and business writing, where letter forms should be conventional and regular. But on some Web sites and in publicity documents, decorative fonts can attract attention, create motion, and reinforce a theme.

Note The point size of a type font is often an unreliable guide to its actual size, as the decorative fonts above illustrate: all the samples are 10 points, but they vary considerably. Before you use a font, print out a sample to be sure it is the size you want.

Highlighting

Within a document's text, underlined, *italic,* **boldface,** or even color type can emphasize key words or sentences. Underlining is rarest these days, having been replaced by italics. Both academic and business writing sometimes use boldface to give strong emphasis—for instance, to a term being defined—and publicity documents often rely extensively on boldface to draw the reader's eye. Neither academic nor business writing generally uses color within passages of text. In Web and publicity documents, however, color may be effective if the color is dark enough to be readable. (See pp. 121–22 for more on color in document design.)

No matter what your writing situation, use highlighting selectively to complement your meaning, not merely to decorate your work. Many readers consider type embellishments to be distracting.

Word spacing

In most writing situations, follow these guidelines for spacing within and between words:

- **Leave one space between words.**
- **Leave one space after all punctuation, with these exceptions:**

Dash (two hyphens or the so-called em dash on a computer)	book--its	book—its
Hyphen	one-half	
Apostrophe within a word	book's	
Two or more adjacent marks	book.")	
Opening quotation mark, parenthesis, or bracket	("book	[book

- **Leave one space before and after an ellipsis mark.** In the examples below, ellipsis marks indicate omissions within a sentence and at the end of a sentence. See pages 477–78 for additional examples.

    book . . . in   book. . . . The

Line breaks

Your word processor will generally insert appropriate breaks between lines of continuous text: it will not, for instance, automatically begin a line with a comma or period, and it will not end a line with an opening parenthesis or bracket. However, you will have to prevent it from breaking a two-hyphen dash or a three-dot ellipsis mark by spacing to push the beginning of each mark to the next line.

When you instruct it to do so (usually under the Tools menu), your word processor will also automatically hyphenate words to prevent very short lines. If you must decide yourself where to break words, follow the guidelines on pages 547–48.

3 | Using lists

Lists give visual reinforcement to the relations between like items—for example, the steps in a process or the elements of a proposal. A list is easier to read than a paragraph and adds white space.

When wording a list, work for parallelism among items—for instance, all complete sentences or all phrases (see also pp. 403–04). Set the list with space above and below. Number the items, or mark them with bullets: centered dots or other devices, such as the squares used in the list above about word spacing. On most word processors you can use the Format menu to create a list automatically.

4 Using headings

Headings are signposts: they direct the reader's attention by focusing the eye on a document's most significant content. In Web and publicity documents, headings may be decorative as well as functional, capturing the reader's attention with large sizes, lots of white space, and unconventional fonts. In academic and much business writing, however, headings are more purely functional. They break the text into discrete parts, create emphasis, and orient the reader.

When you use headings in academic and business writing, follow these guidelines:

- **Use one, two, or three levels of headings** depending on the needs of your material and the length of your document. Some level of heading every two or so pages will help keep readers on track. (A three-page paper probably will not need headings.)
- **Create an outline of your document to plan where headings should go.** Reserve the first level of heading for the main points (and sections). Use a second and perhaps a third level of heading to mark subsections of supporting information.
- **Keep headings as short as possible** while making them specific about the material that follows.
- **Word headings consistently**—for instance, all questions (*What Is the Scientific Method?*), all phrases with -*ing* words (*Understanding the Scientific Method*), or all phrases with nouns (*The Scientific Method*).
- **Indicate the relative importance of headings** with type size, positioning, and highlighting, such as capital letters or boldface.

First-Level Heading

Second-Level Heading

Third-Level Heading

Generally, you can use the same type font and size for headings as for the text.

- **Don't break a page immediately after a heading.** Push the heading to the next page.

Note Document format in psychology and some other social sciences requires a particular treatment of headings. See page 763.

5 Using color

With a computer and a color printer, you can produce documents that use color for bullets, headings, illustrations, and other elements. Web and publicity documents almost always use color, whereas academic and business documents may not need color at all. (Ask your teacher for his or her preferences.) If you do use color in an academic document, follow these guidelines:

- **Print text in black,** not red, blue, or another color.
- **Make sure that color headings are dark enough to be readable.**
- **Stick to the same color for all headings at the same level**—for instance, red for primary headings, black for secondary headings.
- **Use color for bullets, lines, and other nontext elements.** But use no more than a few colors to keep pages clean.
- **Use color to distinguish the parts of illustrations.** Use only as many colors as you need to make your illustration clear.

See also page 127 on the use of color for readers with vision loss.

Exercise 5.1 Redesigning a paper
Save a duplicate copy of a recent paper or one you are currently working on. Then format the duplicate using appropriate elements of design, such as type fonts, lists, and headings. (For a new paper, be sure your teacher will accept your new design.) When you have finished the redesign, share the work with your teacher.

5d Using illustrations

An illustration can often make a point more efficiently than words can. Tables present data. Graphs and charts recast data in visual form. Diagrams, drawings, and photographs can explain processes, show what something looks like, or add emphasis.

Note The Web is an excellent resource for photographs (see pp. 574–75), and you can edit the images with a program such as *Adobe Photoshop*. Your computer may include a program for creating tables, graphs, and other illustrations, or you can work with specialized software such as *Excel* (for graphs and charts) or *Adobe Illustrator* (for diagrams, maps, and the like). Use *PowerPoint* or a similar program for visuals in oral presentations (see pp. 823–25).

1 Using illustrations appropriately for the writing situation

Academic and many business documents tend to use illustrations differently from publicity documents. In the latter, illustrations generally attract attention or emphasize. In academic and business writing, however, illustrations directly reinforce and amplify the text. Follow these guidelines for academic and most business writing:

- **Focus on a purpose for each illustration**—a reason for including it and a point you want it to make. Otherwise, readers may find it irrelevant or confusing.
- **Provide a source note whenever the data or the entire illustration is someone else's independent material** (see pp. 614–15).

Each discipline has a slightly different style for such source notes: those in the illustrations below and on the next three pages reflect MLA style. See also Chapters 46 and 50–52.

- **Number figures, photographs, and other images together**, and label them as figures: Fig. 1, Fig. 2, and so on.
- **Number and label tables separately:** Table 1, Table 2, and so on.
- **Refer to each illustration in your text**—for instance, "See fig. 2." Place the reference at the point(s) in the text where readers will benefit by consulting the illustration.
- **Determine the placement of illustrations.** The social sciences and some other disciplines require each illustration to fall on a page by itself immediately after the text reference to it (see p. 764). You may want to follow this rule in other situations as well if you have a large number of illustrations. Otherwise, you can embed them in your text pages just after you refer to them.

2 Using tables

Tables usually present raw data, making complex information accessible to readers. The data may show how variables relate to one another or how two or more groups contrast, as in the example below. Some tables use rows and columns to present related textual information rather than data. See page 786 for an example.

Table

A self-explanatory title falls above the table.

Self-explanatory headings label horizontal rows and vertical columns.

The layout of rows and columns is clear: headings align with their data, and numbers align vertically down columns.

Table 1

Public- and private-school enrollment of US students age five and older, 2006

	Number of students	Percentage in public school	Percentage in private school
All students	74,220,937	83.2	16.8
Kindergarten	4,012,680	86.0	14.0
Grades 1-4	15,758,734	88.8	11.2
Grades 5-8	16,498,217	89.4	10.6
Grades 9-12	17,500,473	90.5	9.5
College (undergraduate)	17,063,732	77.0	23.0
Graduate and professional school	3,387,101	59.8	40.2

Source: Data from *2006 American Community Survey*; US Census Bureau, n.d.; Web; 10 Oct. 2009; table S1404.

3 | Using figures

Figures represent data or show concepts visually. They include charts, graphs, diagrams, and photographs.

Pie charts

Pie charts show the relations among the parts of a whole. The whole totals 100 percent, and each pie slice is proportional in size to its share of the whole. Use a pie chart when shares, not the underlying data, are your focus.

Pie chart

Color distinguishes segments of the chart. Use distinct shades of gray, black, and white if your paper will not be read in color.

Segment percentages total 100.

Every segment is clearly labeled. You can also use a key, as in the chart on p. 117.

Self-explanatory caption falls below the chart.

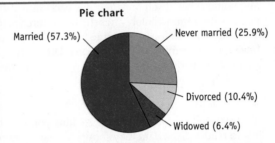

Married (57.3%) Never married (25.9%) Divorced (10.4%) Widowed (6.4%)

Fig. 1. Marital status in 2008 of adults age eighteen and over. Data from *Current Population Survey: 2008 Social and Economic Supplement*; US Census Bureau, Jan. 2009; Web; 2 Feb. 2009.

Bar charts

Bar charts compare groups or time periods on a measure such as quantity or frequency. Use a bar chart when relative size is your focus. Be sure to start with a zero point in the lower left corner so that the values on the vertical axis are clear.

Bar chart

Vertical scale shows and clearly labels the values being measured. Zero point clarifies values.

Horizontal scale shows and clearly labels the groups being compared.

Self-explanatory caption falls below the chart.

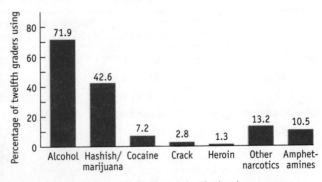

Percentage of twelfth graders using

80 — 60 — 40 — 20 — 0

71.9 42.6 7.2 2.8 1.3 13.2 10.5

Alcohol Hashish/ marijuana Cocaine Crack Heroin Other narcotics Amphet- amines

Fig. 2. Lifetime prevalence of use of alcohol and other drugs, among twelfth graders in 2008. Data from *Monitoring the Future: A Continuing Study of American Youth*; U of Michigan, 11 Dec. 2008; Web; 10 Aug. 2009.

Line graphs

Line graphs show change over time in one or more subjects. They are an economical and highly visual way to compare many points of data. Be sure to start with a zero point in the lower left corner so that the values on the vertical axis are clear.

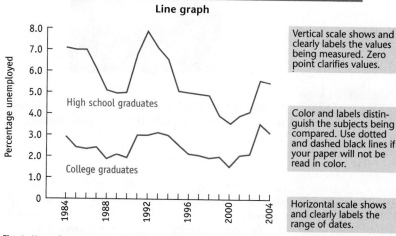

Line graph

Vertical scale shows and clearly labels the values being measured. Zero point clarifies values.

Color and labels distinguish the subjects being compared. Use dotted and dashed black lines if your paper will not be read in color.

Horizontal scale shows and clearly labels the range of dates.

Fig. 3. Unemployment rates of high school graduates and college graduates, 1984-2004. Data from Antony Davies; *The Economics of College Tuition*; Mercatus Center, George Mason U, 3 Mar. 2005; Web; 26 June 2008.

Self-explanatory caption falls below the graph.

Diagrams

Diagrams show concepts visually, such as the structure of an organization, the way something works or looks, or the relations among subjects. (See the example on p. 126.) Often, diagrams show what can't be described economically in words. For other examples of diagrams, see pages 3, 105, and 797.

Photographs and other images

Sometimes you may focus an entire paper on analyzing an image such as a photograph, painting, or advertisement (see pp. 176–78). But most commonly you'll use images to add substance to ideas or to enliven them. You might clarify an astronomy paper with a photograph of Saturn (see page 126), add information to an analysis of a novel with a drawing of the author, or capture the theme of a brochure with a cartoon. Images grab readers' attention, so use them carefully to explain, reinforce, or enhance your writing.

Diagram

Diagram makes concept comprehensible.

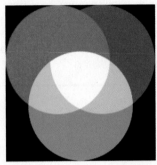

Self-explanatory caption falls below the diagram.

Fig. 4. RGB color theory, applied to televisions and computer monitors, in which all possible colors and white are created from red, green, and blue. From "Color Theory"; *Wikipedia*; Wikimedia, 15 Mar. 2009; Web; 13 May 2009.

Note When using an image prepared by someone else—for instance, a photograph downloaded from the Web—you must verify that the source permits reproduction of the image before you use it. In most documents, but especially in academic papers, you must also fully cite the source of any borrowed image. See page 609 on copyright issues with Internet sources.

Photograph

Photograph shows subject more economically and dramatically than words could.

Self-explanatory caption falls below the image.

Fig. 5. View of Saturn from the *Cassini* spacecraft, showing the planet and its rings. From *Cassini-Huygens: Mission to Saturn and Titan*; US Natl. Atmospheric and Space Administration, Jet Propulsion Laboratory, 24 Feb. 2005; Web; 26 Apr. 2009.

5e | Considering readers with vision loss

Your audience may include readers who have low vision, problems with color perception, or difficulties processing visual information. If so, consider adapting your design to meet these readers' needs. Here are a few pointers:

- **Use large type fonts.** Most guidelines call for 14 points or larger.
- **Use standard type fonts.** Many people with low vision find it easier to read sans serif fonts such as Arial than serif fonts (see p. 119). Avoid decorative fonts with unusual flourishes, even in headings.
- **Avoid words in all-capital letters.**
- **Avoid relying on color alone to distinguish elements.** Label elements, and distinguish them by position or size.
- **Use red and green selectively.** To readers who are red-green colorblind, these colors will appear in shades of gray, yellow, or blue.
- **Use contrasting colors.** To make colors distinct, choose them from opposite sides of the color spectrum—violet and yellow, for instance, or orange and blue.
- **Use only light colors for tints behind type.** Make the type itself black or a very dark color.

PART 2

Reading and Writing in High School

6

Developing Academic Skills

When you take academic classes, you enter a discipline—a community of teachers and students who are studying a particular subject and whose basic goal is to build knowledge about that subject, whether it is English, history, biology, or something else. You participate in a discipline community first by studying a subject, acquiring its vocabulary, and learning to express yourself in its ways. As you gain experience and knowledge, you contribute to the community by asking questions and communicating your answers in writing. This active, involved learning is the core of academic work. It may seem beyond you at first, as you try to grasp the content of assigned reading and identify important ideas. But the transition will be easier if you follow the advice in this chapter for managing your time, getting the most from your classes, understanding assigned reading, being an academic writer, and preparing for exams.

Developing your academic skills

- **Manage your time.** Class assignments often take more time than students anticipate. The tips in the next section will help you schedule regular time for study, organize your workload, and use your study time wisely.
- **Study the course outline, the syllabus, for each class.** This outline lays out the teacher's expectations as well as the course topics, assignments, and deadlines.
- **Participate in class.** Listen carefully, take notes (see p. 133 for tips), ask questions, and join in discussions.
- **Do the assigned reading.** You'll gain experience with the language and ideas used in each of your classes, and you'll become familiar with the kinds of writing expected of you. See pages 133–36 for help with reading.

mycomplab

Visit *mycomplab.com* for more resources as well as exercises on academic skills.

- **Understand each writing assignment.** Knowing the writing situation posed by each assignment—the audience, purpose, options for subjects, and other elements of the situation—will help you meet its expectations. Use the advice in Chapter 8 to understand writing in academic situations.
- **Prepare for exams.** See pages 137–39 in this chapter on study skills and page 784 in Chapter 53 on taking essay exams.
- **Get help when you need it.** Teachers, counselors, tutors, other students—all can help you.

6a Managing your time

Planning and pacing your schoolwork and other activities will help you study more efficiently with less stress.

1 Surveying your activities

How do you spend your days? For a week, keep track of all your activities and the time they absorb. How many of the week's 168 hours do you spend eating, sleeping, watching television, talking on the phone, reading e-mail, attending classes, studying, working at a job, attending religious services, exercising, commuting, doing laundry, socializing, and so on? How much time can you realistically devote to studying?

2 Scheduling your time

One way to organize your time is to use a calendar that divides each day into waking hours. Block out your activities that occur regularly and at specific times, such as school, extracurricular activities, and work. Then fill in the other activities (such as exercise, eating, and studying) that do not necessarily occur at fixed times. Be sure to leave time for relaxing: an unrealistic schedule that assigns all available time to studying will quickly prove too difficult to live by. If you use a computer regularly, consider keeping your schedule online using a calendar program. Set it to remind you of important due dates.

3 Organizing your workload

Use the syllabuses for your classes to estimate the amount of weekly study time required for each class. Generally, plan on several hours of studying for each class. Block out study periods using these guidelines:

- **Schedule study time close to class time.** You'll study more productively if you review notes, read assigned material, or work on projects shortly after school.
- **Pace assignments.** Plan to start early and work regularly on projects requiring extensive time, such as research papers, so that you will not be overwhelmed near the deadline. (See pp. 550–51 for advice on scheduling research projects.)
- **Adjust the weekly plan as needed to accommodate changes in your workload.** Before each week begins, examine its schedule to be sure you've built in enough time to study for a test, finish a paper, or meet other deadlines and commitments.

4 Making the most of study time

When you sit down to study, use your time efficiently:

- **Set realistic study goals.** Divide your study sessions into small chunks, each with a short-term goal, such as previewing a textbook chapter or drafting three paragraphs of a paper. Plan breaks, too, so that you can clear your mind, stretch, and refocus on your goals.
- **Tackle difficult homework first.** Resist any urge to put off demanding jobs, such as working on papers, reading textbooks, and doing math problems. Save easy tasks for when you're less alert.
- **Evaluate how you use your study time.** At the end of each week, ask yourself whether you were as productive as you needed to be. If not, what changes can you make to accomplish your goals for the coming week?

6b Listening and taking notes in class

When you begin each class period, push aside other concerns so that you can focus, listen, and take careful notes.

1 Listening effectively

When you arrive in your classroom, get out your materials so that you are ready to listen when class begins. Use these tips to be an effective listener:

- **Watch the speaker.** Whether the speaker is your teacher or one of your classmates, keep your eyes on the speaker to avoid being distracted.

- **Listen for major ideas.** The speaker may stress important points verbally but not write them on the board.
- **Connect information to what you already know.** As you listen, think about how new material relates to what you already know about the subject.
- **Listen courteously.** Wait until the speaker has finished his or her point before raising your hand to ask a question.

2 | Taking notes

Either on paper or on a computer, record what you hear while sorting out the main ideas from the secondary and supporting ones. Such active note taking will help you understand the teacher's approach to the subject and provide you with complete material for later study. Use the following tips to take notes:

- **Use your own words.** You will understand and retain the material better if you rephrase it. But use the speaker's words if necessary to catch everything.
- **Leave space in your notes if you miss something.** Teachers usually welcome questions about content but not requests for simple repetition, and it's not fair to distract fellow students during class. Ask someone for the missing information as soon as possible after the class ends.
- **Include any reading content mentioned by your teacher.** Use your notes to integrate all the components of the course—your teacher's views, your own thoughts, and the assigned reading, even if you've already read it.
- **Review your notes shortly after class.** Reinforce your new knowledge when it is fresh by underlining key words and ideas, adding headings and comments in the margins, converting your notes to questions, or outlining the lecture based on your notes. If you don't understand something in the notes, consult a classmate for his or her version.

6c | Reading for comprehension

The assigned reading you do for high school classes—such as textbooks, newspaper and journal articles, and works of literature—requires a greater focus on understanding and retention than does the reading you do for entertainment or for practical information. The process discussed here may seem time consuming, but with practice you'll become efficient at it.

Note The following process stresses ways of understanding what you read. In critical reading, covered in the next chapter, you extend this process to analyze and evaluate what you read and see.

1 Writing while reading

Reading for comprehension is an *active* process. Students often believe they are reading actively when they roll a highlighter over the important ideas in a text, but truly engaged reading requires more than that. If you take notes while reading, you "translate" the work into your own words and reconstruct it for yourself.

The substance of your reading notes will change as you preview, read, and summarize. At first, you may jot quick, short notes in the margins, on separate pages, or on a computer. (Use the last two for material you don't own or are reading online.) As you delve into the work, the notes should become more detailed, restating important points, asking questions, connecting ideas. (See p. 144 for an example of a text annotated in this way by a student.) For in-depth critical reading, you may want to keep a reading journal that records both what the work says and what you think about it. (See p. 144.)

2 Previewing

For most course reading, you should **skim** before reading word for word. Skimming gives you an overview of the material that will help you understand any part of it. Your goal is not to comprehend all the details or even the structure of the author's argument. Rather, working as outlined below, aim for a general sense of the length and difficulty of the material, its organization, and its principal ideas.

- **Gauge length and level.** Is the material brief and straightforward enough to read in one sitting, or do you need more time?
- **Examine the title and introduction.** The title and first couple of paragraphs will give you a sense of the topic, the author's approach, and the main ideas. As you read them, ask yourself what you already know about the subject so that you can integrate new information with old.
- **Move from heading to heading or paragraph to paragraph.** Viewing headings as signposts or as the levels of an outline will give you a feeling for which ideas the author sees as primary and which subordinate. In a text without headings, reading the first sentence of each paragraph will give you a sense of the author's important ideas.
- **Note highlighted words.** You will likely need to learn the meanings of terms in **bold**, *italic*, or color.
- **Slow down for pictures, diagrams, tables, graphs, and other illustrations.** They often contain concentrated information.
- **Read the summary or conclusion.** These paragraphs often recap the main ideas.
- **Think over what you've skimmed.** Try to recall the central idea, or thesis, and the sequence of ideas.

3 Reading

After previewing a text, you can settle into it to learn what it has to say.

First reading

The first time through new material, read as steadily and smoothly as possible, trying to get the gist of what the author is saying.

- **Read in a place where you can concentrate.** Choose a quiet environment away from distractions such as music or talking.
- **Give yourself time.** Rushing yourself or worrying about something else you have to do will prevent you from grasping what you read.
- **Try to enjoy the work.** Seek connections between it and what you already know. Appreciate new information, interesting relationships, forceful writing, humor, good examples.
- **Make notes sparingly during this first reading.** Mark major stumbling blocks—such as a paragraph you don't understand—so that you can try to resolve them before rereading.

CULTURE LANGUAGE If English is not your first language and you come across unfamiliar words, don't stop and look up every one. You will lose more in concentration than you will gain in understanding. Instead, try to guess the meanings of unfamiliar words from their contexts, circle them, and look them up later.

Rereading

After the first reading, plan on at least one other. This time read *slowly*. Your main concern should be to grasp the content and how it is constructed. That means rereading a paragraph if you didn't get the point or using a dictionary to look up words you don't know.

Use your pen, pencil, or keyboard freely to highlight and distill the text:

- **Distinguish main ideas from supporting ideas.** Look for the central idea, or thesis, for the main idea of each paragraph or section, and for the evidence supporting ideas.
- **Learn key terms.** Understand both their meanings and their applications.
- **Discern the connections among ideas.** Be sure you see why the author moves from point A to point B to point C and how those points work together to support the central idea. It often helps to outline the text or summarize it (see the next page).
- **Distinguish between facts and opinions.** Especially when reading an argument, tease apart the facts from the author's opinions that may or may not be based on facts. (See pp. 181–82 for more on facts and opinions.)

- **Add your own comments.** In the margins or separately, note links to other readings or to class discussions, questions to explore further, possible topics for your writing, points you find especially strong or weak. (This last category will occupy much of your time when you are expected to read critically. See pp. 147–53.)

4 Summarizing

A good way to master the content of a text is to **summarize** it: reduce it to its main points, in your own words. Some assignments call for brief summaries, as when you summarize the plot in a critical essay about a novel (p. 698). Summary is also an essential tool in research papers and other writing that draws on sources (pp. 597–98). Here, though, we're concerned with summarizing for yourself—for your own enlightenment.

A summary should state in as few words as possible the main ideas of a passage. When you need to summarize a few paragraphs or a brief article, your summary should not exceed one-fifth the length of the original. For longer works, such as chapters of books or whole books, your summary should be quite a bit shorter in proportion to the original. A procedure for drafting a summary appears in the following box.

Writing a summary

- **Understand the meaning.** Look up words or concepts you don't know so that you understand the author's sentences and how they relate to one another.
- **Understand the organization.** Work through the text to identify its sections—single paragraphs or groups of paragraphs focused on a single topic. To understand how parts of a work relate to one another, try drawing a tree diagram or creating an outline (pp. 37–41).
- **Distill each section.** Write a one- or two-sentence summary of each section you identify. Focus on the main point of the section, omitting examples, facts, and other supporting evidence.
- **State the main idea.** Write a sentence or two capturing the author's central idea.
- **Support the main idea.** Write a full paragraph (or more, if needed) that begins with the central idea and supports it with the sentences that summarize sections of the work. The paragraph should concisely and accurately state the thrust of the entire work.
- *Use your own words.* By writing, you re-create the meaning of the work in a way that makes sense for you.

Summarizing even a passage of text can be tricky. The facing page shows one attempt to summarize the following material from an introductory biology textbook.

Original text

As astronomers study newly discovered planets orbiting distant stars, they hope to find evidence of water on these far-off celestial bodies, for water is the substance that makes possible life as we know it here on Earth. All organisms familiar to us are made mostly of water and live in an environment dominated by water. They require water more than any other substance. Human beings, for example, can survive for quite a few weeks without food, but only a week or so without water. Molecules of water participate in many chemical reactions necessary to sustain life. Most cells are surrounded by water, and cells themselves are about 70–95% water. Three-quarters of Earth's surface is submerged in water. Although most of this water is in liquid form, water is also present on Earth as ice and vapor. Water is the only common substance to exist in the natural environment in all three physical states of matter: solid, liquid, and gas.

—Neil A. Campbell and Jane B. Reece, *Biology*

Draft summary

Astronomers look for water in outer space because life depends on it. It is the most common substance on Earth and in living cells, and it can be a liquid, a solid (ice), or a gas (vapor).

This summary accurately restates ideas in the original, but it does not pare the passage to its essence. The work of astronomers and the three physical states of water add color and texture to the original, but they are asides to the key concept that water sustains life because of its role in life. The following revision narrows the summary to this concept:

Revised summary

Water is the most essential support for life—the dominant substance on Earth and in living cells and a component of life-sustaining chemical processes.

Note Do not count on the AutoSummarize function on your word processor for summarizing texts that you may have copied onto your computer. The summaries are rarely accurate, and you will not gain the experience of interacting with the texts on your own.

6d Preparing for exams

Examinations give you a chance to demonstrate what you have learned from listening, reading, and writing. Studying for an exam involves three main steps, each requiring about a third of the preparation time: reviewing the material, organizing summaries of the material, and testing yourself. Your main goals are to strengthen your understanding of the subject, making both its ideas and its details more memorable, and to increase the flexibility of your new knowledge so that you can apply it in new contexts.

The procedure outlined here works for any exam, no matter how much time you have, what material you're studying, or what kind of test you'll be taking. Because an essay exam requires a distinctive approach during the exam itself, it receives special attention in Chapter 53, pages 784–90.

Note Cramming for an exam is about the least effective way of preparing for one. It takes longer to learn under stress, and the learning is shallower, more difficult to apply, and more quickly forgotten. Information learned under stress is even harder to apply in stressful situations such as taking an exam. And the lack of sleep that usually accompanies cramming makes a good performance even more unlikely. If you must cram for a test, face the fact that you can't learn everything. Spend your time reviewing main concepts and facts.

1 Reviewing and memorizing the material

Divide your class notes and reading assignments into manageable units. Reread the material, recite or write out the main ideas and selected supporting ideas and examples, and then skim for an overview. Proceed in this way through all the units of the course, returning to earlier ones as needed to refresh your memory or to relate ideas.

During this stage you should be memorizing what you don't already know by heart. Try these strategies for strengthening your memory:

- **Link new and known information.** For instance, to remember a sequence of four dates in nineteenth-century European history, link the dates to simultaneous and more familiar events in the United States.
- **Create groups of ideas or facts that make sense to you.** For instance, memorize French vocabulary words in related groups, such as words for parts of the body or parts of a house. Keep the groups small: research has shown that we can easily memorize about seven items at a time but have trouble with more.
- **Create narratives and visual images.** You may recall a story or a picture more easily than words. For instance, to remember how the economic laws of supply and demand affect the market for rental housing, you could tie the principles to a narrative about the aftermath of the 1906 San Francisco earthquake, when half the population was suddenly homeless. Or you could visualize a person who has dollar signs for eyes and is converting a spare room into a high-priced rental unit, as many did after the earthquake to meet the new demand for housing.
- **Use *mnemonic devices*, or tricks for remembering.** Say the history dates you want to remember are separated by five years, then four, then nine. By memorizing the first date and recalling $5 + 4 = 9$, you'll have command of all four dates.

2 | Organizing summaries of the material

Allow time to reorganize the material in your own way, creating categories that will help you apply the information in various contexts. For instance, in studying for a biology exam, work to understand a process, such as how a plant develops or how photosynthesis occurs. Or in studying for an American government test, explain the structures of the local, state, and federal levels of government. Other useful categories include causes/effects and advantages/disadvantages. Such analytical thinking will improve your mastery of the class material and may even prepare you directly for specific essay questions.

3 | Testing yourself

Convert each heading in your notes and class reading into a question. Answer in writing, going back to the class material to fill in what you don't yet know. Be sure you can define and explain all key terms. For subjects that require solving problems (such as mathematics or physics), work out a difficult problem for every type on which you will be tested. For all subjects, focus on the main themes and questions of the course. In a psychology class, for example, be certain you understand principal theories and their implications. In a literature class, test your knowledge of literary movements and genres or the relations among specific works.

When you are satisfied with your preparation, stop studying. If your exam is the next day, get as much sleep as your schedule allows. You will be able to think more clearly on exam day if you are rested.

7
Forming a Critical Perspective

Throughout high school and beyond, you will be expected to think, read, and write critically. **Critical** here means "skeptical," "exacting," "creative." When you operate critically, you question,

my**comp**lab

Visit *mycomplab.com* for more resources and exercises on critical thinking and reading.

test, and build on what others say and what you yourself think. The word *critical* does not mean "negative" in this context: you can think critically about something you like, don't like, or just view neutrally.

You already operate critically every day of your life, as when you probe a friendship ("What did she mean by that?"), discuss a movie you just saw ("Don't you think the bad guy was too obvious?"), or attempt to solve a problem ("How can I help my study group make progress on our project?"). Such questioning helps you figure out why things happen to you, what your experiences mean, and how you can create a needed change.

This chapter introduces more formal methods of critical thinking: preparing to read critically (facing page), developing a critical response (p. 147), listening critically (p. 153), and viewing images critically (p. 155). Learning and applying these methods will both engage you in and prepare you for high school classes, college, career, and life in a democratic society:

- **Teachers and employers will expect you to think critically.** In every field, you will need to assess what you read, see, and hear and to make a good case for your own ideas.
- **Critical thinking helps you understand and express yourself.** With it, you gain insight into your actions and ideas, you can weigh them against opposing views, and you can persuasively articulate your reasoning and motivations.
- **Critical thinking improves your problem-solving skills.** Seeing academic and real-life problems from multiple angles can open your mind to creative solutions.
- **Your very independence and freedom depend on your ability to think, read, and write critically.** An open democracy allows as much play for stupid and false claims as for sound ones, and the claims that seem sound often conflict with each other. Critical thinking empowers you to decide rationally for yourself what's useful, fair, and wise—and what's not.

There is no denying that critical thinking, reading, and writing require discipline and hard work. Besides channeling your curiosity, paying attention, and probing, you will often need to consult experts, interpreting and evaluating their ideas. Such an approach also requires a healthy tolerance for doubt or uncertainty—that feeling you may have when the old rules don't seem to apply or when a change is frightening but still attractive. Out of uncertainty, though, comes creativity—the capacity to organize and generate knowledge, to explain, resolve, illuminate, play. Compared to passive, rote learning, creative work is more involving, more productive, and more enjoyable.

7a | Using techniques of critical reading

In high school much of your critical thinking will focus on written texts (a short story, a newspaper article, a blog) or on visual objects (a photograph, a chart, a film). Like all subjects worthy of critical consideration, such works operate on at least three levels: (1) what the creator actually says or shows, (2) what the creator does not say or show but builds into the work (intentionally or not), and (3) what you think. Discovering the first of these levels—reading for comprehension—is discussed in the preceding chapter as part of academic skills (see pp. 133–36). This chapter builds on that material to help you discover the other two levels. The box below summarizes the reading techniques involved.

Techniques of critical reading

For reading a work of literature, which requires a somewhat different approach, see pp. 691–701.

- **Writing:** making notes on your reading throughout the process (next page)
- **Previewing:** getting background; skimming (pp. 142–43)
- **Reading:** interacting with and absorbing the text (pp. 143–45)
- **Summarizing:** distilling and understanding content (pp. 146–47)
- **Forming your critical response** (pp. 147–53)

  Analyzing: separating into parts
  Interpreting: inferring meaning and assumptions
  Synthesizing: reassembling parts; making connections
  Evaluating: judging quality and value

The techniques of critical reading are not steps in a firm sequence. You will not use all of them for all the reading you do. On some occasions, even when a close, critical reading is required, you may simply lack the time to preview, read, and reread. (But if your reading time is continually squeezed by your schedule, you may need to rethink your schedule.) On other occasions your reason for reading (your purpose) will determine which techniques you use.

Even a publication like *People* magazine is open to different methods of reading for different purposes:

Purpose	Learn some gossip while filling time in the dentist's office.
Kind of reading	Quick, uncritical

| Purpose | Examine *People* as an artifact of our popular culture that reflects and perhaps even molds contemporary values. |
| Kind of reading | Close, critical |

Class assignments, too, differ in their requirements. A book report may require writing, previewing, reading, and summarizing but not intense critical reading. An evaluation of a journal article, in contrast, requires all the techniques discussed here.

(CULTURE LANGUAGE) The idea of reading critically may require you to make some adjustments if readers in your native culture tend to seek understanding or agreement more than engagement from what they read. Readers of English use texts for all kinds of reasons, including pleasure, reinforcement, information, and many others. But they also read skeptically, critically, to see the author's motives, test their own ideas, and arrive at new knowledge.

1 Writing while reading

Reading a work for comprehension and then for a critical approach is an *active* process. Making notes on what you read involves you by helping you understand how the text works, why, and what you think about it. The notes help you bring to the work your own experiences, knowledge, and questions.

If you own the material you're reading (a book, a photocopy, or a printout), you can make notes in the margins (see p. 144 for an example). If you don't own the material or if your notes won't fit in the margins, make notes separately using pen and paper or your computer. Many readers keep a **reading journal** in which they regularly work out questions and thoughts about what they read. One technique for keeping such a journal is to divide a page or computer screen into two vertical columns, the left side for the work itself, such as summary and questions, and the right side for what the work makes you think, such as agreements or doubts based on your own experiences, comparisons with other works, and ideas for writing. A two-column journal can encourage you to go beyond summarizing what you read to interacting critically with it because the blank right column will beckon you to respond. See page 144 for an example of this technique.

Note Whenever you photocopy or download a document or take notes separately from the text you're reading, be sure to record all necessary information about the text's location so that you can find it again and cite it fully if you use it. See page 558 for a list of information to record.

2 Previewing the material

To make the most of your reading, it's worthwhile to skim most texts before reading word for word, forming expectations and even preliminary questions. The preview will make your reading more informed and fruitful.

Use the questions in the box below as a guide to previewing a text.

Questions for previewing a text

■ **What kind of work is it?** If the text is nonfiction, is it personal, informative, persuasive, or entertaining? If the text is online, is it fairly static, such as a Web site, or one that changes often, such as a blog? If the text is literary, determine the **genre**: is it fiction, poetry, drama, or a combination?

■ **What is the work's subject and structure?** For nonfiction, follow the steps outlined on page 134 to gauge length and level, read the title and introduction for clues to the topic and main ideas, read the headings, note highlighted words (defined terms), examine illustrations, and read the summary or conclusion. For a literary text, skim several paragraphs or lines to get a feel for the work's subject and the author's writing style.

■ **What are the facts of publication?** Does the date of publication suggest currency or datedness? Does the publisher or publication specialize in a particular kind of material—scholarly articles, say, or popular books? For a literary text, what might the publication date tell you about the author's use of language or the work's cultural context? For a Web document, who or what sponsors the site: an individual? a nonprofit organization? an academic institution? a corporation? a government body? (See pp. 586 and 590 on locating the authors of online sources.)

■ **What do you know about the author?** Does a biography tell you about the author's publications, interests, biases, and reputation in the field? For an online source, which may be posted by an unfamiliar or anonymous author, what can you gather about the author from his or her words? If possible, trace unfamiliar authors to learn more about them.

■ **What is your preliminary response?** What do you already know about the author or the subject? What questions do you have about either the subject or the author's approach to it? What biases of your own might influence your reception of the work—for instance, curiosity, boredom, or an outlook similar or opposed to the author's?

3 | Reading

Reading is itself more than a one-step process. You want to understand the first level on which the text operates—what the author actually says—and begin to form your impressions.

A procedure for this stage appears in the preceding chapter (pp. 135–36). To recap: Read once through fairly smoothly, trying to appreciate the work and keeping your notes to a minimum. Then read again more carefully, this time making detailed notes, to grasp the ideas and their connections and to pose questions.

Following are examples of active reading from a student, Charlene Robinson. She was responding to Thomas Sowell's "Student Loans," reprinted on the next two pages. First Robinson annotated a photocopy of the essay (the first four annotated paragraphs appear below):

> The first lesson of economics is scarcity: There is never enough of anything to fully satisfy all those who want it.
>
> The first lesson of politics is to disregard the first lesson of economics. When politicians discover some group that is being vocal about not having as much as they want, the "solution" is to give them more. Where do politicians get this "more"? They rob Peter to pay Paul.
>
> After a while, of course, they discover that Peter doesn't have enough. Bursting with compassion, politicians rush to the rescue. Needless to say, they do not admit that robbing Peter to pay Paul was a dumb idea in the first place. On the contrary, they now rob Tom, Dick, and Harry to help Peter.
>
> The latest chapter in this long-running saga is that politicians have now suddenly discovered that many college students graduate heavily in debt. To politicians it follows, as the night follows the day, that the government should come to their rescue with the taxpayers' money.

Annotations:
- *Basic contradiction between economics and politics*
- *← biblical reference?*
- *ironic and dismissive language*
- *politicians = fools? or irresponsible*

After reading the text, Robinson wrote about it in the journal she kept on her computer. She divided the journal into two columns, one each for the text and her responses. Here is the portion pertaining to the paragraphs above:

Text	Responses
Economics teaches lessons (1), and politics (politicians) and economics are at odds	Is economics truer or more reliable than politics? More scientific?
Politicians don't accept econ. limits—always trying to satisfy "vocal" voters by giving them what they want (2)	Politicians do spend a lot of our money. Is that what they're elected to do, or do they go too far?
"Robbing Peter to pay Paul" (2)— from the Bible (the Apostles)?	
Politicians support student loan program with taxpayer funds bec. of "vocal" voters (2-4): another ex. of not accepting econ. limits	I support the loan program, too. Are politicians being irresponsible when they do? (Dismissive language underlined on copy.)

You should try to answer the questions about meaning that you raise in your annotations and your journal, and that may take another reading or some digging in other sources, such as dictionaries and encyclopedias. Recording in your journal what you think the author means will help you build an understanding of the text, and a focused attempt to summarize will help even more (see pp. 136–37 and opposite). Such efforts will resolve any confusion you feel, or they will give you the confidence to say that your confusion is the fault of the author, not the reader.

Exercise 7.1 Reading

Below is an essay on the US student-loan program by Thomas Sowell, an economist who writes on economics, politics, and education. The essay was first published in the 1990s, but the debate over student loans has never subsided.

Read this essay at least twice, until you think you understand what the author is saying. Either on these pages or separately, note your questions and reactions in writing.

Student Loans

1   The first lesson of economics is scarcity: There is never enough of anything to fully satisfy all those who want it.

2   The first lesson of politics is to disregard the first lesson of economics. When politicians discover some group that is being vocal about not having as much as they want, the "solution" is to give them more. Where do politicians get this "more"? They rob Peter to pay Paul.

3   After a while, of course, they discover that Peter doesn't have enough. Bursting with compassion, politicians rush to the rescue. Needless to say, they do not admit that robbing Peter to pay Paul was a dumb idea in the first place. On the contrary, they now rob Tom, Dick, and Harry to help Peter.

4   The latest chapter in this long-running saga is that politicians have now suddenly discovered that many college students graduate heavily in debt. To politicians it follows, as the night follows the day, that the government should come to their rescue with the taxpayers' money.

5   How big is this crushing burden of college students' debt that we hear so much about from politicians and media deep thinkers? For those students who graduate from public colleges owing money, the debt averages a little under $7,000. For those who graduate from private colleges owing money, the average debt is a little under $9,000.

6   Buying a very modestly priced automobile involves more debt than that. And a car loan has to be paid off faster than the ten years that college graduates get to repay their student loans. Moreover, you have to keep buying cars every several years, while one college education lasts a lifetime.

7   College graduates of course earn higher incomes than other people. Why, then, should we panic at the thought that they have to repay loans for the education which gave them their opportunities? Even graduates with relatively modest incomes pay less than 10 percent of their annual salary on the loan the first year—with declining percentages in future years, as their pay increases.

Political hysteria and media hype may focus on the low-income student [8] with a huge debt. That is where you get your heart-rending stories— even if they are not at all typical. In reality, the soaring student loans of the past decade have resulted from allowing high-income people to borrow under government programs.

Before 1978, college loans were available through government programs only to students whose family income was below some cut-off level. That cut-off level was about double the national average income, but at least it kept out the Rockefellers and the Vanderbilts. But, in an era of "compassion," Congress took off even those limits.

That opened the floodgates. No matter how rich you were, it still [10] paid to borrow money through the government at low interest rates. The money you had set aside for your children's education could be invested somewhere else, at higher interest rates. Then, when the student loan became due, parents could pay it off with the money they had set aside—pocketing the difference in interest rates.

To politicians and the media, however, the rapidly growing loans [11] showed what a great "need" there was. The fact that many students welshed when time came to repay their loans showed how "crushing" their burden of debt must be. In reality, those who welsh typically have smaller loans, but have dropped out of college before finishing. People who are irresponsible in one way are often irresponsible in other ways.

No small amount of the deterioration of college standards has been [12] due to the increasingly easy availability of college to people who are not very serious about getting an education. College is not a bad place to hang out for a few years, if you have nothing better to do, and if someone else is paying for it. Its costs are staggering, but the taxpayers carry much of that burden, not only for state universities and city colleges, but also to an increasing extent even for "private" institutions.

Numerous government subsidies and loan programs make it possi- [13] ble for many people to use vast amounts of society's resources at low cost to themselves. Whether in money terms or in real terms, federal aid to higher education has increased several hundred percent since 1970. That has enabled colleges to raise their tuition by leaps and bounds and enabled professors to be paid more and more for doing less and less teaching.

Naturally all these beneficiaries are going to create hype and hys- [14] teria to keep more of the taxpayers' money coming in. But we would be fools to keep on writing blank checks for them.

When you weigh the cost of things, in economics that's called [15] "trade-offs." In politics, it's called "mean-spirited." Apparently, if we just took a different attitude, scarcity would go away.

—Thomas Sowell

4 Summarizing

Summarizing a text—distilling it to its essential ideas, in your own words—is an important step for comprehending the text before approaching it critically. Summary is discussed in detail in the previous chapter (pp. 136–37). Here, we'll look at how Charlene

Robinson summarized paragraphs 1–4 of Thomas Sowell's "Student Loans." She first drafted this sentence:

Draft summary

As much as politicians would like to satisfy voters by giving them everything they ask for, the government cannot afford a student loan program.

Rereading the sentence and Sowell's paragraph, Robinson saw that this draft misread the text by asserting that the government cannot afford student loans. She realized that Sowell's point is more complicated than that and rewrote her summary:

Revised summary

As their support of the government's student loan program illustrates, politicians ignore the economic reality that using resources to benefit one group (students in debt) involves taking the resources from another group (taxpayers).

Note Using your own words when writing a summary not only helps you understand the meaning but also constitutes the first step in avoiding plagiarism. The second step is to cite the source when you use it in something written for others. See Chapter 44.

> **Exercise 7.2 Summarizing**
> Start where Robinson's summary of Thomas Sowell's essay ends (at paragraph 5) to summarize the entire essay. Your summary, in your own words, should not exceed one paragraph. For additional exercises in summarizing, see pages 600–01.

7b Developing a critical response

Once you've grasped the content of what you're reading—what the author says—then you can turn to understanding what the author does not say outright but suggests or implies or even lets slip. At this stage you are concerned with the purpose or intention of the author and with how he or she carries it out. Depending on what you are reading and why, you may examine evidence, organization, attitude, use of language, and other elements of the text.

Critical thinking and reading consist of four operations: analyzing, interpreting, synthesizing, and (often) evaluating. Although we'll look at them one by one, these operations interrelate and overlap. Indeed, the first three are often combined under the general label *analysis,* and evaluation is sometimes taken for granted as a result of the process.

In the following pages, we use two quite different examples to show how critical reading can work: *People* magazine and Sowell's "Student Loans."

Guidelines for analysis, interpretation, and synthesis
Guidelines for evaluation appear in the box on page 153.

- **What is the purpose of your reading?**
- **What questions do you have about the work,** given your purpose?
- **What elements does the most interesting question highlight?** What elements might you ignore as a result?
- **How do you interpret the meaning and significance of the elements?** What are your assumptions about the work? What do you infer about the author's assumptions?
- **What patterns can you see in (or synthesize from) the elements?** How do the elements relate? How does this whole work relate to other works?
- **What do you conclude about the work?** What does this conclusion add to the work?

1 Analyzing

Analysis is the separation of something into its parts or elements, the better to understand it. To see these elements in what you are reading, begin with a question that reflects your purpose in analyzing the text: why you're curious about it or what you're trying to make out of it. This question will serve as a kind of lens that highlights some features and not others.

Here are some questions you might ask about *People* magazine, listed along with the elements of the magazine that each question highlights:

Questions for analysis	Elements
Does *People* challenge or perpetuate stereotypes?	Stereotypes: explicit and implicit stereotypes or challenges in the magazine
Does the magazine offer positive role models for its readers?	Role models: text and photographs presenting positive or negative role models
Does the magazine's editorial material (articles and accompanying photographs) encourage readers to consume goods and entertainment?	Encouragement of consumption: references to goods and entertainment, focus on consumers, equation of consumption with happiness or success

As these examples show, a question for analysis concentrates your attention on relevant features and eliminates irrelevant features. To answer the question in the preceding list about *People*'s encouragement of consumption, you would focus on items that feature consumption and the products consumed: photographs of designer clothes and celebrities' well-appointed homes, articles on the authors of best-selling books and the stars of new movies. At the same time, you would skip over items that have little or no relevance to consumption, such as uplifting stories about families or the physically challenged.

Analyzing Thomas Sowell's "Student Loans" (pp. 145–46), you might ask these questions:

Questions for analysis	Elements
What is Sowell's attitude toward politicians?	References to politicians: content, words, tone
How does Sowell support his assertions about the loan program's costs?	Support: evidence, such as statistics and examples

A difference in the kinds of questions asked is a key distinction among academic disciplines. A sociologist neatly outlined three disciplines' approaches to poverty:

> Political science does a wonderful job looking at poverty as a policy issue. Economics does an equally wonderful job looking at it from an income-distribution perspective. But sociology asks how people in poverty live and what they aspire to.

Even within disciplines, approaches may differ. The sociologist quoted above may focus on how people in poverty live, but another may be more interested in the effects of poverty on cities or the changes in the poor population over the last fifty years. (See Chapters 49–52 for more on the disciplines' analytical questions.)

2 Interpreting

Identifying the elements of something is of course only the beginning: you also need to interpret the meaning or significance of the elements and of the whole. Interpretation usually requires you to infer the author's **assumptions,** opinions or beliefs about what is or what could or should be. (**Infer** means to draw a conclusion based on evidence.)

The word *assumption* here has a more specific meaning than it does in everyday usage, where it may stand for expectation (*I assume you'll pay*), speculation (*It was a mere assumption*), or error (*The report was riddled with assumptions*). Defined more strictly as what a person *supposes* to be true, assumptions are unavoidable. We all adhere to certain values and beliefs; we all form opinions. We live our lives by such assumptions.

Though pervasive, assumptions are not always stated outright. Speakers and writers may judge that their audience already understands and accepts their assumptions; they may not even be aware of their assumptions; or they may deliberately refrain from stating their assumptions for fear that the audience will disagree. That is why your job as a critical thinker is to interpret what the assumptions are.

Reasonable inferences

Like an author deciding what to say in an article, the publishers of *People* magazine make assumptions that guide their selection of content for the magazine. One set of assumptions, perhaps the most important, concerns what readers want to see: as a for-profit enterprise, the magazine naturally aims to maintain and even expand its readership (currently about 3.4 million each week). If your analysis of the magazine's editorial material reveals that much of it features consumer products, you might infer the following:

> **Reasonable** The publishers of *People* assume that the magazine's readers are consumers who want to see and hear about goods and entertainment.

Nowhere in *People* will you find a statement of this assumption, but the evidence implies it.

Similarly, Thomas Sowell's "Student Loans" (pp. 145–46) is based on certain assumptions, some obvious, some not so obvious. If you were analyzing Sowell's attitude toward politicians, as suggested earlier, you would focus on his statements about them. Sowell says that they "disregard the first lesson of economics" (paragraph 2), which implies that they ignore important principles (knowing that Sowell is an economist himself makes this a reasonable assumption on your part). Sowell also says that politicians "rob Peter to pay Paul," are "[b]ursting with compassion," "do not admit . . . a dumb idea," are characters in a "long-running saga," and arrive at the solution of spending taxes "as the night follows the day"—that is, inevitably (paragraphs 2–4). From these statements and others, you can infer the following:

> **Reasonable** Sowell assumes that politicians become compassionate when a cause is loud and popular, not necessarily just, and they act irresponsibly by trying to solve the problem with other people's (taxpayers') money.

Unreasonable inferences

Interpreting assumptions gives you greater insight into an author's intentions. But it's crucial that inferences fit the evidence of the text, as those above about *People* and Sowell's essay do. Sometimes it's tempting to read too much into the text, as in the next examples:

> **Faulty** *People*'s publishers deliberately skew the magazine's editorial material to promote products on which they receive kickbacks. [The inference is far-fetched, even absurd. It would be reasonable only if there were hard evidence of kickbacks.]

Faulty   Sowell thinks that politicians should not be entrusted with running the country. [The inference misreads Sowell. Although he does not outline a solution for politicians' irresponsibility, there's no evidence that he would overhaul our democratic political system.]

Faulty inferences like these are often based on the reader's *own* assumptions about the text or its subject. When thinking and reading critically, you need to look hard at *your* ideas, too.

3 Synthesizing

If you stopped at analysis and interpretation, critical thinking and reading might leave you with a pile of elements and possible meanings but no vision of the whole. With **synthesis** you make connections among parts *or* among wholes. You use your perspective—your knowledge and beliefs—to create a new whole by drawing conclusions about relationships and implications.

A key component of academic reading and writing, synthesis receives attention in the next chapter (pp. 164–67) and then in the context of research writing (pp. 693–94). Sometimes you'll respond directly to a text, as in the following two conclusions. The first pulls together the earlier analysis of *People* magazine's editorial content and the interpretation of the publisher's assumptions about readers:

Conclusion   *People* magazine appeals to its readers' urge to consume by displaying, discussing, and glamorizing consumer goods.

The next statement, about Thomas Sowell's essay "Student Loans," connects Sowell's assumptions about politicians to a larger idea also implied by the essay:

Conclusion   Sowell's view that politicians are irresponsible with taxpayers' money reflects his overall opinion that the laws of economics, not politics, should drive government.

Often synthesis will take you outside the text to its surroundings. The following questions can help you investigate the context of a work:

- **How does the work compare with works by others?** For instance, how does *People*'s juxtaposition of articles and advertisements compare with that in similar magazines, such as *Us Weekly, Entertainment Weekly,* and *Interview*? Or how have other writers responded to Sowell's views on student loans?
- **How does the work fit into the context of other works by the same author or group?** What distinguishes *People* from the many other magazines published by Time Inc., such as *Time, Sports Illustrated, Family Circle,* and *Fortune*? How do Sowell's

views on student loans typify, or not, the author's other writings on political and economic issues?

- **What cultural, economic, or political forces influence the work?** Why, for instance, are *People* and other celebrity magazines increasingly popular with readers? What other examples might Sowell have given to illustrate his view that economics, not politics, should determine government spending?
- **What historical forces influence the work?** How does *People* reflect changes in the ways readers choose the magazines they read? How has the indebtedness of college students changed over recent decades?

To create links among the elements of a work or between a work and its context, it helps (again) to write while reading and thinking. The active reading recommended earlier is the place to start, as you note your questions and opinions about the text. You can also create connections with a combination of writing and drawing: start with your notes, expand them as needed to take account of context, and draw connections between related thoughts with lines and arrows. (On a word processor you can use the Highlight function or different colors to link related ideas, or use the Comment function to annotate connections.) You want to open up your thinking, so experiment freely.

With synthesis, you create something different from what you started with. To the supermarket shopper reading *People* while standing in line, the magazine may be entertaining and inconsequential. To you—after a critical reading in which you analyze, interpret, and synthesize—the magazine is (at least in part) a significant vehicle of our consumer culture. The difference depends entirely on the critical reading.

4 | Evaluating

Many critical reading and writing assignments end at analysis, interpretation, and synthesis: you explain your understanding of what the author says and doesn't say. Only if you are expected to evaluate the work will you state and defend the judgments you've made about its quality and its significance.

You'll inevitably form judgments while reading the work: *What a striking series of images* or *That just isn't enough evidence*. In evaluating, you collect your judgments, determine that they are generally applicable and are themselves not trivial, and turn them into assertions: *The poet creates fresh, intensely vivid images. The author does not summon the evidence to support the case he is trying to make.* And you support these statements with examples and citations from the text.

Evaluation takes a certain amount of confidence. You may think that you lack the expertise to cast judgment on another's writing, especially if the text is difficult or the author well known. True, the more informed you are, the better a critical reader you are. But conscientious reading and analysis will give you the internal authority to judge a work *as it stands* and *as it seems to you,* against your own unique bundle of experiences, observations, and attitudes.

The box below gives questions that can help you evaluate many kinds of works. There's more on evaluation (including evaluation of online sources) on pages 580–92. For arguments and in academic disciplines, you'll require additional, more specific criteria. See Chapters 9, 11, and 48–52.

Guidelines for evaluation

- **What are your reactions to the work?** What in the work are you responding to?
- **How sound are the work's central idea and evidence?**
- **How well does the author achieve his or her purpose?** How worthwhile is the purpose?
- **How authoritative, trustworthy, and sincere is the author?**
- **How unified and coherent is the work?** Do its parts all support a central idea and clearly relate to one another?
- **What do color, graphics, or (online) sound or video contribute to the work?** Do such elements add meaning or merely decoration?
- **What is the overall quality and significance of the work?**
- **Do you agree or disagree with the work?** Can you support, refute, or extend it?

Exercise 7.3 Thinking critically

Following are some statements about the communications media. Use systematic critical thinking to understand not only what each statement says but also why its author might have said it. As in the example, do your thinking in writing: the act of writing will help you think, and your notes will help you discuss your ideas with your classmates.

Example:

Statement: Every year sees the disappearance of more book publishers because the larger companies gobble up the smaller ones.

Analysis: Why did the author make this statement? Certain words reveal the author's purpose: *disappearance of _more_ book publishers; because; larger companies _gobble up_ smaller ones.*

Interpretation: *More* book publishers means others have disappeared. *Because* specifies cause. *Gobble up* implies consumption, predator to prey. Author's assumptions: Large publishers behave like predators. The predatory behavior of large companies causes the disappearance of small companies. The more publishing companies there are, the better.

Synthesis: The author objects to the predatory behavior of large publishing companies, which he or she holds responsible for eliminating small companies and reducing the total number of companies.

Evaluation: This biased statement against large publishers holds them responsible for the shrinking number of book publishers. But are the large companies solely responsible? Do they offer value in return? And why is the shrinking necessarily bad?

1. Newspapers and newsmagazines are better news sources than television because they demand reading, not just viewing.
2. Radio call-in shows are the true democratic forum, giving voice to people of all persuasions.
3. Participation in online communities threatens to undermine our ability to interact face to face.

Exercise 7.4   Reading an essay critically

Reread Thomas Sowell's "Student Loans" (pp. 145–46) in order to form your own critical response to it. Follow the guidelines for analysis, interpretation, synthesis, and evaluation in the boxes on pages 148 and 153. Focus on any elements suggested by your question about the text: possibilities are assumptions, evidence, organization, use of language, tone, authority, vision of education or students. Be sure to write while reading and thinking; your notes will help your analysis and enhance your creativity, and they will be essential for writing about the selection (Exercise 8.5, p. 178).

Exercise 7.5   Reading a magazine critically

Do your own critical reading of *People* or another magazine. What do you see beyond the obvious? What questions does your reading raise? Let the guidelines on pages 148 and 153 direct your response, and do your work in writing.

7c   Listening critically

When you listen to a speech, lecture, or other oral presentation, approach it critically, just as you would a text. Critical listening involves all the skills described in the previous two sections. Unlike reading, however, listening requires you to pay attention at the moment the speaker is talking. You need to focus on the speaker, shut out competing talk or thoughts, understand what the speaker is saying, and, often, take notes so that you remember what was said. The questions in the box on the facing page can guide you in listening to an oral presentation.

Techniques of critical listening

- **Identify the subject and purpose of the presentation.** At the beginning of a presentation, listen for a statement of the subject and purpose and try to summarize the main idea of the presentation in a single sentence. Take additional information from any visual aids and nonverbal cues provided by the speaker.

- **Keep track of the speaker's main points.** The speaker will likely emphasize main ideas by repeating them and supporting them with examples, images, audio clips, or video.

- **Note any questions.** If you have questions about the subject or the speaker's approach to it, write them down and ask them after the speech.

- **Gauge your response as you listen.** Consider what beliefs or values of your own might be influencing your reception of the presentation—for instance, curiosity, boredom, or agreement or disagreement with the speaker. If you find yourself disagreeing with a speaker, try to put your resistance aside for the moment in order to remain an engaged listener. Make up your mind after the presentation is over.

7d Viewing images critically

Every day we are bombarded with images—pictures on billboards, commercials on television, graphs and charts in newspapers and textbooks, to name just a few examples. Most images slide by without our noticing them, or so we think. But images, sometimes even more than text, can influence us covertly. Their creators have purposes, some worthy, some not, and understanding those purposes requires critical reading. The method parallels that in the previous sections for reading text critically: write while reading, preview, read for comprehension, analyze, interpret, synthesize, and (often) evaluate.

1 Writing while reading an image

Writing as you read an image helps you view it deliberately and record your impressions precisely. If possible, print a copy of the image or scan it into your reading journal so that you can write your comments in the image margins. The example on the next page shows how one student annotated an image he was reading.

2 Previewing an image

Your first step in exploring an image is to form initial impressions of the work's origin and purpose and to note distinctive features. This previewing process is like the one for previewing a text (p. 143):

Questions for previewing an image

- **What do you see?** What is most striking about the image? What is its subject? What is the gist of any text or symbols? What is the overall effect of the image?
- **What are the facts of publication?** Where did you first see the image? Do you think the image was created especially for that location or for others as well? What can you tell about when the image was created?
- **What do you know about the person or group that created the image?** For instance, was the creator an artist, scholar, news organization, or corporation? What seems to have been the creator's purpose?
- **What is your preliminary response?** What about the image interests, confuses, or disturbs you? Are the form, style, and subject familiar or unfamiliar? How might your knowledge, experiences, and values influence your reception of the image?

3 Reading an image

Reading an image requires the same level of concentration as reading a text. Plan to spend more than one session working with the image to absorb its meaning and purpose and then to analyze and maybe challenge its message.

Try to answer the following questions about the image. If some answers aren't clear at this point, skip the question until later.

- **What is the purpose of the image?** Is it mainly explanatory, conveying information, or is it argumentative, trying to convince readers of something or to persuade them to act? What information or point of view does it seem to want to get across?
- **Who is the intended audience for the image?** What does the source of the image, including its publication facts, tell about the image creator's expectations for readers' knowledge, interests, and attitudes? What do the features of the image itself add to your impression?
- **What do any words or symbols add to the image?** Whether located on the image or outside it (such as in a caption), do words or symbols add information, focus your attention, or alter your impression of the image?
- **What people, places, things, or action does the image show?** Does the image tell a story? Do its characters or other features tap into your knowledge, or are they unfamiliar?
- **What is the form of the image?** Is it a photograph, advertisement, painting, graph, diagram, cartoon, or something else?

How do its content and apparent purpose and audience relate to its form?

The following notes by a student, Matthew Greene, illustrate the results of asking questions like these. Greene first saw this advertisement on a bus shelter and then found it online so that he could examine it more closely. He annotated a copy of the image, shown below. Then he filled out his ideas in his reading journal by writing responses to the details he noticed, shown on the next page.

Annotation of an image

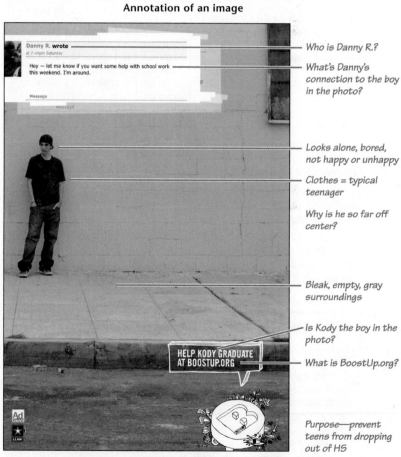

Advertisement for *BoostUp.org*, 2007

Image details	Responses
Gray background: street, sidewalk, wall, blocked-up window	The grim landscape conveys a feeling of emptiness, hopelessness.
Teen dressed in T-shirt, jeans, and a backward baseball cap, standing off to the side with hands in pockets	The clothing seems typical for an urban high school student. Positioned at the edge of the photo, he looks to be on his own, even isolated.
Message from "Danny R." taped to the top of the photo with another message underneath	The message is an offer of help, probably directed at the boy. Danny R. looks to be a friend—is he trying to help the boy stay in school? Is the message underneath also from Danny R.? Taped messages break up the gray = hope for the boy.
Logo at lower right and words "Help Kody graduate at BoostUp.org."	The boy in the picture must be Kody. This is a direct appeal to readers to find out more. What is *BoostUp.org*? How can I or other readers help Kody graduate?

4 Analyzing an image

Elements for analysis

As when analyzing a written work, you analyze an image by identifying its elements. The image elements you might consider appear in the box below. Keep in mind that an image is a visual *composition* whose every element likely reflects a deliberate effort to communicate. Still, few images include all the elements, and you can narrow the list further by posing a question about the image you are reading, as illustrated on the next page.

Elements of images

- **Emphasis:** Most images pull your eyes to certain features: a graph line moving sharply upward, a provocative figure, bright color, thick lines, light against shadow, and so on. The cropping of a photograph or, say, the date range in a chart will also reflect what the image creator considers most important.
- **Narration:** Most images tell stories, whether in a sequence (a TV commercial or a graph showing changes over time) or at a single moment (a photograph, a painting, or a pie chart). Sometimes dialog or a title or caption contributes to the story.
- **Point of view:** The image creator influences responses by taking account of both the viewer's physical relation to the image subject—for

instance, whether it is seen head-on or from above—and the viewer's assumed attitude toward the subject.

- **Arrangement:** Patterns among colors or forms, figures in the foreground and background, and elements that are juxtaposed or set apart contribute to the image's meaning and effect.
- **Color:** An image's colors can direct the viewer's attention and convey the creator's attitude toward the subject. Color may also suggest a mood, an era, a cultural connection, or another frame for viewing the image.
- **Characterization:** The figures and objects in an image have certain qualities—sympathetic or not, desirable or not, and so on. Their characteristics reflect the roles they play in the image's story.
- **Context:** The source of an image or the background in an image affects its meaning, whether it is a graph from a scholarly journal or a photo of a car on a sunny beach.
- **Tension:** Images often communicate a problem or seize attention with features that seem wrong, such as misspelled or misaligned words, distorted figures, or controversial relations between characters.
- **Allusions:** An **allusion** is a reference to something the audience is likely to recognize and respond to. Examples include a cultural symbol such as a dollar sign, a mythological figure such as a unicorn, or a familiar movie character such as Darth Vader from *Star Wars*.

Question for analysis

As discussed on pages 148–49, you can focus your analysis of elements by framing your main interest in the image as a question. Matthew Greene concentrated his analysis of the *BoostUp.org* ad by asking the question *Does the ad move readers to learn more about* BoostUp.org *and how they can help teens to graduate?* The question led Greene to focus on certain elements of the ad and to ignore others, as seen in the following entry from his reading journal:

Image elements	Responses
Emphasis	The ad's grayness and placement of Kody at the far left puts primary emphasis on the boy's isolation. Danny R.'s message, breaking up the gray, receives secondary emphasis.
Narration	The taped-on message suggests a story and connection between Kody and Danny R. Danny R. might be a friend, relative, or mentor. Based on the direct appeal in the word bubble, it appears that Danny R. is trying to help Kody graduate by offering to help him with schoolwork.
Arrangement	The ad places Danny R. and Kody together on the left side of the page, with Danny's message a bright spot on the dull landscape. The appeal to help Kody graduate is subtle and set on its own—the last thing readers look at. It also pulls the elements together so that the ad makes sense.

Image elements	Responses
Color	The lack of color in most of the photo emphasizes Kody's isolation. The whiteness of Danny R.'s message relieves the grayness, like a ray of hope.

Sample images for analysis

The following images give you a chance to analyze selective elements in two kinds of images, a photograph and pages from a Web site. Use the questions in the annotations to help open up your thinking.

Elements in a photograph

Emphasis: What is the focus of the photograph? What are your eyes drawn to?

Characterization: What does the man seem to be feeling? Consider especially his mouth and eyes.

Narration: What story or stories might the photograph tell?

Arrangement: What is interesting about the arrangement of elements?

Color: What does the black-and-white presentation contribute to the image? How might the image differ in full color?

Allusion: What symbol do you see? What meaning does it give to the photograph?

Photograph by Steve Simon

The screen shots opposite are from *AIDS Clock*, an interactive Web site sponsored by the United Nations Population Fund (*www.unfpa.org/aids_clock*). The top image is the home page, displaying a traditional world map. The bottom image appears when viewers click on "Resize the map": now each country's size reflects

Elements of Web pages

Emphasis and color: What elements on these pages draw your attention? How does color distinguish and emphasize elements?

Narration: What story do the two Web pages tell? What does each map contribute to the story? What does the red number contribute? (Notice that the number changes from the first screen to the second.)

Arrangement: What does the arrangement of elements on the pages contribute to the story being told?

Tension: How do you respond to the distorted map in the second image? What does the distortion contribute to your view of the Web site's effectiveness?

Context: How does knowing the Web site's sponsoring organization, the United Nations Population Fund, affect your response to these images?

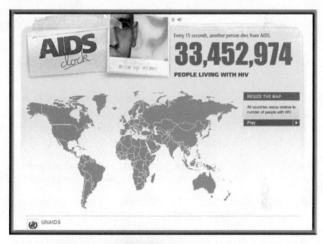

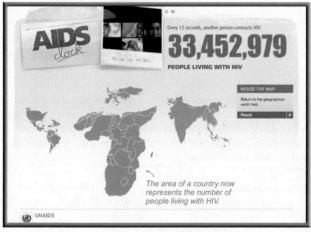

AIDS Clock Web pages, 2008

the number of its people who live with HIV, the virus that causes AIDS. (For example, South Africa grows while the United States shrinks.) The large red number in the upper right changes every fifteen seconds. The "Wake up video" to its left scrolls through photos of people along with text urging viewers to join the World AIDS Campaign.

5 Interpreting an image

The strategies for interpreting an image parallel those for interpreting a written text (pp. 149–51). In this process you look more deeply at the elements, considering them in relation to the image creator's likely assumptions and intentions. You aim to draw reasonable inferences about *why* the image looks as it does. Here's a reasonable inference about the *BoostUp.org* advertisement on page 157:

> Reasonable   The creators of the *BoostUp.org* ad assume that readers want teens to graduate from high school.

This inference is supported by the ad's text: the word bubble connecting to the *BoostUp.org* logo specifically says, "Help Kody graduate at *BoostUp.org*." In contrast, the next inference is *not* reasonable because it leaps to a conclusion that is not supported by the ad:

> Faulty   The creators of the *BoostUp.org* ad want readers to help improve the quality of education in the United States.

The ad implies that readers believe education is important, but it does not suggest that readers should take steps to change the educational system.

6 Synthesizing ideas about an image

As discussed on pages 151–52, with synthesis you take analysis and interpretation a step further to consider how a work's elements and underlying assumptions mesh: How do the elements and assumptions relate to one another? What is the overall message of the image? You may also expand your synthesis to view the whole image in a larger context: How does the work compare with works by others? How does the work fit into the context of other works by the same author or group? What cultural, economic, political, or historical forces influence the work?

Placing an image in its context often requires research. For instance, to learn more about the assumptions underlying the *BoostUp.org* advertisement and the goals of the larger ad campaign, Matthew Greene visited the Web sites of *BoostUp.org* and the Ad Council, one of the ad's sponsors. The following entry from his reading journal synthesizes this research and his own ideas about the ad:

> The *BoostUp.org* magazine ad that features Kody is part of a larger campaign designed to raise public awareness about high school dropouts and encourage pubic support to help teens stay in school. Sponsored by the US Army and the nonprofit Ad Council, *BoostUp.org* profiles high school seniors who are at risk of dropping out and asks individuals to write the students personal messages of support. Ads like "Kody" are the first point of contact between the public and the teens, but they don't by themselves actually help the teens. For that, readers need to visit *BoostUp.org*. Thus the ad's elements work together like pieces of a puzzle, with the solution to be found only on the Web site.

7 Evaluating an image

If your critical reading moves on to evaluation, you'll form judgments about the quality and significance of the image. Questions to ask for evaluation appear in the box on page 153. Briefly: Is the message of the image accurate and fair, or is it distorted and biased? Can you support, refute, or extend the message? Does the image achieve its apparent purpose, and is the purpose worthwhile? How does the image affect you?

See Matthew Greene's paper on pages 176–78 for an evaluation of the *BoostUp.org* advertisement.

Exercise 7.6 Viewing an image critically

Review the list of visual elements on pages 158–59 and then take another close look at the *BoostUp.org* advertisement on page 157. Using the guidelines on the preceding pages, draw your own conclusions about the ad. Write while reading and thinking to help yourself concentrate and develop ideas. A writing suggestion based on this activity appears in Exercise 8.6, page 178.

Exercise 7.7 Viewing an image critically

Select either the photograph on page 160 or the Web pages on page 161 to examine in more detail. Using the guidelines on the preceding pages, read the image(s) methodically and critically. Write down your ideas. A writing suggestion based on this activity appears in Exercise 8.7, page 178.

Exercise 7.8 Comparing images critically

Two images in this section—the advertisement and the photograph—use people as subjects to reinforce their messages. The other images—two Web pages—center on maps and statistics. Using the guidelines on the preceding pages, compare these images, focusing on each one's emphasis. How effective are these emphases? Write down your responses. A writing suggestion based on this activity appears in Exercise 8.8, page 178.

8

Writing in Academic Situations

The academic disciplines differ widely in their subjects and approaches, but they all share the common goal of building knowledge through questioning, research, and communication. The differences among disciplines lie mainly in the kinds of questions asked, the kinds of research done to find the answers, and the types of writing used to communicate the answers, such as case studies, research reports, literary analyses, and reviews of others' research and writings.

Both a discipline's concerns and the kind of writing create an academic writing situation, which in turn shapes a writer's choice of subject, conception of audience, definition of purpose, choice of structure and content, and even choice of language. This chapter introduces academic writing situations in general. Chapters 49–52 detail the particular goals and expectations for writing about literature and in other humanities, the social sciences, and the natural and applied sciences.

8a Writing in response to texts

Academic knowledge building depends on reading, analyzing, and expanding on the work of others. Thus many academic writing assignments require you to respond to one or more texts—not only written products such as short stories and newspaper articles but also visual communications such as images, charts, films, and advertisements. As you form a response to a text, you will integrate, or synthesize, its ideas and information with yours to come to your own conclusions.

Note A common academic assignment, the research paper, expects you to consult and respond to multiple texts in order to support and extend your ideas (see Chapters 41–46). This section focuses on

mycomplab

Visit *mycomplab.com* for more resources and exercises on academic writing.

164

responding directly to a single text, but the skills involved apply to research writing as well.

1 Deciding how to respond

When an assignment asks you to respond directly to a text, you might take one of the following approaches. (Note that the word *author* refers to a photographer, painter, or other creator as well as to a writer.)

- Agree with and extend the author's ideas, exploring related ideas and providing additional examples.
- Agree with the author on some points but disagree on others.
- Disagree with the author on one or more main points.
- Explain how the author achieves a particular effect, such as evoking a historical period or balancing opposing views.
- Analyze the overall effectiveness of a text—for example, how well a writer supports a thesis with convincing evidence or whether an advertisement succeeds in its unstated purpose.

2 Forming a response

You will likely have an immediate response to at least some of the texts you analyze: you may agree or disagree strongly with what the author is saying. But for some other responses, you may need time and thought to determine what the author is saying and what you think about it.

Whatever your assignment, your first task is to examine the text or texts thoroughly so that you're sure you understand what the author says outright and also assumes or implies. You can use the process of critical reading described in the previous chapter to take notes on the text, summarize it, and develop a critical response. Then, as you write, you can use the tips in the following box to convey your response to readers.

Responding to a text

- **Make sure your writing has a point**—a central idea, or thesis, that focuses your response. (For more on developing a thesis, see pp. 29–34.)
- **Include a very brief summary if readers may be unfamiliar with your subject.** But remember that your job is not just to report what the text says or what an image shows; it is to *respond* to the work from your own critical perspective. (For more on summary, see pp. 136–37.)
- **Center each paragraph on an idea of your own that supports your thesis.** Generally, state the idea outright, in your own voice.

(continued)

Responding to a text
(continued)

■ **Support the paragraph idea with evidence from the text**—quotations, paraphrases, details, and examples.

■ **Conclude each paragraph with your interpretation of the evidence.** As a general rule, avoid ending paragraphs with source evidence; instead, end with at least a sentence that explains what the evidence shows.

3 Emphasizing synthesis in your response

Following the suggestions in the preceding box will lead you to show readers the synthesis you achieved by thinking critically about the text. That is, you integrate your perspective with that of the author in order to support a conclusion of your own about the work.

A key to synthesis is deciding how to present evidence from your reading and observation in your writing. Especially when you are writing about a relatively unfamiliar subject, you may be tempted to let a text or other source do the talking for you through extensive summary or quotations. However, your voice is crucial in academic writing, where readers expect to see you managing ideas and information to make your points. A typical paragraph of text-based writing follows the pattern outlined in the box above: the writer's own idea, evidence from the text, and the writer's interpretation of the evidence. You can see this pattern in the following paragraph from an essay that appears later in this chapter (p. 174):

Sowell's portrait of student-loan recipients is questionable. It is based on averages, some statistical and some not, but averages are often deceptive. For example, Sowell cites college graduates' low average debt of $7,000 to $9,000 (131) without acknowledging the fact that many students' debt is much higher or giving the full range of statistics. Similarly, Sowell dismisses "heart-rending stories" of "the low-income student with a huge debt" as "not at all typical" (132), yet he invents his own exaggerated version of the typical loan recipient: an affluent slacker ("Rockefellers" and "Vanderbilts") for whom college is a "place to hang out for a few years" sponging off the government, while his or her parents clear a profit from making use of the loan program (132). Although such students (and parents) may well exist, are they really typical? Sowell does not offer any data one way or the

Writer's idea

Evidence and interpretation

other—for instance, how many loan recipients come from each income group, what percentage of loan funds go to each group, how many loan recipients receive significant help from their parents, and how many receive none. Together, Sowell's statements and omissions cast doubt on the argument that students don't need or deserve the loans.

Writer's conclusion

—Charlene Robinson (student),
"Weighing the Costs"

This example meets an important goal of synthesis in academic writing: Robinson finds **balance** in her own and Sowell's claims so that her claims are reasonable and believable. Disagreeing with Sowell, Robinson might simply have dismissed his claims about loan recipients as "ridiculous" and moved on. Instead, she takes a more serious and impartial approach by giving Sowell's claims a fair hearing, explaining clearly why she faults them, and detailing the omissions she sees. Thus she gives readers a chance to evaluate Sowell's and her own claims for themselves.

Note Effective synthesis requires careful handling of evidence from the text (quotations, paraphrases, and summaries) so that the evidence meshes smoothly into your sentences and yet is clearly distinct from your own ideas. See pages 601–06 on integrating borrowed material.

8b Determining purpose

For most academic writing, your general purpose will be mainly explanatory or mainly argumentative. That is, you will aim to explain your subject so that readers understand it as you do, or you will aim to gain readers' agreement with a debatable idea about the subject. (See p. 10 for more on general purposes and Chapters 9–11 for more on argument.) Although the general purpose for writing may not be stated outright in an assignment, it will probably be implied, as you can see in these two abbreviated assignments:

Explanation
Compare the depiction of war in two films viewed this semester, considering plots, characters, dialog, battle scenes, production designs, and other elements of the films.

Argument
What do you see as a theme in the movies of director Steven Spielberg? What belief about the world do his choices of subject and setting convey, either explicitly or implicitly? Support your claim with evidence from at least four of Spielberg's movies, considering plots, characters, dialog, and other elements such as production designs and camera shots.

Your specific purpose—including your subject and how you hope readers will respond—depends on the kind of writing you're doing. For instance, in a lab report for a biology class, you want readers to understand why you conducted your study, how you conducted it, what the results were, and what their significance is. Not coincidentally, these topics correspond to the major sections of a biology lab report. In following the standard format, you both help to define your purpose and begin to meet the discipline's (and thus your teacher's) expectations.

Your specific purpose will be more complex as well. You take a class to learn about a subject and the ways experts think about it. Your writing, in return, contributes to the discipline through the knowledge you uncover and the lens of your perspective. At the same time, as a student you want to demonstrate your competence with research, evidence, format, and other requirements of the discipline.

8c   Analyzing audience

Many academic writing assignments will specify or assume an educated audience or an academic audience. Such readers look for writing that is clear, balanced, well-organized, and well-reasoned, among other qualities discussed on the opposite page. Other assignments will specify or assume an audience of experts on your subject, readers who look in addition for writing that meets the subject's requirements for claims and evidence, organization, language, format, and other qualities discussed in Chapters 48–52.

Of course, much of your academic writing will have only one reader besides you: the teacher of the class for which you are writing. Teachers fill two main roles as readers:

- **They represent the audience you are addressing.** They may actually be members of the audience, as when you address academic readers or subject experts. Or they may imagine themselves as members of your audience—reading, for instance, as if they sat on the city council. In either case, they're interested in how effectively you write for the audience.
- **They serve as coaches,** guiding you toward achieving the goals of the course and, more broadly, toward the academic aims of building and communicating knowledge.

Like everyone else, teachers have preferences and peeves, but you'll waste time and energy trying to anticipate them. Do attend to written and spoken directions for assignments, of course. But otherwise view your teachers as representatives of the community you are writing for. Their responses will be guided by the community's aims and expectations and by a desire to teach you about them.

8d | Choosing structure and content

Many academic writing assignments will at least imply how you should organize your paper and even how you should develop your ideas. Like the literature review mentioned earlier, the type of paper required will suggest discrete parts, each with its own requirements for content. Even a direct response to a text, whose content depends on the text and the response, still implies certain requirements: you are asked to make a claim and to support the claim with specific evidence. Sometimes you may also be expected to show that you understand what others think about the text.

No matter what type of paper an assignment specifies, the broad academic aims of building and exchanging knowledge determine features that are common across disciplines. Follow these general guidelines for your academic writing, supplementing them as indicated with others elsewhere in this book:

- **Develop a thesis**—a central idea or claim to which everything in the paper clearly relates. Usually, state your thesis near the beginning of the paper. For more on theses, see pages 29–34.
- **Support the thesis with evidence,** drawn usually from reading and sometimes from your own experience. The kinds of evidence will depend on the discipline you're writing in and the type of paper you're doing. For more on evidence in the disciplines, see pages 701–02 (literature), 719–20 (other humanities), 736–37 (social sciences), and 768 (natural and applied sciences).
- **Synthesize.** Put your sources to work for you by thinking critically about them. Integrate them into your own perspective in your own voice. For more on synthesis, see pages 164–67 in this chapter and pages 593–94 in the discussion of research writing.
- **Acknowledge sources fully, including online sources.** *Not* acknowledging sources undermines the knowledge-sharing foundation of academic writing and opens you to charges of plagiarism, which can be punishable. See pages 607–14 on plagiarism and the following pages for details on source-citation styles: 619–63 (MLA style for English and some other humanities), 724–35 (Chicago style for history, philosophy, and some other humanities), 741–61 (APA style for the social sciences), and 773–79 (CSE style for the natural and applied sciences).
- **Organize clearly within the framework of the type of writing you're doing.** Develop your ideas as simply and directly as your purpose and content allow. Clearly relate sentences, paragraphs, and sections so that readers always know where they are in the paper's development.

These features are far from universal. In other cultures, academic writers may be indirect, may expect readers to discover the thesis, or may assume that readers do not require acknowledgment of well-known sources. Recognizing such differences between practices in your native culture and in the United States can help you adapt to US academic writing.

8e Using academic language

American academic writing relies on a dialect called standard American English. The dialect is also used in business, government, the media, and other sites of social and economic power where people of diverse backgrounds must communicate with one another. It is "standard" not because it is better than other forms of English, but because it is accepted as the common language, much as the dollar bill is accepted as the common currency.

You'll recognize standard American English as the dialect used in this handbook, in magazines and newspapers, and on television news. But you might also notice that the dialect varies a great deal, from the formal English of a President's State of the Union address through the middle formality of this handbook to the informal chitchat between anchors on morning TV. Even in academic writing, standard American English allows much room for the writer's own voice, as these passages on the same topic show:

More formal

In *Things Fall Apart,* Chinua Achebe portrays a culture in flux, where ancient rituals of community responsibility and familial loyalty begin to disintegrate. Achebe's central character, a Nigerian tribal chief and a formidable patriarch, finds himself powerless to stop the rising tide of change that floods his home and his village. His son rejects the old traditions, both in the home and among the tribe. Like Shakespeare's King Lear, whose children also confound him, the chief rails against his condition and drifts into madness.

Three complicated sentences

Drawn-out phrasing, such as *finds himself powerless* instead of *can do nothing*

Formal vocabulary, such as *in flux, familial,* and *formidable*

Less formal

Things fall apart in *Things Fall Apart,* by Chinua Achebe. The main character, a Nigerian tribal chief and patriarch, can't stop the world from changing. Even more, he can't count on his son to follow in his footsteps, either at home or

Five shorter sentences

More informal phrasing, such as *Things fall apart in . . .* and *can't stop* in public. The book echoes Shakespeare's *King Lear.* In both works, rulers with ungrateful children lose their minds in the face of events they can't control.

> More informal vocabulary, such as *count on* and *lose their minds*

As different as they are, both examples illustrate several common features of academic language:

- **Its formality varies depending on the writer's voice and audience.** For instance, the first passage might reflect the writer's preference for more formal language and also an audience of experts in the field who expect a serious, measured approach. Addressing peers instead of experts, the same writer might still sound more formal than the second writer does—perhaps retaining the formal vocabulary—but might also shorten sentences and tighten phrasing.
- **It follows the conventions of standard American English for grammar and usage.** These conventions are detailed in guides to the dialect, such as this handbook. Note that standard American English excludes many forms that are encouraged by rapid communication in e-mail and in text or instant messaging, such as incomplete sentences, no capital letters, and abbreviations and shortened spellings (*u* for "you," *b4* for "before," *thru* for "through," *imo* for "in my opinion," and so on). See page 506 for more on these forms.
- **It uses a standard vocabulary,** not one that only some groups understand, such as slang, an ethnic or regional dialect, or another language. See pages 504–05 for more on specialized vocabularies.
- **It creates some distance between writer and reader with the third person (*he, she, it, they*).** The first person (*I, we*) is sometimes appropriate to express personal opinions or invite readers to think along, but not with a strongly explanatory purpose (*When I read* Things Fall Apart, *I felt sorry for the father*). The second person (*you*) is appropriate only in addressing readers directly (as in this handbook), and even then it may seem condescending or too chummy (*You would feel sorry for the father, too*).
- **It is authoritative and neutral.** In the examples on the facing page and above, the writers express themselves confidently, not timidly (as in *One comparison that might be considered in this case is with Shakespeare's* King Lear). They also refrain from hostility (*The father deserves to be punished for his stubbornness*) and enthusiasm (*Achebe's tribal chief is a masterpiece of characterization*).

At first, the diverse demands of academic writing may leave you groping for an appropriate voice. In an effort to sound fresh and confident, you may write too casually:

Too casual
The old guy just can't stop the world, and he can't get his son to see things his way.

In an effort to sound "academic," you may produce wordy and awkward sentences:

Wordy and awkward
In *Things Fall Apart,* a culture in the midst of change is portrayed by author Chinua Achebe. Whereas at one time ancient rituals held sway, which included community responsibility and familial loyalty, the culture is now subject to disintegration in the world that exists today. The central character created by Achebe is a Nigerian tribal chief and formidable patriarch who is seen in a condition of powerlessness to stop his home and his village from being flooded by a rising tide of change. [The passive voice in this example, such as *culture . . . is portrayed* and *who is seen,* adds to its wordiness and indirection. See pp. 306–07 for more on verb voice.]

A cure for writing too informally or too stiffly is to read academic writing so that the language and style become familiar and to edit your writing (see pp. 60–63). With experience and practice, you will develop a voice that is sufficiently formal but still authentic and natural, as in the examples on pages 170–71.

(CULTURE LANGUAGE) If your first language is not English or is an English dialect besides standard American, you know well the power of communicating with others who share your language. Learning to write standard American English in no way requires you to abandon your first language. Like most multilingual people, you are probably already adept at switching between languages as the situation demands—speaking one way with your relatives, say, and another way with an employer. As you practice academic writing, you'll develop the same flexibility with it.

Exercise 8.1 Using academic language
Revise the following paragraph to make the language more academic while keeping the factual information the same.

If you buy into the stereotype of girls chatting away on their cell phones, you should think again. One of the major wireless companies surveyed 1021 cell phone owners for a period of five years and—surprise!—reported that guys talk on cell phones more than girls do. In fact, guys were way ahead of girls, using an average of 571 minutes a month compared to 424 for girls. That's 35 percent more time on the phone! The survey also asked about conversations on home phones, and while girls still beat the field, the guys are catching up.

Exercise 8.2   Considering your past work: Writing in academic situations

Look back at a paper you wrote for one of your high school classes. To what extent does it share the features of academic writing discussed in this chapter? How does it differ? Write a revision plan for making the paper more academic.

Exercise 8.3   Considering your native language or dialect

What main similarities and differences do you notice between writing in your native language or dialect and writing for US high school classes? Consider especially audience, purpose, content, structure, and the expression of ideas. Which differences do you think are easiest to bridge? Which are most difficult? Why?

8f   Examining sample critical responses

A critical response to a text or an image, often called a **critique**, is a common academic writing assignment. The specifics depend on the discipline, but the principles illustrated here apply across disciplines.

Note Critical writing is *not* summarizing. You might write a summary to clarify a text or an image for yourself, and you may briefly summarize a work in your larger piece of writing. But in critical writing you go further to bring your perspective to the work you are responding to.

1   Writing critically about a text

The following essay by the student Charlene Robinson responds to Thomas Sowell's essay "Student Loans" (pp. 145–46). Robinson arrived at her response, an argument, through the process of critical reading outlined in the previous chapter and then by gathering and organizing her ideas, developing a thesis about Sowell's text that synthesized his ideas and hers, and drafting and revising until she believed she had supported her thesis with sufficient evidence from her own experience and from Sowell's text.

Robinson did not assume that her readers would see the same things in Sowell's essay or share her views, so her essay offers evidence of Sowell's ideas in the form of direct quotations, summaries, and paraphrases (restatements in her own words). Robinson documents these borrowings from Sowell using the style of the Modern Language Association (MLA): the numbers in parentheses are page numbers in the book containing Sowell's essay, listed at the end as a "work cited." (See Chapter 46 for more on MLA style.)

Weighing the Costs

Introduction

Summary of Sowell's essay

In the essay "Student Loans," the economist Thomas Sowell challenges the US government's student-loan program for three main reasons:
a scarce resource (taxpayers' money) goes to many undeserving students,
a high number of recipients fail to repay their loans, and the easy availability of money has led to both lower academic standards and higher college tuitions. Sowell wants his readers to "weigh the costs of things"
(133) in order to see, as he does, that the loan program should not re-

Robinson's critical question

Thesis statement

ceive so much government funding. But does he provide the evidence of
cost and other problems to lead the reader to agree with him? The answer
is no, because hard evidence is less common than debatable and unsup-
ported assumptions about students, scarcity, and the value of education.

First main point

Evidence for first point: paraphrases and quotations from Sowell's text

Sowell's portrait of student-loan recipients is questionable. It is
based on averages, some statistical and some not, but averages are often deceptive. For example, Sowell cites college graduates' low average
debt of $7,000 to $9,000 (131) without acknowledging the fact that
many students' debt is much higher or giving the full range of statistics. Similarly, Sowell dismisses "heart-rending stories" of "the low-
income student with a huge debt" as "not at all typical" (132), yet he
invents his own exaggerated version of the typical loan recipient: an
affluent slacker ("Rockefellers" and "Vanderbilts") for whom college is a
"place to hang out for a few years" sponging off the government, while
his or her parents clear a profit from making use of the loan program

Evidence for first point: Sowell's omissions

(132). Although such students (and parents) may well exist, are they
really typical? Sowell does not offer any data one way or the other—for
instance, how many loan recipients come from each income group, what
percentage of loan funds go to each group, how many loan recipients
receive significant help from their parents, and how many receive none.

Conclusion of first point: Robinson's interpretation

Together, Sowell's statements and omissions cast doubt on the argument that students don't need or deserve the loans.

Transition to sec-
ond main point

Second main point

Another set of assumptions in the essay has to do with "scarcity":
"There is never enough of anything to fully satisfy all those who want
it," Sowell says (131). This statement appeals to readers' common
sense, but the "lesson" of scarcity does not necessarily apply to the

Evidence for sec-
ond point: Sowell's omissions

student-loan program. Sowell omits many important figures needed to
prove that the nation's resources are too scarce to support the program,
such as the total cost of the program, its percentage of the total education budget and the total federal budget, and its cost compared to the
cost of defense, Medicare, and other expensive programs. Moreover,
Sowell does not mention the interest paid by loan recipients, even

though the interest must offset some of the costs of running the program and covering unpaid loans. Thus his argument that there isn't
enough money to run the student loan program is unconvincing.

Conclusion of sec-
ond point: Robin-
son's interpretation

The most fundamental and most debatable assumption underlying
Sowell's essay is that higher education is a kind of commodity that not
everyone is entitled to. In order to diminish the importance of graduates'
average debt from education loans, Sowell claims that a car loan will
probably be higher (131). This comparison between education and an automobile implies that the two are somehow equal as products and that an
affordable higher education is no more a right than a new car is. Sowell
also condemns the "irresponsible" students who drop out of school and
"the increasingly easy availability of college to people who are not very serious about getting an education" (132). But he overlooks the value of encouraging education, including the education of those who don't finish
college or who aren't scholars. For many in the United States, education has
a greater value than that of a mere commodity like a car. And even from an
economic perspective such as Sowell's, the cost to society of an uneducated
public needs to be taken into account. By failing to give education its
due, Sowell undermines his argument at its core.

Third main point

Evidence for third
point: paraphrases
and quotations
from Sowell's text

Evidence for third
point: Sowell's
omissions

Conclusion of
third point: Robin-
son's interpreta-
tion

Sowell writes with conviction, and his concerns are valid: high
taxes, waste, unfairness, declining educational standards, obtrusive
government. However, the essay's flaws make it unlikely that Sowell
could convince readers who do not already agree with him. He does
not support his portrait of the typical loan recipient, he fails to
demonstrate a lack of resources for the loan program, and he neglects
the special nature of education compared to other services and products. Sowell may have the evidence to back up his assumptions, but by
omitting it he himself does not truly weigh the costs of the loan program.

Conclusion

Acknowledgment
of Sowell's con-
cerns

Summary of three
main points

Return to theme
of introduction:
weighing costs

Work Cited

Sowell, Thomas. "Student Loans." *Is Reality Optional? and Other Essays.*
Stanford: Hoover, 1993. 131-33. Print.

Work cited in MLA
style (p. 628)

—Charlene Robinson (student)

2 Writing critically about an image

The following essay, by the student Matthew Greene, responds
to the *BoostUp.org* advertisement on page 157. As we saw in the previous chapter, Greene examined the image over several stages, each
time discovering more in it and gradually developing his own ideas.
In his paper Greene takes pains to be sure that readers will see the
image as he does: he reproduces the ad, captions it, and clearly

describes its features. He cites his sources using MLA style (Chapter 46). (All but one of Greene's text citations lack page numbers because the sources themselves are not numbered.)

Note An image is a source just as a written work is, and like a written source it must be acknowledged. Greene cites the *BoostUp.org* ad in the image caption. (MLA style does not require him to cite it again in his list of works cited.) If Greene published his paper online, he would also need to seek the copyright owner's permission to use the image. See pages 609–12 for more about acknowledging sources and pages 612–13 for more about permissions for online publication.

Giving a Boost

<table>
<tr><td>Introduction</td><td rowspan="2">How many commuters paused, as I did, to puzzle over a bus shelter advertisement that shows a teenage boy standing in a sea of gray street, sidewalk, and wall? (See fig. 1.) Were other readers curious about the message from "Danny R.," taped to the top of the photograph, that reads, "Hey—let me know if you want some help with school work this weekend. I'm around"? Did they follow the ad's instruction: "HELP KODY GRADUATE AT BOOSTUP.ORG"? If they did, they probably appreciated how effective the ad is. Through its photograph, taped-on message, and direct appeal, it encourages readers to find out how they can help students stay in high school.</td></tr>
</table>

Introduction

Description of image

Thesis statement

Caption giving the ad's main idea and source

Fig. 1. An advertisement for *BoostUp.org* encourages viewers to visit its Web site and support students who are at risk of dropping out of high school. From "High School Dropout Prevention"; *Ad Council*; Ad Council, 2007; Web; 10 Apr. 2010.

The *BoostUp.org* campaign is sponsored by the nonprofit Ad Council and the US Army. It aims to raise public awareness about high school dropouts and encourage public support to help teens stay in school ("High School"). When people visit *BoostUp.org*, they can learn about particular at-risk seniors and offer them "boost" through e-mail or text messages; users of *YouTube*, *Facebook*, and *MySpace* can send support through those sites ("What"). First, though, people have to visit the site, and that's where "Kody" and similar ads come in. They are very effective at making people curious enough to go to the site and concerned enough to participate in the campaign.

> Background information on the ad campaign

The main image in the *BoostUp.org* ad—the photograph of a teenager wearing a T-shirt, baggy jeans, and a backward baseball cap—presents the boy as especially isolated. The cropping of the photograph pushes him to one side and makes him seem small amid hard gray surfaces. His off-center stance, hands in pockets, and glance to the side all heighten the sense that he is alone, vulnerable, and in need of a friend or help. At the same time, nothing in the photograph suggests that the boy is causing trouble or planning it. He's just very much by himself.

> First main point

> Evidence for first point: analysis of photograph

> Conclusion of first point: Greene's interpretation

The second major element in the ad, Danny R.'s message in the upper left corner, counters the photograph in two ways. First, with the offer to help with school work over the weekend, Danny R. shows that he is someone who knows and cares about the person he's writing to. It isn't immediately clear who this person is, but if it's the boy in the photograph then he isn't as alone as he first seems. Second, Danny R.'s message is literally taped on the photo, over another message that can't be read. This covered message implies that Danny R. is not the only support the boy has. Together, the messages break up the bleak grayness that the photograph depicts as the boy's world, offering hope that the boy has friends who want to help him.

> Second main point

> Evidence for second point: analysis of message

> Conclusion of second point: Greene's interpretation

The third important element in the ad—the word bubble in the lower right—pulls together the other two elements. The word bubble is a direct appeal to readers to get involved. It is less prominent than the other two elements, so it is probably the final place readers look when scanning the ad. It suggests that the boy is named Kody and that he is at risk of not graduating. Yet the text still does not say what *BoostUp.org* is or how readers can help Kody there. Some mystery remains to attract readers to the Web site.

> Third main point

> Evidence for third point: analysis of word bubble

> Conclusion of third point: Greene's interpretation

The creators of this advertisement seem to assume that readers see dropping out as a negative step for high school students. Thus the ad is designed to draw readers in by showing Kody's world, providing an example

> Conclusion

of an encouraging message, and inviting visits to *BoostUp.org*. Once there, readers may be moved, as I was, to offer a "boost" of their own to Kody and his classmates.

Works Cited

"High School Dropout Prevention." *Ad Council*. Ad Council, 2007. Web. 18
Apr. 2010.

"What Is Boost?" *BoostUp.org*. US Army and Ad Council, 2007. Web. 15
Apr. 2010.

—Matthew Greene (student)

Works cited in MLA style

No works-cited entry for advertisement because the caption provides complete source information

Exercise 8.4 Responding to critiques

Read Charlene Robinson's and Matthew Greene's essays carefully. Do you think the authors' critiques are accurate and fair? Are they perceptive? Do the authors provide enough evidence to convince you of their points? Do they miss anything you would have mentioned? Write your responses to one of the essays in a brief critique of your own.

Exercise 8.5 Writing critically about a text

Write an essay based on your own critical reading of Thomas Sowell's "Student Loans" (Exercise 7.4, p. 154). Your critique may be entirely different from Charlene Robinson's, or you may have developed some of the same points. If there are similarities, they should be expressed and supported in your own way, in the context of your own critical perspective.

Exercise 8.6 Writing critically about an image

Write an essay based on your own critical reading of the *BoostUp.org* advertisement (Exercise 7.6, p. 163). Your critique may be entirely different from Matthew Greene's, or you may have developed some of the same points. If there are similarities, they should be expressed and supported in your own way, in the context of your own critical perspective.

Exercise 8.7 Writing critically about an image

Write an essay based on your critical reading of the photograph on page 160 or the Web pages on page 161 (Exercise 7.7, p. 163).

Exercise 8.8 Writing critically about several images

Write an essay based on your critical reading and comparison of the three images in the previous chapter (Exercise 7.8, p. 163).

9

Reading Arguments Critically

Argument is writing that attempts to open readers' minds to an opinion, change readers' own opinions, or move readers to action. A good argument is neither a cold exercise in logic nor an attempt to beat others into submission. It is a work of negotiation and problem solving in which both writer and reader search for the knowledge that will create common ground between them.

Of course, not all arguments are "good." Whether deliberately or not, some are unclear, incomplete, misleading, or downright false. The negotiation fails; the problem remains unsolved. This chapter will help you read written arguments critically, and the next chapter will help you write effective arguments. After that, in Chapter 11, you'll see how to read and use visual arguments.

CULTURE LANGUAGE The ways of reading and writing arguments described in this chapter and the next may be uncomfortable to you if your native culture approaches such writing differently. In some cultures, for example, a writer is expected to begin indirectly, to avoid asserting his or her opinion outright, or to establish a compromise rather than argue a position. In American academic and business settings, readers and writers look or aim for a well-articulated opinion, evidence gathered from many sources, and a direct and concise argument for the opinion.

9a Recognizing the elements of argument

Few arguments are an easy read. Most demand the attentive critical reading discussed in Chapter 7. (If you haven't read pp. 141–53, you should do so before continuing.) As a reader of argument, your purpose will almost always be the same: you'll want to know whether you should be convinced by the argument. This purpose focuses your attention on the elements that make an argument convincing, or not.

Visit *mycomplab.com* for more resources and exercises on reading arguments critically.

In a scheme adapted from the work of the British philosopher Stephen Toulmin, an argument has three main elements:

- **Claims:** positive statements that require support. In a written argument the central claim is stated outright in a **thesis statement** (see p. 29). This central claim is what the argument is about. For instance:

  In both its space and its equipment, the school's chemistry classroom is outdated.

  Several minor claims, such as that the present equipment is inadequate, will contribute to the central assertion.

- **Evidence:** the facts, examples, expert opinions, and other information that support the claims. (Toulmin calls evidence *data* or *grounds,* terms that indicate both its specificity and its work as an argument's foundation.) Evidence to support the preceding claim might include the following:

  The present classroom's square feet
  An inventory of equipment
  The testimony of science teachers

  Like the claims, the evidence is always stated outright.

- **Assumptions:** the writer's underlying (and often unstated) beliefs, opinions, principles, or inferences that tie the evidence to the claims. (Toulmin calls these assumptions *warrants:* they justify making the claims on the basis of the evidence provided.) For instance, the following assumption might connect the evidence of professors' testimony with the claim that a new lab is needed:

  Science teachers are the persons most capable of evaluating the present classroom's quality.

In the following pages, we'll examine each of these elements along with several others: tone and language, reasonableness, and common errors in reasoning. Charlene Robinson's "Weighing the Costs" in the previous chapter (pp. 174–75) provides a good example of critically reading an argument for its claims, evidence, and assumptions.

Note This chapter focuses on reading nonfiction arguments such as those found in speeches, magazines, and books on current issues. Literary works can also be read as arguments in which the author, working from a set of assumptions, tries to persuade readers to accept a point of view by making implicit claims and supporting them with the evidence of character, plot, symbols, and other elements. For more on reading arguments in literary works, see pages 702–03.

Questions for critically reading an argument

■ What **claims** does the writer make?

■ What kinds and quality of **evidence** does the writer provide to support the claims?

■ What **assumptions** underlie the argument, connecting evidence to claims? Are they clear and believable?

■ What is the writer's **tone?** How does the writer use **language?**

■ Is the writer **reasonable?**

■ Is the argument **logical?** Does it contain any **fallacies?**

■ Are you convinced by the argument? Why or why not?

9b Testing claims

The claims or assertions in an argument will likely be statements of opinion, fact, belief, or prejudice. It's important to distinguish between the kinds of statements and to analyze the definitions of terms.

1 Recognizing opinions

An **opinion** is a judgment based on facts and arguable on the basis of facts. Reasonable people could and probably do disagree over opinions, and they are potentially changeable: with more facts, a writer might change opinions partly or wholly.

The thesis statement of an effective argument is an opinion, often one of the following:

■ **A claim about past or present reality:**

In both its space and its equipment, the school's chemistry classroom is outdated.

Academic cheating increases with students' sense of pressure to do well.

■ **A claim of value:**

The new parking fees are unjustified given the lack of student spaces in the lot.

Computer music pirates undermine the system that encourages the very creation of music.

■ **A recommendation for a course of action,** often a solution to a perceived problem:

The school's outdated chemistry classroom should be replaced incrementally over the next five years.

Schools and businesses can help to resolve the region's traffic congestion by implementing car pools and rewarding participants.

The backbone of an argument consists of specific claims that support the thesis statement. These may be statements of opinion, too, or they may state facts or beliefs.

Opinions do not make arguments by themselves. As a critical reader, you must satisfy yourself that the writer has specified the evidence for the opinions and that the assumptions linking claims and evidence are clear and believable.

2 Recognizing facts

A **fact** may be a verifiable statement—that is, one that can be proved as true:

> Last year parking fees increased 16 percent.

Or it may be an inference from verifiable facts:

> Over their lifetimes, four-year college graduates earn almost twice as much as high school graduates.

A claim of fact does not work as the thesis of an argument. Although people often dispute facts, they are not fundamentally arguable because ultimately they can be verified. Facts have another important role in argument, providing crucial evidence for other claims (see p. 184).

3 Recognizing beliefs

A **belief** is a conviction based on cultural or personal faith, morality, or values:

> Abortion is legalized murder.
> Capital punishment is legalized murder.
> The primary goal of government should be to provide equality of opportunity for all.

Such statements are often called opinions because they express viewpoints, but unlike opinions they are not based on facts and other evidence. Since they cannot be disproved by facts or even contested on the basis of facts, they cannot serve as the central or supporting claims of an argument. However, beliefs can play a significant role in argument. Appeals to readers' beliefs can serve as a kind of evidence by tapping into emotions (see pp. 185 and 208–09), and beliefs often form the assumptions that link claims and evidence (see pp. 185 and 188).

4 Recognizing prejudices

One kind of assertion that has no place in argument is a **prejudice**, an opinion based on insufficient or unexamined evidence:

Women are bad drivers.
Fat people are jolly.
Teenagers are irresponsible.
Athletes are unintelligent.
People who use wheelchairs have cognitive disabilities.

Unlike a belief, a prejudice is testable: it can be contested and disproved on the basis of facts. Very often, however, we form prejudices or accept them from others—parents, friends, the communications media—without questioning their meaning or testing their truth. Writers who display prejudice do not deserve your confidence and agreement.

When reading arguments that appear online, you should be especially vigilant for claims of belief or prejudice that pose as considered opinions. Anyone with a computer and an Internet connection can post anything on the Internet, without passing it through an editorial screening like that undergone by books and by articles in journals and magazines. The filtering of such material is entirely up to the reader.

5 Looking for defined terms

In any argument, but especially in arguments about abstract ideas, the clear and consistent definition of terms is essential. In the following claim, the writer is not clear about what she means by the crucial term *justice:*

> Over the past few decades, justice has deteriorated so badly that it almost does not exist anymore.

The word *justice* is **abstract:** it does not refer to anything specific or concrete and in fact has varied meanings. (The five definitions in *The American Heritage Dictionary* include "the principle of moral rightness" and "the administration and procedure of law.") When the writer specifies her meaning, her assertion is much clearer:

> If by *justice* we mean treating people fairly, punishing those who commit crimes, and protecting the victims of those crimes, then justice has deteriorated badly over the past few decades.

Writers who use abstract words such as *justice, equality, success,* and *maturity* have a responsibility to define them. If the word is important to the argument, such a definition may take an entire paragraph. As a reader you have the obligation to evaluate the writer's definitions before you accept his or her assertions. (See pp. 96–97 for more on definition and a paragraph defining the abstract word *quality.*)

9c | Weighing evidence

In argument, evidence demonstrates the validity of the writer's claims. If the evidence is inadequate or questionable, the claims are at best doubtful.

1 | Recognizing kinds of evidence

Writers draw on several kinds of evidence to support their claims.

Evidence for argument

- **Facts:** verifiable statements
- **Statistics:** facts expressed in numbers
- **Examples:** specific cases
- **Expert opinions:** the judgments of authorities
- **Appeals to readers' beliefs or needs**

Facts

Facts are statements whose truth can be verified or inferred (see p. 182). Facts employing numbers are **statistics:**

> Of those polled, 62 percent stated a preference for a flat tax.
>
> In 2005 there were 1,370,237 men and women on active duty in the US armed forces.
>
> The average American household consists of 2.58 persons.

Numbers may be implied:

> Earth is closer to the sun than Saturn is.
> The cost of medical care is rising.

Or a fact may involve no numbers at all:

> The city council adjourned without taking a vote.
> The President vetoed the bill.

Examples

Examples are specific instances of the point being made, including historical precedents and personal experiences. The passage below uses a personal narrative as partial support for the claim in the first sentence:

> Besides broadening students' knowledge, service learning can also introduce students to possible careers that they otherwise would have known

nothing about. Somewhat reluctantly, I volunteered after school at a daycare center to satisfy the service-learning requirement. But what I learned about child development has led me to consider becoming a child psychologist instead of an engineer.

Expert opinions

Expert opinions are the judgments formed by authorities on the basis of their own examination of the facts. In the following passage the writer cites the opinion of an expert to support the claim in the first sentence:

Despite the fact that affirmative action places some individuals at a disadvantage, it remains necessary to right the wrongs inflicted historically on whole groups of people. Howard Glickstein, a past director of the US Commission on Civil Rights, maintains that "it simply is not possible to achieve equality and fairness" unless the previous grounds for discrimination (such as sex, race, and national origin) are now considered as grounds for admission to schools and jobs (26).

As this passage illustrates, a citation of expert opinion should always refer you to the source, here indicated by the author's name, Glickstein, and the page number in parentheses, "(26)." Such a citation is also generally accompanied by a reference to the expert's credentials. See pages 604 and 614–15.

(CULTURE LANGUAGE) In some cultures a person with high standing in government, society, or organized religion may be considered an authority on many different subjects. In American academic and business settings, authority tends to derive from study, learning, and experience: the more knowledge a person can demonstrate about a subject, the more authority he or she has. See page 187 on relevant evidence.

Appeals to beliefs or needs

A writer's **appeal to beliefs or needs** asks you to accept an assertion in part because you already accept it as true without evidence or because it coincides with your needs. Each of the following examples combines such an appeal (second sentence) with a summary of factual evidence (first sentence).

Thus the chemistry classroom is outdated in its equipment. In addition, its shabby, antiquated appearance shames the school, making it seem a second-rate institution. [Appeals to readers' belief that the school is or should be first-rate.]

That police foot patrollers reduce crime has already been demonstrated. Such officers might also restore our sense that our neighborhoods are orderly, stable places. [Appeals to readers' need for order and stability.]

(For more on beliefs, see p. 182. For more on appeals to emotion, see pp. 208–09.)

2 | Judging the reliability of evidence

To be convinced by evidence, you should see it as reliable. The test of reliability for an appeal to beliefs or needs is specific to the situation: whether it is appropriate for the argument and correctly gauges how you, the reader, actually feel (see p. 209). With the other kinds of evidence, the standards are more general, applying to any argument.

Criteria for weighing evidence

- Is it **accurate:** trustworthy, exact, undistorted?
- Is it **relevant:** authoritative, pertinent, current?
- Is it **representative:** true to context?
- Is it **adequate:** plentiful, specific?

Accuracy

Accurate evidence is true:

- It is drawn from trustworthy sources.
- It is quoted exactly.
- It is presented with the original meaning undistorted.

Reading an argument in favor of gun control, you might expect the writer to cite some procontrol sources, which are undoubtedly biased. But you should also look for anticontrol sources (representing the opposite bias) and neutral sources (attempting to be unbiased). If the writer quotes an expert, the quotation should present the expert's true meaning, not just a few words that appear to support the writer's argument. (As a reader you may have difficulty judging the accuracy of quotations if you are not familiar with the expert's opinions.)

Not just opinions but also facts and examples may be misinterpreted or distorted. Suppose you were reading an argument for extending a three-year-old law allowing the police to stop vehicles randomly as a means of apprehending drunk drivers. If the author cited statistics showing that the number of drunk-driving accidents dropped in the first two years of the law but failed to note that the number rose back to the previous level in the third year, then the evidence would be distorted and thus inaccurate. You or any reader would be justified in questioning the entire argument, no matter how accurate the rest seemed.

Relevance

Relevant evidence pertains to the argument:

- **It comes from sources with authority on the subject.**
- **It relates directly to the point the writer is making.**
- **It is current.**

If you are reading an argument against a method of hazardous-waste disposal and the writer offers his church minister's opinion as evidence, you should accept the evidence only if the minister is an authority on the subject and her expertise is up-to-date. If she is an authority on Method A and not Method B, you should accept her authority only about Method A. If the writer relates his own experience of living near a hazardous-waste site, you should accept the story as relevant only if it pertains to his thesis. His authority in this case is that of a close observer and a citizen. (See also p. 194 on the fallacy of false authority.)

Representativeness

Representative evidence is true to its context:

- **It reflects the full range of the sample from which it is said to be drawn.**
- **It does not overrepresent any element of the sample.**

In an essay arguing that schools should not open before Labor Day, a writer might say that "the majority of the school's students favor a later starting date." But that writer would mislead readers if the claim were based only on a poll of seniors in an English class. A few class members could not be said to represent the entire student body, particularly students in other grades. To be representative, the poll would have to take in many more students in proportions that reflect the number of students at each grade level.

Adequacy

Adequate evidence is sufficient:

- **It is plentiful enough to support the writer's assertions.**
- **It is specific enough to support the writer's assertions.**

A writer arguing against animal abuse should not hope to win you over solely with statements about her personal experiences and claims of her opinions. Her experience may indeed be relevant evidence if, say, she has worked with animals or witnessed animal abuse. And her opinions are indeed important to the argument, so that you know what she thinks. But even together her experiences and opinions are not adequate evidence: they cannot substitute entirely for facts, nonpersonal examples, and the opinions of experts to demonstrate abuse and describe the scope of the problem.

9d | Discovering assumptions

Assumptions connect evidence to claims: they are the opinions or beliefs that explain why a particular piece of evidence is relevant to a particular claim. As noted in Chapter 7 on critical thinking, assumptions are not flaws in arguments but necessities: we all acquire beliefs and opinions that shape our view of the world. Here are examples of beliefs that you, or people you know, may hold:

> Criminals should be punished.
> Hard work is virtuous.
> Teachers' salaries are too low.

Assumptions are inevitable in argument, but they aren't neutral. For one thing, an assumption can weaken an argument. Say that a writer claims that real estate development should be prevented in your town. As evidence for this claim, the writer offers facts about past developments that have replaced older buildings. But the evidence is relevant to the claim only if you accept the writer's extreme assumptions that old buildings are always worthy and new development is always bad.

In such a case, the writer's bias may not even be stated. Hence a second problem: in arguments both sound and unsound, assumptions are not always explicit. Following are a claim and evidence forming a reasonable argument. What is the unstated assumption?

> **Claim**
> The town should create a plan to manage building preservation and new development.
>
> **Evidence**
> Examples of how such plans work; expert opinions on how and why both preservation and development are needed.

In this instance the assumption is that neither uncontrolled development nor zero development is healthy for the town. If you can accept this assumption, you should be able to accept the writer's claim (though you might still disagree over particulars).

Here are tips for dealing with assumptions:

Guidelines for analyzing assumptions

- **What are the assumptions underlying the argument?** How does the writer connect claims with evidence?
- **Are the assumptions believable?** Do they express your values? Do they seem true in your experience?
- **Are the assumptions consistent with one another?** Is the argument's foundation solid, not slippery?

9e Watching language, hearing tone

Tone is the expression of the writer's attitudes toward himself or herself, toward the subject, and toward the reader (see pp. 16–17) for a discussion). Tone can tell you quite a bit about the writer's intentions, biases, and trustworthiness. For example:

> Some women cite personal growth as a reason for pursuing careers while raising children. Of course, they are equally concerned with the personal growth of the children they relegate to "child-care specialists" while they work.

In the second sentence this writer is being **ironic,** saying one thing while meaning another. The word *relegate* and the quotation marks with *child-care specialists* betray the writer's belief that working mothers may selfishly neglect their children for their own needs. Irony can sometimes be effective in argument, but here it marks the author as insincere in dealing with the complex issues of working parents and child care.

When reading arguments, you should be alert to the author's language. Look for words that **connote,** or suggest, certain attitudes and evoke certain responses in readers. (Notice your own responses to these word pairs with related meanings but different connotations: *daring/foolhardy, dislike/detest, glad/joyous, angry/rabid, freedom/ license.*) Connotative language is no failure in argument; indeed, the strongest arguments use it skillfully to appeal to readers' hearts as well as their minds (see pp. 208–09). But be suspicious if the language runs counter to the substance of the argument.

Look also for evasive words. **Euphemisms,** such as *attack of a sexual nature* for "rape" or *peace-keeping force* for a war-making army, are supposedly inoffensive substitutes for words that may frighten or offend readers (see pp. 508–09). In argument, though, they are sometimes used to hide or twist the truth. An honest, forthright arguer will avoid them.

Finally, watch carefully for sexist, racist, and other biased language that reveals deep ignorance or, worse, entrenched prejudice on the part of the writer. Obvious examples are *broad* for woman and *fag* for homosexual. (See pp. 509–12 for more on such language.)

9f Judging reasonableness

The **reasonableness** of an argument is the sense you get as a reader that the author is fair and sincere. The reasonable writer does not conceal or distort facts, hide prejudices, mask belief as opinion, manipulate you with language, or resort to any of dozens of devices used unconsciously by those who don't know better and deliberately by those who do.

Reasonableness involves all the elements of argument examined so far: claims, evidence, assumptions, and language. In addition, the fair, sincere argument always avoids so-called fallacies (covered in the next section), and it acknowledges the opposition.

Judging whether a writer deals adequately with his or her opposition is a fairly simple matter for the reader of argument. By definition, an arguable issue has more than one side. Even if you have no preconceptions about a subject, you will know that another side exists. If the writer pretends otherwise or dismisses the opposition too quickly, you are justified in questioning the honesty and fairness of the argument. (For the more complicated business of *writing* an acknowledgment of opposing views, see pp. 210–11.)

Exercise 9.1   Reading arguments critically

Following are two brief arguments. Though not directly opposed, the two arguments do represent different stances on environmental issues. Read each argument critically, following the process outlined in Chapter 7 (pp. 141–53) and answering the questions in the box on page 181 (questions about claims, evidence, assumptions, and the other elements of argument). Develop your responses in writing so that you can refer to them for later exercises and class discussion.

The Environmental Crisis Is Not Our Fault

I am as responsible as most eco-citizens: I bike everywhere; I don't own a   1
car; I recycle newspapers, bottles, cans, and plastics; I have a vegetable garden in the summer; I buy organic products; and I put all vegetable waste into my backyard compost bin, probably the only one in all of Greenwich Village. But I don't at the same time believe that I am saving the planet, or in fact doing anything of much consequence about the various eco-crises around us. What's more, I don't even believe that if "all of us" as individuals started doing the same it would make any but the slightest difference.

Leave aside ozone depletion and rain forest destruction—those are   2
patently corporate crimes that no individual actions can remedy to any degree. Take, instead, energy consumption in this country. In the most recent figures, residential consumption was 7.2 percent of the total, commercial 5.5 percent, and industrial 23.3 percent; of the remainder, 27.8 percent was transportation (about one-third of it by private car) and 36.3 percent was electric generation (about one-third for residential use). Individual energy use, in sum, was something like 28 percent of total consumption. Although you and I cutting down on energy consumption would have some small effect (and should be done), it is surely the energy consumption of industry and other large institutions such as government and agribusiness that needs to be addressed first. And it is industry and government that must be forced to explain what their consumption is for, what is produced by it, how necessary it is, and how it can be drastically reduced.

The point is that the ecological crisis is essentially beyond "our" control, as citizens or householders or consumers or even voters. It is not something that can be halted by recycling or double-pane insulation. It is the inevitable by-product of our modern industrial civilization, dominated by capitalist production and consumption and serviced and protected by various institutions of government, federal to local. It cannot possibly be altered or reversed by simple individual actions, even by the actions of the millions who take part in Earth Day—even if they all go home and fix their refrigerators and from then on walk to work. Nothing less than a drastic overhaul of this civilization and an abandonment of its ingrained gods—progress, growth, exploitation, technology, materialism, anthropocentricity, and power—will do anything substantial to halt our path to environmental destruction, and it's hard to see how life-style solutions will have an effect on that.

What I find truly pernicious about such solutions is that they get people thinking they are actually making a difference and doing their part to halt the destruction of the earth: "There, I've taken all the bottles to the recycling center and used my string bag at the grocery store; I guess that'll take care of global warming." It is the kind of thing that diverts people from the hard truths and hard choices and hard actions, from the recognition that they have to take on the larger forces of society—corporate and governmental—where true power, and true destructiveness, lie.

And to the argument that, well, you have to start somewhere to raise people's consciousness, I would reply that this individualistic approach does not in fact raise consciousness. It does not move people beyond their old familiar liberal perceptions of the world, it does nothing to challenge the belief in technofix or write-your-Congressperson solutions, and it does not begin to provide them with the new vocabulary and modes of thought necessary for a true change of consciousness. We need, for example, to think of recycling centers not as the answer to our waste problems, but as a confession that the system of packaging and production in this society is out of control. Recycling centers are like hospitals; they are the institutions at the end of the cycle that take care of problems that would never exist if ecological criteria had operated at the beginning of the cycle. Until we have those kinds of understandings, we will not do anything with consciousness except reinforce it with the same misguided ideas that created the crisis.

—Kirkpatrick Sale

Myths We Wouldn't Miss

There are tall tales and legends. There are fables and apocryphal stories. And there are myths—a number of which we would like to see disappear. Here are some myths that would not be missed:

MYTH: Offshore drilling would be an ecological disaster.

Truth is, there hasn't been a serious spill in US waters resulting from offshore drilling operations in decades—and even that one, in Santa Barbara Channel in 1969, caused no permanent damage to the environment.

This is why we always have such a problem with the reasoning of those who call for moratoriums or outright bans on such activity while the nation continues to import foreign oil. The fact is, oil industry off-shore drilling operations cause less pollution than urban runoff, atmospheric phenomena, municipal discharges or natural seeps.

Why this nation would choose *not* to drill for oil and *not* to provide 5
the jobs, profits and taxes such activity would mean for the American economy when there are no better alternatives is a mystery we hope puzzles others as much as it does us.

MYTH: America is a profligate waster of energy. 6

The myth makers like to throw around numbers that read like this: 7
with only 5 percent of the world's population, the US uses about 25 percent of the world's energy. But ours is a big country—three thousand miles from one ocean to the next. Transportation accounts for more than 60 percent of US oil use. We could probably cut down if we moved everybody into one corner of the country, but where is the waste?

It certainly isn't the automobiles that are inefficient. They are twice 8
as efficient as the ones we used thirty years ago. If American drivers use more gasoline than their counterparts in Europe and Japan, it may just have something to do with the country's size.

In fact, proof of the country's size may be in our economic output— 9
and may also hold a clue as to why we use the energy we do. Despite having only 5 percent of the world's population, America may indeed use 25 percent of the world's energy. However, according to the latest statistics, we also produce about 25 percent of the world's goods and services. Again, where's the waste?

MYTH: Conservation is *the answer* to America's energy problems. 10

No doubt about it, we all need to be careful of the amount of en- 11
ergy we use. But as long as this nation's economy needs to grow, we are going to need energy to fuel that growth.

For the foreseeable future, there are no viable alternatives to petro- 12
leum as the major source of energy, especially for transportation fuels. Let's face it. Over the past thirty years we *have* learned to conserve—in our factories, our homes, our cars. We probably can—and should—do more. But conservation and new exploration should not be mutually exclusive, because even without an increase in energy consumption, we are using up domestic reserves of oil and gas and must replace them. For the good of the economy, those reserves should be replaced with new domestic production, to the extent economically possible. Otherwise, the only solutions would be additional imports or no growth. And stifling growth would be a gross disservice to the people for whom such growth would provide the opportunity for a better life.

Simply put, America is going to need more energy for all its people. 13
And that is no myth. 14

—Oil corporation advertisement

9g Recognizing fallacies

Fallacies—errors in argument—fall into two groups. Some evade the issue of the argument. Others treat the argument as if it were much simpler than it is.

Checklist of fallacies

Evasions

- **Begging the question:** treating an opinion that is open to question as if it were already proved or disproved.
- **Non sequitur** ("it does not follow"): drawing a conclusion from irrelevant evidence.
- **Red herring:** introducing an irrelevant issue to distract readers.
- **False authority:** citing as expert opinion the views of a person who is not an expert.
- **Inappropriate appeals:**

    Appealing to readers' fear or pity.
    Snob appeal: appealing to readers' wish to be like those who are more intelligent, famous, rich, and so on.
    Bandwagon: appealing to readers' wish to be part of the group.
    Flattery: appealing to readers' intelligence, taste, and so on.
    Argument ad populum ("to the people"): appealing to readers' general values, such as patriotism or love of family.
    Argument ad hominem ("to the man"): attacking the opponent rather than the opponent's argument.

Oversimplifications

- **Hasty generalization (jumping to a conclusion):** asserting an opinion based on too little evidence.
- **Sweeping generalization:** asserting an opinion as applying to all instances when it may apply to some, or to none. **Absolute statements** and **stereotypes** are variations.
- **Reductive fallacy:** generally, oversimplifying causes and effects.
- **Post hoc fallacy:** assuming that A caused B because A preceded B.
- **Either/or fallacy (false dilemma):** reducing a complicated question to two alternatives.
- **False analogy:** exaggerating the similarities in an analogy or ignoring key differences.

---

1 Recognizing evasions

The central claim of an argument defines an issue or question: Should real estate development be controlled? Should drug testing be mandatory in the workplace? An effective argument faces the central issue squarely with relevant opinions, beliefs, and evidence. An ineffective argument dodges the issue.

Begging the question

A writer **begs the question** by treating an opinion that is open to question as if it were already proved or disproved. In essence, the writer begs readers to accept his or her ideas from the start.

> The school's library expenses should be reduced by cutting subscriptions to useless periodicals. [Begged questions: Are some of the library's periodicals useless? Useless to whom?]

> We should stop looking for the "real" Shakespeare and concentrate on understanding his plays. [Begged questions: Does research into Shakespeare's life preclude interpreting the plays? Is there merit in researching Shakespeare's life?]

Non sequitur

A **non sequitur** occurs when no logical relation exists between two or more connected ideas. In Latin *non sequitur* means "it does not follow." In the sentences below, the second thought does not follow from the first:

> She uses a wheelchair, so she must be unhappy. [The second clause does not follow from the first.]

> Kathleen Newsome should be mayor because she has the best-run campaign organization. [Shouldn't support for a candidate be based on his or her qualities, not the campaign's organization?]

Red herring

A **red herring** is literally a kind of fish that might be drawn across a path to distract a bloodhound from a scent it's following. In argument, a red herring is an irrelevant issue intended to distract readers from the relevant issues. The writer changes the subject rather than pursue the argument.

> A school free speech code is essential to protect students, who already have enough problems with academic pressure. [Academic pressure and speech codes are different subjects. What protections do students need that a speech code will provide?]

> How can anyone claim that *King Lear* is a great play when there is evidence that Shakespeare did not write it? [Questions about Shakespeare's authorship do not diminish the play, which needs to be considered on its own merits.]

False authority

Arguments often cite as evidence the opinions of people who are experts on the subject (see p. 185). But writers use **false authority** when they cite as an expert someone whose expertise is doubtful or nonexistent.

> My uncle, a medical doctor, has read *The Scarlet Letter* and considers Roger Chillingworth a reasonable portrait of a physician in colonial America. [Is the uncle an expert in colonial medicine?]

According to Helen Liebowitz, the Food and Drug Administration has approved sixty dangerous drugs in the last two years alone. [Who is Helen Liebowitz? On what authority does she make this claim?]

Inappropriate appeals

Appeals to readers' emotions are common in effective arguments. But such appeals must be relevant and must supplement rather than substitute for facts, examples, and other evidence.

Writers sometimes ignore the question with **appeals to readers' fear or pity.**

By electing Susan Clark to the city council, you will prevent the city's economic collapse. [Trades on people's fears. Can Clark singlehandedly prevent economic collapse? Is collapse even likely?]

She should not have to pay taxes because she is an aged widow with no friends or relatives. [Appeals to people's pity. Should age and loneliness, rather than income, determine a person's tax obligation?]

Sometimes writers ignore the question by appealing to readers' sense of what other people believe or do. One approach is **snob appeal,** inviting readers to accept an assertion in order to be identified with others they admire.

As any literate person knows, James Joyce is the best twentieth-century novelist. [But what qualities of Joyce's writing make him a superior novelist?]

George Clooney has an account at Big City Bank, and so should you. [A celebrity's endorsement does not guarantee the worth of a product, a service, an idea, or anything else.]

A similar tactic invites readers to accept an assertion because everybody else does. This is the **bandwagon approach.**

As everyone knows, marijuana use leads to heroin addiction. [What is the evidence?]

Yet another diversion involves **flattery** of readers, in a way inviting them to join in a conspiracy.

We all understand our school's problems well enough to see the disadvantages of such a policy. [What are the disadvantages of the policy?]

The **argument ad populum** ("argument to the people") asks readers to accept a conclusion based on shared values or even prejudices and nothing else.

Any truly patriotic American will support the President's action. [But why is the action worth taking?]

One final and very common kind of inappropriate emotional appeal addresses *not* the pros and cons of the issue itself but the real or imagined negative qualities of the people who hold the opposing view. This kind of argument is called **ad hominem,** Latin for "to the man."

One of the scientists has been treated for emotional problems, so his pessimism about nuclear waste merits no attention. [Do the scientist's previous emotional problems invalidate his current views?]

2 Recognizing oversimplifications

To **oversimplify** is to conceal or ignore complexities in a vain attempt to create a neater, more convincing argument than reality allows.

Hasty generalization

A **hasty generalization,** also called **jumping to a conclusion,** is a claim based on too little evidence or on evidence that is unrepresentative. (See also p. 187.)

It is disturbing that several of the youths who shot up schools were users of violent video games. Obviously, these games can breed violence, and they should be banned. [A few cases do not establish the relation between the games and violent behavior. Most youths who play violent video games do not behave violently.]

From the way it handled this complaint, we can assume that the consumer protection office has little intention of protecting consumers. [One experience with the office does not demonstrate its intention or overall performance.]

Sweeping generalization

Whereas a hasty generalization comes from inadequate evidence, a **sweeping generalization** probably is not supportable at all. One kind of sweeping generalization is the **absolute statement** involving words such as *all, always, never,* and *no one* that allow no exceptions. Rarely can evidence support such terms. Moderate words such as *some, sometimes, rarely,* and *few* are more reasonable.

Another common sweeping generalization is the **stereotype,** a conventional and oversimplified characterization of a group of people.

People who live in cities are unfriendly.
Californians are fad-crazy.
Women are emotional.
Men can't express their feelings.

(See also pp. 509–12 on sexist and other biased language.)

Reductive fallacy

The **reductive fallacy** oversimplifies (or reduces) the relation between causes and their effects. The fallacy (sometimes called **oversimplification**) often involves linking two events as if one caused the other directly, whereas the causes may be more complex or the relation may not exist at all. For example:

Poverty causes crime. [If so, then why do people who are not poor commit crimes? And why aren't all poor people criminals?]

The better a school's athletic facilities are, the worse its academic programs are. [The sentence assumes a direct cause-and-effect link between athletics and scholarship.]

Post hoc fallacy

Related to the reductive fallacy is the assumption that because *A* preceded *B*, then *A* must have caused *B*. This fallacy is called in Latin *post hoc, ergo propter hoc,* meaning "after this, therefore because of this," or the **post hoc fallacy** for short.

In the two months since he took office, Mayor Holcomb has allowed crime in the city to increase 12 percent. [The increase in crime is probably attributable to conditions existing before Holcomb took office.]

The town council erred in permitting the adult bookstore to open, for shortly afterward two women were assaulted. [It cannot be assumed without evidence that the women's assailants visited or were influenced by the bookstore.]

Either/or fallacy

In the **either/or fallacy** (also called **false dilemma**), the writer assumes that a complicated question has only two answers, one good and one bad, both bad, or both good.

City police officers are either brutal or corrupt. [Most city police officers are neither.]

Conflicts in novels are between characters or within a character's own mind. [Conflicts are not necessarily one or the other.]

False analogy

An **analogy** is a comparison between two essentially unlike things for the purpose of definition or illustration. In arguing by analogy, a writer draws a likeness between things on the basis of a single shared feature and then extends the likeness to other features. For instance, the "war on drugs" equates a battle against a foe with a program to eradicate (or at least reduce) sales and use of illegal drugs. Both involve an enemy, a strategy of overpowering the enemy, a desired goal, officials in uniform, and other similarities.

Analogy can only illustrate a point, never prove it: just because things are similar in one respect, they are not *necessarily* alike in other respects. In the fallacy called **false analogy**, the writer assumes such a complete likeness. Here is the analogy of the war on drugs taken to its false extreme:

To win the war on drugs, we must wage more of a military-style operation. Prisoners of war are locked up without the benefit of a trial by jury, and drug dealers should be, too. Soldiers shoot their enemy on sight, and officials who encounter big drug operators should be allowed to shoot them, too. Military traitors may be executed, and corrupt law enforcers could be, too.

Literary analysis sometimes uses false analogies, too. In an attempt to connect with a current cultural issue, the following passage blurs the focus on Gatsby and loses the point.

> Gatsby is clearly a dreamer. He lives in a world that he has crafted from his desire to possess Daisy, the object of his obsession. His quest is like that of corporate executives who lie and cheat to gain the objects of their obsessions—yachts, mansions, companies, and more money. Like the executives, who are punished by the legal system, Gatsby was punished to the full extent of the moral law.

Exercise 9.2 Analyzing advertisements

Leaf through a magazine or watch commercial television for half an hour, looking for advertisements that attempt to sell a product not on the basis of its worth but by snob appeal, flattery, or other inappropriate appeals to emotions. Be prepared to discuss the advertisers' techniques. (See Chapter 11, pp. 228–29, if you need help analyzing the appeals in images.)

Exercise 9.3 Identifying and revising fallacies

Fallacies tend to appear together, as each of the following sentences illustrates. Identify at least one fallacy in each sentence. Then revise the sentences to make them more reasonable.

1. The American government can sell nuclear technology to nonnuclear nations, so why can't individuals, who after all have a God-given right to earn a living as they see fit?
2. A successful marriage demands a maturity that no one under twenty-five possesses.
3. Students' persistent complaints about the grading system prove that it is unfair.
4. People watch television because they are too lazy to talk or read or because they want mindless escape from their lives.
5. Racial tension is bound to occur when people with different backgrounds are forced to live side by side.

Exercise 9.4 Identifying fallacies in arguments

Analyze the two arguments on pages 190–91 for fallacies. To what extent do any fallacies weaken either argument? Explain.

Exercise 9.5 Identifying fallacies online

At *blogsearch.google.com* or *groups.yahoo.com*, find a conversation about drug testing in the workplace, environmental pollution, violence in the media, or any other subject that interests you and that is debatable. Read through the arguments made in the conversation, noting the fallacies you see. List the fallacious statements as well as the types of fallacies they illustrate, keeping in mind that a given statement may illustrate more than a single type.

10

Writing an Argument

In one way or another, most writing attempts to persuade readers. The author of a research report wants readers to view the findings as significant. The author of a literary analysis wants readers to accept his or her insights into a work. Even the author of a novel wants readers to see the depicted characters or situations in a certain way.

Argument is a special kind of persuasion, a deliberate and straightforward attempt to make a claim, develop it with evidence, and convince readers to agree or to act. In composing an argument, you try to clarify an issue or solve a problem by finding the common ground between you and your readers. Using critical thinking, you develop and test your own ideas. Using a variety of techniques, you engage readers in an attempt to narrow the distance between your views and theirs.

This chapter introduces the process and techniques of composing a written argument. The next chapter discusses the use of images, such as photographs and charts, as effective tools for argument.

10a Finding a subject

An argument subject must be arguable—that is, reasonable people will disagree over it and be able to support their positions with evidence. This sentence implies the *do*s and *don't*s listed in the box on the next page.

Additional help on subjects for writing appears earlier in this book:

- Working with a specific assignment, page 7.
- Working with a general assignment, pages 7–8.
- Narrowing a subject to a question, pages 8–9.

(CULTURE LANGUAGE) Choosing a subject for argument may seem difficult if you're not familiar with what people in the United States find debatable. One way to find a subject is to scout

mycomplab

Visit *mycomplab.com* for more resources and exercises on writing arguments.

Tests for an argument subject

A good subject:

- Concerns a matter of opinion—a conclusion drawn from evidence.
- Can be disputed: others might take a different position.
- *Will* be disputed: it is controversial.
- Is something you care about and know about or want to research.
- Is narrow enough to argue in the space and time available.

A bad subject:

- Cannot be disputed because it concerns a fact, such as the distance to Saturn or the functions of the human liver.
- Cannot be disputed because it concerns a personal preference or belief, such as a liking for a certain vacation spot or a moral commitment to vegetarianism.
- *Will not* be disputed because few if any disagree over it—the virtues of a secure home, for instance.

online discussion groups, such as those listed at *groups.yahoo.com*, for subjects on which there is a range of opinion. Another approach is to read a newspaper every day for at least a week, looking for issues that involve or interest you. Following the development of the issues in articles, editorials, and letters to the editor will give you a sense of how controversial they are, what the positions are, and what your position might be.

Exercise 10.1 Finding a subject for argument

Explain why each subject below is or is not appropriate for argument. Refer to the box above if you need help.

1. Granting of athletic scholarships to first-year college students
2. Care of automobile tires
3. Censoring the Web sites of hate groups
4. History of the town park
5. Housing for the homeless
6. Billboards in urban residential areas or in rural areas
7. Animal testing for cosmetics research
8. Cats versus dogs as pets
9. Ten steps in recycling wastepaper
10. Benefits of having siblings

10b Conceiving a thesis statement

The **thesis** is the main idea of your paper (see pp. 29–34). In an argument the **thesis statement** makes the claim that you want your readers to accept or act on. Here are two thesis statements on the same subject:

> The end of Dickens's novel fails because of its predictability.
>
> If one scene were left out, readers would be happily surprised by the end of Dickens's novel instead of bored by its predictability.

Your thesis statement must satisfy the same requirements as your subject (see the box on the previous page). But it must also specify the basis for your claim. In both thesis statements above, the writer makes clear that the judgment of Dickens's ending is based on its predictability.

Exercise 10.2 Conceiving a thesis statement

For each subject in Exercise 10.1 that you deemed arguable, draft a tentative thesis statement that specifies the basis for an argument. If you prefer, choose five arguable subjects of your own and draft a thesis statement for each one. One thesis statement should interest you enough to develop into a complete argument in later exercises.

10c Analyzing your purpose and your audience

Your purpose in argument is, broadly, to engage readers in order to convince them of your position or persuade them to act. But arguments have more specific purposes as well, such as the following:

> To strengthen the commitment of existing supporters
> To win new supporters from the undecided or uninformed
> To get the opposition to reconsider
> To inspire supporters to act
> To deter the undecided from acting

It's no accident that each of these purposes characterizes the audience (*existing supporters, the undecided,* and so on). In argument, even more than in other kinds of writing, achieving your purpose depends on the response of your readers, so you need a sense of who they are and where they stand. The "Questions About Audience" on page 14 can help you identify readers' knowledge, beliefs, and other pertinent information. In addition, you need to know how readers stand on your subject—not only whether they agree or disagree generally, but also which specific assertions and which appeals they will find more or less convincing. (For more on appeals in argument, see pp. 208–09.)

Your purpose can help you fill in this information. If you decide to address supporters or opponents, you essentially select readers with certain inclinations and ignore other readers who may tune in. If you decide to win new supporters from those who are undecided on your topic, you'll have to imagine skeptical readers who will be convinced only by an argument that is detailed, logical, and fair. Like you when you read an argument critically, these skeptical readers seek to be reasoned with, not manipulated into a position or hammered over the head.

> **Exercise 10.3 Analyzing purpose and audience**
> Specify a purpose and a likely audience for the thesis statement you chose to develop in Exercise 10.2. What do purpose and audience suggest about the way you should develop the argument?

10d Using reason

As a reader of argument, you seek evidence for the writer's claims and clear reasoning about the relationship of evidence to claims. As a writer of argument, you seek to provide what the reader needs in a way that furthers your case.

The thesis of your argument is a conclusion you reach by reasoning about evidence. Two common processes of reasoning are induction and deduction—methods of thinking that you use all the time even if you don't know their names. You can think of induction and deduction as two different ways of moving among claims, evidence, and assumptions—the elements of argument derived from Stephen Toulmin's work (p. 180).

1 Reasoning inductively

When you're about to buy a used car, you consult friends, relatives, and consumer guides before deciding what kind of car to buy. Using **inductive reasoning,** you make specific observations about cars (your evidence) and you induce, or infer, a **generalization** (or claim) that Model X is the most reliable. Writing a paper on the effectiveness of print advertising, you might also use inductive reasoning:

> First analyze statistics on advertising in print and in other media (evidence).
> Then read comments by advertisers and publishers (more evidence).
> Finally, form a conclusion that print is the most cost-effective advertising medium (generalization).

This reasoning builds from the evidence to the claim, with assumptions connecting evidence to claim. By predicting something about the unknown based on what you know, you create new knowledge out of old.

The more evidence you accumulate, the more probable it is that your generalization is true. Note, however, that absolute certainty is not possible. At some point you must *assume* that your evidence justifies your generalization, for yourself and your readers. Most

Inductive reasoning

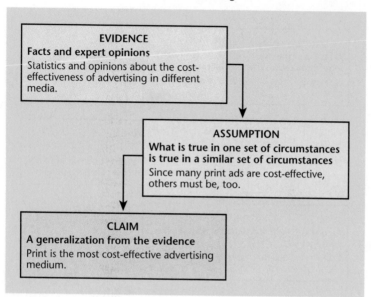

EVIDENCE
Facts and expert opinions
Statistics and opinions about the cost-effectiveness of advertising in different media.

ASSUMPTION
What is true in one set of circumstances is true in a similar set of circumstances
Since many print ads are cost-effective, others must be, too.

CLAIM
A generalization from the evidence
Print is the most cost-effective advertising medium.

errors in inductive reasoning involve oversimplifying either the evidence or the generalization. See pages 192–98 on fallacies.

2 Reasoning deductively

You use **deductive reasoning** when you proceed from your generalization that Model X is the most reliable used car to your own specific circumstances (you want to buy a used car) to the conclusion (or claim) that you should buy a Model X car. Like induction, deduction uses the elements of argument—claims, evidence, and assumptions—but with it you apply old information to new.

The deductive syllogism

The conventional way of displaying a deductive argument is in a **syllogism**:

> **Premise:** All human beings are mortal. [A generalization, fact, principle, or belief that you assume to be true.]
> **Premise:** I am a human being. [New information: a specific case of the first premise.]
> **Conclusion:** Therefore, I am mortal.

As long as the premises of a syllogism are true, the conclusion derives logically and certainly from them. If you want the school

Deductive reasoning

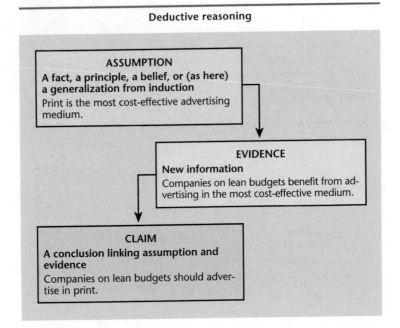

administration not to raise fees for participation in the debate team, your deductive argument might be expressed in this syllogism:

> **Premise:** The administration should not raise fees on student activities that have had no increase in expenses.
> **Premise:** The debate team's expenses have not increased.
> **Conclusion:** Therefore, the administration should not raise fees for the debate team.

The force of deductive reasoning depends on the reliability of the premises and the care taken to apply them in drawing conclusions. The reasoning process is **valid** if the premises lead logically to the conclusion. It is **true** if the premises are believable.

Problems with syllogisms

Sometimes the reasoning in a deductive argument is true because the premises are believable, but it is *not* valid because the conclusion doesn't derive logically from the premises:

> **Premise:** The administration should not raise fees on student activities that have had no increase in expenses.
> **Premise:** The soccer team is a student activity.
> **Conclusion:** Therefore, the administration should not raise fees for the soccer team.

Tests for inductive and deductive reasoning

Induction
- Have you stated your evidence clearly?
- Is your evidence complete enough and good enough to justify your claim? What is the assumption that connects evidence and claim? Is it believable?
- Have you avoided fallacies?

Deduction
- What are the premises leading to your conclusion? Look especially for unstated premises.
- What does the first premise assume? Is the assumption believable?
- Does the first premise necessarily apply to the second premise?
- Is the second premise believable?
- Have you avoided fallacies?

Both premises may be true, but the first does not *necessarily* apply to the second, so the conclusion is invalid.

Sometimes, too, deductive reasoning is valid but *not* true:

> **Premise:** All high school administrators are indifferent to students' needs.
> **Premise:** The administration of Central High is a high school administration.
> **Conclusion:** Therefore, the administration of Central High is indifferent to students' needs.

This syllogism is valid but useless: the first premise is an untrue assumption, so the entire argument is untrue. Invalid and untrue syllogisms underlie many of the fallacies discussed on pages 192–98.

A particular hazard of deductive reasoning is the **unstated premise**: the basic assumption linking evidence and conclusion is not stated but implied. Here the unstated premise is believable and the argument is reasonable:

> Ms. Stein has worked with drug addicts for fifteen years, so she knows a great deal about their problems. [Unstated premise: Anyone who has worked fifteen years with drug addicts knows about their problems.]

But when the unstated premise is wrong or unfounded, the argument is false. For example:

> Since Jane Lightbow is a senator, she must receive money illegally from lobbyists. [Unstated premise: All senators receive money illegally from lobbyists.]

To avoid such false conclusions, you may be tempted to make your claims sound more reasonable. But even a conclusion that sounds reasonable must be supportable. For instance, changing *must* to *might* modifies the unstated assumption about Senator Lightbow:

> Since Jane Lightbow is a senator, she might receive money illegally from lobbyists. [Unstated premise: *Some* senators receive money illegally from lobbyists.]

But it does not necessarily follow that Senator Lightbow is one of the "some." The sentence, though logical, is not truly reasonable unless evidence demonstrates that Senator Lightbow should be linked with illegal activities.

Exercise 10.4 Reasoning inductively

Study the facts below and then evaluate each of the numbered conclusions following them. Which of the generalizations are reasonable given the evidence, and which are not? Why?

In 2006–07 each American household viewed an average of 57 hours and 12 minutes of television, DVDs, or videos weekly.

Each individual viewed an average of 16 hours and 23 minutes every week.

Those viewing the most television per week (36 hours and 58 minutes) were women over age 55.

Those viewing the least television per week (23 hours and 34 minutes) were teens, ages 12–17.

Households earning under $30,000 a year watched an average of 59 hours and 55 minutes a week.

Households earning more than $60,000 a year watched an average of 55 hours and 7 minutes a week.

1. Households with incomes under $30,000 tend to watch more television than average.
2. Women watch more television than men.
3. Nonaffluent people watch less television than affluent people.
4. Women over age 55 tend to watch more television than average.
5. Teens watch less television than critics generally assume.

Exercise 10.5 Reasoning deductively

Convert each of the following statements into a syllogism. (You may have to state unstated assumptions.) Use the syllogism to evaluate both the validity and the truth of the statement.

> *Example:*
> DiSantis is a banker, so he does not care about the poor.
> **Premise:** Bankers do not care about the poor.
> **Premise:** DiSantis is a banker.
> **Conclusion:** Therefore, DiSantis does not care about the poor.
>
> The statement is untrue because the first premise is untrue.

1. The mayor opposed pollution controls when he was president of a manufacturing company, so he may not support new controls or

vigorously enforce existing ones.
2. Information on corporate Web sites is unreliable because the sites are sponsored by for-profit entities.
3. Schroeder is a good artist because she trained at Parsons, like many other good artists.
4. Wealthy athletes who use their resources to help others deserve our particular appreciation.
5. Jimson is clearly a sexist because she has hired only one woman.

10e Using evidence

Whether your argument is reasonable or not depends heavily on the evidence you marshal to support it. The kinds of evidence and the criteria for evaluating evidence are discussed in detail on pages 184–87. Finding evidence is discussed under research writing on pages 564–78. Evaluating sources of evidence, including online sources, is discussed under research writing on pages 580–92.

The kind and quantity of evidence you use should be determined by your purpose, your subject, and the needs of your audience. Some arguments, such as an appeal for volunteer help in a soup kitchen, will rely most heavily on examples (including perhaps a narrative of your own experience) and on appeals to readers' beliefs. Other arguments, such as a proposal for mandatory side air bags in cars, will rely much more on statistics and expert opinions. Most arguments, including these, will mingle facts, examples, expert opinions, and appeals to readers' beliefs and needs.

In using evidence for argument, you'll need to be especially wary of certain traps that carelessness or zeal can lure you into. These traps are listed in the following box.

Responsible use of evidence

- **Don't distort.** You mislead readers when you twist evidence to suit your argument—for instance, when you claim that crime in your city occurs five times more often than it did in 1955, without mentioning that the population is also seven times larger.
- **Don't stack the deck.** Ignoring the evidence that doesn't support your argument is like cheating at cards. You must deal forthrightly with the opposition. (See pp. 210–11.)
- **Don't exaggerate.** Watch your language. Don't attempt to manipulate readers by characterizing your own evidence as *pure* and *rock-solid* and the opposition's as *ridiculous* and *half-baked*. Make the evidence speak for itself.
- **Don't oversimplify.** Avoid forcing the evidence to support more than it can. (See also pp. 196–98.)
- **Don't misquote.** When you cite experts, quote them accurately and fairly.

Exercise 10.6 Using reason and evidence in your argument
Develop the structure and evidence for the argument you began in Exercises 10.2 and 10.3 (pp. 201 and 202). (You may want to begin drafting at this stage.) Is your argument mainly inductive or mainly deductive? Use the box on page 205 to test the reasoning of the argument. Use the boxes on pages 186 and 207 to test your evidence.

10f Reaching your readers

To reach your readers in argument, you appeal directly to their reason and emotions, you present yourself as someone worth heeding, and you account for views opposing your own.

1 Appealing to readers

In forming convictions about arguable issues, we generally interpret the factual evidence through the filter of our values, beliefs, tastes, desires, and feelings. You may object to placing the new town dump in a particular wooded area because the facts suggest that the site is not large enough and that prevailing winds will blow odors back through the town. But you may also have fond memories of playing in the wooded area as a child, feelings that color your interpretation of the facts and strengthen your conviction that the dump should be placed elsewhere. Your conviction is partly logical, because it is based on evidence, and partly emotional, because it is also based on feelings.

Logical and emotional appeals

Almost all arguments combine logical and emotional appeals. **Logical appeals** (called *logos* in classical rhetoric) stem from reasoning logically between evidence and claims. **Emotional appeals** (*pathos*) tap into readers' beliefs and feelings. The following passages, all arguing the same view on the same subject, illustrate how either a primarily logical or a primarily emotional appeal may be weaker than an approach that uses both:

Logical appeal
Advertising should show more physically challenged people. The millions of Americans with disabilities have considerable buying power, yet so far advertisers have made no attempt to tap that power. [Appeals to the logic of financial gain.]

Emotional appeal
Advertising should show more physically challenged people. By keeping people with disabilities out of the mainstream depicted in ads, advertisers encourage widespread prejudice against disability, prejudice that frightens and demeans those who hold it. [Appeals to a sense of fairness and open-mindedness.]

Logical and emotional appeals

Advertising should show more physically challenged people. The millions of Americans with disabilities have considerable buying power, yet so far advertisers have made no attempt to tap that power. Further, by keeping people with disabilities out of the mainstream depicted in ads, advertisers encourage widespread prejudice against disability, prejudice that frightens and demeans those who hold it.

The third passage, in combining both kinds of appeal, gives readers both logical and emotional bases for agreeing with the writer.

For an emotional appeal to be successful, it must be appropriate for the audience and the argument:

- **It must not misjudge readers' actual feelings.**
- **It must not raise emotional issues that are irrelevant to the claims and the evidence.** See pages 195–96 for a discussion of specific inappropriate appeals, such as the bandwagon approach.

One further caution: Photographs and other images can reinforce your claims with a strong emotional appeal, but they must be relevant to your claims, and you must explain their relevance in your text and captions. See pages 228–29 for more on the appeals in images.

Ethical appeal

A third kind of approach to readers is the **ethical appeal** (*ethos*), the sense you give of being a competent, fair, trustworthy person. A sound argument backed by ample evidence—a logical appeal—will convince readers of your knowledge and reasonableness. (So will your acknowledging the opposition. See the next page.) Appropriate emotional appeals will demonstrate that you share readers' beliefs and needs. An argument that is concisely written and correct in grammar, spelling, and other matters will underscore your competence. In addition, a sincere and even tone will assure readers that you are a balanced person who wants to reason with them.

A sincere and even tone need not exclude language with emotional appeal—words such as *frightens* and *demeans* at the end of the third example on the previous page. But avoid certain forms of expression that will mark you as unfair:

- **Insulting words,** such as *idiotic* or *fascist.*
- **Biased language,** such as *rednecks* or *fags.* (See pp. 509–12.)
- **Sarcasm**—for instance, using the phrase *What a brilliant idea* to indicate contempt for the idea and its originator.
- **Exclamation points!** They'll make you sound shrill!

See also page 189 on tone.

2 Responding to opposing views

A good test of your fairness in argument is how you handle possible objections. Assuming your thesis is indeed arguable, then others can marshal their own evidence to support a different view or views. By dealing squarely with these opposing views, you show yourself to be honest and fair. You strengthen your ethical appeal and thus your entire argument.

Before or while you draft your essay, list for yourself all the opposing views you can think of. You'll find them in your research, by talking to friends and classmates, and by critically thinking about your own ideas. You can also look for a range of views in an online discussion that deals with your subject. Two places to start are the *Yahoo!* archive of discussion groups at *groups.yahoo.com* and the *Google* blog directory at *blogsearch.google.com.*

Rebutting opposing views

A common way to handle opposing views is to state them, refute those you can, grant the validity of others, and demonstrate why, despite their validity, the opposing views are less compelling than your own. The following paragraph illustrates this approach:

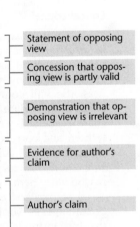

For Springfield to become a first-rate academic institution, it will need to reduce its funding of intercollegiate sports in favor of academic programs. The athletic director argues against a reduction on the grounds that the team programs more than pay for themselves. ⟶ Statement of opposing view

It is true that the surpluses from the team programs have gone into the general university fund. ⟶ Concession that opposing view is partly valid

However, this argument misses the point that the team programs demand too many resources to begin with for an institution whose main priorities should be academic. ⟶ Demonstration that opposing view is irrelevant

Some members of the athletic department have acknowledged that intercollegiate sports could manage with budget cuts of 20 percent. ⟶ Evidence for author's claim

Committing the savings to academic programs would establish a more appropriate balance between the competing goals of athletic power and academic strength. ⟶ Author's claim

Finding common ground

A somewhat different approach to addressing opposing views, developed by the psychologist Carl Rogers, emphasizes the search for common ground. A **Rogerian argument** can be especially helpful when you expect readers to resist your claims. You start by showing that you understand readers' views and by establishing points on which you and readers agree and disagree. Creating a connection in this way can encourage readers to hear you out as you argue your own claims. Recast as a Rogerian argument, the preceding example might read as follows:

> The Springfield community thus seems united in the goal of making the university a first-rate academic institution, but it differs over whether to help pay for the needed improvements by reducing funds for intercollegiate sports. Most of us who support this step do value the sports, and we appreciate the athletic director's point that the team programs more than pay for themselves, contributing surpluses to the general university fund. We certainly do not propose that the university abandon the sports altogether or even dramatically cut their funding. However, some members of the athletic department have acknowledged that intercollegiate sports could manage with budget cuts of 20 percent. Thus we seek this manageable reduction so that Springfield can continue as a sports power while also putting more resources to work for academic excellence.

(Annotations:) Focus on points of agreement — Rejection of more extreme solutions — Evidence for author's claim — Author's claim

Exercise 10.7 Identifying appeals

Identify each passage below as primarily a logical appeal or primarily an emotional appeal. Which passages make a strong ethical appeal as well?

1. Use of the Web may contribute to the global tendency toward breadth rather than depth of knowledge. Relying on those most essential skills—pointing and clicking—our brightest minds may now never encounter, much less read, the works of Plato and Shakespeare.
2. Thus the data collected by these researchers indicate that a mandatory sentence for illegal possession of handguns may lead to a reduction in handgun purchases.
3. Most broadcasters worry that further government regulation of television programming could breed censorship—certainly, an undesirable outcome. Yet most broadcasters also accept that children's television is a fair target for regulation.
4. Anyone who cherishes life in all its diversity could not help being appalled by the mistreatment of laboratory animals. The so-called scientists who run the labs are misguided.
5. Many experts in constitutional law have warned that the rule violates the right to free speech. Yet other experts have viewed the rule, however regretfully, as necessary for the good of the community as a whole.

Exercise 10.8 Reaching your readers

Continuing your argument-in-progress from Exercise 10.6 (p. 208), analyze whether your claims are logical or emotional and whether the mix is appropriate for your audience and argument. Analyze your ethical appeal, too, considering whether it can be strengthened. Then make a list of possible opposing views. Think freely at first, not stopping to censor views that seem far-fetched or irrational. When your list is complete, decide which views must be taken seriously and why, and develop a response to each one.

10g Organizing your argument

All arguments include the same parts, but depending on the type of argument the organization can vary:

- **Introduction:** Commonly, the introduction establishes the significance of the subject or the scope of the problem, provides the background, and usually includes the thesis statement. However, if you think your readers may have difficulty accepting your thesis statement before they see at least some support for it, then it may come later in the paper. A Rogerian argument uses the introduction to emphasize the common ground between writer and readers, saving the thesis for the conclusion.

- **Body:** The body paragraphs state and develop the claims supporting the thesis, using clearly relevant evidence. The arrangement of the claims can vary widely, as can their position relative to the response to opposing views. See the facing page.

- **Response to opposing views:** The response to opposing views details and addresses those views, finding common ground, demonstrating the arguments' greater strengths, or conceding the opponent's points. For some arguments, readers will be satisfied to see opposing views dealt with at the end. For others, each claim will invite its own objections, and those opposing views will need to be addressed claim by claim. In a Rogerian argument, a concession to opposing views appears right after the introduction, before the claims get under way, in order to establish common ground.

- **Conclusion:** The conclusion completes the argument. Often it restates the thesis, summarizes the supporting claims, and makes a final appeal to readers. In a Rogerian argument, the conclusion states the thesis as a solution, giving ground and inviting the audience to do the same.

For more on introductions and conclusions, see pages 105–10.

You may want to experiment with various organizations—for instance, trying out your strongest claims first or last in the body, stating claims outright or letting the evidence build to them, answering the opposition near the beginning or near the end or claim by claim. You can do this experimentation on paper, of course, but it's easier on a computer. Try rearranging your outline as described on page 39. Or try rearranging your draft (work with a copy) by cutting and pasting parts of it for different emphases.

Organizing an argument's body and response to opposing views

A common scheme
Claim 1 and evidence
Claim 2 and evidence
Claim X and evidence
Response to opposing views

A variation
Claim 1 and evidence
Response to opposing views
Claim 2 and evidence
Response to opposing views
Claim X and evidence
Response to opposing views

The Rogerian scheme
Common ground and concession to opposing views
Claim 1 and evidence
Claim 2 and evidence
Claim X and evidence

The problem-solution scheme
The problem: claims and evidence
The solution: claims and evidence
Response to opposing views

Exercise 10.9 Organizing your argument
Continuing from Exercise 10.8 (p. 211), develop a structure for your argument. Consider especially how you will introduce it, how you will arrange your claims, where you will place your responses to opposing views, and how you will conclude.

10h Revising your argument

When you revise your argument, do it in at least two stages—revising underlying meaning and structure, and editing more superficial elements. The checklists on page 56 and 61–62 can be a guide. Supplement them with the checklist below, which encourages you to think critically about your own argument.

Checklist for revising an argument

Thesis
- What is your thesis? Where is it stated?
- In what ways is your thesis statement an arguable claim?

(continued)

Checklist for revising an argument

(continued)

Reasoning

- If your thesis derives from induction, where have you related the evidence to your generalization?
- If your thesis derives from deduction, is your syllogism both true and valid?
- Have you avoided fallacies in reasoning?

Evidence

- Where have you provided the evidence readers need?
- Where might your evidence not be accurate, relevant, representative, or adequate? (Answer this question from the point of view of a neutral or even skeptical reader.)

Appeals

- Where have you considered readers' probable beliefs and values?
- How are your rational appeals and emotional appeals appropriate for your readers?
- What is your ethical appeal? How can you improve it?

Opposing views

- What opposing views have you answered?
- How successfully have you conceded or refuted opposing views? (Again, consider the neutral, skeptical, or hostile reader.)

Organization

- Will readers be able to follow your argument? How clearly does it move from one point to the next?
- How appropriate is your organization given the likely views of your readers?

Exercise 10.10 Writing and revising your argument

Draft and revise the argument you have developed in the exercises in this chapter. Use the revision checklists on page 56 and above to review your work.

10i Examining a sample argument

The following essay by the student Craig Holbrook illustrates the principles discussed in this chapter. As you read the essay, notice especially the organization, the relation of claims and supporting evidence (including illustrations), the mix of logical, emotional, and ethical appeals, and the ways Holbrook responds to opposing views.

TV Can Be Good for You

Television wastes time, pollutes minds, destroys brain cells, and turns some viewers into murderers. Thus runs the prevailing talk about the medium, supported by serious research as well as simple belief. However, television has at least one strong virtue, too: it can ease loneliness, spark healthful laughter, and even educate young children by providing voices that supplement those of real people.

Almost everyone who has lived alone understands the curse of silence, when the only sound is the buzz of unhappiness or anxiety inside one's own head. Although people of all ages who live alone can experience intense loneliness, the elderly are especially vulnerable to solitude. For example, they may suffer increased confusion or depression when left alone for long periods but then rebound when they have steady companionship (Bondevik and Skogstad 329-30).

A study of elderly men and women in New Zealand found that television can actually serve as a companion by assuming "the role of social contact with the wider world," reducing "feelings of isolation and loneliness because it directs viewers' attention away from themselves" ("Television Programming"). (See fig. 1.) Thus television's voices can provide comfort because they distract from a focus on being alone.

Fig. 1. Television can be a source of companionship for people whose living situations and limited mobility leave them lonely. Photograph by Jean Michel Foujols; *Corbis*; Corbis, 2005; Web; 13 Oct. 2008.

The absence of real voices can be most damaging when it means a lack of laughter. Here, too, research shows that television can have a

Side annotations:

Introduction

Identification and modification of prevailing view

Thesis statement: three claims for TV

Background for claim 1: effects of loneliness

Evidence for effects of loneliness

Evidence for effects of television on loneliness

Statement of claim 1

Illustration supporting claim 1

Background for claim 2: effects of laughter

Evidence for effects of laughter

Evidence for comedy on television

Illustration supporting healthful effects of laughter

positive effect on health. Laughter is one of the most powerful calming forces available to human beings, proven in many studies to reduce heart rate, lower blood pressure, and ease other stress-related ailments (Burroughs, Mahoney, and Lippman 172; Griffiths 18). (See fig. 2.) Television offers plenty of laughter: the recent listings for a single Friday night included more than twenty comedy programs running on the networks and on basic cable.

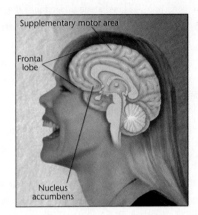

Fig. 2. According to the Society for Neuroscience, the process of understanding and being amused by something funny stimulates at least three main areas of the brain. The society makes no recommendation about TV watching, but other studies show the healthful effects of the activity. Illustration by Lydia Kibiuk from *Brain Briefings*; Soc. for Neuroscience, Dec. 2001; Web; 12 Oct. 2008.

Evidence for effects of laughter in response to television

A study reported in a health magazine found that laughter inspired by television and video is as healthful as the laughter generated by live comedy. Volunteers laughing at a video comedy routine "showed significant improvements in several immune functions, such as natural killer-cell activity" (Laliberte 78). Further, the effects of the comedy were so profound that "merely anticipating watching a funny video improved mood, depression, and anger as much as two days beforehand" (Laliberte 79). Clearly, television's voices can have healthful effects by causing laughter.

Statement of claim 2

Background for claim 3: educational effects

Evidence for educational programming on television

Television also provides information about the world. This service can be helpful to everyone but especially to children, whose natural curiosity can exhaust their caretakers. While the TV may be baby-sitting children, it can also enrich them. For example, educational programs such as those on the Discovery Channel and PBS offer a steady stream of information at various cognitive levels. (See fig. 3.) Even many cartoons, which are generally dismissed as mindless or worse, familiarize children with the material of literature, including strong characters enacting classic narratives.

Illustration supporting claim 3

Fig. 3. Educational television programs such as *Sesame Street* are an important source of learning for children. Characters such as Elmo (shown here) promote reading, learning, and healthy behaviors. Photograph from *The State of the World's Children*; United Nations Children's Fund, 2002; Web; 12 Oct. 2008.

Three researchers conducting a review of studies involving children and television found that TV can inspire imaginative play, which psychologists describe as important for children's cognitive development (Thakkar, Garrison, and Christakis 2028). In the studies reviewed, children who watched *Mister Rogers' Neighborhood*, a show that emphasized make-believe, demonstrated significant increases in imaginative play (2029). Thus high-quality educational programming can both inform young viewers and improve their cognitive development.

Evidence for educational effects of television on children

Statement of claim 3

The value of television voices should not be oversold. Almost everyone agrees that too much TV does no one any good and may cause much harm. Many studies show that excessive TV watching increases violent behavior, especially in children, and can cause, rather than ease, other antisocial behaviors (Reeks 114; Walsh 34). In addition, human beings require the give and take of actual interaction. Steven Pinker, an expert in children's language acquisition, warns that children cannot develop language properly by watching television. They need to interact with actual speakers who respond directly to their needs (282). Television voices are not real voices and in the end can do only limited good.

Anticipation of objection: harm of television

Anticipation of objection: need for actual interaction

Response to objections: qualification of claims

But even limited good is something, especially for those who are lonely or neglected. Television is not an entirely positive force, but neither is it an entirely negative one. Its voices stand by to provide company, laughter, and information whenever they're needed.

Conclusion

Works Cited

Bondevik, Margareth, and Anders Skogstad. "The Oldest Old, ADL, Social Network, and Loneliness." *Western Journal of Nursing Research* 20.3 (1998): 325-43. Print.

Burroughs, W. Jeffrey, Diana L. Mahoney, and Louis G. Lippman. "Attributes of Health-Promoting Laughter: Cross-Generational Comparison." *Journal of Psychology* 136.2 (2004): 171-81. Print.

Griffiths, Joan. "The Mirthful Brain." *Omni* Aug. 1996: 18-19. Print.

Laliberte, Richard W. "The Benefits of Laughter." *Shape* Sept. 2003: 78-79. Print.

Pinker, Steven. *The Language Instinct: How the Mind Creates Language.* New York: Harper, 1994. Print.

Reeks, Anne. "Kids and TV: A Guide." *Parenting* Apr. 2005: 110-15. Print.

"Television Programming for Older People: Summary Research Report." *NZ on Air.* NZ on Air, 25 July 2004. Web. 15 Oct. 2008.

Thakkar, Rupin R., Michelle M. Garrison, and Dimitri A. Christakis. "A Systematic Review for the Effects of Television Viewing by Infants and Preschoolers." *Pediatrics* 18.5 (2006): 2025-31. Web. 12 Oct. 2008.

Walsh, Teri. "Too Much TV Linked to Depression." *Prevention* Feb. 2001: 34-36. Print.

—Craig Holbrook (student)

Works cited in MLA style

No works-cited entries for illustrations because captions provide complete source information

Exercise 10.11   Critically reading an argument

Analyze the construction and effectiveness of the preceding essay by answering the following questions.

1. Where does Holbrook make claims related to his thesis statement, and where does he provide evidence to support the claims?
2. Where does Holbrook appeal primarily to reason, and where does he appeal primarily to emotion? What specific beliefs and values of readers does he appeal to?
3. How would you characterize Holbrook's ethical appeal?
4. How effective do you find the illustrations as support for Holbrook's claims? What appeals do they make? (For an analysis of Holbrook's first illustration, see p. 229.)
5. What objections to his argument does Holbrook anticipate? How does he respond to them?
6. How effective do you find this argument? To what extent does Holbrook convince you that television has virtues? Do some claims seem stronger or weaker than others? Does Holbrook respond adequately to objections?
7. Write a critical evaluation of "TV Can Be Good for You." First summarize Holbrook's views. Then respond to those views by answering the questions posed in number 6 above.

11

Reading and Using Visual Arguments

Visual arguments use images to engage and convince readers. Visual arguments can be strong because their claims are immediate and often emotional. Advertisements often provide the most vivid and memorable examples, but writers in almost every field—from astronomy to music to physiology—support their claims with images. In this chapter you'll learn how to read visual arguments critically (below) and how to use images to strengthen your own arguments (p. 226).

Note This chapter builds on Chapters 7 and 9–10, which discuss forming a critical perspective (including viewing images critically), reading an argument critically, and writing an argument. If you haven't already done so, read those chapters before this one.

11a Reading visual arguments critically

Chapter 9 explains the three main elements of any argument: claims, evidence, and assumptions. To read visual arguments critically, you'll analyze all three elements.

1 Testing claims

Claims are positive statements that require support (see pp. 180, 181–83). In a visual argument, claims may be made by composition as well as by content, with or without accompanying words. Here are a few examples of visual claims:

Image   A magnetic sticker shaped like a ribbon and decorated with the colors and symbols of the American flag, positioned prominently on a car.

Claim   I support American troops overseas, and you should, too.

Image   A photograph framing hundreds of chickens crammed into small cages, resembling familiar images of World War II concentration camps.

Claim   Commercial poultry-raising practices are cruel and unethical.

Image   A chart with dramatically contrasting bars that represent the optimism, stress, and weight reported by people before and after they participated in a program of daily walking.

Claim   Daily exercise leads to a healthier and happier life.

Image   A cartoon featuring affluent-looking young adults on an affluent-looking college campus, conversing and frowning sadly as they gaze downhill at rough-looking teens in a dilapidated schoolyard. The caption reads, "Yes, it's sad what's happening to schools today. But everyone knows that throwing money at the problem isn't the solution."

Claim   Better funding makes for better schools.

The following image is one of a series of advertisements featuring well-known people as milk drinkers. The celebrity here is Serena Williams, a tennis champion. The advertisement makes several claims both in the photograph and in the text.

Claims in an image

Image claim: Strong, shapely women drink milk.

Image claim: Attractive people drink milk.

Image claim: Athletes drink milk.

Text claim: Milk can help dieters reduce to a healthy weight.

Advertisement by the Milk Processor
Education Program

2 Weighing evidence

The kinds of evidence provided in images parallel those found in written arguments (see pp. 184–86):

- **Facts** can be verified by observation or research. In visual arguments they may be data, as in a graph showing a five-year rise in oil prices. Or they may be inferences drawn from data, as in the statement in the preceding ad that milk can help dieters "lose more weight and burn more fat." Sometimes images serve as facts themselves, objects that are analyzed in accompanying writing, as the milk ad is examined by this text or as the *BoostUp.org* ad is examined by Matthew Greene in the essay on pages 176–78.

- **Examples** illustrate and reinforce a point. Visual arguments often focus on an instance of the argument's claims, as the milk ad does on Serena Williams. Another ad might feature multiple images as examples: a Sizzler TV commercial, for instance, shows a sequence of luscious-looking foods to be had at the restaurant. An image might also illustrate a claim made in accompanying writing, as the milk ad does in this text.

- **Expert opinions** are the findings of subject-matter authorities based on their research and experience. A visual argument might present a chart from an expert showing a trend in, say, unemployment among high school graduates. The familiar TV ad that features a doctor recommending a particular medicine to a patient offers the doctor as an expert.

- **Appeals to beliefs or needs** reinforce readers' values or truths. Many visual arguments make such appeals by depicting how things clearly ought to be (an antidrug ad featuring a teenager who is confidently refusing peer pressure) or, in contrast, by showing how things clearly should not be (a Web site for an antihunger campaign featuring images of emaciated children).

The evidence in a visual argument should be judged by the same criteria used to judge a written argument (pp. 186–87):

- **Is the evidence accurate?** Images can be manipulated just as words can, and like words they should be analyzed for their fairness, precision, and trustworthiness. For example, a graph claiming to show changes in students' living expenses between 1998 and 2008 should identify the source and purpose of the research, supply data for all the years, and clarify the definition of *living expenses*.

- **Is the evidence relevant and adequate?** An image should pertain to the claims made in the larger argument and should sufficiently demonstrate its own claims. In an article on eating disorders, for instance, relevant and adequate images might include a medical diagram showing the liver damage from malnutrition and a photograph of a frail-bodied person suffering from anorexia. However, a photograph of a skinny model or actor would be neither relevant nor adequate, merely sensationalistic, unless the subject had publicly confirmed that his or her low weight resulted from an eating disorder.

■ **Does the evidence represent the context?** Representative visual evidence reflects the full range of the sample it's drawn from and does not overrepresent or hide important elements of the subject. For example, a photographic essay claiming to document the poor working conditions of migrant farm workers might reasonably include images of one worker's scarred hands and another worker suffering from heat prostration. But to be representative, the essay would also need to illustrate the full range of migrant workers' experiences.

The annotations on the graph below demonstrate one way of analyzing visual evidence for this claim: *The teen birthrate has dropped steadily since 1990.* The data come from the Centers for Disease Control and Prevention (CDC), a US agency and a reputable source. But the data are incomplete, so the graph is misleading.

Evidence in an image

Accuracy and representativeness: The data are trustworthy because they come from a US government agency.

Relevance and adequacy: The graph shows a steady decrease in birthrate, as claimed, but 2005 is not very recent. In fact, later data (for 2006) show a 3 percent *increase* over 2005, information that undermines the claim.

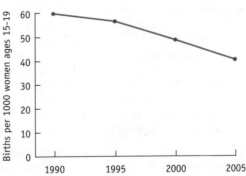

Fig. 1. Decrease in birthrate among women ages 15 to 19 in the United States, 1990-2005. Data from Stephanie J. Ventura et al.; *National Vital Statistics Reports*; US Dept. of Health and Human Services, Centers for Disease Control and Prevention, 22 Apr. 2007; Web; 10 July 2008.

3 Discovering assumptions

Like a written argument, a visual argument is based on **assumptions**—the creator's ideas, often unstated, about why the evidence relates to the claims (see p. 188). In visual arguments many assumptions involve the creator's beliefs about the audience, as detailed below. The examples analyze the milk ad on page 220, featuring the tennis player Serena Williams.

- **Who readers are and where they will see the argument.** The Williams ad first appeared in sports magazines, so the advertiser could assume readers who are interested in sports and athletes.
- **What readers already know about the subject.** To sports fans, Williams would be a familiar subject. The advertiser presumably considers readers less familiar with the benefits of milk or with its appeal to celebrities like Williams.
- **How familiar readers are with the purpose, format, and style of the argument.** With more than two hundred print and TV ads since 1994, the milk-mustache campaign has become a fixture of US popular culture. Each new ad fits into the framework established by its predecessors.
- **Whether readers are likely to lean toward the argument's claims.** The advertiser clearly assumes that the endorsement of a sports star like Williams will influence readers who are interested in healthy weight loss. At the same time, it seems to assume that the benefits of milk still need selling to readers.
- **What kinds of information, ideas, and images readers will find persuasive.** The advertiser seems to assume that a strictly factual claim about the health benefits of milk would not be persuasive enough to readers, so it shows that attractive and talented people like Williams consume milk. The photograph of Williams emphasizes qualities that the advertiser presumably thinks will appeal to readers: strength, shapeliness, beauty, even glamour.

4 Recognizing fallacies

Fallacies, or errors in argument, are sometimes accidental, but they are often used deliberately to manipulate readers' responses. All the fallacies of written arguments discussed on pages 192–98 may appear in visual arguments as well. Here we'll focus on examples of the two main categories.

Evasions

Evasions attempt to deflect the reader from the central claim of the argument. One evasion is **snob appeal,** inviting readers to think or be like someone they admire. Look again at the Williams milk ad on page 220. Like all celebrity ads in the milk-mustache campaign, this one appeals to the reader's wish to emulate a famous person. If you drink milk, the ad says subtly, you too may become strong, beautiful, and fearless (notice that Williams looks unguardedly into the camera). The ad does have some substance in its specific and verifiable claim that drinking "24 ounces a day of lowfat or fat free milk" could help people reduce to a healthy weight, but Williams herself, with her milk mustache, makes a stronger claim.

Oversimplifications

Oversimplifications imply that subjects are less complex than they are. An example is the **hasty generalization,** a claim that is based on too little evidence or that misrepresents the facts. This fallacy appears in the following graph, which is intended to support this claim: *After a steep decline over the preceding five years, the teen birthrate shot up in 2006.* At first, the graph appears to demonstrate the claim, but a close look reveals that it badly misrepresents the data.

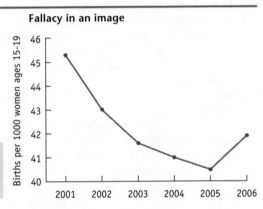

The vertical axis lacks a zero point and covers a small span, thus misrepresenting and exaggerating both the decline and the increase in the birthrate.

Fig. 2. Steep decline and sharp increase in the birthrate among women ages 15 to 19 in the United States, 2001-06. Data from Brady E. Hamilton et al.; *National Vital Statistics Reports*; US Dept. of Health and Human Services, Centers for Disease Control and Prevention, 1 May 2008; Web; 10 July 2008.

The corrected graph below uses exactly the same data, but they tell a different story because they are presented without manipulation.

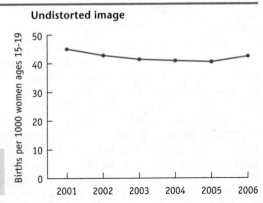

The vertical axis starts at zero and covers a large span, thus showing accurately just a gradual decline and a slight increase.

Exercise 11.1   Reading a visual argument critically

The image below is an e-card found on the Web site of Big Brothers Big Sisters of America, a community organization that brings children and mentors together. The organization invites site visitors to send its cards "to encourage friends and family members to support Big Brothers Big Sisters." Examine the card's visual argument closely, and jot down your answers to the following questions.

1. Who appears to be the intended audience? What aspects of the text and photograph seem best suited to that audience?
2. What can you tell about Big Brothers Big Sisters from this e-card?
3. What claims does the image make?
4. What evidence supports the claims? How effective is it?
5. What assumptions underlie the argument, connecting evidence to claims?
6. How does the visual organization (cropping of the photograph, placement of the text) make the argument more or less effective?
7. Is the argument persuasive to you? Why or why not?

E-card from the Web site of
Big Brothers Big Sisters of America

Exercise 11.2   Identifying fallacies in visual arguments

Locate a current or historical source with extreme views on a subject, such as the Web site of an outspoken political commentator, a sensationalist tabloid newspaper, or a collection of wartime propaganda (from any nation or era). Photocopy or print an image that seems especially rife with fallacies and, referring to the complete list of fallacies on page 193, find as many as possible in the image. The following sites can help you begin your search:

Political commentators
Keith Olbermann: *msn.com*
Rush Limbaugh: *rushlimbaugh.com*

Tabloids
National Enquirer (US): *nationalenquirer.com*
Daily Mail (Great Britain): *www.dailymail.co.uk*

World War II propaganda
Northwestern University (American images): *www.library.northwestern.edu/ govinfo/collections/wwii-posters*
Calvin College (German images): *www.calvin.edu/academic/cas/gpa*

11b Using visual arguments effectively

Visual images can make strong arguments. Sometimes they work by themselves, as a painting might, to convince viewers of an idea. More often in academic situations, they serve as evidence for verbal claims.

Note Any visual you include in a paper requires the same detailed citation as a written source. If you plan to publish your argument online, you will also need to seek permission from the author. See pages 612–14 for more on acknowledging sources and obtaining permissions.

1 Choosing images

You can wait until you've drafted an argument before concentrating on what images to include. This approach keeps your focus on the research and writing needed to craft the best argument from sources. But you can also begin thinking visually at the beginning of a project, as you might if your initial interest in the subject was sparked by a compelling image. Either way, ask yourself some basic questions as you consider visual options:

- **Which parts of your argument require visual evidence or can use visual reinforcement?** Do readers need a visual to understand your argument? Can a claim be explained better visually than verbally? Can a graph or chart present data compactly and interestingly? Can a photograph appeal effectively to readers' beliefs and values?
- **What are the limitations or requirements of your writing situation?** What do the type of writing you're doing and its format allow? Look through examples of similar writing to gauge the kinds of illustrations readers will expect.
- **What kinds of visuals are readily available on your subject?** As you researched your subject, what images seemed especially effective? What sources have you not yet explored? Tips for locating images, whether printed or online, appear on pages 575–76.
- **Should you create original images tailored to your argument?** Instead of searching for existing images, would your time be better spent taking your own photographs or generating visual explanations, such as diagrams, charts, and graphs? Tips for creating images appear on pages 122–26.

2 Using images as evidence

An image can attract readers' attention, but if it stops there it will amount to mere decoration or, worse, it will distract readers from the substance of your argument. When you use images as *evidence* for your argument, you engage readers both intellectually and visually.

Images can work in various ways as evidence. In an evaluation of an advertisement, the ad itself would support the claim. In a paper arguing for earthquake preparedness, a photograph could provide a visual record of earthquake damage and a chart could show levels of current preparedness. The two images here supported an argument with this thesis: *Despite proof that the depiction of smoking in movies encourages children and teens to smoke, studios continue to release youth-oriented movies that show stars smoking.*

To make an image work hard as evidence, ensure that it relates directly to a point in your argument, adds to that point, and gives readers something to think about. Always include a caption that explicitly ties the image to your text, so that readers don't have to puzzle out your intentions, and that provides source information. Number images in sequence (Fig. 1, Fig. 2, and so on), and refer to them by number at the appropriate points in your text. (See Chapter 5, pp. 122–26, for more on captioning and numbering illustrations.)

Image as evidence

Photograph of an actress smoking in a PG-13 movie —a visual example of the claim that youth-oriented movies depict smoking

Fig. 1. The actress Kate Hudson in *Raising Helen,* one of many PG-13 movies released each year in which characters smoke. Photograph by Peggy Storm; *gettyimages.com*; Getty Images, 2003; Web; 21 Apr. 2010.

Caption explaining the image, tying it to the text of the paper and providing source information

Image as evidence

Advertisement by a reputable research and advocacy group, reinforcing the thesis and providing data about depictions of smoking in movies

[One in a Series]

Eighty percent of this year's nominated movies feature smoking. And the winner is

the global tobacco industry. It gains at least $4 billion in lifetime sales revenue, in the U.S. alone, from the new teen smokers recruited to smoke by films each year. In 2007, two-thirds of new U.S. releases featured smoking: 39% of G/PG movies, 66% of PG-13 films, 84% of R-rated films. Together, these movies delivered **6.6 billion tobacco impressions** to North American theater audiences. R-rating smoking is reasonable, responsible—and inevitable. You'll still be able to include smoking in any film, just like this year's R-rated nominees for Best Picture. Yet by keeping smoking out of the G/PG/PG-13 films that kids see most, you'll save 60,000 lives a year. So who's trying to stop the "R"? Must be somebody with a lot to lose.

SMOKE FREE MOVIES

SmokeFreeMovies.ucsf.edu

Caption interpreting the ad and providing source information

Fig. 2. Advertisement by the research and advocacy group Smoke Free Movies, providing data on the depiction of smoking in movies and linking the tobacco industry to the practice. From "Our Ads"; *Smoke Free Movies*; U of California, San Francisco, Cardiovascular Research Inst., 2008; Web; 23 Apr. 2010.

3 Considering images' appeals to readers

Images can help to strengthen your argument's appeals to readers. The appeals are discussed in detail on pages 208–09. The following summary suggests how they apply to images:

- **Logical appeals target readers' capacity for reasoning rationally.** Images can strengthen the evidence for an argument if they come from reliable sources, present information fairly and accurately, and relate clearly to the paper's claims.
- **Emotional appeals tap into readers' beliefs and feelings.** Images can appeal to a host of ideas and emotions, including

patriotism, curiosity, moral values, sympathy, and anger. Any such appeal should correctly gauge readers' beliefs and feelings and should be clearly relevant to the argument.

■ **Ethical appeals show readers that you are a competent, fair, and trustworthy source of information.** Images make ethical appeals largely by making appropriate logical and emotional appeals. In addition, they can show that you are aware of readers' knowledge, prove your seriousness, and demonstrate your neutrality.

To see how all three appeals can work in images, look again at a photograph used in the sample argument paper on pages 215–18. This image illustrates the writer's claim that television can ease loneliness.

Appeals in an image

Logical appeal: Backs up the writer's claim that TV can ease loneliness: the man appears to live alone (only one chair is visible) and is interacting enthusiastically with the TV

Emotional appeal: Reinforces the benefits of TV watching: the man's isolation may be disturbing, but his excitement is pleasing

Ethical appeal: Conveys the writer's competence through the appropriateness of the image for the point being made

Fig. 1. Television can be a source of companionship for people whose living situations and limited mobility leave them lonely. Photograph by Jean Michel Foujols; *Corbis*; Corbis, 2005; Web; 13 Oct. 2008.

Exercise 11.3 Brainstorming images for a visual argument

Working on your own or with others in a small group, apply the four questions for choosing images (p. 226) to the following argument subjects. Which subject would most likely benefit from images? Which would be most difficult to illustrate? Why?

1. A program to help senior citizens adopt and care for a pet would improve seniors' lives and benefit the community.
2. Smoking cigarettes is a good way to meet interesting people.

3. Today's military-recruitment advertising targets certain kinds of people more than others.
4. Our school needs a better recycling program.
5. Listening to music while studying helps one retain crucial information.

Exercise 11.4 Filling gaps in a visual argument

Take another look at the photograph and the advertisement on pages 227–28, taken from a paper claiming that movie studios continue to release youth-oriented movies that show stars smoking despite proof that showing smoking in movies encourages children and teens to smoke. What additional images might bolster the argument? Consider especially how you might supplement the data in the ad to connect the number of movies that depict smoking with the number of children and teens who start smoking.

Exercise 11.5 Creating a deliberately bad visual argument

Purposely breaking the rules of argument can be fun and illuminating, building your knowledge about what works best and why. Using one of the topics listed in Exercise 11.3 or a new one, create a visual argument and an accompanying paragraph of text that deliberately antagonize readers instead of appealing to them. Do your best to do your worst: instead of demonstrating logic, use flawed reasoning or confusing examples; instead of appealing to readers' values and emotions, let your argument be boring or hostile; instead of communicating your credibility and expertise, display ignorance or ineptness.

Exercise 11.6 Revising an ineffective visual argument

Locate an ineffective visual argument, and use the guidelines on pages 228–29 to improve its likely appeal to readers. If your classmates completed Exercise 11.5, you could revise another student's deliberately bad argument.

PART 3

Grammatical
Sentences

12

Understanding Sentence Grammar

Grammar describes how language works. Following the rules of standard English grammar is what allows you to communicate with others across barriers of personality, region, class, or ethnic origin. If you are a native English speaker, you follow these rules mostly unconsciously. But when you're trying to improve your communication, making the rules conscious and learning the language for them can help.

Grammar reveals a lot about a sentence, even if you don't know the meanings of all the words:

The rumfrums prattly biggled the pooba.

You don't know what this sentence means, but you can infer that some things called *rumfrums* did something to a *pooba*. They *biggled* it, whatever that means, in a *prattly* way. Two grammatical cues, especially, make this sentence like *The students easily passed the test:*

- **Word forms.** The ending *-s* means more than one *rumfrum*. The ending *-ed* means that *biggled* is an action that happened in the past. The ending *-ly* means that *prattly* probably describes *how* the rumfrums biggled.
- **Word order.** *Rumfrums biggled pooba* resembles a common sequence in English: something (*rumfrums*) performed some action (*biggled*) to or on something else (*pooba*). Since *prattly* comes right before the action, it probably describes the action.

This chapter explains how such structures work and shows how practicing with them can help you communicate more effectively.

Grammar checkers A grammar checker can both offer assistance and cause problems as you compose sentences. Look for the cautions and tips for using a checker in this and the next five parts of this book. For more information about grammar checkers, see pages 65–66.

12a Understanding the basic sentence

The **sentence** is the basic unit of thought. Its grammar consists of words with specific forms and functions arranged in specific ways.

1 Identifying subjects and predicates

Most sentences make statements. First the **subject** names something; then the **predicate** makes an assertion about the subject or describes an action by the subject.

Subject	Predicate
Art	thrives.

The **simple subject** consists of one or more nouns or pronouns, whereas the **complete subject** also includes any modifiers. The **simple predicate** consists of one or more verbs, whereas the **complete predicate** adds any words needed to complete the meaning of the verb plus any modifiers.

Sometimes, as in the short example *Art thrives*, the simple and complete subject and predicate are the same. More often, they are different:

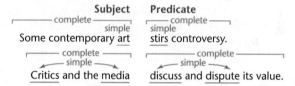

In the second example, the simple subject and simple predicate are both **compound**: in each, two words joined by *and* serve the same function.

Note If a sentence contains a word group such as *that makes it into established museums* or *because viewers finally agree about its quality*, you may be tempted to mark the subject and verb in the word group as the subject and verb of the sentence. But these word groups are subordinate clauses, made into modifiers by the words they begin with: *that* and *because*. See pages 252–53 for more on subordinate clauses.

CULTURE LANGUAGE The subject of an English sentence may be a noun (*art*) or a pronoun that refers to the noun (*it*), but not both. (See pp. 235 and 237.)

Faulty	Some art it stirs controversy.
Revised	Some art stirs controversy.

Tests to find subjects and predicates

The tests below use the following example:

Art that makes it into museums has often survived controversy.

Identify the subject.

- Ask *who* or *what* is acting or being described in the sentence.

    Complete subject   art that makes it into museums

- Isolate the simple subject by deleting modifiers—words or word groups that don't name the actor of the sentence but give information about it. In the example, the word group *that makes it into museums* does not name the actor but modifies it.

    Simple subject   art

Identify the predicate.

- Ask what the sentence asserts about the subject: what is its action, or what state is it in? In the example, the assertion about *art* is that it *has often survived controversy.*

    Complete predicate   has often survived controversy

- Isolate the verb, the simple predicate, by changing the time of the subject's action. The simple predicate is the word or words that change as a result.

    Example   Art . . . has often survived controversy.
    Present   Art . . . often survives controversy.
    Future   Art . . . will often survive controversy.
    Simple predicate   has survived

2 | Identifying the basic words: Nouns and verbs

The following five simple sentences consist almost entirely of two quite different kinds of words:

Subject	Predicate
The earth	trembled.
The earthquake	destroyed the city.
The result	was chaos.
The government	sent the city aid.
The citizens	considered the earthquake a disaster.

The words in the subject position name things, such as *earth, earthquake,* and *government.* In contrast, the words in the predicate position express states or actions, such as *trembled, destroyed,* and *sent.*

These two groups of words work in different ways. *Citizen* can become *citizens,* but not *citizened. Destroyed* can become *destroys,* but not *destroyeds.* Grammar reflects such differences by identifying

The parts of speech

Nouns name persons, places, things, ideas, or qualities: *Roosevelt, girl, Kip River, coastline, Koran, table, strife, happiness.* (See below.)

Pronouns usually substitute for nouns and function as nouns: *I, you, he, she, it, we, they, myself, this, that, who, which, everyone.* (See p. 237.)

Verbs express actions, occurrences, or states of being: *run, bunt, inflate, become, be.* (See the next page.)

Adjectives describe or modify nouns or pronouns: *gentle, small, helpful.* (See p. 242.)

Adverbs describe or modify verbs, adjectives, other adverbs, or whole groups of words: *gently, helpfully, almost, really, someday.* (See p. 242.)

Prepositions relate nouns or pronouns to other words in a sentence: *about, at, down, for, of, with.* (See pp. 244–45.)

Conjunctions link words, phrases, and clauses. **Coordinating conjunctions** and **correlative conjunctions** link words, phrases, or clauses of equal importance: *and, but, or, nor; both . . . and, not only . . . but also, either . . . or.* (See pp. 258–59.) **Subordinating conjunctions** introduce subordinate clauses and link them to main clauses: *although, because, if, whenever.* (See p. 253.)

Interjections express feeling or command attention, either alone or in a sentence: *hey, oh, darn, wow.*

the **parts of speech** or **word classes** shown in the box above. Except for *the* and *a*, which simply point to and help identify the words after them, the five sentences about the earthquake consist entirely of nouns and verbs.

Nouns

Meaning

Nouns name. They may name a person (*Angelina Jolie, Jesse Jackson, astronaut*), a thing (*chair, book, Mt. Rainier*), a quality (*pain, mystery, simplicity*), a place (*city, Washington, ocean, Red Sea*), or an idea (*reality, peace, success*).

Form

Most nouns form the **possessive** to indicate ownership or source. Singular nouns usually add an apostrophe plus -*s* (*Auden's poems*); plural nouns usually add just an apostrophe (*citizens' rights*).

Nouns also change form to distinguish between singular (one) and plural (more than one). Most nouns add -*s* or -*es* for the plural: *earthquake, earthquakes; city, cities.* Some nouns have irregular plurals: *woman, women; child, children.*

CULTURE LANGUAGE Some useful rules for forming noun plurals appear on pages 539–40. The irregular plurals must be memorized. Note that some nouns (noncount nouns) do not form plurals in English—for instance, *equality, anger, oxygen, equipment.* (See p. 325.)

Nouns with *the, a,* and *an*

Nouns are often preceded by *the* or *a* (*an* before a vowel sound: *an apple*). These words are usually called **articles** or **determiners** and always indicate that a noun follows.

 See pages 323–27 for the rules governing the use of *the, a/an,* or no article at all before a noun.

Verbs

Meaning

Verbs express an action (*bring, change, grow*), an occurrence (*become, happen*), or a state of being (*be, seem*).

Form

Most verbs can be recognized by two changes in form:

- Most verbs add *-d* or *-ed* to indicate a difference between present and past time: *They play today. They played yesterday.* Some verbs indicate past time irregularly: *eat, ate; begin, began* (see pp. 277–79).

- Most present-time verbs add *-s* or *-es* with subjects that are singular nouns: *The bear escapes. It runs. The woman begins. She sings.* The exceptions are *be* and *have,* which change to *is* and *has.*

(See Chapter 14, pp. 274–90, for more on verb forms.)

Helping verbs

Certain forms of all verbs can combine with other words such as *do, have, can, might, will,* and *must.* These other words are called **helping verbs** or **auxiliary verbs.** In phrases such as *could run, will be running,* and *has escaped,* they help to convey time and other attributes. (See Chapter 14, pp. 276, 285–89.)

A note on form and function

In different sentences an English word may serve different functions, take correspondingly different forms, and belong to different word classes. For example:

> The government sent the city aid. [*Aid* functions as a noun.]
> Governments aid citizens. [*Aid* functions as a verb.]

Because words can function in different ways, we must always determine how a particular word works in a sentence before we can identify what part of speech it is. **The *function* of a word in a sentence always determines its part of speech in that sentence.**

Pronouns

Most **pronouns** substitute for nouns and function in sentences as nouns do. In the following sentence all three pronouns—*who, they, their*—refer to *nurses:*

> Some nurses <u>who</u> have families prefer the night shift because <u>they</u> have more time with <u>their</u> children.

The most common pronouns are the **personal pronouns** (*I, you, he, she, it, we, they*) and the **relative pronouns** (*who, whoever, which, that*). Most of them change form to indicate their function in the sentence—for instance, *He called me. I called him back.* (See Chapter 13 for a discussion of these form changes.)

Exercise 12.1 Identifying subjects and predicates

In the following sentences, insert a vertical line between the complete subject and the complete predicate. Underline each simple subject once and each simple predicate twice. Then use each sentence as a model to create a sentence of your own.

Example:

The <u>pony</u>, the light <u>horse</u>, and the draft <u>horse</u>|<u><u>are</u></u> three types of domestic horses.

Sample imitation: Toyota, Honda, and Nissan are three brands of Japanese cars.

1. The leaves fell.
2. October ends soon.
3. The orchard owners made apple cider.
4. They examined each apple carefully for quality.
5. Over a hundred people will buy cider at the roadside stand.

Exercise 12.2 Identifying nouns, verbs, and pronouns

In the following sentences identify all words functioning as nouns with *N*, all words functioning as verbs with *V*, and all pronouns with *P*.

Example:

P V N N
They took the tour through the museum.

1. The trees died.
2. They caught a disease.
3. The disease was a fungus.
4. It ruined a special grove.
5. Our great-grandfather planted the grove in the last century.

Exercise 12.3 Using nouns and verbs

Identify each of the following words as a noun, as a verb, or as both. Then create sentences of your own, using each word in each possible function.

Example:

fly
Noun and verb.
The <u>fly</u> sat on the meat loaf. [Noun.] The planes <u>fly</u> low. [Verb.]

1. wish	6. label
2. tie	7. door
3. swing	8. company
4. mail	9. whistle
5. spend	10. glue

3 | Forming sentence patterns with nouns and verbs

English builds all sentences on the five basic patterns shown in the box on the facing page. As the diagrams indicate, the patterns differ in their predicates because the relation between the verb and the remaining words is different.

CULTURE LANGUAGE Word order in English sentences may not correspond to word order in the sentences of your native language. English, for instance, strongly prefers subject first, then verb, then any other words, whereas some other languages prefer the verb first. The main exceptions to the word patterns discussed here appear on pages 262–63. See also pages 361–67 on positioning modifiers in sentences.

Pattern 1: The earth trembled.

In the simplest pattern the predicate consists only of the verb. Verbs in this pattern do not require following words to complete their meaning and thus are called **intransitive** (from Latin words meaning "not passing over").

Subject	Predicate
	Intransitive verb
The earth	trembled.
The hospital	may close.

Pattern 2: The earthquake destroyed the city.

In pattern 2 the predicate consists of a verb followed by a noun that identifies who or what receives the action of the verb. This noun is a **direct object**. Verbs that require direct objects to complete their meaning are called **transitive** ("passing over"): the verb transfers the action from subject to object.

Subject	Predicate	
	Transitive verb	*Direct object*
The earthquake	destroyed	the city.
Education	opens	doors.

The five basic sentence patterns

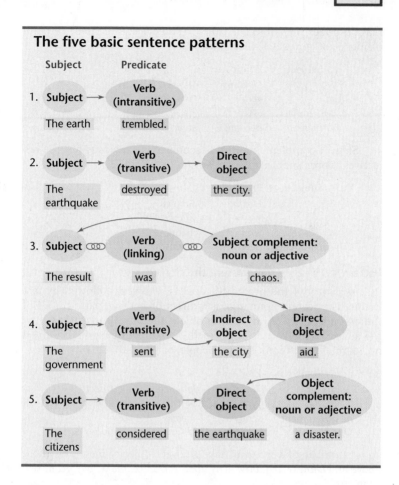

Subject · Predicate

1. Subject → Verb (intransitive)
   The earth · trembled.

2. Subject → Verb (transitive) → Direct object
   The earthquake · destroyed · the city.

3. Subject ⟵ Verb (linking) → Subject complement: noun or adjective
   The result · was · chaos.

4. Subject → Verb (transitive) → Indirect object → Direct object
   The government · sent · the city · aid.

5. Subject → Verb (transitive) → Direct object → Object complement: noun or adjective
   The citizens · considered · the earthquake · a disaster.

CULTURE LANGUAGE The distinction between transitive verbs and intransitive verbs like those in pattern 1 is important because only transitive verbs may be used in the passive voice (*The city was destroyed*). (See pp. 300–01.) Your dictionary says whether a verb is transitive or intransitive. Some verbs (*begin, learn, read, write,* and others) are both.

Pattern 3: The result was chaos.

In pattern 3 the predicate also consists of a verb followed by a noun, but here the noun renames or describes the subject. We could write the sentence *The result = chaos*. The verb serving as an equal sign is a **linking verb** because it links the subject and the following description. The linking verbs include *be, seem, appear, become, grow, remain, stay, prove, feel, look, smell, sound,* and *taste*. The word that describes the subject is called a **subject complement** (it complements, or completes, the subject).

Subject	Predicate	
	Linking verb	*Subject complement*
The result	was	chaos.
The man	became	an accountant.

Subject complements in this sentence pattern may also be adjectives, words such as *tall* and *hopeful* (see p. 242):

Subject	Predicate	
	Linking verb	*Subject complement*
The result	was	chaotic.
The apartments	seem	expensive.

Pattern 4: The government sent the city aid.

In pattern 4 the predicate consists of a verb followed by two nouns. The second noun, *aid*, is a direct object (see pattern 2). But the first noun, *city*, is an **indirect object**, identifying to or for whom the action of the verb is performed. The direct object and indirect object refer to different things, people, or places.

Subject	Predicate		
	Transitive verb	*Indirect object*	*Direct object*
The government	sent	the city	aid.
One company	offered	its employees	bonuses.

A number of verbs can take indirect objects, including those above and *allow, bring, buy, deny, find, get, leave, make, pay, read, sell, show, teach,* and *write.*

CULTURE LANGUAGE With some verbs that express action done to or for someone, the indirect object must be turned into a phrase beginning with *to* or *for*. These verbs include *admit, announce, demonstrate, explain, introduce, mention, prove, recommend, say,* and *suggest.* The *to* or *for* phrase then falls after the direct object.

Faulty The manual explains workers the new procedure.

Revised The manual explains the new procedure to workers.

Pattern 5: The citizens considered the earthquake a disaster.

In pattern 5, as in pattern 4, the predicate consists of a verb followed by two nouns. But in pattern 5 the first noun is a direct object and the second noun renames or describes it. Here the second noun is an **object complement** (it complements, or completes, the object):

Subject	Predicate		
	Transitive verb	*Direct object*	*Object complement*
The citizens	considered	the earthquake	a disaster.
The class	elected	Joan O'Day	president.

Like a subject complement (pattern 3), an object complement may be a noun or an adjective, as below:

Subject	Predicate		
	Transitive verb	*Direct object*	*Object complement*
The citizens	considered	the earthquake	disastrous.
Success	makes	some people	nervous.

Exercise 12.4 Identifying sentence patterns

In the following sentences, identify each verb as intransitive, transitive, or linking. Then identify each direct object (DO), indirect object (IO), subject complement (SC), and object complement (OC).

Example:

transitive
verb   IO   DO   DO
Children <u>give</u> their <u>parents</u> both <u>headaches</u> and <u>pleasures</u>.

1. Many people find New York City exciting.
2. Tourists flock to New York each year.
3. Often they visit Times Square first.
4. The square's lights are astounding.
5. The flashing signs sell visitors everything from TVs to underwear.

Exercise 12.5 Creating sentences

Create sentences by using each of the following verbs in the pattern indicated. (For the meanings of the abbreviations, see the directions for Exercise 12.4.) You may want to change the form of the verb.

Example:
give (S-V-IO-DO)
Sam gave his brother a birthday card.

1. laugh (S-V)
2. elect (S-V-DO-OC)
3. steal (S-V-DO)
4. catch (S-V-DO)
5. bring (S-V-IO-DO)
6. seem (S-V-SC)
7. call (S-V-DO-OC)
8. become (S-V-SC)
9. buy (S-V-IO-DO)
10. study (S-V)

12b Expanding the basic sentence with single words

Most of the sentences we read, write, or speak are more complex and also more informative and interesting than those examined so far. Most sentences contain one or more of the following: (1) modifying words (discussed here); (2) word groups, called phrases and clauses (p. 244); and (3) combinations of two or more words or word groups of the same kind (p. 258).

1 Using adjectives and adverbs

The simplest expansion of sentences occurs when we add modifying words to describe or limit the nouns and verbs. Modifying words add details:

> <u>Recently</u>, the earth trembled.
> The earthquake <u>nearly</u> destroyed the <u>old</u> city.
> The <u>federal</u> government <u>soon</u> sent the city aid.
> The grant was a <u>very generous</u> one but disappeared <u>too quickly</u>.

The underlined words represent two different parts of speech:

■ **Adjectives** describe or modify nouns and pronouns. They specify which one, what quality, or how many.

old	city		generous	one		two	pears
adjective	noun		adjective	pronoun		adjective	noun

■ **Adverbs** describe or modify verbs, adjectives, other adverbs, and whole groups of words. They specify when, where, how, and to what extent.

nearly	destroyed		too	quickly
adverb	verb		adverb	adverb

very	generous		Unfortunately,	taxes will rise.
adverb	adjective		adverb	word group

An *-ly* ending often signals an adverb, but not always: *friendly* is an adjective; *never, not,* and *always* are adverbs. The only way to tell whether a word is an adjective or an adverb is to determine what it modifies.

Adjectives and adverbs appear in three forms:

■ The **positive** form is the basic form, the one listed in the dictionary: *good, green, angry; badly, quickly, angrily.*

■ The **comparative** form indicates a greater degree of the quality named by the word: *better, greener, angrier; worse, more quickly, more angrily.*

■ The **superlative** form indicates the greatest degree of the quality named: *best, greenest, angriest; worst, most quickly, most angrily.*

(For further discussion of these forms, see p. 320.)

2 Using other words as modifiers

Nouns and special forms of verbs may sometimes serve as modifiers of other nouns. In combinations such as *office buildings*, *Thanksgiving prayer*, and *shock hazard*, the first noun modifies the second. In combinations such as *singing birds*, *corrected papers*, and *broken finger*, the first word is a verb form modifying the following noun. (These modifying verb forms are discussed in more detail on pp. 247–49.) Again, the part of speech to which we assign a word always depends on its function in a sentence.

Exercise 12.6 Identifying and using adjectives and adverbs

Identify the adjectives and adverbs in the following sentences. Then use each sentence as a model for creating a sentence of your own.

> *Example:*
>
>   adjective   adverb   adjective
> The red barn sat uncomfortably among modern buildings.
>
> *Sample imitation:* The little girl complained loudly to her busy mother.

1. The blue water glistened in the hot afternoon sunlight.
2. Happily, children dipped their toes in the cool lake.
3. Excitedly, some of the children hopped into the water.
4. Cautious parents watched from their shady porches.
5. The children played contentedly until the day finally ended.

Exercise 12.7 Using verb forms as modifiers

Use each of the following verb forms to modify a noun in a sentence of your own.

> *Example:*
> smoking
> Only a smoking cigar remained.

1. scrambled
2. twitching
3. rambling
4. typed
5. painted
6. written
7. charging
8. ripened
9. known
10. driven

Exercise 12.8 Sentence combining: Single-word modifiers

To practice expanding the basic sentence patterns with single-word modifiers, combine each group of sentences below into one sentence. You will have to delete and rearrange words.

> *Example:*
> Paris offers tourists food. Paris offers food proudly. The food is delicious.
>
> Paris proudly offers tourists delicious food.

1. The turn of the century ushered in technology and materials. The century was the twentieth. The technology was improved. The materials were new.
2. A skeleton made the construction of skyscrapers possible. The skeleton was sturdy. It was made of steel.
3. By 1913 the Woolworth Building, with its ornaments, stood 760 feet (55 stories). The building was towering. The ornaments were Gothic.
4. At 1450 feet the Sears Tower in Chicago doubles the height of the Woolworth Building. The doubling is now. The Woolworth height is puny. The puniness is relative.
5. Skyscrapers became practical in 1857 when Elisha Graves Otis built the elevator. It was the first elevator. The elevator was safe. It served passengers.

12c Expanding the basic sentence with word groups

Most sentences we read or write contain word groups that serve as nouns and modifiers. Such word groups enable us to combine several bits of information into one sentence and to make the relations among them clear, as in the following sentence:

> subject
> When the experiment succeeded, the <u>researchers</u>, excited by the
> verb   object
> results, <u>expanded</u> the <u>study</u> to enroll more patients.

Attached to *researchers expanded the study*, the skeleton of this sentence, are three groups of words that add related information: *When the experiment succeeded, excited by the results, to enroll more patients.* These constructions are phrases and clauses:

- A *phrase* is a group of related words that lacks either a subject or a predicate or both: *excited by the results, to enroll more patients.*
- A *clause* contains both a subject and a predicate: *When the experiment succeeded* and *the researchers expanded the study* are both clauses, though only the second can stand alone as a sentence.

1 Using prepositional phrases

Prepositions are connecting words. Unlike nouns, verbs, and modifiers, which may change form, prepositions never change form. As the box opposite shows, many prepositions signal relationships of time or space; others signal relationships such as addition, comparison or contrast, cause or effect, concession, condition, opposition, possession, and source. Notice that some prepositions consist of more than one word.

Common prepositions

Time or space (position or direction)			Other relationships (addition, comparison, etc.)	
about	by	outside	according to	in spite of
above	down	over	as	instead of
across	during	past	as for	like
after	for	since	aside from	of
against	from	through	because of	on account of
along	in	throughout	concerning	regarding
along with	inside	till	despite	regardless of
among	inside of	to	except	unlike
around	into	toward	except for	with
at	near	under	excepting	without
before	next to	underneath	in addition to	
behind	off	until		
below	on	up		
beneath	onto	upon		
beside	on top of	within		
between	out			
beyond	out of			

A preposition connects a noun or pronoun to another word in the sentence: *Robins nest in trees*. The noun or pronoun so connected (*trees*) is the **object of the preposition**. The preposition plus its object and any modifiers is a **prepositional phrase**:

Preposition	Object
on	the surface
upon	entering the room
from	where you are standing
except for	ten employees

Prepositional phrases function as adjectives (modifying nouns) or as adverbs (modifying verbs, adjectives, or other adverbs). As modifiers, they add details that make sentences clearer and more interesting for readers.

Life on a raft was an opportunity for adventure.
adjective phrase   adjective phrase

Huck Finn rode the raft by choice.
adverb phrase

CULTURE LANGUAGE The meanings and idiomatic uses of English prepositions can be difficult to master; most must be memorized or looked up in a dictionary. (A list of dictionaries for English as a second language appears on p. 515.) See pages 289–90 for the uses of prepositions in two-word verbs such as *look after* and pages 520–21 for the uses of prepositions in idioms.

Punctuating prepositional phrases

Since a prepositional phrase lacks a subject and a predicate, it should not be punctuated as a complete sentence. If it is, the result is a **sentence fragment** (Chapter 17):

> **Fragment**   Toward the sun.

The phrase must be attached to another group of words containing both a subject and a predicate:

> **Revised**   The plane turned <u>toward the sun</u>.

A prepositional phrase that introduces a sentence is set off with punctuation, usually a comma, unless it is short (see p. 427):

> <u>According to the newspaper and other sources</u>, the governor has reluctantly decided to veto the bill.
>
> <u>In 1865</u> the Civil War finally ended.

A prepositional phrase that interrupts or concludes a sentence is *not* set off with punctuation when it is essential to the meaning of the word or words it modifies (see p. 431):

> The announcement <u>of a tuition increase</u> surprised no one.
>
> Students expected new fees <u>for the coming year</u>.

When an interrupting or concluding prepositional phrase is *not* essential to meaning, but merely adds information to the sentence, then it *is* set off with punctuation, usually a comma or commas (see p. 430):

> The governor, <u>according to the newspaper and other sources</u>, has reluctantly decided to veto the bill.

As all the preceding examples illustrate, a preposition and its object are not separated by a comma.

Exercise 12.9   Identifying prepositional phrases

Identify the prepositional phrases in the following passage. Indicate whether each phrase functions as an adjective or as an adverb, and underline the word that the phrase modifies.

> *Example:*
>
> ┌—adverb—┐   ┌—adverb—┐ ┌—adjective—┐
> After an hour I finally <u>arrived</u> at the <u>home</u> of my professor.

On July 3, 1863, at Gettysburg, Pennsylvania, General Robert E. Lee gambled unsuccessfully for a Confederate victory in the American Civil War. The battle of Pickett's Charge was one of the most disastrous conflicts of the war. Confederate and Union forces faced each other on parallel ridges separated by almost a mile of open fields. After an artillery bombardment of the Union position, nearly 12,000 Confederate infantry marched toward the Union ridge. The Union guns had been silent but suddenly roared against the approaching Confederates. Within an hour, perhaps half of the Confederate soldiers lay wounded or dead.

Exercise 12.10 Sentence combining: Prepositional phrases

To practice writing sentences with prepositional phrases, combine each group of sentences below into one sentence that includes one or two prepositional phrases. You will have to add, delete, and rearrange words. Some items have more than one possible answer.

> *Example:*
> I will start working. The new job will pay the minimum wage.
> I will start working <u>at a new job</u> <u>for the minimum wage.</u>

1. The slow loris protects itself well. Its habitat is Southeast Asia. It possesses a poisonous chemical.
2. The loris frightens predators when it exudes this chemical. The chemical comes from a gland. The gland is on the loris's upper arm.
3. The loris's chemical is highly toxic. The chemical is not like a skunk's spray. Even small quantities of the chemical are toxic.
4. A tiny dose can affect a human. The dose would get in the mouth. The human would be sent into shock.
5. Predators probably can sense the toxin. They detect it at a distance. They use their nasal organs.

2 Using verbals and verbal phrases

Verbals are special verb forms such as *smoking* or *hidden* or *to win* that can function as nouns (*smoking is dangerous*) or as modifiers (*the hidden money, the urge to win*).

Note A verbal *cannot* stand alone as the complete verb in the predicate of a sentence. For example, *The man smoking* and *The money hidden* are not sentences but sentence fragments (see p. 332). Any verbal must combine with a helping verb to serve as the predicate of a sentence: *The man was smoking. The money is hidden.*

Because verbals cannot serve alone as sentence predicates, they are sometimes called **nonfinite verbs** (in essence, they are "unfinished"). **Finite verbs**, in contrast, can make an assertion or express a state of being without a helping verb (they are "finished"). Either of the following two tests can distinguish finite and nonfinite verbs.

Tests for finite and nonfinite verbs (verbals)

Test 1 Does the word require a change in form when a third-person subject changes from singular to plural?

> **Yes** Finite verb: *It sings. They sing.*
>
> **No** Nonfinite verb (verbal): *bird singing, birds singing*

(continued)

> ## Tests for finite and nonfinite verbs (verbals)
> *(continued)*
>
> **Test 2** Does the word require a change in form to show the difference in present, past, and future?
>
> > Yes   Finite verb: *It sings. It sang. It will sing.*
> > No   Nonfinite verb (verbal): *The bird singing is a robin.*
> >   *The bird singing was a robin.*
> >   *The bird singing will be a robin.*

There are three kinds of verbals: participles, gerunds, and infinitives.

Participles

All verbs have two participle forms, a present and a past. The **present participle** consists of the dictionary form of the verb plus the ending *-ing: beginning, completing, hiding.* The **past participle** of most verbs consists of the dictionary form plus *-d* or *-ed: believed, completed.* Some common verbs have an irregular past participle, such as *begun* or *hidden.* (See pp. 277–79.)

Both present and past participles function as adjectives to modify nouns and pronouns:

Shopping malls sometimes frustrate shoppers.

Shoppers may feel trapped.

CULTURE LANGUAGE   For English verbs expressing feeling, the present and past participles have different meanings: *It was a boring lecture. The bored students slept.* See pages 324–25.

Gerunds

Gerund is the name given to the *-ing* form of the verb when it serves as a noun:

subject
Strolling through stores can exhaust the hardiest shopper.

object
Many children learn to hate shopping.

Present participles and gerunds can be distinguished *only* by their function in a sentence. When the *-ing* form functions as an adjective (*a teaching degree*), it is a present participle. When the *-ing* form functions as a noun (*Teaching is difficult*), it is a gerund.

CULTURE LANGUAGE   In English, always use a gerund, not any other verb form, as the object of a preposition: *Diners are prohibited from smoking.* See also the culture-language note opposite.

Infinitives

The **infinitive** is the *to* form of the verb, the dictionary form preceded by the infinitive marker *to: to begin, to hide, to run*. Infinitives may function as adjectives, nouns, or adverbs:

⌐adjective¬
The question to answer is why shoppers endure mall fatigue.

⌐noun¬
The solution for mall fatigue is to leave.

⌐adverb¬
Still, shoppers find it difficult to quit.

CULTURE LANGUAGE Infinitives and gerunds may follow some English verbs and not others and may differ in meaning after a verb: *The cowboy stopped to sing. The cowboy stopped singing.* (See pp. 287–88.)

Verbal phrases

Participles, gerunds, and infinitives—like other verb forms—may take subjects, objects, or complements, and they may be modified by adverbs. The verbal and all the words immediately related to it make up a **verbal phrase**. With verbal phrases, we can create concise sentences packed with information.

Like participles, **participial phrases** always serve as adjectives, modifying nouns or pronouns:

Buying things, most shoppers feel themselves in control.

They make selections determined by personal taste.

Gerund phrases, like gerunds, always serve as nouns:

⌐————— subject —————¬
Shopping for clothing and other items satisfies personal needs.

⌐object of preposition¬
Malls are good at creating such needs.

Infinitive phrases may serve as nouns, adverbs, or adjectives:

⌐sentence subject¬ ⌐———subject complement———¬
To design a mall is to create an artificial environment.
   noun phrase   noun phrase

Malls are designed to make shoppers feel safe.
                     adverb phrase

The environment supports the impulse to shop for oneself.
                     adjective phrase

Note When an infinitive or infinitive phrase serves as a noun after verbs such as *hear, help, let, make, see,* and *watch,* the infinitive marker *to* is omitted: *We all heard her tell* [not *to tell*] *the story.*

Punctuating verbals and verbal phrases

Verbal phrases punctuated as complete sentences are sentence fragments (Chapter 17). A complete sentence must contain a subject and a finite verb (p. 247):

Fragment   <u>Treating</u> the patients kindly.
Revised   <u>She treats</u> the patients kindly.

A verbal or verbal phrase serving as a modifier is almost always set off with a comma when it introduces a sentence (see p. 427):

<u>To pay tuition</u>, some students work at two jobs.

A modifying verbal or verbal phrase that interrupts or concludes a sentence is *not* set off with punctuation when it is essential to the meaning of the word or words it modifies (see p. 430):

Jobs <u>paying well</u> are hard to find.

When an interrupting or concluding verbal modifier is *not* essential to meaning but merely adds information to the sentence, it *is* set off with punctuation, usually a comma or commas (see p. 430):

One good job, <u>paying twelve dollars an hour</u>, was filled in fifteen minutes.

Exercise 12.11   Identifying verbals and verbal phrases

The following sentences contain participles, gerunds, and infinitives as well as participial, gerund, and infinitive phrases. First underline each verbal or verbal phrase. Then indicate whether it is used as an adjective, an adverb, or a noun.

Example:

adjective   adverb
<u>Laughing</u>, the talk-show host prodded her guest <u>to speak</u>.

1. Written in 1850 by Nathaniel Hawthorne, *The Scarlet Letter* tells the story of Hester Prynne.
2. Shunned by the community, Hester endures her loneliness.
3. Hester is humble enough to withstand her Puritan neighbors' cutting remarks.
4. Enduring the cruel treatment, the determined young woman refuses to leave her home.
5. By living a life of patience and unselfishness, Hester eventually becomes the community's angel.

Exercise 12.12   Sentence combining: Verbals and verbal phrases

To practice writing sentences with verbals and verbal phrases, combine each of the following pairs of sentences into one sentence. You will have to add, delete, change, and rearrange words. Each item has more than one possible answer.

Example:

My father took pleasure in mean pranks. For instance, he hid the neighbor's cat.

My father took pleasure in mean pranks such as <u>hiding the neighbor's cat.</u>

1. Air pollution is a health problem. It affects millions of Americans.
2. The air has been polluted mainly by industries and automobiles. It contains toxic chemicals.
3. Environmentalists pressure politicians. They think politicians should pass stricter laws.
4. Many politicians waver. They are not necessarily against environmentalism.
5. The problems are too complex. They cannot be solved easily.

2 Using absolute phrases

Absolute phrases consist of a noun or pronoun and a participle, plus any modifiers:

```
            ┌──────── absolute phrase ────────┐
```
Many ethnic groups, their own place established, are making way for new arrivals.

```
┌──────absolute phrase──────┐┌────── absolute phrase ──────┐
```
Their native lands left behind, an uncertain future looming, immigrants face many obstacles.

These phrases are called *absolute* (from a Latin word meaning "free") because they have no specific grammatical connection to a noun, verb, or any other word in the rest of the sentence. Instead, they modify the entire rest of the sentence, adding information.

Notice that absolute phrases, unlike participial phrases, always contain a subject. Compare the following sentences:

```
               ┌─┬participial phrase┐
```
For many immigrants learning English, the language introduces American culture.

```
┌──────────── absolute phrase ────────────┐
```
The immigrants having learned English, their opportunities widen.

We often omit the participle from an absolute phrase when it is some form of *be*, such as *being* or *having been:*

```
┌──────── absolute phrase ────────┐
```
Two languages [being] at hand, bilingual citizens in fact have many cultural and occupational advantages.

Punctuating absolute phrases

Absolute phrases are always set off from the rest of the sentence with punctuation, usually a comma or commas (see also p. 434):

<u>Their future more secure,</u> these citizens will make room for new arrivals.
These citizens<u>, their future more secure,</u> will make room for new arrivals.

Exercise 12.13 Sentence combining: Absolute phrases

To practice writing sentences with absolute phrases, combine each pair of sentences below into one sentence that contains an absolute phrase. You will have to add, delete, change, and rearrange words.

Example:

The flower's petals wilted. It looked pathetic.
Its petals wilted, the flower looked pathetic.

1. Geraldine Ferraro's face beamed. She enjoyed the crowd's cheers after her nomination for Vice President.
2. A vacancy had occurred. Sandra Day O'Connor was appointed the first female Supreme Court justice.
3. Her appointment was confirmed. Condoleezza Rice became the first female national security adviser.
4. The midterm elections were over. Nancy Pelosi was elected the first female minority leader of the House of Representatives.
5. The election was won. Elizabeth Dole was the first woman to become a US senator from North Carolina.

4 Using subordinate clauses

A **clause** is any group of words that contains both a subject and a predicate. There are two kinds of clauses, and the distinction between them is important:

- A *main* or *independent clause* makes a complete statement and can stand alone as a sentence: *The sky darkened.*
- A *subordinate* or *dependent clause* is just like a main clause *except* that it begins with a subordinating word: *when the sky darkened; because he wants it; whoever calls.* The subordinating word reduces the clause to a single part of speech—an adjective, an adverb, or a noun—that supports the idea in a main clause. Because it only modifies or names something, a subordinate clause cannot stand alone as a sentence (see the discussion of punctuation on p. 255). (The word *subordinate* means "secondary" or "controlled by another." It comes from the Latin *sub,* "under," and *ordo,* "order.")

The following examples show the differences between main and subordinate clauses:

┌──────── main clause ────────┐┌─ main clause ─┐
The school teaches parents. It is unusual.

┌──────── subordinate clause ────────┐┌─ main clause ─┐
Because the school teaches parents, it is unusual.

┌──────────── main clause ────────────┐┌──────── main clause ────────┐
Some parents avoid their children's schools. They are often illiterate.

┌──────────────── main clause ────────────────┐
Parents who are illiterate often avoid their children's schools.
└ subordinate clause ┘

Two kinds of subordinating words introduce subordinate clauses: subordinating conjunctions and relative pronouns.

Subordinating conjunctions

Subordinating conjunctions, like prepositions, never change form in any way. In the following box they are arranged by the relationships they signal. (Some fit in more than one group.)

Common subordinating conjunctions

Cause or effect	Condition	Comparison or contrast	Space or time
as	even if	as	after
because	if	as if	as long as
in order that	if only	as though	before
since	provided	rather than	now that
so that	since	than	once
	unless	whereas	since
Concession	when	whether	till
although	whenever	while	until
as if	whether		when
even if		**Purpose**	whenever
even though		in order that	where
though		so that	wherever
		that	while

CULTURE LANGUAGE Subordinating conjunctions convey their meaning without help from other function words, such as the coordinating conjunctions *and, but, for,* and *so* (p. 259).

Faulty   Even though the parents are illiterate, but their children may read well. [*Even though* and *but* have the same meaning, so both are not needed.]

Revised   Even though the parents are illiterate, their children may read well.

Relative pronouns

Unlike subordinating conjunctions, **relative pronouns** usually act as subjects or objects in their own clauses, and two of them (*who* and *whoever*) change form accordingly (see pp. 271–72).

Relative pronouns

which	what	who (whose, whom)
that	whatever	whoever (whomever)

Subordinate clauses

Subordinate clauses function as adjectives, adverbs, or nouns.

Adjective clauses

Adjective clauses modify nouns and pronouns. They usually begin with the relative pronoun *who, whom, whose, which,* or *that,* although a few adjective clauses begin with *when* or *where* (standing for *in which, on which,* or *at which*). The pronoun is the subject or object of the clause it begins. The clause ordinarily falls immediately after the noun or pronoun it modifies:

Parents who are illiterate often have bad memories of school.

Schools that involve parents are more successful with children.

One school, which is open year-round, helps parents learn to read.

The school is in a city where the illiteracy rate is high.

Adverb clauses

Like adverbs, **adverb clauses** modify verbs, adjectives, other adverbs, and whole groups of words. They usually tell how, why, when, where, under what conditions, or with what result. They always begin with subordinating conjunctions.

The school began teaching parents when adult illiteracy gained national attention.

At first the program was not as successful as its founders had hoped.

Because it was directed at people who could not read, advertising had to be inventive.

Noun clauses

Noun clauses function as subjects, objects, and complements in sentences. They begin with *that, what, whatever, who, whom, whoever, whomever, when, where, whether, why,* or *how.* Unlike adjective and adverb clauses, noun clauses *replace* a word (a noun) within a clause; therefore, they can be difficult to identify.

——— sentence subject ———
Whether the program would succeed depended on door-to-door advertising.

——— object of verb ———
Teachers explained in person how the program would work.

——— object of preposition———
A few parents were anxious about what their children would think.

Elliptical clauses

A subordinate clause that is grammatically incomplete but clear in meaning is an **elliptical clause** (*ellipsis* means "omission"). The meaning of the clause is clear because the missing element can be supplied from the context. Most often the elements omitted are the pronouns *that, which,* and *whom* or the predicate from the second part of a comparison.

> Skepticism and fear were among the feelings [that] the parents voiced.
>
> The parents knew their children could read better than they [could read].

Punctuating subordinate clauses

Subordinate clauses punctuated as complete sentences are sentence fragments (Chapter 17). Though a subordinate clause contains a subject and a predicate and thus resembles a complete sentence, it also begins with a subordinating word that makes it into an adjective, adverb, or noun. A single part of speech cannot stand alone as a complete sentence.

> Fragment Because a door was ajar.
> Revised   A door was ajar.
> Revised   The secret leaked because a door was ajar.

A subordinate clause serving as an adverb is almost always set off with a comma when it introduces a sentence (see p. 427):

> Although the project was almost completed, it lost its funding.

A modifying subordinate clause that interrupts or concludes a main clause is *not* set off with punctuation when it is essential to the meaning of the word or words it modifies (see p. 431):

> The woman who directed the project lost her job.
> The project lost its funding because it was not completed on time.

When an interrupting or concluding subordinate clause is *not* essential to meaning, but merely adds information to the sentence, it *is* set off with punctuation, usually a comma or commas (see pp. 430–31):

> The project lost its funding, although it was almost completed.
> The director, who holds a PhD, sought new funding.

Exercise 12.14 Identifying subordinate clauses

Identify the subordinate clauses in the following sentences. Then indicate whether each is used as an adjective, an adverb, or a noun. If the clause is a noun, indicate what function it performs in the sentence.

Example:
noun
The article explained how one could build an underground house.
[Object of *explained*.]

1. Scientists who want to catch the slightest signals from space use extremely sensitive receivers.
2. Even though they have had to fight for funding, these scientists have persisted in their research.
3. The research is called SETI, which stands for Search for Extraterrestrial Intelligence.
4. The theory is that intelligent beings in space are trying to get in touch with us.
5. Scientists do not yet know what frequency these beings would use to send signals.

Exercise 12.15 Sentence combining: Subordinate clauses

To practice writing sentences with subordinate clauses, combine each pair of main clauses into one sentence. Use either subordinating conjunctions or relative pronouns as appropriate, referring to the lists on page 253 if necessary. You will have to add, delete, and rearrange words. Each item has more than one possible answer.

Example:
She did not have her tire irons with her. She could not change her bicycle tire.

Because she did not have her tire irons with her, she could not change her bicycle tire.

1. Moviegoers expect something. Movie sequels should be as exciting as the original films.
2. A few sequels are good films. Most sequels are poor imitations of the originals.
3. A sequel to a blockbuster film arrives in the theater. Crowds quickly line up to see it.
4. Viewers pay to see the same villains and heroes. They remember these characters fondly.
5. Afterward, viewers often grumble about filmmakers. The filmmakers rehash tired plots and characters.

5 Using appositives

An **appositive** is usually a noun that renames another noun nearby, most often the noun just before the appositive. (The word *appositive* derives from a Latin word that means "placed near to" or "applied to.") An **appositive phrase** includes modifiers as well.

Bizen ware, a dark stoneware, has been produced in Japan since the fourteenth century.

The name Bizen comes from the location of the kilns used to fire the pottery.

All appositives can replace the words they refer to: *A dark stoneware has been produced in Japan.*

Appositives are often introduced by words and phrases such as *or, that is, such as, for example,* and *in other words:*

> Bizen ware is used in the Japanese tea ceremony, that is, <u>the Zen Buddhist observance that links meditation and art.</u>

Appositives are economical alternatives to adjective clauses containing a form of *be,* as shown in the next example.

> Bizen ware, [which is] <u>a dark stoneware</u>, has been produced in Japan since the fourteenth century.

Although most appositives are nouns that rename other nouns, they may also be and rename other parts of speech, such as the verb *thrown* in the sentence below:

> The pottery is thrown, or <u>formed on a potter's wheel.</u>

Punctuating appositives

Appositives punctuated as complete sentences are sentence fragments (see Chapter 17). To correct such fragments, you can usually connect the appositive to the main clause containing the word referred to:

> **Fragment**   An exceedingly tall man with narrow shoulders.
> **Revised**   He stood next to a basketball player, <u>an exceedingly tall man with narrow shoulders.</u>

An appositive is *not* set off with punctuation when it is essential to the meaning of the word it refers to (see p. 431):

> The verb *howl* comes from the Old English verb *houlen.*

When an appositive is *not* essential to the meaning of the word it refers to, it *is* set off with punctuation, usually a comma or commas (see p. 431):

> <u>An aged elm,</u> the tree was struck by lightning.
> The tree, <u>an aged elm,</u> was struck by lightning.
> Lightning struck the tree, <u>an aged elm.</u>

A nonessential appositive is sometimes set off with a dash or dashes, especially when it contains commas (see p. 473):

> Three people—Will, Erica, and Alex—object to the new procedure.

A concluding appositive is sometimes set off with a colon (see p. 471):

> Two principles guide the judge's decisions: <u>justice and mercy.</u>

Exercise 12.16 Sentence combining: Appositives

To practice writing sentences with appositives, combine each pair of sentences into one sentence that contains an appositive. You will have to delete and rearrange words. Some items have more than one possible answer.

Example:

The largest land animal is the elephant. The elephant is also one of the most intelligent animals.

The largest land animal, <u>the elephant</u>, is also one of the most intelligent animals.

1. Some people perform amazing feats when they are very young. These people are geniuses from birth.
2. John Stuart Mill was a British philosopher. He had written a history of Rome by age seven.
3. Two great artists began their work at age four. They were Paul Klee and Gustav Mahler.
4. Mahler was a Bohemian composer of intensely emotional works. He was also the child of a brutal father.
5. Paul Klee was a Swiss painter. As a child he was frightened by his own drawings of devils.

12d Compounding words, phrases, and clauses

A **compound construction** combines words that are closely related and equally important. It makes writing clearer and more economical because it pulls together linked information.

Headaches can be controlled by biofeedback. Heart rate can be controlled by biofeedback.

┌──── compound subject ────┐
Headaches and heart rate can be controlled by biofeedback.

Without medication, biofeedback cures headaches. It steadies heart rate. It lowers blood pressure. It relaxes muscles.

┌──── compound predicate ────┐
Without medication, biofeedback cures headaches, steadies heart

rate, lowers blood pressure, and relaxes muscles.

1 Using coordinating conjunctions and correlative conjunctions

Two kinds of words create compound constructions: coordinating and correlative conjunctions. **Coordinating conjunctions** are few and do not change form. In the following box the relationship that each conjunction signals appears in parentheses.

Coordinating conjunctions

and (*addition*)	nor (*alternative*)	for (*cause*)	yet (*contrast*)
but (*contrast*)	or (*alternative*)	so (*effect*)	

To remember the coordinating conjunctions, use the word *fanboys: for, and, nor, but, or, yet, so.*

The coordinating conjunctions *and, but, nor,* and *or* always connect words or word groups of the same kind—that is, two or more nouns, verbs, adjectives, adverbs, phrases, subordinate clauses, or main clauses:

> Biofeedback or simple relaxation can relieve headaches.
> Biofeedback is effective but costly.
> Relaxation also works well, and it is inexpensive.

The conjunctions *for* and *so* connect only main clauses. *For* indicates cause; *so* indicates effect.

> Biofeedback can be costly, for the training involves technical equipment and specialists.
>
> Relaxation can be difficult to learn alone, so some people do seek help from specialists.

Some coordinating conjunctions pair up with other words to form **correlative conjunctions.** In the following box the relationship each conjunction signals appears in parentheses.

Common correlative conjunctions

both . . . and (*addition*)	neither . . . nor (*negation*)
not only . . . but also (*addition*)	whether . . . or (*alternative*)
not . . . but (*substitution*)	as . . . as (*comparison*)
either . . . or (*alternative*)	

> Both biofeedback and relaxation can relieve headaches.
>
> The techniques require neither psychotherapy nor medication.
>
> The headache sufferer learns not only to recognize the causes of headaches but also to control those causes.

Punctuating compounded words, phrases, and clauses

Two words, phrases, or subordinate clauses that are connected by a coordinating conjunction are *not* separated by a comma (see pp. 441–42):

The library needs <u>renovation and rebuilding</u>.

The work will begin <u>after spring term but before fall term</u>.

When two *main* clauses are joined into one sentence with a coordinating conjunction, a comma precedes the conjunction (see p. 424):

The project will be lengthy, <u>and</u> everyone will suffer some inconvenience.

When two main clauses are joined *without* a coordinating conjunction, they must be separated with a semicolon to avoid the error called a comma splice (see p. 340):

The work cannot be delayed; it's already overdue.

In a series of three or more items, commas separate the items, with *and* usually preceding the last item (see p. 435):

The renovated library will feature <u>new study carrels, new shelving, and a larger reference section</u>.

Semicolons sometimes separate the items in a series if they are long or contain commas (see p. 450).

A comma also separates two or more adjectives when they modify a noun equally and are not joined by a coordinating conjunction (see p. 435):

<u>Cracked, crumbling</u> walls will be repaired.

The comma does *not* separate adjectives when the one nearer the noun is more closely related to it in meaning (see p. 436):

<u>New reading</u> lounges will replace the old ones.

2 Using conjunctive adverbs

One other kind of connecting word, called a **conjunctive adverb**, relates only main clauses, not words, phrases, or subordinate clauses. In the box opposite, the conjunctive adverbs are arranged by the relationships they signal.

It's important to distinguish between conjunctive adverbs and conjunctions (coordinating and subordinating) because they demand different punctuation (see the next page). Conjunctive adverbs are *adverbs:* they describe the relation of ideas in two clauses, and, like most adverbs, they can move around in their clause:

Relaxation techniques have improved; <u>however,</u> few people know them.
Relaxation techniques have improved; few people know them, <u>however</u>.

In contrast, conjunctions bind two clauses into a single grammatical unit, and they cannot be moved.

Common conjunctive adverbs

Addition	Emphasis	Comparison or contrast	Cause or effect	Time
also	certainly	however	accordingly	finally
besides	indeed	in comparison	as a result	meanwhile
further	in fact	in contrast	consequently	next
furthermore	still	instead	hence	now
in addition	undoubtedly	likewise	similarly	then
incidentally		nevertheless	therefore	thereafter
moreover		nonetheless	thus	
		otherwise		
		rather		

Although few people know them, relaxation techniques have improved. [The subordinating conjunction can't be moved: *Few people know them although, relaxation techniques have improved.*]

Relaxation techniques have improved, but few people know them. [The coordinating conjunction can't be moved: *Relaxation techniques have improved, few people know them but.*]

Note Some connecting words have more than one use. *After, until,* and some other words may be either prepositions or subordinating conjunctions. Some prepositions, such as *behind* and *in,* can serve also as adverbs, as in *He trailed behind.* And some conjunctive adverbs, particularly *however,* may also serve simply as adverbs in sentences such as *However much the books cost, we must have them for our classes.* Again, the part of speech of a word depends on its function in a sentence.

Punctuating sentences containing conjunctive adverbs

Because the two main clauses related by a conjunctive adverb remain independent units, they must be separated by a semicolon. If they are separated by a comma, the result is a comma splice (Chapter 18):

Comma splice   Interest rates rose, therefore, real estate prices declined.

Revised   Interest rates rose; therefore, real estate prices declined.

A conjunctive adverb is almost always set off from its clause with a comma or commas (see p. 432):

The decline was small; however, some home owners suffered unexpected losses.

The decline was small; some home owners, however, suffered unexpected losses.

Exercise 12.17 Sentence combining: Compound constructions

To practice compounding words, phrases, and clauses, combine each of the following pairs of sentences into one sentence that is as short as possible without altering meaning. Use an appropriate connecting word of the type specified in parentheses, referring to the lists on pages 259 and 261 as necessary. You will have to add and delete words, and you may have to change or add punctuation.

Example:

The encyclopedia had some information. It was not detailed enough. (*Conjunctive adverb.*)

The encyclopedia had some information; <u>however,</u> it was not detailed enough.

1. All too often people assume that old age is not a productive time. Many people in their nineties have had great achievements. (*Conjunctive adverb.*)
2. In his nineties the philosopher Bertrand Russell spoke vigorously for international peace. He spoke for nuclear disarmament. (*Correlative conjunction.*)
3. Grandma Moses did not retire to an easy chair. She began painting at age seventy-six and was still going at one hundred. (*Conjunctive adverb.*)
4. The British general George Higginson published his memoirs after he was ninety. The British archaeologist Margaret Murray published her memoirs after she was ninety. (*Coordinating conjunction.*)
5. The architect Frank Lloyd Wright designed his first building at age twenty. He designed his last building at age ninety. (*Coordinating conjunction.*)

12e Changing the usual word order

So far, all the examples of basic sentence structure have been similar: the subject of the sentence comes first, naming the performer of the predicate's action, and the predicate comes second. This arrangement describes most English sentences, but four kinds of sentences change the order.

Questions

In most questions the predicate verb or a part of it precedes the subject:

verb   subject ⌐—verb—⌐
Have interest rates been rising?

verb subject verb
Did rates rise?

verb subject verb
Why did rates rise today?

subject verb
What is the answer? [Normal subject-verb order.]

Commands

In commands the subject *you* is omitted:

verb   verb
Think of the options.   Watch the news.

Passive sentences

Generally, the subject performs the action of a verb in the **active voice.** But sometimes the subject *receives* the action of a verb in the **passive voice:**

subject verb
Active   Kyong wrote the paper.

subject ⌐—verb—⌐
Passive The paper was written by Kyong.

See pages 300–01 for more on forming the passive voice, and see pages 301–02 on overuse of the passive voice.

Sentences with postponed subjects

The subject follows the predicate in two sentence patterns. The normal order may be reversed for emphasis:

Henry comes here. [Normal order.]
Here comes Henry. [Reversed order.]

Or the word *there, here,* or *it* may postpone the subject:

verb   subject
There will be eighteen people attending the meeting.

verb   ⌐————subject————⌐
It was surprising that Marinetti was nominated.

verb   subject
Here are the reasons why.

There, it, and *here* in such sentences are called **expletives.** Expletive sentences have their uses, but they can also be wordy and unemphatic (see p. 531).

CULTURE LANGUAGE   When you use an expletive construction, be careful to include *there, here,* or *it.* Only commands and some questions can begin with verbs.

Faulty   No one predicted the nomination. Were no polls showing Marinetti ahead.

Revised No one predicted the nomination. There were no polls showing Marinetti ahead.

Exercise 12.18 Forming questions and commands

Form a question and a command from the following noun and verb pairs.

Example:
wood, split
Did you split all this wood? Split the wood for our fire.

1. water, boil
2. music, stop
3. table, set
4. dice, roll
5. telephone, use

Exercise 12.19 Rewriting passives and expletives

Rewrite each passive sentence below as active, and rewrite each expletive construction to restore normal subject-predicate order. (For additional exercises with the passive voice and with expletives, see pp. 302, 382, and 532.)

Example:
All the trees in the park were planted by the city.
The city planted all the trees in the park.

1. The screenplay for *Monster's Ball* was cowritten by Milo Addica and Will Rokos.
2. The film was directed by Marc Foster.
3. There was only one performance in the movie that received an Academy Award.
4. It was Halle Berry who won the award for best actress.
5. Berry was congratulated by the press for being the first African American to win the award.

12f Classifying sentences

We describe and classify sentences in two different ways: by function (statement, question, command, exclamation, and so on) or by structure. Four basic sentence structures are possible: simple, compound, complex, and compound-complex. Each structure gives different emphasis to the sentence's main idea or ideas and to any supporting information.

1 Writing simple sentences

A **simple sentence** consists of a single main clause and no subordinate clause:

———main clause———
Last summer was unusually hot.

————main clause————
The summer made many farmers leave the area for good or reduced them to bare existence.

2 Writing compound sentences

A **compound sentence** consists of two or more main clauses and no subordinate clause. The clauses may be joined by a coordinating conjunction and a comma, by a semicolon alone, or by a conjunctive adverb and a semicolon.

```
┌──main clause─┐   ┌────────main clause────────┐
```
Last July was hot, but August was even hotter.
```
┌─────────────main clause─────────────┐┌────────────main clause────────────┐
```
The hot sun scorched the earth; the lack of rain killed many crops.

3 Writing complex sentences

A **complex sentence** contains one main clause and one or more subordinate clauses:
```
┌──main clause──┐┌─────────── subordinate clause ───────────┐
```
Rain finally came, although many had left the area by then.
```
┌─────────────────── main clause───────────────────┐┌── subordinate clause──
```
Those who remained were able to start anew because the government
subordinate clause
```

```
came to their aid.

Notice that length does not determine whether a sentence is complex or simple; both kinds can be short or long.

4 Writing compound-complex sentences

A **compound-complex sentence** has the characteristics of both the compound sentence (two or more main clauses) and the complex sentence (at least one subordinate clause):
```
┌──────────subordinate clause──────────┐┌──────────── main clause───────────
```
When government aid finally came, many people had already been re-
```
──────────────────────┐   ┌────────────main clause───────────┐
```
duced to poverty and others had been forced to move.

Exercise 12.20 Identifying sentence structures

Mark the main clauses and subordinate clauses in the following sentences. Identify each sentence as simple, compound, complex, or compound-complex.

Example:
```
┌──────────────main clause──────────────┐┌── subordinate clause──
```
The police began patrolling more often when crime in the neigh-

borhood increased. [Complex sentence.]

1. Joseph Pulitzer endowed the Pulitzer Prizes.
2. Pulitzer, incidentally, was the publisher of the New York newspaper The World.
3. Although the first prizes were for journalism and letters only, Pulitzers are now awarded in music and other areas.
4. For example, Berke Breathed won for his *Bloom County* comic strip, and Roger Reynolds won for his musical composition *Whispers Out of Time*.
5. Although only one prize is usually awarded in each category, in 1989 Taylor Branch's *Parting the Waters* won a history prize, and it shared the honor with James M. McPherson's *Battle Cry of Freedom*.

Exercise 12.21   Sentence combining: Sentence structures

Combine each set of simple sentences below to produce the kind of sentence specified in parentheses. You will have to add, delete, change, and rearrange words.

> *Example:*
> The traffic passed the house. It never stopped. (*Complex.*)
> The traffic that passed the house never stopped.

1. Recycling takes time. It reduces garbage in landfills. (*Compound.*)
2. People begin to recycle. They generate much less trash. (*Complex.*)
3. White tissues and paper towels biodegrade more easily than dyed ones. People still buy dyed papers. (*Complex.*)
4. The cans are aluminum. They bring recyclers good money. (*Simple.*)
5. Environmentalists have hope. Perhaps more communities will recycle newspaper and glass. Many citizens refuse to participate. (*Compound-complex.*)

13

Case of Nouns and Pronouns

Case is the form of a noun or pronoun that shows the reader how it functions in a sentence—that is, whether it functions as a subject, as an object, or in some other way. As shown in the box on the next page, only *I, we, he, she, they,* and *who* change form for each case. Thus these pronouns are the focus of this chapter.

The **subjective case** generally indicates that the word is a subject or a subject complement. (See pp. 233 and 239–40.)

subject
She and Novick discussed the proposal.

subject
The proposal ignores many who need help.

subject complement
The disgruntled planners were she and Novick.

---

mycomplab

Visit *mycomplab.com* for more resources and exercises on noun and pronoun case.

Case forms of nouns and pronouns

	Subjective	Objective	Possessive
Nouns	boy	boy	boy's
	Jessie	Jessie	Jessie's
Personal pronouns			
Singular			
1st person	I	me	my, mine
2nd person	you	you	your, yours
3rd person	he	him	his
	she	her	her, hers
	it	it	its
Plural			
1st person	we	us	our, ours
2nd person	you	you	your, yours
3rd person	they	them	their, theirs
Relative and interrogative pronouns			
	who	whom	whose
	whoever	whomever	—
	which, that, what	which, that, what	—
Indefinite pronouns	everybody	everybody	everybody's

The **objective case** generally indicates that the word is the object of a verb or preposition. (See pp. 238–41 and 244–45.)

object of verb
The proposal disappointed her and Novick.

object — object
of verb — of verb
A colleague whom they respected let them down.

object of preposition
Their opinion of him suffered.

The **possessive case** generally indicates ownership or source:

Her counterproposal is in preparation.
Theirs is the more defensible position.
The problem is not his.

Do not use an apostrophe to form the possessive of personal pronouns: *yours* (not *your's*); *theirs* (not *their's*). (See p. 458. See also p. 454 for the possessive forms of nouns, which do use apostrophes.)

Grammar checkers A grammar checker may flag some problems with pronoun case, but it will also miss a lot. For instance, one checker spotted the error in *We asked whom would come* (should be *who would come*), but it overlooked *We dreaded them coming* (should be *their coming*).

CULTURE LANGUAGE In standard American English, *-self* pronouns do not change form to show function. Their only forms are *myself, yourself, himself, herself, itself, ourselves, yourselves, themselves.* Avoid nonstandard forms such as *hisself, ourself,* and *theirselves.*

13a Use the subjective case for compound subjects and for subject complements.

In compound subjects use the same pronoun form you would use if the pronoun stood alone as a subject:

subject
She and Novick will persist.

subject
The others may lend their support when she and Novick get a hearing.

If you are in doubt about the correct form, try the test in the box below.

After a linking verb, such as a form of *be*, a pronoun renaming the subject (a subject complement) should be in the subjective case:

subject complement
The ones who care most are she and Novick.

subject complement
It was they whom the mayor appointed.

If this construction sounds stilted to you, use the more natural order: *She and Novick are the ones who care most. The mayor appointed them.*

A test for case forms in compound constructions

1. **Identify a compound construction** (one connected by *and, but or, nor*).

   [He, Him] and [I, me] won the prize.
   The prize went to [he, him] and [I, me].

2. **Write a separate sentence for each part of the compound.**

   [He, Him] won the prize. [I, Me] won the prize.
   The prize went to [he, him]. The prize went to [I, me].

3. **Choose the pronouns that sound correct.**

   He won the prize. I won the prize. [Subjective.]
   The prize went to him. The prize went to me. [Objective.]

4. **Put the separate sentences back together.**

   He and I won the prize.
   The prize went to him and me.

13b Use the objective case for compound objects.

In compound objects use the same pronoun form you would use if the pronoun stood alone as an object:

direct object
The mayor nominated <u>Zhu and him</u>.

indirect object
The mayor gave <u>Zhu and him</u> awards.

object of preposition
Credit goes equally to <u>them and the mayor</u>.

If you are in doubt about the correct form, try the test in the box opposite.

Exercise 13.1 **Choosing between subjective and objective pronouns**

From the pairs in brackets, select the appropriate subjective or objective pronoun(s) for each of the following sentences.

Example:
"Between you and [I, me]," the seller said, "this deal is a steal."
"Between you and <u>me</u>," the seller said, "this deal is a steal."

1. Lisa and [I, me] were competing for places on the relay team.
2. The fastest runners at our school were [she, her] and [I, me], so [we, us] expected to make the team.
3. [She, Her] and [I, me] were friends but also intense rivals.
4. The time trials went badly, excluding both [she, her] and [I, me] from the team.
5. Next season we are determined to earn at least one place between [she, her] and [I, me].

13c Use the appropriate case when the plural pronoun *we* or *us* occurs with a noun.

Whether to use *we* or *us* with a noun depends on the use of the noun:

object of preposition
Freezing weather is welcomed by us skaters.

subject
We skaters welcome freezing weather.

13d In appositives the case of a pronoun depends on the function of the word described or identified.

object of verb · appositive identifies object
The class elected two representatives, DeShawn and me.

subject appositive
identifies subject
Two representatives, DeShawn and I, were elected.

If you are in doubt about case in an appositive, try the sentence without the word the appositive identifies: *The class elected DeShawn and me. DeShawn and I were elected.*

Exercise 13.2 Choosing between subjective and objective pronouns

From the pairs in brackets, select the appropriate subjective or objective pronoun for each of the following sentences.

Example:
Convincing [we, us] veterans to vote yes will be difficult.
Convincing us veterans to vote yes will be difficult.

1. Obtaining enough protein is important to [we, us] vegetarians.
2. Instead of obtaining protein from meat, [we, us] vegetarians get our protein from other sources.
3. Jeff claims to know only two vegetarians, Helena and [he, him], who avoid all animal products, including milk.
4. Some of [we, us] vegetarians eat fish, which is a good source of protein.
5. [We, Us] vegetarians in my family, my parents and [I, me], drink milk and eat fish.

13e | **The case of a pronoun after *than* or *as* in a comparison depends on the meaning.**

When a pronoun follows *than* or *as* in a comparison, the case of the pronoun indicates what words may have been omitted. When the pronoun is subjective, it must serve as the subject of an omitted verb:

subject
Some critics like Glass more than he [does].

When the pronoun is objective, it must serve as the object of an omitted verb:

object
Some critics like Glass more than [they like] him.

13f | **Use the objective case for pronouns that are subjects or objects of infinitives.**

subject of
infinitive
The school asked him to speak.

object of
infinitive
Students chose to invite him.

13g Use *who* or *whom* depending on function.

To choose between *who* and *whom*, *whoever* and *whomever*, you need to figure out whether the word serves as a subject or as an object. Use *who* where you would use *he* or *she*—all ending in vowels. Use *whom* where you would use *him* or *her*—all ending in consonants.

1 At the beginning of a question, use *who* for a subject and *whom* for an object.

subject→
Who wrote the policy?

object ←——————
Whom does it affect?

A test for *who* versus *whom* in questions

1. **Pose the question.**

   [Who, Whom] makes that decision?
   [Who, Whom] does one ask?

2. **Answer the question, using a personal pronoun.** Choose the pronoun that sounds correct, and note its case.

   [She, Her] makes that decision. She makes that decision. [Subjective.]
   One asks [she, her]. One asks her. [Objective.]

3. **Use the same case (*who* or *whom*) in the question.**

   Who makes that decision? [Subjective.]
   Whom does one ask? [Objective.]

Note In speech the subjective case *who* is commonly used whenever it is the first word of a question, regardless of whether it is a subject or an object. But formal writing requires a distinction between the forms:

Spoken Who should we credit?

object ←——————
Written Whom should we credit?

2 In a subordinate clause, use *who* or *whoever* for the subject, *whom* or *whomever* for an object.

The case of a pronoun in a subordinate clause depends on its function in the clause, regardless of whether the clause itself functions as a subject, an object, or a modifier:

subject →
Credit whoever wrote the policy.

object ←⎯⎯⎯⎯⎯
Research should reveal whom to credit.

Note Don't let expressions such as *I think* and *she says* confuse you when they come between the subject *who* and its verb:

subject ⎯⎯⎯⎯⎯⎯⎯⎯⎯⎯⎯↘
He is the one who the polls say will win.

To choose between *who* and *whom* in such constructions, delete the interrupting phrase: *He is the one who will win.*

A test for *who* versus *whom* in subordinate clauses

1. **Locate the subordinate clause.**

   Few people know [who, whom] they should ask.
   They are unsure [who, whom] makes the decision.

2. **Rewrite the subordinate clause as a separate sentence, substituting a personal pronoun for *who, whom*.** Choose the pronoun that sounds correct, and note its case.

   They should ask [she, her]. They should ask her. [Objective.]
   [She, Her] makes the decision. She makes the decision. [Subjective.]

3. **Use the same case (*who* or *whom*) in the subordinate clause.**

   Few people know whom they should ask. [Objective.]
   They are unsure who makes the decision. [Subjective.]

Exercise 13.3 Choosing between *who* and *whom*

From the pairs in brackets, select the appropriate form of the pronoun in each of the following sentences.

   Example:
   My mother asked me [who, whom] I was going out with.
   My mother asked me whom I was going out with.

1. The judges awarded first prize to Inez, [who, whom] they believed gave the best performance.
2. Inez beat the other contestants [who, whom] competed against her.
3. She is a consummate performer, singing to [whoever, whomever] would listen.
4. [Who, Whom] in the school has not heard Inez sing?
5. [Who, Whom] has she not performed for?

Exercise 13.4 Sentence combining: *Who* versus *whom*

Combine each of the following pairs of sentences into one sentence that contains a clause beginning with *who* or *whom*. Be sure to use the appropriate case form. You will have to add, delete, and rearrange words. Each item may have more than one possible answer.

Example:
David is the candidate. We think David deserves to win.
David is the candidate <u>who</u> we think deserves to win.

1. Some children have undetected hearing problems. These children may do poorly in school.
2. They may not hear important instructions and information from teachers. Teachers may speak softly.
3. Classmates may not be audible. The teacher calls on those classmates.
4. Some hearing-impaired children may work harder to overcome their disability. These children get a lot of encouragement at home.
5. Some hearing-impaired children may take refuge in fantasy friends. They can rely on these friends not to criticize or laugh.

13h Ordinarily, use a possessive pronoun or noun immediately before a gerund.

A **gerund** is the *-ing* form of a verb (*running, sleeping*) used as a noun (p. 248). Like nouns, gerunds are commonly preceded by possessive nouns and pronouns: *our vote* (noun), *our voting* (gerund).

The coach disapproved of <u>their</u> lifting weights.

The <u>coach's</u> disapproving was a surprise.

A noun or pronoun before an *-ing* verb form is not always possessive. Sometimes the *-ing* form will be a present participle modifying the preceding word:

Everyone had noticed <u>him</u> weightlifting. [Emphasis on *him*.]
        objective participle
        pronoun

Everyone had noticed <u>his</u> weightlifting. [Emphasis on the activity.]
        possessive gerund
        pronoun

Note that a gerund usually is not preceded by the possessive when the possessive would create an awkward construction:

Awkward	A rumor spread about <u>everybody's</u> on the team wanting to quit.
Less awkward	A rumor spread about <u>everybody</u> on the team wanting to quit.
Better	A rumor spread <u>that everybody</u> on the team <u>wanted</u> to quit.

Exercise 13.5 Revising: Case

Revise all inappropriate case forms in the following paragraph, and explain the function of each case form.

Written four thousand years ago, *The Epic of Gilgamesh* tells of the friendship of Gilgamesh and Enkidu. Gilgamesh was a bored king who his people thought was too harsh. Then he met Enkidu, a wild man whom had lived with the animals in the mountains. Immediately, him and Gilgamesh wrestled to see whom was more powerful. After hours of struggle, Enkidu admitted that Gilgamesh was stronger than him. Now the friends needed adventures worthy of the two strongest men on earth. Gilgamesh said, "Between you and I, mighty deeds will be accomplished, and our fame will be everlasting." Among their acts, Enkidu and him defeated a giant bull, Humbaba, and cut down the bull's cedar forests. Them bringing back cedar logs to Gilgamesh's treeless land won great praise from the people. When Enkidu died, Gilgamesh mourned his death, realizing that no one had been a better friend than him. When Gilgamesh himself died many years later, his people raised a monument praising Enkidu and he for their friendship and their mighty deeds of courage.

Note See page 329 for an exercise involving case along with other aspects of grammar.

14

Verbs

The verb is the most complicated part of speech in English, changing form to express a wide range of information.

──────── Verb Forms ────────

All verbs except *be* have five basic forms. The first three are the verb's **principal parts.**

- **The *plain form* is the dictionary form of the verb.** When the subject is a plural noun or the pronoun *I, we, you,* or *they,* the plain form indicates action that occurs in the present, occurs habitually, or is generally true.

mycomplab

Visit *mycomplab.com* for more resources and exercises on verb forms.

Terms used to describe verbs

Tense

The time of the verb's action—for instance, present (*kick*), past (*kicked*), future (**will** *kick*). (See p. 291.)

Mood

The attitude of the verb's speaker or writer—the difference, for example, in *I kick the ball*, *Kick the ball*, and *I suggested that she kick the ball*. (See p. 298.)

Voice

The distinction between the **active**, in which the subject performs the verb's action (*I kick the ball*), and the **passive**, in which the subject is acted upon (*The ball is kicked by me*). (See p. 300.)

Person

The verb form that reflects whether the subject is speaking (*I/we kick the ball*), spoken to (*You kick the ball*), or spoken about (*She kicks the ball*). (See p. 304.)

Number

The verb form that reflects whether the subject is singular (*The girl kicks the ball*) or plural (*Girls kick the ball*). (See p. 304.)

A few artists <u>live</u> in town today.
They <u>hold</u> classes downtown.

- The *past-tense form* indicates that the action of the verb occurred before now. It usually adds *-d* or *-ed* to the plain form, although some irregular verbs form it in other ways (see p. 277).

Many artists <u>lived</u> in town before this year.
They <u>held</u> classes downtown. [Irregular verb.]

- The *past participle* is the same as the past-tense form, except in most irregular verbs. It combines with forms of *have* or *be* (*has <u>climbed</u>*, *was <u>created</u>*), or by itself it modifies nouns and pronouns (*the <u>sliced</u> apples*).

Artists have <u>lived</u> in town for decades.
They have <u>held</u> classes downtown. [Irregular verb.]

- The *present participle* adds *-ing* to the verb's plain form. It combines with forms of *be* (*is <u>buying</u>*), modifies nouns and pronouns (*the <u>boiling</u> water*), or functions as a noun (*<u>Running</u> exhausts me*).

A few artists are <u>living</u> in town today.
They are <u>holding</u> classes downtown.

■ **The *-s form* ends in *-s* or *-es*.** When the subject is a singular noun, a pronoun such as *everyone*, or the personal pronoun *he*, *she*, or *it*, the *-s* form indicates action that occurs in the present, occurs habitually, or is generally true.

The artist lives in town today.
She holds classes downtown.

The verb *be* has eight forms rather than the five forms of most other verbs:

Plain form	be		
Present participle	being		
Past participle	been		
	I	*he, she, it*	*we, you, they*
Present tense	am	is	are
Past tense	was	was	were

CULTURE LANGUAGE If standard American English is not your native language or dialect, you may have difficulty with verbs' *-s* forms (including those for *be: is, was*) or with the forms that indicate time (such as the past-tense form). See pages 281–82 and 292–94, respectively, for more on these forms.

Helping verbs

Helping verbs, also called **auxiliary verbs,** combine with some verb forms to indicate time and other kinds of meaning, as in *can run*, *was sleeping*, *had been eaten*. These combinations are **verb phrases.** Since the plain form, present participle, or past participle in any verb phrase always carries the principal meaning, it is sometimes called the **main verb.**

Verb phrase

Helping   *Main*

Artists can   train others to draw.
The techniques have   changed little.

These are the most common helping verbs:

Forms of *be:* be, am, is, are, was, were, been, being
Forms of *have:* have, has, had, having
Forms of *do:* do, does, did

be able to	had better	must	used to
be supposed to	have to	ought to	will
can	may	shall	would
could	might	should	

CULTURE LANGUAGE The helping verbs of standard American English may be problematic if you are used to speaking another language or dialect. See pages 282–86 for more on helping verbs.

14a Use the correct forms of regular and irregular verbs.

Most verbs are **regular;** that is, they form their past tense and past participle by adding *-d* or *-ed* to the plain form.

Plain form	Past tense	Past participle
live	lived	lived
act	acted	acted

Since the past tense and past participle are the same, the forms of regular verbs do not often cause problems (but see pp. 281–82).

About two hundred English verbs are **irregular;** that is, they form their past tense and past participle in some irregular way.

Plain form	Past tense	Past participle
begin	began	begun
break	broke	broken
sleep	slept	slept

You can see the difference between a regular and an irregular verb in these examples:

Plain form	Today the birds twitter.
	Today the birds sing.
Past tense	Yesterday the birds twittered.
	Yesterday the birds sang.
Past participle	In the past the birds have twittered.
	In the past the birds have sung.

The box on the next two pages lists the forms of many irregular verbs. Check this box or a dictionary if you have any doubt about a verb's principal parts. If a dictionary lists only the plain form, the verb is regular: both the past tense and the past participle add *-d* or *-ed* to the plain form. If the verb is irregular, the dictionary will list the plain form, the past tense, and the past participle in that order (*go, went, gone*). If the dictionary gives only two forms (as in *think, thought*), then the past tense and the past participle are the same.

Grammar checkers A grammar checker may flag incorrect forms of irregular verbs, but it may also fail to do so. For example, a checker did not flag *The runner had steal second base* (*stolen* is correct). When in doubt about the forms of irregular verbs, refer to the box on the next page or consult a dictionary.

CULTURE LANGUAGE Some English dialects use distinctive verb forms that differ from those of standard American English: for instance, *drug* for *dragged, growed* for *grew,* *come* for *came,* or *went* for *gone.* In situations requiring standard American English, use the forms in the list on the next page or in a dictionary.

Principal parts of common irregular verbs

Plain form	Past tense	Past participle
arise	arose	arisen
be	was, were	been
become	became	become
begin	began	begun
bid	bid	bid
bite	bit	bitten, bit
blow	blew	blown
break	broke	broken
bring	brought	brought
burst	burst	burst
buy	bought	bought
catch	caught	caught
choose	chose	chosen
come	came	come
cut	cut	cut
dive	dived, dove	dived
do	did	done
draw	drew	drawn
dream	dreamed, dreamt	dreamed, dreamt
drink	drank	drunk
drive	drove	driven
eat	ate	eaten
fall	fell	fallen
find	found	found
flee	fled	fled
fly	flew	flown
forget	forgot	forgotten, forgot
freeze	froze	frozen
get	got	got, gotten
give	gave	given
go	went	gone
grow	grew	grown
hang (suspend)	hung	hung
hang (execute)	hanged	hanged
have	had	had
hear	heard	heard
hide	hid	hidden
hold	held	held
keep	kept	kept
know	knew	known
lay	laid	laid
lead	led	led
leave	left	left
lend	lent	lent
let	let	let
lie	lay	lain

Plain form	Past tense	Past participle
lose	lost	lost
pay	paid	paid
prove	proved	proved, proven
ride	rode	ridden
ring	rang	rung
rise	rose	risen
run	ran	run
say	said	said
see	saw	seen
set	set	set
shake	shook	shaken
shrink	shrank, shrunk	shrunk, shrunken
sing	sang, sung	sung
sink	sank, sunk	sunk
sit	sat	sat
sleep	slept	slept
slide	slid	slid
speak	spoke	spoken
spring	sprang, sprung	sprung
stand	stood	stood
steal	stole	stolen
swim	swam	swum
swing	swung	swung
take	took	taken
teach	taught	taught
tear	tore	torn
throw	threw	thrown
wear	wore	worn
write	wrote	written

Exercise 14.1 Using irregular verbs

For each irregular verb in brackets, give either the past tense or the past participle, as appropriate, and identify the form you used.

Example:

Though we had [hide] the cash box, it was [steal].

Though we had hidden the cash box, it was stolen. [Two past participles.]

1. The world population has [grow] by two-thirds of a billion people in less than a decade.
2. In 2000 it [break] the 6 billion mark.
3. Experts have [draw] pictures of a crowded future.
4. They predict that the world population may have [slide] up to as much as 10 billion by the year 2050.
5. Though the food supply [rise] in the last decade, the share to each person [fall].

14b Distinguish between *sit* and *set*, *lie* and *lay*, and *rise* and *raise*.

The forms of *sit* and *set*, *lie* and *lay*, and *rise* and *raise* are easy to confuse:

Plain form	Past tense	Past participle
sit	sat	sat
set	set	set
lie	lay	lain
lay	laid	laid
rise	rose	risen
raise	raised	raised

In each of these confusing pairs, one verb is **intransitive** (it does not take an object) and one is **transitive** (it does take an object). (See pp. 238–41 for more on this distinction.)

Intransitive

The patients lie in their beds. [*Lie* means "recline" and takes no object.]

Visitors sit with them. [*Sit* means "be seated" or "be located" and takes no object.]

Patients' temperatures rise. [*Rise* means "increase" or "get up" and takes no object.]

Transitive

Orderlies lay the dinner trays on tables. [*Lay* means "place" and takes an object, here *trays*.]

Orderlies set the trays down. [*Set* means "place" and takes an object, here *trays*.]

Nursing aides raise the shades. [*Raise* means "lift" or "bring up" and takes an object, here *shades*.]

Exercise 14.2 Distinguishing *sit/set*, *lie/lay*, *rise/raise*

Choose the correct verb from the pair given in brackets. Then supply the past tense or past participle, as appropriate.

Example:

After I washed all the windows, I [lie, lay] down the squeegee and then I [sit, set] the table.

After I washed all the windows, I laid down the squeegee and then I set the table.

1. Yesterday afternoon the child [lie, lay] down for a nap.
2. The child has been [rise, raise] by her grandparents.
3. Most days her grandfather has [sit, set] with her, reading her stories.
4. She has [rise, raise] at dawn most mornings.
5. Her toys were [lie, lay] out on the floor.

14c Use the -s and -ed forms of the verb when they are required. CULTURE LANGUAGE

Speakers of some English dialects and nonnative speakers of English sometimes omit the -s and -ed verb endings when they are required in standard American English.

Grammar checkers A grammar checker will flag many omitted -s and -ed endings from verbs, such as in *he ask* and *was ask*. But it will miss many omissions, too.

Required -s ending

Use the -s form of a verb when *both* of these situations hold:

- **The subject is a singular noun** (*boy*), **an indefinite pronoun** (*everyone*), **or** *he, she,* **or** *it*. These subjects are **third person**, used when someone or something is being spoken about.
- **The verb's action occurs in the present.**

> The letter asks [not ask] for a quick response.
> Delay costs [not cost] money.

Be especially careful with the -s forms of *be* (*is*), *have* (*has*), and *do* (*does, doesn't*). These forms should always be used to indicate present time with third-person singular subjects.

> The company is [not be] late in responding.
> It has [not have] problems.
> It doesn't [not don't] have the needed data.
> The contract does [not do] depend on the response.

In addition, *be* has an -s form in the past tense with *I* and with third-person singular subjects:

> The company was [not were] in trouble before.

I, you, and plural subjects do *not* take the -s form of verbs:

> I am [not is] a student.
> You are [not is] also a student.
> They are [not is] students, too.

Required -ed or -d ending

The -ed or -d verb form is required in *any* of these situations:

- **The verb's action occurred in the past:**

> Yesterday the company asked [not ask] for more time.

- **The verb form functions as a modifier:**

> The data concerned [not concern] should be retrievable.

■ **The verb form combines with a form of *be* or *have*:**

The company is <u>supposed</u> [not <u>suppose</u>] to be the best.
It has <u>developed</u> [not <u>develop</u>] an excellent reputation.

Watch especially for a needed *-ed* or *-d* ending when it isn't pronounced clearly in speech, as in *asked, discussed, mixed, supposed, walked,* and *used.*

Exercise 14.3 Using *-s* and *-ed* verb endings

Supply the correct form of each verb in brackets. Be careful to include *-s* and *-ed* (or *-d*) endings where they are needed for standard English.

A teacher sometimes [ask] too much of a student. In high school I was once [punish] for being sick. I had [miss] some school, and I [realize] that I would fail a test unless I had a chance to make up the classwork. I [discuss] the problem with the teacher, but he said I was [suppose] to make up the work while I was sick. At that I [walk] out of the class. I [receive] a failing grade then, but it did not change my attitude. Today I still balk when a teacher [make] unreasonable demands or [expect] miracles.

| **14d** | Use helping verbs with main verbs appropriately. | |

Helping verbs combine with main verbs to form verb phrases (see p. 276).

Common helping verbs

Forms of *be:* be, am, is, are, was, were, been, being
Forms of *have:* have, has, had, having
Forms of *do:* do, does, did

be able to	had better	must	used to
be supposed to	have to	ought to	will
can	may	shall	would
could	might	should	

Grammar checkers A grammar checker often spots omitted helping verbs and incorrect main verbs with helping verbs, but sometimes it does not. A checker flagged *Many been fortunate* and *She working* but overlooked other examples on the following pages.

1 Use helping verbs when they are required.

Standard American English requires helping verbs in certain situations:

- **The main verb ends in -*ing*:**

  Researchers <u>are</u> conducting fieldwork all over the world. [Not <u>Researchers</u> <u>conducting</u>. . . .]

- **The main verb is *been* or *be*:**

  Many <u>have</u> been fortunate in their discoveries. [Not <u>Many been</u>. . . .]
  Some <u>could</u> be real-life Indiana Joneses. [Not <u>Some be</u>. . . .]

- **The main verb is a past participle, such as *talked, begun*, or *thrown*.**

  Their discoveries <u>were</u> covered in newspapers and magazines. [Not <u>Their</u> <u>discoveries covered</u>. . . .]

  Often the researchers <u>have</u> done TV interviews. [Not <u>the researchers</u> <u>done</u>. . . .]

In every example above, omitting the helping verb would create an incomplete sentence, or **sentence fragment** (see Chapter 17). In a complete sentence, some part of the verb (helping or main) must be capable of changing form to show changes in time: *I run, I ran; you are running, you were running* (see p. 332). But a present participle (*conducting*), an irregular past participle (*been*), and the infinitive *be* cannot change form in this way. They need helping verbs to work as sentence verbs.

2 **Combine helping verbs and main verbs appropriately for your meaning.**

Helping verbs and main verbs combine into verb phrases in specific ways.

Note The main verb in a verb phrase (the one carrying the main meaning) does not change to show a change in subject or time: *she has <u>studied</u>, you had <u>studied</u>*. Only the helping verb may change.

Form of *be* + present participle

The **progressive tenses** indicate action in progress (see p. 294). Create them with *be, am, is, are, was, were*, or *been* followed by the main verb's present participle:

She <u>is working</u> on a new book.

Be and *been* always require additional helping verbs to form the progressive tenses:

can	might	should	} be working	have	} been working
could	must	will		has	
may	shall	would		had	

When forming the progressive tenses, be sure to use the *-ing* form of the main verb:

Faulty   Her ideas are <u>grow</u> more complex. She is <u>developed</u> a new approach to ethics.

Revised   Her ideas are <u>growing</u> more complex. She is <u>developing</u> a new approach to ethics.

Form of *be* + past participle

The **passive voice** of the verb indicates that the subject *receives* the action of the verb (see p. 300). Create the passive voice with *be, am, is, are, was, were, being,* or *been* followed by the main verb's past participle:

Her latest book <u>was completed</u> in four months.

Be, being, and *been* always require additional helping verbs to form the passive voice:

have ⎫
has ⎬ <u>been</u> completed
had ⎭

am was ⎫
is   were ⎬ <u>being</u> completed
are   ⎭

will <u>be</u> completed

Be sure to use the main verb's past participle for the passive voice:

Faulty   Her next book will be <u>publish</u> soon.

Revised   Her next book will be <u>published</u> soon.

Note Only transitive verbs may form the passive voice:

Faulty   A philosophy conference <u>will be occurred</u> in the same week. [*Occur* is not a transitive verb.]

Revised   A philosophy conference <u>will occur</u> in the same week.

See pages 301–02 for advice on when to use and when to avoid the passive voice.

Forms of *have*

Four forms of *have* serve as helping verbs: *have, has, had, having*. One of these forms plus the main verb's past participle creates one of the **perfect tenses**, those expressing action completed before another specific time or action (see p. 293):

Some students <u>have complained</u> about the laboratory.
Others <u>had complained</u> before.

Will and other helping verbs sometimes accompany forms of *have* in the perfect tenses:

Several more students <u>will have complained</u> by the end of the week.

Forms of do

Do, does, and *did* have three uses as helping verbs, always with the plain form of the main verb:

- **To pose a question:** *How did the trial end?*
- **To emphasize the main verb:** *It did end eventually.*
- **To negate the main verb, along with** *not* **or** *never:* The judge *did not withdraw*.

Be sure to use the main verb's plain form with any form of *do:*

Faulty   The judge did remained in court.
Revised   The judge did remain in court.

Modals

The modal helping verbs include *can, could, may,* and *might,* along with several two- and three-word combinations, such as *have to* and *be able to.* (See p. 282 for a list of helping verbs.) Use the plain form of the main verb with a modal unless the modal combines with another helping verb (usually *have*):

Faulty   The equipment can detects small vibrations. It should have detect the change.
Revised   The equipment can detect small vibrations. It should have detected the change.

Modals convey various meanings, with these being most common:

- **Ability:** *can, could, be able to*

The equipment can detect small vibrations. [Present.]
The equipment could detect small vibrations. [Past.]
The equipment is able to detect small vibrations. [Present. Past: was able to. Future: will be able to.]

- **Possibility:** *could, may, might; could/may/might have* + past participle

The equipment could fail. [Present.]
The equipment may fail. [Present or future.]
The equipment might fail. [Present or future.]
The equipment may have failed. [Past.]

- **Necessity or obligation:** *must, have to, be supposed to*

The lab must purchase a backup. [Present or future.]
The lab has to purchase a backup. [Present or future. Past: had to.]
The lab will have to purchase a backup. [Future.]
The lab is supposed to purchase a backup. [Present. Past: was supposed to.]

- **Permission:** *may, can, could*

The lab <u>may spend</u> the money. [Present or future.]
The lab <u>can spend</u> the money. [Present or future.]
The lab <u>could spend</u> the money. [Present or future, more tentative.]
With budget approval, the lab <u>could have spent</u> the money. [Past.]

- **Intention:** *will, shall, would*

The lab <u>will spend</u> the money. [Future.]
<u>Shall</u> we <u>offer</u> advice? [Future. Use *shall* for questions requesting opinion or consent.]
We <u>would have offered</u> advice. [Past.]

- **Request:** *could, can, would*

<u>Could</u> [or <u>Can</u> or <u>Would</u>] you please <u>obtain</u> a bid? [Present or future.]

- **Advisability:** *should, had better, ought to; should have* + past participle

You <u>should obtain</u> three bids. [Present or future.]
You <u>had better obtain</u> three bids. [Present or future.]
You <u>ought to obtain</u> three bids. [Present or future.]
You <u>should have obtained</u> three bids. [Past.]

- **Past habit:** *would, used to*

In years past we <u>would obtain</u> five bids.
We <u>used to obtain</u> five bids.

Exercise 14.4 Using helping verbs

Add helping verbs in the following sentences where they are needed for standard English.

> *Example:*
> The story been told for many years.
> The story <u>has</u> been told for many years.

1. Each year thousands of new readers been discovering Agatha Christie's mysteries.
2. The books written by a prim woman who had worked as a nurse during World War I.
3. Christie never expected that her play *The Mousetrap* be performed for decades.
4. During her life Christie always complaining about movie versions of her stories.
5. Readers of her stories been delighted to be baffled by her.

Exercise 14.5 Revising: Helping verbs plus main verbs

Revise the following sentences so that helping verbs and main verbs are used correctly. Mark the number preceding any sentence that is already correct.

Example:

The college testing service has test as many as five hundred students at one time.

The college testing service has <u>tested</u> as many as five hundred students at one time.

1. A report from the Bureau of the Census has confirm a widening gap between rich and poor.
2. As suspected, the percentage of people below the poverty level did increased over the last decade.
3. More than 17 percent of the population is make 5 percent of all the income.
4. About 1 percent of the population will keeping an average of $500,000 apiece after taxes.
5. The other 99 percent all together will retain about $300,000.

14e Use a gerund or an infinitive after a verb as appropriate.

Nonnative speakers of English sometimes stumble over using a gerund or an infinitive after a verb. A **gerund** is the *-ing* form of a verb used as a noun (*opening*). An **infinitive** is the plain form of a verb preceded by *to* (*to open*). (See pp. 248–49 for more on these forms.)

Gerunds and infinitives may follow certain verbs but not others. And sometimes the use of a gerund or infinitive with the same verb changes the meaning.

Grammar checkers A grammar checker will spot some but not all errors in matching gerunds or infinitives with verbs. For example, a checker failed to flag *I practice to swim* and *I promise helping out*. Use the lists given here and a dictionary of English as a second language to determine whether an infinitive or a gerund is appropriate. (See p. 515 for a list of ESL dictionaries.)

Either gerund or infinitive

A gerund or an infinitive may follow these verbs with no significant difference in meaning:

begin	hate	love
can't bear	hesitate	prefer
can't stand	intend	start
continue	like	

The pump began <u>working</u>.
The pump began <u>to work</u>.

Meaning change with gerund or infinitive

With four verbs, a gerund has quite a different meaning from an infinitive:

forget	stop
remember	try

The engineer stopped <u>eating</u>. [He no longer ate.]
The engineer stopped <u>to eat</u>. [He stopped in order to eat.]

Gerund, not infinitive

Do not use an infinitive after these verbs:

admit	discuss	mind	recollect
adore	dislike	miss	resent
appreciate	enjoy	postpone	resist
avoid	escape	practice	risk
consider	finish	put off	suggest
deny	imagine	quit	tolerate
detest	keep	recall	understand

Faulty   He finished <u>to eat</u> lunch.
Revised   He finished <u>eating</u> lunch.

Infinitive, not gerund

Do not use a gerund after these verbs:

agree	decide	mean	refuse
appear	expect	offer	say
ask	have	plan	wait
assent	hope	pretend	want
beg	manage	promise	wish
claim			

Faulty   He decided <u>checking</u> the pump.
Revised   He decided <u>to check</u> the pump.

Noun or pronoun + infinitive

Some verbs may be followed by an infinitive alone or by a noun or pronoun and an infinitive. The presence of a noun or pronoun changes the meaning.

ask	dare	need	wish
beg	expect	promise	would like
choose	help	want	

He expected <u>to watch</u>.
He expected <u>his workers to watch</u>.

Some verbs *must* be followed by a noun or pronoun before an infinitive:

admonish	allow	challenge	convince
advise	cause	command	encourage

forbid	oblige	remind	tell
force	order	request	train
hire	permit	require	urge
instruct	persuade	teach	warn
invite			

He instructed <u>his workers</u> <u>to watch</u>.

Do not use *to* before the infinitive when it follows one of these verbs and a noun or pronoun:

feel	make ("force")
have	see
hear	watch
let	

He let his workers <u>learn</u> by observation.

Exercise 14.6 Revising: Verbs plus gerunds or infinitives

Revise the following sentences so that gerunds or infinitives are used correctly with verbs. Mark the number preceding any sentence that is already correct.

> *Example:*
> A politician cannot avoid to alienate some voters.
> A politician cannot avoid <u>alienating</u> some voters.

1. A program called HELP Wanted tries to encourage citizens take action on behalf of American competitiveness.
2. Officials working on this program hope improving education for work.
3. American businesses find that their workers need learning to read.
4. In the next ten years the United States expects facing a shortage of 350,000 scientists.
5. HELP Wanted suggests creating a media campaign.

 Use the appropriate particles with two-word verbs.

Standard American English includes some verbs that consist of two words: the verb itself and a **particle**, a preposition or adverb that affects the meaning of the verb. For example:

<u>Look up</u> the answer. [Research the answer.]
<u>Look over</u> the answer. [Examine the answer.]

The meanings of these two-word verbs are often quite different from the meanings of the individual words that make them up. (There are some three-word verbs, too, such as *put up with* and *run out of*.)

A dictionary of English as a second language will define two-word verbs and say whether the verb may be separated in a sentence, as explained below. (See p. 515 for a list of ESL dictionaries.) A grammar checker will rarely recognize misused two-word verbs.

Note Many two-word verbs are more common in speech than in more formal academic or business writing. For formal writing, consider using *research* instead of *look up, examine* or *inspect* instead of *look over.*

Inseparable two-word verbs

Verbs and particles that may not be separated by any other words include the following:

call on	go out with	run across	stay away
catch on	go over	run into	stay up
come across	grow up	run out of	take care of
get along	keep on	speak up	turn out
get up	look for	speak with	turn up at
give in	look into	stand up	work for
go on	play around		

Faulty	Children <u>grow</u> quickly <u>up</u>.
Revised	Children <u>grow up</u> quickly.

Separable two-word verbs

Most two-word verbs that take direct objects may be separated by the object:

Parents <u>help out</u> their children.
Parents <u>help</u> their children <u>out</u>.

If the direct object is a pronoun, the pronoun *must* separate the verb from the particle:

Faulty	Parents <u>help out</u> them.
Revised	Parents <u>help</u> them <u>out</u>.

The separable two-word verbs include the following:

bring up	give back	make up	throw out
call off	hand in	point out	try on
call up	hand out	put away	try out
drop off	help out	put back	turn down
fill out	leave out	put off	turn on
fill up	look over	take out	wrap up
give away	look up	take over	

Exercise 14.7 Revising: Verbs plus particles

The two- and three-word verbs in the following sentences are underlined. Some are correct as given, and some are not because they should or should not be separated by other words. Revise the verbs and other words that are incorrect. Consult the lists on the preceding page or an ESL dictionary if necessary to determine whether verbs are separable.

Example:

Hollywood producers never seem to <u>come up with</u> entirely new plots, but they also never <u>run</u> new ways <u>out of</u> to present old ones.

Hollywood producers never seem to come up with [correct] entirely new plots, but they also never <u>run out of</u> new ways to present old ones.

1. American movies treat everything from <u>going out with</u> someone to <u>making up</u> an ethnic identity, but few people <u>look</u> their significance <u>into</u>.
2. While some viewers <u>stay away from</u> topical films, others <u>turn</u> at the theater <u>up</u> simply because a movie has sparked debate.
3. Some movies attracted rowdy spectators, and the theaters had to <u>throw out</u> them.
4. Filmmakers have always been eager to <u>point</u> their influence <u>out</u> to the public.
5. Everyone agrees that filmmakers will <u>keep</u> creating controversy <u>on</u>, if only because it can <u>fill up</u> theaters.

Tense

Tense shows the time of a verb's action. The box on the next page defines and illustrates the tense forms for a regular verb in the active voice. (See pp. 277 and 300 on regular verbs and voice.)

Grammar checkers A grammar checker can provide little help with incorrect verb tenses and tense sequences because correctness usually depends on meaning. You'll have to proofread carefully yourself to catch errors in tense or tense sequence.

CULTURE LANGUAGE In standard American English, a verb conveys time and sequence through its form. In some other languages and English dialects, various markers besides verb form may indicate the time of a verb. For instance, in African American dialect *I be attending class on Wednesday* means that the speaker attends class every Wednesday. To a speaker of standard American English, however, the sentence may be unclear: last Wednesday? this Wednesday? every Wednesday? The intended meaning must be indicated by verb tense: *I <u>attended</u> class on Wednesday. I <u>will attend</u> class on Wednesday. I <u>attend</u> class on Wednesday.*

my**comp**lab

Visit *mycomplab.com* for more resources and exercises on verb tense.

Tenses of a regular verb (active voice)

Present Action that is occurring now, occurs habitually, or is generally true

Simple present Plain form or -s form	**Present progressive** *Am, is,* or *are* plus *-ing* form
I walk. You/we/they walk. He/she/it walks.	I am walking. You/we/they are walking. He/she/it is walking.

Past Action that occurred before now

Simple past Past-tense form (-d or -ed)	**Past progressive** *Was* or *were* plus *-ing* form
I/he/she/it walked. You/we/they walked.	I/he/she/it was walking. You/we/they were walking.

Future Action that will occur in the future

Simple future Plain form plus *will*	**Future progressive** *Will be* plus *-ing* form
I/you/he/she/it/we/they will walk.	I/you/he/she/it/we/they will be walking.

Present perfect Action that began in the past and is linked to the present

Present perfect *Have* or *has* plus past participle (-d or -ed)	**Present perfect progressive** *Have been* or *has been* plus *-ing* form
I/you/we/they have walked. He/she/it has walked.	I/you/we/they have been walking. He/she/it has been walking.

Past perfect Action that was completed before another past action

Past perfect *Had* plus past participle (-d or -ed)	**Past perfect progressive** *Had been* plus *-ing* form
I/you/he/she/it/we/they had walked.	I/you/he/she/it/we/they had been walking.

Future perfect Action that will be completed before another future action

Future perfect *Will have* plus past participle (-d or -ed)	**Future perfect progressive** *Will have been* plus *-ing* form
I/you/he/she/it/we/they will have walked.	I/you/he/she/it/we/they will have been walking.

14g Use the appropriate tense to express your meaning.

Many errors in verb tense are actually errors in verb form like those discussed earlier. Still, the present tense, the perfect tenses, and the progressive tenses can cause problems.

1 Observe the special uses of the present tense.

The present tense has several distinctive uses:

Action occurring now

She <u>understands</u> the problem.
We <u>define</u> the problem differently.

Habitual or recurring action

Banks regularly <u>undergo</u> audits.
The audits <u>monitor</u> the banks' activities.

A general truth

The mills of the gods <u>grind</u> slowly.
The earth <u>is</u> round.

Discussion of literature, film, and so on (see also p. 704)

Huckleberry Finn <u>has</u> adventures we all envy.
In that article, the author <u>examines</u> several causes of crime.

Future time

Next week we <u>draft</u> a new budget.
Funding <u>ends</u> in less than a year.

(In the last two examples, time is really indicated by *Next week* and *in less than a year*.)

2 Observe the uses of the perfect tenses.

The perfect tenses generally indicate action completed before another specific time or action. (The term *perfect* derives from the Latin *perfectus*, "completed.") The present perfect tense also indicates action begun in the past and continued into the present. The perfect tenses consist of a form of *have* plus the verb's past participle.

present perfect
The dancer <u>has performed</u> here only once. [The action is completed at the time of the statement.]

present perfect
Critics <u>have written</u> about the performance ever since. [The action began in the past and continues now.]

past perfect
The dancer <u>had trained</u> in Asia before his performance. [The action was completed before another past action.]

future perfect
He <u>will have danced</u> here again by the end of the year. [The action begins now or in the future and will be completed by a specified time in the future.]

CULTURE LANGUAGE With the present perfect tense, the words *since* and *for* are followed by different information. After *since*, give a specific point in time: *The United States has been a* *member of the United Nations <u>since 1945</u>*. After *for*, give a span of time: *The United States has been a member of the United Nations <u>for many decades</u>*.

3 Observe the uses of the progressive tenses. CULTURE LANGUAGE

The progressive tenses indicate continuing (therefore progressive) action. In standard American English the progressive tenses consist of a form of *be* plus the verb's *-ing* form (present participle). (The words *be* and *been* must be combined with other helping verbs. See pp. 283–84.)

present progressive
The economy <u>is improving</u>.

past progressive
Last year the economy <u>was stagnating</u>.

future progressive
Economists <u>will be watching</u> for signs of growth.

present perfect progressive
The government <u>has been expecting</u> an upturn.

past perfect progressive
Various indicators <u>had been suggesting</u> improvement.

future perfect progressive
By the end of this month, investors <u>will have been pushing</u> the markets up for half a year.

Note Verbs that express unchanging states (especially mental states) rather than physical actions do not usually appear in the progressive tenses. These verbs include *adore, appear, believe, belong, care, doubt, hate, have, hear, imagine, know, like, love, mean, need, own, prefer, realize, remember, see, sound, taste, think, understand,* and *want*.

Faulty   She <u>is wanting</u> to study ethics.
Revised   She <u>wants</u> to study ethics.

14h Use the appropriate sequence of verb tenses.

The term **sequence of tenses** refers to the relation between the verb tense in a main clause and the verb tense in a subordinate clause or phrase. The tenses should change when necessary to reflect changes in actual or relative time. (For a discussion of tense shifts—changes *not* required by meaning—see p. 357.)

1 Use the appropriate tense sequence with infinitives.

The **present infinitive** is the verb's plain form preceded by *to*. It indicates action *at the same time* as or *later* than that of the verb:

verb: infinitive:
present perfect   present

She <u>would have liked</u> <u>to see</u> [not to have seen] change before now.

The verb's **perfect infinitive** consists of *to have* followed by the past participle, as in *to have talked, to have won*. It indicates action *earlier* than that of the verb:

verb: infinitive:
present   perfect

Other researchers <u>would like</u> [not would have liked] <u>to have seen</u> change as well.

2 Use the appropriate tense sequence with participles.

The present participle shows action occurring *at the same time* as that of the verb:

participle: verb:
present   past perfect

<u>Testing</u> a large group, the researcher <u>had posed</u> multiple-choice questions.

The past participle and the present perfect participle show action occurring *earlier* than that of the verb:

participle: verb:
past   past

<u>Prepared</u> by earlier failures, she <u>knew</u> not to ask open questions.

participle: verb:
present perfect   past

<u>Having tested</u> many people, she <u>understood</u> the process.

3 Use the appropriate tense sequence with the past or past perfect tense.

When the verb in the main clause is in the past or past perfect tense, the verb in the subordinate clause must also be past or past perfect:

main clause: subordinate clause:
past   past

The researchers <u>discovered</u> that people <u>varied</u> widely in their knowledge of public events.

main clause: subordinate clause:
past   past perfect

The variation <u>occurred</u> because respondents <u>had been born</u> in different decades.

main clause: subordinate clause:
past perfect   past

None of them <u>had been born</u> when Warren G. Harding <u>was</u> President.

Exception Always use the present tense for a general truth, such as *The earth is round:*

main clause: subordinate clause:
past   present

Most <u>understood</u> that popular Presidents <u>are</u> not necessarily good Presidents.

4 Use the appropriate tense sequence in conditional sentences.

A **conditional sentence** states a factual relation between cause and effect, makes a prediction, or speculates about what might happen. Such a sentence usually contains a subordinate clause beginning with *if, when,* or *unless* along with a main clause stating the result. The three kinds of conditional sentences use distinctive verbs.

Factual relation

Statements linking factual causes and effects use matched tenses in the subordinate and main clauses:

> subordinate clause: main clause:
> present   present
> When a voter <u>casts</u> a ballot, he or she <u>has</u> complete privacy.

> subordinate clause: main clause:
> past   past
> When voters <u>registered</u> in some states, they <u>had</u> to pay a poll tax.

Prediction

Predictions generally use the present tense in the subordinate clause and the future tense in the main clause:

> subordinate clause: main clause:
> present   future
> Unless citizens <u>regain</u> faith in politics, they <u>will</u> not <u>vote</u>.

Sometimes the verb in the main clause consists of *may, can, should,* or *might* plus the verb's plain form: *If citizens <u>regain</u> faith, they <u>may vote</u>.*

Speculation

The verbs in speculations depend on whether the linked events are possible or impossible. For possible events in the present, use the past tense in the subordinate clause and *would, could,* or *might* plus the verb's plain form in the main clause:

> subordinate clause: main clause:
> past   *would* + plain form
> If voters <u>had</u> more confidence, they <u>would vote</u> more often.

Use *were* instead of *was* in the subordinate clause, even when the subject is *I, he, she, it* or a singular noun. (See p. 299 for more on this distinctive verb form.)

> subordinate clause: main clause:
> past   *would* + plain form
> If the voter <u>were</u> more confident, he or she <u>would vote</u> more often.

For impossible events in the present—events that are contrary to fact—use the same forms as above (including the distinctive *were* when applicable):

> subordinate clause: main clause:
> past   *might* + plain form
> If Lincoln <u>were</u> alive, he <u>might inspire</u> confidence.

For impossible events in the past, use the past perfect tense in the subordinate clause and *would, could,* or *might* plus the present perfect tense in the main clause:

subordinate clause: main clause:
past perfect   *might* + present perfect

If Lincoln had lived past the Civil War, he might have helped stabilize the country.

Exercise 14.8 Adjusting tense sequence: Past or past perfect tense

The tenses in each sentence below are in correct sequence. Change the tense of one verb as instructed. Then change the tense of infinitives, participles, and other verbs to restore correct sequence. Some items have more than one possible answer.

Example:

Delgado will call when he reaches his destination. (*Change will call to called.*)

Delgado called when he reached [or had reached] his destination.

1. Diaries that Adolf Hitler is supposed to have written have surfaced in Germany. (*Change have surfaced to had surfaced.*)
2. Many people believe that the diaries are authentic because a well-known historian has declared them so. (*Change believe to believed.*)
3. However, the historian's evaluation has been questioned by other authorities, who call the diaries forgeries. (*Change has been questioned to was questioned.*)
4. They claim, among other things, that the paper is not old enough to have been used by Hitler. (*Change claim to claimed.*)
5. Eventually, the doubters will win the debate because they have the best evidence. (*Change will win to won.*)

Exercise 14.9 Revising: Tense sequence with conditional sentences

Supply the appropriate tense for each verb in brackets below.

Example:

If Babe Ruth or Jim Thorpe [be] athletes today, they [remind] us that even sports heroes must contend with a harsh reality.

If Babe Ruth or Jim Thorpe were athletes today, they might [or could or would] remind us that even sports heroes must contend with a harsh reality.

1. When an athlete [turn] professional, he or she [commit] to a grueling regimen of mental and physical training.
2. If athletes [be] less committed, they [disappoint] teammates, fans, and themselves.
3. If professional athletes [be] very lucky, they [play] until age forty.
4. Unless an athlete [achieve] celebrity status, he or she [have] few employment choices after retirement.
5. If professional sports [be] less risky, athletes [have] longer careers and more choices after retirement.

Mood

Mood in grammar is a verb form that indicates the writer's or speaker's attitude toward what he or she is saying. The **indicative mood** states a fact or opinion or asks a question:

> The theater needs help. [Opinion.]
> The ceiling is falling. [Fact.]
> Will you contribute to the theater? [Question.]

The **imperative mood** expresses a command or gives a direction. It omits the subject of the sentence, *you:*

> Help the theater. [Command.]
> Send contributions to the theater. [Direction.]

The **subjunctive mood** expresses a suggestion, a requirement, or a desire, or it states a condition that is contrary to fact (that is, imaginary or hypothetical). The subjunctive mood uses distinctive verb forms.

■ **Suggestion or requirement: plain form with all subjects.**

> The manager asked that he donate money. [Suggestion.]
> Rules require that every donation be mailed. [Requirement.]

■ **Desire or present condition contrary to fact: past tense; for *be*,** the past tense *were* for all subjects, singular as well as plural.

> We wish that the theater had more money. [Desire.]
> It would be in better shape if it were better funded. [Present condition contrary to fact.]

■ **Past condition contrary to fact: past perfect.**

> The theater could have been better funded if it had been better managed.

Note that with conditions contrary to fact, the verb in the main clause also expresses the imaginary or hypothetical with the helping verb *could, would,* or *might.* (See also p. 296.)

For a discussion of keeping mood consistent within and among sentences, see page 357.

14i Use the subjunctive verb forms appropriately.

Contemporary English uses distinctive subjunctive verb forms in only a few constructions and idioms. (For the sequence of tenses in many subjunctive sentences, see pp. 296–97.)

mycomplab

Visit *mycomplab.com* for more resources and exercises on verb mood.

Grammar checkers A grammar checker may spot some simple errors in the subjunctive mood, but it may miss others. For example, a checker flagged *I wish I <u>was</u> home* (should be <u>were</u> *home*) but not *If I had a hammer, I <u>will</u> hammer in the morning* (should be <u>would</u> *hammer*).

1 Use the subjunctive in contrary-to-fact clauses beginning with *if* or expressing desire.

If the theater <u>were</u> saved, the town would benefit.
We all wish the theater <u>were</u> not so decrepit.
I wish I <u>were</u> able to donate money.

Note The indicative form *was* (*We all wish the theater <u>was</u> not so decrepit*) is common in speech and in some informal writing, but the subjunctive *were* is usual in formal English.

Not all clauses beginning with *if* express conditions contrary to fact. In the sentence *If Joe <u>is</u> out of town, he hasn't heard the news*, the verb *is* is correct because the clause refers to a condition presumed to exist.

2 Use *would, could,* or *might* only in the main clause of a conditional statement.

The helping verb *would, could,* or *might* appears in the main clause of a sentence expressing a condition contrary to fact. The helping verb does not appear in the subordinate clause beginning with *if:*

Not   Many people would have helped if they <u>would have</u> known.
But   Many people would have helped if they <u>had</u> known.

3 Use the subjunctive in *that* clauses following verbs that demand, request, or recommend.

Verbs such as *ask, demand, insist, mandate, recommend, request, require, suggest,* and *urge* indicate demand or suggestion. They often precede subordinate clauses beginning with *that* and containing the substance of the demand or suggestion. The verb in such a *that* clause should be in the subjunctive mood:

The board urged that everyone <u>contribute</u>.
The members insisted that they themselves <u>be</u> donors.
They suggested that each <u>donate</u> both time and money.

Note These constructions have widely used alternative forms that do not require the subjunctive, such as *The board urged everyone to contribute* and *The members insisted on donating*.

Exercise 14.10 Revising: Subjunctive mood

Revise the following sentences with appropriate subjunctive verb forms.

Example:

I would help the old man if I was able to reach him.
I would help the old man if I <u>were</u> able to reach him.

1. If John Hawkins would have known of the dangerous side effects of smoking tobacco, would he have introduced the dried plant to England in 1565?
2. Hawkins noted that if a Florida Indian was to travel for several days, he would have smoked tobacco to satisfy his hunger and thirst.
3. Early tobacco growers feared that their product would not gain acceptance unless it was perceived as healthful.
4. To prevent fires, in 1646 the General Court of Massachusetts passed a law requiring that colonists smoked tobacco only if they were five miles from any town.
5. To prevent decadence, in 1647 Connecticut passed a law mandating that one's smoking of tobacco was limited to once a day in one's own home.

Voice

The **voice** of a verb tells whether the subject of the sentence performs the action (**active voice**) or is acted upon (**passive voice**). In the passive voice, the actual actor may be named in a prepositional phrase (such as *by the city*) or may be omitted.

> **CULTURE LANGUAGE** A passive verb always consists of a form of *be* plus the past participle of the main verb: *rents <u>are controlled</u>*. Other helping verbs must also be used with *be, being,* and *been: rents <u>have been controlled</u>*. Only a transitive verb (one that takes an object) may be used in the passive voice. (See p. 284.)

Converting passive to active

To change a passive verb to active, name the verb's actor as the subject, use an active verb form, and convert the old subject into an object:

	subject	passive verb	
Passive	Tenants	are protected	by leases.
	new subject	active verb	old subject = object
Active	Leases	protect	tenants.

mycomplab

Visit *mycomplab.com* for more resources and exercises on verb voice.

Active and passive voice

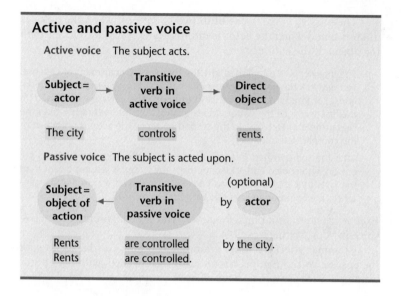

Active voice The subject acts.

Subject = actor	Transitive verb in active voice	Direct object
The city	controls	rents.

Passive voice The subject is acted upon.

Subject = object of action	Transitive verb in passive voice	(optional) by actor
Rents	are controlled	by the city.
Rents	are controlled.	

Converting active to passive

To change a transitive verb from active to passive voice, convert either an indirect object or a direct object into the subject of the sentence, and use the passive verb form:

	subject	transitive verb	indirect object	direct object
Active	The city	gives	tenants	leases.

	new subject	passive verb	direct object	
Passive	Tenants	are given	leases.	

	new subject	passive verb	old indirect object	old subject
	Leases	are given	to tenants	by the city.

14j Generally, prefer the active voice. Use the passive voice when the actor is unknown or unimportant.

Because the passive omits or de-emphasizes the actor (the performer of the verb's action), it can deprive writing of vigor and is often vague or confusing. The active voice is usually stronger, clearer, and more forthright.

Weak passive	The library is used by students and teachers for studying and research, and the plan to expand it has been praised by many.
Strong active	Students and teachers use the library for studying and research, and many have praised the plan to expand it.

The passive voice is useful in two situations: when the actor is unknown and when the actor is unimportant or less important than the object of the action.

> The Internet <u>was established</u> in 1969 by the US Department of Defense. The network <u>has been extended</u> internationally to governments, foundations, corporations, educational institutions, and private individuals. [In the first sentence the writer wishes to stress the Internet rather than the Department of Defense. In the second sentence the actor is unknown or too complicated to name.]

> After the solution <u>had been cooled</u> to 10°C, the acid <u>was added</u>. [The person who cooled and added, perhaps the writer, is less important than the facts that the solution was cooled and acid was added. Passive sentences are common in scientific writing. See p. 770.]

Except in such situations, however, you should prefer the active voice in your writing.

Grammar checkers Most grammar checkers can be set to spot the passive voice. (See pp. 65–66.) But the checkers will flag appropriate passives as well, such as when the actor is unknown.

Exercise 14.11 Converting between active and passive voices

To practice using the two voices of the verb, convert the following sentences from active to passive or from passive to active. (In converting from passive to active, you may have to add a subject for the new sentence.) Which version of each sentence seems more effective, and why? For additional exercises with the passive voice, see pages 264 and 382.

Example:
The aspiring actor was discovered in a nightclub.
A <u>talent scout</u> <u>discovered</u> the aspiring actor in a nightclub.

1. When the Eiffel Tower was built in 1889, it was thought by the French to be ugly.
2. At that time many people still resisted industrial technology.
3. The tower's naked steel construction epitomized this technology.
4. Beautiful ornament was expected to grace fine buildings.
5. Further, the tower could not even be called a building because it had no solid walls.

Exercise 14.12 Revising: Verb forms, tense, mood

Mark all the verbs and verbals in the following paragraph and correct their form, tense, or mood if necessary.

For centuries the natives of Melanesia, a group of islands laying northeast of Australia, have practice an unusual religion. It began in the eighteenth century when European explorers first have visited the islands. The natives were fascinated by the rich goods or "cargo" possessed by the explorers. They saw the wealth as treasures of the gods, and cargo cults eventually had arised among them. Over the centuries some Melanesians turned to Christianity in the belief that the white man's religion will bring them the white man's treasures. During World War II, US soldiers, having arrived by boat and airplane to have occupied some of the islands, introduced new and even more wonderful cargo. Even today some leaders of the cargo cults insist that the airplane is worship as a vehicle of the Melanesians' future salvation.

Note See page 329 for an exercise involving verbs along with other aspects of grammar.

15

Agreement

Agreement helps readers understand the relations between elements in a sentence. Subjects and verbs agree in number and person:

More Japanese Americans live in Hawaii and California than elsewhere.
subject · · · · · verb

Daniel Inouye was the first Japanese American in Congress.
subject · · · verb

Pronouns and their **antecedents**—the words they refer to—agree in person, number, and gender:

Inouye makes his home in Hawaii.
antecedent · · pronoun

Hawaiians value his work for them.
antecedent · · · · · pronoun

15a Make subjects and verbs agree in number.

Most subject-verb agreement problems arise when endings are omitted from subjects or verbs or when the relation between sentence parts is uncertain.

Visit *mycomplab.com* for more resources and exercises on subject-verb and pronoun-antecedent agreement.

Person and number in subject-verb agreement

	Number	
Person	Singular	Plural
First	I eat.	We eat.
Second	You eat.	You eat.
Third	He/she/it eats.	They eat.
	The bird eats.	Birds eat.

Grammar checkers A grammar checker will catch many simple errors in subject-verb agreement, such as *Addie and John is late,* and some more complicated errors, such as *Is Margaret and Tom going with us?* (should be *are* in both cases). But a checker failed to flag *The old group has gone their separate ways* (should be *have*) and offered a wrong correction for *The old group have gone their separate ways,* which is already correct.

1 **The -s and -es endings work differently for nouns and verbs.**

An *-s* or *-es* ending does opposite things to nouns and verbs: it usually makes a noun *plural,* but it always makes a present-tense verb *singular.* Thus a singular noun as subject will not end in *-s,* but its verb will. A plural noun as subject will end in *-s,* but its verb will not. **Between them, subject and verb use only one -s ending.**

Singular	Plural
The boy plays.	The boys play.
The bird soars.	The birds soar.

The only exceptions to these rules involve the nouns that form irregular plurals, such as *child/children, woman/women.* The irregular plural still requires a plural verb: The *children play.*

CULTURE LANGUAGE If your first language or dialect is not standard American English, subject-verb agreement may be problematic, especially for these reasons:

■ **Some English dialects follow different rules for subject-verb agreement,** such as omitting the *-s* ending for singular verbs or using the *-s* ending for plural verbs.

Nonstandard	The voter resist change.
Standard	The voter resists change.
Standard	The voters resist change.

The verb *be* changes spelling for singular and plural in both present and past tenses. (See also p. 276.)

Nonstandard	Taxes is high. They was raised just last year.
Standard	Taxes are high. They were raised just last year.

Summary of subject-verb agreement

- **Basic subject-verb agreement** (opposite):

  singular singular   plural plural
  subject verb   subject verb
  The kite flies.   The kites fly.

- **Words between subject and verb** (p. 306):

  The kite with two tails flies badly. The tails of the kite compete.

- **Subjects joined by** *and* (p. 306):

  The kite and the bird are almost indistinguishable.

- **Subjects joined by** *or* **or** *nor* (p. 307):

  The kite or the bird dives. Kites or birds fill the sky.

- **Indefinite pronoun as subject** (p. 307):

  No one knows. All the spectators wonder.

- **Collective noun as subject** (p. 308):

  A flock appears. The flock disperse.

- **Verb preceding subject** (p. 309):

  Is the kite or the bird blue? Are the kite and the bird both blue?

- **Linking verb** (p. 309):

  The kite is a flier and a dipper.

- ***Who, which, that*** **as subject** (p. 309):

  The kite that flies longest wins. Kites that fall lose.

- **Subject with plural form and singular meaning** (p. 310):

  Aeronautics plays a role in kite flying.

- **Title or word named as word** (p. 310):

  Kite Dynamics is one title. *Vectors* is a key word.

Have also has a distinctive *-s* form, *has:*

| Nonstandard | The new tax have little chance of passing. |
| Standard | The new tax has little chance of passing. |

- Some other languages change all *parts of* verb phrases to match their subjects. In English verb phrases, however, only the helping verbs *be, have,* and *do* change for different subjects. The modal helping verbs—*can, may, should, will,* and others—do not change:

| Nonstandard | The tax <u>mays</u> pass next year. |
| Standard | The tax <u>may</u> pass next year. |

The main verb in a verb phrase also does not change for different subjects:

| Nonstandard | The tax may <u>passes</u> next year. |
| Standard | The tax may <u>pass</u> next year. |

2 **Subject and verb should agree even when other words come between them.**

When the subject and verb are interrupted by other words, make sure the verb agrees with the subject:

A catalog of courses and requirements often <u>baffles</u> [not <u>baffle</u>] students.

The requirements stated in the catalog <u>are</u> [not <u>is</u>] unclear.

Note Phrases beginning with *as well as, together with, along with,* and *in addition to* do not change the number of the subject:

The president, as well as the deans, <u>has</u> [not <u>have</u>] agreed to revise the catalog.

If you really mean *and* in such a sentence, use it. Then the subject is compound, and the verb should be plural: *The <u>president and the deans have agreed</u> to revise the catalog.*

3 **Subjects joined by *and* usually take plural verbs.**

Two or more subjects joined by *and* usually take a plural verb, whether one or all of the subjects are singular:

Frost and Roethke <u>were</u> contemporaries.

Frost, Roethke, Stevens, and Pound <u>are</u> among the great American poets.

Exceptions When the parts of the subject form a single idea or refer to a single person or thing, they take a singular verb:

Avocado and bean sprouts <u>is</u> a California sandwich.

When a compound subject is preceded by the adjective *each* or *every,* the verb is usually singular:

Each man, woman, and child <u>has</u> a right to be heard.

But a compound subject *followed* by *each* takes a plural verb:

The man and the woman each <u>have</u> different problems.

4 When parts of a subject are joined by *or* or *nor*, the verb agrees with the nearer part.

When all parts of a subject joined by *or* or *nor* are singular, the verb is singular; when all parts are plural, the verb is plural.

Either the painter or the carpenter <u>knows</u> the cost.

The cabinets or the bookcases <u>are</u> too costly.

When one part of the subject is singular and the other plural, avoid awkwardness by placing the plural part closer to the verb so that the verb is plural:

| Awkward | Neither the owners nor the contractor <u>agrees</u>. |
| Revised | Neither the contractor nor the owners <u>agree</u>. |

When the subject consists of nouns and pronouns of different person requiring different verb forms, the verb agrees with the nearer part of the subject. Reword if this construction is awkward:

| Awkward | Either Juarez or I <u>am</u> responsible. |
| Revised | Either Juarez <u>is</u> responsible, or I <u>am</u>. |

5 With an indefinite pronoun such as *anybody* or *all*, use a singular or plural verb as appropriate.

An **indefinite pronoun** is one that does not refer to a specific person or thing. Most indefinite pronouns take a singular verb, but some take a plural verb and some take a singular *or* a plural verb.

Common indefinite pronouns

Singular			Singular or plural	Plural
anybody	everyone	nothing	all	both
anyone	everything	one	any	few
anything	much	somebody	more	many
each	neither	someone	most	several
either	nobody	something	none	
everybody	no one		some	

The singular indefinite pronouns refer to a single unspecified person or thing, and they take a singular verb:

Something smells.   Neither is right.

The plural indefinite pronouns refer to more than one unspecified thing, and they take a plural verb:

Both are correct.   Several were invited.

The other indefinite pronouns take a singular or a plural verb depending on whether the word they refer to is singular or plural. The word may be stated in the sentence:

All of the money is reserved for emergencies.

All of the funds are reserved for emergencies.

The word referred to by the pronoun may also be implied:

All are planning to attend. [*All* implies "all the people."]

All is lost. [*All* implies "everything."]

> **CULTURE LANGUAGE** See page 328 for the distinction between *few* ("not many") and *a few* ("some").

6 Collective nouns *such as group* take singular or plural verbs depending on meaning.

A **collective noun** has singular form but names a group of individuals or things—for example, *army, audience, committee, crowd, family, group, team.* As a subject, a collective noun may take a singular or plural verb, depending on the context. When the group acts as one unit, use a singular verb:

The group agrees that action is necessary.

But when considering the group's members as individuals who act separately, use the plural form of the verb:

The old group have gone their separate ways.

The collective noun *number* may be singular or plural. Preceded by *a*, it is plural; preceded by *the*, it is singular.

A number of people are in debt.

The number of people in debt is very large.

> **CULTURE LANGUAGE** In English some noncount nouns (nouns that don't form plurals) are collective nouns because they

name groups: for instance, *furniture, clothing, mail*. These noncount nouns usually take singular verbs: *Mail arrives daily.* But some of these nouns take plural verbs, including *clergy, military, people, police*, and any collective noun that comes from an adjective, such as *the poor, the rich, the young, the elderly*. If you mean one representative of the group, use a singular noun such as *police officer* or *poor person*.

7 The verb agrees with the subject even when it precedes the subject.

The verb precedes the subject mainly in questions and in constructions beginning with *there* or *here* and a form of *be:*

Is voting a right or a privilege?

Are a right and a privilege the same thing?

There are differences between them.

In constructions beginning with *there or here*, you may use *is* before a compound subject when the first element in the subject is singular:

Here lies both the problem and its solution.

Word order may sometimes be reversed for emphasis. The verb still agrees with its subject:

From the mountains comes an eerie, shimmering light.

8 A linking verb agrees with its subject, not the subject complement.

A linking verb such as *is* or *are* should agree with its subject, usually the first element in the sentence, not with the noun or pronoun serving as a subject complement (see pp. 239–40):

The child's sole support is her court-appointed guardians.

Her court-appointed guardians are the child's sole support.

9 *Who, which,* and *that* take verbs that agree with their antecedents.

When used as subjects, *who, which,* and *that* refer to another word in the sentence, called the **antecedent**. The verb agrees with the antecedent:

Mayor Garber ought to listen to the people who work for her.

Bardini is the only aide who has her ear.

Agreement problems often occur with who, which, or that when the sentence includes *one of the* or *the only one of the:*

Bardini is one of the aides who work unpaid. [Of the aides who work unpaid, Bardini is one.]

Bardini is the only one of the aides who knows the community. [Of the aides, only one, Bardini, knows the community.]

CULTURE LANGUAGE In phrases like those above beginning with *one of the*, be sure the noun is plural: *Bardini is one of the aides* [not *aide*] *who work unpaid.*

10 **Nouns with plural form but singular meaning, *such as news*, take singular verbs.**

Some nouns with plural form (that is, ending in -s) are usually regarded as singular in meaning. They include *athletics, economics, mathematics, measles, mumps, news, physics, politics,* and *statistics,* as well as place names such as *Athens, Wales,* and *United States.*

After so long a wait, the news has to be good.

Statistics is required of psychology majors.

A few of these words take plural verbs only when they describe individual items rather than whole bodies of activity or knowledge: *The statistics prove him wrong.*

Measurements and figures ending in -s may also be singular when the quantity they refer to is a unit:

Three years is a long time to wait.

Three-fourths of the library consists of reference books.

11 **Titles and words named as words take singular verbs.**

When your sentence subject is the name of a corporation, the title of a work (such as a book), or a word you are defining or describing, the verb should be singular even if the name, title, or word is plural:

Hakada Associates is a new firm.

Dream Days remains a favorite book.

Folks is a down-home word for *people.*

Exercise 15.1 Revising: Subject-verb agreement

Revise the verbs in the following sentences as needed to make subjects and verbs agree in number. If the sentence is already correct as given, mark the number preceding it.

Example:
Each of the job applicants type sixty words per minute.
Each of the job applicants <u>types</u> sixty words per minute.

1. Weinstein & Associates are a consulting firm that try to make businesspeople laugh.
2. Statistics from recent research suggests that humor relieves stress.
3. Reduced stress in businesses in turn reduce illness and absenteeism.
4. Reduced stress can also reduce friction within an employee group, which then work more productively.
5. In special conferences held by one consultant, each of the participants practice making the others laugh.
6. One consultant to many companies suggest cultivating office humor with practical jokes such as a rubber fish in the water cooler.
7. When employees or their manager regularly post cartoons on the bulletin board, office spirit usually picks up.
8. When someone who has seemed too easily distracted is entrusted with updating the cartoons, his or her concentration often improves.
9. In the face of levity, the former sourpuss becomes one of those who hides bad temper.
10. Every one of the consultants caution, however, that humor has no place in life-affecting corporate situations such as employee layoffs.

15b Make pronouns and their antecedents agree in person, number, and gender.

The **antecedent** of a pronoun is the noun or other pronoun to which the pronoun refers.

Homeowners fret over their tax bills.
antecedent   pronoun

Its constant increases make the tax bill a dreaded document.
pronoun   antecedent

Since a pronoun derives its meaning from its antecedent, the two must agree in person, number, and gender.

Person, number, and gender in pronoun-antecedent agreement

	Number	
Person	*Singular*	*Plural*
First	*I*	*we*
Second	*you*	*you*
Third	*he, she, it,* indefinite pronouns, singular nouns	*they,* plural nouns

(continued)

Person, number, and gender in pronoun-antecedent agreement
(continued)

Gender

Masculine	*he*, nouns naming males
Feminine	*she*, nouns naming females
Neuter	*it*, all other nouns

Grammar checkers A grammar checker cannot help with agreement between pronoun and antecedent because it cannot recognize the intended relation between the two.

⟨CULTURE LANGUAGE⟩ The gender of a pronoun should match its antecedent, not a noun that the pronoun may modify: *Sara Young invited her* [not *his*] *son to join the company's staff.* Also, nouns in English have only neuter gender unless they specifically refer to males or females. Thus nouns such as *book, table, sun,* and *earth* take the pronoun *it*.

Summary of pronoun-antecedent agreement

■ **Basic pronoun-antecedent agreement:**

antecedent   pronoun
Old Faithful spews its columns of water, each of them over 115 feet high.

■ **Antecedents joined by *and* (opposite):**

Old Faithful and Giant are geysers known for their height.

■ **Antecedents joined by *or* or *nor* (opposite):**

Either Giant or Giantess ejects its column the highest.

■ **Indefinite words as antecedents (opposite):**

Each of the geysers has its own personality.

Each person who visits has his or her favorites.

Some return to their favorites year after year.

■ **Collective nouns as antecedents (p. 315):**

A crowd amuses itself watching Old Faithful.

Afterward the crowd go their separate ways.

1 **Antecedents joined by *and* usually take plural pronouns.**

Two or more antecedents joined by *and* usually take a plural pronoun, whether one or all of the antecedents are singular:

Mr. Bartos and I cannot settle our dispute.

The dean and my adviser have offered their help.

Exceptions When the compound antecedent refers to a single idea, person, or thing, then the pronoun is singular:

My friend and adviser offered her help.

When the compound antecedent follows *each* or *every*, the pronoun is singular:

Every girl and woman took her seat.

2 **When parts of an antecedent are joined by *or* or *nor*, the pronoun agrees with the nearer part.**

When the parts of an antecedent are connected by *or* or *nor*, the pronoun should agree with the part closer to it:

Tenants or owners must present their grievances.

Either the tenant or the owner will have her way.

When one subject is plural and the other singular, the sentence will be awkward unless you put the plural one second:

Awkward   Neither the tenants nor the owner has yet made her case.

Revised   Neither the owner nor the tenants have yet made their case.

3 **With an indefinite word as antecedent, such as *anyone* or *person*, use a singular or plural pronoun as appropriate.**

Indefinite words do not refer to any specific person or thing. They include **indefinite pronouns** such as *anyone, everybody*, and *no one* (see p. 307 for a list). They also include **generic nouns,** or singular nouns that refer to typical members of a group, as in *The individual has rights* or *The job requires a person with computer skills*.

Most indefinite pronouns and all generic nouns are singular in meaning. When they serve as antecedents of pronouns, the pronouns should be singular.

Everyone on the women's team now has her own locker.
indefinite
pronoun

Every person on the women's team now has her own locker.
generic
noun

Six indefinite pronouns—*all, any, more, most, none, some*—may be singular or plural in meaning depending on what they refer to:

Few women athletes had changing spaces, so most had to change in their rooms.

Most of the changing space was dismal, its color a drab olive green.

Four indefinite pronouns—*both, few, many, several*—are always plural in meaning:

Few realize how their athletic facilities have changed.

Most agreement problems arise with the singular indefinite words. We often use these words to mean something like "many" or "all" rather than "one" and then refer to them with plural pronouns, as in *Everyone has their own locker* or *A person can padlock their locker*. Often, too, we mean indefinite words to include both masculine and feminine genders and thus resort to *they* instead of the **generic *he***—the masculine pronoun referring to both genders, as in *Everyone deserves his privacy*. (For more on the generic *he*, which many readers view as sexist, see p. 511.)

Ways to correct agreement with indefinite words

■ **Change the indefinite word to a plural, and use a plural pronoun to match:**

Faulty   Every athlete deserves their privacy.
Revised   **Athletes** deserve their privacy.

■ **Rewrite the sentence to omit the pronoun:**

Faulty   Everyone is entitled to their own locker.
Revised   Everyone is entitled to **a** locker.

■ **Use *he or she* (*him or her, his or her*) to refer to the indefinite word:**

Faulty   Now everyone has their private space.
Revised   Now everyone has **his or her** private space.

However, used more than once in several sentences, *he or she* quickly becomes awkward. (Many readers do not accept the alternative *he/she*.) Using the plural or omitting the pronoun will usually correct agreement problems and create more readable sentences.

Although some experts accept *they, them,* and *their* with singular indefinite words, most do not, and many teachers and employers regard the plural as incorrect. To be safe, work for agreement between singular indefinite words and the pronouns that refer to them, using the options in the preceding box.

4 With a collective noun as antecedent, such as *group* or *team,* use a singular or plural pronoun depending on meaning.

Collective nouns such as *army, committee, family, group,* and *team* have singular form but may be referred to by singular or plural pronouns, depending on the meaning intended. When the group acts as a unit, the pronoun is singular:

The committee voted to disband itself.

When the members of the group act separately, the pronoun is plural:

The old group have gone their separate ways.

In the last example, note that the verb and pronoun are consistent in number (see also p. 356).

Inconsistent   The old group has gone their separate ways.
Consistent   The old group have gone their separate ways.

CULTURE LANGUAGE In standard American English, collective nouns that are noncount nouns (they don't form plurals) usually take singular pronouns: *The mail sits in its own basket.* A few noncount nouns take plural pronouns, including *clergy, military, people, police, the rich,* and *the poor: The police support their unions.* (See also pp. 308–09.)

Exercise 15.2   Revising: Pronoun-antecedent agreement
Revise the following sentences so that pronouns and their antecedents agree in person and number. Some items have more than one possible answer. Try to avoid the generic *he* (see opposite). If you change the subject of a sentence, be sure to change verbs as necessary for agreement. If the sentence is already correct as given, mark the number preceding it.

Example:
Each of the Boudreaus' children brought their friends to the party.

All of the Boudreaus' children brought their friends to the party. *Or:* Each of the Boudreaus' children brought friends to the party. *Or:* Each of the Boudreaus' children brought his or her friends to the party.

1. Each girl raised in a Mexican American family in the Rio Grande Valley of Texas hopes that one day they will be given a *quinceañera* party for their fifteenth birthday.
2. Such celebrations are very expensive because it entails a religious service followed by a huge party.
3. A girl's immediate family, unless they are wealthy, cannot afford the party by themselves.
4. The parents will ask each close friend or relative if they can help with the preparations.
5. Surrounded by her family and attended by her friends and their escorts, the *quinceañera* is introduced as a young woman eligible for Mexican American society.

Exercise 15.3 Adjusting for agreement

In the sentences below, subjects agree with verbs and pronouns agree with antecedents. Make the change specified in parentheses after each sentence, and then revise the sentence as necessary to maintain agreement. Some items have more than one possible answer.

> *Example:*
>
> The student attends weekly conferences with her teacher. (*Change The student to Students.*)
>
> Students attend weekly conferences with their teacher.

1. The giant panda is endangered. (*Change The giant panda to Giant pandas.*)
2. A conservationist estimates that fewer than two thousand giant pandas live in central China, their natural habitat, because the bamboo forests there are shrinking. (*Change A conservationist to Conservationists.*)
3. The giant panda eats bamboo and gains most of its nutrition from its leaves and stalks. (*Change The giant panda to Giant pandas.*)
4. At the Wolong Wildlife Refuge in China, researchers breed pandas in captivity and release a cub into the wild when it is old enough to survive on its own. (*Change a cub to the cubs.*)
5. A zoo in the United States wishes to raise awareness of the giant panda's plight by breeding a pair of adults and allowing the public to view the adorable cub while it is young. (*Change A zoo to Zoos, a pair to pairs, and cub to the cubs.*)

Exercise 15.4 Revising: Agreement

Revise the sentences in the following paragraphs to correct errors in agreement between subjects and verbs or between pronouns and their antecedents. Try to avoid the generic *he.*

The writers Richard Rodriguez and Maxine Hong Kingston, despite their differences, shares one characteristic: their parents was immigrants to California. A frequent theme of their writings are the difficulties of growing up with two languages and two cultures.

A child whose first language is not English is often ridiculed because they cannot communicate "properly." Rodriguez learned Spanish at home, but at school everyone expected him to use their language, English. He remembers his childish embarrassment because of his parents' poor English.

College and graduate school, which usually expands one's knowledge, widened the gap between Rodriguez and his Latino culture. His essays suggests that he lost a part of himself, a loss that continue to bother him.

Kingston spoke Chinese at home and also learned her first English at school. She sometimes write of these experiences, but more often she write to recover and preserve her Chinese culture. *The Woman Warrior*, which offer a blend of autobiography, family history, and mythic tales, describe the struggle of Kingston's female relatives. *China Men* focus on Kingston's male ancestors; each one traveled to Hawaii or California to make money for their wife back in China. Kingston's work, like Rodriguez's essays, reflect the tension and confusion that the child of immigrants often feel when they try to blend two cultures.

Note See page 329 for an exercise involving agreement along with other aspects of grammar.

16

Adjectives and Adverbs

Adjectives and adverbs are modifiers that describe, restrict, or otherwise qualify the words to which they relate.

Functions of adjectives and adverbs

Adjectives modify	nouns:	serious student
	pronouns:	ordinary one
Adverbs modify	verbs:	warmly greet
	adjectives:	only three people
	adverbs:	quite seriously
	phrases:	nearly to the edge of the cliff
	clauses:	just when we arrived
	sentences:	Fortunately, she is employed.

mycomplab

Visit *mycomplab.com* for more resources and exercises on adjectives and adverbs.

Many of the most common adjectives are familiar one-syllable words such as *bad, strange, large,* and *wrong.* Many others are formed by adding endings such as *-al, -able, -ful, -less, -ish, -ive,* and *-y* to nouns or verbs: *optional, fashionable, beautiful, fruitless, self-ish, expressive, dreamy.*

Most adverbs are formed by adding *-ly* to adjectives: *badly, strangely, largely, beautifully.* But note that we cannot depend on *-ly* to identify adverbs, since some adjectives also end in *-ly* (*fatherly, lonely*) and since some common adverbs do not end in *-ly* (*always, here, not, now, often, there*). Thus the only sure way to distinguish between adjectives and adverbs is to determine what they modify.

Grammar checkers A grammar checker will spot some but not all problems with misused adjectives and adverbs. For instance, a checker flagged *Some children suffer bad* and *Chang was the most wisest person in town* and *Jenny did not feel nothing.* But it did not flag *Educating children good is everyone's focus.*

CULTURE LANGUAGE In standard American English an adjective does not change along with the noun it modifies to show plural number: *white* [not *whites*] *shoes, square* [not *squares*] *spaces.* Only nouns form plurals.

16a Use adjectives only to modify nouns and pronouns.

Adjectives modify only nouns and pronouns. Do not use adjectives instead of adverbs to modify verbs, adverbs, or other adjectives:

Faulty   The groups view family values different.

Revised   The groups view family values differently.

Be especially careful not to use *good* and *bad* in place of *well* and *badly.*

Faulty   Educating children good is everyone's focus.

Revised   Educating children well is everyone's focus.

Faulty   Some children suffer bad.

Revised   Some children suffer badly.

CULTURE LANGUAGE To negate a verb or an adjective, use the adverb *not:*

They are not learning. They are not stupid.

To negate a noun, use the adjective *no:*

No child should fail to read.

16b Use an adjective after a linking verb to modify the subject. Use an adverb to modify a verb.

A **linking verb** is one that links, or connects, a subject and its complement, either a noun (*They are golfers*) or an adjective (*He is lucky*). (See also pp. 239–40.) Linking verbs are forms of *be*, the verbs associated with our five senses (*look, sound, smell, feel, taste*), and a few others (*appear, seem, become, grow, turn, prove, remain, stay*).

Some of these verbs may or may not be linking, depending on their meaning in the sentence. When the word after the verb modifies the subject, the verb is linking and the word should be an adjective: *He feels strong*. When the word modifies the verb, however, it should be an adverb: *He feels strongly about that*.

Two word pairs are especially troublesome in this context. One is *bad* and *badly:*

The weather grew bad.
linking adjective
verb

She felt bad.
linking adjective
verb

Flowers grow badly in such soil.
verb adverb

The other pair is *good* and *well. Good* serves only as an adjective. *Well* may serve as an adverb with a host of meanings or as an adjective meaning only "fit" or "healthy."

Decker trained well.
verb adverb

She felt well.
linking adjective
verb

Her health was good.
linking adjective
verb

16c After a direct object, use an adjective to modify the object and an adverb to modify the verb.

After a direct object, an adjective modifies the object, whereas an adverb modifies the verb of the sentence. (See p. 238 for more on direct objects.)

School politics made Mungo angry.
adjective

Mungo repeated the words angrily.
adverb

You can test whether a modifier should be an adjective or an adverb by trying to separate it from the direct object. If you can separate it, it should be an adverb: *Mungo angrily repeated the words*. If you cannot separate it, it is probably an adjective.

The teacher considered the student's work thorough. [The adjective can be moved in front of *work* (*student's thorough work*), but it cannot be separated from *work*.]

The teacher considered the student's work thoroughly. [The adverb can be separated from *work*. Compare *The teacher thoroughly considered the student's work*.]

Exercise 16.1   Revising: Adjectives and adverbs

Revise the following sentences so that adjectives and adverbs are used appropriately. If any sentence is already correct as given, mark the number preceding it.

Example:
The announcer warned that traffic was moving very slow.
The announcer warned that traffic was moving very slowly.

1. King George III of England declared Samuel Johnson suitably for a pension.
2. Johnson was taken serious as a critic and dictionary maker.
3. Thinking about his meeting with the king, Johnson felt proudly.
4. Johnson was relieved that he had not behaved badly in the king's presence.
5. After living cheap for over twenty years, Johnson finally had enough money from the pension to eat and dress good.

16d   Use the comparative and superlative forms of adjectives and adverbs appropriately.

Adjectives and adverbs can show degrees of quality or amount with the endings *-er* and *-est* or with the words *more* and *most* or *less* and *least*. Most modifiers have three forms:

Positive The basic form listed in the dictionary	Comparative A greater or lesser degree of the quality	Superlative The greatest or least degree of the quality
Adjectives		
red	redder	reddest
awful	more/less awful	most/least awful
Adverbs		
soon	sooner	soonest
quickly	more/less quickly	most/least quickly

If sound alone does not tell you whether to use *-er/-est* or *more/most*, consult a dictionary. If the endings can be used, the dictionary will list them. Otherwise, use *more* or *most*.

1 Use the correct forms of irregular adjectives and adverbs.

Certain adjectives and adverbs are irregular: they change the spelling of their positive form to show comparative and superlative degrees.

Degrees of irregular adjectives and adverbs

Positive	Comparative	Superlative
Adjectives		
good	better	best
bad	worse	worst
little	littler, less	littlest, least
many some much	more	most
Adverbs		
well	better	best
badly	worse	worst

2 Use either *-er/-est* or *more/most,* not both.

A double comparative or double superlative combines the *-er* or *-est* ending with the word *more* or *most.* It is redundant.

Chang was the wisest [not most wisest] person in town.
He was smarter [not more smarter] than anyone else.

3 Use the comparative for comparing two things and the superlative for comparing three or more things.

It is the shorter of her two books. [Comparative.]
The Yearling is the most popular of the six books. [Superlative.]

In conversation the superlative form is often used to compare only two things: *When two people argue, the angriest one is usually wrong.* But the distinction between the forms should be observed in writing.

4 Use comparative or superlative forms only for modifiers that can logically be compared.

Some adjectives and adverbs cannot logically be compared—for instance, *perfect, unique, dead, impossible, infinite.* These absolute words can be preceded by adverbs like *nearly* and *almost* that mean "approaching," but they cannot logically be modified by *more* or *most* (as in *most perfect*). This distinction is sometimes ignored in speech, but it should always be made in writing:

Not	He was the <u>most unique</u> teacher we had.
But	He was a <u>unique</u> teacher.

Exercise 16.2 Revising: Comparatives and superlatives

Revise the sentences below so that the comparative and superlative forms of adjectives and adverbs are appropriate for formal usage. Mark the number preceding any sentence that is already correct.

Example:

Attending high school and working at two jobs was the most impossible thing I ever did.

Attending high school and working at two jobs was <u>impossible</u> [or the hardest thing I ever did].

1. Charlotte was the older of the three Brontë sisters, all of whom were novelists.
2. Some readers think Emily Brontë's *Wuthering Heights* is the most saddest novel they have ever read.
3. Of the other two sisters, Charlotte and Anne, Charlotte was probably the more talented.
4. Critics still argue about whether Charlotte or Emily wrote more better.
5. Certainly this family of women novelists was the most unique.

16e Watch for double negatives.

In a **double negative** two negative words such as *no, not, none, neither, barely, hardly,* or *scarcely* cancel each other out. Some double negatives are intentional: for instance, *She was <u>not unhappy</u>* indicates with understatement that she was indeed happy. But most double negatives say the opposite of what is intended: *Sophie did <u>not feel nothing</u>* asserts that Sophie felt other than nothing, or something. For the opposite meaning, one of the negatives must be eliminated or changed to a positive: *She felt <u>nothing</u>* or *She did <u>not feel anything</u>*.

Faulty	The IRS <u>cannot hardly</u> audit all tax returns. <u>None</u> of its audits <u>never</u> touch many cheaters.
Revised	The IRS <u>cannot</u> audit all tax returns. Its audits <u>never</u> touch many cheaters.

Exercise 16.3 Revising: Double negatives

Identify and revise the double negatives in the following paragraph. Each error may have more than one correct revision.

Interest in books about the founding of the United States seems to vary with the national mood. Americans show hardly no interest in books about the founders when things are going well in the United

States. However, when Americans can't barely agree on major issues, sales of books about the Revolutionary War era increase. During such periods, one cannot go to no bookstore without seeing several new volumes about John Adams, Thomas Jefferson, and other founders. When Americans feel they don't have nothing in common, their increased interest in the early leaders may reflect a desire for unity.

16f Use nouns sparingly as modifiers.

We often use one noun to modify another. For example:

child care   flood control   security guard

Such phrases can be both clear and concise, but overuse of noun modifiers can lead to flat, even senseless, writing. To avoid awkwardness or confusion, observe two principles. First, prefer possessives or adjectives as modifiers:

Not	A student takes the state medical <u>board</u> exams to become a <u>dentist</u> technician.
But	A student takes the state medical <u>board's</u> exams to become a <u>dental</u> technician.

Second, use only short nouns as modifiers and use them only in two- or three-word sequences:

Confusing	Minimex maintains a <u>plant employee relations improvement program</u>.
Revised	Minimex maintains a program <u>for improving</u> relations <u>among plant employees</u>.

16g Distinguish between present and past participles as adjectives.

Both present participles and past participles may serve as adjectives: *a <u>burning</u> building, a <u>burned</u> building*. As in the examples, the two participles usually differ in the time they indicate.

But some present and past participles—those derived from verbs expressing feeling—can have altogether different meanings. The present participle modifies something that causes the feeling: *That was a <u>frightening</u> storm* (the storm frightens). The past participle modifies something that experiences the feeling: *They quieted the <u>frightened</u> horses* (the horses feel fright).

The following participles are among those likely to be confused:

amazing/amazed   astonishing/astonished
amusing/amused   boring/bored
annoying/annoyed   confusing/confused

depressing/depressed	interesting/interested
embarrassing/embarrassed	pleasing/pleased
exciting/excited	satisfying/satisfied
exhausting/exhausted	shocking/shocked
fascinating/fascinated	surprising/surprised
frightening/frightened	tiring/tired
frustrating/frustrated	worrying/worried

Exercise 16.4 Revising: Present and past participles

Revise the adjectives in the following sentences as needed to distinguish between present and past participles. If the sentence is already correct as given, mark the number preceding it.

> *Example:*
> The subject was embarrassed to many people.
> The subject was <u>embarrassing</u> to many people.

1. Several critics found Alice Walker's *The Color Purple* to be a fascinated book.
2. One confused critic wished that Walker had deleted the scenes set in Africa.
3. Another critic argued that although the book contained many depressed episodes, the overall impact was excited.
4. Since other readers found the book annoyed, this critic pointed out its many surprised qualities.
5. In the end most critics agreed that the book was a satisfied novel.

16h Use *a, an, the,* and other determiners appropriately.

Determiners are special kinds of adjectives that mark nouns because they always precede nouns. Some common determiners are *a, an,* and *the* (called **articles**) and *my, their, whose, this, these, those, one, some,* and *any.* They convey information to readers—for instance, by specifying who owns what, which one of two is meant, or whether a subject is familiar or unfamiliar.

Native speakers of standard American English can rely on their intuition when using determiners, but speakers of other languages and dialects often have difficulty with them. In standard English the use of determiners depends on the context they appear in and the kind of noun they precede:

- A **proper noun** names a particular person, place, or thing and begins with a capital letter: *February, Joe Allen, Red River.* Most proper nouns are not preceded by determiners.
- A **count noun** names something that is countable in English and can form a plural: *girl/girls, apple/apples, child/children.* A

singular count noun is always preceded by a determiner; a plural count noun sometimes is.

- **A noncount noun** names something not usually considered countable in English, and so it does not form a plural. A noncount noun is sometimes preceded by a determiner. Here is a sample of noncount nouns, sorted into groups by meaning:

Abstractions: confidence, democracy, education, equality, evidence, health, information, intelligence, knowledge, luxury, peace, pollution, research, success, supervision, truth, wealth, work

Food and drink: bread, candy, cereal, flour, meat, milk, salt, water, wine

Emotions: anger, courage, happiness, hate, joy, love, respect, satisfaction

Natural events and substances: air, blood, dirt, gasoline, gold, hair, heat, ice, oil, oxygen, rain, silver, smoke, weather, wood

Groups: clergy, clothing, equipment, furniture, garbage, jewelry, junk, legislation, machinery, mail, military, money, police, vocabulary

Fields of study: architecture, accounting, biology, business, chemistry, engineering, literature, psychology, science

A dictionary of English as a second language will tell you whether a noun is a count noun, a noncount noun, or both. (See p. 515 for recommended dictionaries.)

Note Many nouns can be both count and noncount nouns:

The library has a room for readers. [*Room* is a count noun meaning "walled area."]

The library has room for reading. [*Room* is a noncount noun meaning "space."]

Grammar checkers Partly because the same noun may fall into different groups, a grammar checker is an unreliable guide to missing or misused articles and other determiners. For instance, a checker flagged the omitted *a* before *Scientist* in *Scientist developed new processes;* it did not flag the omitted *a* before *new* in *A scientist developed new process;* and it mistakenly flagged the correctly omitted article *the* before *Vegetation* in *Vegetation suffers from drought.*

1 Use *a, an,* and *the* where they are required.

With singular count nouns

A or *an* precedes a singular count noun when the reader does not already know its identity, usually because you have not mentioned it before:

A scientist in the school's chemistry department developed a process to strengthen metals. [*Scientist* and *process* are being introduced for the first time.]

The precedes a singular count noun that has a specific identity for the reader, for one of the following reasons:

- **You have mentioned the noun before:**

  A scientist in the school's chemistry department developed a process to strengthen metals. The scientist patented the process. [*Scientist* and *process* were identified in the preceding sentence.]

- **You identify the noun immediately before or after you state it:**

  The most productive laboratory is the research center in the chemistry department. [*Most productive* identifies *laboratory. In the chemistry department* identifies *research center.* And *chemistry department* is a shared facility.]

- **The noun names something unique—the only one in existence:**

  The sun rises in the east. [*Sun* and *east* are unique.]

- **The noun names an institution or facility that is shared by the community of readers:**

  Many men and women aspire to the presidency. [*Presidency* is a shared institution.]

  The cell phone has changed communication. [*Cell phone* is a shared facility.]

The is not used before a singular noun that names a general category:

  Sherman said that war is hell. [*War* names a general category.]

  The war in Iraq left many wounded. [*War* names a specific war.]

With plural count nouns

A or *an* never precedes a plural noun. *The* does not precede a plural noun that names a general category. *The* does precede a plural noun that names specific representatives of a category.

  Men and women are different. [*Men* and *women* name general categories.]

  The women formed a team. [*Women* refers to specific people.]

With noncount nouns

A or *an* never precedes a noncount noun. *The* does precede a noncount noun when it names specific representatives of a general category:

  Vegetation suffers from drought. [*Vegetation* names a general category.]

  The vegetation in the park withered or died. [*Vegetation* refers to specific plants.]

With proper nouns

A or *an* never precedes a proper noun. *The* generally does not precede a proper noun:

<u>Garcia</u> lives in <u>Boulder</u>.

There are exceptions, however. For instance, we generally use *the* before plural proper nouns (<u>*the*</u> *Murphys*, <u>*the*</u> *New England Patriots*) and the names of groups and organizations (<u>*the*</u> *Department of Justice*, <u>*the*</u> *Sierra Club*), ships (<u>*the*</u> *Lusitania*), oceans (<u>*the*</u> *Pacific*), mountain ranges (<u>*the*</u> *Alps*), regions (<u>*the*</u> *Middle East*), rivers (<u>*the*</u> *Mississippi*), and some countries (<u>*the*</u> *United States*, <u>*the*</u> *Netherlands*).

2 Use other determiners appropriately.

The uses of English determiners besides articles also depend on context and kind of noun. The following determiners may be used as indicated with singular count nouns, plural count nouns, or noncount nouns.

With any kind of noun (singular count, plural count, noncount)

my, our, your, his, her, its, their
possessive nouns (*boy's, boys'*)
whose, which(ever), what(ever)
some, any, the other
no

<u>Their</u> account is overdrawn. [Singular count.]
<u>Their</u> funds are low. [Plural count.]
<u>Their</u> money is running out. [Noncount.]

Only with singular nouns (count and noncount)

this, that

<u>This</u> account has some money. [Count.]
<u>That</u> information may help. [Noncount.]

Only with noncount nouns and plural count nouns

most, enough, other, such, all, all of the, a lot of

<u>Most</u> money is needed elsewhere. [Noncount.]
<u>Most</u> funds are committed. [Plural count.]

Only with singular count nouns

one, every, each, either, neither, another

<u>One</u> car must be sold. [Singular count.]

Only with plural count nouns

> *these, those*
> *both, many, few, a few, fewer, fewest, several*
> *two, three,* and so forth

> <u>Two</u> cars are unnecessary. [Plural count.]

Note *Few* means "not many" or "not enough." *A few* means "some" or "a small but sufficient quantity."

> <u>Few</u> committee members came to the meeting.
> <u>A few</u> members can keep the committee going.

Do not use *much* with a plural count noun:

> <u>Many</u> [not <u>Much</u>] members want to help.

Only with noncount nouns

> *much, more, little, a little, less, least, a large amount of*

> <u>Less</u> luxury is in order. [Noncount.]

Note *Little* means "not many" or "not enough." *A little* means "some" or "a small but sufficient quantity."

> <u>Little</u> time remains before the conference.
> The members need <u>a little</u> help from their colleagues.

Do not use *many* with a noncount noun:

> <u>Much</u> [not <u>Many</u>] work remains.

Exercise 16.5   Revising: Articles   (CULTURE LANGUAGE)

For each blank below, indicate whether *a, an, the,* or no article should be inserted.

From _____ native American Indians who migrated from _____ Asia 20,000 years ago to _____ new arrivals who now come by _____ planes, _____ United States is _____ nation of foreigners. It is _____ country of immigrants who are all living under _____ single flag.

Back in _____ seventeenth and eighteenth centuries, at least 75 percent of the population came from _____ England. However, between 1820 and 1975 more than 38 million immigrants came to this country from elsewhere in _____ Europe. Many children of _____ immigrants were self-conscious and denied their heritage; many even refused to learn _____ native language of their parents and grandparents. They tried to "Americanize" themselves. The so-called Melting Pot theory of _____ social change stressed _____ importance of blending everyone together into _____ kind of stew. Each nationality would contribute its own flavor, but _____ final stew would be something called "American."

This Melting Pot theory was never completely successful. In the last half of the twentieth century, _____ ethnic revival changed _____ metaphor. Many people now see _____ American society as _____ mosaic. Americans are once again proud of their heritage, and _____ ethnic differences make _____ mosaic colorful and interesting.

Exercise 16.6 Revising: Adjectives and adverbs

Revise the following paragraph so that it conforms to formal usage of adjectives and adverbs.

Americans often argue about which professional sport is better: basketball, football, or baseball. Basketball fans contend that their sport offers more action because the players are constant running and shooting. Because it is played indoors in relative small arenas, basketball allows fans to be more closer to the action than the other sports do. Fans point to how graceful the players fly through the air to the hoop. Football fanatics say they don't hardly stop yelling once the game begins. They cheer when their team executes a real complicated play good. They roar more louder when the defense stops the opponents in a goal-line stand. They yell loudest when a fullback crashes in for a score. In contrast, the supporters of baseball believe that it might be the most perfect sport. It combines the one-on-one duel of pitcher and batter struggling valiant with the tight teamwork of double and triple plays. Because the game is played slow and careful, fans can analyze and discuss the manager's strategy. Besides, they don't never know when they might catch a foul ball as a souvenir. However, no matter what the sport, all fans feel happily only when their team wins.

Exercise on Chapters 13–16 Revising: Grammatical sentences

The following paragraphs contain errors in pronoun case, verb forms, subject-verb agreement, pronoun-antecedent agreement, and the forms of adjectives and adverbs. Revise the paragraphs to correct the errors.

Occasionally, musicians become "crossover artists" whom can perform good in more than one field of music. For example, Wynton and Branford Marsalis was train in jazz by their father, the great pianist Ellis Marsalis. Both of the sons has became successful classical artists. Branford's saxophone captures the richness of pieces by Ravel and Stravinsky. Wynton's albums of classical trumpet music from the Baroque period has brung him many awards. Still, if he was to choose which kind of music he likes best, Wynton would probable choose jazz. In contrast to the Marsalises, violinist Nigel Kennedy growed up studying and performing classical music. In his teens he began playing jazz and even rock music. Today he is known almost as good for his interpretations of Miles Davis and Jimi Hendrix as he is for his classical performances.

Such crossovers are often more harder for vocalists. Each type of music has their own style and feel that is hard to learn. For example, Kiri te Kanawa, one of the great opera sopranos, have sang popular music and folk songs in concerts and on albums. On each occasion, her technique was the most perfect, yet she sounded as if she was simply trying to sing proper. It is even more difficulter for pop or country vocalists to sing opera, as Linda Ronstadt and Gary Morris founded when they appear in

La Bohème. Each of them have a clear, pure voice, but a few critics said that him and her lacked the vocal power necessary for opera. However, Bobby McFerrin been successful singing both pop and classical pieces. He won pop Grammy awards, but he is equal able to sing classical pieces *a cappella* (without musical accompaniment). His voice's remarkable range and clarity allows him to imitate many musical instruments.

No matter how successful, all of these musicians has shown great courage by performing in a new field. They are willing to test and stretch their talents, and each of we music fans benefit.

PART 4

Clear Sentences

17

Sentence Fragments

A **sentence fragment** is part of a sentence that is set off as if it were a whole sentence by an initial capital letter and a final period or other end punctuation. Although writers occasionally use fragments deliberately and effectively (see p. 339), readers perceive most fragments as serious errors because, expecting complete sentences, they find partial sentences distracting or confusing. (Before reading further, you may find it helpful to review pp. 233–41 and 252–55 on sentences and clauses.)

Complete sentence versus sentence fragment

A complete sentence or **main clause**

- contains a subject and a predicate verb (*The wind blows*)
- and is not a subordinate clause (beginning with a word such as *because* or *who*).

A sentence fragment

- lacks a predicate verb (*The wind <u>blowing</u>*)
- or lacks a subject (*And blows*)
- or is a subordinate clause not attached to a complete sentence (*<u>Because the wind blows</u>*).

Grammar checkers A grammar checker can spot many but not all sentence fragments, and it may flag sentences that are actually correct commands, such as *Continue reading*.

17a Test your sentences for completeness, and revise any fragments.

The following three tests will help you determine whether a word group punctuated as a sentence is actually a complete sentence. If the word group does not pass *all three* tests, it is a fragment and needs to be revised.

Visit *mycomplab.com* for more resources and exercises on sentence fragments.

Tests for complete sentences

Perform *all three* of the following tests to be sure your sentences are complete.

1. Find the predicate verb.
2. Find the subject.
3. Make sure the clause is not subordinate.

Test 1: Find the predicate verb.

Look for a predicate verb in the group of words. Some fragments lack any verb at all:

Fragment	Uncountable numbers of sites on the World Wide Web.
Revised	Uncountable numbers of sites make up the World Wide Web.

Other fragments may include a verb form but not a **finite verb,** one that changes form as indicated below. A verbal does not change; it cannot serve as a predicate verb without the aid of a helping verb.

	Finite verbs in complete sentences	Verbals in sentence fragments
Singular	The network grows.	The network growing.
Plural	Networks grow.	Networks growing.
Present	The network grows.	
Past	The network grew.	The network growing.
Future	The network will grow.	

CULTURE · LANGUAGE Some languages allow forms of *be* to be omitted as helping or linking verbs. But English requires stating forms of *be:*

Fragments	The network growing. It much larger than its developers anticipated.
Revised	The network is growing. It is much larger than its developers anticipated.

Test 2: Find the subject.

If you find a finite, predicate verb, look for its subject by asking *who* or *what* performs the action or makes the assertion of the verb. The subject of the sentence will usually come before the verb. If there is no subject, the word group is probably a fragment:

Fragment	And has great popular appeal.
Revised	And the Web has great popular appeal.

In one kind of complete sentence, a command, the subject *you* is understood: [*You*] *Experiment with the Web.*

CULTURE·LANGUAGE Some languages allow the omission of the sentence subject, especially when it is a pronoun. But in English, except in commands, the subject is always stated:

Fragments Web shopping has expanded dramatically. Has hurt traditional stores.

Revised Web shopping has expanded dramatically. <u>It</u> has hurt traditional stores.

Test 3: Make sure the clause is not subordinate.

A subordinate clause usually begins with a subordinating word:

Subordinating conjunctions			Relative pronouns	
after	once	until	that	who/whom
although	since	when	which	whoever/whomever
as	than	where		whose
because	that	whereas		
if	unless	while		

(See p. 253 for a longer list of subordinating conjunctions.)

Subordinate clauses serve as parts of sentences (as nouns or modifiers), not as whole sentences:

Fragment When the government devised the Internet.

Revised The government devised the Internet.

Revised When the government devised the Internet, <u>no expansive computer network existed.</u>

Fragment The reason that the government devised the Internet.

Revised The reason that the government devised the Internet <u>was to provide secure links among departments and defense contractors.</u>

Note Questions beginning with *how, what, when, where, which, who, whom, whose,* and *why* are not sentence fragments: *Who was responsible? When did it happen?*

Revising sentence fragments

Almost all sentence fragments can be corrected in one of the two ways shown in the following box. The choice depends on the importance of the information in the fragment.

Revision of sentence fragments

Option 1

Rewrite the fragment as a complete sentence. This revision gives the information in the fragment the same importance as that in other complete sentences.

Fragment	A major improvement in public health occurred with the widespread use of vaccines. <u>Which protected children against life-threatening diseases.</u>
Revised	A major improvement in public health occurred with the widespread use of vaccines. They protected children against life-threatening diseases.

Two main clauses may be separated by a semicolon instead of a period (p. 447).

Option 2

Combine the fragment with a main clause. This revision subordinates the information in the fragment to the information in the main clause.

Fragment	The polio vaccine eradicated the disease from most of the globe. <u>The first vaccine to be used widely.</u>
Revised	The polio vaccine, the first to be used widely, eradicated the disease from most of the globe.

Punctuating corrected fragments

In the last example in the box, commas separate the inserted phrase from the rest of the sentence because the phrase is not essential to the meaning of any word in the main clause but simply adds information (see p. 429). When a phrase or subordinate clause *is* essential to the meaning of a word in the main clause, a comma or commas do *not* separate the two elements:

Fragment	High school students often use the Web to research colleges. <u>That they might want to visit in person.</u>
Revised	High school students often use the Web to research colleges that they might want to visit in person.

Sometimes a fragment may be combined with the main clause using a colon or a dash (see pp. 471 and 473–74, respectively):

Fragment	Some colleges recruit students from all over the United States. <u>Large cities, suburbs, small towns, and rural areas.</u>
Revised	Some colleges recruit students from all over the United States: large cities, suburbs, small towns, and rural areas.
Fragment	The colleges strive to bring together diverse groups of students. <u>Young people with different backgrounds, experiences, and dreams for the future.</u>
Revised	The colleges strive to bring together diverse groups of students—young people with different backgrounds, experiences, and dreams for the future.

Exercise 17.1 Identifying and revising sentence fragments

Apply the tests for completeness to each of the following word groups. If a word group is a complete sentence, mark the number preceding it. If it is a sentence fragment, revise it in two ways: by making it a complete sentence, and by combining it with a main clause written from the information given in other items.

> *Example:*
> And could not find his money. [The word group has a verb (*could . . . find*) but no subject.]
>
> *Revised into a complete sentence:* And <u>he</u> could not find his money.
>
> *Combined with a new main clause:* <u>He was lost</u> and could not find his money.

1. In an interesting article about vandalism against works of art.
2. The motives of the vandals varying widely.
3. Those who harm artwork are usually angry.
4. But not necessarily at the artist or the owner.
5. For instance, a man who hammered at Michelangelo's *Pietà*.
6. And knocked off the Virgin Mary's nose.
7. Because he was angry at the Roman Catholic Church.
8. Which knew nothing of his grievance.
9. Although many damaged works can be repaired.
10. Usually even the most skillful repairs are forever visible.

17b A subordinate clause is not a complete sentence.

Subordinate clauses contain both subjects and verbs, but they always begin with a subordinating conjunction (*although, if,* and so on) or a relative pronoun (*who, which, that,* and so on). (See pp. 252–53.) Subordinate clauses serve as nouns or modifiers, but they cannot stand alone as complete sentences.

To correct a subordinate clause set off as a sentence, combine it with the main clause or remove or change the subordinating word to create a main clause.

Fragment	Many pine trees bear large cones. <u>Which appear in August.</u>
Revised	Many pine trees bear large cones, which appear in August.
Revised	Many pine trees bear large cones. <u>They</u> appear in August.

17c A verbal phrase or a prepositional phrase is not a complete sentence.

A **verbal phrase** consists of an infinitive (*to choose*), a past participle (*chosen*), or a present participle or gerund (*choosing*) together with any objects and modifiers it may have (see p. 249). A verbal phrase is a noun or modifier and cannot serve as the verb in a complete sentence:

Fragment	For many of the elderly, their house is their only asset. <u>Offering some security but no income.</u>
Revised	For many of the elderly, their house is their only asset, offering some security but no income.
Revised	For many of the elderly, their house is their only asset. It offers some security but no income.

A **prepositional phrase** is a modifier consisting of a preposition (such as *in, on, to,* or *with*) together with its object and any modifiers (see pp. 244–45). A prepositional phrase cannot stand alone as a complete sentence:

Fragment	<u>In a squeeze between a valuable asset and little income.</u> Eventually many elderly people sell their homes.
Revised	In a squeeze between a valuable asset and little income, eventually many elderly people sell their homes.
Revised	<u>Many elderly people are</u> in a squeeze between a valuable asset and little income. Eventually they may sell their homes.

⟨CULTURE LANGUAGE⟩ Some English prepositions consist of two or three words: *as well as, along with, in addition to, on top of,* and others. Don't let prepositions of more than one word mislead you into writing sentence fragments.

Fragment	In today's retirement communities, the elderly may have health care, housekeeping, and new friends. <u>As well as financial security.</u>
Revised	In today's retirement communities, the elderly may have health care, housekeeping, and new friends, as well as financial security.

17d Any word group lacking a subject or a verb or both is not a complete sentence.

We often follow a noun with a modifier. No matter how long the noun and its modifier are, they cannot stand alone as a sentence:

Fragments	<u>People waving flags and cheering. Lined the streets for the parade.</u>
Revised	People waving flags and cheering lined the streets for the parade.
Fragment	<u>Veterans who fought in Vietnam.</u> They are finally being honored.
Revised	Veterans who fought in Vietnam are finally being honored.

Appositives are nouns, or nouns and their modifiers, that rename or describe other nouns (see pp. 256–57). They cannot stand alone as sentences:

Fragment	When I was a child, my favorite adult was an old uncle. <u>A retired sea captain who always told me long stories of wild adventures in faraway places.</u>
Revised	When I was a child, my favorite adult was an old uncle, a retired sea captain who always told me long stories of wild adventures in faraway places.

Compound predicates are predicates made up of two or more verbs and their objects, if any (see p. 258). A verb or its object cannot stand alone as a sentence:

Fragment	Uncle Marlon drew out his tales. <u>And embellished them.</u>
Revised	Uncle Marlon drew out his tales and embellished them.

Fragment	He described characters he had met. <u>And storms at sea.</u>
Revised	He described characters he had met and storms at sea.

Note Beginning a sentence with a coordinating conjunction such as *and* or *but* can lead to a sentence fragment. Check every sentence you begin with a coordinating conjunction to be sure it is complete.

Exercise 17.2 Revising: Sentence fragments

Correct any sentence fragment below either by combining it with a main clause or by making it a main clause. If an item contains no sentence fragment, mark the number preceding it.

Example:

Jujitsu is good for self-protection. Because it enables one to overcome an opponent without the use of weapons.

Jujitsu is good for self-protection because it enables one to overcome an opponent without the use of weapons.

1. Human beings who perfume themselves. They are not much different from other animals.
2. Animals as varied as insects and dogs release *pheromones*. Chemicals that signal other animals.
3. Human beings have a diminished sense of smell. And do not consciously detect most of their own species' pheromones.
4. The human substitute for pheromones may be perfumes. Especially musk and other fragrances derived from animal oils.
5. Some sources say that humans began using perfume to cover up the smell of burning flesh. During sacrifices to the gods.
6. Perfumes became religious offerings in their own right. Being expensive to make, they were highly prized.

7. The earliest historical documents from the Middle East record the use of fragrances. Not only in religious ceremonies but on the body.
8. In the nineteenth century chemists began synthesizing perfume oils. Which previously could be made only from natural sources.
9. The most popular animal oil for perfume today is musk. Although some people dislike its heavy, sweet odor.
10. Synthetic musk oil would help conserve a certain species of deer. Whose gland is the source of musk.

17e Be aware of the acceptable uses of incomplete sentences.

A few word groups lacking the usual subject-predicate combination are not sentence fragments because they conform to the expectations of most readers. They include commands (*Move along. Shut the window.*); exclamations (*Oh no!*); questions and answers (*Where next? To Kansas.*); and descriptions in employment résumés (*Weekly volunteer in a soup kitchen.*). Another kind of incomplete sentence, occurring in special situations, is the transitional phrase (*So much for the causes, now for the results. One final point.*).

Experienced writers sometimes use sentence fragments when they want to achieve a special effect. Such fragments appear more in informal than in formal writing. Unless you are experienced and thoroughly secure in your own writing, you should avoid all fragments and concentrate on writing clear, well-formed sentences.

Exercise 17.3 Revising: Sentence fragments
Revise the following paragraph to eliminate sentence fragments by combining them with main clauses or rewriting them as main clauses.

Baby red-eared slider turtles are brightly colored. With bold patterns on their yellowish undershells. Which serve as a warning to predators. The bright colors of skunks and other animals. They signal that the animals will spray nasty chemicals. In contrast, the turtle's colors warn largemouth bass. That the baby turtle will actively defend itself. When a bass gulps down a turtle. The feisty baby claws and bites. Forcing the bass to spit it out. To avoid a similar painful experience. The bass will avoid other baby red-eared slider turtles. The turtle loses its bright colors as it grows too big. For a bass's afternoon snack.

Note See page 378 for an exercise involving sentence fragments along with comma splices, fused sentences, and other sentence errors.

18

Comma Splices and Fused Sentences

A sentence or main clause contains at least a subject and a predicate, which together express a complete thought that can stand alone (see p. 233). When two main clauses fall together, readers need a signal that one clause is ending and another is beginning. The following box shows the ways to provide this signal.

Punctuation of two or more main clauses

■ **Separate main clauses with periods.**

> Main clause ● Main clause ●

Hybrid cars are popular with consumers. Automakers are releasing new models.

■ **Link main clauses with a coordinating conjunction and a comma.**

> Main clause , for and or | so but nor | yet main clause ●

Hybrid cars are popular with consumers, and automakers are releasing new models.

■ **Link main clauses with a semicolon.**

> Main clause ; main clause ●

Hybrid cars are popular with consumers; automakers are releasing new models.

---

mycomplab

Visit *mycomplab.com* for more resources and exercises on comma splices and fused sentences.

340

> ■ **Relate main clauses with a semicolon and a conjunctive adverb or transitional expression.**
>
> Main clause **;** *however,* / *for example,* / *etc.* **,** main clause **.**
>
> Hybrid cars are popular with consumers**;** as a result**,** automakers are releasing new models.

With a comma splice or a fused sentence, two main clauses run together without one of the signals listed in the box, and readers often must reread for sense. A **comma splice** joins (or splices) main clauses *only* with a comma, not with a coordinating conjunction as well:

Comma splice
The ship was huge, its mast stood eighty feet high.

A **fused sentence** (or **run-on sentence**) joins main clauses with no punctuation at all:

Fused sentence
The ship was huge its mast stood eighty feet high.

Exception Experienced writers sometimes use a comma without a coordinating conjunction between very brief main clauses that are grammatically parallel:

He's not a person, he's a monster.

However, many readers view such punctuation as incorrect. Unless you are certain that your readers will not object to the comma in a sentence like this one, separate the clauses with periods or semicolons, as described in this chapter.

Grammar checkers A grammar checker can detect many comma splices, but it will miss most fused sentences. For example, a checker flagged *Money is tight, we need to spend carefully* but not *Money is tight we need to spend carefully*. A checker may also question sentences that are actually correct, such as *Money being tighter now than before, we need to spend carefully*. Verify that revision is actually needed on any flagged sentence.

CULTURE LANGUAGE An English sentence may not include more than one main clause unless the clauses are separated by a comma and a coordinating conjunction or by a semicolon or colon. If your native language does not have such a rule or has accustomed you to writing long sentences, you may need to edit your English writing especially for comma splices and fused sentences.

Revision of comma splices and fused sentences

1. **Underline the main clauses in your draft.**

Sailors trained on the ship they learned about wind and sails. Trainees who took the course ranged from high school students to Navy officers. The ship was built in 1910, it had sailed ever since. In almost a century, it had circled the globe forty times. It burned in 2001 its cabins and decks were destroyed.

2. **Focus on sentences that contain two or more main clauses.**

3. **If nothing falls between the clauses or only a comma does, revise in one of the following ways.** The choice depends on the relation you want to establish between the clauses, as explained below and opposite.

■ **Separate main clauses with a period.**

Sailors trained on the ship. They learned about wind and sails.

■ **Separate main clauses with a comma and a coordinating conjunction.**

The ship was built in 1910, and it had sailed ever since.

■ **Separate main clauses with a semicolon.**

The ship was built in 1910; it had sailed ever since.

■ **Subordinate one clause to the other,** depending on which clause is more important.

When it burned in 2001, its cabins and decks were destroyed.

Comma Splices

18a Separate two main clauses with a comma *only* when they are joined by a coordinating conjunction.

A comma cannot separate main clauses unless they are linked by a coordinating conjunction (*and, but, or, nor, for, so, yet*). Readers expect the same main clause to continue after a comma alone. When they find themselves reading a second main clause before they realize they have finished the first, they may have to reread.

You have several options for revising comma splices.

Making separate sentences

Revising a comma splice by making separate sentences from the main clauses will always be correct. The period is not only correct but preferable when the ideas expressed in the two main clauses are only loosely related:

Comma splice	Chemistry has contributed much to our understanding of foods, many foods such as wheat and beans can be produced in the laboratory.
Revised	Chemistry has contributed much to our understanding of foods. Many foods such as wheat and beans can be produced in the laboratory.

(CULTURE LANGUAGE) Making separate sentences may be the best option if you are used to writing very long sentences in your native language and often write comma splices in English.

Inserting a coordinating conjunction

When the ideas in the main clauses are closely related and equally important, you may correct a comma splice by inserting the appropriate coordinating conjunction immediately after the comma to join the clauses:

Comma splice	Some laboratory-grown foods taste good, they are nutritious.
Revised	Some laboratory-grown foods taste good, and they are nutritious.

Using a semicolon

If the relation between the ideas expressed in the main clauses is very close and obvious without a conjunction, you can separate the clauses with a semicolon.

Comma splice	Good taste is rare in laboratory-grown vegetables, they are usually bland.
Revised	Good taste is rare in laboratory-grown vegetables; they are usually bland.

Subordinating one clause

When the idea in one clause is more important than that in the other, you can express the less important idea in a phrase or a subordinate clause. (See p. 253 for a list of subordinating conjunctions and pp. 393–95 for more on subordination.) Subordination is often more effective than forming separate sentences because it defines the relation between ideas more precisely:

Comma splice	The vitamins are adequate, the flavor is deficient.
Revised	The vitamins are adequate. The flavor is deficient. [Both ideas receive equal weight.]
Improved	Even though the vitamins are adequate, the flavor is deficient. [Emphasis on the second idea.]

18b Separate main clauses related by *however,* *for example,* and so on.

Two kinds of words that are not conjunctions describe how one main clause relates to another:

- **Conjunctive adverbs,** such as *consequently, finally, hence, however, indeed, therefore,* and *thus.* (See p. 261 for a longer list.)
- Other **transitional expressions,** such as *even so, for example, in fact, of course, to the right,* and *to this end.* (See pp. 89–90 for a longer list.)

When two main clauses are related by a conjunctive adverb or a transitional expression, they must be separated by a period or by a semicolon. The adverb or expression is also generally set off by a comma or commas (see p. 432):

Comma splice	Healthcare costs are higher in the United States than in many other countries, <u>consequently</u> health insurance is also more costly.
Revised	Healthcare costs are higher in the United States than in many other countries. <u>Consequently,</u> health insurance is also more costly.
Revised	Healthcare costs are higher in the United States than in many other countries; <u>consequently,</u> health insurance is also more costly.

Conjunctive adverbs and transitional expressions are different from coordinating conjunctions (*and, but,* and so on) and subordinating conjunctions (*although, because,* and so on):

- Unlike conjunctions, conjunctive adverbs and transitional expressions do not join two clauses into a grammatical unit. They merely describe the way two clauses relate in meaning.
- Unlike conjunctions, conjunctive adverbs and transitional expressions can be moved within a clause (see also pp. 260–61). No matter where in the clause an adverb or expression falls, though, the clause must be separated from another main clause by a period or semicolon.

Comma splice

The increased time devoted to watching television is not the only cause of the decline in reading ability, <u>however,</u> it is one of the important causes.

Revised with a period

The increased time devoted to watching television is not the only cause of the decline in reading ability. <u>However,</u> it is one of the important causes.

Revised with a semicolon

The increased time devoted to watching television is not the only cause of the decline in reading ability; however, it is one of the important causes.

The increased time devoted to watching television is not the only cause of the decline in reading ability; it is, however, one of the important causes.

Exercise 18.1 Identifying and revising comma splices

Correct each comma splice below in *two* of the ways described on pages 342–43. If an item contains no comma splice, mark the number preceding it.

Example:

Carolyn still had a headache, she could not get the child-proof cap off the aspirin bottle.

Carolyn still had a headache because she could not get the child-proof cap off the aspirin bottle. [Subordination.]

Carolyn still had a headache, for she could not get the child-proof cap off the aspirin bottle. [Coordinating conjunction.]

1. Money has a long history, it goes back at least as far as the earliest records.
2. Many of the earliest records concern financial transactions, indeed, early history must often be inferred from commercial activity.
3. Every known society has had a system of money, though the objects serving as money have varied widely.
4. Sometimes the objects have had real value, in modern times, however, their value has been more abstract.
5. Cattle, fermented beverages, and rare shells have served as money, each one had actual value for the society.

—————— Fused Sentences ——————

 Combine two main clauses only with an appropriate conjunction or punctuation mark between them.

When two main clauses are joined without a word to connect them or a punctuation mark to separate them, the result is a **fused** or **run-on sentence.** Fused sentences can rarely be understood on first reading, and they are never acceptable in standard written English.

Fused   Our foreign policy is not well defined it confuses many countries.

Fused sentences may be corrected in the same ways as comma splices. See pages 342–43.

Separate sentences

Our foreign policy is not well defined. It confuses many countries.

Comma and coordinating conjunction

Our foreign policy is not well defined, and it confuses many countries.

Semicolon

Our foreign policy is not well defined; it confuses many countries.

Subordinating conjunction

Because our foreign policy is not well defined, it confuses many countries.

Exercise 18.2 Identifying and revising fused sentences

Revise each of the fused sentences below in *two* of the four ways shown above.

> *Example:*
> Tim was shy he usually refused invitations.
> Tim was shy, so he usually refused invitations.
> Tim was shy; he usually refused invitations.

1. Throughout history money and religion were closely linked there was little distinction between government and religion.
2. The head of state and the religious leader were often the same person all power rested in one ruler.
3. These powerful leaders decided what objects would serve as money their backing encouraged public faith in the money.
4. Coins were minted of precious metals the religious overtones of money were then strengthened.
5. People already believed the precious metals to be divine their use in money intensified its allure.

Exercise 18.3 Sentence combining to avoid comma splices and fused sentences

Combine each pair of sentences below into one sentence without creating a comma splice or fused sentence. Combine sentences by (1) supplying a comma and coordinating conjunction, (2) supplying a semicolon, or (3) subordinating one clause to the other. You will have to add, delete, or change words as well as punctuation.

> *Example:*
> The sun sank lower in the sky. The colors gradually faded.
> As the sun sank lower in the sky, the colors gradually faded. [The first clause is subordinated to the second.]

1. The exact origin of paper money is unknown. It has not survived as coins, shells, and other durable objects have.
2. Perhaps goldsmiths were also bankers. Thus they held the gold of their wealthy customers.
3. The goldsmiths probably gave customers receipts for their gold. These receipts were then used in trade.

4. The goldsmiths were something like modern-day bankers. Their receipts were something like modern-day money.
5. The goldsmiths became even more like modern-day bankers. They began issuing receipts for more gold than they actually held in their vaults.

Exercise 18.4   Revising: Comma splices and fused sentences

Identify and revise the comma splices and fused sentences in the following paragraph.

All those parents who urged their children to eat broccoli were right, the vegetable really is healthful. Broccoli contains sulforaphane, moreover, this mustard oil can be found in kale and Brussels sprouts. Sulforaphane causes the body to make an enzyme that attacks carcinogens, these substances cause cancer. The enzyme speeds up the work of the kidneys then they can flush harmful chemicals out of the body. Other vegetables have similar benefits however, green, leafy vegetables like broccoli are the most efficient. Thus wise people will eat their broccoli it could save their lives.

Note See page 378 for an exercise involving comma splices and fused sentences along with other sentence errors.

19

Pronoun Reference

A **pronoun** such as *it* or *they* derives its meaning from its **antecedent,** the noun it substitutes for. Therefore, a pronoun must refer clearly and unmistakably to its antecedent in order for the meaning to be clear. A sentence such as *Jim told Mark he was not invited* is not clear because the reader does not know whether *he* refers to Jim or to Mark.

One way to make pronoun reference clear is to ensure that the pronoun and antecedent agree in person, number, and gender (see pp. 311–12). The other way is to ensure that the pronoun refers unambiguously to a single, close, specific antecedent.

Visit *mycomplab.com* for more resources and exercises on pronoun reference.

Principal causes of unclear pronoun reference

- **More than one possible antecedent** (below):

Confusing	To keep birds from eating seeds, soak <u>them</u> in blue food coloring.
Clear	To keep birds from eating seeds, soak the seeds in blue food coloring.

- **Antecedent too far away** (facing page):

Confusing	Employees should consult with their supervisor <u>who</u> require personal time.
Clear	Employees who require personal time should consult with their supervisor.

- **Antecedent only implied** (p. 350):

Confusing	Many children begin reading on their own by watching television, but <u>this</u> should probably be discounted in government policy.
Clear	Many children begin reading on their own by watching television, but such self-instruction should probably be discounted in government policy.

See also pages 352–53.

Grammar checkers A grammar checker cannot recognize unclear pronoun reference. For instance, a checker did not spot any of the problems in Exercise 19.2 on page 353.

CULTURE LANGUAGE An English pronoun does need a clear antecedent nearby, but don't use both a pronoun and its antecedent as the subject of the same sentence or clause: *Jim* [not *Jim he*] *told Mark to go alone.* (See also pp. 372–73.)

19a Make a pronoun refer clearly to one antecedent.

When either of two nouns can be a pronoun's antecedent, the reference will not be clear:

Confusing	Emily Dickinson is sometimes compared with Jane Austen, but <u>she</u> was quite different.

Revise such a sentence in one of two ways:

- **Replace the pronoun with the appropriate noun:**

Clear	Emily Dickinson is sometimes compared with Jane Austen, but <u>Dickinson</u> [or <u>Austen</u>] was quite different.

- **Avoid repetition by rewriting the sentence.** If you use the pronoun, make sure it has only one possible antecedent:

Clear	Despite occasional comparison, Emily Dickinson and Jane Austen were quite different.
Clear	Though sometimes compared with her, Emily Dickinson was quite different from Jane Austen.

Sentences that report what someone said, using verbs such as *said* or *told*, often require direct rather than indirect quotation:

Confusing	Juliet Noble told Ashley Torre that she was next in line for the job.
Clear	Juliet Noble told Ashley Torre, "I am next in line for the job."
Clear	Juliet Noble told Ashley Torre, "You are next in line for the job."

Note Avoid the awkward device of using a pronoun followed by the appropriate noun in parentheses, as in the following example:

Weak	Noble and Torre had both hoped for the job, so she (Noble) was disappointed.
Improved	Noble was disappointed because she and Torre had both hoped for the job.

19b Place a pronoun close enough to its antecedent to ensure clarity.

A clause beginning *who, which,* or *that* generally should fall immediately after the word to which it refers:

Confusing	Kara found a lamp in the attic that her aunt had used.
Clear	In the attic Kara found a lamp that her aunt had used.

Even when only one word could possibly serve as the antecedent of a pronoun, the relationship between the two may still be unclear if they are widely separated:

Confusing	Jane Austen had little formal education but was well educated at home. Far from living an isolated life in the English countryside, the Austens were a large family with a wide circle of friends who provided entertainment and cultural enrichment. They also provided material for her stories.
Clear	Jane Austen had little formal education but was well educated at home. Far from living an isolated life in the English countryside, the Austens were a large family with a wide circle of friends who provided entertainment and cultural enrichment. They also provided material for Jane Austen's stories.

Exercise 19.1 Revising: Ambiguous and remote pronoun reference

Rewrite the following sentences to eliminate unclear pronoun reference. If you use a pronoun in your revision, be sure that it refers to only one antecedent and that it falls close enough to its antecedent to ensure clarity.

Example:

Saul found an old gun in the rotting shed that was just as his grandfather had left it.

In the rotting shed Saul found an old <u>gun that</u> was just as his grandfather had left it.

1. There is a difference between the heroes of the twentieth century and the heroes of earlier times: they have flaws in their characters.
2. Sports fans still admire Pete Rose, Babe Ruth, and Joe Namath even though they could not be perfect.
3. Fans liked Rose for having his young son serve as batboy when he was in Cincinnati.
4. The reputation Rose earned as a gambler and tax evader may overshadow his reputation as a ballplayer, but it will survive.
5. Rose amassed an unequaled record as a hitter, using his bat to do things no one else has ever done. It stands even though Rose was banned from baseball.

19c Make a pronoun refer to a specific antecedent, not an implied one.

A pronoun should refer to a specific noun or other pronoun. The reader can only guess at the meaning of a pronoun when its antecedent is implied by the context, not stated outright.

1 Use *this, that, which,* and *it* cautiously.

The most common kind of implied reference occurs when the pronoun *this, that, which,* or *it* refers to a whole idea or situation described in the preceding clause, sentence, or even paragraph. Such reference, often called **broad reference**, is acceptable only when the pronoun refers clearly to the entire preceding clause. In the following sentence, *which* could not possibly refer to anything but the whole preceding clause:

I can be kind and civil to people, <u>which</u> is more than you can.
—George Bernard Shaw

But if a pronoun might confuse a reader, you should avoid using it or provide an appropriate noun:

Confusing   The British knew little of the American countryside, and they had no experience with the colonists' guerilla tactics. This gave the colonists an advantage.

Clear   The British knew little of the American countryside, and they had no experience with the colonists' guerrilla tactics. This ignorance and inexperience gave the colonists an advantage.

2 *It* and *they* should have definite antecedents.

Although common in speech, using *it* and *they* to refer to indefinite antecedents is inappropriate in writing.

Confusing   In Chapter 4 of this book, it describes the early flights of the Wright brothers.
Clear   Chapter 4 of this book describes the early flights of the Wright brothers.

Confusing   Even in reality TV shows, they present a false picture of life.
Clear   Even reality TV shows present a false picture of life.

3 Implied nouns are not clear antecedents.

A noun may be implied in some other word or phrase, as *happiness* is implied in *happy*, *driver* is implied in *drive*, and *mother* is implied in *mother's*. But a pronoun cannot refer clearly to an implied noun, only to a specific, stated one:

Confusing   Cohen's report brought her a lawsuit.

Clear   Cohen was sued over her report.

Confusing   Her reports on psychological development generally go unnoticed outside it.

Clear   Her reports on psychological development generally go unnoticed outside the field.

4 Titles of papers are not clear antecedents.

The title of a paper is entirely separate from the paper itself, so a pronoun should not be used in the opening sentence of a paper to refer to the title:

Title	How to Row a Boat
Confusing	<u>This</u> is not as easy as it looks.
Revised	<u>Rowing a boat</u> is not as easy as it looks.

19d Use *you* only to mean "you, the reader."

You should clearly mean "you, the reader." The context must be appropriate for such a meaning:

Inappropriate	In the fourteenth century <u>you</u> had to struggle simply to survive.
Revised	In the fourteenth century <u>one</u> [or <u>a person</u>] had to struggle simply to survive.

Writers sometimes drift into *you* because *one, a person, the individual,* or a similar indefinite word can be difficult to sustain. Sentence after sentence, the indefinite word may sound stuffy, and it requires the sexist *he* or the awkward *he or she* for pronoun-antecedent agreement (see pp. 313–15). To avoid these difficulties, try using plural nouns and pronouns:

Original	In the fourteenth century <u>one</u> had to struggle simply to survive.
Revised	In the fourteenth century <u>people</u> had to struggle simply to survive.

19e Use the pronoun *it* only one way in a sentence.

We use *it* idiomatically in expressions such as *It is raining.* We use *it* to postpone the subject in sentences such as *It is true that more jobs are available to women today.* And we use *it* as a personal pronoun in sentences such as *Nicole wanted the book, but she couldn't find it.* All these uses are standard, but two of them in the same passage can confuse the reader:

Confusing	It is true that the Constitution sets limits, but it is also flexible.
Clear	<u>The Constitution</u> does set limits, but it is also flexible.

19f Use *who, which,* and *that* for appropriate antecedents.

The relative pronouns *who, which,* and *that* commonly refer to persons, animals, or things. *Who* refers most often to persons but may also refer to animals that have names:

Dorothy is the girl <u>who</u> visits Oz.
Her dog, Toto, <u>who</u> accompanies her, gives her courage.

Which refers to animals and things:

The Orinoco River, <u>which</u> is 1600 miles long, flows through Venezuela into the Atlantic Ocean.

That refers to animals and things and occasionally to persons when they are collective or anonymous:

The rocket <u>that</u> failed cost millions.
Infants <u>that</u> walk need constant tending.

(See also p. 431 for the use of *which* and *that* in nonessential and essential clauses.)

The possessive *whose* generally refers to people but may refer to animals and things to avoid awkward and wordy *of which* constructions:

The book <u>whose</u> binding broke was rare. [Compare *The book <u>of which</u> the binding broke was rare.*]

Exercise 19.2   Revising: Indefinite and inappropriate pronoun reference

Many of the pronouns in the following sentences do not refer to specific, appropriate antecedents. Revise the sentences as necessary to make them clear.

Example:

In Glacier National Park, they have moose, elk, and wolves.
<u>Moose, elk, and wolves live</u> in Glacier National Park.

1. "Life begins at forty" is a cliché many people live by, and this may well be true.
2. When she was forty, Pearl Buck's novel *The Good Earth* won the Pulitzer Prize.
3. Buck was a novelist which wrote primarily about China.
4. In *The Good Earth* you have to struggle, but fortitude is rewarded.
5. Buck received much critical praise and earned over $7 million, but she was very modest about it.
6. Kenneth Kaunda, past president of Zambia, was elected to it in 1964, at age forty.
7. When Catherine I became empress of Russia at age forty, they feared more than loved her.
8. At forty, Paul Revere made his famous ride to warn American revolutionary leaders that the British were going to arrest them. This gave the colonists time to prepare for battle.
9. In the British House of Commons they did not welcome forty-year-old Nancy Astor as the first female member when she entered in 1919.
10. In 610 CE, Muhammad, age forty, began to have a series of visions that became the foundation of the Muslim faith. Since then, millions of people have become one.

Exercise 19.3 Revising: Pronoun reference

Revise the following paragraph so that each pronoun refers clearly to a single specific and appropriate antecedent.

In Charlotte Brontë's *Jane Eyre,* she is a shy young woman that takes a job as governess. Her employer is a rude, brooding man named Rochester. He lives in a mysterious mansion on the English moors, which contributes an eerie quality to Jane's experience. Eerier still are the fires, strange noises, and other unexplained happenings in the house; but Rochester refuses to discuss this. Eventually, they fall in love. On the day they are to be married, however, she learns that he has a wife hidden in the house. She is hopelessly insane and violent and must be guarded at all times, which explains his strange behavior. Heartbroken, Jane leaves the moors, and many years pass before they are reunited.

Note See page 378 for an exercise involving unclear pronoun reference along with sentence fragments, comma splices, and other sentence errors.

20

Shifts

Inconsistencies in grammatical elements will confuse your readers and distort your meaning. The box on the facing page shows ways to correct inconsistencies, or **shifts,** in nouns, pronouns, and verbs.

Shifts are likely to occur while you are trying to piece together meaning during drafting. But during editing you should make the grammatical elements of your sentences consistent.

Grammar checkers A grammar checker cannot recognize most shifts in sentences. Proofread your work on your own, looking carefully for inconsistencies.

my**comp**lab

Visit *mycomplab.com* for more resources and exercises on shifts.

Ways to correct shifts

First draft

A bank owes more to its customers than is held in
reserve. It kept enough assets to meet reasonable
withdrawals, but panicked customers may demand
all their deposits. Then demands will exceed supplies, and banks will fail. These days, a person's
losses are not likely to be great because the government insures your deposits.

Shift in verb voice

Shift in verb tense

Shift in number

Shifts in number
and person

Revised

A bank owes more to its customers than **it holds** in reserve. It **keeps** enough assets to meet reasonable withdrawals, but panicked customers may demand all their deposits. Then demands will exceed supplies, and **the bank** will fail. These days, the losses of **customers** are not likely to be great because the government insures **their** deposits.

20a Keep a sentence or related sentences consistent in person and number.

Person in grammar refers to the distinction among the person talking (first person), the person spoken to (second person), and the person, object, or concept being talked about (third person). **Number** refers to the distinction between one (singular) and more than one (plural).

Shifts in person

Most shifts in person occur because we can refer to people in general, including our readers, either in the third person (*a person, one; people, they*) or in the second person (*you*):

People should not drive when they have been drinking.
One should not drive when he or she has been drinking.
You should not drive when you have been drinking.

Although any one of these possibilities is acceptable in an appropriate context, a mixture of them is inconsistent:

Inconsistent	If a person works hard, you can gain satisfaction.
Revised	If you work hard, you can gain satisfaction.
Revised	If a person works hard, he or she can gain satisfaction.
Better	If people work hard, they can gain satisfaction.

Shifts in number

Inconsistency in number occurs most often between a pronoun and its antecedent (see p. 311):

Inconsistent	If a <u>student</u> does not understand a problem, <u>they</u> should consult the teacher.
Revised	If a <u>student</u> does not understand a problem, <u>he or she</u> should consult the teacher.
Better	If <u>students</u> do not understand a problem, <u>they</u> should consult the teacher.
Or	A <u>student who</u> does not understand a problem should consult the teacher.

Note Generic nouns and most indefinite pronouns take singular pronouns with a definite gender: *he, she,* or *it.* When we use a generic noun like *student* or *person* or an indefinite pronoun like *everyone* or *each,* we often mean to include both males and females. To indicate this meaning, use *he or she* rather than *he* (as in the first of the preceding revisions) or, better still, rewrite in the plural or rewrite to avoid the inconsistent pronoun (as in the second and third of the revisions). See pages 313–15 for more discussion and examples.

Inconsistency in number can also occur between other words (usually nouns) that relate to each other in meaning.

Inconsistent	All the <u>boys</u> have a good <u>reputation</u>.
Revised	All the <u>boys</u> have good <u>reputations</u>.

The consistency in the revised sentence is called **logical agreement** because the nouns are consistent (the *boys* have *reputations,* not a single *reputation*).

Exercise 20.1 Revising: Shifts in person and number

Revise the following sentences to make them consistent in person and number.

Example:

A plumber will fix burst pipes, but they won't repair waterlogged appliances.

<u>Plumbers</u> will fix burst pipes, but they won't repair waterlogged appliances.

1. When a taxpayer is waiting to receive a tax refund from the Internal Revenue Service, you begin to notice what time the mail carrier arrives.
2. If the taxpayer does not receive a refund check within six weeks of filing a return, they may not have followed the rules of the IRS.
3. If a taxpayer does not include a Social Security number on a return, you will have to wait for a refund.

4. When taxpayers do not file their return early, they will not get a refund quickly.
5. If one makes errors on the tax form, they might even be audited, thereby delaying a refund even longer.

20b Keep a sentence or related sentences consistent in tense and mood.

Shifts in tense

Within a sentence or from one sentence to another, certain changes in tense may be required to indicate changes in actual or relative time (see pp. 294–95). The following changes are necessary:

Ramon will graduate from high school thirty-one years after his father arrived in the United States.

But changes that are not required by meaning distract readers. Unnecessary shifts between past and present in passages narrating a series of events are particularly confusing:

Inconsistent   Immediately after Booth shot Lincoln, Major Rathbone threw himself upon the assassin. But Booth pulls a knife and plunges it into the major's arm.

Revised   Immediately after Booth shot Lincoln, Major Rathbone threw himself upon the assassin. But Booth pulled a knife and plunged it into the major's arm.

Use the present tense consistently to describe what an author has written, including the action in literature or a film:

Inconsistent   The main character in the novel suffers psychologically because he has a clubfoot, but he eventually triumphed over his disability.

Revised   The main character in the novel suffers psychologically because he has a clubfoot, but he eventually triumphs over his disability.

Shifts in mood

Shifts in the mood of verbs occur most frequently in directions when the writer moves between the imperative mood (*Unplug the appliance*) and the indicative mood (*You should unplug the appliance*). (See p. 298.) Directions are usually clearer and more concise in the imperative, as long as its use is consistent:

Inconsistent   Cook the mixture slowly, and you should stir it until the sugar is dissolved.

Revised   Cook the mixture slowly, and stir it until the sugar is dissolved.

Exercise 20.2 Revising: Shifts in tense and mood

Revise each of the following sentences to make it consistent in tense and mood.

Example:

Jenna ran to first, rounded the base, and keeps running until she slides into second.

Jenna ran to first, rounded the base, and kept running until she slid into second.

1. When your cholesterol count is too high, adjusting your diet and exercise level reduced it.
2. After you lowered your cholesterol rate, you decrease the chances of heart attack and stroke.
3. First eliminate saturated fats from your diet; then you should consume more whole grains and raw vegetables.
4. To avoid saturated fats, substitute turkey and chicken for beef, and you should use cholesterol-free salad dressing and cooking oil.
5. A regular program of aerobic exercise, such as walking or swimming, improves your cholesterol rate and made you feel much healthier.

20c Keep a sentence or related sentences consistent in subject and voice.

When a verb is in the **active voice**, the subject names the actor: *Linda passed the peas.* When a verb is in the **passive voice**, the subject names the receiver of the action: *The peas were passed* [*by Linda*]. (See pp. 300–02.)

A shift in voice may sometimes help focus the reader's attention on a single subject, as in *The candidate campaigned vigorously and was nominated on the first ballot.* However, most shifts in voice also involve shifts in subject. They are unnecessary and confusing.

Inconsistent	Internet blogs cover an enormous range of topics. Opportunities for people to discuss pet issues are provided on these sites.
Revised	Internet blogs cover an enormous range of topics and provide opportunities for people to discuss pet issues.

Exercise 20.3 Revising: Shifts in subject and voice

Make the following sentences consistent in subject and voice.

Example:
At the reunion they ate hot dogs and volleyball was played.
At the reunion they ate hot dogs and played volleyball.

1. If students learn how to study efficiently, much better grades will be made on tests.
2. Conscientious students begin to prepare for tests immediately after the first class is attended.
3. Before each class all reading assignments are completed, and the students outline the material and answer any study questions.
4. In class they listen carefully and good notes are taken.
5. Questions are asked by the students when they do not understand the professor.

20d Keep a quotation or a question consistently direct or indirect.

Direct quotations or questions report the exact words of a quotation or question:

"I am the greatest," bragged Muhammad Ali.
In his day few people asked, "Is he right?"

Indirect quotations or questions report that someone said or asked something, but not in the exact words:

Muhammad Ali bragged that he was the greatest.
In his day few people asked whether he was right.

Shifts between direct and indirect quotations or questions are difficult to follow.

Shift in quotation	Kapek reported that the rats avoided the maze and "as of this writing, none responds to conditioning."
Revised (indirect)	Kapek reported that the rats avoided the maze and that as of his writing none responded to conditioning.
Revised (direct)	Kapek reported, "The rats avoid the maze. As of this writing, none responds to conditioning."
Shift in question	The reader wonders whether the experiment failed or did it perhaps succeed?
Revised (indirect)	The reader wonders whether the experiment failed or whether it perhaps succeeded.
Revised (direct)	Did the experiment fail? Or did it perhaps succeed?

For more on quotations, see pages 438–40 (commas with signal phrases such as *she said*), 461–68 (quotation marks), and 601–06 (integrating quotations into your writing). For more on questions, see pages 421–22.

Exercise 20.4 Revising: Shifts in direct and indirect quotations and questions

Revise each of the following sentences twice, once to make it consistently direct, once to make it consistently indirect. You will have to guess at the exact wording of direct quotations and questions that are now stated indirectly.

Example:

We all wonder what the next decade will bring and will we thrive or not?

Direct: What will the next decade bring? Will we thrive or not?

Indirect: We all wonder what the next decade will bring and whether we will thrive or not.

1. One anthropologist says that the functions of marriage have changed and "nowhere more dramatically than in industrialized cultures."
2. The question even arises of whether siblings may marry and would the union be immoral?
3. The author points out, "Sibling marriage is still illegal everywhere in the United States" and that people are still prosecuted under the law.
4. She says that incest could be considered a universal taboo and "the questions asked about the taboo vary widely."
5. Some ask is the taboo a way of protecting the family or whether it may be instinctive.

Exercise 20.5 Revising: Shifts

Revise the following paragraph to eliminate unnecessary shifts in person, number, tense, mood, and voice.

Driving in snow need not be dangerous if you practice a few rules. First, one should avoid fast starts, which prevent the wheels from gaining traction and may result in the car's getting stuck. Second, drive more slowly than usual, and you should pay attention to the feel of the car: if the steering seemed unusually loose or the wheels did not seem to be grabbing the road, slow down. Third, avoid fast stops, which lead to skids. One should be alert for other cars and intersections that may necessitate that the brakes be applied suddenly. If you need to slow down, the car's momentum can be reduced by downshifting as well as by applying the brakes. When braking, press the pedal to the floor only if you have antilock brakes; otherwise, the pedal should be pumped in short bursts. If you feel the car skidding, the brakes should be released and the wheel should be turned into the direction of the skid, and then the brakes should be pressed or pumped again. If one repeated these motions, the skid would be stopped and the speed of the car would be reduced.

Note See page 378 for an exercise involving shifts along with sentence fragments, comma splices, and other sentence errors.

21

Misplaced and Dangling Modifiers

When reading a sentence in English, we depend principally on the arrangement of the words to tell us how they are related. In writing, we may create confusion if we fail to connect modifiers to the words they modify.

Grammar checkers A grammar checker cannot recognize most problems with modifiers. For instance, a checker failed to flag the misplaced modifiers in *Gasoline high prices affect usually car sales* or the dangling modifier in *The vandalism was visible passing the building.*

Misplaced Modifiers

A modifier is **misplaced** if readers can't easily relate it to the word it modifies. Misplaced modifiers may be awkward, confusing, or even unintentionally funny.

21a Place modifiers where they will clearly modify the words intended.

Readers tend to link a modifying word, phrase, or clause to the nearest word it could modify: *I saw a man in a green hat*. Thus the writer must place the phrase so that it clearly modifies the intended word and not some other.

Confusing	He served steak to the men on paper plates.
Revised	He served the men steak on paper plates.
Confusing	Many dogs are killed by cars and trucks roaming unleashed.
Revised	Many dogs roaming unleashed are killed by cars and trucks.

mycomplab

Visit *mycomplab.com* for more resources and exercises on misplaced and dangling modifiers.

361

Ways to revise misplaced modifiers

■ **Place modifiers clearly** (previous page and below).

| Confusing | Listening to music can cause hearing loss <u>at high levels</u>. |
| Revised | Listening to music at high levels can cause hearing loss. |

■ **Place limiting modifiers carefully** (facing page).

| Confusing | The women <u>only</u> reached the summit on their last climb. |
| Revised | The women reached the summit only on their last climb. |

■ **Make each modifier refer to only one grammatical unit** (facing page).

Confusing	Students who fail to complete assignments <u>often</u> receive poor grades.
Revised	Students who often fail to complete assignments receive poor grades.
Revised	Students who fail to complete assignments receive poor grades often.

■ **Keep grammatical units together** (pp. 364–65).

| Awkward | The owner ordered the dog to not bark. |
| Revised | The owner ordered the dog **not to bark**. |

■ **Place adverbs and adjectives conventionally** (pp. 366–67).

| Awkward | Once endangered, bald eagles were spotted <u>seldom</u> in the eastern United States. |
| Revised | Once endangered, bald eagles were seldom spotted in the eastern United States. |

| Confusing | This is the only chocolate chip cookie in a bag that tastes like Mom's. [Actual advertisement.] |
| Revised | This is the only <u>bagged</u> [or <u>packaged</u>] chocolate chip cookie that tastes like Mom's. |

Exercise 21.1 Revising: Misplaced phrases and clauses

Revise the following sentences so that phrases and clauses clearly modify the appropriate words.

Example:

I came to enjoy flying over time.
Over time I came to enjoy flying.

1. Women have contributed much to knowledge and culture of great value.

2. Emma Willard founded the Troy Female Seminary, the first institution to provide a college-level education for women in 1821.
3. Sixteen years later Mary Lyon founded Mount Holyoke Female Seminary, the first true women's college with directors and a campus who would sustain the college even after Lyon's death.
4. Una was the first US newspaper, which was founded by Pauline Wright Davis in 1853, that was dedicated to gaining women's rights.
5. Mitchell's Comet was discovered in 1847, which was named for Maria Mitchell.

21b Place limiting modifiers carefully.

Limiting modifiers include *almost, even, exactly, hardly, just, merely, nearly, only, scarcely,* and *simply.* In speech these modifiers often occur before the verb, regardless of the words they are intended to modify. In writing, however, these modifiers should fall immediately before the word or word group they modify to avoid any ambiguity:

Unclear   She only found that fossil on her last dig.

Revised   She found only that fossil on her last dig.

Revised   She found that fossil only on her last dig.

Exercise 21.2 Using limiting modifiers

Use each of the following limiting modifiers in two versions of the same sentence.

Example:

only

He is the only one I like. He is the one only I like.

1. almost   3. hardly   5. nearly
2. even   4. simply

21c Make each modifier refer to only one grammatical element.

A modifier can modify only *one* element in a sentence—the subject, the verb, or some other element. A **squinting modifier** seems confusingly to refer to either of two words:

Squinting   Snipers who fired on the soldiers often escaped capture.

Clear   Snipers who often fired on the soldiers escaped capture.

Clear   Snipers who fired on the soldiers escaped capture often.

When an adverb modifies an entire main clause, as in the last example, it can usually be moved to the beginning of the sentence: *Often, snipers who fired on the soldiers escaped capture.*

Exercise 21.3 Revising: Squinting modifiers

Revise each sentence twice so that the squinting modifier applies clearly first to one element and then to the other.

Example:
The work that he hoped would satisfy him completely frustrated him.
The work that he hoped would <u>completely</u> satisfy him frustrated him.
The work that he hoped would satisfy him frustrated him <u>completely</u>.

1. People who sunbathe often can damage their skin.
2. Sunbathers who apply a sunscreen frequently block some of the sun's harmful ultraviolet rays.
3. Men and women who lie out in the sun often have leathery, dry skin.
4. Doctors tell sunbathers when they are older they risk skin cancer.
5. People who stay out of the sun usually will have better skin and fewer chances of skin cancer.

21d Keep subjects, verbs, and objects together.

English sentences tend to move from subject to verb to object. The movement is so familiar that modifiers between these elements can be awkward.

A subject and verb may be separated by an adjective that modifies the subject: *The hurricane, which hit the city with ferocious winds, damaged many homes and public buildings.* But an adverb of more than a word usually stops the flow of the sentence:

Awkward The city, after the hurricane, began massive rebuilding.

Revised After the hurricane, the city began massive rebuilding.

Even a one-word adverb will be awkward between a verb and its object:

Awkward The hurricane had damaged <u>badly</u> many homes in the city.

Revised The hurricane had <u>badly</u> damaged many homes in the city.

21e Keep parts of infinitives or verb phrases together.

An **infinitive** consists of the marker *to* plus the plain form of a verb: *to produce, to enjoy.* The two words in an infinitive are widely regarded as a grammatical unit that should not be split apart by a modifier:

γ infinitive γ
Awkward The weather service expected temperatures to <u>not</u> rise.

infinitive
Revised The weather service expected temperatures <u>not</u> to rise.

A split infinitive may sometimes be natural and preferable, though it may still bother some readers:

— infinitive —
Several US industries expect to <u>more than</u> triple their use of robots.

Here the split infinitive is more economical than the alternatives, such as *Several US industries expect to increase their use of robots by more than three times.*

A **verb phrase** consists of a helping verb plus a main verb, as in *will call, was going, had been writing* (see p. 276). A single-word adverb may be inserted after the helping verb in a verb phrase (or the first helping verb if more than one): *Scientists have <u>lately</u> been using spacecraft to study the sun.* But when longer adverbs interrupt verb phrases, the result is almost always awkward:

helping
verb ┌——— adverb ———
Awkward People who have osteoporosis can, by increasing their daily
└——————————————┐ main verb
intake of calcium and vitamin D, improve their bone density.
┌————————— adverb ——————————┐
Revised By increasing their daily intake of calcium and vitamin D,
verb phrase
people who have osteoporosis can improve their bone density.

CULTURE LANGUAGE In an English question, place a one-word adverb after the first helping verb and the subject:

helping   rest of
verb   subject   adverb   verb phrase
Will spacecraft <u>ever</u> be able to leave the solar system?

Exercise 21.4 Revising: Separated sentence parts

Revise the following sentences to connect separated parts (subject-predicate, verb-object, verb phrase, infinitive).

Example:
Most children have by the time they are seven lost a tooth.
<u>By the time they are seven</u>, most children have lost a tooth.

1. Myra Bradwell founded in 1868 the *Chicago Legal News*.
2. Bradwell was later denied, although she had qualified, admission to the Illinois Bar Association.
3. In an attempt to finally gain admission to the bar, she carried the case to the Supreme Court, but the justices decided against her.
4. Bradwell was determined that no other woman would, if she were qualified, be denied entrance to a profession.

5. The Illinois legislature finally passed, in response to Bradwell's persuasion, a bill ensuring that no one on the basis of gender would be restricted from a profession.

21f Position adverbs with care.

A few adverbs are subject to conventions that can trouble nonnative speakers of English.

Adverbs of frequency

Adverbs of frequency include *always, never, often, rarely, seldom, sometimes,* and *usually.* They appear at the beginning of a sentence, before a one-word verb, or after the helping verb in a verb phrase:

	verb phrase adverb
Awkward	Robots have put <u>sometimes</u> humans out of work.

	helping verb adverb main verb
Revised	Robots have <u>sometimes</u> put humans out of work.

	adverb verb phrase
Revised	<u>Sometimes</u> robots have put humans out of work.

Adverbs of frequency always follow the verb *be:*

	adverb verb
Awkward	Robots <u>often</u> are helpful to workers.

	verb adverb
Revised	Robots are <u>often</u> helpful to workers.

Adverbs of degree

Adverbs of degree include *absolutely, almost, certainly, completely, especially, extremely, hardly,* and *only.* They fall just before the word modified (an adjective, another adverb, sometimes a verb).

	adjective adverb
Awkward	Robots have been useful <u>especially</u> in making cars.

	adverb adjective
Revised	Robots have been <u>especially</u> useful in making cars.

Adverbs of manner

Adverbs of manner include *badly, sweetly, tightly,* and others that describe how something is done. They usually fall after the verb:

	adverb verb
Awkward	Robots <u>smoothly</u> work on assembly lines.

	verb adverb
Revised	Robots work <u>smoothly</u> on assembly lines.

The adverb *not*

When the adverb *not* modifies a verb, place it after the helping verb (or the first helping verb if more than one):

<table>
<tr><td></td><td>helping
verb</td><td>main
verb</td></tr>
</table>

	helping verb	main verb
Awkward	Robots do think <u>not</u>.	

	helping verb	main verb
Revised	Robots do <u>not</u> think.	

Place *not* after a form of *be: Robots are <u>not</u> thinkers.*

When *not* modifies another adverb or an adjective, place it before the other modifier: *Robots are <u>not</u> sleek machines.*

21g Arrange adjectives appropriately.

English follows distinctive rules for arranging two or three adjectives before a noun. (A string of more than three adjectives before a noun is rare.) The order depends on the meaning of the adjectives, as indicated in the following table:

Determiner	Opinion	Size or shape	Color	Origin	Material	Noun used as adjective	Noun
many						st ate	laws
	striking		green	Thai			birds
a	fine			German			camera
this		square			wooden		table
all						business	reports
the			blue		litmus		paper

See pages 435–36 on punctuating adjectives before a noun.

Exercise 21.5 **Revising: Placement of adverbs and adjectives**

Revise the sentences below to correct the positions of adverbs or adjectives. If a sentence is already correct as given, mark the number preceding it.

Example:
Gasoline high prices affect usually car sales.
<u>High</u> gasoline prices <u>usually</u> affect car sales.

1. Some years ago Detroit cars often were praised.
2. Luxury large cars especially were prized.
3. Then a serious oil shortage led drivers to value small foreign cars that got good mileage.
4. When gasoline ample supplies returned, consumers bought again American large cars and trucks.
5. Consumers not were loyal to the big vehicles when gasoline prices dramatically rose.

--- **Dangling Modifiers** ---

21h Relate dangling modifiers to their sentences.

A **dangling modifier** does not sensibly modify anything in its sentence:

Dangling Passing the building, the vandalism became visible.

Dangling modifiers usually introduce sentences, contain a verb form, and imply but do not name a subject. In the preceding example, the implied subject is the someone or something passing the building. Readers assume that this implied subject is the same as the subject of the sentence (*vandalism* in the example), but vandalism does not pass buildings. The modifier "dangles" because it does not connect sensibly to the rest of the sentence.

Certain kinds of modifiers are the most likely to dangle:

■ **Participial phrases:**

Dangling Passing the building, the vandalism became visible.
Revised   As we passed the building, the vandalism became visible.

■ **Infinitive phrases:**

Dangling To understand the causes, vandalism has been studied.
Revised   To understand the causes, researchers have studied vandalism.

■ **Prepositional phrases in which the object of the preposition is a gerund:**

Dangling After studying the problem, vandals are now thought to share certain characteristics.
Revised   After studying the problem, researchers think that vandals share certain characteristics.

■ **Elliptical clauses in which the subject and perhaps the verb are omitted:**

Dangling When destructive, researchers have learned that vandals are more likely to be in groups.
Revised   When vandals are destructive, researchers have learned, they are more likely to be in groups.

Dangling modifiers are especially likely when the verb in the main clause is in the **passive voice** instead of the **active voice**, as in *vandalism has been investigated* and *vandals are thought*. (See pp. 300–02 for more on the passive voice.)

Identifying and revising dangling modifiers

■ **Identify the modifier's subject.** If the modifier lacks a stated subject (as *when in diapers* does), identify what the modifier describes.

■ **Compare the subject of the modifier and the subject of the sentence.** Verify that what the modifier describes is in fact the subject of the main clause. If it is not, the modifier probably dangles.

■ **Revise as needed.** Either (*a*) recast the dangling modifier with a stated subject of its own, or (*b*) change the subject of the main clause to be what the modifier describes.

	┌─── modifier ───┐ subject
Dangling	When in diapers, my mother remarried.
Revision *a*	When I was in diapers, my mother remarried.
Revision *b*	When in diapers, I attended my mother's second wedding.

Note A modifier may be dangling even when the sentence elsewhere contains a word the modifier might seem to describe, such as *vandals* below:

Dangling   When destructive, researchers have learned that vandals are more likely to be in groups.

In addition, a dangling modifier may fall at the end of a sentence:

Dangling   The vandalism was visible passing the building.

Revising dangling modifiers

Revise most dangling modifiers in one of two ways, depending on what you want to emphasize in the sentence.

■ **Change the subject of the main clause to a word the modifier properly describes:**

Dangling   To express themselves, graffiti decorate walls.

Revised   To express themselves, some youths decorate walls with graffiti.

■ **Rewrite the dangling modifier as a complete clause with its own stated subject and verb:**

Revised   Because some youths need to express themselves, they decorate walls with graffiti.

Exercise 21.6   Revising: Dangling modifiers

Revise the following sentences to eliminate any dangling modifiers. Each item has more than one possible answer.

Example:

Driving north, the vegetation became increasingly sparse.

Driving north, we noticed that the vegetation became increasingly sparse.

As we drove north, the vegetation became increasingly sparse.

1. After accomplishing many deeds of valor, Andrew Jackson's fame led to his election to the presidency in 1828 and 1832.
2. By the age of fourteen, both of Jackson's parents had died.
3. To aid the American Revolution, service as a mounted courier was chosen by Jackson.
4. Though not well educated, a successful career as a lawyer and judge proved Jackson's ability.
5. Winning many military battles, the American public believed in Jackson's leadership.

Exercise 21.7 Sentence combining: Placing modifiers

Combine each pair of sentences below into a single sentence by rewriting one as a modifier. Make sure the modifier applies clearly to the appropriate word. You will have to add, delete, and rearrange words, and you may find that more than one answer is possible in each case.

Example:

Eric demanded a hearing from the principal. He wanted to appeal the decision.

Wanting to appeal the decision, Eric demanded a hearing from the principal.

1. Evening falls in the Central American rain forests. The tungara frogs begin their croaking chorus.
2. Male tungara frogs croak loudly at night. The "songs" they sing are designed to attract female frogs.
3. But predators also hear the croaking. They gather to feast on the frogs.
4. The predators are lured by their croaking dinners. The predators include bullfrogs, snakes, bats, and opossums.
5. The frogs hope to mate. Their nightly chorus can result in death instead.

Exercise 21.8 Revising: Misplaced and dangling modifiers

Revise the following paragraph to eliminate any misplaced or dangling modifiers.

Central American tungara frogs silence several nights a week their mating croaks. When not croaking, the chance that the frogs will be eaten by predators is reduced. The frogs seem to fully believe in "safety in numbers." They more than likely will croak along with a large group rather than by themselves. By forgoing croaking on some nights, the frogs' behavior prevents the species from "croaking."

Note See page 378 for an exercise involving misplaced and dangling modifiers along with other sentence errors.

22

Mixed and Incomplete Sentences

Mixed Sentences

A **mixed sentence** contains two or more parts that are incompatible—that is, the parts do not fit together. The misfit may be in grammar or in meaning.

Grammar checkers A grammar checker may recognize a simple mixed construction such as *reason is because*, but it will fail to flag most mixed sentences.

22a Untangle sentences that are mixed in grammar.

Sentences mixed in grammar combine two or more incompatible grammatical structures.

1 Make sure subject and verb fit together grammatically.

A mixed sentence may occur when you start a sentence with one plan and end it with another:

> ┌────── modifier (prepositional phrase) ──────┐ verb
> **Mixed** By paying more attention to impressions than facts leads us to misjudge others.

> ┌────── modifier (prepositional phrase) ──────┐ subject + verb
> **Revised** By paying more attention to impressions than facts, we misjudge others.

> ┌────── subject (gerund phrase) ──────┐ verb
> **Revised** Paying more attention to impressions than facts leads us to misjudge others.

Constructions that use *Just because* clauses as subjects are common in speech but should be avoided in writing.

Visit *mycomplab.com* for more resources on mixed and incomplete sentences.

| modifier (subordinate clause) | verb |

Mixed Just because no one is watching doesn't mean we have license to break the law.

| modifier (subordinate clause) | subject + verb |

Revised Even when no one is watching, we don't have license to break the law.

In some mixed sentences the grammar is so jumbled that the writer has little choice but to start over:

Mixed My long-range goal is through law school and government work I hope to help people deal with those problems we all deal with more effectively.

Revised My long-range goal is to go to law school and then work in government so that I can help people deal more effectively with problems we all face.

A mixed sentence is especially likely when you are working on a computer and connect parts of two sentences or rewrite half a sentence but not the other half. A mixed sentence may also occur when you don't make the subject and the predicate verb carry the principal meaning. (See pp. 380–82.) If you need help identifying the subject and predicate, see pages 233–36.

2 State parts of sentences, such as subjects, only once.

In some languages other than English, certain parts of sentences may be repeated. These include the subject in any kind of clause and an object or adverb in an adjective clause. In English, however, these parts are stated only once in a clause.

Repetition of subject

You may be tempted to restate a subject as a pronoun before the verb. But the subject needs stating only once in its clause.

Faulty The liquid it reached a temperature of 180°F.
Revised The liquid reached a temperature of 180°F.

Faulty Gases in the liquid they escaped.
Revised Gases in the liquid escaped.

Repetition in an adjective clause

Adjective clauses begin with *who, whom, whose, which, that, where,* and *when* (see p. 254). The beginning word replaces another word: the subject (*He is the person who called*), an object of a verb or preposition (*He is the person whom I mentioned*), or a preposition and pronoun (*He knows the office where [in which] the conference will occur*).

Do not state the word that *who, whom,* and so on replace in an adjective clause:

> Faulty   The technician <u>whom</u> the test depended on <u>her</u> was burned.
> [*Whom* should replace *her.*]
>
> Revised   The technician <u>whom</u> the test depended on was burned.

Adjective clauses beginning with *where* or *when* do not need an adverb such as *there* or *then:*

> Faulty   Gases escaped at a moment <u>when</u> the technician was unprepared <u>then</u>.
>
> Revised   Gases escaped at a moment <u>when</u> the technician was unprepared.

22b Match subjects and predicates in meaning.

In a sentence with mixed meaning, the subject is said to be or do something illogical. Such a mixture is sometimes called **faulty predication** because the predicate conflicts with the subject.

Illogical equation with *be*

When a form of *be* connects a subject and a word that describes the subject (a complement), the subject and complement must be logically related:

> Mixed   A <u>compromise</u> between the city and the country would be the ideal <u>place</u> to live.
>
> Revised   A <u>community</u> that offered the best qualities of both city and country would be the ideal <u>place</u> to live.

Is when, is where

Definitions require nouns on both sides of *be*. Definition clauses beginning with *when* or *where* are common in speech but should be avoided in writing:

> Mixed   An <u>examination</u> is <u>when you are tested</u> on what you know.
>
> Revised   An <u>examination</u> is a <u>test</u> of what you know.

Reason is because

The commonly heard construction *reason is because* is redundant since *because* means "for the reason that":

> Mixed   The <u>reason</u> the temple requests donations <u>is because</u> the school needs expansion.

Revised   The <u>reason</u> the temple requests donations <u>is that</u> the school needs expansion.

Revised   The temple requests donations <u>because</u> the school needs expansion.

Other mixed meanings

Mismatched subjects and predicates are not confined to sentences with *be:*

Mixed   The <u>use</u> of emission controls <u>was created</u> to reduce air pollution.

Revised   Emission <u>controls were created</u> to reduce air pollution.

Exercise 22.1 Revising: Sentences mixed in grammar or meaning

Revise the following sentences so that their parts fit together both in grammar and in meaning. Each item has more than one possible answer.

Example:
When they found out how expensive pianos are is why they were discouraged.
They were discouraged <u>because</u> they found out how expensive pianos are.
When they found out how expensive pianos are, <u>they</u> were discouraged.

1. A hurricane is when the winds in a tropical depression rotate counterclockwise at more than seventy-four miles per hour.
2. Because hurricanes can destroy so many lives and so much property is why people fear them.
3. Through high winds, storm surge, floods, and tornadoes is how a hurricane can kill thousands of people.
4. Many scientists observe that hurricanes in recent years they have become more ferocious and destructive.
5. However, in the last half-century, with improved communications systems and weather satellites have made hurricanes less deadly.

Exercise 22.2 Revising: Repeated sentence parts

Revise the following sentences to eliminate any unnecessary repetition of sentence parts.

Example:
Over 87 percent of Americans they have heard of global warming.
Over 87 percent of <u>Americans have</u> heard of global warming.

1. Global warming it is caused by the gradual erosion of the ozone layer that protects the earth from the sun.
2. Scientists who study this problem they say that the primary causes of erosion are the use of fossil fuels and the reduction of forests.
3. Many nonscientists they mistakenly believe that aerosol spray cans are the primary cause of erosion.

4. One scientist whom others respect him argues that Americans have effectively reduced their use of aerosol sprays.
5. He argues that we will stop global warming only when the public learns the real causes then.

Incomplete Sentences

The most serious kind of incomplete sentence is the fragment (see Chapter 17). But sentences are also incomplete when they omit one or more words needed for clarity.

Grammar checkers A grammar checker will not flag most kinds of incomplete sentences discussed in this section.

22c | Omissions from compound constructions should be consistent with grammar and idiom.

In both speech and writing, we commonly omit words not necessary for meaning, such as those bracketed in the examples below. Notice that all the sentences contain compound constructions (see p. 258):

By 2015 automobile-emission standards will be tougher, and by 2020 [automobile-emission standards will be] tougher still.

Some cars run on electricity and some [run] on methane or another alternative fuel.

Environmentalists have hopes for alternative fuels and [for] public transportation.

Such omissions are possible only when you omit words that are common to all the parts of a compound construction. When the parts differ in either grammar or idiom, all words must be included in all parts:

One new car gets eighty miles per gallon of gasoline; some old cars get as little as five miles per gallon. [One verb is singular, the other plural.]

Environmentalists were invited to submit proposals and were eager to do so. [Each *were* has a different grammatical function: the first is a helping verb; the second is a linking verb.]

They believe in and work for fuel conservation. [Idiom requires different prepositions with *believe* and *work*.]

In the sentence *My brother and friend moved to Dallas*, the omission of *my* before *friend* indicates that *brother* and *friend* are the same person. If two different persons are meant, the modifier or article must be repeated: *My brother and my friend moved to Dallas*.

(See pp. 520–21 for a list of English idioms with prepositions and pp. 400–03 for a discussion of grammatical parallelism.)

22d All comparisons should be complete and logical.

Comparisons make statements about the relation between two or more things, as in *Dogs are more intelligent than cats.*

1 State a comparison fully enough to ensure clarity.

Unclear	Automakers worry about their industry more than environmentalists.
Clear	Automakers worry about their industry more than environmentalists <u>do</u>.
Clear	Automakers worry about their industry more than <u>they worry about</u> environmentalists.

2 The items being compared should in fact be comparable.

| Illogical | The cost of a hybrid car can be greater than a gasoline-powered car. [Illogically compares a cost and a car.] |
| Revised | The cost of a hybrid car can be greater than <u>the cost of</u> [or that of] a gasoline-powered car. |

3 Use *any* or *any other* appropriately in comparisons.

Comparing a person or thing with all others in the same group creates two units: (1) the individual person or thing and (2) all *other* persons or things in the group. The two units need to be distinguished:

| Illogical | Los Angeles is larger than <u>any</u> city in California. [The sentence seems to say that Los Angeles is larger than itself.] |
| Logical | Los Angeles is larger than <u>any other</u> city in California. |

Comparing a person or thing with the members of a *different* group assumes separate units to begin with. The two units do not need to be distinguished with *other:*

| Illogical | Los Angeles is larger than <u>any other</u> city in Canada. [Canadian cities are a group to which Los Angeles does not belong.] |
| Logical | Los Angeles is larger than <u>any</u> city in Canada. |

4 Comparisons should state what is being compared.

Brand X gets clothes <u>whiter</u>. [Whiter than what?]
Brand Y is so much <u>better</u>. [Better than what?]

22e Include all needed prepositions, articles, and other words.

In haste or carelessness we sometimes omit small words such as prepositions and articles that are needed for clarity:

Incomplete	Regular payroll deductions are a type painless savings. You hardly notice missing amounts, and after period of years the contributions can add a large total.
Revised	Regular payroll deductions are a type of painless savings. You hardly notice the missing amounts, and after a period of years the contributions can add up to a large total.

Be careful not to omit *that* when the omission is confusing:

Incomplete	The personnel director expects many employees will benefit from the plan. [*Many employees* seems to be the object of *expects*.]
Revised	The personnel director expects that many employees will benefit from the plan.

Attentive proofreading is the best insurance against the kinds of omissions described in this section. *Proofread all your papers carefully.* See page 67 for tips.

CULTURE LANGUAGE If your native language or dialect is not standard American English, you may have difficulty knowing when to use the English articles *a, an,* and *the.* For guidelines on using articles, see pages 324–27.

Exercise 22.3   Revising: Incomplete sentences

Revise the following sentences so that they are complete, logical, and clear. Some items have more than one possible answer.

Example:
Our house is closer to the bank than the subway stop.
Our house is closer to the bank than it is to the subway stop.
Our house is closer to the bank than the subway stop is.

1. The first ice cream, eaten in China in about 2000 BC, was more lumpy than the modern era.
2. The Chinese made their ice cream of milk, spices, and overcooked rice and packed in snow to solidify.
3. In the fourteenth century ice milk and fruit ices appeared in Italy and the tables of the wealthy.
4. At her wedding in 1533 to the king of France, Catherine de Médicis offered more flavors of fruit ices than any hostess offered.
5. Modern sherbets resemble her ices; modern ice cream her soft dessert of thick, sweetened cream.

Exercise 22.4   Revising: Mixed and incomplete sentences

Revise the following paragraph to eliminate mixed or incomplete constructions.

The Hancock Tower in Boston is thin mirror-glass slab that rises almost eight hundred feet. When it was being constructed was when its windows began cracking, and some fell crashing to the ground. In order to minimize risks is why the architects and owners replaced over a third the huge windows with plywood until the problem could be found and solved. With its plywood sheath, the building was homelier than any skyscraper, the butt of many jokes. Eventually, however, it was discovered that the reason the windows cracked was because joint between the double panes of glass was too rigid. The solution of thicker single-pane windows was installed, and the silly plywood building crystallized into reflective jewel.

Exercise on Chapters 17–22   Revising: Clear sentences

Clarify meaning in the following paragraphs by revising sentence fragments, comma splices, fused sentences, problems with pronoun reference, awkward shifts, misplaced and dangling modifiers, and mixed and incomplete sentences. Most errors can be corrected in more than one way.

Many people who are physically challenged. They have accomplished much. Which proves that they are not "handicapped." Confined to wheelchairs, successful careers were forged by Bob Sampson and Stephen Hawking. Despite Sampson's muscular dystrophy, he earned a law degree he also worked for United Airlines for more than thirty years. Stephen Hawking most famous for his book *A Brief History of Time*. Unable to speak, Hawking's voice synthesizer allows him to dictate his books and conduct public lectures. And teach mathematics classes at Cambridge University.

Franklin D. Roosevelt, Ann Adams, and Itzhak Perlman all refused let polio destroy their lives. Indeed, Roosevelt led the United States during two of the worst periods of its history as President. The Great Depression and World War II. Reassured by his strong, firm voice, Roosevelt inspired hope and determination in the American people. Ann Adams, who was talented in art before polio paralyzed her, knew she had to continue to be one. Having retrained herself to draw with a pencil grasped in her teeth. She produces sketches of children and pets. That were turned into greeting cards. The profits from the cards sustained her. Roosevelt and Adams were stricken with polio when they were adults; Itzhak Perlman when a child. He was unable to play sports, instead he studied the violin, now many think he is greater than any violinist in the world.

Like Perlman, many physically challenged individuals turn to the arts. Perhaps the reason is because the joy of artistic achievement compensates for other pleasures they cannot experience. Stevie Wonder, José Feliciano, and Andrea Bocelli all express, through their music, their souls. Although unable to see physically, their music reveals truly how well they see. Hearing impairment struck Ludwig van Beethoven and Marlee Matlin it did not stop them from developing their talents. Already a successful composer, many of Beethoven's most powerful pieces were written after he became deaf. Similarly, Matlin has had excellent acting roles in movies, plays, and television programs, indeed she won an Oscar for *Children of a Lesser God*. She encourages others to develop their ability, and many hearing-impaired actors have been inspired by her.

PART 5

Effective Sentences

23

Emphasizing Ideas

When you emphasize the main ideas in your sentences, you hold and channel readers' attention.

Grammar checkers A grammar checker may spot some problems with emphasis, such as nouns made from verbs, passive voice, wordy phrases, and long sentences that may also be flabby and unemphatic. However, no checker can help you identify the important ideas in your sentences or determine whether those ideas receive appropriate emphasis.

Ways to emphasize ideas

- Use the subjects and verbs of sentences to state key actors and actions (below).
- Use the beginnings and endings of sentences to pace and stress information (p. 382).
- Arrange series items in order of increasing importance (p. 385).
- Use an occasional balanced sentence (p. 385).
- Carefully repeat key words and phrases (p. 386).
- Set off important ideas with punctuation (p. 387).
- Write concisely (p. 388).

23a Using subjects and verbs effectively

The heart of every sentence is its subject, which usually names the actor, and its predicate verb, which usually specifies the subject's action: *Children* [subject] *grow* [verb]. When these elements do not identify the sentence's key actor and action, readers must find that information elsewhere and the sentence may be wordy and unemphatic.

In the following sentences, the subjects and verbs are underlined.

Visit *mycomplab.com* for more resources and exercises on emphasis.

| Unemphatic | The intention of the company was to expand its workforce. A proposal was also made to diversify the backgrounds and abilities of employees. |

These sentences are unemphatic because their key ideas do not appear in their subjects and verbs. Revised, the sentences are not only clearer but more concise:

| Revised | The company intended to expand its workforce. It also proposed to diversify the backgrounds and abilities of employees. |

The constructions below usually drain meaning from a sentence's subject and verb.

Nouns made from verbs

Nouns made from verbs can obscure the key actions of sentences and add words. These nouns include *intention* (from *intend*), *proposal* (from *propose*), *decision* (from *decide*), *expectation* (from *expect*), *persistence* (from *persist*), *argument* (from *argue*), and *inclusion* (from *include*).

| Unemphatic | After the company made a decision to hire more workers with disabilities, its next step was the construction of wheelchair ramps and other facilities. |
| Revised | After the company decided to hire more workers with disabilities, it next constructed wheelchair ramps and other facilities. |

Weak verbs

Weak verbs, such as *made* and *was* in the unemphatic sentence above, tend to stall sentences just where they should be moving and often bury key actions:

| Unemphatic | The company is now the leader among businesses in complying with the 1990 Americans with Disabilities Act. Its officers make speeches on the act to business groups. |
| Revised | The company now leads other businesses in complying with the 1990 Americans with Disabilities Act. Its officers speak on the act to business groups. |

Passive voice

Verbs in the passive voice state actions received by, not performed by, their subjects. Thus the passive de-emphasizes the true actor of the sentence, sometimes omitting it entirely. Generally, prefer the active voice, in which the subject performs the verb's action. (See also pp. 300–02.)

Unemphatic	The 1990 law is seen by most businesses as fair, but the costs of complying have sometimes been objected to.
Revised	Most businesses see the 1990 law as fair, but some have objected to the costs of complying.

Exercise 23.1 Revising: Emphasis of subjects and verbs

Rewrite the following sentences so that their subjects and verbs identify their key actors and actions.

Example:

The issue of students making a competition over grades is a reason why their focus on learning may be lost.

Students who compete over grades may lose their focus on learning.

1. The work of many heroes was crucial in helping to emancipate the slaves.
2. The contribution of Harriet Tubman, an escaped slave herself, included the guidance of hundreds of other slaves to freedom on the Underground Railroad.
3. A return to slavery was risked by Tubman or possibly death.
4. During the Civil War she was also a carrier of information from the South to the North.
5. After the war needy former slaves were helped by Tubman's raising of money for refugees.

23b Using sentence beginnings and endings

Readers automatically seek a writer's principal meaning in the main clause of a sentence—essentially, in the subject that names the actor and the verb that usually specifies the action (see the preceding pages). Thus you can help readers understand your intended meaning by controlling the information in your subjects and the relation of the main clause to any modifiers attached to it.

Old and new information

Generally, readers expect the beginning of a sentence to contain information that they already know or that you have already introduced. They then look to the sentence ending for new information. In the unemphatic passage below, the second and third sentences both begin with new topics, while the old topics appear at the ends of the sentences. The pattern of the passage is A→B. C→B. D→A.

	A B
Unemphatic	Education often means controversy these days, with rising

costs and constant complaints about its inadequacies.
C
But the value of schooling should not be obscured by the

B   D
controversy. The single best means of economic advance-
                                    A
ment, despite its shortcomings, remains education.

In the more emphatic revision, old information begins each sentence and new information ends the sentence. The passage follows the pattern A→B. B→C. A→D.

Revised	^AEducation often means ^Bcontroversy these days, with rising costs and constant complaints about its inadequacies. But the ^Bcontroversy should not obscure the ^Cvalue of schooling. ^AEducation remains, despite its shortcomings, the single best means of economic ^Dadvancement.

Cumulative and periodic sentences

You can call attention to information by placing it first or last in a sentence, reserving the middle for incidentals:

Unemphatic	Education remains the single best means of economic advancement, despite its shortcomings. [Emphasizes shortcomings.]
Revised	Despite its shortcomings, education remains the single best means of economic advancement. [Emphasizes advancement more than shortcomings.]
Revised	Education remains, despite its shortcomings, the single best means of economic advancement. [De-emphasizes shortcomings.]

Many sentences begin with the main clause and then add modifiers to explain, amplify, or illustrate it. Such sentences are called **cumulative** (because they accumulate information as they proceed) or **loose** (because they are not tightly structured). They parallel the way we naturally think.

Cumulative	Education has no equal in opening minds, instilling values, and creating opportunities.
Cumulative	Most of the Great American Desert is made up of bare rock, rugged cliffs, mesas, canyons, mountains, separated from one another by broad flat basins covered with sunbaked mud and alkali, supporting a sparse and measured growth of sagebrush or creosote or saltbush, depending on location and elevation.
	—Edward Abbey

The opposite kind of sentence, called **periodic**, saves the main clause until just before the end (the period) of the sentence. Everything before the main clause points toward it.

Periodic   In opening minds, instilling values, and creating opportunities, education has no equal.

Periodic   With people from all over the world—Korean doctors, Jamaican cricket players, Vietnamese engineers, Haitian cabdrivers, Chinese athletes, Indian grocers—the American mosaic is continually changing.

The periodic sentence creates suspense for readers by reserving important information for the end. But readers should already have an idea of the sentence's subject—because it was discussed or introduced in the preceding sentence—so that they know what the opening modifiers describe. A variation of the periodic sentence names the subject at the beginning, follows it with a modifier, and then completes the main clause:

Dick Hayne, who works in jeans and loafers and likes to let a question cure in the air for a while before answering it, bears all the markings of what his generation used to call a laid-back kind of guy.

—George Rush

Exercise 23.2 Sentence combining: Beginnings and endings

Locate the main idea in each group of sentences below. Then combine each group into a single sentence that emphasizes that idea by placing it at the beginning or the end. For sentences 2–5, determine the position of the main idea by considering its relation to the previous sentences: if the main idea picks up a topic that's already been introduced, place it at the beginning; if it adds new information, place it at the end.

Example:

The storm blew roofs off buildings. It caused extensive damage. It knocked down trees. It severed power lines.

Main idea at beginning: The storm caused extensive damage, blowing roofs off buildings, knocking down trees, and severing power lines.

Main idea at end: Blowing roofs off buildings, knocking down trees, and severing power lines, the storm caused extensive damage.

1. Pat Taylor strode into the room. The room was packed. He greeted students called "Taylor's Kids." He nodded to their parents and teachers.
2. This was a wealthy Louisiana oilman. He had promised his "Kids" free college educations. He was determined to make higher education available to all qualified but disadvantaged students.
3. The students welcomed Taylor. Their voices joined in singing. They sang "You Are the Wind Beneath My Wings." Their faces beamed with hope. Their eyes flashed with self-confidence.
4. The students had thought a college education was beyond their dreams. It seemed too costly. It seemed too demanding.

5. Taylor had to ease the costs and the demands of getting to college. He created a bold plan. The plan consisted of scholarships, tutoring, and counseling.

23c Arranging parallel elements effectively

Series

With parallelism, you use similar grammatical structures for ideas linked by *and, but,* and similar words: *Blustery winds and upturned leaves often signal thunderstorms.* (See Chapter 25.) In addition, you should arrange the parallel ideas in order of their importance:

Unemphatic	The storm ripped the roofs off several buildings, killed ten people, and knocked down many trees in town. [Buries the most serious damage—deaths—in the middle.]
Emphatic	The storm knocked down many trees in town, ripped the roofs off several buildings, and killed ten people. [Arranges items in order of increasing importance.]

You may want to use an unexpected item at the end of a series for humor or for another special effect:

Early to bed and early to rise makes a man healthy, wealthy, and dead.

—James Thurber

But be careful when creating such a series. The following series seems thoughtlessly random rather than intentionally humorous:

Unemphatic	The painting has subdued tone, intense feeling, and a height of about three feet.
Emphatic	The painting, about three feet high, has subdued tone and intense feeling.

Balanced sentences

A sentence is **balanced** when its clauses are parallel—that is, matched in grammatical structure (Chapter 25). When used carefully, balanced sentences can be especially effective in alerting readers to a strong comparison between two ideas. Read the following examples aloud to hear their rhythm.

The fickleness of the women I love is equalled only by the infernal constancy of the women who love me.   —George Bernard Shaw

In a pure balanced sentence two main clauses are exactly parallel: they match item for item.

Scratch a lover, and find a foe.   —Dorothy Parker

But the term is commonly applied to sentences that are only approximately parallel or that have only some parallel parts:

> If thought corrupts language, language can also corrupt thought.
> —George Orwell

> As the traveler who has once been from home is wiser than he who has never left his own doorstep, so a knowledge of one other culture should sharpen our ability to scrutinize more steadily, to appreciate more lovingly, our own. —Margaret Mead

Exercise 23.3 Revising: Series and balanced elements

Revise the following sentences so that elements in a series or balanced elements are arranged to give maximum emphasis to main ideas.

Example:

The campers were stranded without matches, without food or water, and without a tent.

The campers were stranded without matches, without a tent, and without food or water.

1. Remembering her days as a "conductor" on the Underground Railroad made Harriet Tubman proud, but she got angry when she remembered her years as a slave.
2. Tubman wanted freedom regardless of personal danger, whereas for her husband, John, personal safety was more important than freedom.
3. Tubman proved her fearlessness in many ways: she led hundreds of other slaves to freedom, she was a spy for the North during the Civil War, and she disobeyed John's order not to run away.
4. To conduct slaves north to freedom, Tubman risked being returned to slavery, being hanged for a huge reward, and being caught by Southern patrollers.
5. After the war Tubman worked tirelessly for civil rights and women's suffrage; raising money for homes for needy former slaves was something else she did.

23d Repeating ideas

Repetition of words and phrases often clutters and weakens sentences, as discussed on pages 529–30. But carefully planned repetition can be an effective means of emphasis. Such repetition often combines with parallelism. It may occur in a series of sentences (see p. 86) or in a series of words, phrases, or clauses within a sentence, as in the following examples:

> There is something uneasy in the Los Angeles air this afternoon, some unnatural stillness, some tension. —Joan Didion

> We have the tools, all the tools—we are suffocating in tools—but we cannot find the actual wood to work or even the actual hand to work it.
> —Archibald MacLeish

23e | Separating ideas

When you save important information for the end of a sentence, you can emphasize it even more by setting it off from the rest of the sentence, as in the second example below:

> Mothers and housewives are the only workers who do not have regular time off, so they are the great vacationless class.

> Mothers and housewives are the only workers who do not have regular time off. They are the great vacationless class.
> —Anne Morrow Lindbergh

You can vary the degree of emphasis by varying the extent to which you separate one idea from the others. A semicolon provides more separation than a comma, and a period provides still more separation. Compare the following sentences:

> Most of the reading which is praised for itself is neither literary nor intellectual, but narcotic.

> Most of the reading which is praised for itself is neither literary nor intellectual; it is narcotic.

> Most of the reading which is praised for itself is neither literary nor intellectual. It is narcotic. —Donald Hall

Sometimes a dash or a pair of dashes will isolate and thus emphasize a part of a statement (see also pp. 472–73):

> His schemes were always elaborate, ingenious, and exciting—and wholly impractical.

> Athletics—that is, winning athletics—has become a profitable university operation.

Exercise 23.4 Emphasizing with repetition or separation

Emphasize the main idea in each of the following sentences or groups of sentences by following the instructions in parentheses: either combine sentences so that parallelism and repetition stress the main idea, or place the main idea in a separate sentence. Each item has more than one possible answer.

Example:

I try to listen to other people's opinions. When my mind is closed, I find that other opinions open it. And they can change my mind when it is wrong. (*Parallelism and repetition.*)

I try to listen to other people's opinions, for they can open my mind when it is closed and they can change my mind when it is wrong.

1. One of the few worthwhile habits is daily reading. One can read for information. One can read for entertainment. Reading can give one a broader view of the world. (*Parallelism and repetition.*)

2. Reading introduces new words. One encounters unfamiliar styles of expression through reading. (*Parallelism and repetition.*)
3. Students who read a great deal will more likely write vividly, coherently, and grammatically, for they will have learned from other authors. (*Separation.*)
4. Reading gives knowledge. One gets knowledge about other cultures. One will know about history and current events. One gains information about human nature. (*Parallelism and repetition.*)
5. As a result of reading, writers have more resources and more flexibility, and thus reading creates better writers. (*Separation.*)

23f Being concise

Conciseness—brevity of expression—aids emphasis no matter what the sentence structure. Unnecessary words detract from necessary words. They clutter sentences and obscure ideas.

Weak   In my opinion the competition in the area of grades is distracting. It distracts many students from their goal, which is to obtain an education that is good. There seems to be a belief among a few students that grades are more important than what is measured by them.

Emphatic   The competition for grades distracts many students from their goal of obtaining a good education. A few students seem to believe that grades are more important than what they measure.

Techniques for tightening sentences are listed in the following box. Some of these techniques appear earlier in this chapter. All of them are covered in Chapter 39 on writing concisely.

Ways to achieve conciseness

■ **Make the subject and verb of each sentence identify its actor and action** (pp. 380, 526–27):

Avoid nouns made from verbs.
Use strong verbs.
Rewrite the passive voice as active.

■ **Cut or shorten empty words or phrases** (pp. 527–28):

Shorten filler phrases, such as *by virtue of the fact that.*
Cut all-purpose words, such as *area, factor.*
Cut unneeded qualifiers, such as *in my opinion, for the most part.*

■ **Cut unnecessary repetition** (p. 529).
■ **Reduce clauses to phrases and phrases to single words** (p. 530).

■ **Avoid constructions beginning with** *there is, here is,* **or** *it is* (p. 531).
■ **Combine sentences** (p. 531).
■ **Cut or rewrite jargon** (pp. 531–32).

Exercise 23.5 Revising: Conciseness

Revise the following sentences to make them more emphatic by eliminating wordiness.

> *Example:*
>
> The problem in this particular situation is that we owe more money than we can afford under present circumstances.
>
> The problem is that we owe more money than we can afford.

1. As far as I am concerned, customers who are dining out in restaurants in our country must be wary of suggestive selling, so to speak.
2. In suggestive selling, diners are asked by the waiter to buy additional menu selections in addition to what was ordered by them.
3. For each item on the menu, there is another food that will naturally complement it.
4. For example, customers will be presented with the question of whether they want to order french fries along with a sandwich or whether they want to order a salad along with a steak dinner.
5. Due to the fact that customers often give in to suggestive selling, they often find that their restaurant meals are more costly than they had intended to pay.

Exercise 23.6 Revising: Emphasizing ideas

Drawing on the advice in this chapter, rewrite the following paragraph to emphasize main ideas and to de-emphasize less important information.

> In preparing pasta, there is a requirement for common sense and imagination rather than for complicated recipes. The key to success in this area is fresh ingredients for the sauce and perfectly cooked pasta. The sauce may be made with just about any fresh fish, meat, cheese, herb, or vegetable. As for the pasta itself, it may be dried or fresh, although fresh pasta is usually more delicate and flavorful, as many experienced cooks find. Dried pasta is fine with zesty sauces; with light oil and cream sauces fresh pasta is the best choice. There is a difference in the cooking time for dried and fresh pasta, with dried pasta taking longer. It is important that the cook follow the package directions and that the pasta be tested before the cooking time is up. The pasta is done when the texture is neither tough nor mushy but *al dente,* or "firm to the bite," according to the Italians, who ought to know.

Note See page 415 for an exercise involving emphasis along with parallelism and other techniques for effective sentences.

24

Using Coordination and Subordination

When clearly written, your sentences show the relations between ideas and stress the more important ideas over the lesser ones. Two techniques can help you achieve such clarity:

- *Coordination* shows that two or more elements in a sentence are equally important in meaning. You signal coordination with words such as *and, but,* and *or.*

  equally important
  Car insurance is costly, but health insurance seems a luxury.

- *Subordination* shows that some elements in a sentence are less important than other elements for your meaning. Usually, the main idea appears in the main clause, and supporting information appears in single words, phrases, and subordinate clauses.

  less important   more important
  (subordinate clause)   (main clause)
  Because accidents and thefts occur frequently, car insurance is costly.

Grammar checkers A grammar checker may spot some errors in punctuating coordinated and subordinated elements, and it can usually flag long sentences that may contain excessive coordination or subordination. But otherwise it can provide little help because it cannot recognize the relations among ideas in sentences.

24a Coordinating to relate equal ideas

By linking equally important information, you can emphasize the relations for readers. Compare the following passages:

String of simple sentences
We should not rely so heavily on oil. Coal and uranium are also overused. We have a substantial energy resource in the moving waters of our rivers.

mycomplab

Visit *mycomplab.com* for more resources and exercises on coordination and subordination.

Ways to coordinate information in sentences

- **Link main clauses with a comma and a coordinating conjunction:** *and, but, or, nor, for, so, yet* (p. 424).

  Independence Hall in Philadelphia is faithfully restored, but many years ago it was in bad shape.

- **Relate main clauses with a semicolon alone or a semicolon and a conjunctive adverb:** *however, indeed, thus,* etc. (pp. 447, 448).

  The building was standing; however, it suffered from neglect.

- **Within clauses, link words and phrases with a coordinating conjunction:** *and, but, or, nor* (pp. 258–59).

  The people and officials of the nation were indifferent to Independence Hall or took it for granted.

- **Link main clauses, words, or phrases with a correlative conjunction:** *both . . . and, not only . . . but also,* etc. (p. 259).

  People not only took the building for granted but also neglected it.

Smaller streams add to the total volume of water. The resource renews itself. Oil and coal are irreplaceable. Uranium is also irreplaceable. The cost of water does not increase much over time. The costs of coal, oil, and uranium rise dramatically.

Ideas coordinated

We should not rely so heavily on oil, coal, and uranium, for we have a substantial energy resource in the moving waters of our rivers and streams. Oil, coal, and uranium are irreplaceable and thus subject to dramatic cost increases; water, however, is self-renewing and more stable in cost.

The second passage is shorter and considerably easier to understand because it links coordinate ideas with the underlined words.

Punctuating coordinated words, phrases, and clauses

Most coordinated words, phrases, and subordinate clauses are not punctuated with commas (see pp. 441–42). The exceptions are items in a series and coordinate adjectives:

We rely heavily on coal, oil, and uranium. [A series; see p. 435.]
Dirty, unhealthy air is one result. [Coordinate adjectives; see pp. 435–36.]

In a sentence consisting of two main clauses, punctuation depends on whether a coordinating conjunction, a conjunctive adverb, or no connecting word links the clauses:

Oil is irreplaceable, but water is self-renewing. [See pp. 424–26.]
Oil is irreplaceable; however, water is self-renewing. [See p. 448.]
Oil is irreplaceable; water is self-renewing. [See p. 447.]

1 Using coordination effectively

A string of coordinated elements—especially main clauses—creates the same effect as a string of simple sentences: it obscures the relative importance of ideas and details.

| Excessive coordination | The weeks leading up to the resignation of President Richard Nixon were eventful, and the Supreme Court and the Congress closed in on him, and the Senate Judiciary Committee voted to begin impeachment proceedings, and finally the President resigned on August 9, 1974. |

Such a passage needs editing to stress the important points (underlined below) and to de-emphasize the less important information:

| Revised | The weeks leading up to the resignation of President Richard Nixon were eventful, as the Supreme Court and the Congress closed in on him and the Senate Judiciary Committee voted to begin impeachment proceedings. Finally, the President resigned on August 9, 1974. |

2 Coordinating logically

Coordinated sentence elements should be logically equal and related, and the relation between them should be the one expressed by the connecting word. If either principle is violated, the result is **faulty coordination**.

Faulty	John Stuart Mill was a nineteenth-century utilitarian, and he believed that actions should be judged by their usefulness or by the happiness they cause. [The two clauses are not separate and equal: the second expands on the first by explaining what a utilitarian such as Mill believed.]
Revised	John Stuart Mill, a nineteenth-century utilitarian, believed that actions should be judged by their usefulness or by the happiness they cause.
Faulty	Mill is recognized as a utilitarian, and he did not found the utilitarian school of philosophy. [The two clauses seem to contrast, requiring *but* or *yet* between them.]
Revised	Mill is recognized as a utilitarian, but he did not found the utilitarian school of philosophy.

Exercise 24.1 Sentence combining: Coordination

Combine sentences in the following passages to coordinate related ideas in the ways that seem most effective to you. You will have to supply coordinating conjunctions or conjunctive adverbs and the appropriate punctuation.

1. Many chronic misspellers do not have the time to master spelling rules. They may not have the motivation. They may rely on dictionaries to catch misspellings. Most dictionaries list words under their correct spellings. One kind of dictionary is designed for chronic

misspellers. It lists each word under its common misspellings. It then provides the correct spelling. It also provides the definition.

2. Henry Hudson was an English explorer. He captained ships for the Dutch East India Company. On a voyage in 1610 he passed by Greenland. He sailed into a great bay in today's northern Canada. He thought he and his sailors could winter there. The cold was terrible. Food ran out. The sailors mutinied. The sailors cast Hudson adrift in a small boat. Eight others were also in the boat. Hudson and his companions perished.

Exercise 24.2 Revising: Excessive or faulty coordination

Revise the following sentences to eliminate excessive or faulty coordination. Relate ideas effectively by adding or subordinating information or by forming more than one sentence. Each item has more than one possible answer.

Example:

My dog barks, and I have to keep her inside.

Because my dog's barking <u>disturbs my neighbors</u>, I have to keep her inside.

1. Often soldiers admired their commanding officers, and they gave them nicknames, and these names frequently contained the word "old," but not all of the commanders were old.
2. General Thomas "Stonewall" Jackson was also called "Old Jack," and he was not yet forty years old.
3. Another Southern general in the Civil War was called "Old Pete," and his full name was James Longstreet.
4. The Union general Henry W. Halleck had a reputation as a good military strategist, and he was an expert on the work of a French military authority, Henri Jomini, and Halleck was called "Old Brains."
5. General William Henry Harrison won the Battle of Tippecanoe, and he received the nickname "Old Tippecanoe," and he used the name in his presidential campaign slogan "Tippecanoe and Tyler, Too," and he won the election in 1840, but he died of pneumonia a month after taking office.

24b Subordinating to distinguish main ideas

With **subordination** you use words or word groups to indicate that some ideas in a sentence are less important than the idea in the main clause. In the following sentence, it is difficult to tell what is most important:

Excessive coordination	Computer prices have dropped, and production costs have dropped more slowly, and computer manufacturers have had to contend with shrinking profits.

The following revision places the point of the sentence (shrinking profits) in the main clause and reduces the rest of the information to a modifier (underlined):

Revised Because production costs have dropped more slowly than prices, computer manufacturers have had to contend with shrinking profits.

No rules can specify what information in a sentence you should make primary and what you should subordinate; the decision will depend on your meaning. But, in general, you should consider using subordinate structures for details of time, cause, condition, concession, purpose, and identification (size, location, and the like). You can subordinate information with the structures listed in the box opposite.

In general, the shorter a subordinate structure is, the less emphasis it has. The following examples show how subordinate structures may convey various meanings with various weights. (Some appropriate subordinating words for each meaning appear in parentheses.)

Space or time (*after, before, since, until, when, while; at, in, on, until*)
The mine explosion killed six workers. The owners adopted safety measures.
After the mine explosion killed six workers, the owners adopted safety measures. [Subordinate clause.]
After six deaths in a mine explosion, the owners adopted safety measures. [Prepositional phrases.]

Cause or effect (*as, because, since, so that; because of, due to*)
Jones had been without work for six months. He was having trouble paying his bills.
Because Jones had been without work for six months, he was having trouble paying his bills. [Subordinate clause.]
Having been jobless for six months, Jones could not pay his bills. [Verbal phrase.]

Condition (*if, provided, since, unless, whenever; with, without*)
Forecasters predict a mild winter. Farmers hope for an early spring.
Whenever forecasters predict a mild winter, farmers hope for an early spring. [Subordinate clause.]
With forecasts for a mild winter, farmers hope for an early spring. [Prepositional phrase.]

Concession (*although, as if, even though, though; despite, except for, in spite of*)
The horse looked gentle. It proved hard to manage.
Although the horse looked gentle, it proved hard to manage. [Subordinate clause.]
The horse, a gentle-looking animal, proved hard to manage. [Appositive.]
The gentle-looking horse proved hard to manage. [Single word.]

Purpose (*in order that, so that, that; for, toward*)
Congress passed new immigration laws. Many Vietnamese refugees could enter the United States.

Ways to subordinate information in sentences

- **Use a subordinate clause beginning with a subordinating conjunction:** *although, because, if, whereas,* etc. (p. 253).

  Although some citizens had tried to rescue Independence Hall, they had not gained substantial public support.

- **Use a subordinate clause beginning with a relative pronoun:** *who, whoever, which, that* (p. 253).

  The first strong step was taken by the federal government, which made the building a national monument.

- **Use a phrase** (p. 244).

  Like most national monuments, Independence Hall is protected by the National Park Service. [Prepositional phrase.]

  Protecting many popular tourist sites, the service is a highly visible government agency. [Verbal phrase.]

- **Use an appositive** (p. 256).

  The National Park Service, a branch of the Department of Interior, also runs Yosemite and other wilderness parks.

- **Use a short modifier.**

  At the red brick Independence Hall, park rangers give guided tours and protect the irreplaceable building from vandalism.

Congress passed new immigration laws so that many Vietnamese refugees could enter the United States. [Subordinate clause.]

Congress passed new immigration laws, permitting many Vietnamese refugees to enter the United States. [Verbal phrase.]

Identification (*that, when, where, which, who; by, from, of*)

Old barns are common in New England. They are often painted red.

Old barns, which are often painted red, are common in New England. [Subordinate clause.]

Old barns, often painted red, are common in New England. [Verbal phrase.]

Old red barns are common in New England. [Single word.]

Punctuating subordinate constructions

A modifying word, phrase, or clause that introduces a sentence is usually set off from the rest of the sentence with a comma (see pp. 427–28):

Unfortunately, the bank failed.
In a little over six months, the bank became insolvent.
When the bank failed, many reporters investigated.

A modifier that interrupts or concludes a main clause is *not* set off with punctuation when it is essential to the meaning of a word or words in the clause (see p. 429):

One article *about the bank failure* won a prize.
The article *that won the prize* appeared in the local newspaper.
The reporter wrote the article *because the bank failure affected many residents of the town.*

When an interrupting or concluding modifier is *not* essential to meaning, but simply adds information to the sentence, it *is* set off with punctuation, usually a comma or commas (see p. 429):

The bank, *over forty years old,* never reopened after its doors were closed.
The bank managers, *who were cleared of any wrongdoing,* all found new jobs.
Some customers of the bank never recovered all their money, *though most of them tried to do so.*

Like a modifier, an appositive is set off with punctuation (usually a comma or commas) only when it is *not* essential to the meaning of the word it refers to (see p. 431):

The bank, *First City,* was the oldest in town.
Our newspaper, *the Chronicle,* was one of several reporting the story.

A dash or dashes may also be used to set off a nonessential appositive, particularly when it contains commas (see p. 473). A concluding appositive is sometimes set off with a colon (see p. 471).

1 Subordinating logically

Use subordination only for the less important information in a sentence. **Faulty subordination** reverses the dependent relation the reader expects:

Faulty Ms. Angelo was in her first year of teaching, although she was a better teacher than others with many years of experience. [The sentence suggests that Angelo's inexperience is the main idea, whereas the writer meant to stress her skill *despite* her inexperience.]

Revised Although Ms. Angelo was in her first year of teaching, she was a better teacher than others with many years of experience.

2 Using subordination effectively

Subordination can do much to organize and emphasize information. But it loses that power when you try to cram too much loosely related detail into one long sentence:

| Overloaded | The boats that were moored at the dock when the hurricane, which was one of the worst in three decades, struck were ripped from their moorings, because the owners had not been adequately prepared, since the weather service had predicted that the storm would blow out to sea, which storms do at this time of year. |

Such sentences usually have more than one idea that deserves a main clause, so they are best revised by sorting their details into more than one sentence:

| Revised | Struck by one of the worst hurricanes in three decades, <u>the boats at the dock were ripped from their moorings.</u> <u>The owners were unprepared</u> because the weather service had said that storms at this time of year blow out to sea. |

A common form of excessive subordination occurs with a string of adjective clauses, each beginning with *which, who,* or *that:*

| Stringy | The company opened a new plant outside Louisville, which is in Kentucky and which is on the Ohio River, which forms the border between Kentucky and Ohio. |

To revise such sentences, recast some of the subordinate clauses as other kinds of modifying structures:

| Revised | The company opened a new plant outside Louisville, <u>Kentucky</u>, <u>a city across the Ohio River from Ohio.</u> |

Exercise 24.3   Sentence combining: Subordination

Combine each of the following pairs of sentences twice, each time using one of the subordinate structures in parentheses to make a single sentence. You will have to add, delete, change, and rearrange words.

Example:

During the late eighteenth century, workers carried beverages in brightly colored bottles. The bottles had cork stoppers. (*Clause beginning* <u>that</u>. *Phrase beginning* <u>with</u>.)

During the late eighteenth century, workers carried beverages in brightly colored bottles <u>that had cork stoppers</u>.

During the late eighteenth century, workers carried beverages in brightly colored bottles <u>with cork stoppers</u>.

1. The bombardier beetle sees an enemy. It shoots out a jet of chemicals to protect itself. (*Clause beginning* <u>when</u>. *Phrase beginning* <u>seeing</u>.)
2. The beetle's spray is very potent. It consists of hot and irritating chemicals. (*Phrase beginning* <u>consisting</u>. *Phrase beginning* <u>of</u>.)
3. The spray's two chemicals are stored separately in the beetle's body and mixed in the spraying gland. The chemicals resemble a nerve-gas weapon. (*Phrase beginning* <u>stored</u>. *Clause beginning* <u>which</u>.)

4. The tip of the beetle's abdomen sprays the chemicals. The tip re-volves like a turret on a World War II bomber. (*Phrase beginning re-volving*. Phrase beginning *spraying*.)
5. The beetle defeats most of its enemies. It is still eaten by spiders and birds. (*Clause beginning although*. Phrase beginning *except*.)

Exercise 24.4 Revising: Subordination

Rewrite the following paragraph in the way you think most effective to subordinate the less important ideas to the more important ones. Use subordinate clauses, phrases, and single words as you think appropriate.

Fewer students entering college are planning to major in the liberal arts. I mean by "liberal arts" such subjects as history, English, and the social sciences. Students think a liberal arts degree will not help them get jobs. They are wrong. They may not get practical, job-related experience from the liberal arts, but they will get a broad education, and it will never again be available to them. Many employers look for more than a technical, professional education. They think such an education can make an employee's views too narrow. The employers want open-minded employees. They want employees to think about problems from many angles. The liberal arts curriculum instills such flexibility. The flexibility is vital to the health of our society.

Exercise 24.5 Revising: Faulty or excessive subordination

Revise the following sentences to eliminate faulty or excessive subordination. Correct faulty subordination by reversing main and subordinate structures. Correct excessive subordination by coordinating equal ideas or by making separate sentences.

Example:
Terrified to return home, he had driven his mother's car into a corn-field.

Having driven his mother's car into a cornfield, he was terrified to return home.

1. Genaro González is a successful writer, which means that his stories and novels have been published to critical acclaim.
2. He loves to write, although he has also earned a doctorate in psychology.
3. His first story, which reflects his consciousness of his Aztec heritage and place in the world, is titled "Un Hijo del Sol."
4. González, who writes equally well in English and Spanish, received a large fellowship that enabled him to take a leave of absence from the University of Texas–Pan American, where he teaches psychology, so that he could write without worrying about an income.
5. González wrote the first version of "Un Hijo del Sol" while he was a sophomore at Pan American, which is in the Rio Grande valley of southern Texas, which González calls "el Valle" in the story.

24c | Choosing clear connectors

Most connecting words signal specific and unambiguous relations; for instance, *but* clearly indicates contrast, and *because* clearly indicates cause. A few connectors, however, require careful use, either because they are ambiguous in many contexts or because they are often misused.

1 Using *as* and *while* clearly

The subordinating conjunction *as* can indicate several relations, including comparison and time:

| Comparison | The technicians work quickly, as they are required to do. |
| Time | One shift starts as the other stops. |

Avoid using *as* to indicate cause. It is unclear.

Unclear	As the experiment was occurring, the laboratory was sealed. [Time or cause intended?]
Revised	When the experiment was occurring, the laboratory was sealed. [Time.]
Revised	Because the experiment was occurring, the laboratory was sealed. [Cause.]

The subordinating conjunction *while* can indicate either time or concession. Unless the context makes the meaning of *while* unmistakably clear, choose a more exact connector:

Unclear	While technicians work in the next room, they cannot hear the noise. [Time or concession intended?]
Revised	When technicians work in the next room, they cannot hear the noise. [Time.]
Revised	Although technicians work in the next room, they cannot hear the noise. [Concession.]

2 Using *as* and *like* correctly

The use of *as* as a substitute for *whether* or *that* is considered nonstandard (it does not conform to spoken and written standard English):

| Nonstandard | They are not sure as the study succeeded. |
| Revised | They are not sure whether [or that] the study succeeded. |

Although the preposition *like* is often used as a conjunction in informal speech and in advertising (*Dirt-Away works like a soap should*), writing generally requires the conjunction *as, as if, as though,* or *that:*

| Speech | It seemed like it did succeed. |
| Writing | It seemed as if [or as though or that] it did succeed. |

Exercise 24.6 Revising: Coordination and subordination
The following paragraph consists entirely of simple sentences. Use coordination and subordination to combine sentences in the ways you think most effective to emphasize main ideas.

Sir Walter Raleigh personified the Elizabethan Age. That was the period of Elizabeth I's rule of England. The period occurred in the last half of the sixteenth century. Raleigh was a courtier and poet. He was also an explorer and entrepreneur. Supposedly, he gained Queen Elizabeth's favor. He did this by throwing his cloak beneath her feet at the right moment. She was just about to step over a puddle. There is no evidence for this story. It does illustrate Raleigh's dramatic and dynamic personality. His energy drew others to him. He was one of Elizabeth's favorites. She supported him. She also dispensed favors to him. However, he lost his queen's goodwill. Without her permission he seduced one of her maids of honor. He eventually married the maid of honor. Elizabeth died. Then her successor imprisoned Raleigh in the Tower of London. Her successor was James I. The king falsely charged Raleigh with treason. Raleigh was released after thirteen years. He was arrested again two years later on the old treason charges. At the age of sixty-six he was beheaded.

Note See page 415 for an exercise involving coordination and subordination along with parallelism and other techniques for effective sentences.

25
Using Parallelism

Parallelism gives similar grammatical form to sentence elements that have similar function and importance.

The air is dirtied by ||| factories belching smoke
and ||| cars spewing exhaust.

Parallel structure reinforces and highlights a close relation between compound sentence elements, whether words, phrases, or clauses.

mycomplab

Visit *mycomplab.com* for more resources and exercises on parallelism.

The principle underlying parallelism is that form should reflect meaning: since the parts of compound constructions have the same function and importance, they should have the same grammatical form.

Grammar checkers A grammar checker cannot recognize problems with parallelism because it cannot recognize the relations among ideas.

25a Using parallelism for coordinate elements

Use parallelism in all the situations illustrated in the box on the next page.

Note Parallel elements match each other in structure, but they do not always match word for word:

The pioneers passed ‖ through the town
         and ‖ into the vast, unpopulated desert.

1 Using parallelism for elements linked by coordinating conjunctions

The coordinating conjunctions *and, but, or, nor,* and *yet* always signal a need for parallelism:

The industrial base was shifting and shrinking.

Politicians rarely acknowledged the problem or proposed alternatives.

Industrial workers were understandably disturbed that they were losing their jobs and that no one seemed to care.

If sentence elements linked by coordinating conjunctions are not parallel in structure, the resulting sentence will be awkward and distracting:

Nonparallel	Three reasons why steel companies kept losing money were that their plants were inefficient, high labor costs, and foreign competition was increasing.
Revised	Three reasons why steel companies kept losing money were inefficient plants, high labor costs, and increasing foreign competition.

All the words required by idiom or grammar must be stated in compound constructions (see also p. 258).

Nonparallel	Given training, workers can acquire the skills and interest in other jobs. [*Skills* and *interest* require different prepositions, so both must be stated.]
Revised	Given training, workers can acquire the skills for and interest in other jobs.

Patterns of parallelism

■ **Use parallel structures for elements connected by coordinating conjunctions** (*and, but, or,* etc.) **or correlative conjunctions** (*both . . . and, neither . . . nor,* etc.):

In 1988 a Greek cyclist, backed up by ‖ engineers,
‖ physiologists,
and ‖ athletes,

broke the world's record for human flight
with neither ‖ a boost
nor ‖ a motor.

■ **Use parallel structures for elements being compared or contrasted:**

‖ Pedal power
rather than ‖ horse power
propelled the plane.

■ **Use parallel structures for lists, outlines, or headings:**

The four-hour flight was successful because
‖ (1) the cyclist was very fit,
‖ (2) he flew a straight course over water,
and ‖ (3) he kept the aircraft near the water's surface.

Often, a word must be repeated to avoid confusion:

Confusing	Thoreau stood up for his principles <u>by not paying</u> his taxes and <u>spending</u> a night in jail. [Did he spend a night in jail or not?]
Revised	Thoreau stood up for his principles by not paying his taxes and <u>by</u> spending a night in jail.

Be sure that clauses beginning *who* or *which* are coordinated only with other *who* or *which* clauses, even when the pronoun is not repeated:

Nonparallel	Thoreau is the nineteenth-century essayist <u>who retired</u> to the woods and <u>he wrote</u> about nature.
Revised	Thoreau is the nineteenth-century essayist who retired to the woods and [<u>who</u>] <u>wrote</u> about nature.

2 Using parallelism for elements linked by correlative conjunctions

Correlative conjunctions are pairs of connectors. For example:

both . . . and	neither . . . nor	not only . . . but also
either . . . or	not . . . but	whether . . . or

Correlative conjunctions stress equality and balance and thus emphasize the relation between elements, even long phrases and clauses. The elements should be parallel to confirm their relation:

> It is not a tax bill but a tax relief bill, providing relief not for the needy but for the greedy.   —Franklin Delano Roosevelt

> At the end of the novel, Huck Finn both rejects society's values by turning down money and a home and affirms his own values by setting out for "the territory."

Most errors in parallelism with correlative conjunctions occur when the element after the second connector does not match the element after the first connector.

Nonparallel Mark Twain refused either to ignore the moral blindness of his society or spare the reader's sensibilities. [*To* follows *either,* so it must also follow *or.*]

Revised Mark Twain refused either to ignore the moral blindness of his society or to spare the reader's sensibilities.

Nonparallel Huck Finn learns not only that human beings have an enormous capacity for folly but also enormous dignity. [The first element includes *that human beings have;* the second element does not.]

Revised Huck Finn learns that human beings have not only an enormous capacity for folly but also enormous dignity.

3 Using parallelism for elements being compared or contrasted

Elements being compared or contrasted should ordinarily be cast in the same grammatical form.

> It is better to live rich than to die rich.   —Samuel Johnson

Weak The study found that most welfare recipients wanted to work rather than handouts.

Revised The study found that most welfare recipients wanted work rather than handouts.

Revised The study found that most welfare recipients wanted to work rather than to accept handouts.

4 Using parallelism for lists, outlines, and headings

The elements of a list or outline that divides a larger subject are coordinate and should be parallel in structure. Parallelism is essential in the headings that divide a paper into sections (see p. 121) and in a formal topic outline (see p. 41).

Faulty	Improved
Changes in Renaissance England	Changes in Renaissance England
1. Extension of trade routes	1. Extension of trade routes
2. Merchant class became more powerful	2. Increased power of the merchant class
3. The death of feudalism	3. Death of feudalism
4. Upsurging of the arts	4. Upsurge of the arts
5. The sciences were encouraged	5. Encouragement of the sciences
6. Religious quarrels began	6. Rise of religious quarrels

Exercise 25.1 Identifying parallel elements

Identify the parallel elements in the following sentences. How does parallelism contribute to the effectiveness of each sentence?

1. Eating an animal has not always been an automatic or an everyday affair; it has tended to be done on solemn occasions and for a special treat. —Margaret Visser

2. They [pioneer women] rolled out dough on the wagon seats, cooked with fires made out of buffalo chips, tended the sick, and marked the graves of their children, their husbands and each other. —Ellen Goodman

3. The mornings are the pleasantest times in the apartment, exhaustion having set in, the sated mosquitoes at rest on ceiling and walls, sleeping it off, the room a swirl of tortured bedclothes and abandoned garments, the vines in their full leafiness filtering the hard light of day, the air conditioner silent at last, like the mosquitoes. —E. B. White

4. Aging paints every action gray, lies heavy on every movement, imprisons every thought. —Sharon Curtin

Exercise 25.2 Revising: Parallelism

Revise the following sentences to make coordinate, compared, or listed elements parallel in structure. Add or delete words or rephrase as necessary.

Example:

After emptying her bag, searching the apartment, and she called the library, Emma realized she had lost the book.

After emptying her bag, searching the apartment, and calling the library, Emma realized she had lost the book.

1. The ancient Greeks celebrated four athletic contests: the Olympic Games at Olympia, the Isthmian Games were held near Corinth, at Delphi the Pythian Games, and the Nemean Games were sponsored by the people of Cleonae.

2. Each day of the games consisted of either athletic events or holding ceremonies and sacrifices to the gods.

3. In the years between the games, competitors were taught wrestling, javelin throwing, and how to box.
4. Competitors participated in running sprints, spectacular chariot and horse races, and running long distances while wearing full armor.
5. The purpose of such events was developing physical strength, demonstrating skill and endurance, and to sharpen the skills needed for war.
6. Events were held for both men and for boys.
7. At the Olympic Games the spectators cheered their favorites to victory, attended sacrifices to the gods, and they feasted on the meat not burned in offerings.
8. The athletes competed less to achieve great wealth than for gaining honor both for themselves and their cities.
9. Of course, exceptional athletes received financial support from patrons, poems and statues by admiring artists, and they even got lavish living quarters from their sponsoring cities.
10. With the medal counts and flag ceremonies, today's Olympians sometimes seem to be proving their countries' superiority more than to demonstrate individual talent.

25b Using parallelism to increase coherence

Effective parallelism will enable you to combine in a single, well-ordered sentence related ideas that you might have expressed in separate sentences. Compare the following three sentences with the original single sentence written by H. L. Mencken:

> Slang originates in the effort of ingenious individuals to make the language more pungent and picturesque. They increase the store of terse and striking words or widen the boundaries of metaphor. Thus a vocabulary for new shades and differences in meaning is provided by slang.

> Slang originates in the effort of ingenious individuals to make the language more pungent and picturesque—to increase the store of terse and striking words, to widen the boundaries of metaphor, and to provide a vocabulary for new shades and differences in meaning.   —H. L. Mencken

Parallel structure works as well to emphasize the connections among related sentences in a paragraph:

> *Lewis Mumford stands* high in the company of [twentieth-century] sages. A scholar of cosmic cultural reach and conspicuous public conscience, a distinguished critic of life, arts, and letters, an unequaled observer of cities and civilizations, *he is* secure in the modern pantheon of great men. *He is* also an enigma and an anachronism. A legend of epic proportions in intellectual and academic circles, *he is* surprisingly little known to the public.   —Ada Louise Huxtable

Here, Huxtable tightly binds her sentences with two layers of parallelism: the subject-verb patterns of all four sentences (italic and underlined) and the appositives of the second and fourth sentences (underlined). (See pp. 86–87 for another illustration of parallelism among sentences.)

Exercise 25.3 Sentence combining: Parallelism

Combine each group of sentences below into one concise sentence in which parallel elements appear in parallel structures. You will have to add, delete, change, and rearrange words. Each item has more than one possible answer.

Example:
The new process works smoothly. It is efficient, too.
The new process works smoothly and efficiently.

1. People can develop post-traumatic stress disorder (PTSD). They develop it after experiencing a dangerous situation. They will also have felt fear for their survival.
2. The disorder can be triggered by a wide variety of events. Combat is a typical cause. Similarly, natural disasters can result in PTSD. Some people experience PTSD after a hostage situation.
3. PTSD can occur immediately after the stressful incident. Or it may not appear until many years later.
4. Sometimes people with PTSD will act irrationally. Moreover, they often become angry.
5. Other symptoms include dreaming that one is reliving the experience. They include hallucinating that one is back in the terrifying place. In another symptom one imagines that strangers are actually one's former torturers.

Exercise 25.4 Revising: Parallelism

Revise the following paragraph to create parallelism wherever it is required for grammar or for coherence.

The great white shark has an undeserved bad reputation. Many people consider the great white not only swift and powerful but also to be a cunning and cruel predator on humans. However, scientists claim that the great white attacks humans not by choice but as a result of chance. To a shark, our behavior in the water is similar to that of porpoises, seals, and sea lions—the shark's favorite foods. These sea mammals are both agile enough and can move fast enough to evade the shark. Thus the shark must attack with swiftness and noiselessly to surprise the prey and giving it little chance to escape. Humans become the shark's victims not because the shark has any preference or hatred of humans but because humans can neither outswim nor can they outmaneuver the shark. If the fish were truly a cruel human-eater, it would prolong the terror of its attacks, perhaps by circling or bumping into its intended victims before they were attacked.

Note See page 415 for an exercise involving parallelism along with other techniques for effective sentences.

26

Achieving Variety

In a paragraph or an essay, each sentence stands in relation to those before and after it. To make sentences work together effectively, you need to vary their length, structure, and word order to reflect the importance and complexity of ideas. Variety sometimes takes care of itself, but you can practice established techniques for achieving varied sentences:

Ways to achieve variety among sentences

- Vary the length and structure of sentences so that important ideas stand out (next page).
- Vary the beginnings of sentences with modifiers, transitional words and expressions, and occasional expletive constructions (p. 410).
- Occasionally, invert the normal order of subject, verb, and object or complement (p. 412).
- Occasionally, use a command, question, or exclamation (p. 412).

A series of similar sentences will prove monotonous and ineffective, as the following passage illustrates.

> Ulysses S. Grant and Robert E. Lee met on April 9, 1865. Their meeting place was the parlor of a modest house at Appomattox Court House, Virginia. They met to work out the terms for the surrender of Lee's Army of Northern Virginia. One great chapter of American life ended with their meeting, and another began. Grant and Lee were bringing the Civil War to its virtual finish. Other armies still had to surrender, and the fugitive Confederate government would struggle desperately and vainly. It would try to find some way to go on living with its chief support gone. Grant and Lee had signed the papers, however, and it was all over in effect.

These eight sentences are all between twelve and sixteen words long (counting initials and dates), they are about equally detailed, and they all begin with the subject. We get a sense of names, dates, and

mycomplab

Visit *mycomplab.com* for more resources and exercises on sentence variety.

events but no immediate sense of how they relate or what is most important.

Now compare the preceding passage with the actual passage written by Bruce Catton. Here the four sentences range from eleven to fifty-five words, and only one sentence begins with its subject:

> When Ulysses S. Grant and Robert E. Lee met in the parlor of a modest house at Appomattox Court House, Virginia, on April 9, 1865, to work out the terms for the surrender of Lee's Army of Northern Virginia, a great chapter in American life came to a close, and a great new chapter began.

Suspenseful periodic sentence (pp. 383–84) focuses attention on meeting; details of place, time, and cause are in opening subordinate clause

> These men were bringing the Civil War to its virtual finish.

Short sentence sums up

> To be sure, other armies had yet to surrender, and for a few days the fugitive Confederate government would struggle desperately and vainly, trying to find some way to go on living now that its chief support was gone.

Cumulative sentence (p. 383) reflects lingering obstacles to peace

> But in effect it was all over when Grant and Lee signed the papers.

Short final sentence indicates futility of further struggle

—Bruce Catton, "Grant and Lee"

The rest of this chapter suggests how you can vary your sentences for the kind of interest and clarity that Catton achieves in this passage.

Grammar checkers Some grammar checkers will flag long sentences, and you can check for appropriate variety in a series of such sentences. But generally these programs cannot help you see where variety may be needed because they cannot recognize the relative importance and complexity of your ideas.

26a Varying sentence length and structure

The sentences of a stylistically effective essay will vary most obviously in their length and the arrangement of main clauses and modifiers. The variation in length and structure makes writing both readable and clear.

1 Varying length

In most contemporary writing, sentences vary from about ten to about forty words. When sentences are all at one extreme or the other, readers may have difficulty focusing on main ideas and seeing the relations among them:

- **Long sentences.** If most of your sentences contain thirty-five words or more, your main ideas may not stand out from the details that support them. Break some of the long sentences into shorter, simpler ones.

- **Short sentences.** If most of your sentences contain fewer than ten or fifteen words, all your ideas may seem equally important and the links between them may not be clear. Try combining them with coordination (p. 390) and subordination (p. 393) to show relationships and to stress main ideas over supporting information.

2 Rewriting strings of brief and simple sentences

A series of brief and simple sentences is both monotonous and hard to understand because it forces the reader to sort out relations among ideas. If you find that you depend on brief, simple sentences, work to increase variety by combining some of them into longer units that emphasize and link important ideas while de-emphasizing incidental information. (See Chapter 24.)

The following examples show how a string of simple sentences can be revised into an effective piece of writing:

Monotonous	The moon is now drifting away from the earth. It moves away at the rate of about one inch a year. This movement is lengthening our days. They increase a thousandth of a second every century. Forty-seven of our present days will someday make up a month. We might eventually lose the moon altogether. Such great planetary movement rightly concerns astronomers, but it need not worry us. It will take 50 million years.
Revised	The moon is now drifting away from the earth <u>about one inch a year</u>. <u>At a thousandth of a second every century</u>, this movement is lengthening our days. Forty-seven of our present days will someday make up a month, <u>if we don't eventually lose the moon altogether</u>. Such great planetary movement rightly concerns astronomers, but it need not worry us. It will take 50 million years.

In the revision, underlining indicates subordinate structures that were simple sentences in the original. With five sentences instead of the original eight, the revision emphasizes the moon's movement, our lengthening days, and the enormous span of time involved.

3 Rewriting strings of compound sentences

Compound sentences are usually just simple sentences linked with conjunctions. Thus a series of them will be as weak as a series of brief, simple sentences, especially if the clauses of the compound sentences are all about the same length:

Monotonous	Physical illness may involve more than the body, for the mind may also be affected. Disorientation is common among sick people, but they are often unaware of it. They may reason abnormally, or they may behave immaturely.
Revised	Physical illness may involve the mind <u>as well as the body</u>. <u>Though often unaware of it</u>, sick people are commonly disoriented. They may reason abnormally <u>or behave immaturely</u>.

The first passage creates a seesaw effect. The revision, with some main clauses shortened or changed into modifiers (underlined), is both clearer and more emphatic. (See p. 392 for more on avoiding excessive coordination.)

> **Exercise 26.1 Revising: Varied sentence structures**
>
> Rewrite the following paragraph to increase variety so that important ideas receive greater emphasis than supporting information does. You will have to change some main clauses into modifiers and then combine and reposition the modifiers and the remaining main clauses.
>
> Charlotte Perkins Gilman was a leading intellectual in the women's movement during the first decades of the twentieth century. She wrote *Women and Economics.* This book challenged Victorian assumptions about differences between the sexes, and it explored the economic roots of women's oppression. Gilman wrote little about gaining the vote for women, but many feminists were then preoccupied with this issue, and historians have since focused their analyses on this issue. As a result, Gilman's contribution to today's women's movement has often been overlooked.

26b Varying sentence beginnings

An English sentence often begins with its subject, which generally captures old information from a preceding sentence (see pp. 382–83):

> The defendant's <u>lawyer</u> was determined to break the prosecution's witness. <u>She</u> relentlessly cross-examined the stubborn witness for a week.

However, an unbroken sequence of sentences beginning with the subject quickly becomes monotonous, as shown by the unvaried passage on Grant and Lee that opened this chapter (p. 407). You can vary this subject-first pattern by adding modifiers or other elements before the subject.

Note The final arrangement of sentence elements should always depend on two concerns: the relation of a sentence to those preceding and following it and the emphasis required by your meaning.

Adverb modifiers

Adverbs modify verbs, adjectives, other adverbs, and whole clauses. They can often fall in a variety of spots in a sentence. Consider these different emphases:

For a week, the defendant's lawyer relentlessly cross-examined the stubborn witness.

Relentlessly, the defendant's lawyer cross-examined the stubborn witness for a week.

Relentlessly, for a week, the defendant's lawyer cross-examined the stubborn witness.

Notice that the last sentence, with both modifiers at the beginning, is periodic and thus highly emphatic (see pp. 383–84).

CULTURE LANGUAGE In standard American English, placing certain adverb modifiers at the beginning of a sentence requires you to change the normal subject-verb order as well. The most common of these modifiers are negatives, including *seldom, rarely, in no case, not since,* and *not until.*

adverb   subject verb phrase
Faulty   Seldom a witness has held the stand for so long.

helping   main
adverb verb subject verb
Revised Seldom has a witness held the stand for so long.

Adjective modifiers

Adjectives, modifying nouns and pronouns, may include participles and participial phrases, as in *flying* geese or *money well spent* (see pp. 247–49). These modifiers may sometimes fall at the beginning of a sentence to postpone the subject:

The witness was exhausted from his testimony, and he did not cooperate.

Exhausted from his testimony, the witness did not cooperate.

Coordinating conjunctions and transitional expressions

When the relation between two successive sentences demands, you may begin the second with a coordinating conjunction such as *and* or *but* (p. 259) or with a transitional expression such as *first, for instance, however,* or *therefore* (pp. 89–90).

The witness had expected to be dismissed after his first long day of cross-examination. But he was not.

The price of a college education has risen astronomically. For example, tuition at one state university climbed from $4500 to $7000 in just four years.

Occasional expletive constructions

An expletive construction—*it, there,* or *here* plus a form of *be*—may occasionally be useful to delay and thus emphasize the subject of the sentence:

His judgment seems questionable, not his desire.
It is his judgment that seems questionable, not his desire.

However, expletive constructions are more likely to flatten writing by adding extra words. You should use them rarely, only when you can justify doing so. (See also p. 531.)

Exercise 26.2 Revising: Varied sentence beginnings

Follow the instructions in parentheses to revise each group of sentences below: either create a single sentence that begins with an adverb or adjective modifier, or make one sentence begin with an appropriate connector.

Example:
The *Seabird* took first place. It moved quickly in the wind. (*One sentence with adjective modifier beginning Moving.*)
Moving quickly in the wind, the *Seabird* took first place.

1. Some people are champion procrastinators. They seldom complete their work on time. (*Two sentences with transitional expression.*)
2. Procrastinators may fear criticism. They may fear rejection. They will delay completing an assignment. (*One sentence with adverb modifier beginning If.*)
3. Procrastinators often desire to please a boss or a teacher. They fear failure so much that they cannot do the work. (*Two sentences with coordinating conjunction.*)
4. Procrastination seems a hopeless habit. It is conquerable. (*One sentence with adverb modifier beginning Although.*)
5. Teachers or employers can be helpful. They can encourage procrastinators. They can give procrastinators the confidence to do good work on time. (*One sentence with adjective modifier beginning Helpfully encouraging.*)

Exercise 26.3 Revising: Varied sentence beginnings

Revise the following paragraph to vary sentence beginnings by using each of the following at least once: an adverb modifier, an adjective modifier, a coordinating conjunction, and a transitional expression.

Scientists in Egypt dug up 40-million-year-old fossil bones. They had evidence of primitive whales. The whale ancestors are called mesonychids. They were small, furry land mammals with four legs. These limbs were complete with kneecaps, ankles, and little toes. Gigantic modern whales have tiny hind legs inside their bodies and flippers instead of front legs. Scientists are certain that these two very different creatures share the same family tree.

26c | Inverting the normal word order

The word order of subject, verb, and object or complement is strongly fixed in English (see pp. 238–41). Thus an inverted sentence can be emphatic:

> Voters once had some faith in politicians, and they were fond of incumbents. But now <u>all politicians</u>, especially incumbents, <u>voters seem to detest</u>. [The object *all politicians* precedes the verb *detests*.]

Inverting the normal order of subject, verb, and complement can be useful in two successive sentences when the second expands on the first:

> Critics have not been kind to Presidents who have tried to apply the ways of private business to public affairs. Particularly <u>explicit was the curt verdict</u> of one critic of President Hoover: Mr. Hoover was never President of the United States; he was four years chairman of the board.
> —Adapted from Emmet John Hughes, "The Presidency vs. Jimmy Carter"

Inverted sentences used without need are artificial. Avoid descriptive sentences such as *Up came Ben and down went Katie's spirits.*

26d | Mixing types of sentences

Most written sentences make statements. Occasionally, however, you may want to use questions, commands, or exclamations to enhance variety.

Questions may set the direction of a paragraph, as in *What does a detective do?* or *How is the percentage of unemployed workers calculated?* More often, though, the questions used in exposition or argument do not require answers but simply emphasize ideas that readers can be expected to agree with. Such **rhetorical questions** are illustrated in the following passage:

> Another word that has ceased to have meaning due to overuse is *attractive. Attractive* has become verbal chaff. Who, by some stretch of language and imagination, cannot be described as attractive? And just what is it that attractive individuals are attracting? —Diane White

Commands occur frequently in an explanation of a process, particularly in directions, as this passage on freewriting illustrates:

> The idea is simply to write for ten minutes (later on, perhaps fifteen or twenty). Don't stop for anything. Go quickly, without rushing. Never stop to look back, to cross something out, to wonder how to spell something, to wonder what word or thought to use, or to think about what you are doing. —Peter Elbow

Notice that the authors of these examples use questions and commands to achieve some special purpose. Variety occurs because a particular sentence type is effective for the context, not because the writer set out to achieve variety for its own sake.

Exercise 26.4 Writing varied sentences

Imagine that you are writing an essay on a transportation problem at your school. Practice varying your sentences by composing a sentence or passage to serve each purpose listed below.

1. Write a question that could open the essay.
2. Write a command that could open the essay.
3. Write an exclamation that could open the essay.
4. For the body of the essay, write an appropriately varied paragraph of at least five sentences, including at least one short and one long sentence beginning with the subject; at least one sentence beginning with an adverb modifier; at least one sentence beginning with a coordinating conjunction or transitional expression; and one rhetorical question or command.

Exercise 26.5 Analyzing variety

Examine the following paragraph for sentence variety. By analyzing your own response to each sentence, try to explain why the author wrote each short or long sentence, each cumulative or periodic sentence, each sentence beginning with its subject or beginning some other way, and each question.

My earliest memory of learning to read is sitting with my grandmother on her livingroom sofa as her finger underlined the words of *Go, Dog. Go!* and I struggled to decipher them. Why did she spend so much time with me when she knew I would have every opportunity to finish high school and go to college? She listened patiently because she didn't take my education—or anyone's—for granted. The only one of her ten siblings to graduate from college, she had beaten the odds. She finished high school at the top of her class, held a full-time job while commuting to her college classes, and graduated with honors. Then she then took a job at a public high school where she taught for more than thirty years. She knew that I was unaware of my opportunities, and she did not assume that I would succeed as she had. In her years of teaching, she had seen enough students struggle and drop out to know that failure often comes more easily than success. She was determined that I would be one of the successes—indeed, that I would soar. And soar I did.

Exercise 26.6 Revising: Variety

The following paragraph consists entirely of simple sentences that begin with their subjects. As appropriate, use the techniques discussed in this chapter to vary sentences. Your goal is to make the paragraph more readable and make its important ideas stand out clearly. You will have to delete, add, change, and rearrange words.

The Italian volcano Vesuvius had been dormant for many years. It then exploded on August 24 in the year AD 79. The ash, pumice, and mud from the volcano buried two busy towns. Herculaneum is one. The more famous is Pompeii. Both towns lay undiscovered for many centuries. Herculaneum and Pompeii were discovered in 1709 and 1748, respectively. The excavation of Pompeii was the more systematic. It was the occasion for initiating modern methods of conservation and restoration. Herculaneum was simply looted of its most valuable finds. It was then left to disintegrate. Pompeii appears much as it did before the eruption. A luxurious house opens onto a lush central garden. An election poster decorates a wall. A dining table is set for breakfast.

Exercise on Chapters 23–26   Revising: Effective sentences

Revise the paragraphs below to emphasize main ideas, de-emphasize supporting information, and achieve a pleasing, clear variety in sentences. As appropriate, employ the techniques discussed in Chapters 23–26, such as using subjects and verbs effectively, subordinating and coordinating, creating parallelism, and varying sentence beginnings. Edit the finished product for punctuation.

Modern Americans owe many debts to Native Americans. Several pleasures are among the debts. Native Americans originated two fine junk foods. They discovered popcorn. Potato chips were also one of their contributions.

The introduction of popcorn to the European settlers came from Native Americans. Massasoit provided popcorn at the first Thanksgiving feast. The Aztecs offered popcorn to the Spanish explorer Hernando Cortés. The Aztecs wore popcorn necklaces. So did the natives of the West Indies. There were three ways that the Native Americans popped the corn. First, they roasted an ear over fire. The ear was skewered on a stick. They ate only some of the popcorn. They ate the corn that fell outside the flames. Second, they scraped the corn off the cob. The kernels would be thrown into the fire. Of course, the fire had to be low. Then the popped kernels that did not fall into the fire were eaten. The third method was the most sophisticated. It involved a shallow pottery vessel. It contained sand. The vessel was heated. The sand soon got hot. Corn kernels were stirred in. They popped to the surface of the sand and were eaten.

A Native American chef was responsible for devising the crunchy potato chip. His name was George Crum. In 1853 Crum was cooking at Moon Lake Lodge. The lodge was in Saratoga Springs, New York. Complaints were sent in by a customer. The man thought Crum's french-fried potatoes were too thick. Crum tried a thinner batch. These were also unsuitable. Crum became frustrated. He deliberately made the potatoes thin and crisp. They could not be cut with a knife and fork. Crum's joke backfired. The customer raved about the potato chips. The chips were named Saratoga Chips. Soon they appeared on the lodge's menu. They also appeared throughout New England. Crum later opened his own restaurant. Of course, he offered potato chips.

Now all Americans munch popcorn in movies. They crunch potato chips at parties. They gorge on both when alone and bored. They can be grateful to Native Americans for these guilty pleasures.

Punctuation

Commas, semicolons, colons, dashes, parentheses

(For explanations, consult the pages in parentheses.)

Sentences with two main clauses

The bus stopped, but no one got off. (p. 424)

The bus stopped; no one got off. (p. 447)

The bus stopped; however, no one got off. (p. 448)

The mechanic replaced the battery, the distributor cap, and the starter; but still the car would not start. (p. 450)

Her duty was clear: she had to locate the problem. (p. 470)

Introductory elements

Modifiers (p. 427)

After the argument was over, we laughed at ourselves.

Racing over the plain, the gazelle escaped the lion.

To dance in the contest, he had to tape his knee.

Suddenly, the door flew open.

With 125 passengers aboard, the plane was half full.

In 1983 he won the Nobel Prize.

Absolute phrases (p. 434)

Its wing broken, the bird hopped around on the ground.

Interrupting and concluding elements

Nonessential modifiers (p. 429)

Jim's car, which barely runs, has been impounded.

We consulted the dean, who had promised to help us.

The boy, like his sister, wants to be a pilot.

They moved across the desert, shielding their eyes from the sun.

The men do not speak to each other, although they share a car.

Nonessential appositives

Bergen's only daughter, Candice, became an actress. (p. 431)

The residents of three counties—Suffolk, Springfield, and Morrison—were urged to evacuate. (p. 473)

My father demanded one promise: that we not lie to him. (p. 470)

Essential modifiers (p. 429)

The car that hit mine was uninsured.

We consulted a teacher who had promised to help us.

The boy in the black hat is my cousin.

They were surprised to find the desert teeming with life.

The men do not speak to each other because they are feuding.

Essential appositives (p. 431)

Shaw's play *Saint Joan* was performed last year.

Their sons Tony, William, and Steve all chose military careers, leaving only Matthew to run the family business.

Transitional or parenthetical expressions

We suspect, however, that he will not come. (p. 432)

Jessica is respected by many people—including me. (p. 473)

George Balanchine (1904–83) was a brilliant choreographer of classical ballet. (p. 474)

Absolute phrases (p. 434)

The bird, its wing broken, hopped about on the ground.

The bird hopped about on the ground, its wing broken.

Phrases expressing contrast (p. 434)

The humidity, not just the heat, gives me headaches.

My headaches are caused by the humidity, not just the heat.

Concluding summaries and explanations

The movie opened to bad notices: the characters were judged shallow and unrealistic. (p. 470)

We had gumbo and jambalaya for dinner—a Cajun feast. (p. 473)

Items in a series

Three or more items

Chimpanzees, gorillas, orangutans, and gibbons are all apes. (p. 435)

The cities singled out for praise were Birmingham, Alabama; Lincoln, Nebraska; Austin, Texas; and Troy, New York. (p. 450)

Two or more adjectives before a noun (p. 435)

Dingy, smelly clothes decorated their room.

Dessert consisted of one tiny scoop of ice cream.

Introductory series (p. 473)

Appropriateness, accuracy, and necessity—these criteria should govern your selection of words.

Concluding series

Every word should be appropriate, accurate, and necessary. (p. 441)

Every word should meet three criteria: appropriateness, accuracy, and necessity. (p. 470)

Pay attention to your words—to their appropriateness, their accuracy, and their necessity. (p. 473)

27
End Punctuation

End punctuation marks—the period, the question mark, and the exclamation point—signal the ends of sentences.

Grammar checkers A grammar checker may flag missing question marks after direct questions or incorrect combinations of marks (such as a question mark and a period at the end of a sentence), but it cannot do much else.

27a Use periods after most sentences and with some abbreviations.

1 Use a period to end a statement, mild command, or indirect question.

Statements
These are exciting and trying times.
The airline went bankrupt.

Mild commands
Please do not smoke.
Think of the possibilities.

If you are unsure whether to use an exclamation point or a period after a command, use a period. The exclamation point should be used only rarely (see p. 423).

An **indirect question** reports what someone has asked but not in the form or the exact words of the original:

Indirect questions
Students sometimes wonder whether their teachers read the papers they write.
Abused children eventually stop asking why they are being punished.

 In standard American English, an indirect question uses the wording and subject-verb order of a

---

Visit *mycomplab.com* for more resources and exercises

on end punctuation.

statement: *The reporter asked why the negotiations failed*, not *why did the negotiations fail*.

2 Use periods with some abbreviations.

Use periods with abbreviations that consist of or end in small letters. Otherwise, omit periods from abbreviations.

Dr.	Mr., Mrs.	e.g.	Feb.	ft.
St.	Ms.	i.e.	p.	a.m., p.m.
PhD	BC, BCE	USA	IBM	AM, PM
BA	AD, CE	US	USMC	AIDS

Note When a sentence ends in an abbreviation with a period, don't add a second period: *My first class is at 8 a.m.*

See also pages 494–97 on uses of abbreviations in writing.

Exercise 27.1 Revising: Periods

Revise the following sentences so that periods are used correctly.

Example:
Several times I wrote to ask when my subscription ended?
Several times I wrote to ask when my subscription ended.

1. The teacher asked when Plato wrote *The Republic*?
2. Give the date within one century
3. The exact date is not known, but it is estimated at 370 BCE
4. Dr Arn will lecture on Plato at 7:30 p.m..
5. The area of the lecture hall is only 1600 sq ft

27b Use question marks after direct questions and sometimes to indicate doubt.

1 Use a question mark with a direct question.

What is the difference between these two people?
Will economists ever really understand the economy?

After an indirect question, use a period: *The senator asked why the bill had passed.* (See opposite.)

Questions in a series are each followed by a question mark:

The officer asked how many times the suspect had been arrested. Three times? Four times? More than that?

The use of capital letters for questions in a series is optional (see p. 485).

Note Question marks are never combined with other question marks, exclamation points, periods, or commas:

| Faulty | "What is the point?," readers ask. |
| Revised | "What is the point?" readers ask. |

2 Use a question mark within parentheses to indicate doubt about a number or date.

The Greek philosopher Socrates was born in 470 (?) BC and died in 399 BC from drinking poison after having been condemned to death.

Note Don't use a question mark within parentheses to express sarcasm or irony. Express these attitudes through sentence structure and word choice. (See Chapters 23 and 38.)

| Faulty | Stern's friendliness (?) bothered Crane. |
| Revised | Stern's insincerity bothered Crane. |

Exercise 27.2 Revising: Question marks

Revise the following sentences so that question marks (along with other punctuation marks) are used correctly.

Example:
"Why should I vote for you?," the woman asked the candidate.
"Why should I vote for you?" the woman asked the candidate.

1. In Homer's *Odyssey,* Odysseus took seven years to travel from Troy to Ithaca. Or was it eight years. Or more?
2. Odysseus must have wondered whether he would ever make it home?
3. "What man are you and whence?," asks Odysseus's wife, Penelope.
4. Why does Penelope ask, "Where is your city? Your family?"?
5. Penelope does not recognize Odysseus and asks who this stranger is?

27c Use an exclamation point after an emphatic statement, interjection, or command.

No! We must not lose this election!
Come here immediately!

Follow mild interjections and commands with commas or periods, as appropriate:

No, the response was not terrific.
To prolong your car's life, change its oil regularly.

Use exclamation points sparingly, not to express sarcasm, irony, or amazement. Rely on sentence structure and word choice to express these attitudes. (See Chapters 23 and 38.)

| Faulty | After traveling 4.4 billion miles through space, *Voyager 2* was off-target by 21 miles (!). |
| Revised | After traveling 4.4 billion miles through space, *Voyager 2* was off-target by a mere 21 miles. |

Relying on the exclamation point for emphasis is like crying wolf: the mark loses its power to impress the reader. Frequent exclamation points can also make writing sound overemotional:

Overused exclamation points

Our city government is a mess! After just six months in office, the mayor has had to fire four city officials! In the same period the city councilors have done nothing but argue! And city services decline with each passing day!

Note Exclamation points are never combined with other exclamation points, question marks, periods, or commas:

Faulty   "This will not be endured!," he roared.
Revised   "This will not be endured!" he roared.

Exercise 27.3 Revising: Exclamation points

Revise the following sentences so that exclamation points (along with other punctuation marks) are used correctly. If a sentence is punctuated correctly as given, mark the number preceding it.

Example:
"Well, now!," he said loudly.
"Well, now!" he said loudly.

1. As the firefighters moved their equipment into place, the police shouted, "Move back!".
2. A child's cries could be heard from above: "Help me. Help."
3. When the child was rescued, the crowd called, "Hooray."
4. The rescue was the most exciting event of the day!
5. Let me tell you about it.

Exercise 27.4 Revising: End punctuation

Insert appropriate punctuation (periods, question marks, or exclamation points) where needed in the following paragraph.

When visitors first arrive in Hawaii, they often encounter an unexpected language barrier Standard English is the language of business and government, but many of the people speak Pidgin English Instead of an excited "Aloha" the visitors may be greeted with an excited Pidgin "Howzit" or asked if they know "how fo' find one good hotel" Many Hawaiians question whether Pidgin will hold children back because it prevents communication with the *haoles,* or Caucasians, who run businesses Yet many others feel that Pidgin is a last defense of ethnic diversity on the islands To those who want to make standard English the official language of the state, these Hawaiians may respond, "Just 'cause I speak Pidgin no mean I dumb" They may ask, "Why you no listen" or, in standard English, "Why don't you listen"

Note See page 481 for a punctuation exercise combining periods with other marks of punctuation.

28

The Comma

Commas usually function within sentences to separate elements (see the box on the next page). Omitting needed commas or inserting needless ones can confuse the reader:

Comma needed	Though very tall Abraham Lincoln was not an overbearing man.
Revised	Though very tall, Abraham Lincoln was not an overbearing man.
Unneeded commas	The hectic pace of Beirut, broke suddenly into frightening chaos when the city became, the focus of civil war.
Revised	The hectic pace of Beirut broke suddenly into frightening chaos when the city became the focus of civil war.

Grammar checkers A grammar checker will ignore many comma errors. For example, a checker failed to catch the missing commas in *The boat ran aground and we were stranded* and in *We cooked lasagna spinach and apple pie.* At the same time the checker overlooked the misused commas in *The trip was short but, the weather was perfect* and *The travelers were tempted by, the many shops, and varied restaurants.*

28a Use a comma before *and, but,* or another coordinating conjunction linking main clauses.

The coordinating conjunctions are *and, but, or, nor, for, so,* and *yet.* When one of them links words or phrases, do not use a comma: *Dugain plays and sings Irish and English folk songs.* However, *do* use a comma when a coordinating conjunction joins main clauses. A **main clause** has a subject and a predicate (but no subordinating word at the beginning) and makes a complete statement (see p. 252).

mycomplab

Visit *mycomplab.com* for more resources and exercises
424   on the comma.

Principal uses of the comma

■ **Separate main clauses linked by a coordinating conjunction** (opposite and next page):

| Main clause | **,** | for and or
so but nor
yet | main clause | **.** |

The building is finished**,** but it has no tenants.

■ **Set off most introductory elements** (p. 427):

| Introductory element | **,** | main clause | **.** |

Unfortunately**,** the only tenant pulled out.

■ **Set off nonessential elements** (p. 429):

| Main clause | **,** | nonessential element | **.** |

The empty building symbolizes a weak local economy**,** which affects everyone.

| Beginning of main clause | **,** | nonessential element | **,** | end of main clause | **.** |

The primary cause**,** the decline of local industry**,** is not news.

■ **Separate items in a series** (p. 435):

| . . . | item 1 | **,** | item 2 | **,** | and
or | item 3 | . . . |

The city needs healthier businesses**,** new schools**,** and improved housing.

■ **Separate coordinate adjectives** (p. 435):

| . . . | first adjective | **,** | second adjective | word modified | . . . |

A tall**,** sleek skyscraper is not needed.

Other uses of the comma:

Set off absolute phrases (p. 434).
Set off phrases expressing contrast (p. 434).
Separate parts of dates, addresses, long numbers (p. 437).
Separate quotations and signal phrases (p. 438).
Prevent misreading (p. 440).

See also page 441 for when *not* to use the comma.

Caffeine can keep coffee drinkers alert, and it may elevate their mood.

Caffeine was once thought to be safe, but now researchers warn of harmful effects.

Coffee drinkers may suffer sleeplessness, for the drug acts as a stimulant to the nervous system.

Note Do not add a comma *after* a coordinating conjunction between main clauses (see also pp. 441–42):

Not Caffeine increases the heart rate, and, it constricts blood vessels.

But Caffeine increases the heart rate, and it constricts blood vessels.

Exceptions When the main clauses in a sentence are very long or grammatically complicated, or when they contain internal punctuation, a semicolon before the coordinating conjunction will clarify the division between clauses (see p. 445):

Caffeine may increase alertness, elevate mood, and provide energy; but it may also cause irritability, anxiety, stomach pains, and other ills.

When main clauses are very short and closely related in meaning, you may omit the comma between them as long as the resulting sentence is clear:

Caffeine helps but it also hurts.

If you are in doubt about whether to use a comma in such a sentence, use it. It will always be correct.

Exercise 28.1 Punctuating linked main clauses

Insert a comma before each coordinating conjunction that links main clauses in the following sentences.

Example:

I would have attended the concert and the reception but I had to baby-sit for my niece.

I would have attended the concert and the reception, but I had to baby-sit for my niece.

1. Parents once automatically gave their children the father's surname but some no longer do.
2. Instead, they bestow the mother's name for they believe that the mother's importance should be recognized.
3. The child's surname may be just the mother's or it may link the mother's and the father's with a hyphen.
4. Sometimes the first and third children will have the mother's surname and the second child will have the father's.
5. Occasionally the mother and father combine parts of their names and a new hybrid surname is born.

Exercise 28.2 Sentence combining: Linked main clauses

Combine each group of sentences below into one sentence that contains only two main clauses connected by the coordinating conjunction in parentheses. Separate the main clauses with a comma. You will have to add, delete, and rearrange words.

Example:

The circus had come to town. The children wanted to see it. Their parents wanted to see it. (*and*)

The circus had come to town, and the children and their parents wanted to see it.

1. Parents were once legally required to bestow the father's surname on their children. These laws have been contested in court. They have been found invalid. (*but*)
2. Parents may now give their children any surname they choose. The arguments for bestowing the mother's surname are often strong. They are often convincing. (*and*)
3. Critics sometimes question the effects of unusual surnames on children. They wonder how confusing the new surnames will be. They wonder how fleeting the surnames will be. (*or*)
4. Children with surnames different from their parents' may suffer embarrassment. They may suffer identity problems. Giving children their father's surname is still very much the norm. (*for*)
5. Hyphenated names are awkward. They are also difficult to pass on. Some observers think they will die out in the next generation. Or they may die out before. (*so*)

28b Use a comma to set off most introductory elements.

An introductory element modifies a word or words in the main clause that follows. These elements are usually set off from the rest of the sentence with a comma:

Subordinate clause (p. 252)

Even when identical twins are raised apart, they grow up very like each other.

Because they are similar, such twins interest scientists.

Verbal or verbal phrase (p. 247)

Explaining the similarity, some researchers claim that one's genes are one's destiny.

Concerned, other researchers deny the claim.

Prepositional phrase (p. 244)

In a debate that has lasted centuries, scientists use identical twins to argue for or against genetic destiny.

Transitional or parenthetical expression (pp. 89–90)

Of course, scientists can now look directly at the genes themselves.

The comma may be omitted after short introductory elements if its omission does not create confusion. (If you are in doubt, however, the comma is always correct.)

Clear	In a hundred years genetics may no longer be a mystery.
Confusing	Despite intensive research scientists still have more questions than answers.
Clear	Despite intensive research, scientists still have more questions than answers.

Commas may also be omitted after some transitional expressions when they start sentences. (See p. 432.)

Thus the debate continues.

Note Take care to distinguish *-ing* words used as modifiers from *-ing* words used as subjects, as shown in the following examples. The former almost always take a comma; the latter never do.

┌──── modifier ────┐   subject   verb
Studying identical twins, geneticists learn about inheritance.

┌──── subject ────┐   verb
Studying identical twins helps geneticists learn about inheritance.

Exercise 28.3 Punctuating introductory elements

Insert commas where needed after introductory elements in the following sentences. If a sentence is punctuated correctly as given, mark the number preceding it.

Example:
After the new library opened the old one became a student union.
After the new library opened, the old one became a student union.

1. Moving in a fluid mass is typical of flocks of birds and schools of fish.
2. Because it is sudden and apparently well coordinated the movement of flocks and schools has seemed to be directed by a leader.
3. However new studies have discovered that flocks and schools are leaderless.
4. When each bird or fish senses a predator it follows individual rules for fleeing.
5. Multiplied over hundreds of individuals these responses look as if they have been choreographed.

Exercise 28.4 Sentence combining: Introductory elements

Combine each pair of sentences below into one sentence that begins with an introductory phrase or clause as specified in parentheses. Follow the introductory element with a comma. You will have to add, delete, change, and rearrange words.

Example:

The girl was humming to herself. She walked upstairs. (*Phrase beginning Humming.*)

<u>Humming to herself</u>, the girl walked upstairs.

1. Scientists have made an effort to explain the mysteries of flocks and schools. They have proposed bizarre magnetic fields and telepathy. (*Phrase beginning <u>In</u>.*)
2. Scientists developed computer models. They have abandoned earlier explanations. (*Clause beginning <u>Since</u>.*)
3. The movement of a flock or school starts with each individual. It is rapidly and perhaps automatically coordinated among individuals. (*Phrase beginning <u>Starting</u>.*)
4. One zoologist observes that human beings seek coherent patterns. He suggests that investigators saw purpose in the movement of flocks and schools where none existed. (*Phrase beginning <u>Observing</u>.*)
5. One may want to study the movement of flocks or schools. Then one must abandon a search for purpose or design. (*Phrase beginning <u>To</u>.*)

28c Use a comma or commas to set off nonessential elements.

Commas around part of a sentence often signal that the element is not essential to the meaning of the sentence:

Nonessential element

The company, <u>which is located in Oklahoma</u>, has a good reputation.

This **nonessential element** may modify or rename the word it refers to (*company* in the example), but it does not limit the word to a particular individual or group. (Because it does not restrict meaning, a nonessential element is also called a **nonrestrictive element**.) Nonessential elements are *not* essential, but punctuation *is*.

In contrast, an **essential** (or **restrictive**) element *does* limit the word it refers to:

Essential element

The company rewards employees <u>who work hard</u>.

In this example the underlined essential element cannot be omitted without leaving the meaning of *employees* too general. Because it is essential, such an element is *not* set off with commas. The element *is* essential, but punctuation is *not*.

Meaning and context

The same element in the same sentence may be essential or nonessential depending on your intended meaning and the context in which the sentence appears. For example, look at the second sentence in each of the following passages:

Essential
Not all the bands were equally well received, however. The band playing old music held the audience's attention. The other groups created much less excitement. [*Playing old music* identifies a particular band.]

Nonessential
A new band called Fats made its debut on Saturday night. The band, playing old music, held the audience's attention. If this performance is typical, the group has a bright future. [*Playing old music* adds information about a band already named.]

Punctuation of interrupting nonessential elements

When a nonessential element falls in the middle of a sentence, be sure to set it off with a pair of commas, one *before* and one *after* the element. Dashes or parentheses may also set off nonessential elements (see pp. 472 and 474).

1 Use a comma or commas to set off nonessential clauses and phrases.

Clauses and phrases serving as adjectives and adverbs may be either nonessential or essential. In the following examples the underlined clauses and phrases are nonessential: they could be omitted without changing the meaning of the words they modify.

Nonessential
Elizabeth Blackwell was the first woman to graduate from an American medical school, in 1849.

A test for essential and nonessential elements

1. **Identify the element.**

   Hai Nguyen who emigrated from Vietnam lives in Denver.
   Those who emigrated with him live elsewhere.

2. **Remove the element. Does the fundamental meaning of the sentence change?**

   Hai Nguyen lives in Denver. *No.*
   Those live elsewhere. *Yes.* [Who are *Those?*]

3. **If *no*, the element is *nonessential* and should be set off with punctuation.**

   Hai Nguyen, who emigrated from Vietnam, lives in Denver.

   If *yes*, the element is *essential* and should *not* be set off with punctuation.

   Those who emigrated with him live elsewhere.

She was a medical pioneer, helping to found the first medical college for women.
She taught at the school, which was affiliated with the New York Infirmary.
Blackwell, who published books and papers on medicine, practiced pediatrics and gynecology.
She moved to England in 1869, when she was forty-eight.

Note Most adverb clauses are essential because they describe conditions necessary to the main clause. They are set off by a comma only when they introduce sentences (see p. 427) and when they are truly nonessential, adding incidental information (as in the last example above) or expressing a contrast beginning *although, even though, though, whereas,* and the like.

In the following sentences, the underlined elements limit the meaning of the words they modify. Removing the elements would leave the meaning too general.

Essential

The history of aspirin began with the ancient Greeks.
Physicians who sought to relieve their patients' pains recommended chewing willow bark.
Willow bark contains a chemical that is similar to aspirin.

Note Whereas both nonessential and essential clauses may begin with *which,* only essential clauses begin with *that.* Some writers prefer *that* exclusively for essential clauses and *which* exclusively for nonessential clauses. See the Glossary of Usage, page 859, for advice on the use of *that* and *which.*

2 Use a comma or commas to set off nonessential appositives.

An **appositive** is a noun or noun substitute that renames another noun just before it. (See p. 256.) Many appositives are nonessential; thus they are set off, usually with commas.

Nonessential

Toni Morrison's fifth novel, *Beloved,* won the Pulitzer Prize in 1988.
Morrison, a native of Ohio, won the Nobel Prize in 1993.

Take care *not* to set off essential appositives; like other essential elements, they limit or define the word to which they refer.

Essential

Morrison's novel *The Bluest Eye* is about an African American girl who longs for blue eyes.
The critic Michiko Kakutani says that Morrison's work "stands radiantly on its own as an American epic."

3 Use a comma or commas to set off transitional or parenthetical expressions.

Transitional expressions

Transitional expressions form links between ideas. They include conjunctive adverbs such as *however* and *moreover* as well as other words or phrases such as *for example* and *of course*. (See pp. 89–90 for a list of transitional words and phrases.) Transitional expressions are nonessential, and most of them are set off with a comma or commas:

> US workers, for example, receive fewer holidays than European workers do.

When a transitional expression links main clauses, precede it with a semicolon and follow it with a comma. (See p. 448.)

> European workers often have long paid vacations; indeed, they may receive a full month.

Exceptions The conjunctions *and, but,* and *yet* are sometimes used as transitional expressions but are never followed by commas (see p. 443). Usage varies with some other transitional expressions, depending on the expression and the writer's judgment. Many writers omit commas with expressions that we read without pauses, such as *also, hence, next, now, then,* and *thus*. The same applies to *therefore* and *instead* when they fall inside or at the ends of clauses.

> US workers therefore put in more work days. But the days themselves may be shorter.
> Then the total hours worked come out roughly the same.

Parenthetical expressions

Parenthetical expressions provide comments, explanations, digressions, or other supplementary information not essential to meaning—for example, *fortunately, unfortunately, all things considered, to be frank, in other words*. Like transitional expressions, most parenthetical expressions are set off, sometimes with commas:

> Surprisingly, the most celebrated holiday in the world is New Year's Day.

Dashes and parentheses may also set off parenthetical expressions. (See pp. 472 and 474, respectively.)

4 Use a comma or commas to set off *yes* and *no*, tag questions, words of direct address, and mild interjections.

Yes and *no*

> Yes, the editorial did have a point.
> No, that can never be.

Tag questions

They don't stop to consider others, do they?
Beatriz should be allowed to vote, shouldn't he?

Direct address

Cody, please bring me the newspaper.
With all due respect, sir, I will not do that.

Mild interjections

Well, you will never know who did it.
Oh, they forgot all about the science fair.

(You may want to use an exclamation point to set off a forceful interjection. See p. 422.)

Exercise 28.5 Punctuating essential and nonessential elements

Insert commas in the following sentences to set off nonessential elements, and delete any commas that incorrectly set off essential elements. If a sentence is correct as given, mark the number preceding it.

> *Example:*
>
> Our language has adopted the words, *garage* and *fanfare,* from the French.
>
> Our language has adopted the words *garage* and *fanfare* from the French.

1. Italians insist that Marco Polo the thirteenth-century explorer did not import pasta from China.
2. Pasta which consists of flour and water and often egg existed in Italy long before Marco Polo left for his travels.
3. A historian who studied pasta says that it originated in the Middle East in the fifth century.
4. Most Italians dispute this account although their evidence is shaky.
5. Wherever pasta originated, the Italians are now the undisputed masters, in making and cooking it.
6. Marcella Hazan, who has written several books on Italian cooking, insists that homemade and hand-rolled pasta is the best.
7. Most cooks must buy dried pasta lacking the time to make their own.
8. The finest pasta is made from semolina, a flour from hard durum wheat.
9. Pasta manufacturers choose hard durum wheat, because it makes firmer cooked pasta than common wheat does.
10. Pasta, made from common wheat, tends to get soggy in boiling water.

Exercise 28.6 Sentence combining: Essential and nonessential elements

Combine each pair of sentences below into one sentence that uses the element described in parentheses. Insert commas as appropriate. You will have to add, delete, change, and rearrange words. Some items have more than one possible answer.

Example:

Mr. Ward's oldest sister helped keep him alive. She was a nurse in the hospital. (*Nonessential clause beginning who.*)

Mr. Ward's oldest sister, who was a nurse in the hospital, helped keep him alive.

1. American colonists first imported pasta from the English. The English had discovered it as tourists in Italy. (*Nonessential clause beginning who.*)
2. The English returned from their grand tours of Italy. They were called *macaronis* because of their fancy airs. (*Essential phrase beginning returning.*)
3. A hair style was also called *macaroni*. It had elaborate curls. (*Essential phrase beginning with.*)
4. The song "Yankee Doodle" refers to this hairdo. It reports that Yankee Doodle "stuck a feather in his cap and called it macaroni." (*Essential clause beginning when.*)
5. The song was actually intended to poke fun at unrefined American colonists. It was a creation of the English. (*Nonessential appositive beginning a creation.*)

28d Use a comma or commas to set off absolute phrases.

An **absolute phrase** modifies a whole main clause rather than any word in the clause, and it usually consists of at least a participle (such as *done* or *having torn*) and its subject (a noun or pronoun). (See p. 251.) Absolute phrases can occur at almost any point in the sentence, and they are always set off by a comma or commas:

Household recycling having succeeded, the city now wants to extend the program to businesses.

Many businesses, their profits already squeezed, resist recycling.

28e Use a comma or commas to set off phrases expressing contrast.

The essay needs less wit, more pith.
The substance, not the style, is important.
Substance, unlike style, cannot be faked.

Note Writers often omit commas around contrasting phrases beginning with *but: A full but hazy moon shone down.*

Exercise 28.7 Punctuating absolute phrases and phrases of contrast

Insert commas in the following sentences to set off absolute phrases and phrases of contrast.

Example:

The recording contract was canceled the band having broken up.
The recording contract was canceled, the band having broken up.

1. Prices having risen rapidly the government debated a price freeze.
2. A price freeze unlike a rise in interest rates seemed a sure solution.
3. The President would have to persuade businesses to accept a price freeze his methods depending on their resistance.
4. No doubt the President his advisers having urged it would first try a patriotic appeal.
5. The President not his advisers insisted on negotiations with businesses.

28f Use commas between items in a series and between coordinate adjectives.

1 Use commas between words, phrases, or clauses forming a series.

Place commas between all elements of a **series**—that is, three or more items of equal importance:

Anna Spingle married at the age of seventeen, had three children by twenty-one, and divorced at twenty-two.
She worked as a cook, a baby-sitter, and a crossing guard.

Some writers omit the comma before the coordinating conjunction in a series (*Breakfast consisted of coffee, eggs and kippers*). But the final comma is never wrong, and it always helps the reader see the last two items as separate:

Confusing   Spingle's new job involves typing, filing and answering correspondence.

Clear   Spingle's new job involves typing, filing, and answering correspondence.

Exception When items in a series are long and grammatically complicated, they may be separated by semicolons. When the items contain commas, they must be separated by semicolons. (See p. 450.)

2 Use commas between two or more adjectives that equally modify the same words.

When two or more adjectives modify the same word equally, they are said to be **coordinate**. The adjectives may be separated either by *and* or by a comma, as in the following examples.

Spingle's scratched and dented car is old, but it gets her to work.
She has dreams of a sleek, shiny car.

Punctuating two or more adjectives

1. **Identify the adjectives.**

   She was a <u>faithful sincere</u> friend.
   They are <u>dedicated volunteer</u> tutors.

2. **Can the adjectives be reversed without changing meaning?**

   She was a <u>sincere faithful</u> friend. *Yes.*
   They are <u>volunteer dedicated</u> tutors. *No.*

3. **Can the word *and* be sensibly inserted between the adjectives?**

   She was a <u>faithful and sincere</u> friend. *Yes.*
   They are <u>dedicated and volunteer</u> tutors. *No.*

4. **If *yes* to both questions, the adjectives *are* coordinate and *should* be separated by a comma.**

   She was a <u>faithful **,** sincere</u> friend.

   If *no* to both questions, the adjectives are *not* coordinate and should *not* be separated by a comma.

   They are <u>dedicated volunteer</u> tutors.

Adjectives are not coordinate—and should *not* be separated by commas—when the one nearer the noun is more closely related to the noun in meaning. In each of the next examples, the second adjective and the noun form a unit that is modified by the first adjective:

> Spingle's children work at <u>various part-time</u> jobs.
> They all expect to go to a <u>nearby community</u> college.

See the box above for a test to use in punctuating adjectives.

Note Numbers are not coordinate with other adjectives:

Faulty	Spingle has <u>three, teenaged</u> children.
Revised	Spingle has <u>three teenaged</u> children.

Do not use a comma between the final adjective and the noun:

Faulty	The children hope to achieve <u>good, well-paying,</u> jobs.
Revised	The children hope to achieve <u>good, well-paying</u> jobs.

Exercise 28.8 Punctuating series and coordinate adjectives

Insert commas in the following sentences to separate elements in series and coordinate adjectives. Mark the number preceding any sentence whose punctuation is already correct.

Example:
Quiet by day, the club became a noisy smoky dive at night.
Quiet by day, the club became a noisy **,** smoky dive at night.

1. Shoes with high heels originated to protect feet from the mud garbage and animal waste in the streets.
2. The first known high heels worn strictly for fashion appeared in the sixteenth century.
3. The heels were worn by men and made of colorful silk brocades soft suedes or smooth leathers.
4. High-heeled shoes received a boost when the short powerful King Louis XIV of France began wearing them.
5. Eventually only wealthy fashionable French women wore high heels.

28g Use commas according to convention in dates, addresses, place names, and long numbers.

Use commas to separate most parts of dates, addresses, and place names: *June 20, 1950; 24 Fifth Avenue, Suite 601; Cairo, Illinois*. Within a sentence, any element preceded by a comma should be followed by a comma as well, as in the examples below:

Dates

July 4, 1776, is the date the Declaration of Independence was signed.

The bombing of Pearl Harbor on Sunday, December 7, 1941, prompted American entry into World War II.

Do not use commas between the parts of a date in inverted order: *Their anniversary on 15 December 2005 was their fiftieth.* You need not use commas in dates consisting of a month or season and a year: *For the United States the war ended in August 1945.*

Addresses and place names

Columbus, Ohio, is the state capital and the location of Ohio State University.

The population of Garden City, Long Island, New York, is 30,000.

Use the address 220 Cornell Road, Woodside, California 94062, for all correspondence.

Do not use a comma between a state and a zip code.

Long numbers

Use the comma to separate the figures in long numbers into groups of three, counting from the right. With numbers of four digits, the comma is optional.

A kilometer is 3,281 feet [*or* 3281 feet].

The new assembly plant cost $7,535,000 to design and build.

CULTURE LANGUAGE Usage in American English differs from that in some other languages and dialects, which use a period, not a comma, to separate the figures in long numbers.

Exercise 28.9 **Punctuating dates, addresses, place names, numbers**

Insert commas as needed in the following sentences.

Example:
The house cost $27000 thirty years ago.
The house cost $27,000 thirty years ago.

1. The festival will hold a benefit dinner and performance on March 10 2009 in Asheville.
2. The organizers hope to raise more than $100000 from donations and ticket sales.
3. Performers are expected from as far away as Milan Italy and Kyoto Japan.
4. All inquiries sent to Mozart Festival PO Box 725 Asheville North Carolina 28803 will receive a quick response.
5. The deadline for ordering tickets by mail is Monday December 3 2008.

28h Use commas with quotations according to standard practice.

The words *he said, she writes, he claims,* and so on identify the source of a quotation. These **signal phrases** may come before, after, or in the middle of the quotation. A signal phrase must always be separated from the quotation by punctuation, usually a comma or commas.

Note Additional issues with quotations are discussed elsewhere in this book:

- Using quotation marks conventionally, pages 461–68.
- Choosing and transcribing quotations from sources, pages 599–600.
- Integrating source material into your text, pages 601–06.
- Acknowledging the sources of quotations to avoid plagiarism, pages 610–12 and 614–15.
- Formatting long prose quotations and poetry quotations in MLA style, pages 665–66, and APA style, page 763.

1 Ordinarily, use a comma with a signal phrase before or after a quotation.

Eleanor Roosevelt said, "You must do the thing you think you cannot do."
"Knowledge is power," writes Francis Bacon.

Exceptions Do not use a comma when a signal phrase follows a quotation ending in an exclamation point or a question mark:

"Claude!" Mrs. Harrison called.
"Why must I come home?" he asked.

Do not use commas with a quotation introduced by *that* or with a quotation that is integrated into your sentence structure:

> James Baldwin insists that "one must never, in one's life, accept . . . injustices as commonplace."

> Baldwin thought that the violence of a riot "had been devised as a corrective" to his own violence.

Use a colon instead of a comma between a signal phrase and a quotation when the signal phrase is actually a complete sentence, with its own subject and predicate:

> The Bill of Rights is unambiguous: "Congress shall make no law respecting an establishment of religion, or prohibiting the free exercise thereof."

2 **With an interrupted quotation, precede the signal phrase with a comma and follow it with the punctuation required by the quotation.**

Original quotation

"The shore has a dual nature, changing with the swing of the tides."

Signal phrase interrupts at comma, ends with comma

"The shore has a dual nature," observes Rachel Carson, "changing with the swing of the tides."

Original quotation

"However mean your life is, meet it and live it; do not shun it and call it hard names."

Signal phrase interrupts at semicolon, ends with semicolon

"However mean your life is, meet it and live it," Thoreau advises in *Walden*; "do not shun it and call it hard names."

Original quotation

"This is the faith with which I return to the South. With this new faith we will be able to hew out of the mountain of despair a stone of hope."

Signal phrase interrupts at end of sentence, ends with period

"This is the faith with which I return to the South," Martin Luther King, Jr., proclaimed. "With this new faith we will be able to hew out of the mountain of despair a stone of hope."

Note Using a comma instead of a semicolon or a period after the Thoreau and King signal phrases would result in the error called a comma splice: two main clauses separated only by a comma. (See pp. 342–45.)

3 Place commas that follow quotations within quotation marks.

"Death is not the greatest loss in life," claims Norman Cousins. "The greatest loss," Cousins says, "is what dies inside us while we live."

Exercise 28.10 Punctuating quotations

Insert commas or semicolons in the following sentences to correct punctuation with quotations. Mark the number preceding any sentence whose punctuation is already correct.

Example:
The shoplifter declared "I didn't steal anything."
The shoplifter declared, "I didn't steal anything."

1. The writer and writing teacher Peter Elbow proposes an "open-ended writing process" that "can change you, not just your words."
2. "I think of the open-ended writing process as a voyage in two stages" Elbow says.
3. "The sea voyage is a process of divergence, branching, proliferation, and confusion" Elbow continues "the coming to land is a process of convergence, pruning, centralizing, and clarifying."
4. "Keep up one session of writing long enough to get loosened up and tired" advises Elbow "long enough in fact to make a bit of a voyage."
5. "In coming to new land" Elbow says "you develop a new conception of what you are writing about."

28i Use commas to prevent misreading.

In some sentences words may run together in unintended and confusing ways unless a comma separates them:

Confusing	Soon after the business closed its doors.
Clear	Soon after, the business closed its doors.

Always check whether a comma added to prevent misreading might cause some other confusion or error. In the first example below, the comma prevents *pasta* and *places* from running into each other as *pasta places*, but it separates the subject (*historian*) and the verb (*places*). The revision solves both problems.

Faulty	A historian who studied pasta, places its origin in the Middle East.
Revised	A historian who studied pasta says that it originated in the Middle East.

Exercise 28.11 Punctuating to prevent misreading

Insert commas in the following sentences to prevent misreading.

Example:
To Laura Ann symbolized decadence.
To Laura, Ann symbolized decadence.

1. Though happy people still have moments of self-doubt.
2. In research subjects have reported themselves to be generally happy people.
3. Among those who have life has included sufferings as well as joys.
4. Of fifty eight subjects reported bouts of serious depression.
5. For half the preceding year had included at least one personal crisis.

28j Use commas only where required.

Commas can make sentences choppy and even confusing if they are used more often than needed. The main misuses of commas are summarized in the box on the next page.

1 Delete any comma after a subject or a verb.

Commas interrupt the movement from subject to verb to object or complement, as in the following faulty examples.

Faulty	The returning soldiers, received a warmer welcome than they expected. [Separation of subject and verb.]
Revised	The returning soldiers received a warmer welcome than they expected.
Faulty	They had chosen, to fight for their country. [Separation of verb *chosen* and object *to fight*.]
Revised	They had chosen to fight for their country.

Exception Use commas between subject, verb, and object or complement only when other words between these elements require punctuation:

Americans, who are preoccupied with other sports, have only recently developed an interest in professional soccer. [Commas set off a nonessential clause.]

2 Delete any comma that separates a pair of words, phrases, or subordinate clauses joined by a coordinating conjunction.

When linking elements with *and, or,* or another coordinating conjunction, do not use a comma unless the elements are main clauses (see p. 424):

| Faulty | Banks could, and should help older people manage their money. [Compound helping verb.] |
| Revised | Banks could and should help older people manage their money. |

Principal misuses of the comma

■ **Don't use a comma after a subject or verb:**

Faulty   Anyone with breathing problems, should not exercise during smog alerts.

Revised   Anyone with breathing problems should not exercise during smog alerts.

■ **Don't separate a pair of words, phrases, or subordinate clauses joined by** *and, or,* **or** *nor:*

Faulty   Asthmatics are affected by ozone, and sulfur oxides.

Revised   Asthmatics are affected by ozone and sulfur oxides.

■ **Don't use a comma after** *and, but, although, because,* **or another conjunction:**

Faulty   Smog is dangerous and, sometimes even fatal.

Revised   Smog is dangerous and sometimes even fatal.

■ **Don't set off essential elements:**

Faulty   Even people, who are healthy, should be careful.

Revised   Even people who are healthy should be careful.

Faulty   Bruce Springsteen's song, "Born in the USA," is an anthem.

Revised   Bruce Springsteen's song "Born in the USA" is an anthem.

■ **Don't set off a series:**

Faulty   Cars, factories, and even bakeries, contribute to smog.

Revised   Cars, factories, and even bakeries contribute to smog.

■ **Don't set off an indirect quotation:**

Faulty   Experts say, that the pollutant ozone is especially damaging.

Revised   Experts say that the pollutant ozone is especially damaging.

Faulty   Older people need special assistance because they live on fixed incomes, and because they are not familiar with new accounts, and rates. [Compound subordinate clauses *because . . . because* and compound object of preposition *with*.]

Revised   Older people need special assistance because they live on fixed incomes and because they are not familiar with new accounts and rates.

Faulty   Banks, and community groups can assist the elderly, and eliminate the confusion they often feel. [Compound subject and compound predicate.]

Revised   Banks and community groups can assist the elderly and eliminate the confusion they often feel.

3 Delete any comma after a conjunction.

The coordinating conjunctions (*and, but,* and so on) and the subordinating conjunctions (*although, because,* and so on) are not followed by commas:

Faulty	Parents of adolescents notice increased conflict at puberty, <u>and</u>, they complain of bickering.
Revised	Parents of adolescents notice increased conflict at puberty, and they complain of bickering.
Faulty	<u>Although,</u> other primates leave the family at adolescence, humans do not.
Revised	Although other primates leave the family at adolescence, humans do not.

4 Delete any commas that set off essential elements.

Commas do not set off an essential element, which limits the meaning of the word to which it refers (see p. 429):

Faulty	Hawthorne's work, *The Scarlet Letter,* was the first major American novel. [The title is essential to distinguish the novel from the rest of Hawthorne's work.]
Revised	Hawthorne's work *The Scarlet Letter* was the first major American novel.
Faulty	The symbols, <u>that Hawthorne uses,</u> have influenced other novelists. [The clause identifies which symbols have been influential.]
Revised	The symbols that Hawthorne uses have influenced other novelists.

Quoted or italicized words are essential appositives when they limit the word they refer to (see p. 431). Do not use commas around an essential appositive:

Faulty	James Joyce's short story, "The Dead," was made into an affecting film. [The commas imply wrongly that Joyce wrote only one story.]
Revised	James Joyce's short story "The Dead" was made into an affecting film.
Faulty	The word, *open,* can be either a verb or an adjective.
Revised	The word *open* can be either a verb or an adjective.

The following sentence requires commas because the quoted title is a nonessential appositive:

Her only poem about death, "Mourning," was printed in *The New Yorker.*

5 Delete any comma before or after a series unless a rule requires it.

Commas separate the items *within* a series (p. 435) but do not separate the series from the rest of the sentence:

> Faulty   The skills of, hunting, herding, and agriculture, sustained the Native Americans.
>
> Revised   The skills of hunting, herding, and agriculture sustained the Native Americans.

In the sentence below, the commas around the series are appropriate because the series is a nonessential appositive (p. 431):

> The four major broadcast networks, ABC, CBS, Fox, and NBC, face fierce competition from the cable and satellite networks.

However, many writers prefer to use dashes rather than commas to set off series functioning as appositives (see p. 473).

6 Delete any comma setting off an indirect quotation.

> Faulty   The report concluded, that dieting could be more dangerous than overeating.
>
> Revised   The report concluded that dieting could be more dangerous than overeating.

Exercise 28.12   Revising: Needless or misused commas

Revise the following sentences to eliminate needless or misused commas. Mark the number preceding any sentence that is already punctuated correctly.

> *Example:*
> The portrait of the founder, that hung in the dining hall, was stolen by pranksters.
> The portrait of the founder that hung in the dining hall was stolen by pranksters.

1. Nearly 32 million US residents, speak a first language other than English.
2. After English the languages most commonly spoken in the United States are, Spanish, French, and German.
3. Almost 75 percent of the people, who speak foreign languages, used the words, "good" or "very good," when judging their proficiency in English.
4. Recent immigrants, especially those speaking Spanish, Chinese, and Korean, tended to judge their English more harshly.
5. The states with the highest proportion of foreign language speakers, are New Mexico, and California.

Exercise 28.13 Revising: Commas

Insert commas in the following paragraphs wherever they are needed, and eliminate any misused or needless commas.

Ellis Island New York reopened for business in 1990 but now the customers are tourists not immigrants. This spot which lies in New York Harbor was the first American soil seen, or touched by many of the nation's immigrants. Though other places also served as ports of entry for foreigners none has the symbolic power of, Ellis Island. Between its opening in 1892 and its closing in 1954, over 20 million people about two-thirds of all immigrants were detained there before taking up their new lives in the United States. Ellis Island processed over 2000 newcomers a day when immigration was at its peak between 1900 and 1920.

As the end of a long voyage and the introduction to the New World Ellis Island must have left something to be desired. The "huddled masses" as the Statue of Liberty calls them indeed were huddled. New arrivals were herded about kept standing in lines for hours or days yelled at and abused. Assigned numbers they submitted their bodies to the pokings and proddings of the silent nurses and doctors, who were charged with ferreting out the slightest sign of sickness, disability or insanity. That test having been passed the immigrants faced interrogation by an official through an interpreter. Those, with names deemed inconveniently long or difficult to pronounce, often found themselves permanently labeled with abbreviations, of their names, or with the names, of their hometowns. But, millions survived the examination humiliation and confusion, to take the last short boat ride to New York City. For many of them and especially for their descendants Ellis Island eventually became not a nightmare but the place where life began.

Note See page 481 for a punctuation exercise combining commas with other marks of punctuation.

29

The Semicolon

The semicolon separates equal and balanced sentence elements, usually main clauses (pp. 447–50), sometimes items in series (p. 450).

mycomplab

Visit *mycomplab.com* for more resources and exercises on the semicolon.

Grammar checkers A grammar checker can spot a few errors in the use of semicolons. For example, a checker suggested using a semicolon after *perfect* in *The set was perfect, the director had planned every detail,* thus correcting a comma splice. But it missed the incorrect semicolon in *The set was perfect; deserted streets, dark houses, and gloomy mist* (a colon would be correct; see pp. 470–71).

Distinguishing the comma, the semicolon, and the colon

Comma

The *comma* chiefly separates both equal and unequal sentence elements.

- It separates main clauses when they are linked by a coordinating conjunction (p. 424):

  An airline once tried to boost sales by advertising the tense alertness of its crews, but nervous fliers did not want to hear about pilots' sweaty palms.

- It separates subordinate information that is part of or attached to a main clause, such as an introductory element or a nonessential modifier (pp. 427, 429):

  Although the airline campaign failed, many advertising agencies, including some clever ones, copied its underlying message.

Semicolon

The *semicolon* chiefly separates equal and balanced sentence elements. Often the first clause creates an expectation, and the second clause fulfills the expectation.

- It separates complementary main clauses that are *not* linked by a coordinating conjunction (facing page):

  The airline campaign had highlighted only half the story; the other half was buried in the copy.

- It separates complementary main clauses that are related by a conjunctive adverb or other transitional expression (p. 448):

  The campaign should not have stressed the pilots' insecurity; instead, the campaign should have stressed the improved performance resulting from that insecurity.

Colon

The *colon* chiefly separates unequal sentence elements.

- It separates a main clause from a following explanation or summary, which may or may not be a main clause (pp. 469–70):

  Many successful advertising campaigns have used this message: the anxious seller is harder working and smarter than the competitor.

29a Use a semicolon between main clauses not joined by *and, but,* or another coordinating conjunction.

Main clauses contain a subject and a predicate and do not begin with a subordinating word (see p. 252). When you join two main clauses in a sentence, you have two primary options for separating them:

■ **Insert a comma and a coordinating conjunction:** *and, but, or, nor, for, so, yet.* (See p. 424.)

The drug does little to relieve symptoms, and it can have side effects.

■ **Insert a semicolon:**

The side effects are not minor; some leave the patient quite ill.

Note If you do not link main clauses with a coordinating conjunction and you separate them only with a comma or with no punctuation at all, you will produce a comma splice or a fused sentence. (See Chapter 18.)

Exercise 29.1 Punctuating between main clauses

Insert semicolons to separate main clauses in the following sentences.

Example:

One man at the auction bid prudently another spent his bank account.

One man at the auction bid prudently; another spent his bank account.

1. More and more musicians are playing computerized instruments more and more listeners are worrying about the future of acoustic instruments.
2. The computer is not the first new technology in music the pipe organ and saxophone were also technological breakthroughs in their day.
3. Musicians have always experimented with new technology audiences have always resisted the experiments.
4. Most computer musicians are not merely following the latest fad they are discovering new sounds and new ways to manipulate sound.
5. Few musicians have abandoned acoustic instruments most value acoustic sounds as much as electronic sounds.

Exercise 29.2 Sentence combining: Related main clauses

Combine each set of three sentences below into one sentence containing only two main clauses, and insert a semicolon between the clauses. You will have to add, delete, change, and rearrange words. Most items have more than one possible answer.

Example:

The painter Andrew Wyeth is widely admired. He is not universally admired. Some critics view his work as sentimental.

The painter Andrew Wyeth is widely but not universally admired; some critics view his work as sentimental.

1. Electronic instruments are prevalent in jazz. They are also prevalent in rock music. They are less common in classical music.
2. Jazz and rock change rapidly. They nourish experimentation. They nourish improvisation.
3. Traditional classical music does not change. Its notes and instrumentation were established by a composer. The composer was writing decades or centuries ago.
4. Contemporary classical music can not only draw on tradition. It can also respond to innovations. These are innovations such as jazz rhythms and electronic sounds.
5. Much contemporary electronic music is more than just one type of music. It is more than just jazz, rock, or classical. It is a fusion of all three.

29b Use a semicolon between main clauses related by *however, for example,* and so on.

Two kinds of words can relate main clauses: **conjunctive adverbs,** such as *consequently, hence, however, indeed,* and *thus* (see p. 261), and other **transitional expressions,** such as *even so, for example,* and *of course* (see pp. 89–90). When either of these connects two main clauses, the clauses should be separated by a semicolon:

An American immigrant, Levi Strauss, invented blue jeans in the 1860s; eventually, his product clothed working men throughout the West.

The position of the semicolon between main clauses never changes, but the conjunctive adverb or transitional expression may move around within a clause. The adverb or expression is usually set off with a comma or commas (see p. 430):

Blue jeans have become fashionable all over the world; however, the American originators still wear more jeans than anyone else.

Blue jeans have become fashionable all over the world; the American originators, however, still wear more jeans than anyone else.

Its mobility distinguishes a conjunctive adverb or transitional expression from other connecting words, such as coordinating and subordinating conjunctions. See pages 260–61 on this distinction.

Note If you use a comma or no punctuation at all between main clauses connected by a conjunctive adverb or transitional expression, you will produce a comma splice or a fused sentence. (See Chapter 18.)

Exercise 29.3 Punctuating main clauses related by conjunctive adverbs or transitional expressions

Insert a semicolon in each of the following sentences to separate main clauses related by a conjunctive adverb or transitional expression. Also insert a comma or commas where needed to set off the adverb or expression.

Example:

He knew that tickets for the concert would sell quickly therefore he arrived at the box office hours before it opened.

He knew that tickets for the concert would sell quickly**;** therefore**,** he arrived at the box office hours before it opened.

1. Music is a form of communication like language the basic elements however are not letters but notes.
2. Computers can process any information that can be represented numerically as a result they can process musical information.
3. A computer's ability to process music depends on what software it can run it must moreover be connected to a system that converts electrical vibration into sound.
4. Computers and their sound systems can produce many different sounds indeed the number of possible sounds is infinite.
5. The powerful music computers are very expensive therefore they are used only by professional musicians.

Exercise 29.4 Sentence combining: Main clauses related by conjunctive adverbs or transitional expressions

Combine each set of three sentences below into one sentence containing only two main clauses. Connect the clauses with the conjunctive adverb or transitional expression in parentheses, and separate them with a semicolon. Be sure the adverbs and expressions are punctuated appropriately. You will have to add, delete, change, and rearrange words. Each item has more than one possible answer.

Example:

The Albanians censored their news. We got little news from them. And what we got was unreliable. (*therefore*)

The Albanians censored their news**;** therefore**,** the little news we got from them was unreliable.

1. Most music computers are too expensive for the average consumer. Digital keyboard instruments can be inexpensive. They are widely available. (*however*)
2. Inside the keyboard is a small computer. The computer controls a sound synthesizer. The instrument can both process and produce music. (*consequently*)
3. The person playing the keyboard presses keys or manipulates other controls. The computer and synthesizer convert these signals. The signals are converted into vibrations and sounds. (*immediately*)
4. The inexpensive keyboards can perform only a few functions. To the novice computer musician, the range is exciting. The range includes drum rhythms and simulated instruments. (*still*)

5. Would-be musicians can orchestrate whole songs. They start from just the melody lines. They need never again play "Chopsticks." (*thus*)

29c Use a semicolon to separate main clauses when they are long or contain commas, even with a coordinating conjunction.

We normally use a comma with a coordinating conjunction such as *and* or *but* between main clauses (see p. 424). But a semicolon makes a sentence easier to read when the main clauses are long and complicated or contain commas:

> By a conscious effort of the mind, we can stand aloof from actions and their consequences; and all things, good and bad, go by us like a torrent.
> —Henry David Thoreau

> I doubt if the texture of Southern life is any more grotesque than that of the rest of the nation, but it does seem evident that the Southern writer is particularly adept at recognizing the grotesque; and to recognize the grotesque, you have to have some notion of what is not grotesque and why.
> —Flannery O'Connor

29d Use semicolons to separate items in a series when they are long or contain commas.

We normally use commas to separate items in a series (see p. 435). But when the items are long or contain commas, semicolons help readers identify the items:

> The custody case involved Amy Dalton, the child; Ellen and Mark Dalton, the parents; and Ruth and Hal Blum, the grandparents.

> One may even reasonably advance the claim that the sort of communication that really counts, and is therefore embodied into permanent records, is primarily written; that "words fly away, but written messages endure," as the Latin saying put it two thousand years ago; and that there is no basic significance to at least fifty percent of the oral interchange that goes on among all sorts of persons, high and low.
> —Mario Pei

Exercise 29.5 Punctuating long main clauses and series items

Substitute semicolons for commas in the following sentences to separate main clauses or series items that are long or contain commas.

Example:
He debated whether to attend college in San Francisco, which was temperate but far from his parents, New York City, which was exciting but expensive, or Atlanta, which was close to home but already familiar.

He debated whether to attend college in San Francisco, which was temperate but far from his parents; New York City, which was exciting but expensive; or Atlanta, which was close to home but already familiar.

1. The Indian subcontinent is separated from the rest of the world by clear barriers: the Bay of Bengal and the Arabian Sea to the east and west, respectively, the Indian Ocean to the south, and 1600 miles of mountain ranges to the north.
2. In the north of India are the world's highest mountains, the Himalayas, and farther south are fertile farmlands, unpopulated deserts, and rain forests.
3. India is a nation of ethnic and linguistic diversity, with numerous religions, including Hinduism, Islam, and Christianity, with distinct castes and ethnic groups, and with sixteen languages, including the official Hindi and the "associate official" English.
4. Between the seventeenth and nineteenth centuries, the British colonized most of India, taking control of government, the bureaucracy, and industry, and they assumed a social position above all Indians.
5. During British rule the Indians' own unresolved differences and their frustrations with the British erupted in violent incidents such as the Sepoy Mutiny, which began on February 26, 1857, and lasted two years, the Amritsar Massacre on April 13, 1919, and violence between Hindus and Muslims during World War II that resulted in the separation of Pakistan from India.

29e Use the semicolon only where required.

Semicolons do not separate unequal sentence elements and should not be overused.

1 Delete or replace any semicolon that separates a subordinate clause or a phrase from a main clause.

The semicolon does not separate subordinate clauses from main clauses or phrases from main clauses:

| Faulty | Pygmies are in danger of extinction; <u>because of encroaching development.</u> |
| Revised | Pygmies are in danger of extinction because of encroaching development. |

| Faulty | <u>According to African authorities;</u> only about 35,000 Pygmies exist today. |
| Revised | According to African authorities, only about 35,000 Pygmies exist today. |

Note Many readers regard a phrase or subordinate clause set off with a semicolon as a kind of sentence fragment. (See Chapter 17.)

2 Delete or replace any semicolon that introduces a series or explanation.

Colons and dashes, not semicolons, introduce series, explanations, and so forth. (See pp. 470 and 473.)

Faulty	Teachers have heard all sorts of reasons why students do poorly; <u>psychological problems, family illness, too much work, too little time.</u>
Revised	Teachers have heard all sorts of reasons why students do poorly**:** psychological problems, family illness, too much work, too little time.
Revised	Teachers have heard all sorts of reasons why students do poorly**—**psychological problems, family illness, too much work, too little time.

3 Use the semicolon sparingly.

Use the semicolon only occasionally. Many semicolons in a passage, even when they are required by rule, often indicate repetitive sentence structure. To revise a passage with too many semicolons, you'll need to restructure your sentences, not just remove the semicolons. (See Chapter 26 for tips on varying sentences.)

Semicolon overused

The Make-a-Wish Foundation helps sick children; it grants the wishes of children who are terminally ill. The foundation learns of a child's wish; the information usually comes from parents, friends, or hospital staff; the wish may be for a special toy, a trip to the circus, or a visit to Disneyland. The foundation grants some wishes with its own funds; for other wishes it appeals to those who have what the child desires.

Revised

The Make-a-Wish Foundation grants the wishes of children who are terminally ill. From parents, friends, or hospital staff, the foundation learns of a child's wish for a special toy, a trip to the circus, or a visit to Disneyland. It grants some wishes with its own funds; for other wishes it appeals to those who have what the child desires.

Exercise 29.6 Revising: Misused or overused semicolons

Revise the following sentences to eliminate misused or overused semicolons, substituting other punctuation as appropriate.

Example:

The doctor gave everyone the same advice; get exercise.
The doctor gave everyone the same advice**:** get exercise.

1. The main religion in India is Hinduism; a way of life as well as a theology and philosophy.
2. Unlike Christianity and Judaism; Hinduism is a polytheistic religion; with deities numbering in the hundreds.

3. Hinduism is unlike many other religions; it allows its creeds and practices to vary widely from place to place and person to person. Other religions have churches; Hinduism does not. Other religions have principal prophets and holy books; Hinduism does not. Other religions center on specially trained priests or other leaders; Hinduism promotes the individual as his or her own priest.
4. In Hindu belief there are four types of people; reflective, emotional, active, and experimental.
5. Each type of person has a different technique for realizing the true, immortal self; which has infinite existence, infinite knowledge, and infinite joy.

Exercise 29.7 Revising: Semicolons

Insert semicolons in the following paragraph wherever they are needed. Eliminate any misused or needless semicolons, substituting other punctuation as appropriate.

The set, sounds, and actors in the movie captured the essence of horror films. The set was ideal; dark, deserted streets, trees dipping their branches over the sidewalks, mist hugging the ground and creeping up to meet the trees, looming shadows of unlighted, turreted houses. The sounds, too, were appropriate, especially terrifying was the hard, hollow sound of footsteps echoing throughout the film. But the best feature of the movie was its actors; all of them tall, pale, and thin to the point of emaciation. With one exception, they were dressed uniformly in gray and had gray hair. The exception was an actress who dressed only in black; as if to set off her pale yellow, nearly white, long hair; the only color in the film. The glinting black eyes of another actor stole almost every scene, indeed, they were the source of all the film's mischief.

Note See page 481 for a punctuation exercise combining semicolons with other marks of punctuation.

30

The Apostrophe

Unlike other punctuation marks, which separate words, the apostrophe (') appears as *part* of a word to indicate possession or the omission of one or more letters.

my**comp**lab

Visit *mycomplab.com* for more resources and exercises on the apostrophe.

Uses and misuses of the apostrophe

Uses of the apostrophe

■ **Use an apostrophe to form the possessives of nouns and indefinite pronouns** (opposite).

Singular	Plural
Ms. Park's	the Parks'
lawyer's	lawyers'
everyone's	two weeks'

■ **Use an apostrophe to form contractions** (p. 458).

it's a girl	shouldn't
you're	won't

■ **The apostrophe is optional for plurals of abbreviations, dates, and words or characters named as words** (p. 460).

MAs or MA's	Cs or C's
1960s or 1960's	ifs or if's

Misuses of the apostrophe

■ **Do not use an apostrophe plus -s to form the possessives of plural nouns ending in -s** (p. 456). Instead, use an apostrophe alone after the -s that forms the plural.

Not	But
the Kim's car	the Kims' car
boy's fathers	boys' fathers
babie's care	babies' care

■ **Do not use an apostrophe to form plurals of nouns** (p. 457).

Not	But
book's are	books are
the Freed's	the Freeds

■ **Do not use an apostrophe with verbs ending in -s** (p. 457).

Not	But
swim's	swims

■ **Do not use an apostrophe to form the possessives of personal pronouns** (p. 458).

Not	But
it's toes	its toes
your's	yours

Grammar checkers A grammar checker usually has mixed results in recognizing apostrophe errors. For instance, it may flag missing apostrophes in contractions (as in *isnt*) but may not distinguish between *its* and *it's, their* and *they're, your* and *you're, whose* and *who's.* A checker may identify some apostrophe errors in possessives but overlook others, and it may flag correct plurals. Instead of relying on your checker, try using your computer's Search or Find function to hunt for all words you have ended in *-s.* Then check each one to ensure that you have used apostrophes correctly.

30a Use the apostrophe to show possession.

In English the **possessive case** shows ownership or possession of one person or thing by another. For nouns and indefinite pronouns, possession may be shown with an *of* phrase (*the hair of the dog, the interest of everyone*), or it may be shown with the addition of an apostrophe and, usually, an *-s* (*the dog's hair, everyone's interest*). Only the pronouns *mine, yours, his, hers, its, ours, theirs,* and *whose* do not use apostrophes for possession (p. 458).

Note Apostrophes are easy to misuse. Always check your drafts to ensure the following:

- Every word ending in *-s* neither omits a needed apostrophe nor adds an unneeded one.
- The apostrophe or apostrophe-plus-*s* is an *addition.* Before this addition, always spell the name of the owner or owners without dropping or adding letters: *girls* becomes *girls',* not *girl's.*

1 Add *-'s* to singular nouns and indefinite pronouns.

Bill Boughton's skillful card tricks amaze children.

Anyone's eyes would widen. [Indefinite pronoun.]

Most tricks will pique an adult's curiosity, too.

Add *-'s* as well to singular nouns that end in *-s:*

Henry James's novels reward the patient reader.

Los Angeles's weather is mostly warm.

The business's customers filed suit.

Exception We often do not pronounce the possessive *-s* of a few singular nouns ending in an *s* or *z* sound: names with more than one *s* sound (*Moses*), names that sound like plurals (*Rivers, Bridges*), and nouns followed by a word beginning in *s.* In these cases, many writers add only the apostrophe to show possession.

Moses' mother concealed him in the bulrushes.

Joan Rivers' jokes offend many people.

For conscience' sake she confessed her lie.

However, usage varies widely, and the final -*s* is not wrong with words like these (*Moses's*, *Rivers's*, *conscience's*).

2 Add -'s to plural nouns not ending in -s.

The bill establishes children's rights.

Publicity grabbed the media's attention.

3 Add only an apostrophe to plural nouns ending in -s.

Workers' incomes have not risen much over the past decade.

Many students benefit from several years' work after high school.

The Jameses' talents are extraordinary.

Note the difference in the possessives of singular and plural words ending in -*s*. The singular form usually takes the apostrophe and -*s*: *James's*. The plural takes only the apostrophe: *Jameses'*.

4 Add -'s only to the last word of compound words or word groups.

The council president's speech was a bore.

The brother-in-law's business failed.

Taxes are always somebody else's fault.

5 With two or more words, add -'s to one or both depending on meaning

Individual possession

Zimbale's and Mason's comedy techniques are similar. [Each comedian has his own technique.]

Joint possession

The child recovered despite her mother and father's neglect. [The mother and father were jointly neglectful.]

Exercise 30.1   Forming possessives

Form the possessive case of each word or word group in brackets.

Example:

The [men] blood pressures were higher than the [women].

The men's blood pressures were higher than the women's.

1. In the myths of the ancient Greeks, the [goddesses] roles vary widely.
2. [Demeter] responsibility is the fruitfulness of the earth.
3. [Athena] role is to guard the city of Athens.
4. [Artemis] function is to care for wild animals and small children.
5. [Athena and Artemis] father, Zeus, is the king of the gods.

6. Even a single [goddess] responsibilities are often varied.
7. Over several [centuries] time, Athena changes from a [mariner] goddess to the patron of crafts.
8. Athena is also concerned with fertility and with [children] well-being, since [Athens] strength depended on a large and healthy population.
9. Athena often changes into [birds] forms.
10. In [Homer] Odyssey she assumes a [sea eagle] form.
11. In ancient Athens the myths of Athena were part of [everyone] knowledge and life.
12. A cherished myth tells how Athena fights to retain possession of her [people] land when the god Poseidon wants it.
13. [Athena and Poseidon] skills are different, and each promises a special gift to the Athenians.
14. At the [contest] conclusion, Poseidon has given water and Athena has given an olive tree, for sustenance.
15. The other gods decide that the [Athenians] lives depend more on Athena than on Poseidon.

30b Delete or replace any apostrophe in a plural noun, a singular verb, or a possessive personal pronoun.

Not all words ending in -*s* take an apostrophe. Three kinds of words are especially likely to attract unneeded apostrophes.

Plural nouns

Form most plural nouns by adding -*s* or -*es* (*boys, Smiths, families, Joneses*). Never add an apostrophe to form the plural:

Faulty	The unleashed dog's began traveling in a pack.
Revised	The unleashed dogs began traveling in a pack.

Faulty	The Jones' and Bass' were feuding.
Revised	The Joneses and Basses were feuding.

Singular verbs

Do not add an apostrophe to present-tense verbs used with *he, she, it,* and other third-person singular subjects. These verbs always end in -*s* but *never* with an apostrophe:

Faulty	The subway break's down less often now.
Revised	The subway breaks down less often now.

Faulty	It run's more reliably.
Revised	It runs more reliably.

Possessive personal pronouns

His, hers, its, ours, yours, theirs, and *whose* are possessive forms of the pronouns *he, she, it, we, you, they,* and *who.* They do not take apostrophes:

Faulty	The credit is her's not their's.
Revised	The credit is hers, not theirs.

The personal pronouns are often confused with contractions, such as *it's, you're,* and *who's.* See below.

Exercise 30.2 Distinguishing between plurals and possessives

Supply the appropriate form—possessive or plural—of each word given in brackets. Some answers require apostrophes, and some do not.

Example:

A dozen Hawaiian [shirt], each with [it] own loud design, hung in the window.

A dozen Hawaiian shirts, each with its own loud design, hung in the window.

1. Demeter may be the oldest of the Greek [god], older than Zeus.
2. Many prehistoric [culture] had earth [goddess] like Demeter.
3. In myth she is the earth mother, which means that the responsibility for the fertility of both [animal] and [plant] is [she].
4. The [goddess] festival came at harvest time, with [it] celebration of bounty.
5. The [people] [prayer] to Demeter thanked her for grain and other [gift].

30c Use an apostrophe to indicate the omission in a standard contraction.

it is, it has	it's	let us	let's
he is	he's	does not	doesn't
she is	she's	were not	weren't
they are	they're	class of 2009	class of '09
you are	you're	of the clock	o'clock
who is, who has	who's	madam	ma'am

Contractions are common in speech and in informal writing. They may also be used to relax style in more formal kinds of writing, as they are in this handbook. But be aware that many people disapprove of contractions in any kind of formal writing.

Note Contractions are easily confused with the possessive personal pronouns:

Contraction	Possessive pronoun
it's	its
they're	their
you're	your
who's	whose

Faulty   Legislators know their going to have to cut the budget to eliminate it's deficit.

Revised   Legislators know they're going to have to cut the budget to eliminate its deficit.

If you tend to confuse these forms, search for both spellings throughout your drafts. Then test for correctness:

- **Use an apostrophe when you intend the word to contain the sentence verb *is, are,* or *has,*** as in *It is [It's] a shame, It has [It's] happened, They are [They're] to blame, You are [You're] right, Who is [Who's] coming? Who has [Who's] responded?*
- **Don't use an apostrophe when you intend the word to indicate possession,** as in *Its tail was wagging, Their car broke down, Your eyes are blue, Whose book is that?*

Exercise 30.3   Forming contractions

Form contractions from each set of words below. Use each contraction in a complete sentence.

Example:
we are: we're
We're open to ideas.

1. she would
2. could not
3. they are
4. he is
5. do not
6. she will
7. hurricane of 1962
8. is not
9. it is
10. will not

Exercise 30.4   Revising: Contractions and personal pronouns

Revise the following sentences to correct mistakes in the use of contractions and personal pronouns. Mark the number preceding any sentence that is already correct.

Example:
The agencies give they're employees they're birthdays off.
The agencies give their employees their birthdays off.

1. In Greek myth the goddess Demeter has a special fondness for Eleusis, near Athens, and it's people.
2. She finds rest among the people and is touched by their kindness.
3. Demeter rewards the Eleusians with the secret for making they're land fruitful.

4. The Eleusians begin a cult in honor of Demeter, whose worshiped in secret ceremonies.
5. Its unknown what happened in the ceremonies, for no participant ever revealed their rituals.

30d | The apostrophe is optional to mark plural abbreviations, dates, and words or characters named as words.

You'll sometimes see apostrophes used to form the plurals of abbreviations (BA's), dates (1900's), and words or characters named as words (*but's*). However, most current style guides do not recommend the apostrophe in these cases.

BAs	PhDs
1990s	2000s

The sentence has too many *buts*.
Two 3s end the zip code.

Note Italicize or underline a word or character named as a word (see p. 492), but not the added -s.

Exercise 30.5 Revising: Apostrophes

In the following paragraph correct any mistakes in the use of the apostrophe or any confusion between contractions and possessive personal pronouns.

People who's online experiences include blogging, Web cams, and social-networking sites are often used to seeing the details of other peoples private lives. Many are also comfortable sharing they're own opinions, photographs, and videos with family, friend's, and even stranger's. However, they need to realize that employers and even the government can see they're information, too. Employers commonly put applicants names through social-networking Web sites such as *MySpace* and *Facebook*. Many large companies read their employees outbound e-mail. People can take steps to protect their personal information by adjusting the privacy settings on their social-networking pages. They can avoid posting photos of themselves that they wouldnt want an employer to see. They can avoid sending personal e-mail while their at work. Its the individuals responsibility to keep certain information private.

Note See page 481 for a punctuation exercise involving apostrophes along with other marks of punctuation.

31

Quotation Marks

Quotation marks—either double (" ") or single (' ')—mainly enclose direct quotations from speech and from writing. The box on the next two pages summarizes this use and the combination of quotation marks with commas, semicolons, ellipsis marks, and other punctuation. Additional information on using quotations appears elsewhere in this book:

- **Using commas with signal phrases introducing quotations,** pages 438–40.
- **Using brackets and the ellipsis mark to indicate changes in quotations,** pages 476–79.
- **Quoting sources versus paraphrasing or summarizing them,** pages 597–600.
- **Integrating quotations into your text,** pages 601–06.
- **Acknowledging the sources of quotations to avoid plagiarism,** pages 610–12 and 614–15.
- **Formatting long prose quotations and poetry quotations in MLA style, pages 665–66, and APA style, page 763.**

Note Always use quotation marks in pairs, one at the beginning of a quotation and one at the end.

Grammar checkers A grammar checker will help you use quotation marks in pairs by flagging a lone mark. It may also look for punctuation inside or outside quotation marks (see p. 467), but it may still fail to detect some errors.

31a Use double quotation marks to enclose direct quotations.

Direct quotations report what someone has said or written in the exact words of the original. Always enclose direct quotations in quotation marks.

Visit *mycomplab.com* for more resources and exercises on quotation marks.

Handling quotations from speech or writing

Direct and indirect quotation

Direct quotation

According to Lewis Thomas, "We are, perhaps uniquely among the earth's creatures, the worrying animal. We worry away our lives."

Note Do not use quotation marks with a direct quotation that is set off from your text. See pages 665–66 (MLA style) and 763 (APA style).

Quotation within quotation

Quoting a phrase by Lewis Thomas, the author adds, "We are 'the worrying animal.'"

Indirect quotation

Lewis Thomas says that human beings are unique among animals in their worrying.

Quotation marks with other punctuation marks

Commas and periods

Human beings are the "worrying animal," says Thomas.
Thomas calls human beings "the worrying animal."

Semicolons and colons

Machiavelli says that "the majority of men live content"; in contrast, Thomas calls us "the worrying animal."
Thomas believes that we are "the worrying animal": we spend our lives afraid and restless.

Question marks, exclamation points, dashes

When part of your own sentence:

Who said that human beings are "the worrying animal"?
Imagine saying that we human beings "worry away our lives"!
Thomas's phrase—"the worrying animal"—seems too narrow.

When part of the original quotation:

"Will you discuss this with me?" she asked.
"I demand that you discuss this with me!" she yelled.
"Please, won't you—" She paused.

Altering quotations

Brackets for additions

"We [human beings] worry away our lives," says Thomas.

Brackets for altered capitalization

"[T]he worrying animal" is what Thomas calls us. He says that "[w]e worry away our lives."

Ellipsis marks for omissions

"We are . . . the worrying animal," says Thomas.

Worrying places us "uniquely among the earth's creatures. . . . We worry away our lives."

Punctuating signal phrases with quotations

Introductory signal phrase

He says, "We worry away our lives."

An answer is in these words by Lewis Thomas: "We are, perhaps uniquely among the earth's creatures, the worrying animal."

Thomas says that "the worrying animal" is afraid and restless.

Concluding signal phrase

We are "the worrying animal," says Thomas.

"Who says?" she demanded.

"I do!" he shouted.

Interrupting signal phrase

"We are," says Thomas, "perhaps uniquely among the earth's creatures, the worrying animal."

"I do not like the idea," she said; "however, I agree with it."

Human beings are "the worrying animal," says Thomas. "We worry away our lives."

"Fortunately," said the psychoanalyst Karen Horney, "analysis is not the only way to resolve inner conflicts. Life itself still remains a very effective therapist."

Indirect quotations report what has been said or written, but not in the exact words of the person being quoted. Indirect quotations are *not* enclosed in quotation marks:

The psychoanalyst Karen Horney remarked that analysis is but one solution to personal problems, for life is a good therapist.

(See also pp. 598–99 on paraphrasing quotations.)

31b Use single quotation marks to enclose a quotation within a quotation.

When you quote a writer or speaker, use double quotation marks. When the material you quote contains yet another quotation, distinguish the two by enclosing the second one in single quotation marks:

"In formulating any philosophy," Woody Allen writes, "the first consideration must always be: What can we know? Descartes hinted at the problem when he wrote, 'My mind can never know my body, although it has become quite friendly with my leg.'"

Notice that two different quotation marks appear at the end of the sentence—one single (to finish the interior quotation) and one double (to finish the main quotation).

Exercise 31.1 Using double and single quotation marks

Insert double and single quotation marks as needed in the following sentences. Mark the number preceding any sentence that is already correct.

Example:
The purpose of this book, explains the preface, is to examine the meaning of the expression Dance is poetry.

"The purpose of this book," explains the preface, "is to examine the meaning of the expression 'Dance is poetry.'"

1. Why, the lecturer asked, do we say Bless you! or something else when people sneeze but not acknowledge coughs, hiccups, and other eruptions?
2. She said that sneezes have always been regarded differently.
3. Sneezes feel more uncontrollable than some other eruptions, she said.
4. Unlike coughs and hiccups, she explained, sneezes feel as if they come from inside the head.
5. She concluded, People thus wish to recognize a sneeze, if only with a Gosh.

31c Set off quotations of dialog according to standard practice.

When quoting conversations, begin a new paragraph for each speaker:

"What shall I call you? Your name?" Andrews whispered rapidly, as with a high squeak the latch of the door rose.
"Elizabeth," she said. "Elizabeth."
—Graham Greene, *The Man Within*

When you quote a single speaker for more than one paragraph, put quotation marks at the beginning of each paragraph but at the end of only the last paragraph. The absence of quotation marks at the end of a paragraph tells readers that the speech is continuing.

Note Quotation marks are optional for quoting unspoken thoughts or imagined dialog:

I asked myself, "How can we solve this?"
I asked myself, How can we solve this?

31d Put quotation marks around the titles of works that are parts of other works.

Use quotation marks to enclose the titles of works that are published or released within larger works: see the box below. As in the second article title in the box, use single quotation marks for a quotation within a quoted title, and enclose all punctuation in the title within the quotation marks. Use italics or underlining for all other titles, such as books, plays, periodicals, and movies. (See p. 491.)

Titles to be enclosed in quotation marks

Other titles should be italicized or underlined. (See p. 491.)

Songs
"Lucy in the Sky with Diamonds"
"America the Beautiful"

Short poems
"Stopping by Woods on a Snowy Evening"
"Sunday Morning"

Articles in periodicals
"Comedy and Tragedy Transposed"
"Does 'Scaring' Work?"

Essays
"Politics and the English Language"
"Joey: A 'Mechanical Boy'"

Short stories
"The Battler"
"The Gift of the Magi"

Page or document on a Web site
"Readers' Page" (on site *Friends of Prufrock*)

Episodes of television and radio programs
"The Mexican Connection" (on *60 Minutes*)
"Cooking with Clams" (on *Eating In*)

Subdivisions of books
"Voyage to the Houyhnhnms" (Part IV of *Gulliver's Travels*)
"The Mast Head" (Chapter 35 of *Moby-Dick*)

Note Some academic disciplines do not require quotation marks for titles within source citations. See pages 747 (APA style) and 775 (CSE style).

Exercise 31.2 Quoting titles

Insert quotation marks as needed for titles in the following sentences. If quotation marks should be used instead of italics, insert them.

Example:

She published an article titled Marriage in Grace Paley's An Interest in Life.

She published an article titled "Marriage in Grace Paley's 'An Interest in Life.'"

1. In Chapter 8, titled *How to Be Interesting,* the author explains the art of conversation.
2. The Beatles' song Let It Be reminds Martin of his uncle.
3. The article that appeared in *Mental Health* was titled *Children of Divorce Ask, "Why?"*
4. In the encyclopedia the discussion under Modern Art fills less than a column.
5. One prizewinning essay, *Cowgirls on Wall Street,* first appeared in *Entrepreneur* magazine.

31e Quotation marks may be used to enclose words used in a special sense.

On movie sets movable *"wild walls"* make a one-walled room seem four-walled on film.

Writers often put quotation marks around a word they are using with irony—that is, with a different or even opposite meaning than usual:

With all the *"compassion"* it could muster, the agency turned away two-thirds of those seeking help.   —Joan Simonson

Readers quickly tire of such irony, though, so use it sparingly. Prefer language that expresses your meaning exactly. (See Chapter 38.)

Note For words you are defining, use italics or underlining. (See p. 492.)

31f Use quotation marks only where they are required.

Don't use quotation marks in the titles of your papers unless they contain or are themselves direct quotations:

Not   *"*The Death Wish in One Poem by Robert Frost*"*

But   The Death Wish in One Poem by Robert Frost

Or   The Death Wish in *"*Stopping by Woods on a Snowy Evening*"*

Don't use quotation marks to enclose common nicknames or technical terms that are not being defined:

Not   As President, "Jimmy" Carter preferred to use his nickname.

But   As President, Jimmy Carter preferred to use his nickname.

Not   "Mitosis" in a cell is fascinating to watch.

But   Mitosis in a cell is fascinating to watch.

Don't use quotation marks in an attempt to justify or apologize for slang and trite expressions that are inappropriate to your writing. If slang is appropriate, use it without quotation marks.

Not	We should support the President in his "hour of need" rather than "wimp out" on him.
But	We should give the President the support he needs rather than turn away like cowards.

(See pp. 506 and 524 for more on slang and trite expressions.)

31g Place other punctuation marks inside or outside quotation marks according to standard practice.

The position of another punctuation mark inside or outside a closing quotation mark depends on what the other mark is, whether it appears in the quotation, and whether a source citation immediately follows the quotation.

1 Place commas and periods inside quotation marks.

Commas or periods fall *inside* closing quotation marks, even when (as in the third example) single and double quotation marks are combined:

> Swift uses irony in his essay "A Modest Proposal."
>
> Many first-time readers are shocked to see infants described as "delicious."
>
> "'A Modest Proposal,'" writes one critic, "is so outrageous that it cannot be believed."

(See pp. 438–40 for the use of commas, as in the preceding example, to separate a quotation from a signal phrase such as *writes one critic*.)

Exception When a parenthetical source citation immediately follows a quotation, place any period or comma *after* the citation:

> One critic calls the essay "outrageous" (Olms 26).
>
> Partly because of "the cool calculation of its delivery" (Olms 27), Swift's satire still chills a modern reader.

See page 626 for more on placing parenthetical citations.

2 Place colons and semicolons outside quotation marks.

> Some years ago the slogan in elementary education was "learning by playing"; now educators are concerned with basic skills.
>
> We all know what is meant by "inflation": more money buys less.

3 Place dashes, question marks, and exclamation points inside quotation marks only if they belong to the quotation.

When a dash, question mark, or exclamation point is part of the quotation, put it *inside* quotation marks. Don't use any other punctuation such as a period or comma:

"But must you——" Marcia hesitated, afraid of the answer.

"Go away!" I yelled.

Did you say, "Who is she?" [When both your sentence and the quotation would end in a question mark or exclamation point, use only the mark in the quotation.]

When a dash, question mark, or exclamation point applies only to the larger sentence, not to the quotation, place it *outside* quotation marks—again, with no other punctuation:

One evocative line in English poetry—"After many a summer dies the swan"—comes from Alfred, Lord Tennyson.

Who said, "Now cracks a noble heart"?

The woman called me "stupid"!

Exercise 31.3 Revising: Quotation marks

The italic words in the following sentences are titles or direct quotations. Insert quotation marks where italics should not be used. Be sure that other marks of punctuation are correctly placed inside or outside the quotation marks.

> *Example:*
> The award-winning essay is *Science and Values.*
> The award-winning essay is "Science and Values."

1. In the title essay of her book *The Death of the Moth and Other Essays,* Virginia Woolf describes the last moments of a *frail and diminutive body.*
2. An insect's death may seem insignificant, but the moth is, in Woolf's words, *life, a pure bead.*
3. The moth's struggle against death, *indifferent, impersonal,* is heroic.
4. Where else but in such a bit of life could one see a protest so *superb*?
5. At the end Woolf sees the moth lying *most decently and uncomplainingly composed*; in death it finds dignity.

Exercise 31.4 Revising: Quotation marks

Insert quotation marks as needed in the following paragraph.
In one class we talked about a passage from I Have a Dream, the speech delivered by Martin Luther King, Jr., on the steps of the Lincoln Memorial on August 28, 1963:

> When the architects of our republic wrote the magnificent words of the Constitution and the Declaration of Independence, they were signing a promissory note to which every American was to fall heir. This note was a promise that all men would be guaranteed the unalienable rights of life, liberty, and the pursuit of happiness.

What did Dr. King mean by this statement? the teacher asked. Perhaps we should define promissory note first. Then she explained that a person who signs such a note agrees to pay a specific sum of money on a particular date or on demand by the holder of the note. One student suggested, Maybe Dr. King meant that the writers of the Constitution and Declaration promised that all people in America should be equal. He and over 200,000 people had gathered in Washington, DC, added another student. Maybe their purpose was to demand payment, to demand those rights for African Americans. The whole discussion was an eye opener for those of us (including me) who had never considered that those documents make promises that we should expect our country to fulfill.

Note See page 481 for a punctuation exercise involving quotation marks along with other marks of punctuation.

32

Other Punctuation Marks

This chapter covers the colon (below), the dash (p. 472), parentheses (p. 474), brackets (p. 476), the ellipsis mark (p. 477), and the slash (p. 480).

Grammar checkers A grammar checker may flag a lone parenthesis or bracket so that you can match it with another parenthesis or bracket. But most checkers cannot recognize other misuses of the marks covered here and instead simply ignore the marks.

32a Use the colon to introduce and to separate.

The colon is mainly a mark of introduction: it signals that the words following will explain or amplify. The colon also has several conventional uses, such as in expressions of time.

In its main use as an introducer, a colon is *always* preceded by a complete **main clause**—a word group that can stand alone as a

mycomplab

Visit *mycomplab.com* for more resources and exercises on the colon, the dash, parentheses, brackets, the ellipsis mark, and the slash.

Distinguishing the colon and the semicolon

Colon

The colon is a mark of introduction that separates elements of *unequal* importance, such as statements and explanations or introductions and quotations. The first element must be a complete main clause; the second element need not be.

The business school caters to working students: it offers special evening courses in business writing, finance, and management.

The school has one goal: to train students to be responsible, competent businesspeople.

Semicolon

The semicolon separates elements of *equal* importance, almost always complete main clauses. (See p. 445.)

Few enrolling students know exactly what they want from the school ; most hope generally for a managerial career.

---

sentence because it contains a subject and a predicate and does not start with a subordinating word (see p. 252 for more on main clauses). A colon may or may not be followed by a main clause. This is one way the colon differs from the semicolon (see the box above). The colon is interchangeable with the dash, though the dash is more informal and more abrupt (see p. 472).

Note Don't use a colon more than once in a sentence. The sentence should end with the element introduced by the colon.

1 Use a colon to introduce a concluding explanation, a series, an appositive, and some quotations.

Depending on your preference, a complete sentence *after* the colon may begin with a capital letter or a small letter. Just be consistent throughout an essay.

Explanation
Soul food is a varied cuisine: it includes spicy gumbos, black-eyed peas, and collard greens.

Soul food has a deceptively simple definition: the ethnic cooking of African Americans.

Sometimes a concluding explanation is preceded by *the following* or *as follows* and a colon:

A more precise definition might be the following: soul food draws on ingredients, cooking methods, and dishes that originated in Africa, were brought to the New World by slaves, and were modified or supplemented in the Caribbean and the American South.

Series (p. 435)
At least three soul food dishes are familiar to most Americans: fried chicken, barbecued spareribs, and sweet potato pie.

Appositive (p. 256)
Soul food has one disadvantage: fat.

Certain expressions commonly introduce appositives, such as *namely* and *that is*. These expressions should *follow* the colon: *Soul food has one disadvantage: namely, fat.*

Quotation

The comma generally separates a signal phrase from a quotation (see p. 438). But when you introduce a quotation with a complete sentence, use a colon instead:

One soul food chef has a solution: "Soul food doesn't have to be greasy to taste good. Instead of using ham hocks to flavor beans, I use smoked turkey wings. The soulful, smoky taste remains, but without all the fat of pork."

2 Use a colon to separate titles and subtitles and the subdivisions of time.

Titles and subtitles	Time
Charles Dickens: An Introduction to His Novels	1:30 AM
Eros and Civilization: An Inquiry into Freud	12:26 PM

3 Use the colon only where required.

Use the colon only at the *end* of a main clause. Do not use it directly after a verb or preposition.

Not   Two critically acclaimed movies directed by Steven Spielberg are: *Schindler's List* and *Saving Private Ryan.*

But   Two critically acclaimed movies directed by Steven Spielberg are *Schindler's List* and *Saving Private Ryan.*

Not   Shakespeare had the qualities of a Renaissance thinker, such as: humanism and an interest in Greek and Roman literature.

But   Shakespeare had the qualities of a Renaissance thinker, such as humanism and an interest in Greek and Roman literature.

Exercise 32.1   Revising: Colons
Insert colons as needed in the following sentences, or delete colons that are misused.

Example:
Mix the ingredients as follows sift the flour and salt together, add the milk, and slowly beat in the egg yolk.

Mix the ingredients as follows: sift the flour and salt together, add the milk, and slowly beat in the egg yolk.

1. In remote areas of many developing countries, simple signs mark human habitation a dirt path, a few huts, smoke from a campfire.
2. In the built-up sections of industrialized countries, nature is all but obliterated by signs of human life, such as: houses, factories, skyscrapers, and highways.
3. The spectacle makes many question the words of Ecclesiastes 1.4 "One generation passeth away, and another cometh; but the earth abideth forever."
4. Yet many scientists see the future differently they hold that human beings have all the technology necessary to clean up the earth and restore the cycles of nature.
5. All that is needed is: a change in the attitudes of those who use technology.

32b   Use a dash to indicate shifts in tone or thought and to set off some sentence elements.

The dash is mainly a mark of interruption: it signals an insertion or break.

Note In your papers, form a dash with two hyphens (--) or use the character called an em dash on your word processor. Do not add extra space around or between the hyphens or around the em dash.

1 Use a dash or dashes to indicate shifts and hesitations.

Shift in tone
The novel—if one can call it that—appeared in 2009.

Unfinished thought
If the book had a plot—but a plot would be conventional.

Hesitation in dialog
"I was worried you might think I had stayed away because I was influenced by—" He stopped and lowered his eyes.
Astonished, Howe said, "Influenced by what?"
"Well, by—" Blackburn hesitated and for an answer pointed to the table.   —Lionel Trilling

2 Use a dash or dashes to emphasize nonessential elements.

Dashes may be used in place of commas or parentheses to set off and emphasize nonessential elements. (See the box on the facing page.) Dashes are especially useful when these elements are internally punctuated. Be sure to use a pair of dashes when the element interrupts a main clause.

Distinguishing dashes, commas, and parentheses

Dashes, commas, and parentheses may all set off nonessential elements.

Dashes
Dashes give the information the greatest emphasis (facing page):

Many students—including some on the advisory board—disapprove of the new dress code.

Commas
Commas are less emphatic (p. 437):

Many students, including some on the advisory board, disapprove of the new dress code.

Parentheses
Parentheses are the least emphatic, signaling that the information is just worth a mention (next page):

Many students (including some on the advisory board) disapprove of the new dress code.

Appositive (p. 456)
The qualities Monet painted—bright sunlight, rich shadows, deep colors—abounded near the rivers and gardens he used as subjects.

Modifier
Though they are close together—separated by only a few blocks—the two neighborhoods could be in different countries.

Parenthetical expression (p. 474)
At any given time there exists an inventory of undiscovered embezzlement in—or more precisely not in—the country's businesses and banks.
—John Kenneth Galbraith

3 Use a dash to set off introductory series and concluding series and explanations.

Introductory series
Shortness of breath, skin discoloration or the sudden appearance of moles, persistent indigestion, the presence of small lumps—all these may signify cancer.

A dash sets off concluding series and explanations more informally and more abruptly than a colon does (see p. 470):

Concluding series
The patient undergoes a battery of tests—MRI, bronchoscopy, perhaps even biopsy.

Concluding explanation
Many patients are disturbed by the MRI—by the need to keep still for long periods in an exceedingly small space.

4 **Use the dash only where needed.**

Don't use the dash when commas, semicolons, and periods are more appropriate. And don't use too many dashes. They can create a jumpy or breathy quality in writing.

> **Not** In all his life—eighty-seven years—my great-grandfather never allowed his picture to be taken—not even once. He claimed the "black box"—the camera—would steal his soul.
>
> **But** In all his eighty-seven years my great-grandfather did not allow his picture to be taken even once. He claimed the "black box"—the camera—would steal his soul.

Exercise 32.2 Revising: Dashes

Insert dashes as needed in the following sentences.

> *Example:*
> What would we do if someone like Adolf Hitler that monster appeared among us?
> What would we do if someone like Adolf Hitler—that monster—appeared among us?

1. The movie-theater business is undergoing dramatic changes changes that may affect what movies are made and shown.
2. The closing of independent theaters, the control of theaters by fewer and fewer owners, and the increasing ownership of theaters by movie studios and distributors these changes may reduce the availability of noncommercial films.
3. Yet at the same time the number of movie screens is increasing primarily in multiscreen complexes so that smaller films may find more outlets.
4. The number of active movie screens that is, screens showing films or booked to do so is higher now than at any time since World War II.
5. The biggest theater complexes seem to be something else as well art galleries, amusement arcades, restaurants, spectacles.

32c **Use parentheses to enclose parenthetical expressions and labels for lists within sentences.**

Parentheses *always* come in pairs: one before and one after the punctuated material.

1 **Use parentheses to enclose parenthetical expressions.**

Parenthetical expressions include explanations, digressions, and examples that may be helpful or interesting but are not essential to meaning. They are emphasized least when set off with a pair of parentheses instead of commas or dashes. (See the box on p. 473.)

> The population of Philadelphia (now about 1.5 million) has declined since 1950.
>
> *Ariel* (published in 1965) contains Sylvia Plath's last poems.

Note Don't put a comma before a parenthetical expression enclosed in parentheses:

> **Not** The population of Philadelphia compares with that of Phoenix, (just over 1.5 million).
>
> **But** The population of Philadelphia compares with that of Phoenix (just over 1.5 million).

If you use a comma, semicolon, or period after a parenthetical expression, place the mark *outside* the closing parenthesis:

> Philadelphia has a larger African American population (over 40 percent), while Phoenix has a larger Latino population (over 40 percent).

If you enclose a complete sentence in parentheses, capitalize the sentence and place the closing period *inside* the closing parenthesis:

> In general, coaches will tell you that scouts are just guys who can't coach. (But then, so are brain surgeons.)
> —Roy Blount

2 Use parentheses to enclose labels for lists within sentences.

> Outside the Middle East, the countries with the largest oil reserves are (1) Venezuela (63 billion barrels), (2) Russia (57 billion barrels), and (3) Mexico (51 billion barrels).

When you set a list off from your text, do not enclose such labels in parentheses.

Exercise 32.3 Revising: Parentheses

Insert parentheses as needed in the following sentences.

> *Example:*
> Shoppers can find good-quality, inexpensive furniture for example, desks, tables, chairs, sofas, even beds in junk stores.
> Shoppers can find good-quality, inexpensive furniture (for example, desks, tables, chairs, sofas, even beds) in junk stores.

1. Many of those involved in the movie business agree that multiscreen complexes are good for two reasons: 1 they cut the costs of exhibitors, and 2 they offer more choices to audiences.
2. Those who produce and distribute films and not just the big studios argue that the multiscreen theaters give exhibitors too much power.

3. The major studios are buying movie theaters to gain control over important parts of the distribution process what gets shown and for how much money.
4. For twelve years 1938–50 the federal government forced the studios to sell all their movie theaters.
5. But because they now have more competition television and DVD players, for instance, the studios are permitted to own theaters.

32d Use brackets within quotations to indicate your own comments or changes.

Brackets have specialized uses in mathematical equations, but their main use for all kinds of writing is to indicate that you have altered a quotation. If you need to explain, clarify, or correct the words of the writer you quote, place your additions in a pair of brackets:

"That Texaco station [just outside Chicago] is one of the busiest in the nation," said a company spokesperson.

Use brackets if you need to alter the capitalization of a quotation so that it will fit into your sentence. (See also p. 485.)

"[O]ne of the busiest in the nation" is how a company spokesperson described the station.

You may also use a bracketed word or words to substitute for parts of a quotation that would otherwise be unclear. In the following sentence, the bracketed word substitutes for *they* in the original:

"Despite considerable achievements in other areas, [humans] still cannot control the weather and probably will never be able to do so."

See page 602 for additional examples of using brackets with quotations.

The word *sic* (Latin for "in this manner") in brackets indicates that an error in the quotation appeared in the original and was not made by you. When following MLA style, do not italicize *sic* in brackets. Most other styles—including Chicago, APA, and CSE—do italicize *sic*.

According to the newspaper report, "The car slammed thru [sic] the railing and into oncoming traffic."

Don't use *sic* to make fun of a writer or to note errors in a passage that is clearly nonstandard or illiterate.

Note Always acknowledge the sources of quotations in order to avoid plagiarism. (See pp. 610–12 and 614–15.)

32e | Use the ellipsis mark to indicate omissions from quotations and pauses in speech.

The **ellipsis mark** consists of three periods separated by space (. . .). The ellipsis mark usually indicates an omission from a quotation, although it may also show an interruption in dialog.

Note Additional issues with quotations are discussed elsewhere in this book:

- **Choosing and editing quotations,** pages 599–600.
- **Integrating source material into your text,** pages 601–06.
- **Acknowledging the sources of quotations to avoid plagiarism,** pages 610–12 and 614–15. See also example 3 below.

1 The ellipsis mark substitutes for omissions from quotations.

When you omit a part of a quotation, show the omission with an ellipsis mark. All the following examples quote from the passage below about environmentalism.

Original quotation

"At the heart of the environmentalist world view is the conviction that human physical and spiritual health depends on sustaining the planet in a relatively unaltered state. Earth is our home in the full, genetic sense, where humanity and its ancestors existed for all the millions of years of their evolution. Natural ecosystems—forests, coral reefs, marine blue waters—maintain the world exactly as we would wish it to be maintained. When we debase the global environment and extinguish the variety of life, we are dismantling a support system that is too complex to understand, let alone replace, in the foreseeable future." —Edward O. Wilson, "Is Humanity Suicidal?"

1. Omission of the middle of a sentence

"Natural ecosystems . . . maintain the world exactly as we would wish it to be maintained."

2. Omission of the end of a sentence, without source citation

"Earth is our home. . . ." [The sentence period, closed up to the last word, precedes the ellipsis mark.]

3. Omission of the end of a sentence, with source citation

"Earth is our home . . ." (Wilson 27). [The sentence period follows the source citation.]

4. Omission of parts of two or more sentences

Wilson writes, "At the heart of the environmentalist world view is the conviction that human physical and spiritual health depends on sustaining the planet . . . where humanity and its ancestors existed for all the millions of years of their evolution."

5. Omission of one or more sentences

As Wilson puts it, "At the heart of the environmentalist world view is the conviction that human physical and spiritual health depends on sustaining the planet in a relatively unaltered state. . . . When we debase the global environment and extinguish the variety of life, we are dismantling a support system that is too complex to understand, let alone replace, in the foreseeable future."

6. Omission from the middle of a sentence through the end of another sentence

"Earth is our home. . . . When we debase the global environment and extinguish the variety of life, we are dismantling a support system that is too complex to understand, let alone replace, in the foreseeable future."

7. Omission of the beginning of a sentence, leaving a complete sentence

a. Bracketed capital letter
"[H]uman physical and spiritual health," Wilson writes, "depends on sustaining the planet in a relatively unaltered state." [No ellipsis mark is needed because the brackets around the *H* indicate that the letter was not capitalized originally and thus that the beginning of the sentence has been omitted.]

b. Small letter
According to Wilson, "human physical and spiritual health depends on sustaining the planet in a relatively unaltered state." [No ellipsis mark is needed because the small *h* indicates that the beginning of the sentence has been omitted.]

c. Capital letter from the original
Hami comments, ". . . Wilson argues eloquently for the environmentalist world view." [An ellipsis mark is needed because the quoted part of the sentence begins with a capital letter and it is not clear that the beginning of the original sentence has been omitted.]

8. Use of a word or phrase

Wilson describes the earth as "our home." [No ellipsis mark needed.]

Note the following features of the examples:

- **Use an ellipsis mark when it is not otherwise clear that you have left out material from the source,** as when you omit one or more sentences (examples 5 and 6) or when the words you quote form a complete sentence that is different in the original (examples 1–4 and 7c).
- **You don't need an ellipsis mark when it is obvious that you have omitted something,** such as when a bracketed letter or a small letter indicates omission (example 7b) or when a phrase clearly comes from a larger sentence (example 8).

■ Place an ellipsis mark after a sentence period *except* when a parenthetical source citation follows the quotation, as in example 3. Then the sentence period falls after the citation.

If you omit one or more lines of poetry or paragraphs of prose from a quotation, use a separate line of ellipsis marks across the full width of the quotation to show the omission:

> In "Song: Love Armed" from 1676, Aphra Behn contrasts two lovers' experiences of a romance:
>
> > Love in fantastic triumph sate,
> >
> > Whilst bleeding hearts around him flowed,
> >
> > . . . .
> >
> > But my poor heart alone is harmed,
> >
> > Whilst thine the victor is, and free. (lines 1-2, 15-16)

(See pp. 665–66 for the format of displayed quotations like this one. And see pp. 624–25 on the source-citation form illustrated here.)

2 The ellipsis mark indicates pauses or unfinished statements.

When writing dialog or when writing informally (not in academic writing), you can show hesitation or interruption with an ellipsis mark instead of a dash (p. 472).

"I wish . . ." His voice trailed off.

Exercise 32.4 Using ellipsis marks

Use ellipsis marks and any other needed punctuation to follow the numbered instructions for quoting from the following paragraph.

> Women in the sixteenth and seventeenth centuries were educated in the home and, in some cases, in boarding schools. Men were educated at home, in grammar schools, and at the universities. The universities were closed to female students. For women, "learning the Bible," as Elizabeth Joceline puts it, was an impetus to learning to read. To be able to read the Bible in the vernacular was a liberating experience that freed the reader from hearing only the set passages read in the church and interpreted by the church. A Protestant woman was expected to read the scriptures daily, to meditate on them, and to memorize portions of them. In addition, a woman was expected to instruct her entire household in "learning the Bible" by holding instructional and devotional times each day for all household members, including the servants.
>
> —Charlotte F. Otten, *English Women's Voices, 1540–1700*

1. Quote the fifth sentence, but omit everything from *that freed the reader* to the end.
2. Quote the fifth sentence, but omit the words *was a liberating experience that.*
3. Quote the first and sixth sentences.

| **32f** | Use the slash between options, between lines of poetry, and in electronic addresses. |

Option

I don't know why some teachers oppose pass/fail courses.

Between options, the slash is not surrounded by extra space.

Note The options *and/or* and *he/she* should be avoided. (See the Glossary of Usage, pp. 846 and 852.)

Poetry

Many readers have sensed a reluctant turn away from death in Frost's lines "The woods are lovely, dark and deep, / But I have promises to keep" (13–14).

When you run lines of poetry into your text, separate them with a slash surrounded by space. (See pp. 665–66 for more on quoting poetry.)

Electronic address

http:/www.stanford.edu/depts/spc/spc.html

Exercise 32.5 Revising: Colons, dashes, parentheses, brackets, ellipsis marks, slashes

Insert colons, dashes, parentheses, brackets, ellipsis marks, or slashes as needed in the following paragraph. When different marks would be appropriate in the same place, be able to defend the choice you make.

"Let all the learned say what they can, 'Tis ready money makes the man." These two lines of poetry by the Englishman William Somerville 1645–1742 may apply to a current American economic problem. Non-American investors with "ready money" pour some of it as much as $1.3 trillion in recent years into the United States. The investments of foreigners are varied stocks and bonds, savings deposits, service companies, factories, art works, even the campaigns of political candidates. Proponents of foreign investment argue that it revives industry, strengthens the economy, creates jobs more than 3 million, they say, and encourages free trade among nations. Opponents discuss the risks of heavy foreign investment it makes the American economy vulnerable to outsiders, sucks profits from the country, and gives foreigners an influence in governmental decision making. On both sides, it seems, "the learned say 'Tis ready money makes the man or country." The question is, whose money?

Exercise on Chapters 27–32 Revising: Punctuation

The following paragraphs are unpunctuated except for end-of-sentence periods. Insert periods, commas, semicolons, apostrophes, quotation marks, colons, dashes, or parentheses where they are required. When different marks would be appropriate in the same place, be able to defend the choice you make.

Brewed coffee is the most widely consumed beverage in the world. The trade in coffee beans alone amounts to well over $6000000000 a year and the total volume of beans traded exceeds 4250000 tons a year. Its believed that the beverage was introduced into Arabia in the fifteenth century CE probably by Ethiopians. By the middle or late sixteenth century the Arabs had introduced the beverage to the Europeans who at first resisted it because of its strong flavor and effect as a mild stimulant. The French Italians and other Europeans incorporated coffee into their diets by the seventeenth century the English however preferred tea which they were then importing from India. Since America was colonized primarily by the English Americans also preferred tea. Only after the Boston Tea Party 1773 did Americans begin drinking coffee in large quantities. Now though the US is one of the top coffee-consuming countries consumption having been spurred on by familiar advertising claims Good till the last drop Rich hearty aroma Always rich never bitter and by ubiquitous coffee bars.

Produced from the fruit of an evergreen tree coffee is grown primarily in Latin America southern Asia and Africa. Coffee trees require a hot climate high humidity rich soil with good drainage and partial shade consequently they thrive on the east or west slopes of tropical volcanic mountains where the soil is laced with potash and drains easily. The coffee beans actually seeds grow inside bright red berries. The berries are picked by hand and the beans are extracted by machine leaving a pulpy fruit residue that can be used for fertilizer. The beans are usually roasted in ovens a chemical process that releases the beans essential oil caffeol which gives coffee its distinctive aroma. Over a hundred different varieties of beans are produced in the world each with a different flavor attributable to three factors the species of plant *Coffea arabica* and *Coffea robusta* are the most common and the soil and climate where the variety was grown.

Mechanics

33

Capitals

Generally, capitalize a word only when a dictionary or conventional use says you must. Consult one of the style guides listed on pages 741–42 and 773 for special uses of capitals in the social, natural, and applied sciences.

Grammar checkers A grammar checker will flag overused capital letters and missing capitals at the beginnings of sentences. It will also spot missing capitals at the beginnings of proper nouns and adjectives—*if* the nouns and adjectives are in the checker's dictionary. For example, a checker caught *christianity* and *europe* but not *china* (for the country) or *Stephen king*.

CULTURE LANGUAGE Conventions of capitalization vary from language to language. English, for instance, is the only language to capitalize the first-person singular pronoun (*I*), and its practice of capitalizing proper nouns but not most common nouns also distinguishes it from some other languages.

33a Capitalize the first word of every sentence.

> Every writer should own a good dictionary.
> Will inflation be curbed?
> Watch out!

When quoting other writers, you must either reproduce the capital letters beginning their sentences or indicate with brackets that you have altered the source. Whenever possible, integrate the quotation into your own sentence so that its capital letters coincide with your own:

> "Psychotherapists often overlook the benefits of self-deception," the author argues.

> The author argues that "the benefits of self-deception" are not always recognized by psychotherapists.

mycomplab

If you need to alter the capitalization in the source, indicate the change with brackets (see p. 476):

> "[T]he benefits of self-deception" are not always recognized by psychotherapists, the author argues.

> The author argues that "[p]sychotherapists often overlook the benefits of self-deception."

Note Capitalization of questions in a series is optional. Both examples below are correct:

> Is the population a hundred? Two hundred? More?
> Is the population a hundred? two hundred? more?

Also optional is capitalization of the first word in a complete sentence after a colon (see p. 469).

33b Capitalize most words in titles and subtitles of works.

Within your text, capitalize all the words in a title *except* the following: articles (*a, an, the*), *to* in infinitives, and connecting words (prepositions and coordinating and subordinating conjunctions) of fewer than five letters. Capitalize even these short words when they are the first or last word in a title or when they fall after a colon or semicolon.

The Sound and the Fury	*Management: A New Theory*
"Courtship Through the Ages"	"Once More to the Lake"
A Diamond Is Forever	*An End to Live For*
"Knowing Whom to Ask"	"Power: How to Get It"
Learning from Las Vegas	*File Under Architecture*
"The Truth About AIDS"	*Only when I Laugh*

Always capitalize the prefix or first word in a hyphenated word within a title. Capitalize the second word only if it is a noun or an adjective or is as important as the first word.

"Applying Stage Make-up"	*Through the Looking-Glass*
The Pre-Raphaelites	

Note The style guides of the academic disciplines have their own rules for capitals in titles. For instance, MLA style for English and some other humanities capitalizes all subordinating conjunctions but no prepositions. In addition, APA style for the social sciences and CSE style for the sciences capitalize only the first word and proper names in book and article titles within source citations. See pages 747 (APA) and 775 (CSE).

33c Always capitalize the pronoun *I* and the interjection *O*. Capitalize *oh* only when it begins a sentence.

I love to stay up at night, but, oh, I hate to get up in the morning.
He who thinks himself wise, O heavens, is a great fool.   —Voltaire

33d Capitalize proper nouns, proper adjectives, and words used as essential parts of proper nouns.

Proper nouns name specific persons, places, and things: *Shakespeare, California, World War I.* **Proper adjectives** are formed from some proper nouns: *Shakespearean, Californian.*

1 Capitalize proper nouns and proper adjectives.

Capitalize all proper nouns and proper adjectives but not the articles (*a, an, the*) that precede them.

Proper nouns and adjectives to be capitalized

Specific persons and things

Stephen King	the Leaning Tower of Pisa
Napoleon Bonaparte	Boulder Dam
Doris Lessing	the Empire State Building

Specific places and geographical regions

New York City	the Mediterranean Sea
China	Lake Victoria
Europe	the Northeast, the South
North America	the Rocky Mountains

But: northeast of the city, going south

Days of the week, months, holidays

Monday	Yom Kippur
May	Christmas
Thanksgiving	Columbus Day

Historical events, documents, periods, movements

World War II	the Middle Ages
the Vietnam War	the Age of Reason
the Boston Tea Party	the Renaissance
the Treaty of Ghent	the Great Depression
the Constitution	the Romantic Movement
the Bill of Rights	the Cultural Revolution

Government offices or departments and institutions

House of Representatives	Polk Municipal Court
Department of Defense	Warren County Hospital
Appropriations Committee	Northeast High School
Sequoia Hospital	Central State College

Political, social, athletic, and other organizations and associations and their members

Democratic Party, Democrats	Rotary Club, Rotarians
Sierra Club	League of Women Voters
Girl Scouts of America, Scout	Boston Celtics
B'nai B'rith	Chicago Symphony Orchestra

Races, nationalities, and their languages

Native American	Germans
African American	Swahili
Caucasian	Italian

But: blacks, whites

Religions and their followers

Christianity, Christians	Judaism, Orthodox Jews
Protestantism, Protestants	Hinduism, Hindus
Catholicism, Catholics	Islam, Muslims

Religious terms for the sacred

God	Buddha
Allah	the Bible [**but** biblical]
Christ	the Koran, the Qur'an

Note Follow your own preference in capitalizing *he, his,* or *him* when referring to God or Allah.

2 Capitalize common nouns used as essential parts of proper nouns.

Common nouns name general classes of persons, places, or things, and they usually are not capitalized. However, capitalize common nouns such as *street, avenue, park, river, ocean, lake, company, college, county,* and *memorial* when they are part of proper nouns naming specific places or institutions:

Main Street	Crum Creek
Park Avenue	Lake Superior
Garland Place	Ford Motor Company
Central Park	Madison College
Mississippi River	San Mateo County
Pacific Ocean	George Washington Memorial

3 Capitalize trade names.

Trade names identify individual brands of certain products. When a trade name loses its association with a brand and comes to refer to a product in general, it is not capitalized. Refer to a dictionary for current usage when you are in doubt about a name.

Scotch tape	Xerox
Chevrolet	Bunsen burner

But: nylon, thermos

33e Capitalize most titles of persons only when they precede proper names.

Professor Otto Osborne	Otto Osborne, a professor of English
Doctor Jane Covington	Jane Covington, a medical doctor
Governor Ella Moore	Ella Moore, the governor

Not   The Senator supported the bill.
But   The senator supported the bill.
Or   Senator Carmine supported the bill.

Exception Many writers capitalize a title denoting very high rank even when it follows a proper name or is used alone:

Ronald Reagan, past President of the United States, died in 2004.
John Roberts is Chief Justice of the United States.

33f Avoid common misuses of capital letters.

1 Use small letters for common nouns replacing proper nouns.

Not   I am determined to take a World History class before I graduate from High School.
But   I am determined to take a world history class before I graduate from high school.
Or   I am determined to take World History I before I graduate from Grimsley High School.

2 Capitalize compass directions only when they refer to specific geographical areas.

The storm blew in from the northeast and then veered south along the coast. [Here *northeast* and *south* refer to general directions.]

Students from the South have trouble adjusting to the Northeast's bitter winters. [Here *South* and *Northeast* refer to specific regions.]

3 Use small letters for the names of seasons and the names of academic years and terms.

spring   autumn   senior year
summer   fall quarter   winter term

4 Capitalize the names of relationships only when they form part of or substitute for proper names.

my <u>mother</u>   the <u>father</u> of my friend
my <u>uncle</u> Brad   Brad's <u>brother</u>

I remember how <u>Dad</u> scolded us.
<u>Aunt</u> Annie and <u>Uncle</u> Jake died within two months of each other.

5 Use capitals according to convention in online communication.

Online messages written in all-capital letters or with no capital letters are difficult to read. Further, messages in all-capital letters may be considered rude. Use capital letters according to rules 33a–33f in all your online communication.

Exercise 33.1 Revising: Capitals

Capitalize words as necessary in the following sentences, or substitute small letters for unnecessary capitals. Consult a dictionary if you are in doubt. If the capitalization in a sentence is already correct, mark the number preceding the sentence.

Example:

The first book on the reading list is mark twain's *a connecticut yankee in king arthur's court.*

The first book on the reading list is Mark Twain's *A Connecticut Yankee in King Arthur's Court.*

1. San Antonio, texas, is a thriving city in the southwest.
2. The city has always offered much to tourists interested in the roots of spanish settlement of the new world.
3. The alamo is one of five Catholic Missions built by Priests to convert native americans and to maintain spain's claims in the area.
4. But the alamo is more famous for being the site of an 1836 battle that helped to create the republic of Texas.
5. Many of the nearby Streets, such as Crockett street, are named for men who gave their lives in that Battle.
6. The Hemisfair plaza and the San Antonio river link new tourist and convention facilities developed during mayor Cisneros's terms.
7. Restaurants, Hotels, and shops line the River. the haunting melodies of "Una paloma blanca" and "malagueña" lure passing tourists into Casa rio and other excellent mexican restaurants.
8. The university of Texas at San Antonio has expanded, and a Medical Center has been developed in the Northwest part of the city.

9. Sea World, on the west side of San Antonio, entertains grandparents, fathers and mothers, and children with the antics of dolphins and seals.
10. The City has attracted high-tech industry, creating a corridor of economic growth between san antonio and austin and contributing to the texas economy.

Note See page 500 for an exercise involving capitals along with italics or underlining and other mechanics.

34

Italics or Underlining

Italic type and <u>underlining</u> indicate the same thing: the word or words are being distinguished or emphasized. Italic type is now used almost universally in academic and business writing, and it has recently become the preferred style of the Modern Language Association. Some teachers recommend underlining, so ask your teacher for his or her preference.

Always use either italics or underlining consistently throughout a document in both text and source citations. If you are using italics, make sure that the italic characters are clearly distinct from the regular type. If you are using underlining and you underline two or more words in a row, underline the space between the words, too: <u>Criminal Statistics: Misuses of Numbers</u>.

Grammar checkers A grammar checker cannot recognize problems with italics or underlining. Use the guidelines in this chapter to edit your work.

34a Italicize or underline the titles of works that appear independently.

Within your text, italicize or underline the titles of works that are published, released, or produced separately from other works (see the box opposite). Use quotation marks for all other titles (see p. 465).

mycomplab

Visit *mycomplab.com* for more resources and exercises on italics and underlining.

Titles to be italicized or underlined

Other titles should be placed in quotation marks. (See p. 465.)

Books
War and Peace
Psychology: An Introduction

Plays
Hamlet
The Phantom of the Opera

Computer software
Microsoft Internet Explorer
Acrobat Reader

Web sites
Google
Friends of Prufrock

Pamphlets
The Truth About Alcoholism
Plants of the Desert

Long musical works
Tchaikovsky's *Swan Lake*
The Beatles' *Revolver*
But: Symphony in C

Television and radio programs
All Things Considered
NBC Sports Hour

Long poems
Beowulf
Paradise Lost

Periodicals
Time
Boston Globe
Yale Law Review

Published speeches
Lincoln's *Gettysburg Address*
Pericles's *Funeral Oration*

Movies, DVDs, and videos
Schindler's List
How to Relax

Works of visual art
Michelangelo's *David*
Picasso's *Guernica*

Note Italicize or underline a mark of punctuation only when it is part of the title. In newspaper titles, highlight the name of the city only when it is part of the title. And for all periodical titles, do not capitalize or highlight the article *the* when it begins the title.

Who is the publisher of the Manchester *Guardian*?

The national edition of the *New York Times* often differs substantially from the late edition.

Exceptions Legal documents, the Bible, the Koran, and their parts are generally not italicized or underlined.

Not   They registered their *deed*.
But   They registered their deed.

Not   We studied the *Book of Revelation* in the *Bible*.
But   We studied the Book of Revelation in the Bible.

Many sciences do not use italics or underlining for some or all titles within source citations. (See p. 775 on CSE style.)

34b Italicize or underline the names of ships, aircraft, spacecraft, and trains.

Queen Elizabeth 2   *Orient Express*   *Apollo XI*
Challenger   *Spirit of St. Louis*   *Montrealer*

34c Italicize or underline foreign words and phrases that have not been absorbed into English.

English has adopted many foreign words and phrases—such as the French "bon voyage"—and they need not be italicized or underlined. Do italicize or underline words considered foreign, consulting a dictionary if needed.

> The scientific name for the brown trout is *Salmo trutta.* [The Latin scientific names for plants and animals are always italicized or underlined.]
>
> What a life he led! He was a true *bon vivant.*
>
> The Latin *De gustibus non est disputandum* translates roughly as "There's no accounting for taste."

34d Italicize or underline words or characters named as words.

Use italics or underlining to indicate that you are citing a character or word as a word rather than using it for its meaning. Words you are defining fall under this convention:

> The word *syzygy* refers to a straight line formed by three celestial bodies, as in the alignment of the earth, sun, and moon.
>
> Some people say *th,* as in *thought,* with a faint *s* or *f* sound.
>
> Carved into the column, twenty feet up, was a mysterious *7.*

34e Occasionally, italics or underlining may be used for emphasis.

Italics or underlining can stress an important word or phrase, especially in reporting how someone said something:

> "Why on earth would *you* do that?" she cried.

But use such emphasis very rarely. Excessive underlining or italics will make your writing sound immature or hysterical:

> The settlers had *no* firewood and *no* food. Many of them *starved* or *froze to death* that first winter.

34f In online communication, use alternatives for italics or underlining.

Some forms of online communication do not allow italics or underlining for the purposes described in this chapter. On Web sites, for instance, underlining often indicates a link to another site.

To distinguish elements that usually require italics or underlining, type an underscore before and after the element: *Measurements coincide with those in _Joule's Handbook_.* You can also emphasize words with asterisks: *I *will not* be able to attend.*

Avoid using all-capital letters for emphasis. (See also p. 489.)

Exercise 34.1 Revising: Italics or underlining

In the following sentences, circle (1) the words and phrases that need highlighting with italics or underlining and (2) the words and phrases that are highlighted unnecessarily. Note that some highlighting is correct as given.

Example:
Of Hitchcock's movies, Psycho is the scariest.
Of Hitchcock's movies, *Psycho* is the scariest.

1. Of the many Vietnam veterans who are writers, Oliver Stone is perhaps the most famous for writing and directing the films Platoon and Born on the Fourth of July.
2. Tim O'Brien has written short stories for Esquire, GQ, and Massachusetts Review.
3. Going After Cacciato is O'Brien's dreamlike novel about the horrors of combat.
4. The word Vietnam is technically two words (*Viet* and *Nam*), but most American writers spell it as *one* word.
5. American writers use words or phrases borrowed from Vietnamese, such as di di mau ("go quickly") or dinky dau ("crazy").
6. Philip Caputo's *gripping* account of his service in Vietnam appears in the book A Rumor of War.
7. Caputo's book was made into a television movie, also titled *A Rumor of War.*
8. David Rabe's plays—including The Basic Training of Pavlo Hummel, Streamers, and Sticks and Bones—depict the effects of the war *not only* on the soldiers *but also* on their families.
9. Called the *poet laureate of the Vietnam war*, Steve Mason has published two collections of poems: Johnny's Song and Warrior for Peace.
10. The Washington Post published *rave* reviews of Veteran's Day, an autobiography by Rod Kane.

Note See page 500 for an exercise involving italics or underlining along with capitals and other mechanics.

35

Abbreviations

The following guidelines on abbreviations pertain to the text of a nontechnical document. All academic disciplines use abbreviations in source citations, and much technical writing, such as in the sciences and engineering, uses many abbreviations in the document text. For the requirements of the discipline you are writing in, consult one of the style guides listed on pages 724 (humanities), 741–42 (social sciences), and 773 (natural and applied sciences).

Usage varies, but writers increasingly omit periods from abbreviations that consist of or end in capital letters: *US, BA, USMC, PhD*. See page 421 on punctuating abbreviations.

Grammar and spelling checkers A grammar checker may flag some abbreviations, such as *ft.* (for *foot*) and *st.* (for *street*). A spelling checker will flag abbreviations it does not recognize. But neither checker can tell you whether an abbreviation is appropriate for your writing situation or will be clear to your readers.

35a	Use standard abbreviations for titles immediately before and after proper names.

Before the name	After the name
Dr. James Hsu	James Hsu, MD
Mr., Mrs., Ms., Hon., St., Rev., Msgr., Gen.	DDS, DVM, PhD, EdD, OSB, SJ, Sr., Jr.

Use abbreviations such as *Rev., Hon., Prof., Rep., Sen., Dr.,* and *St.* (for *Saint*) only if they appear before a proper name. Spell them out in the absence of a proper name:

Not   We learned to trust the <u>Dr.</u>

But   We learned to trust the <u>doctor.</u>

Or   We learned to trust <u>Dr. Kaplan.</u>

The abbreviations for academic degrees—*PhD, MA, BA,* and the like—may be used without a proper name: *My brother took*

Visit *mycomplab.com* for more resources and exercises
494 on abbreviations.

> ## Abbreviations for nontechnical writing
>
> ■ Titles before or after proper names: *Dr. Jorge Rodriguez; Jorge Rodriguez, PhD.*
> ■ Familiar abbreviations and acronyms: *USA, AIDS.*
> ■ *BC, BCE, AD, CE, AM, PM, no.,* and *$* with dates and numbers.
> ■ *I.e., e.g.,* and other Latin abbreviations within parentheses and in source citations.
> ■ *Inc., Bros., Co.,* and *&* with names of business firms.

seven years to get his <u>PhD</u>. *It will probably take me just as long to earn my* <u>BA</u>.

35b Familiar abbreviations and acronyms are acceptable in most writing.

An **acronym** is an abbreviation that spells a pronounceable word, such as WHO, NATO, and AIDS. These and other abbreviations that use initials are acceptable in most writing as long as they are familiar to readers. Abbreviations of two or more words written in all capital letters may be written without periods (see p. 421):

Institutions	LSU, UCLA, TCU
Organizations	CIA, FBI, YMCA, AFL-CIO
Corporations	IBM, CBS, ITT
People	JFK, LBJ, FDR
Countries	US, USA

Note If a name or term (such as *operating room*) appears often in a piece of writing, then its abbreviation (*OR*) can cut down on extra words. Spell out the full term at its first appearance, give its abbreviation in parentheses, and use the abbreviation from then on.

35c Use *BC, BCE, AD, CE, AM, PM, no.,* and *$* only with specific dates and numbers.

44 BC	AD 1492	8:05 PM (*or* p.m.)	no. 36 (*or* No. 36)
44 BCE	1492 CE	11:26 AM (*or* a.m.)	$7.41

Not	Hospital routine is easier to follow in the <u>AM</u> than in the <u>PM</u>.
But	Hospital routine is easier to follow in the <u>morning</u> than in the <u>afternoon or evening</u>.

Note The abbreviation BC ("before Christ") always follows a date, whereas AD (*anno Domini,* Latin for "in the year of the Lord") precedes a date. Increasingly, these abbreviations are being replaced by BCE ("before the common era") and CE ("common era"), respectively. Both follow the date.

35d Generally, reserve Latin abbreviations for source citations and comments in parentheses.

The following common Latin abbreviations are generally not italicized or underlined.

i.e.	*id est:* that is	
cf.	*confer:* compare	
e.g.	*exempli gratia:* for example	
et al.	*et alii:* and others	
etc.	*et cetera:* and so forth	
NB	*nota bene:* note well	

He said he would be gone a fortnight (i.e., two weeks).
Trees, too, are susceptible to disease (e.g., Dutch elm disease).
Bloom et al., editors, *Anthology of Light Verse*

Some writers avoid these abbreviations in formal writing, even within parentheses.

35e Use *Inc., Bros., Co.,* or & (for *and*) only in official names of business firms.

Not	The Santini bros. operate a large moving firm in New York City.
But	The Santini brothers operate a large moving firm in New York City.
Or	Santini Bros. is a large moving firm in New York City.
Not	We read about the Hardy Boys & Nancy Drew.
But	We read about the Hardy Boys and Nancy Drew.

35f Spell out most units of measurement and names of places, calendar designations, people, and courses.

In most academic, general, and business writing, certain words should always be spelled out. (In source citations and technical writing, however, these words are more often abbreviated.)

Units of measurement
The dog is thirty inches [not in.] high.
The building is 150 feet [not ft.] tall.

Exception Long phrases such as *miles per hour (m.p.h.)* or *cycles per second (c.p.s.)* are usually abbreviated, with or without periods: *The speed limit on that road was once 75 m.p.h.* [or *mph*].

Geographical names
The publisher is in Massachusetts [not Mass. or MA].
He came from Auckland, New Zealand [not NZ].
She lived on Morrissey Boulevard [not Blvd.].

Exceptions The United States is often referred to as the USA or the US. In writing of the US capital, use the abbreviation DC for District of Columbia when it follows the city's name: Washington, DC.

Names of days, months, and holidays
The truce was signed on Tuesday [not Tues.], April [not Apr.] 16.
The Christmas [not Xmas] holidays were uneventful.

Names of people
Virginia [not Va.] Woolf was British.
Robert [not Robt.] Frost wrote accessible poems.

Courses of instruction
I'm majoring in political science [not poli. sci.] in college.
Economics [not Econ.] is a difficult course.

Exercise 35.1 Revising: Abbreviations
Revise the following sentences as needed to correct inappropriate use of abbreviations for nontechnical writing. Mark the number preceding any sentence in which abbreviations are appropriate as written.

Example:
One prof. lectured for five hrs.
One professor lectured for five hours.

1. In the Sept. 17, 2003, issue of *Science* magazine, Virgil L. Sharpton discusses a theory that could help explain the extinction of dinosaurs.
2. About 65 mill. yrs. ago, a comet or asteroid crashed into the earth.
3. The result was a huge crater about 10 km. (6.2 mi.) deep in the Gulf of Mex.
4. Sharpton's new measurements suggest that the crater is 50 pct. larger than scientists previously believed.
5. Indeed, 20-yr.-old drilling cores reveal that the crater is about 186 mi. wide, roughly the size of Conn.
6. The space object was traveling more than 100,000 m.p.h. and hit earth with the impact of 100 to 300 million megatons of TNT.
7. On impact, 200,000 cubic km. of rock and soil were vaporized or thrown into the air.
8. That's the equivalent of 2.34 bill. cubic ft. of matter.
9. The impact would have created 400-ft. tidal waves across the Atl. Ocean, temps. higher than 20,000 degs., and powerful earthquakes.

10. Sharpton theorizes that the dust, vapor, and smoke from this impact blocked the sun's rays for mos., cooled the earth, and thus resulted in the death of the dinosaurs.

Note See page 500 for an exercise involving abbreviations along with capitals and other mechanics.

36

Numbers

This chapter addresses the use of numbers (numerals versus words) in the text of a document. All disciplines use many more numerals in source citations.

Grammar checkers A grammar checker will flag numerals beginning sentences and can be customized to ignore or to look for numerals (see p. 65). But it can't tell you whether numerals or spelled-out numbers are appropriate for your writing situation.

36a Use numerals according to standard practice in the field you are writing in.

Always use numerals for numbers that require more than two words to spell out:

The leap year has <u>366</u> days.
The population of Minot, North Dakota, is about <u>36,500</u>.

In nontechnical academic writing, spell out numbers of one or two words:

<u>Twelve</u> nations signed the treaty.
The ball game drew <u>forty-two thousand</u> people. [A hyphenated number may be considered one word.]

my**comp**lab

Visit *mycomplab.com* for more resources and exercises on numbers.

In much business writing, use numerals for all numbers over ten (*five reasons, 11 participants*). In technical academic and business writing, such as in science and engineering, use numerals for all numbers over ten, and use numerals for zero through nine when they refer to exact measurements (*2 liters, 1 hour*). (Consult one of the style guides listed on pp. 741–42 and 773 for more details.)

Note Use a combination of numerals and words for round numbers over a million: *26 million, 2.45 billion*. And use either all numerals or all words when several numbers appear together in a passage, even if convention would require a mixture:

Inconsistent	The satellite Galatea is about twenty-six thousand miles from Neptune. It is 110 miles in diameter and orbits Neptune in just over ten hours.
Revised	The satellite Galatea is about 26,000 miles from Neptune. It is 110 miles in diameter and orbits Neptune in just over 10 hours.

CULTURE LANGUAGE In American English a comma separates the numerals in long numbers (*26,000*), and a period functions as a decimal point (*2.06*).

36b Use numerals according to convention for dates, addresses, and other information.

Even when a number requires one or two words to spell out, we conventionally use numerals in the following situations:

Days and years
June 18, 2000   AD 12   456 BCE   1999

Exception The day of a month may be expressed in words when it is not followed by a year (*June fifth; October first*).

Pages, chapters, volumes, acts, scenes, lines
Chapter 9, page 123
Hamlet, act 5, scene 3, lines 35–40

Decimals, percentages, and fractions
22.5
48% (*or* 48 percent)
3½

Addresses
RD 2
419 Stonewall Street
Washington, DC 20036

Scores and statistics
21 to 7
a mean of 26
a ratio of 8 to 1

Exact amounts of money
$4.50
$3.5 million (*or* $3,500,000)

The time of day
9:00 AM
2:30 PM

Exceptions Round dollar or cent amounts of only a few words may be expressed in words: *seventeen dollars; fifteen hundred dollars; sixty cents.* When the word *o'clock* is used for the time of day, also express the number in words: *two o'clock* (not *2 o'clock*).

36c | Always spell out numbers that begin sentences.

For clarity, spell out any number that begins a sentence. If the number requires more than two words, reword the sentence so that the number falls later and can be expressed as a numeral:

Not   3.9 billion people live in Asia.
But   The population of Asia is 3.9 billion.

Exercise 36.1 Revising: Numbers

Revise the following sentences so that numbers are used appropriately for nontechnical writing. Mark the number preceding any sentence in which numbers are already used appropriately.

Example:
Christine paid two hundred five dollars for used scuba gear.
Christine paid $205 for used scuba gear.

1. The planet Saturn is nine hundred million miles, or nearly one billion five hundred million kilometers, from the sun.
2. A year on Saturn equals almost thirty of our years.
3. Thus, Saturn orbits the sun only two and four-tenths times during the average human life span.
4. It travels in its orbit at about twenty-one thousand six hundred miles per hour.
5. 15 to 20 times denser than Earth's core, Saturn's core measures 17,000 miles across.
6. The temperature at Saturn's cloud tops is minus one hundred seventy degrees Fahrenheit.
7. In nineteen hundred thirty-three, astronomers found on Saturn's surface a huge white spot 2 times the size of Earth and 7 times the size of Mercury.
8. Saturn's famous rings reflect almost seventy percent of the sunlight that approaches the planet.
9. The ring system is almost forty thousand miles wide, beginning 8800 miles from the planet's visible surface and ending forty-seven thousand miles from that surface.
10. Saturn generates about one hundred thirty trillion kilowatts of electricity.

Exercise on Chapter 33–36 Revising: Mechanics

Revise the following paragraphs to correct any errors in the use of capital letters, italics or underlining, abbreviations, and numbers. (For abbreviations and numbers, follow standard practice for nontechnical writing.) Consult a dictionary as needed.

According to many sources—e.g., the Cambridge Ancient History and Gardiner's Egypt of the Pharaohs—the ancient egyptians devoted much attention to making Life more convenient and pleasurable for themselves.

Our word pharaoh for the ancient egyptian rulers comes from the egyptian word pr'o, meaning "great house." Indeed, the egyptians placed great emphasis on family residences, adding small bedrms. as early as 3500 yrs. bce. By 3000 bce, the egyptians made ice through evaporation of water at night and then used it to cool their homes. About the same time they used fans made of palm fronds or papyrus to cool themselves in the day. To light their homes, the egyptians abandoned the animal-fat lamps Humans had used for 50 thousand yrs. Instead, around 1300 bce the people of Egt. devised the 1st oil lamps.

egyptians found great pleasure in playing games. Four thousand three hundred yrs. ago or so they created one of the oldest board games known. the game involved racing ivory or stone pieces across a papyrus playing board. By three thousand bce, egyptian children played marbles with semi-precious stones, some of which have been found in gravesites at nagada, EG. Around one thousand three hundred sixty bce, small children played with clay rattles covered in silk and shaped like animals.

To play the game of love, egyptian men and women experimented with cosmetics applied to skin and eyelids. kohl, history's first eyeliner, was used by both sexes to ward off evil. 5000 yrs. ago egyptians wore wigs made of vegetable fibers or human hair. In 9 hundred bce, queen Isimkheb wore a wig so heavy that she needed assistance in walking. To adjust their make-up and wigs, egyptians adapted the simple metal mirrors devised by the sumerians in the bronze age, ornamenting them with carved handles of ivory, gold, or wood. Feeling that only those who smelled sweet could be attractive, the egyptians made deodorants from perfumed oils, e.g., cinnamon and citrus.

PART 8

Effective Words

37

Using Appropriate Language

Appropriate language suits your writing situation—your subject, purpose, and audience. Like everyone, you vary your words depending on the context in which you are speaking and writing. Look, for example, at the underlined words in these two sentences:

> Some patients decide to <u>bag</u> counseling because their <u>shrinks</u> seem <u>strung out</u>.

> Some patients decide to <u>abandon</u> counseling because their <u>therapists</u> seem <u>disturbed</u>.

The first sentence might be addressed to friends in casual conversation. The second is more suitable for an academic audience.

The more formal language of the second example is typical of **standard American English.** This is the dialect of English normally expected and used in school, business, government, the professions, and the communications media. (For more on its role in academic writing, see pp. 170–72.)

The vocabulary of standard American English is huge, allowing expression of an infinite range of ideas and feelings; but it does exclude words that only some groups of people use, understand, or find inoffensive. Some of those more limited vocabularies should be avoided altogether; others should be used cautiously and in special situations, as when aiming for a special effect with an audience you know will appreciate it. Whenever you doubt a word's status, consult a dictionary (see p. 514).

Grammar checkers A grammar checker can often be set to flag potentially inappropriate words, such as nonstandard dialect, slang, colloquialisms, and gender-specific terms (*manmade, mailman*). However, the checker can flag only words listed in its dictionary of questionable words. For example, a checker flagged *businessman* as potentially sexist in *A successful businessman puts clients first*, but the checker did not flag *his* in *A successful businessperson*

Visit *mycomplab.com* for more resources and exercises
504 on appropriate language.

Appropriate language in academic writing

- **Use standard American English,** the dialect recommended by this handbook. Slang, colloquial language, and other vocabularies are sometimes appropriate in academic writing. Nonstandard dialect, online shortcuts, and pretentious writing are rarely or never appropriate. (See below and pp. 506–09.)

| Inappropriate | With a little help, Web-shy folks can get to be hotshot surfers. |
| Revised | With a little help, people reluctant to explore the Web can become capable users. |

- **Avoid stereotypes.** (See pp. 509–10.)

| Stereotype | Football players need tutors and counselors. |
| Revised | Football players with poor grades need tutors and counselors. |

- **Avoid sexist language.** (See pp. 510–12.)

| Sexist | Teenage girls are ideal babysitters. |
| Revised | Teenagers who enjoy young children are ideal babysitters. |

- **Be sensitive when labeling groups.** (See p. 512.)

| Inappropriate | The hurricane victims needed immediate help. |
| Revised | The people affected by the hurricane needed immediate help. |

listens to his clients. If you use a checker to review your language, you'll need to determine whether a flagged word is or is not appropriate for your writing situation. (See pp. 65–66 for tips on customizing a grammar checker.)

37a Revising nonstandard dialect

Like many countries, the United States consists of scores of regional, social, and ethnic groups with their own distinct dialects, or versions of English. Standard American English is one of these dialects, and so are African American English, Appalachian English, Creole, and the English of coastal Maine. All the dialects of English share many features, but each also has its own vocabulary, pronunciation, and grammar.

If you speak a dialect of English besides standard American English, be careful about using your dialect in situations where standard English is the norm, such as in academic or public writing. Dialects are not wrong in themselves, but forms imported from one dialect into another may still be perceived as unclear or incorrect. When you know standard English is expected in your writing, edit to eliminate expressions in your dialect that you know (or have been told) differ from standard English. These expressions may include *theirselves, hisn, them books,* and others labeled "non-standard" by a dictionary. They may also include certain verb forms, as discussed on pages 277–90. For help identifying and editing nonstandard language, see "⟨CULTURE LANGUAGE⟩ Guide" on pages 952–53.

Your participation in the community of standard English does not require you to abandon your own dialect. You may want to use it in writing you do for yourself, such as journals, notes, and drafts, which should be composed as freely as possible. You may want to quote it in an academic paper, as when analyzing or reporting conversation in dialect. And, of course, you will want to use it with others who speak it.

37b | Revising the shortcuts of online communication

Rapid communication by e-mail and text or instant messaging encourages some informalities that are inappropriate for academic writing. If you use these media frequently, you may need to proofread your academic papers especially to identify and revise errors such as the following:

- **Sentence fragments.** Make sure every sentence has a subject and a predicate. Avoid fragments such as *Observing the results* and *After the meeting.* For more on fragments, see pages 332–38.
- **Missing punctuation.** Between and within sentences, use standard punctuation marks. Check especially for missing commas within sentences and missing apostrophes in possessives and contractions. See pages 424–40 and 454–59.
- **Missing capital letters.** Use capital letters at the beginnings of sentences, for proper nouns and adjectives, and in titles. See pages 484–88.
- **Nonstandard abbreviations and spellings.** Avoid forms such as *2* for *to* or *too, b4* for *before, bc* for *because, ur* for *you are* or *you're,* and *+* or *&* for *and.* See pages 540–46.

37c | Using slang only when appropriate

All groups of people—from musicians and computer scientists to vegetarians and golfers—create novel and colorful expressions called **slang.** The following quotation, for instance, is from an essay on the slang of "skaters" (skateboarders):

> Curtis slashed ultra-punk crunchers on his longboard, while the Rubeman flailed his usual Gumbyness on tweaked frontsides and lofty fakie ollies.
> —Miles Orkin, "Mucho Slingage by the Pool"

Among those who understand it, slang may be vivid and forceful. It often occurs in dialog, and an occasional slang expression can enliven an informal essay. Some slang, such as *dropout* (*She was a high school dropout*), has proved so useful that it has passed into the general vocabulary.

But most slang is too flippant and imprecise for effective communication, and it is generally inappropriate for college or business writing. Notice the gain in seriousness and precision achieved in the following revision:

| Slang | Many students start out <u>pretty together</u> but then <u>get weird</u>. |
| Revised | Many students start out <u>with clear goals</u> but then <u>lose their direction</u>. |

37d Using colloquial language only when appropriate

Colloquial language designates the words and expressions appropriate to everyday spoken language. Regardless of our backgrounds and how we live, we all try to *get along with* each other. We play with *kids, go crazy* for something, and in our worst moments try to *get back at* someone who has made us do the *dirty work*.

When you write informally, colloquial language may be appropriate to achieve the casual, relaxed effect of conversation. An occasional colloquial word dropped into otherwise more formal writing can also help you achieve a desired emphasis. But colloquial language does not provide the exactness needed in more formal academic, public, and professional writing. In such writing you should generally avoid any words and expressions labeled "informal" or "colloquial" in your dictionary. Take special care to avoid **mixed diction,** a combination of standard and colloquial words:

| Mixed diction | According to a Native American myth, the Great Creator <u>had a dog hanging around with him</u> when he created the earth. |
| Revised | According to a Native American myth, the Great Creator <u>was accompanied by a dog</u> when he created the earth. |

37e Using regionalisms only when appropriate

Regionalisms are expressions or pronunciations peculiar to a particular area. Southerners may say they *reckon,* meaning "think" or "suppose." People in Maine invite their Boston friends to come *down* rather than *up* (north) to visit. New Yorkers stand *on* rather than *in* line for a movie.

Regional expressions are appropriate in writing addressed to local readers and may lend realism to regional description, but they should be avoided in writing intended for a general audience.

37f Revising neologisms

Neologisms are words created (or coined) so recently that they have not come into established use. An example is *prequel* (made up of *pre-,* meaning "before," and the ending of *sequel*), a movie or book that takes the story of an existing movie or book back in time. Some neologisms do become accepted as part of our general vocabulary—*motel,* coined from *motor* and *hotel,* is an example. But most neologisms pass quickly from the language. Unless such words serve a special purpose in your writing and are sure to be understood by your readers, you should avoid them.

37g Using technical words with care

All disciplines and professions rely on special words or give common words special meanings. Chemists speak of *esters* and *phosphatides,* geographers and mapmakers refer to *isobars* and *isotherms,* and literary critics write about *motifs* and *subtexts.* Such technical language allows specialists to communicate precisely and economically with other specialists who share their vocabulary. But without explanation these words are meaningless to nonspecialists. When you are writing for nonspecialists, avoid unnecessary technical terms and carefully define terms you must use.

37h Revising indirect or pretentious writing

In most writing, small, plain, and direct words are preferable to big, showy, or evasive words. Avoid euphemisms, double talk, and pretentious writing.

A **euphemism** is a presumably inoffensive word that a writer or speaker substitutes for a word deemed potentially offensive or too blunt, such as *passed away* for "died." Euphemisms appear whenever a writer or speaker wants to soften the truth, as when a governor mentions the *negative growth* (meaning "decline") in her state. Use euphemisms only when you know that blunt, truthful words would needlessly hurt or offend members of your audience.

A kind of euphemism that deliberately evades the truth is **double talk** (also called **doublespeak** or **weasel words**): language intended to confuse or to be misunderstood. Today double talk is unfortunately common in politics and advertising—the *revenue enhancement* that is really a tax, the *biodegradable* bags that last decades. Double talk has no place in honest writing.

Euphemism and sometimes double talk seem to keep company with fancy writing. Any writing that is more elaborate than its subject requires will sound **pretentious**—that is, excessively showy. Choose your words for their exactness and economy. The big, ornate word may be tempting, but pass it up. Your readers will be grateful.

Pretentious	To perpetuate our endeavor of providing funds for our elderly citizens as we do at the present moment, we will face the exigency of enhanced contributions from all our citizens.
Revised	We cannot continue to fund Social Security and Medicare for the elderly unless we raise taxes.

37i | Revising sexist and other biased language

Even when we do not mean it to, our language can reflect and perpetuate hurtful prejudices toward groups of people, especially racial, ethnic, religious, age, and sexual groups. Such biased language can be obvious—words such as *nigger, whitey, mick, kike, fag, dyke*, and *broad*. But it can also be subtle, generalizing about groups in ways that may be familiar but that are also inaccurate or unfair. For instance, people with physical disabilities are as varied a group as any other: the only thing they have in common is some form of impairment. To assume that people with disabilities share certain attitudes (shyness, helplessness, victimization, whatever) is to disregard the uniqueness of each person.

Biased language reflects poorly on the user, not on the person or persons whom it mischaracterizes or insults. Unbiased language does not submit to false generalizations. It treats people as individuals and labels groups as they wish to be labeled.

1 | Avoiding stereotypes of race, ethnicity, religion, age, and other characteristics

A **stereotype** is a generalization based on poor evidence, a kind of formula for understanding and judging people simply because of their membership in a group:

Men are uncommunicative.
Women are emotional.
Liberals want to raise taxes.
Conservatives are affluent.

At best, stereotypes betray an uncritical writer, one who is not thinking beyond notions received from others. Worse, they betray a writer who does not mind hurting others or even *wants* to hurt others.

In your writing, be alert for any general statements about people based on only one or a few characteristics. Be especially cautious about substituting such statements for the evidence you should be providing instead.

Stereotype	Elderly drivers should have their licenses limited to daytime driving. [Implies that all elderly people are poor night drivers.]
Revised	Drivers with impaired night vision should have their licenses limited to daytime driving.

Some stereotypes have become part of the language, but they are still potentially offensive.

Stereotype	The administrators are too blind to see the need for a new gymnasium. [Equates vision disability and lack of understanding.]
Revised	The administrators do not understand the need for a new gymnasium.

2 Avoiding sexist language

Among the most subtle and persistent biased language is that expressing narrow ideas about men's and women's roles, position, and value in society. This **sexist language** distinguishes needlessly between men and women in such matters as occupation, ability, behavior, temperament, and maturity. Like other stereotypes, it can wound or irritate readers, and it indicates the writer's thoughtlessness or unfairness. The following box suggests ways of eliminating sexist language.

Eliminating sexist language

■ **Avoid demeaning and patronizing language**—for instance, identifying women and men differently or trivializing either gender:

Sexist	Dr. Keith Kim and Lydia Hawkins wrote the article.
Revised	Dr. Keith Kim and Dr. Lydia Hawkins wrote the article.
Revised	Keith Kim and Lydia Hawkins wrote the article.
Sexist	Ladies are entering formerly male occupations.
Revised	Women are entering formerly male occupations.

- **Avoid occupational or social stereotypes,** assuming that a role or profession is exclusively male or female:

  Sexist   The considerate doctor commends a nurse when <u>she</u> provides <u>his</u> patients with good care.

  Revised   The considerate doctor commends a nurse who provides good care for patients.

- **Avoid referring needlessly to gender:**

  Sexist   Marie Curie, <u>a woman chemist</u>, discovered radium.

  Revised   Marie Curie, a chemist, discovered radium.

  Sexist   The patients were tended by <u>a male nurse</u>.

  Revised   The patients were tended by a nurse.

- **Avoid using *man* or words containing *man* to refer to all human beings.** Here are a few alternatives:

businessman	businessperson
chairman	chair, chairperson
congressman	representative in Congress, legislator
craftsman	craftsperson, artisan
layman	layperson
mankind	humankind, humanity, human beings, people
policeman	police officer
salesman	salesperson

  Sexist   <u>Man</u> has not reached the limits of social justice.

  Revised   Humankind [or Humanity] has not reached the limits of social justice.

  Sexist   The furniture consists of <u>manmade</u> materials.

  Revised   The furniture consists of synthetic materials.

- **Avoid the generic *he,*** the male pronoun used to refer to both genders. (See also pp. 313–15.)

  Sexist   The newborn child explores <u>his</u> world.

  Revised   Newborn children explore their world. [Use the plural for the pronoun and the word it refers to.]

  Revised   The newborn child explores the world. [Avoid the pronoun altogether.]

  Revised   The newborn child explores his or her world. [Substitute male and female pronouns.]

  Use the last option sparingly—only once in a group of sentences and only to stress the singular individual.

(CULTURE LANGUAGE) Forms of address vary widely from culture to culture. In some cultures, for instance, one shows respect by referring to all older women as if they were married, using the equivalent of the title *Mrs.* Usage in the United States is changing toward making no assumptions about marital status, rank, or other characteristics—for instance, using the title *Ms.* for a woman unless she is known to prefer *Mrs.* or *Miss.*

3 | Using appropriate labels

We often need to label groups: *swimmers, politicians, mothers, Christians, westerners, students.* But labels can be shorthand stereotypes that slight the person labeled and ignore the preferences of the group members themselves. Showing sensitivity when applying labels reveals that you are alert to readers' needs and concerns. Although sometimes dismissed as "political correctness," such sensitivity hurts no one and helps gain your readers' trust and respect.

- **Avoid labels that (intentionally or not) disparage the person or group you refer to.** A person with emotional problems is not a *mental patient.* A person with cancer is not a *cancer victim.* A person using a wheelchair is not *wheelchair-bound.*
- **Use names for racial, ethnic, and other groups that reflect the preferences of each group's members,** or at least many of them. Examples of current preferences include *African American* or *black, latino/latina* (for Americans and American immigrants of Spanish-speaking descent), and *people with disabilities* (rather than *the handicapped*). But labels change often. To learn how a group's members wish to be labeled, ask them directly, attend to usage in reputable periodicals, or check a recent dictionary.
- **Identify a person's group only when it is relevant to the point you're making.** Consider the context of the label: Is it a necessary piece of information? If not, don't use it.

A helpful reference for appropriate labels is *Guidelines for Bias-Free Writing,* by Marilyn Schwartz and the Task Force on Bias-Free Language of the Association of American University Presses.

Exercise 37.1 Revising: Appropriate words

Rewrite the following sentences as needed for standard American English. Consult a dictionary to determine whether particular words are appropriate and to find suitable substitutes.

Example:

If negotiators get hyper during contract discussions, they may mess up chances for a settlement.

If negotiators <u>become excited or upset</u> during contract discussions, they may <u>harm</u> chances for a settlement.

1. Acquired immune deficiency syndrome (AIDS) is a major deal all over the world.
2. The disease gets around primarily by sexual intercourse, exchange of bodily fluids, shared needles, and blood transfusions.

3. Those who think the disease is limited to homos, druggies, and foreigners are quite mistaken.

4. Stats suggest that in the United States one in every five hundred college kids carries the virus.

5. A person with AIDS does not deserve to be subjected to exclusionary behavior or callousness on the part of his fellow citizens. Instead, he has the necessity for all the compassion, medical care, and financial assistance due those who are in the extremity of illness.

6. An AIDS victim often sees a team of doctors or a single doctor with a specialized practice.

7. The doctor may help his patients by obtaining social services for them as well as by providing medical care.

8. The AIDS sufferer who loses his job may need public assistance.

9. For someone who is very ill, a full-time nurse may be necessary. She can administer medications and make the sick person as comfortable as possible.

10. Some people with AIDS have insurance, but others lack the bread for premiums.

38

Using Exact Language

To write clearly and effectively, you will want to find the words that fit your meaning exactly and convey your attitude precisely. Don't worry too much about choosing exact words while you are drafting an essay. If the right word doesn't come to you, leave a blank. Revision (p. 52) or editing (p. 60) is the stage to consider tone, specificity, and precision.

Grammar checkers A grammar checker can provide some help with inexact language. For instance, you can set it to flag commonly confused words (such as *continuous/continual*), misused prepositions in idioms (such as *accuse for* instead of *accuse of*), and clichés. (See p. 65 on setting a checker.) But the checker can flag only words stored in its dictionary. It can't help you at all with inappropriate connotation, excessive abstraction, or other problems discussed in this chapter.

mycomplab

Visit *mycomplab.com* for more resources on exact language.

Avoiding common mistakes in word choice

- **Make sure words have the meanings you intend.** Check the meanings of words whose meanings you aren't sure of. (See below for more on dictionaries.)

  Incorrect   Increased global temperatures will effect everyone.

  Revised   Increased global temperatures will affect everyone.

- **Make sure that any word suggested by a spelling checker is the one you mean.** (See pp. 64–65 for more on spelling checkers.)

  Incorrect   The results were defiant: the experiment was a failure.

  Revised   The results were definite: the experiment was a failure.

- **Use idioms correctly.** (See pp. 519–21 for more on idioms.)

  Incorrect   The planners agreed over the details of the evacuation plan.

  Revised   The planners agreed on the details of the evacuation plan.

38a Using a dictionary and a thesaurus

For writing exactly, a dictionary is essential and a thesaurus can be helpful.

1 Using a desk dictionary

A desk dictionary defines about 150,000 to 200,000 words and provides pronunciation, grammatical functions, etymology (word history), and other information. The sample below is from *Merriam-Webster's Collegiate Dictionary*.

Dictionary entry for *reckon*

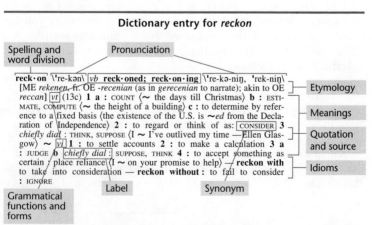

Good desk dictionaries, in addition to *Merriam-Webster's,* include the *American Heritage College Dictionary,* the *Random House Webster's College Dictionary,* and *Webster's New World Dictionary.* Most of these dictionaries are available in both print and electronic form (CD-ROM or online). In addition, several Web sites provide online dictionaries or links to online dictionaries. *Dictionary.com* allows you to search for word meanings in more than a dozen general and specialized dictionaries, including *American Heritage.*

CULTURE LANGUAGE If English is not your native language, you probably should have a dictionary prepared especially for students using English as a second language (ESL). Such a dictionary contains special information on prepositions, count versus noncount nouns, and many other matters. Reliable ESL dictionaries include *COBUILD English Language Dictionary, Longman Dictionary of Contemporary English,* and *Oxford Advanced Learner's Dictionary.*

2 Using a thesaurus

To find a word with the exact shade of meaning you intend, you may want to consult a thesaurus, or book of **synonyms**—words with approximately the same meaning. A thesaurus such as *Roget's International Thesaurus* lists most imaginable synonyms for thousands of words. The word *news,* for instance, has half a page of synonyms in *Roget's International,* including *tidings, dispatch, gossip,* and *journalism.*

Since a thesaurus aims to open up possibilities, its lists of synonyms include approximate as well as precise matches. The thesaurus does not define synonyms or distinguish among them, however, so you need a dictionary to discover exact meanings. In general, don't use a word from a thesaurus—even one you like the sound of—until you are sure of its appropriateness for your meaning.

Note Many Web sites, such as *Thesaurus.com,* provide tools for finding synonyms. Your word processor may also include a thesaurus, making it easy to look up synonyms and insert the chosen word into your text. But still you should consult a dictionary unless you are certain of the word's meaning.

Exercise 38.1 Using a dictionary

Consult your dictionary on five of the following words. For each word, write down (*a*) the division into syllables, (*b*) *the pronunciation,* (*c*) the grammatical functions and forms, (*d*) the etymology, (*e*) each meaning, and (*f*) any special uses indicated by labels. Finally, use the word in at least two sentences of your own.

1. depreciation	4. manifest	7. potlatch	10. toxic
2. secretary	5. assassin	8. plain (*adj.*)	11. steal
3. grammar	6. astrology	9. ceremony	12. obelisk

38b Using the right word for your meaning

Precisely expressing your meaning requires understanding both the denotations and the connotations of words. A word's **denotation** is the thing or idea it refers to, the meaning listed in the dictionary without reference to the emotional associations it may arouse in a reader. Using words according to their established denotations is essential if readers are to grasp your meaning. Here are a few guidelines:

- **Consult a dictionary whenever you are unsure of a word's meaning.**
- **Distinguish between similar-sounding words that have widely different denotations:**

  Inexact   Older people often suffer <u>infirmaries</u> [places for the sick].

  Exact   Older people often suffer <u>infirmities</u> [disabilities].

Some words, called **homonyms** (from the Greek meaning "same name"), sound exactly alike but differ in meaning: for example, *principal/principle* and *rain/reign/rein*. (See pp. 534–35 for a list of commonly confused homonyms.)

- **Distinguish between words with related but distinct denotations:**

  Inexact   Television commercials <u>continuously</u> [unceasingly] interrupt programming.

  Exact   Television commercials <u>continually</u> [regularly] interrupt programming.

In addition to their emotion-free denotations, many words carry related meanings that evoke specific feelings. These **connotations** can shape readers' responses and are thus a powerful tool for writers. (At the same time they are a potential snare for readers. See p. 189.) Some connotations are personal: the word *dog,* for instance, may have negative connotations for the letter carrier who has been bitten three times. Usually, though, people agree about connotations. The following word pairs are just a few of many that have related denotations but very different connotations:

> *pride:* sense of self-worth
> *vanity:* excessive regard for oneself
>
> *firm:* steady, unchanging, unyielding
> *stubborn:* unreasonable, bullheaded
>
> *enthusiasm:* excitement
> *mania:* excessive interest or desire
>
> *statesman* or *stateswoman:* responsible, high-minded public servant
> *politician:* self-serving elected official
>
> *quiet:* peacefully silent
> *taciturn:* stubbornly silent

Understanding connotation is especially important in choosing among synonyms, or words with approximately the same meanings. For instance, *cry* and *weep* both denote the shedding of tears, but *cry* more than *weep* connotes a sobbing sound accompanying the tears. *Sob* itself connotes broken, gasping crying, with tears, whereas *wail* connotes sustained sound, perhaps without tears.

Exercise 38.2   Revising: Denotation

Revise any underlined word below that is not used according to its established denotation. Circle any word used correctly. Consult a dictionary if you are uncertain of a word's precise meaning.

Example:

Sam and Dave are going to Bermuda and Hauppauge, respectfully, for spring vacation.

Sam and Dave are going to Bermuda and Hauppauge, respectively, for spring vacation.

1. Maxine Hong Kingston was rewarded many prizes for her first two books, *The Woman Warrior* and *China Men*.
2. Kingston sites her mother's tales about ancestors and ancient Chinese customs as the sources of these memoirs.
3. In her childhood Kingston was greatly effected by her mother's tale about a pregnant aunt who was ostracized by villagers.
4. The aunt gained avengeance by drowning herself in the village's water supply.
5. Kingston decided to make her nameless relative infamous by giving her immortality in *The Woman Warrior*.

Exercise 38.3   Considering the connotations of words

Fill the blank in each sentence below with the most appropriate word from the list in parentheses. Consult a dictionary to be sure of your choice.

Example:

Channel 5 _____ Oshu the winner before the polls closed. (*advertised, declared, broadcast, promulgated*)

Channel 5 declared Oshu the winner before the polls closed.

1. AIDS is a serious health _____. (*problem, worry, difficulty, plight*)
2. Once the virus has entered the blood system, it _____ T-cells. (*murders, destroys, slaughters, executes*)
3. The _____ of T-cells is to combat infections. (*ambition, function, aim, goal*)
4. Without enough T-cells, the body is nearly _____ against infections. (*defenseless, hopeless, desperate*)
5. To prevent exposure to the disease, one should be especially _____ in sexual relationships. (*chary, circumspect, cautious, calculating*)

38c Balancing the abstract and concrete, the general and specific

To understand a subject as you understand it, your readers need ample guidance from your words. When you describe a building as *beautiful* and nothing more, you force readers to provide their own ideas of what makes a building beautiful. If readers bother (and they may not), they surely will not conjure up the image you had in mind. Use words to tell readers what you want them to know, that the beautiful building is *a sleek, silver skyscraper with blue-tinted windows,* for instance, or *a Victorian brick courthouse with tall, arched windows.*

Clear, exact writing balances abstract and general words, which outline ideas and objects, with concrete and specific words, which sharpen and solidify.

- **Abstract words** name ideas: *beauty, inflation, management, culture, liberal.* **Concrete words** name qualities and things we can know by our five senses of sight, hearing, touch, taste, and smell: *sleek, humming, rough, salty, musty.*

- **General words** name classes or groups of things, such as *buildings, weather,* and *birds,* and include all the varieties of the class. **Specific words** limit a general class, such as *buildings,* by naming a variety, such as *skyscraper, Victorian courthouse,* or *hut.*

Note that *general* and *specific* are relative terms: the same word may be more general than some words but more specific than others.

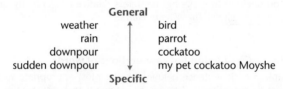

	General	
weather	↑	bird
rain		parrot
downpour		cockatoo
sudden downpour	↓	my pet cockatoo Moyshe
	Specific	

Abstract and general words are useful in the broad statements that set the course for your writing:

The wild horse in America has a <u>romantic</u> history.

We must be <u>free</u> from <u>government interference</u> in our <u>affairs</u>.

<u>Relations</u> between the sexes today are only a <u>little</u> more <u>relaxed</u> than they were in the past.

But the sentences following these would have to develop the ideas with concrete and specific details. When your meaning calls for an abstract or general word, make sure you define it, explain it, and narrow it. Look at how concrete and specific information turns vague sentences into exact ones in the following examples:

Vague The size of his hands made his smallness real. [How big were his hands? How small was he?]

Idioms | **exact** 38d

Exact   Not until I saw his delicate, doll-like hands did I realize that he stood a full head shorter than most other men.

Vague   The long flood caused a lot of awful destruction in the town. [How long did the flood last? What destruction did it cause? Why was the destruction awful?]

Exact   The flood waters, which rose swiftly and then stayed stubbornly high for days, made life a misery for the hundreds who had to evacuate their ruined homes and stores.

Note You can use your computer's Find function to help you find and revise abstract and general words that you tend to overuse. Examples of such words might include *nice, interesting, things, very, good, a lot, a little,* and *some.*

Exercise 38.4 Revising: Concrete and specific words

Make the following paragraph vivid by expanding the sentences with appropriate details of your own choosing. Substitute concrete and specific words for the abstract and general ones that are underlined.

    I remember clearly how awful I felt the first time I attended Mrs. Murphy's second-grade class. I had recently moved from a small town in Missouri to a crowded suburb of Chicago. My new school looked big from the outside and seemed dark inside as I walked down the long corridor toward the classroom. The class was noisy as I neared the door; but when I entered, everyone became quiet and looked at me. I felt uncomfortable and wanted a place to hide. However, in a loud voice Mrs. Murphy directed me to the front of the room to introduce myself.

Exercise 38.5 Using concrete and specific words

For each abstract or general word below, give at least two other words or phrases that illustrate increasing specificity or concreteness. Consult a dictionary as needed. Use the most specific or concrete word from each group in a sentence of your own.

    Example:
awake, watchful, vigilant
Vigilant guards patrol the buildings.

1. fabric	6. green	11. teacher
2. delicious	7. walk (verb)	12. nice
3. car	8. flower	13. virtue
4. narrow-minded	9. serious	14. angry
5. reach (verb)	10. pretty	15. crime

38d Using idioms

Idioms are expressions in any language whose meanings cannot be determined simply from the words in them or whose component words cannot be predicted by any rule of grammar; often, they violate conventional grammar. Examples of English idioms include *put up with, plug away at,* and *make off with.*

Idioms involving prepositions can be especially confusing for both native and nonnative speakers of English. A number of these idioms appear in the box below.

Idioms with prepositions

abide **by** a rule
    in a place or state
accords **with**
according **to**
accuse **of** a crime
adapt **from** a source
    to a situation
afraid **of**
agree **on** a plan as a group
    to someone else's plan
    with a person
angry **with**
aware **of**
based **on**
capable **of**
certain **of**
charge **for** a purchase
    with a crime
concur **in** an opinion
    with a person
contend **for** a principle or prize
    with an obstacle
dependent **on**
differ **about** or **over** a question
    from in some quality
    with a person
disappointed **by** or **in** a person
    in or **with** a thing

familiar **with**
identical **with** or **to**
impatient **for** a raise
    with a person
independent **of**
infer **from**
inferior **to**
involved **in** a task
    with a person
oblivious **of** or **to** one's surroundings
    of something forgotten
occupied **by** a person
    in study
    with a thing
opposed **to**
part **from** a person
    with a possession
prior **to**
proud **of**
related **to**
rewarded **by** the judge
    for something done
    with a gift
similar **to**
superior **to**
wait **at** a place
    for a train, a person
    on a customer

CULTURE LANGUAGE If you are learning standard American English, you are justified in stumbling over its prepositions: their meanings can shift depending on context, and they have many idiomatic uses. In mastering the prepositions of standard English, you probably can't avoid memorization. But you can help yourself by memorizing related groups, such as those following for the very common *at, in, on, for,* and *since.*

At, in, or *on* in expressions of time

■ Use *at* before actual clock time: *at 8:30.*

■ Use *in* before a month, year, century, or period: *in April, in 2007, in the twenty-first century, in the next month.*

■ Use *on* before a day or date: *on Tuesday, on August 3, on Labor Day.*

At, in, or *on* in expressions of place

■ Use *at* before a specific place or address: *at the school, at 511 Iris Street.*

■ Use *in* before a place with limits or before a city, state, country, or continent: *in the house, in a box, in Oklahoma City, in China, in Asia.*

■ Use *on* to mean "supported by" or "touching the surface of": *on the table, on Iris Street, on page 150.*

For or *since* in expressions of time

■ Use *for* before a period of time: *for an hour, for two years.*

■ Use *since* before a specific point in time: *since 1999, since the war began.*

A dictionary of English as a second language is the best source for the meanings of prepositions; see the recommendations on page 515. In addition, some reference works focus on prepositions. See, for instance, volume 1 (*Verbs with Prepositions and Particles*) of the *Oxford Dictionary of Current Idiomatic English*.

Exercise 38.6 Using prepositions in idioms

Insert the preposition that correctly completes each idiom in the following sentences. Consult the box on the previous page or a dictionary as needed.

Example:

I disagree _____ many feminists who say women should not be homemakers.

I disagree with many feminists who say women should not be homemakers.

1. Children are waiting longer to become independent _____ their parents.

2. According _____ US Census data for young adults ages eighteen to twenty-four, 57 percent of men and 47 percent of women live full-time with their parents.

3. Some of these adult children are dependent _____ their parents financially.

4. In other cases, the parents charge their children _____ housing, food, and other living expenses.

5. Many adult children are financially capable _____ living independently but prefer to save money rather than contend _____ high housing costs.

38e Using figurative language

Figurative language (or a **figure of speech**) departs from the literal meanings (the denotations) of words. It is common in speech. Having *slept like a log,* you may get up to find it *raining cats and dogs* and have to *run like the wind* to get to school on time.

The rapid exchange of speech leaves little time for inventiveness, and most figures of daily conversation, like those above, are worn and hackneyed. Writing gives you time to reject the tired figure and to search out fresh, concrete words and phrases that capture meaning precisely and feelingly:

> Literal   As I try to write, I can think of nothing to say.
> Figurative   As I try to write, my mind is a slab of black slate.

The following are some common figures of speech. (Others appear in the Glossary of Terms, pp. 862–88.)

- **Simile and metaphor** compare two things of different classes, often one abstract and the other concrete. A **simile** makes the comparison explicit and usually begins with *like* or *as:*

> Whenever we grow, we tend to feel it, as a young seed must feel the weight and inertia of the earth when it seeks to break out of its shell on its way to becoming a plant.   —Alice Walker

> To hold America in one's thoughts is like holding a love letter in one's hand—it has so special a meaning.   —E. B. White

A **metaphor** implies a comparison instead of stating it, omitting words such as *like* or *as:*

> I cannot and will not cut my conscience to fit this year's fashions.
> —Lillian Hellman

> A school is a hopper into which children are heaved while they are young and tender; therein they are pressed into certain standard shapes and covered from head to heels with official rubber stamps.
> —H. L. Mencken

Similes are usually limited to a sentence, but metaphors can extend throughout a paragraph or even an entire essay. Metaphors and similes work effectively when they draw readers in through the comparison, and they often subtly express the writer's attitude about the subject. The Mencken quotation above, for example, shows the writer's attitude about schooling.

- **Personification** treats ideas and objects as if they were human:

> I could hear the whisper of snowflakes, nudging each other as they fell.
> Because I could not stop for Death—
> He kindly stopped for me—   —Emily Dickinson

■ **Hyperbole** deliberately exaggerates:

> She appeared in a mile of billowing chiffon, flashing a rhinestone as big as an ostrich egg.
>
> He yelled so loud that his voice carried to the next county.

■ **Synecdoche** names a part of something to refer to the whole:

> I traded in my junker for a new set of wheels.
>
> If everyone lends a hand, the job will be done quickly.

■ **Metonymy** uses a name to refer to a complete entity:

> The White House issued a statement about its health policy.
>
> The citizens criticized the press for not reporting the details of the crime wave.

■ **Irony** states the opposite of the literal meaning:

> The new center on the basketball team is over seven feet tall. Where do they find these little players?
>
> Snow flurries, sleet, and freezing rain—just another April in the upper Midwest.

See page 875 for more examples of irony.

To be successful, figurative language must be fresh and unstrained, calling attention not to itself but to the writer's meaning. One kind of figurative language gone wrong is the **mixed metaphor,** in which the writer combines two or more incompatible figures. Since metaphors often generate visual images in the reader's mind, a mixed metaphor can be laughable:

> **Mixed** Various thorny problems that we try to sweep under the rug continue to bob up all the same.

To revise a mixed metaphor, follow through with just one image:

> **Improved** Various thorny problems that we try to weed out continue to thrive all the same.

Exercise 38.7 Analyzing figurative language

Identify each figure of speech in the following sentences as a simile or a metaphor, and analyze how it adds to the writer's meaning.

1. A distant airplane, a delta wing out of nightmare, made a gliding shadow on the creek's bottom that looked like a stingray crossing upstream. —Annie Dillard
2. Her roots ran deep into the earth, and from those roots she drew strength enough to hold still against all the forces of chance and disorder. —N. Scott Momaday
3. As a member of the winning team (the graduating class of 1940) I had outdistanced unpleasant sensations by miles. I was headed for the freedom of open fields. —Maya Angelou

4. All artists quiver under the lash of adverse criticism.
—Catherine Drinker Bowen
5. Every writer, in a roomful of writers, wants to be the best, and the judge, or umpire, or referee is soon overwhelmed and shouted down like a chickadee trying to take charge of a caucus of crows.
—James Thurber

Exercise 38.8 Using figurative language

Invent appropriate figurative language of your own (simile, metaphor, hyperbole, personification, synecdoche, metonymy, or irony) to describe each of the following scenes or qualities, and use each figure in a sentence.

Example:
The attraction of a lake on a hot day
The small waves <u>like fingers beckoned</u> us irresistibly.

1. The sound of a kindergarten classroom
2. People waiting in line to buy tickets to a rock concert
3. The politeness of strangers meeting for the first time
4. A streetlight seen through dense fog
5. The effect of watching television for ten hours straight

38f Using fresh, not trite, expressions

Trite expressions, or **clichés**, are phrases so old and so often repeated that they have become stale. They include the following:

acid test	ladder of success
add insult to injury	moving experience
better late than never	needle in a haystack
beyond the shadow of a doubt	point with pride
brought back to reality	ripe old age
cold, hard facts	shoulder the burden
cool as a cucumber	sneaking suspicion
crushing blow	sober as a judge
easier said than done	stand in awe
face the music	strong as an ox
flat as a pancake	thin as a rail
green with envy	tired but happy
hard as a rock	tried and true
heavy as lead	untimely death
hour of need	wise as an owl

Besides these old phrases, stale writing may also depend on fashionable words that are losing their effect: for instance, *lifestyle, enhance, awesome, fantastic,* and *caring.*

Many of these expressions were once fresh and forceful, but constant use has dulled them. They, in turn, will dull your writing by suggesting that you have not thought about what you are saying and have resorted to the easiest phrase.

Clichés may slide into your drafts while you are trying to express your meaning. In editing, then, be wary of any expression you have heard or used before. Substitute fresh words of your own or restate the idea in plain language.

Trite	A healthful <u>lifestyle enhances</u> your ability to <u>go for the gold</u>, allows you <u>to enjoy life to the fullest</u>, and helps you live <u>to a ripe old age</u>.
Revised	Living <u>healthfully</u> helps you <u>perform well</u>, enjoy life <u>thoroughly</u>, and <u>live long</u>.

Exercise 38.9   Revising: Trite expressions

Revise the following sentences to eliminate trite expressions.

Example:

The basketball team had almost seized victory, but it faced the test of truth in the last quarter of the game.

The basketball team <u>seemed about to win</u>, but the <u>real test</u> came in the last quarter of the game.

1. The disastrous consequences of the war have shaken the small nation to its roots.
2. Prices for food have shot sky high, and citizens have sneaking suspicions that others are making a killing on the black market.
3. Medical supplies are so few and far between that even civilians who are as sick as dogs cannot get treatment.
4. With most men fighting or injured or killed, women have had to bite the bullet and bear the men's burden in farming and manufacturing.
5. Last but not least, the war's heavy drain on the nation's pocketbook has left the economy in a shambles.

39

Writing Concisely

Concise writing makes every word count. Conciseness is not the same as mere brevity: detail and originality should not be cut along with needless words. Rather, the length of an expression should be appropriate to the thought.

mycomplab

Visit *mycomplab.com* for more resources and exercises on writing concisely.

You may find yourself writing wordily when you are unsure of your subject or when your thoughts are tangled. It's fine, even necessary, to stumble and grope while drafting. But you should straighten out your ideas and eliminate wordiness during revision and editing.

Ways to achieve conciseness

Wordy (87 words)

The highly pressured nature of critical-care nursing is due to the fact that the patients have life-threatening illnesses. Critical-care nurses must have possession of steady nerves to care for patients who are critically ill and very sick. The nurses must also have possession of interpersonal skills. They must also have medical skills. It is considered by most health-care professionals that these nurses are essential if there is to be improvement of patients who are now in critical care from that status to the status of intermediate care.

Focus on subject and verb, and cut or shorten empty words and phrases.

Avoid nouns made from verbs.

Cut unneeded repetition.

Combine sentences.

Change passive voice to active voice.

Revise *there is* constructions.

Cut unneeded repetition, and reduce clauses and phrases.

Concise (37 words)

Critical-care nursing is highly pressured because the patients have life-threatening illnesses. Critical-care nurses must possess steady nerves and interpersonal and medical skills. Most health-care professionals consider these nurses essential if patients are to improve to intermediate care.

Grammar checkers Any grammar checker will identify at least some wordy structures, such as repeated words, weak verbs, passive voice, and *there is* and *it is* constructions. But a checker can't identify all potentially wordy structures, nor can it tell you whether a structure is appropriate for your ideas.

⬭ **CULTURE LANGUAGE** As you'll see in the examples that follow, wordiness is not a problem of incorrect grammar. A sentence may be perfectly grammatical but still contain unneeded words that interfere with your idea.

39a Focusing on the subject and verb

Using the subjects and verbs of your sentences for the key actors and actions will reduce words and emphasize important ideas. (See pp. 380–82 for more on this topic.)

Wordy	The <u>reason</u> why most of the country shifts to daylight time <u>is</u> that winter days are much shorter than summer days.
Concise	Most of the <u>country shifts</u> to daylight time because winter days are much shorter than summer days.

Focusing on subjects and verbs will also help you avoid several other causes of wordiness (also discussed further on pp. 380–82):

Nouns made from verbs

Wordy	The <u>occurrence</u> of the winter solstice, the shortest day of the year, <u>is</u> an event occurring about December 22.
Concise	The winter <u>solstice</u>, the shortest day of the year, <u>occurs</u> about December 22.

Weak verbs

Wordy	The earth's axis <u>has</u> a tilt as the planet <u>is</u> in orbit around the sun so that the northern and southern hemispheres <u>are</u> alternately in alignment toward the sun.
Concise	The earth's axis <u>tilts</u> as the planet <u>orbits</u> the sun so that the northern and southern hemispheres alternately <u>align</u> toward the sun.

Passive voice

Wordy	During its winter the northern hemisphere <u>is tilted</u> farthest away from the sun, so the nights <u>are made</u> longer and the days <u>are made</u> shorter.
Concise	During its winter the northern hemisphere <u>tilts</u> away from the sun, <u>making</u> the nights longer and the days shorter.

See also pages 300–01 on changing the passive voice to the active voice, as in the example above.

39b Cutting or shortening empty words and phrases

Empty words and phrases walk in place, gaining little or nothing in meaning. When you cut or shorten them, your writing will move faster and work harder.

Many empty phrases can be cut entirely:

all things considered	in a manner of speaking
as far as I'm concerned	in my opinion
for all intents and purposes	last but not least
for the most part	more or less

Wordy	<u>In my opinion</u>, the council's proposal to improve the city center is inadequate, <u>all things considered</u>.
Revised	The council's proposal to improve the city center is inadequate.

Other empty words can be cut along with some words around them:

angle	character	kind	situation
area	element	manner	thing
aspect	factor	nature	type
case	field		

Wordy   The type of large expenEditures on advertising that manufacturers must make is a very important aspect of the cost of detergents.

Concise   Manufacturers' large advertising expenditures increase the
cost of detergents.

Still other empty phrases can be reduced from several words to a
single word:

For	Substitute
at all times	always
at the present time	now
at this point in time	now
in today's society	now
in the nature of	like
for the purpose of	for
in order to	to
until such time as	until
for the reason that	because
due to the fact that	because
because of the fact that	because
by virtue of the fact that	because
despite the fact that	although
in the event that	if
by means of	by
in the final analysis	finally

Wordy   At this point in time, the software is expensive due to the fact
that it has no significant competition.

Revised   The software is expensive now because it has no significant
competition.

**Exercise 39.1   Revising: Subjects and verbs; empty words
and phrases**

Revise the following sentences to achieve conciseness by focusing on
subjects and verbs and by cutting or reducing empty words and phrases.
See also page 380 for an additional exercise in focusing on subjects and
verbs.

Example:

I am making college my destination because of many factors, but
most of all because of the fact that I want a career in medicine.

I am going to college mainly because I want a career in medicine.

1. *Gerrymandering* refers to a situation in which the lines of a voting district are redrawn so that a particular party or ethnic group has benefits.
2. The name is a reference to the fact that Elbridge Gerry, the governor of Massachusetts in 1812, redrew voting districts in Essex County.
3. On the map one new district was seen to resemble something in the nature of a salamander.
4. Upon seeing the map, a man who was for all intents and purposes a critic of Governor Gerry's administration cried out, "Gerrymander!"
5. At the present time, changes may be made in the character of a district's voting pattern by a political group by gerrymandering to achieve the exclusion of rival groups' supporters.

39c Cutting unnecessary repetition

Planned repetition and restatement can make writing more coherent (p. 86) or emphatic (p. 386). But unnecessary repetition weakens sentences:

Wordy	Many <u>unskilled</u> workers <u>without training in a particular job</u> are unemployed <u>and do not have any work.</u>
Concise	Many unskilled workers are unemployed.

The use of one word two different ways within a sentence is confusing:

Confusing	Preschool instructors play a <u>role</u> in the child's understanding of male and female <u>roles</u>.
Clear	Preschool instructors <u>contribute</u> to the child's understanding of male and female roles.

The simplest kind of useless repetition is the phrase that says the same thing twice. In the following examples, the unneeded words are underlined:

biography <u>of his life</u>	habitual custom
circle <u>around</u>	<u>important</u> [basic] essentials
consensus <u>of opinion</u>	large <u>in size</u>
continue <u>on</u>	puzzling <u>in nature</u>
cooperate <u>together</u>	repeat <u>again</u>
few <u>in number</u>	return <u>again</u>
<u>final</u> completion	revert <u>back</u>
frank <u>and</u> honest exchange	square [round] <u>in shape</u>
the future <u>to come</u>	<u>surrounding</u> circumstances

CULTURE LANGUAGE Phrases like those above are redundant because the main word already implies the underlined word or words. The repetition is not emphatic but tedious. A dictionary will tell you what meanings a word implies. *Assassinate*, for instance, means "murder someone well known," so the following sentence is redundant: *Julius Caesar was assassinated and killed.*

Exercise 39.2 Revising: Unnecessary repetition

Revise the following sentences to achieve conciseness. Concentrate on eliminating repetition and redundancy.

> *Example:*
>
> Because the circumstances surrounding the cancellation of classes were murky and unclear, the editor of the student newspaper assigned a staff reporter to investigate and file a report on the circumstances.
>
> Because the circumstances <u>leading to</u> the cancellation of classes were <u>unclear</u>, the editor of the student newspaper assigned a <u>staffer</u> to investigate and <u>report the story</u>.

1. Some Vietnam veterans coming back to the United States after their tours of duty in Vietnam had problems readjusting again to life in America.
2. Afflicted with post-traumatic stress disorder, a psychological disorder that sometimes arises after a trauma, some veterans had psychological problems that caused them to have trouble holding jobs and maintaining relationships.
3. Some who used to use drugs in Vietnam could not break their drug habits after they returned back to the United States.
4. The few veterans who committed crimes and violent acts gained so much notoriety and fame that many Americans thought all veterans were crazy, insane maniacs.
5. As a result of such stereotyping of Vietnam-era veterans, veterans are included in the same antidiscrimination laws that protect other victims of discrimination.

39d Reducing clauses to phrases, phrases to single words

Modifiers—subordinate clauses, phrases, and single words—can be expanded or contracted depending on the emphasis you want to achieve. (See pp. 244–56 on phrases and clauses and 393–95 on working with modifiers.) When editing your sentences, consider whether any modifiers can be reduced without loss of emphasis or clarity:

Wordy	The Channel Tunnel, <u>which runs between Britain and France,</u> bores through <u>a bed of solid chalk that is twenty-three miles across.</u>
Concise	The Channel Tunnel <u>between Britain and France</u> bores through <u>twenty-three miles of solid chalk.</u>

39e | Revising *there is, here is,* and *it is* constructions

You can postpone the sentence subject with the words *there, here,* and *it: There are three points made in the text. Here is the main problem. It was not fair that only seniors could vote.* (See p. 263.) These constructions can be useful to emphasize the subject (as when introducing it for the first time) or to indicate a change in direction. But often they just add words and create limp sentences:

Wordy   There were delays and cost overruns that plagued construction of the Channel Tunnel. It had been the expectation of investors that they would see earnings soon after there were trains passing through the tunnel, but profits took years to materialize.

Concise   Delays and cost overruns plagued construction of the Channel Tunnel. Investors had expected to see earnings soon after trains began passing through the tunnel, but profits took years to materialize.

39f | Combining sentences

Often the information in two or more sentences can be combined into one tight sentence:

Wordy   An unexpected problem with the Channel Tunnel is stowaways. The stowaways are mostly illegal immigrants. They are trying to smuggle themselves into England. They cling to train roofs and undercarriages.

Concise   An unexpected problem with the Channel Tunnel is stowaways, mostly illegal immigrants who are trying to smuggle themselves into England by clinging to train roofs and undercarriages.

A number of exercises in this handbook give you practice in sentence combining. For a list, see "Sentence combining" in this book's index.

39g | Rewriting jargon

Jargon can refer to the special vocabulary of any discipline or profession (see p. 508). But it has also come to describe vague, inflated language that is overcomplicated, even incomprehensible. When such language comes from government or business, we call it *bureaucratese.*

Jargon	The weekly social gatherings stimulate networking by members of management from various divisions, with the aim of developing contacts and maximizing the flow of creative information.
Translation	The weekly parties give managers from different divisions a chance to meet and to share ideas.

Exercise 39.3 Revising: Conciseness

Rewrite each passage below into a single concise sentence, using the techniques described in this chapter.

Example:

He was taking some exercise in the park. Then several thugs were suddenly ahead of him in his path.

He was <u>exercising</u> [or <u>jogging</u> or <u>strolling</u>] in the park <u>when</u> several thugs suddenly <u>loomed</u> in his path.

1. Chewing gum was originally introduced to the United States by Antonio López de Santa Anna. He was the Mexican general.
2. After he had been defeated by the Texans in 1845, the general, who was exiled, made the choice to settle in New York.
3. A piece of chicle had been stashed by the general in his baggage. Chicle is the dried milky sap of the Mexican sapodilla tree.
4. There was more of this resin brought into the country by Santa Anna's friend Thomas Adams. Adams had a plan to make rubber.
5. The plan failed. Then the occasion arose for Adams to get a much more successful idea on the basis of the use to which the resin was put by General Santa Anna. That is, Adams decided to make a gum that could be chewed.

Exercise 39.4 Revising: Conciseness

Make the following passage as concise as possible. Be merciless.

At the end of a lengthy line of reasoning, he came to the conclusion that the situation with carcinogens [cancer-causing substances] should be regarded as similar to the situation with the automobile. Instead of giving in to an irrational fear of cancer, we should consider all aspects of the problem in a balanced and dispassionate frame of mind, making a total of the benefits received from potential carcinogens (plastics, pesticides, and other similar products) and measuring said total against the damage done by such products. This is the nature of most discussions about the automobile. Instead of responding irrationally to the visual, aural, and air pollution caused by automobiles, we have decided to live with them (while simultaneously working to improve on them) for the benefits brought to society as a whole.

40

Spelling and the Hyphen

English spelling is difficult, even for some very experienced and competent writers. You can train yourself to spell better, and this chapter will help you. But you can also improve instantly by acquiring the habits listed in the following box.

Ways to improve your spelling

- **Carefully proofread all your writing.** Use the proofreading tips on page 67 to help you find spelling errors.
- **Check a dictionary *every time* you doubt a spelling.** Being suspicious of your spellings and relying on a dictionary will take care of many potential spelling errors.
- **Create a list of your spelling errors.** Keep a record of words you misspell, and check the list every time you write a paper. With experience, you'll learn to recognize and correct the words you typically misspell.
- **Use a spelling checker critically.** A spelling checker can help you find spelling errors in your papers. However, its usefulness is limited because it can't spot the common error of confusing words with similar spellings, such as *now/not, to/too, their/they're/there,* and *principal/principle.* See pages 64–65 for more on spelling checkers.

40a Recognizing typical spelling problems

Spelling well involves recognizing situations that commonly lead to misspelling: pronunciation can mislead you in several ways; different forms of the same word may have different spellings; and some words have more than one acceptable spelling.

mycomplab

Visit *mycomplab.com* for more resources and exercises on spelling and the hyphen.

1 Being wary of pronunciation

In English, unlike some other languages, pronunciation of words is an unreliable guide to their spelling. The same letter or combination of letters may have different sounds in different words. (Say aloud these different ways of pronouncing the letters *ough: tough, dough, cough, through, bough.*) In addition, some words contain letters that are not pronounced clearly or at all, such as the *ed* in *asked,* the silent *e* in *swipe,* or the unpronounced *gh* in *tight.*

Pronunciation is a particularly unreliable guide in spelling **homonyms,** words pronounced the same though they have different spellings and meanings: *great/grate, to/too/two.* Some commonly confused homonyms and near-homonyms, such as *accept/except,* are listed below. (See p. 542 for tips on how to use spelling lists.)

Words commonly confused

accept (to receive)
except (other than)

affect (to have an influence on)
effect (a result)

all ready (prepared)
already (by this time)

allude (to refer to indirectly)
elude (to avoid)

allusion (an indirect reference)
illusion (an erroneous belief or
    perception)

ascent (a movement up)
assent (to agree, or an agreement)

bare (unclothed)
bear (to carry, or an animal)

board (a plane of wood)
bored (uninterested)

born (brought into life)
borne (carried)

brake (to stop)
break (to smash)

buy (to purchase)
by (next to)

capital (the seat of a government)
capitol (the building where a
    legislature meets)

cite (to quote an authority)
sight (the ability to see)
site (a place)

desert (to abandon)
dessert (after-dinner course)

discreet (reserved, respectful)
discrete (individual or distinct)

elicit (to bring out)
illicit (illegal)

eminent (well known)
imminent (soon to happen)

fair (average, or lovely)
fare (a fee for transportation)

forth (forward)
fourth (after *third*)

gorilla (a large primate)
guerrilla (a kind of soldier)

hear (to perceive by ear)
here (in this place)

heard (past tense of *hear*)
herd (a group of animals)

hole (an opening)
whole (complete)

its (possessive of *it*)
it's (contraction of *it is* or
    it has)

lead (heavy metal)
led (past tense of *lead*)

lessen (to make less)
lesson (something learned)

meat (flesh)
meet (to encounter, or a
   competition)

no (the opposite of *yes*)
know (to be certain)

passed (past tense of *pass*)
past (after, or a time gone by)

patience (forbearance)
patients (persons under medical
   care)

peace (the absence of war)
piece (a portion of something)

persecute (to oppress, to harass)
prosecute (to pursue, to take legal
   action against)

plain (clear)
plane (a carpenter's tool, or an
   airborne vehicle)

presence (the state of being at
   hand)
presents (gifts)

principal (most important, or the
   head of a school)
principle (a basic truth or law)

rain (precipitation)
reign (to rule)
rein (a strap for controlling an
   animal)

raise (to build up)
raze (to tear down)

right (correct)
rite (a religious ceremony)
write (to make letters)

road (a surface for driving)
rode (past tense of *ride*)

scene (where an action occurs)
seen (past participle of *see*)

seam (a junction)
seem (to appear)

stationary (unmoving)
stationery (writing paper)

straight (unbending)
strait (a water passageway)

their (possessive of *they*)
there (opposite of *here*)
they're (contraction of *they are*)

to (toward)
too (also)
two (following *one*)

waist (the middle of the body)
waste (discarded material)

weak (not strong)
week (Sunday through Saturday)

weather (climate)
whether (*if*, or introducing a
   choice)

which (one of a group)
witch (a sorcerer)

who's (contraction of *who is* or
   who has)
whose (possessive of *who*)

your (possessive of *you*)
you're (contraction of *you are*)

---

2 **Distinguishing between different forms of the same word**

Spelling problems may occur when forms of the same word have different spellings, as in the following examples.

Verbs and nouns

Verb	Noun	Verb	Noun
advise	advice	enter	entrance
describe	description	marry	marriage
speak	speech	omit	omission

Nouns and adjectives

Noun	Adjective	Noun	Adjective
comedy	comic	height	high
courtesy	courteous	Britain	British
generosity	generous		

Irregular verbs

begin, began, begun   know, knew, known
break, broke, broken   ring, rang, rung

Irregular nouns

child, children   shelf, shelves
goose, geese   tooth, teeth
mouse, mice   woman, women

Other differences

four, forty   thief, theft

3 Using preferred spellings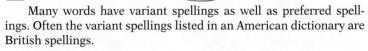

Many words have variant spellings as well as preferred spellings. Often the variant spellings listed in an American dictionary are British spellings.

American	British
color, humor	colour, humour
theater, center	theatre, centre
canceled, traveled	cancelled, travelled
judgment	judgement
realize	realise

40b Following spelling rules

Misspelling is often a matter of misspelling a syllable rather than the whole word. The following general rules focus on troublesome syllables, with notes for the occasional exceptions.

1 Distinguishing between *ie* and *ei*

Words like *believe* and *receive* sound alike in the second syllable, but the syllable is spelled differently. Use the familiar jingle to distinguish between *ie* and *ei:*

> *I* before *e*, except after *c,* or when pronounced "ay" as in *neighbor* and *weigh.*

i before *e*	believe	bier	hygiene
	grief	thief	friend

ei after *c*	ceiling	conceive	perceive
	receive	deceit	conceit
ei sounded	neighbor	weight	eight
as "ay"	sleigh	freight	vein

Exceptions In some words an *ei* combination neither follows *c* nor is pronounced "ay." These words include *either, neither, foreign, forfeit, height, leisure, weird, seize,* and *seizure.* This sentence might help you remember some of them: *The weird foreigner neither seizes leisure nor forfeits height.*

Exercise 40.1 Distinguishing between *ie* and *ei*

Insert *ie* or *ei* in the words below. Check doubtful spellings in a dictionary.

1. br__f
2. dec__ve
3. rec__pt
4. s__ze
5. for__gn
6. pr__st
7. gr__vance
8. f__nd
9. l__surely
10. ach__ve
11. pat__nce
12. p__rce
13. h__ght
14. fr__ght
15. f__nt
16. s__ve

---

2 | Keeping or dropping a final *e*

Many words end with an unpronounced or silent *e: move, brave, late, rinse.* Drop the final *e* when adding an ending that begins with a vowel:

advise + able = advisable
force + ible = forcible
surprise + ing = surprising
guide + ance = guidance

Keep the final, silent *e* when adding an ending that begins with a consonant:

battle + ment = battlement
accurate + ly = accurately
care + ful = careful
like + ness = likeness

Exceptions The silent *e* is sometimes retained before an ending beginning with a vowel. It is kept when *dye* becomes *dyeing,* to avoid confusion with *dying.* It is kept to prevent mispronunciation of words like *shoeing* (not *shoing*) and *mileage* (not *milage*). And the final *e* is often retained after a soft *c* or *g,* to keep the sound of the consonant soft rather than hard:

courageous
outrageous
changeable
manageable
noticeable
embraceable

The silent *e* is also sometimes *dropped* before an ending beginning with a consonant, when the *e* is preceded by another vowel:

argue + ment = argument
due + ly = duly
true + ly = truly

Exercise 40.2 Keeping or dropping a final *e*

Combine the following words and endings, keeping or dropping a final *e* as necessary to make correctly spelled words. Check doubtful spellings in a dictionary.

1. malice + ious
2. love + able
3. service + able
4. retire + ment
5. sue + ing
6. virtue + ous
7. note + able
8. battle + ing
9. suspense + ion

3 | Keeping or dropping a final *y*

Words ending in *y* often change their spelling when an ending is added to them. Change the final *y* to an *i* when it follows a consonant:

| beauty, beauties | worry, worried | supply, supplies |
| folly, follies | merry, merrier | deputy, deputize |

But keep the *y* when it follows a vowel, when the ending is -*ing*, or when it ends a proper name:

| day, days | cry, crying | May, Mays |
| obey, obeyed | study, studying | Minsky, Minskys |

Exercise 40.3 Keeping or dropping a final *y*

Combine the following words and endings, changing or keeping a final *y* as necessary to make correctly spelled words. Check doubtful spellings in a dictionary.

1. imply + s
2. messy + er
3. apply + ing
4. delay + ing
5. defy + ance
6. say + s
7. solidify + s
8. Murphy + s
9. supply + ed

4 | Doubling consonants

Whether to double a word's final consonant depends first on the number of syllables in the word. In one-syllable words, double the final consonant when a single vowel precedes the final consonant. Otherwise, don't double the consonant.

| slap, slapping | pair, paired |
| tip, tipping | park, parking |

In words of more than one syllable, double the final consonant when a single vowel precedes the final consonant *and* the consonant ends a stressed syllable once the ending is added. Otherwise, don't double the consonant.

refer, referring	refer, reference
begin, beginning	relent, relented
occur, occurrence	despair, despairing

Exercise 40.4 Doubling consonants

Combine the following words and endings, doubling final consonants as necessary to make correctly spelled words. Check doubtful spellings in a dictionary.

1. repair + ing	4. shop + ed	7. drip + ing
2. admit + ance	5. conceal + ed	8. declaim + ed
3. benefit + ed	6. allot + ed	9. parallel + ing

5 Attaching prefixes

Adding a prefix such as *dis*, *mis*, and *un* does not change the spelling of a word. When adding a prefix, do not drop a letter from or add a letter to the original word:

uneasy	anti-intellectual	defuse	misstate
unnecessary	disappoint	de-emphasize	misspell
antifreeze	dissatisfied	misinform	

(See also p. 547 for when to use hyphens with prefixes: *prehistory* versus *ex-student*.)

6 Forming plurals

Nouns

Most nouns form plurals by adding *s* to the singular form:

boy, boys	table, tables
carnival, carnivals	Murphy, Murphys

Some nouns ending in *f* or *fe* form the plural by changing the ending to *ve* before adding *s:*

leaf, leaves	wife, wives
life, lives	yourself, yourselves

Singular nouns ending in *s*, *sh*, *ch*, or *x* form the plural by adding *es:*

kiss, kisses	church, churches
wish, wishes	Jones, Joneses

(Notice that verbs ending in *s*, *sh*, *ch*, or *x* form the third-person singular in the same way. *Taxes* and *lurches* are examples.)

Nouns ending in *o* preceded by a vowel usually form the plural by adding *s:*

ratio, ratios	zoo, zoos

Nouns ending in *o* preceded by a consonant usually form the plural by adding *es:*

hero, heroes	tomato, tomatoes

Exceptions Some very common nouns form irregular plurals:

child, children   man, men
mouse, mice   woman, women

Some English nouns that were originally Italian, Greek, Latin, or French form the plural according to their original language:

analysis, analyses   datum, data
basis, bases   medium, media
beau, beaux   phenomenon, phenomena
crisis, crises   piano, pianos
criterion, criteria   thesis, theses

A few such nouns may form irregular or regular plurals: for instance, *index, indices, indexes; curriculum, curricula, curriculums.* The regular plural is more contemporary.

CULTURE LANGUAGE Noncount nouns do not form plurals, either regularly (with an added *s*) or irregularly. Examples of noncount nouns include *equipment, courage,* and *wealth.* (See p. 325.)

Compound nouns

Form plurals of compound nouns in one of two ways. Add *s* to the last word when the component words are roughly equal in importance, whether or not they are hyphenated:

city-states   breakthroughs
painter-sculptors   bucket seats

Add *s* to a noun combined with other parts of speech:

fathers-in-law   passersby

Note, however, that most modern dictionaries give the plural of *spoonful* as *spoonfuls.*

Exercise 40.5 Forming plurals

Make the correct plural of each of the following singular words. Check doubtful spellings in a dictionary.

1. pile	5. mile per hour	9. Bales	13. thief
2. donkey	6. box	10. cupful	14. goose
3. beach	7. switch	11. libretto	15. hiss
4. summary	8. sister-in-law	12. video	16. appendix

40c Developing spelling skills

The following techniques can help you improve your spelling. In addition, do not overrely on your computer's spelling checker (see pp. 64–65).

1 Editing and proofreading carefully

If spelling is a problem for you, give it high priority while editing your writing (p. 60) and again while proofreading, your last chance to catch misspelled words (p. 66). Reading a draft backward, word by word, can help you spot mistakes such as switched or omitted letters in words you know. Because the procedure forces you to consider each word in isolation, it can also highlight spellings you may be less sure of. A sense of uncertainty is crucial in spotting and correcting spelling errors, even for good spellers who make relatively few errors. Listen to your own uncertainty, and let it lead you to the dictionary.

2 Using a dictionary

How can you look up a word you can't spell? Start by guessing at the spelling and looking up your guess. If that doesn't work, pronounce the word aloud to come up with other possible spellings, and look them up. Unless the word is too specialized to be included in your dictionary, trial and error will eventually pay off.

If you're using a spelling checker, it may do the guessing for you by providing several choices for misspelled words. But you may still need to check a dictionary to verify your choice.

3 Pronouncing carefully

Careful pronunciation is not always a reliable guide to spelling (see p. 534), but it can keep you from misspelling words that are often mispronounced. For example:

athletics (*not* atheletics)	laboratory (*not* labratory)
disastrous (*not* disasterous)	library (*not* libary)
environment (*not* envirnment)	lightning (*not* lightening)
frustrate (*not* fustrate)	mischievous (*not* mischievious)
government (*not* goverment)	nuclear (*not* nucular)
height (*not* heighth)	recognize (*not* reconize)
history (*not* histry)	representative (*not* representive)
irrelevant (*not* irrevelant)	strictly (*not* stricly)

4 Tracking and analyzing your errors

Keep a list of the words marked "misspelled" or "spelling" or "sp" in your papers. This list will contain hints about your particular spelling problems, such as confusing *affect* and *effect* or forming plurals incorrectly. (If you need help analyzing the list, consult your writing instructor.) The list will also provide a personalized study guide, a focus for your efforts to spell better.

5 Using mnemonics

Mnemonics (pronounced with an initial *n* sound) are techniques for assisting your memory. The *er* in *letter* and *paper* can remind you that *stationery* (meaning "writing paper") has an *er* near the end; *stationary* with an *a* means "standing in place." Or the word *dome* with its long *o* sound can remind you that the building in which the legislature meets is spelled *capitol*, with an *o*. The *capital* city is spelled with *al* like *Albany*, the capital of New York. If you identify the words you have trouble spelling, you can think of your own mnemonics, which may work better for you than someone else's.

6 Studying spelling lists

Learning to spell commonly misspelled words will reduce your spelling errors. For general improvement, work with the following list of commonly misspelled words. Study only six or seven words at a time. If you are unsure of the meaning of a word, look it up in a dictionary and try using it in a sentence. Pronounce the word out loud, syllable by syllable, and write the word out. (The list of similar-sounding words on pp. 534–35 should be considered an extension of the following list.)

absence	aggressive	appropriate
abundance	all right	approximately
acceptable	all together	argument
accessible	allegiance	arrest
accidentally	almost	ascend
accommodate	a lot	assassinate
accomplish	already	assimilation
accumulate	although	assistance
accuracy	altogether	associate
accustomed	amateur	atheist
achieve	among	athlete
acknowledge	amount	attendance
acquire	analysis	audience
across	analyze	average
actually	angel	
address	annual	bargain
admission	answer	basically
adolescent	apology	because
advice	apparent	beginning
advising	appearance	belief
against	appetite	believe
aggravate	appreciate	beneficial

benefited
boundary
breath
Britain
bureaucracy
business

calculator
calendar
caricature
carrying
cede
ceiling
cello
cemetery
certain
changeable
changing
characteristic
chief
chocolate
choose
chose
climbed
coarse
column
coming
commercial
commitment
committed
committee
competent
competition
complement
compliment
conceive
concentrate
concert
condemn
conquer
conscience
conscious
consistency
consistent
continuous

controlled
controversial
convenience
convenient
coolly
course
courteous
criticism
criticize
crowd
cruelty
curiosity
curious
curriculum

deceive
deception
decide
decision
deductible
definitely
degree
dependent
descend
descendant
describe
description
desirable
despair
desperate
destroy
determine
develop
device
devise
dictionary
difference
dining
disagree
disappear
disappoint
disapprove
disastrous
discipline
discriminate

discussion
disease
disgusted
dissatisfied
distinction
divide
divine
division
doctor
drawer

easily
ecstasy
efficiency
efficient
eighth
either
eligible
embarrass
emphasize
empty
enemy
entirely
entrepreneur
environment
equipped
especially
essential
every
exaggerate
exceed
excellent
exercise
exhaust
exhilarate
existence
expense
experience
experiment
explanation
extremely

familiar
fascinate
favorite

February
fiery
finally
forcibly
foreign
foresee
forty
forward
friend
frightening
fulfill

gauge
generally
ghost
government
grammar
grief
guarantee
guard
guidance

happily
harass
height
heroes
hideous
humorous
hungry
hurriedly
hurrying
hypocrisy
hypocrite

ideally
illogical
imaginary
imagine
imitation
immediately
immigrant
incidentally
incredible
independence
independent
individually

inevitably
influential
initiate
innocuous
inoculate
insistent
integrate
intelligence
interest
interference
interpret
irrelevant
irresistible
irritable
island

jealousy
judgment

kindergarten
knowledge

laboratory
leisure
length
library
license
lieutenant
lightning
likelihood
literally
livelihood
loneliness
loose
lose
luxury
lying

magazine
maintenance
manageable
marriage
mathematics
meant
medicine
miniature

minor
minutes
mirror
mischievous
missile
misspelled
morale
morals
mortgage
mournful
muscle
mysterious

naturally
necessary
neighbor
neither
nickel
niece
ninety
ninth
noticeable
nuclear
nuisance
numerous

obstacle
occasion
occasionally
occur
occurrence
official
omission
omit
omitted
opinion
opponent
opportunity
opposite
ordinary
originally

paid
panicky
paralleled
parliament

particularly
peaceable
peculiar
pedal
perceive
perception
performance
permanent
permissible
persistence
personnel
perspiration
persuade
persuasion
physical
physiology
physique
pitiful
planning
playwright
pleasant
poison
politician
pollute
possession
possibly
practically
practice
prairie
precede
preference
preferred
prejudice
preparation
prevalent
primitive
privilege
probably
procedure
proceed
process
professor
prominent
pronunciation
psychology
purpose

pursue
pursuit

quandary
quantity
quarter
questionnaire
quiet
quizzes

realistically
realize
really
rebel
rebelled
recede
receipt
receive
recognize
recommend
reference
referred
relief
relieve
religious
remembrance
reminisce
renown
repetition
representative
resemblance
resistance
restaurant
rhyme
rhythm
ridiculous
roommate

sacrifice
sacrilegious
safety
satellite
scarcity
schedule
science
secretary

seize
separate
sergeant
several
sheriff
shining
shoulder
siege
significance
similar
sincerely
sophomore
source
speak
specimen
speech
sponsor
strategy
strength
strenuous
stretch
strict
strictly
studying
succeed
successful
sufficient
summary
superintendent
supersede
suppress
surely
surprise
suspicious

teammate
technical
technique
temperature
tendency
than
then
thorough
though
throughout
together

tomatoes	unnecessary	weather
tomorrow	until	Wednesday
tragedy	usable	weird
transferred	usually	wherever
truly		whether
twelfth	vacuum	wholly
tyranny	vegetable	woman
	vengeance	women
unanimous	vicious	writing
unconscious	villain	
undoubtedly	visible	yacht

40d Using the hyphen to form or divide words

The hyphen (-) is a mark of punctuation used either to form words or to divide them at the ends of lines.

1 Forming compound adjectives

When two or more words serve together as a single modifier before a noun, a hyphen or hyphens form the modifying words clearly into a unit:

> She is a well-known actor.
> The conclusions are based on out-of-date statistics.
> Some Spanish-speaking students work as translators.

When the same compound adjectives follow the noun, hyphens are unnecessary and are usually left out.

> The actor is well known.
> The statistics were out of date.
> Many students are Spanish speaking.

Hyphens are also unnecessary in compound modifiers containing an -ly adverb, even when the modifiers fall before the noun: *clearly defined terms; swiftly moving train.*

When part of a compound adjective appears only once in two or more parallel compound adjectives, hyphens indicate which words the reader should mentally join with the missing part:

> School-aged children should have eight- or nine-o'clock bedtimes.

2 Writing fractions and compound numbers

Hyphens join the numerator and denominator of fractions and the parts of the whole numbers twenty-one to ninety-nine:

three-fourths   twenty-four
one-half   eighty-seven

3 Forming coined compounds

Writers sometimes create (coin) temporary compounds and join the words with hyphens:

Muhammad Ali gave his opponent a come-and-get-me look.

4 Attaching some prefixes and suffixes

Do not use hyphens with prefixes except as follows:

- With the prefixes *self-, all-,* and *ex-: self-control, all-inclusive, ex-student.*
- With a prefix before a capitalized word: *un-American.*
- With a capital letter before a word: *T-shirt.*
- To prevent misreading: *de-emphasize, anti-intellectual.*

The only suffix that regularly requires a hyphen is *-elect,* as in *president-elect.*

5 Eliminating confusion

Hyphens can prevent possible confusion:

Confusing	Doonesbury is a comic strip character. [Is Doonesbury a comic (funny) character who strips or a character in a comic strip?]
Clear	Doonesbury is a comic-strip character.

Hyphens can also clarify words with added prefixes. For example, *recreation* (*creation* with the prefix *re-*) could mean either "a new creation" or "diverting, pleasurable activity." The use of a hyphen, *re-creation,* limits the word to the first meaning. Without a hyphen the word suggests the second meaning.

6 Dividing words at the ends of lines

You can avoid occasional short lines in your documents by dividing some words between the end of one line and the beginning of the next. On a word processor, you can set the program to divide words automatically at appropriate breaks (in the Tools menu, select Language and then Hyphenation). To divide words manually, follow these guidelines:

- **Divide words only between syllables**—for instance, *win-dows,* not *wi-ndows.* Check a dictionary for correct syllable breaks.

- **Never divide a one-syllable word.**
- **Leave at least two letters on the first line and three on the second line.** If a word cannot be divided to follow this rule (for instance, *a-bus-er*), don't divide it.
- **Break an electronic address only after a slash.** Do not hyphenate, because readers may perceive any added hyphens as part of the address.

Exercise 40.6 **Using hyphens in compound words**

Insert hyphens as needed in the following compounds. Mark all compounds that are correct as given. Consult a dictionary as needed.

1. reimburse
2. deescalate
3. forty odd soldiers
4. little known bar
5. seven eighths

6. seventy eight
7. happy go lucky
8. preexisting
9. senator elect
10. postwar

11. two and six person cars
12. ex songwriter
13. V shaped
14. reeducate

41

Planning a Research Project

Research writing gives you a chance to work like a detective solving a case. The mystery is the answer to a question you care about. The search for the answer leads you to consider what others think about your subject, but you do more than simply report their views. You build on them to develop and support your own opinion, and ultimately you become an expert in your own right.

Your investigation will be more productive and enjoyable if you take some steps described in this chapter: plan your work from the start (below), keep a research journal (facing page), find an appropriate subject and research question (p. 552), develop a strategy for your research (p. 554), and keep a working, annotated bibliography (p. 557).

41a Starting out

Research writing is a *writing* process:

- You work within a particular situation of subject, purpose, audience, and other factors (pp. 4–17).
- You gather ideas and information about your subject (pp. 18–28).
- You focus and arrange your ideas (pp. 29–45).
- You draft to explore your meaning (pp. 48–51).
- You revise and edit to develop, shape, and polish (pp. 52–69).

Although the process seems neatly sequential in this list, you know from experience that the stages overlap—that, for instance, you may begin drafting before you've gathered all the information you expect to find, and then while drafting you may discover a source that causes you to rethink your approach. Anticipating the process of research writing can free you to be flexible in your search and open to discoveries.

Visit *mycomplab.com* for more resources and exercises on planning a research project.

A thoughtful plan and systematic procedures can help you follow through on the diverse activities of research writing. One step is to make a schedule like the one below that apportions the available time to the necessary work. You can estimate that each segment marked off by a horizontal line will occupy *roughly* one-quarter of the total time—for example, a week in a four-week assignment or two weeks in an eight-week assignment. The most unpredictable segments are the first two, so get started early enough to accommodate the unexpected.

Complete
by:

_____ 1. Setting a schedule and beginning a research journal (here and below)

_____ 2. Finding a researchable subject and question (next page)

_____ 3. Developing a research strategy (p. 554)

_____ 4. Finding print and electronic sources (p. 560), and making a working, annotated bibliography (p. 557)

_____ 5. Evaluating and synthesizing sources (pp. 580, 593)

_____ 6. Gathering information from sources (p. 596), often using summary, paraphrase, and direct quotation (p. 597)

_____ 7. Taking steps to avoid plagiarism (p. 607)

_____ 8. Developing a thesis statement and creating a structure (p. 616)

_____ 9. Drafting the paper (p. 617), integrating summaries, paraphrases, and direct quotations into your ideas (p. 601)

_____ 10. Revising and editing the paper (p. 617)

_____ 11. Citing sources in your text (p. 614)

_____ 12. Preparing the list of works cited or references (p. 614)

_____ 13. Preparing the final manuscript (p. 617)

_____   Final paper due

41b Keeping a research journal

While working on a research project, carry a notebook or a computer with you at all times to use as a **research journal,** a place to record your activities and ideas. (See p. 21 on journal keeping.) In the journal's dated entries, you can write about the sources you consult, the leads you want to pursue, and any difficulties you encounter. Most important, you can record your thoughts about sources, leads, dead ends, new directions, relationships, and anything else that strikes you. The very act of writing in the journal can expand and clarify your thinking.

Note The research journal is the place to track and develop your own ideas. To avoid mixing up your thoughts and those of others, keep separate notes on what your sources actually say, using one of the methods discussed on pp. 596–97.

41c Finding a researchable subject and question

Before reading this section, review the suggestions given in Chapter 1 for finding and narrowing a writing subject (pp. 7–9). Generally, the same procedure applies to writing any kind of research paper. However, selecting and limiting a subject for a research paper can present special opportunities and problems. And before you proceed with your subject, you'll want to transform it into a question that can guide your search for sources.

1 Choosing an appropriate subject

Seek a research subject that interests you and that you care about. (It may be a subject you've already written about without the benefit of research.) Starting with your own views will motivate you, and you will be a participant in a dialog when you begin examining sources.

When you settle on a subject, ask the following questions about it. For each requirement, there are corresponding pitfalls.

■ **Are ample sources of information available on the subject?**

Avoid very recent subjects, such as a newly announced medical discovery or a breaking story in today's newspaper.

■ **Does the subject encourage research in the kinds and number of sources required by the assignment?**

Avoid (*a*) subjects that depend entirely on personal opinion and experience, such as the virtues of your hobby, and (*b*) subjects that require research in only one source, such as a straight factual biography.

■ **Will the subject lead you to an objective assessment of sources and to defensible conclusions?**

Avoid subjects that rest entirely on belief or prejudice, such as when human life begins or why women (or men) are superior. Your readers are unlikely to be swayed from their own beliefs.

■ **Does the subject suit the length of paper assigned and the time given for research and writing?**

Avoid broad subjects that have too many sources to survey adequately, such as a major event in history.

2 Posing a research question

Asking a question about your subject can give direction to your research by focusing your thinking on a particular approach. To discover your question, consider what about your subject intrigues or perplexes you, what you'd like to know more about. (See below for suggestions on using your own knowledge.)

Try to narrow your research question so that you can answer it in the time and space you have available. The question *How does human activity affect the environment?* is very broad, encompassing issues as diverse as pollution, distribution of resources, climate change, population growth, land use, biodiversity, and the ozone layer. In contrast, the question *How can buying environmentally friendly products help the environment?* or *How, if at all, should carbon emissions be taxed?* is much narrower. Each question also requires more than a simple *yes* or *no* answer, so that answering, even tentatively, demands thought about pros and cons, causes and effects.

As you read and write, your question will probably evolve to reflect your increasing knowledge of the subject, and eventually its answer will become your main idea, or thesis statement (see p. 616).

Exercise 41.1 Finding a topic and question

Choose three of the following subjects (or three subjects of your own), and narrow each one to at least one subject and question suitable for beginning work on a research paper. (This exercise can be the first step in a research-writing project that continues through Chapters 41–45.)

1. Bilingual education
2. National security and civil rights
3. Distribution of music by conventional versus electronic means
4. Dance in America
5. The history of women's suffrage
6. Genetically modified foods
7. Immigrants in the United States
8. Space exploration
9. Puritan religion and nineteenth-century American literature
10. The effect of television on professional sports
11. Child abuse
12. African Americans and civil rights
13. Tragedy in Greek drama
14. Computer piracy
15. The European exploration of North America before Columbus
16. Villains in the plays of William Shakespeare
17. Television evangelism
18. Science fiction
19. Treatment or prevention of AIDS in the United States or Africa

20. Water pollution
21. Women writers
22. Language in nineteenth-century English poetry
23. Comic film actors
24. An unsolved crime
25. Alternative fuels
26. Male and female heroes in modern fiction
27. Computers and the privacy of the individual
28. Gothic or romance novels in the nineteenth and twenty-first centuries
29. The social responsibility of business
30. Stem-cell research

41d Developing a research strategy

Before you start looking for sources, consider what you already know about your subject and where you are likely to find information on it.

1 Tapping into your own knowledge

Discovering what you already know about your topic will guide you in discovering what you don't know. Take some time to spell out facts you have learned, opinions you have heard or read elsewhere, and of course your own opinions. Use one of the discovery techniques discussed on pages 18–28 to explore and develop your ideas: keeping a journal, observing your surroundings, freewriting, brainstorming, drawing, and asking questions.

When you've explored your thoughts, make a list of questions for which you don't have answers, whether factual (*How much do Americans spend on green products?*) or more open-ended (*Are green products worth the higher prices?*). These questions will give you clues about the sources you need to look for first.

2 Setting goals for sources

For many research projects, you'll want to consult a mix of sources, as described on the next two pages. You may start by seeking the outlines of your topic—the range and depth of opinions about it—in reference works and articles in popular periodicals or through a Web search. Then, as you refine your views and your research question, you'll move on to more specialized sources, such as scholarly books and periodicals and your own interviews or surveys. (See pp. 564–78 for more on each kind of source.)

The mix of sources you choose depends heavily on your subject. For example, a paper on green consumerism would require the use of very recent sources because environmentally friendly products are fairly new to the marketplace. Your mix of sources may also be specified by your teacher or limited by the requirements of your assignment.

Library and Internet sources

The print and electronic sources available through your library—mainly reference works, periodicals, and books—have two big advantages over most of what you'll find on the open Web: they are cataloged and indexed for easy retrieval; and they are generally reliable, having been screened first by their publishers and then by the library's staff. In contrast, the Internet's retrieval systems are more difficult to use effectively, and Internet sources tend to be less reliable because most do not pass through any screening before being posted. (There are many exceptions, such as online scholarly journals and reference works. But these sources are generally available through your library's Web site as well.)

Most teachers expect research writers to consult library sources. But they'll accept Internet sources, too, if you have used them judiciously. Even with its disadvantages, the Internet can be a valuable resource for primary sources, current information, and a diversity of views. For guidelines on evaluating both library and Internet sources, see pages 580–92.

Primary and secondary sources

Use **primary sources** when they are available or are required by your assignment. These sources are firsthand accounts, such as works of literature, historical documents (letters, speeches, and so on), eyewitness reports (including articles by journalists who are on location), reports on experiments or surveys conducted by the writer, and your own interviews, experiments, observations, or correspondence.

Many assignments will allow you to use **secondary sources,** which report and analyze information drawn from other sources, often primary ones. Examples include a reporter's summary of a controversial issue, a historian's account of a battle, a critic's reading of a poem, and a psychologist's evaluation of several studies. Secondary sources may contain helpful summaries and interpretations that direct, support, and extend your own thinking. However, most research-writing assignments expect your own ideas to go beyond those in such sources.

Scholarly and popular sources

The scholarship of acknowledged experts is essential for depth, authority, and specificity. Most teachers expect students to emphasize scholarly sources in their research. But the general-interest views and information of popular sources can help you apply more scholarly approaches to daily life.

- **Check the title.** Is it technical, or does it use a general vocabulary?
- **Check the publisher.** Is it a scholarly journal (such as *Cultural Geographies*) or a publisher of scholarly books (such as Harvard University Press), or is it a popular magazine (such as *Consumer Reports* or *Newsweek*) or a publisher of popular books (such as Little, Brown)?
- **Check the length of periodical articles.** Scholarly articles are generally much longer than magazine and newspaper articles.
- **Check the author.** Have you seen the name elsewhere, which might suggest that the author is an expert?
- **Check the electronic address.** Addresses, or URLs, for Internet sources include an abbreviation that tells you something about the origin of the source: scholarly sources end in *edu, org,* or *gov,* while popular sources usually end in *com.* (See pp. 569–74 for more on types of online sources.)

Older and newer sources

Check the publication date. For most subjects a combination of older, established sources (such as books) and current sources (such as newspaper articles, interviews, or Web sites) will provide both background and up-to-date information. Only historical subjects or very current subjects require an emphasis on one extreme or another.

Impartial and biased sources

Seek a range of viewpoints. Sources that attempt to be impartial can offer an overview of your subject and trustworthy facts. Sources with clear biases can offer a diversity of opinion. Of course, to discover bias, you may have to read the source carefully (see pp. 580–92); but you can infer quite a bit just from a bibliographical listing.

- **Check the author.** You may have heard of the author as a respected researcher (thus more likely to be objective) or as a leading proponent of a certain view (less likely to be objective).
- **Check the title.** It may reveal something about point of view. (Consider these contrasting titles: "Go for the Green" versus "Green Consumerism and the Struggle for Northern Maine.")

Note Sources you find on the Internet must be approached with particular care. See pages 584–92.

Sources with helpful features

Depending on your topic and how far along your research is, you may want to look for sources with features such as illustrations (which can clarify important concepts), bibliographies (which can direct you to other sources), and indexes (which can help you develop keywords for electronic searches; see pp. 562–64).

Exercise 41.2 Developing a research strategy

Following the suggestions on page 554, write what you already know about the topic you selected in Exercise 41.1 (pp. 553–54), and then frame some questions for which you'll need to find answers. Also in writing, consider the kinds of sources you'll probably need to consult, using the categories given on the preceding pages.

41e Keeping a working, annotated bibliography

To track where sources are, compile a **working bibliography** as you uncover possibilities. When you have a substantial file—say, ten to thirty sources—you can decide which ones seem most promising and look them up first.

1 Tracking source information

When you turn in your paper, you will be expected to attach a list of the sources you have used. So that readers can check or follow up on your sources, your list must include all the information needed to find the sources, in a format readers can understand. (See pp. 614–15.) The box on the next page shows the information you should record for each type of source so that you will not have to retrace your steps later.

Note Whenever possible, record source information in the correct format for the documentation style you will be using. Then you will be less likely to omit needed information or to confuse numbers, dates, and other data when it's time to write your citations. This book describes four styles: MLA (p. 619), Chicago (p. 724), APA (p. 741), and CSE (p. 773). For others, consult one of the guides listed on pages 724, 741–42, and 773.

2 Annotating source information

Creating annotations for a working bibliography converts it from a simple list into a tool for assessing sources. When you discover a possible source, record not only its publication information but also the following:

- **What you know about the content of the source.** Periodical databases and book catalogs generally include abstracts, or summaries, of sources that can help with this part of the annotation.

■ **How you think the source may be helpful in your research.** Does it offer expert opinion, statistics, an important example, or a range of views? Does it place your subject in a historical, social, or economic context?

Information for a working bibliography

For books
Library call number
Name(s) of author(s), editor(s), translator(s), or others listed
Title and subtitle
Publication data:
  Place of publication
  Publisher's name
  Date of publication
Other important data, such as edition or volume number
Medium (print, Web, etc.)

For periodical articles
Name(s) of author(s)
Title and subtitle of article
Title of periodical
Publication data:
  Volume number and issue number (if any) in which article appears
  Date of issue
  Page numbers on which article appears
Medium (print, Web, etc.)

For electronic sources
Name(s) of author(s)
Title and subtitle of source
Title of Web site, periodical, or other larger work
Publication data, such as data listed above for a book or article; the publisher or sponsor of a Web site; and the date

of release, revision, or online posting
Any publication data for the source in another medium (print, film, etc.)
Format of online source (Web site or page, podcast, e-mail, etc.)
Date you consulted the source
Title of any database used to reach the source
Complete URL (but see the note below)
Digital Object Identifier, if any (for APA style)
Medium (Web, CD-ROM, etc.)

For other sources
Name(s) of author(s), creator(s), or others listed, such as a government department, recording artist, or photographer
Title of work
Format, such as unpublished letter, live performance, or photograph
Publication or production data:
  Publication title
  Publisher's or producer's name
  Date of publication, release, or production
Identifying numbers (if any)
Medium (print, typescript, etc.)

Note MLA documentation style does not require URLs for citations of most electronic sources; other styles do require them. Recording URLs will ensure that you have them if you need them and will make it easy to track down sources if you want to consult them again. For sources you reach through databases, record URLs only if they are usable by others outside your school. Most database URLs are unique to the search or the subscriber.

Taking the time with your annotations can help you discover gaps that may remain in your sources and will later help you decide which sources to pursue in depth. One student annotated a bibliography entry on his computer with a summary and a note on the source features he thought would be most helpful to him:

Entry for an annotated working bibliography

Gore, Al. *An Inconvenient Truth: The Planetary Emergency of Global Warming and What We Can Do about It*. Emmaus: Rodale, 2006. Print.
— Publication information for source

Book version of the documentary movie supporting Gore's argument that global warming is a serious threat to the planet. Includes summaries of scientific studies, short essays on various subjects, and dozens of images, tables, charts, and graphs. Last chapter offers several suggestions for ways to solve the problem, with an emphasis on changing individual buying habits.
— Summary of source
— Ideas on use of source

As you become more familiar with your sources, you can use your initial annotated bibliography to record your evaluations of them as well as more detailed thoughts on how they fit into your research.

Exercise 41.3 Compiling an annotated working bibliography

Prepare an annotated working bibliography of at least ten sources for a research paper on one of the following people or on someone of your own choosing. Begin by limiting the subject to a manageable size, posing a question about a particular characteristic or achievement of the person. Then consult reference works, periodical indexes, the library's book catalog, and the Web. (See pp. 564–76 for more on these resources.) For each source, record complete publication information as well as a summary and a note on the source's potential use.

1. Steven Jobs (a founder of Apple Computer), or another business entrepreneur
2. Ruth Bader Ginsburg, or another Supreme Court justice
3. Emily Dickinson, or another writer
4. Shaquille O'Neal, or another sports figure
5. Isamu Noguchi, or another artist

42

Finding Sources

This chapter discusses conducting electronic searches (next page) and taking advantage of the range of sources, both print and electronic, that you have access to: reference works (p. 564); books (p. 564); periodicals (p. 565); the Web (p. 569); other online sources (p. 572); government publications (p. 574); images, audio, and video (p. 574); and your own interviews, surveys, and other primary sources (p. 576).

Note As you look for sources, avoid the temptation to seek a "silver bullet"—that is, to locate two or three perfect sources that already say everything you want to say about your subject. Instead of merely repeating others' ideas, read and synthesize many sources so that you develop your own ideas. For more on synthesis, see pages 593–94.

42a | Starting with your library's Web site

As you conduct research, the Web will be your gateway to ideas and information. Always start with your library's Web site, not with a public search engine such as *Google*. The library site will lead you to vast resources, including books, periodical articles, and reference works that aren't available on the open Web. More important, unlike many sources on the open Web, every source you find on the library site will have passed through filters to ensure its value. A scholarly journal article, for instance, undergoes at least three successive reviews: subject-matter experts first deem it worth publishing in the journal; then a database vendor deems the journal worth including in the database; and finally your school's librarians deem the database worth subscribing to.

Google and other search engines may seem more user-friendly than the library's Web site and may seem to return plenty of sources for you to work with. Many of the sources may indeed be reliable and relevant to your research, but many more will not be. In the end, a library Web search will be more efficient and more

mycomplab

Visit *mycomplab.com* for more resources and exercises on finding sources.

A tip for researchers

Take advantage of two valuable resources offered by your library:

- **An orientation,** which introduces the library's resources and explains how to reach and use the Web site and the print holdings.
- **Reference librarians,** whose job it is to help you and others navigate the library's resources. Even very experienced researchers often consult reference librarians.

effective than a direct Web search. (For help with evaluating sources from any resource, see pp. 580–92.)

Note Start with the library's Web site, but don't stop there. Many books, periodicals, and other excellent sources are available only on library shelves, not online, and most instructors expect research papers to be built to some extent on these resources. When you spot promising print sources while browsing the library's online databases, make records of them and then look them up at the library.

42b Searching electronically

Searching electronically requires careful planning. Become familiar with the kinds of electronic resources available to you, understand the different search strategies they demand, and take the time to develop **keywords** that name your subject for databases and Web search engines.

1 Anticipating the kinds of electronic sources

Your school's library, its Web site, and the open Web offer several kinds of electronic resources that are suitable for academic research:

- **The library's catalog of holdings** is a database that lists all the resources that the library owns or subscribes to: books, magazines, newspapers, reference works, and more. The catalog may also include the holdings of other school libraries nearby or in your state.
- **Online databases** include indexes, bibliographies, and other reference works. They are your main route to articles in periodicals, providing publication information, summaries, and often full text. Your library subscribes to the databases and makes them available through its Web site. (You may also discover databases directly on the Web, but, again, the library is a more productive starting place.)

- **Databases on CD-ROM** include the same information as online databases, but they must be read at a library computer terminal. Increasingly, libraries are moving away from CD-ROMs in favor of online databases.
- **Full-text resources** contain the entire contents of articles, book chapters, and even whole books. The library's databases provide access to the full text of many listed sources. In addition, the Web sites of many periodicals and organizations, such as government agencies, offer the full text of articles, reports, and other publications.

2 Searching databases and the open Web

To develop keywords it helps to understand an important difference in how library databases and the open Web work:

- **A database indexes sources by authors, titles, publication years, and its own subject headings.** The subject headings reflect the database's directory of terms and are assigned by people who have read the sources. You can find these subject headings by using your own keywords until you locate a promising source. The information for the source will list the headings under which the database indexes it and other sources like it. (See p. 568 for an illustration.) You can then use those headings for further searches.
- **A Web search engine seeks your keywords in the titles and texts of sites.** The process is entirely electronic, so the results from a search engine will depend on how well your keywords describe your subject and anticipate the words used in sources. If you describe your subject too broadly or describe it specifically but don't match the vocabulary in relevant sources, your search will turn up few relevant sources and probably many that aren't relevant.

Ways to refine keywords

Most databases and many search engines work with **Boolean operators,** terms or symbols that allow you to expand or limit your keywords and thus your search.

- Use *AND* or **+** to narrow the search by including only sources that use all the given words. The keywords *green AND products* request only the sources in the shaded area.

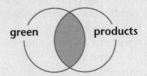

green   products

- Use *NOT* or − ("minus") to narrow the search by excluding irrelevant words. The keywords *green AND products NOT guide* exclude sources that use the word *guide:*

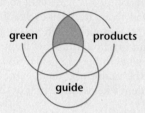

- Use *OR* to broaden the search by giving alternate keywords. The keywords *green AND products OR goods* allow for sources that use a synonym for *products:*

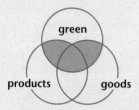

- Use parentheses or quotation marks to form search phrases. For instance, *(green products)* requests the exact phrase, not the separate words. Only sources using *green products* would turn up.
- Use wild cards to permit different versions of the same word. In *consum**, for instance, the wild card * indicates that sources may include *consume, consumer, consumerism,* and *consumption* as well as *consumptive, consumedly,* and *consummate.* The example suggests that you have to consider all the variations allowed by a wild card and whether it opens up your search too much. If you seek only two or three from many variations, you may be better off using *OR: consumption OR consumerism.* (Note that some systems use ?, :, or + for a wild card instead of *.)
- Be sure to spell your keywords correctly. Some search tools will look for close matches or approximations, but correct spelling gives you the best chance of finding relevant sources.

---

3 Refining keywords

Every database and search engine provides a system that you can use to refine your keywords for a productive search. The basic operations appear in the box above, but resources do differ. For instance, some assume that *AND* should link keywords, while others provide options specifying "Must contain all the words" and other equivalents for the operations in the box. You can learn a search engine's system by consulting its Advanced Search page.

Note You will probably have to use trial and error in developing your keywords, sometimes running dry (turning up few or no sources) and sometimes hitting uncontrollable gushers (turning up thousands or millions of mostly irrelevant sources). But the process is not busywork—far from it. Besides leading you eventually to worthwhile sources, it can also teach you a great deal about your subject: how you can or should narrow it, how it is and is not described by others, what others consider interesting or debatable about it, and what the major arguments are. See pages 571–72 for an example of a student's keyword search of the Web.

42c Finding reference works

Reference works, often available online, include encyclopedias, dictionaries, digests, bibliographies, indexes, atlases, almanacs, and handbooks. Your research *must* go beyond these sources, but they can help you decide whether your topic really interests you and whether it meets the requirements for a research paper (pp. 552–53). Preliminary research in reference works can also help you develop keywords for electronic searches and can direct you to more detailed sources on your topic.

You'll find many reference works through your library and directly on the Web. The following list gives general Web references for all disciplines:

Internet Public Library (*www.ipl.org*)
Library of Congress (*lcweb.loc.gov*)
LSU Libraries Webliography (*www.lib.lsu.edu/weblio.html*)
World Wide Web Virtual Library (*vlib.org*)

For Web sites in specific academic disciplines, see pages 705 (literature), 723–24 (other humanities), 740–41 (social sciences), and 771–72 (natural and applied sciences).

Note The Web-based encyclopedia *Wikipedia* (found at *wikipedia .org*) is one of the largest reference sites on the Internet. Like any encyclopedia, *Wikipedia* can provide background information for research on a topic; but unlike other encyclopedias, *Wikipedia* is a **wiki,** a kind of Web site that can be contributed to or edited by anyone. Ask your teacher whether *Wikipedia* is an acceptable source before you use it. If you do use it, you must carefully evaluate any information you find, using the guidelines on pages 584–92.

42d Finding books

Your library's catalog is searchable at a terminal in the library and via the library's Web site. You can search the catalog by author or title, of course, and by your own keywords or the headings found in *Library of Congress Subject Headings* (*LCSH*). The screen shot below shows the complete record for a book, including the *LCSH* headings that can be used to find similar sources.

Book catalog full record

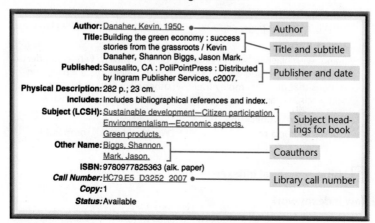

Author: Danaher, Kevin, 1950- — Author
Title: Building the green economy : success stories from the grassroots / Kevin Danaher, Shannon Biggs, Jason Mark. — Title and subtitle
Published: Sausalito, CA : PoliPointPress : Distributed by Ingram Publisher Services, c2007. — Publisher and date
Physical Description: 282 p. ; 23 cm.
Includes: Includes bibliographical references and index.
Subject (LCSH): Sustainable development—Citizen participation. Environmentalism—Economic aspects. Green products. — Subject headings for book
Other Name: Biggs, Shannon. Mark, Jason. — Coauthors
ISBN: 9780977825363 (alk. paper)
Call Number: HC79.E5 D3252 2007 — Library call number
Copy: 1
Status: Available

42e Finding periodicals

Periodicals include newspapers, journals, and magazines. Newspapers, the easiest to recognize, are useful for detailed accounts of past and current events. Journals and magazines can be harder to distinguish, but their differences are important.

Journals	Magazines
Examples	
American Anthropologist, Journal of Black Studies, Journal of Chemical Education	*The New Yorker, Time, Rolling Stone, People*
Availability	
Mainly through academic libraries, either on library shelves or in online databases	Public libraries, newsstands, bookstores, the open Web, and online databases
Purpose	
Advance knowledge in a particular field	Express opinion, inform, or entertain
Authors	
Specialists in the field	May or may not be specialists in their subjects

Journals	Magazines
Readers	
Often specialists in the field	Members of the general public or a subgroup with a particular interest
Source citations	
Source citations always included	Source citations rarely included
Length of articles	
Usually long, ten pages or more	Usually short, fewer than ten pages
Appearance	
Bland, with black-only type, little or no decoration, and only illustrations that directly amplify the text, such as graphs	Generally lively, with color, decoration (headings, sidebars, and other elements), and illustrations (drawings, photographs)
Frequency of publication	
Quarterly or less often	Weekly, biweekly, or monthly

1 Using periodical indexes

How indexes work

Periodical databases index the articles in journals, magazines, and newspapers. Often these databases include abstracts, or summaries, of the articles, and they may offer the full text of the articles as well. Your library subscribes to many periodical databases and to services that offer multiple databases. (See p. 569 for a list.) Most databases and services will be searchable through the library's Web site.

Note The search engine *Google* is developing *Google Scholar*, a search engine at *scholar.google.com* that seeks out scholarly articles. It is particularly useful for subjects that range across disciplines, for which discipline-specific databases can be too limited.

Selection of databases

To decide which databases to consult, you'll need to consider what you're looking for:

- **How broadly and deeply should you search?** Periodical databases vary widely in what they index. Some, such as *ProQuest*, cover many subjects but don't index the full range of periodicals in each subject. Others, such as *Historical Abstracts*, cover a single subject but then include most of the available periodicals. If your subject ranges across disciplines, then start with a broad database. If your subject focuses on a particular discipline, then start with a narrower database.
- **Which databases most likely include the kinds of resources you need?** The Web sites of many libraries allow you to narrow a database search to a particular kind of periodical (such as newspapers or journals) or to a particular discipline. You can

then discover each database's focus by checking the description of the database (sometimes labeled "Help" or "Guide") or the list of indexed resources (sometimes labeled "Publications" or "Index"). The description will also tell you the time period the database covers, so you'll know whether you also need to consult older print indexes at the library.

Database searches

When you first search a database, use your own keywords to locate sources, as illustrated in the following three screen shots. Your

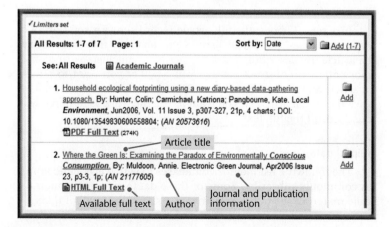

1. Initial keyword search of a periodical database

2. Partial keyword search results

3. Full article record with abstract

Title:	Where the Green Is: Examining the Paradox of Environmentally *Conscious Consumption.* ● —— Article title
	Find More Like This
Authors:	Muldoon, Annie goinggreenottawa@yahoo.ca ● —————— Author
Source:	Electronic Green Journal; Apr2006 Issue 23, p3-3, 1p
Document Type:	Article — Journal and publication information
Subject Terms:	*GREEN marketing *CONSUMERISM *GREEN products *ENVIRONMENTAL economics *CONSUMER protection *RECYCLED products *CONSUMER goods *NATURAL products *MARKETING — Database subject headings
	—— Abstract
Abstract:	The article discusses issues related to green consumerism. It also examines the merits and shortcomings of green consumerism. Green consumerism is defined as the purchasing and non-purchasing decisions made by consumers, based at least partly on environmental or social criteria. There is much debate about the value of green consumerism. Critics claim that environmentally conscientious shopping has negligible effects, does not address wider issues relating to the creation of needs and capitalism, and has been co-opted by advertisers as a **marketing** technique. One of the problems with green consumption, according to its detractors, is that it supports the corporate ideal that places environmental responsibility on the shoulders of individuals. Government regulation needs to be a part of the green consumerism movement. One way for this to happen is for governments to gradually increase the prices of natural resources, until they begin to reflect their full cost. Another possibility is government certified eco-labelling for products that are proven to exert less of a strain on the natural **environment**.
Persistent link to this record:	http://search.ebscohost.com/login.aspx?direct=true&db=aph&AN=21177605&site=ehost-live
Database:	Academic Search Complete ● ———————— Database

goal in using this procedure is to find at least one source that seems just right for your subject, so that you can see what subject headings the database itself uses for such sources. Using one or more of those headings will focus and speed your search.

The use of abstracts

In screen 3 above, the full article record shows a key feature of many databases' periodical listings: an **abstract** that summarizes the article. By describing research methods, conclusions, and other information, an abstract can tell you whether you want to pursue an article and thus save you time. However, the abstract cannot replace the actual article. If you want to use the work as a source, you must consult the full text.

Helpful databases

The following list includes databases to which academic libraries commonly subscribe. Some of these databases cover much the same material, so your library may not subscribe to all of them.

EBSCOhost. A periodical index covering magazines and journals in the social sciences, sciences, arts, and humanities. Many articles are available full-text.

InfoTrac. The Gale Group's general periodical index covering the social sciences, sciences, arts, and humanities as well as national news periodicals. It includes full-text articles.

LexisNexis. An index of news and business, legal, and reference information, with full-text articles. *LexisNexis* includes international, national, and regional newspapers, news magazines, legal and business publications, and court cases.

ProQuest. A periodical index covering the sciences, social sciences, arts, and humanities, including many full-text articles.

2 Locating periodicals

If an index listing does not include or link directly to the full text of an article, you'll need to consult the periodical itself. Recent issues of periodicals are probably held in the library's periodical area. Back issues are usually stored elsewhere, either in bound volumes or on film that requires a special machine to read. A librarian will show you how to operate the machine.

42f Finding sources on the Web

As an academic researcher, you enter the Web in two ways: through your library's Web site, and through public search engines such as *Yahoo!* and *Google.* The library entrance, covered in the preceding sections, is your main path to the books and periodicals that, for most subjects, should make up most of your sources. The public entrance, discussed here, can lead to a wealth of information and ideas, but it also has a number of disadvantages:

- **The Web is a wide-open network.** Anyone with the right hardware and software can place information on the Internet, and even a carefully conceived search can turn up sources with widely varying reliability: journal articles, government documents, scholarly data, term papers written by high school students, sales pitches masked as objective reports, wild theories. You must be especially diligent about evaluating Internet sources (see pp. 584–92).
- **The Web changes constantly.** No search engine can keep up with the Web's daily additions and deletions, and a source you find today may be different or gone tomorrow. You should not put off consulting an online source that you think you may want to use.

- **The Web provides limited information on the past.** Sources dating from before the 1980s or even more recently probably will not appear on the Web.
- **The Web is not all-inclusive.** Most books and many periodicals are available only via the library, not directly via the Web.

Clearly, the Web warrants cautious use. It should not be the only resource you work with.

1 Using a search engine

To find sources on the Web, you use a **search engine** that catalogs Web sites in a series of directories and conducts keyword searches. Generally, use a directory when you haven't yet refined your topic or you want a general overview. Use keywords when you have refined your topic and you seek specific information.

Current search engines

The box below lists popular search engines. To reach any one of them, enter its address in the Address or Location field of your Web browser.

Web search engines

The features of search engines change often, and new ones appear constantly. For the latest on search engines, see the links collected by *Easy Searcher* at *easysearcher.com*.

Directories that review sites

BUBL Link (bubl.ac.uk)
ipl2 (ipl.org)
Internet Scout Project (scout.wisc.edu/archives)
Librarians' Internet Index (lii.org)

Search engines

AlltheWeb (alltheweb.com)
AltaVista (altavista.com)
Ask.com (ask.com)
Bing (bing.com)
Dogpile (dogpile.com)
Factbites (factbites.com)
Google (google.com)
Livesearch.com (livesearch.com)
MetaCrawler (metacrawler.com)
Yahoo! (yahoo.com)

Note For a good range of reliable sources, try out more than a single search engine, perhaps as many as four or five. No search engine can catalog the entire Web—indeed, even the most powerful engine may not include half the sites available at any given time, and most engines include only a fifth or less. In addition, most search engines accept paid placements, giving higher billing to sites that pay a fee. These so-called sponsored links are usually marked as such, but they can compromise a search engine's method for arranging sites in response to your keywords.

Customized searches

The home page of a search engine includes a field for you to type your keywords into. Generally, it will also include an Advanced Search link that you can use to customize your search. For instance, you may be able to select a range of dates, a language, or a number of results to see. Advanced Search will also explain how to use operators such as *AND* and *NOT* to limit or expand your search.

Search records

Your Web browser includes functions that allow you to keep track of Web sources and your search:

- Use *Favorites* or *Bookmarks* **to save site addresses as links.** Click one of these terms near the top of the browser screen to add a site you want to return to. A favorite or bookmark remains on file until you delete it.
- Use *History* **to locate sites you have visited before.** The browser records visited sites for a certain period, such as a single online session or a week's sessions. (After that period, the history is deleted.) If you forgot to bookmark a site, you can click History or Go to locate your search history and recover the site.

2 Following a sample search

The sample Web search that follows illustrates how the refinement of keywords can narrow a search to maximize the relevant hits and minimize the irrelevant ones. Justin Malik, a student researching the environmental effects of green consumer products, first used the keywords *green consumption* on *Google*. But, as shown on screen 1 on the next page, the search produced more than 3.4 *million* hits, an unusably large number and a sure sign that Malik's keywords needed revision.

After several tries, Malik arrived at *"green consumption" "environmental issues"* to describe his subject more precisely. He then added *site:.org* to limit the results to nonprofit organizations. Narrowed in this way, Malik's search still produced 387 hits, but this large number included many potential sources on the first few screens, as shown on screen 2 on the next page.

1. First *Google* search results

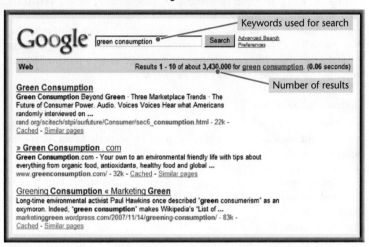

2. *Google* results with refined keywords

42g Finding other online sources

Several online sources can put you directly in touch with experts and others whose ideas and information may inform your research. Because these sources, like Web sites, are unfiltered, you must always evaluate them carefully. (See pp. 589–92.)

1 Using e-mail

As a research tool, e-mail allows you to communicate with others who are interested in your topic. You might, for instance, carry on an e-mail conversation with a teacher at your school or interview an expert in another state to follow up on a scholarly article he or she published. (See pp. 790–93 for more on using e-mail.)

2 Using blogs

Blogs (Web logs) are personal sites on which an author posts time-stamped comments, generally centering on a common theme, in a format that allows readers to respond to the author or to each other. You can find a directory of blogs at *blogcatalog.com*.

Like all other online media discussed in this section, blogs consulted as potential sources must be evaluated carefully. Some are reliable sources of opinion, news, or evolving scholarship, and many refer to worthy books, articles, Web sites, and other resources. But lots of blogs are little more than outlets for their authors' gripes and prejudices. See pages 589–92 for tips on telling the good from the bad.

3 Using discussion lists

A **discussion list** (sometimes called a **listserv** or just a **list**) uses e-mail to connect individuals who are interested in a common subject, often with a scholarly or technical focus. By sending a question to an appropriate list, you may be able to reach scores of people who know something about your topic. For an index of discussion lists, see *tile.net/lists*.

When conducting research on a discussion list, follow the guidelines for writing e-mail (pp. 790–93) as well as these:

- *Lurk* for a while—read without posting messages. Make sure the discussion is relevant to your topic, and get a sense of how the group interacts.
- **Consult the list's archive.** Your question may already have been answered.
- **Don't ask for information you can find elsewhere.** Most list members are glad to help with legitimate questions but resent messages that rehash familiar debates or that ask them to do someone else's work.
- **Evaluate messages carefully.** Many list subscribers are passionate experts with fair-minded approaches to their topics, but almost anyone with an Internet connection can post a message to a list. See pages 589–92 on evaluating online sources.

4 Using Web forums and newsgroups

Web forums and newsgroups are more open and less scholarly than discussion lists, so their messages require even more diligent evaluation. **Web forums** allow participants to join a conversation simply by selecting a link on a Web page. For a directory of forums, see *delphiforums.com*. **Newsgroups** are organized under subject headings such as *soc* for social issues and *biz* for business. For a directory of newsgroups, see *groups.google.com*.

42h Finding government publications

Government publications provide a vast array of data, reports, policy statements, public records, and other historical and contemporary information. For US government publications, consult the Government Printing Office's *GPO Access* at *www.gpoaccess.gov*. Also helpful is *Google US Government Search* (*google.com/unclesam*) because it returns *.gov* (government) and *.mil* (military) documents and its ranking system emphasizes the most useful documents. Many federal, state, and local government agencies post important publications—legislation, reports, press releases—on their own Web sites. You can find lists of sites for various federal agencies by using the keywords *United States federal government* with a search engine. Use the name of a state, city, or town with *government* for state and local information.

42i Finding images, audio, and video

Images, audio, and video can be used as both primary and secondary sources in a research project. A painting, an advertisement, or a video of a speech might be the subject of a paper and thus a primary source. A podcast of a radio interview with an expert on your subject or a college lecture might serve as a secondary source. Because many of these sources are unfiltered—they can be posted by anyone—you must always evaluate them as carefully as you would any source you find on the open Web.

Note You must also cite every image, audio, and video source fully in your paper, just as you cite text sources, with author, title, and publication information. In addition, some sources will require that you seek permission from the copyright holder, either the source itself or a third party such as a photographer or the creator of video. Permission is especially likely to be required if you are submitting your paper on the public Web. See pages 613–14 for more about online publication.

1 Finding images

The use of images to support an argument is discussed on pages 226-29. To find images, you have a number of options.

- **Scout for images while reading sources.** Your sources may include charts, graphs, photographs, and other images that can support your ideas. When you find an image you may want to use, photocopy or download it so you'll have it available later.
- **Create your own images,** such as photographs or charts. See pages 123–26 for examples.
- **Use an image search engine.** *Google, Yahoo!, AlltheWeb,* and some other search engines conduct specialized image searches. They can find scores of images, but the results may be inaccurate or incomplete because the sources surveyed often do not include descriptions of the images. (The engines will search file names and any text accompanying the images.)
- **Use a public image database.** The following sites generally conduct accurate searches because their images are filed with information such as a description of the image, the artist's name, and the image's date:

  Adflip (adflip.com): Historical and contemporary print advertisements
  Duke University, *Ad*Access (library.duke.edu/digitalcollections/adaccess):* Print advertisements spanning 1911–55
  Library of Congress, *American Memory (memory.loc.gov/ammem):* Maps, photographs, and prints documenting the American experience
  Library of Congress, *Prints and Photographs Online Catalog (loc.gov/rr/print/catalog.html):* Images from the library's collection, including those available through *American Memory*
  New York Public Library Digital Gallery (digitalgallery.nypl.org/nypldigital): Maps, drawings, photographs, and paintings from the library's collection
  Political Cartoons (politicalcartoons.com): Cartoons on contemporary issues and events

- **Use a public image directory.** The following sites collect links to image sources:

  Art Source (ilpi.com/artsource/general.html): Sources on art and architecture
  Museum Computer Network (mcn.edu/resources/sitesonline.htm): Museum collections
  MuseumLink's Museum of Museums (museumlink.com): Links to museums all over the world
  Washington State University, *Popular Culture: Resources for Critical Analysis (wsu.edu/~amerstu/pop):* Sources on advertising, fashion, magazines, toys, and other artifacts of popular culture
  Yale University Arts Library, *Image Resources (library.yale.edu/art):* Sources on the visual and performing arts

■ **Use a subscription database.** Your library may subscribe to the following resources:

ARTstor: Museum collections and a database of images typically used in art history courses

Associated Press, *AccuNet/AP Multimedia Archives*: Historical and contemporary news images

Grove Art Online: Art images and links to museum sites

Many images you find will be available for free, but some sources do charge a fee for use. Before paying for an image, check with a librarian to see if it is available elsewhere for free.

2 | Finding audio and video

Audio and video, widely available on the Web and on CD-ROM, can provide your readers with the experience of "being there." For example, if you are researching the media response to Martin Luther King's famous "I Have a Dream" speech and you are publishing your paper electronically, you might insert links to the speech and to TV and radio coverage of it.

■ **Audio files** such as podcasts, Webcasts, and CDs record radio programs, interviews, speeches, lectures, and music. They are available on the Web and through your library. Online sources of audio include Congress's *American Memory* (see the previous page) and podcasts at www.podcastdirectory.com.

■ **Video files** capture performances, public presentations and speeches, news events, and other activities. They are available on the Web and through your library on DVD. Online sources of video include the Library of Congress's *American Memory* (see the previous page); *YouTube*, which includes commercials, historical footage, current events, and much more (*youtube.com*); and search engines such as *Google* (*video.google.com*).

42j | Generating your own sources

Academic writing will often require you to conduct primary research for information of your own. For instance, you may need to analyze a poem, conduct an experiment, or interview an expert. Three common forms of primary research are observation, personal interviews, and surveys.

1 | Observing

Observation can be an effective way to gather fresh information on your subject. You may observe in a controlled setting—for instance, watching the behavior of children playing in a child-development lab. Or you may observe in a more open setting—for instance, watching the interactions among students at a cafeteria on your campus. Be sure your observation has a well-defined purpose that relates to your research project. Throughout the observation, take careful notes, either on paper or on a handheld computer, and always record the date, time, and location for each session.

2 Conducting personal interviews

An interview can be especially helpful for a research project because it allows you to ask questions precisely geared to your topic. You can conduct an interview in person, over the telephone, or online. A personal interview is preferable if you can arrange it, because you can see the person's expressions and gestures as well as hear his or her tone.

Here are a few guidelines for interviews:

- **Call or write for an appointment.** Tell the person exactly why you are calling, what you want to discuss, and how long you expect the interview to take. Be true to your word on all points.
- **Prepare a list of open-ended questions to ask**—perhaps ten or twelve for a one-hour interview. Plan on doing some research for these questions to discover background on the issues and your subject's published views on the issues.
- **Pay attention to your subject's answers** so that you can ask appropriate follow-up questions. Take care in interpreting answers, especially if you are online and thus can't depend on facial expressions, gestures, and tone of voice to convey the subject's attitudes.
- **Keep thorough notes.** Take notes during an in-person or telephone interview, or record the interview if you have the equipment and your subject agrees. For online interviews, save the discussion in a file of its own.
- **Verify quotations.** Before you quote your subject in your paper, check with him or her to ensure that the quotations are accurate.
- **Send a thank-you note immediately after the interview.** Promise your subject a copy of your finished paper, and send the paper promptly.

3 Conducting surveys

Asking questions of a defined group of people can provide information about respondents' attitudes, behavior, backgrounds, and expectations. Use the following tips to plan and conduct a survey:

- **Decide what you want to find out.** The questions you ask should be dictated by your purpose. Formulating a **hypothesis** about your subject—a generalization that can be tested—will help you refine your purpose.

- **Define your population.** Think about the kinds of people your hypothesis is about—for instance, elderly women or preschool children. Plan to sample this population so that your findings will be representative.
- **Write your questions.** Surveys may contain closed questions that direct the respondent's answers (checklists and multiple-choice, true/false, or yes/no questions) or open-ended questions that allow brief, descriptive answers. Avoid loaded questions that reveal your own biases or make assumptions about subjects' answers.
- **Test your questions.** Use a few respondents with whom you can discuss the answers. Eliminate or recast questions that respondents find unclear, discomforting, or unanswerable.
- **Tally the results.** Count the actual numbers of answers, including any nonanswers.
- **Seek patterns in the raw data.** Such patterns may confirm or contradict your hypothesis. Revise the hypothesis or conduct additional research if necessary.

Exercise 42.1 Using the library

To become familiar with the research sources available through your library, visit both the library and its Web site for answers to the following questions. Ask a librarian for help whenever necessary.

1. Which resources does the library include on its Web site? Which resources require a visit to the library?
2. Where are reference books stored in the library? How are they cataloged and arranged? Which ones are available through the Web site? Where and in what format(s) are (a) *Contemporary Authors,* (b) *Encyclopaedia Britannica,* and (c) *Congressional Quarterly?*
3. Where is the catalog of the library's periodicals? Where and in what format(s) does the library have current and back issues of the following periodicals: (a) the *New York Times,* (b) *Time* magazine, and (c) *Psychology Today?*
4. What tools does the library's Web site offer for finding periodical databases that are appropriate for a particular research subject?
5. Research the focus and indexed publications of two periodical databases, such as *Academic Search Complete, LexisNexis,* or *ProQuest.* What disciplines does each database seem most suited for?
6. Does the book catalog cover all of the library's book holdings? If not, which books are not included, and where are they cataloged?
7. What are the library call numbers of the following books: (a) *The Power Broker,* by Robert Caro; (b) *Heart of Darkness,* by Joseph Conrad; and (c) *The Hero with a Thousand Faces,* by Joseph Campbell?

Exercise 42.2 Finding library sources

Locate at least six promising articles and books for the subject you began working on in the previous chapter (Exercise 41.1, p. 553, and Exercise 41.2, p. 557). Consider the sources "promising" if they seem directly to address your central research question. Following the guidelines on pages 557–59, make an annotated working bibliography of the sources. Be sure to include all the information you will need to acknowledge the sources in your final paper.

Exercise 42.3 Finding Web sources

Use at least two Web search engines to locate six or seven promising sources for your research project. Begin by developing a list of keywords that can be used to query one of the search engines (see pp. 562–63). Then try your keywords on the other search engine as well. How do the results differ? What keyword strategies worked best for finding relevant information? Add promising sources to your annotated working bibliography.

43

Working with Sources

Research writing is much more than finding sources and reporting their contents. The challenge and interest come from interacting with and synthesizing sources: reading them critically to discover their meanings, judge their relevance and reliability, and create relationships among them; and using them to extend and support your own ideas so that you make your subject your own.

CULTURE LANGUAGE Making a subject your own requires thinking critically about sources and developing independent ideas. These goals may at first be uncomfortable if your native culture emphasizes understanding and respecting established authority more than questioning and enlarging it. The information here will help you work with sources so that you can become an expert in your own right and convincingly convey your expertise to others.

mycomplab

Visit *mycomplab.com* for more resources and exercises on working with sources.

43a Evaluating sources

Before you gather information and ideas from sources, scan them to evaluate what they have to offer and how you might use them.

Note In evaluating sources, you need to consider how they come to you. The sources you find through the library, both in print and on the Web, have been previewed for you by their publishers and by the library's staff. They still require your critical reading, but you can have some confidence in the information they contain. With online sources you reach directly, however, you can't assume similar previewing, so your critical reading must be especially rigorous. Special tips for evaluating Web sites and other online sources begin on page 584.

1 Judging relevance and reliability

Not all the sources you find will prove worthwhile: some may be irrelevant to your subject, and others may be unreliable. Gauging the relevance and reliability of sources is the essential task of evaluating them. If you haven't already done so, read this book's chapter on critical thinking and reading (pp. 139–63). It provides a foundation for answering the questions in the following box.

Questions for evaluating sources

For online sources, supplement these questions with those on pages 584 and 589.

Relevance

- **Does the source devote some attention to your subject?** Does it focus on your subject or cover it marginally? How does it compare to other sources you've found?
- **Is the source appropriately specialized for your needs?** Check the source's treatment of a topic you know something about, to ensure that it is neither too superficial nor too technical.
- **Is the source up to date enough for your subject?** When was it published? If your subject is current, your sources should be, too.

Reliability

- **Where does the source come from?** Did you find it through your library or directly through the Internet? (If the latter, see pp. 584–92.) Is the source popular or scholarly?
- **Is the author an expert in the field?** Check the author's credentials in a biography (if the source includes one), in a biographical reference, or by a keyword search of the Web.

- **What is the author's bias?** How do the author's ideas relate to those in other sources? What areas does the author emphasize, ignore, or dismiss?
- **Is the source fair, reasonable, and well written?** Does it provide sound reasoning and a fair picture of opposing views? Is the tone calm and objective? Is the source logically organized and error-free?
- **Are the author's claims well supported?** Does the author provide accurate, relevant, representative, and adequate evidence to back up his or her claims? Does the author cite sources, and if so are they reliable?

2 Evaluating library sources

To evaluate sources you find through your library, either in print or on the library's Web site, look at dates, titles, summaries, introductions, headings, author biographies, and any source notes. The following criteria expand on the most important tips in the preceding box. On the next two pages you can see how Justin Malik applied these criteria to two print sources, a magazine article and a journal article, that he consulted while researching green consumerism.

Identify the origin of the source.

Check whether a library source is popular or scholarly. Scholarly sources, such as refereed journals and university press books, are generally deeper and more reliable, though some popular sources, such as first-hand newspaper accounts and books for a general audience, are often appropriate for research projects.

Check the author's expertise.

The authors of scholarly publications tend to be experts whose authority can be verified. Check the source to see whether it contains a biographical note about the author, check a biographical reference, or check the author's name in a keyword search of the Web. Look for other publications by the author and for his or her job and any affiliation, such as teacher at a university, researcher with a nonprofit organization, author of general-interest books, or writer for popular magazines.

Identify the author's bias.

Every author has a point of view that influences the selection and interpretation of evidence. You may be able to learn about an author's bias from biographies, citation indexes, and review indexes. But also look at the source itself. How do the author's ideas relate to those in other sources? What areas does the author emphasize, ignore, or dismiss? When you're aware of sources' biases, you can attempt to balance them.

(continued on p. 584)

Evaluating library sources

Opposite are sample pages from two library sources that Justin Malik considered for his paper on green consumerism. Malik evaluated the sources using the questions and guidelines on pages 580–81.

Makower	Jackson
Origin	
Interview with Joel Makower published in *Vegetarian Times*, a popular magazine.	Article by Tim Jackson published in *Journal of Industrial Ecology*, a scholarly journal sponsored by two reputable universities: MIT and Yale.
Author	
Gives Makower's credentials at the beginning of the interview: the author of a book on green products and of a monthly newsletter on green businesses. Quotes another source that calls Makower the "guru of green business practice."	Includes a biography at the end of the article that describes Jackson as a professor at the University of Surrey (UK) and lists his professional activities related to the environment.
Bias	
Describes and promotes green products. Concludes with an endorsement of a for-profit Web site that tracks and sells green products.	Presents multiple views of green consumerism. Argues that a solution to environmental problems will involve green products and less consumption but in different ways than currently proposed.
Reasonableness and writing	
Presents Makower's data and perspective on distinguishing good from bad green products, using conversational writing in an informal presentation.	Presents and cites opposing views objectively, using formal academic writing.
Source citations	
Lacks source citations for claims and data.	Includes more than three pages of source citations, many of scholarly and government sources and all cited within the article.
Assessment	
Probably unreliable: Despite Makower's reputation, the article comes from a nonscholarly source, takes a one-sided approach to consumption, and depends on statistics credited only to Makower.	**Probably reliable:** The article comes from a scholarly journal, the author is an expert in the field, he discusses many views and concedes some, and his source citations confirm evidence from reliable sources.

First and last pages of an interview with Joel Makower, published in *Vegetarian Times*

Largest manufacturer of renewable energy equipment in the United States?	Largest buyer of green energy in the United States?	Largest buyer of fair-trade coffee in the world?
General Electric	Johnson & Johnson	Starbucks

q:
Who are they?

q:
Can we really do too much in our own homes?

a:
Sure. I live in the house where I grew up. We've made a series of eco-friendly renovations, using wood that is harvested in a sustainable way...

green-rated products

go for the green

buying beer? sneakers? a car?
the most eco-conscious companies
aren't always the most obvious

interview by alan pell crawford

www.vegetariantimes.com *87*

STATE OF THE DEBATE

Live Better by Consuming Less?

Is There a "Double Dividend" in Sustainable Consumption?

Tim Jackson

Keywords
consumer behavior
consumer choice
consumer culture
evolutionary psychology
industrial ecology
symbolic interactionism

...This article explores some of these wider debates. In particular, it draws attention to a fundamental disagreement that runs through the literature on consumption and haunts the debate on sustainable consumption: the question of whether or to what extent, consumption can be taken as 'good for us.' Some approaches assume that increasing consumption is more or less synonymous with improved well-being: the more we consume the better off we are. Others argue, just as vehemently, that the scale of consumption in modern society is both environmentally and psychologically damaging, and that we could reduce consumption significantly without threatening the quality of our lives. This second viewpoint suggests that a kind of 'double dividend' is inherent in sustainable consumption: the ability to live better by consuming less and reduce our impact on the environment in the process. In the final analysis, this article argues, such 'win-win' solutions may exist but will require a concerted societal effort to realize.

UNEP (United Nations Development Programme) 1998. Human development report 1998. Oxford, UK: Oxford University Press.
UNEP (United Nations Environment Programme) 2001. Consumption opportunities: Strategies for change. Paris: UNEP.
Van den Bergh, J. C. J. M., A. Ferrer-i-Carbonell, and G. Munda. 2000. Alternative models of individual behaviour and implications for environmental policy. Ecological Economics 32(1): 43–61.

About the Author
Tim Jackson is Professor of Sustainable Development at the Centre for Environmental Strategy (CES) in the University of Surrey, Guildford, United Kingdom. He currently holds a research fellowship in sustainable consumption funded by the Economic and Social Research Council and leads the Ecological Economics Research Group at CES. He is also chair of the Economics Steering Group of the U.K. Sustainable Development Commission and sits on the U.K. Round Table on Sustainable Consumption.

First and last pages of an article by Tim Jackson, published in the *Journal of Industrial Ecology*

(continued from p. 581)

Determine whether the source is fair, reasonable, and well written.

Even a strongly biased work should present solid reasoning and give balanced coverage to opposing views—all in an objective tone. Any source should be organized logically and should be written in clear, error-free sentences. The absence of any of these qualities should raise a warning flag.

Analyze support for the author's claims.

Evidence should be accurate, relevant to the argument, representative of its context, and adequate for the point being made (see p. 184). The author's sources should themselves be reliable.

3 Evaluating Web sites

To a great extent, the same critical reading that helps you evaluate library sources will help you evaluate Web sites that you reach directly. But most Web sites have not undergone prior screening by editors and librarians. On your own, you must distinguish scholarship from corporate promotion, valid data from invented statistics, well-founded opinion from clever propaganda.

The strategy summarized in the box below can help you make such distinctions. On pages 586–87 you can see how Justin Malik applied this strategy to two Web sites that he consulted while researching green consumerism.

Questions for evaluating Web sites

Supplement these questions with those on pages 580–81.

- **What type of site are you viewing?** What does the type lead you to expect about the site's purpose and content?
- **Who is the author or sponsor?** How credible is the person or group responsible for the site?
- **What is the purpose of the site?** What does the site's author or sponsor intend to achieve?
- **What does context tell you?** What do you already know about the site's subject that can inform your evaluation? What kinds of support or other information do the site's links provide?
- **What does presentation tell you?** Is the site's design well thought out and effective? Is the writing clear and error-free?
- **How worthwhile is the content?** Are the site's claims well supported by evidence? Is the evidence from reliable sources? When was the site last updated?

Note To evaluate a Web document, you'll often need to travel to the site's home page to discover the author or sponsor, date of publication, and other relevant information. The page you're reading may include a link to the home page. If it doesn't, you can find it by editing the URL in the Address or Location field of your browser. Working backward, delete the end of the URL up to the last slash and hit Enter. Repeat this step until you reach the home page. There you may also find a menu option, often labeled "About," that will lead you to a description of the site's author or sponsor.

Determine the type of site.

When you search the Web, you're likely to encounter various types of sites. Although they overlap—a primarily informational site may include scholarship as well—the types can usually be identified by their content and purposes. Here are the main types:

- **Scholarly sites:** These sites have a knowledge-building interest and include research reports with supporting data and extensive documentation of scholarly sources. The URLs of the sites generally end in *edu* (originating from an educational institution), *org* (a nonprofit organization), or *gov* (a government department or agency). Such sites are more likely to be reliable than the others described below.

- **Informational sites:** Individuals, nonprofit organizations, corporations, schools, and government bodies all produce sites intended to centralize information on particular subjects. The sites' URLs may end in *edu, org, gov,* or *com* (originating from a commercial organization). Such sites generally do not have the knowledge-building focus of scholarly sites and may omit supporting data and documentation, but they can provide useful information and often include links to scholarly sources.

- **Advocacy sites:** Many sites promote certain policies or actions. Their URLs usually end in *org,* but they may end in *edu* or *com*. Some advocacy sites include serious, well-documented research to support their positions, but others select or distort evidence.

- **Commercial sites:** Corporations and other businesses maintain Web sites to explain or promote themselves or to sell goods and services. The URLs of commercial sites end in *com*. The information on such a site furthers the sponsor's profit-making purpose, but it can include reliable data.

- **Personal sites:** The sites maintained by individuals range from diaries of a family's travels to opinions on political issues to reports on evolving scholarship. The sites' URLs usually end in *com* or *edu*. Personal sites are only as reliable as their authors, but some do provide valuable eyewitness accounts, links to worthy sources, and other usable information. A particular kind of personal site, the blog, is discussed on pages 573 and 589–92.

(continued on p. 588)

Evaluating Web sites

Opposite are screen shots from two Web sites that Justin Malik considered for his paper on green consumerism. Malik evaluated the sources using the questions in the boxes on pages 580–81 and 584.

Allianz Knowledge Partnersite	*Nature Reports: Climate Change*
Author and sponsor	
Site sponsor is the Allianz Group, a global insurance company partnering with well-known organizations to provide information on a variety of issues. Author of article is identified as an editor, not a scientist.	Listed authors are scientists, experts on climate change. (Biographies appear at the end of the article.) Site sponsor is the Nature Publishing Group, which also publishes the reputable science journal *Nature*.
Purpose and bias	
Educational page on a corporate-sponsored Web site with the self-stated purpose of gathering information about global issues and making it available to an international audience.	Informational site with the self-stated purpose of providing "authoritative, in-depth reporting on climate change and its wider implications for policy, society and the economy." Article expresses bias toward reducing pollution to stop climate change.
Context	
One of many sites publishing current information on climate issues.	One of many sites publishing current research on climate issues.
Presentation	
Clean, professionally designed site with mostly error-free writing.	Clean, professionally designed site with error-free writing.
Content	
Article gives basic information about climate change and provides links to other pages that expand on its claims. Probably because of the intended general (nonscientist) audience, the pages do not include citations of scholarly research.	Article is current (date above the title) and clearly explains the science of climate change with references and links to scholarly sources. Other links connect to hundreds of articles elsewhere on the site about climate-related topics.
Assessment	
Probably unreliable: Despite the wealth of information in the article and its links, the material lacks the scholarly source citations necessary for its use as evidence in an academic paper.	**Probably reliable:** The article has an explicit bias toward stopping climate change, but the site sponsor has a scholarly reputation, the authors are climate-change experts, and the references cite many scholarly and government sources.

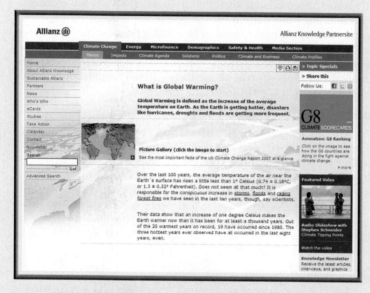

Article published on the Web site *Allianz Knowledge Partnersite*

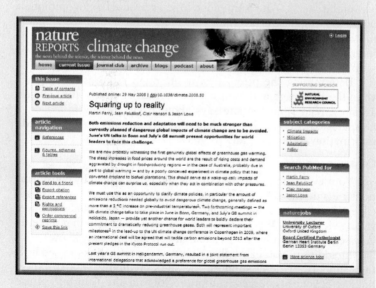

Article published on the Web site *Nature Reports: Climate Change*

(continued from p. 585)

Note Informational sites called wikis allow anyone to contribute and edit information on the site. Older entries on reputable wikis, such as *Wikipedia*, tend to be reliable because they have been reviewed and edited by experts, but recent entries may contain errors and even misinformation. Ask your teacher whether wikis are acceptable sources. If so, evaluate them carefully against other, more reliable sources using the following guidelines.

Identify the author and sponsor.

A reputable site will list its authors, will name the group responsible for the site, and will provide information or a link for contacting the author and the sponsor. If none of this information is provided, you should not use the source. If you have only the author's or the sponsor's name, you may be able to discover more in a biographical dictionary, through a keyword search, or in your other sources. Make sure the author and the sponsor have expertise on the subject they're presenting: if an author is a doctor, for instance, what is he or she a doctor of?

Gauge purpose and bias.

A Web site's purpose determines what ideas and information it offers. Inferring that purpose tells you how to interpret what you see on the site. If a site is intended to sell a product or an opinion, it will likely emphasize favorable ideas and information while ignoring or even distorting what is unfavorable. In contrast, if a site is intended to build knowledge—for instance, a scholarly project or journal—it will likely acknowledge diverse views and evidence.

Determining the purpose of a site often requires looking beyond the first page and beneath the surface of words and images. To start, read what the site says about itself, usually found on a page labeled "About." Be suspicious of any site that doesn't provide information about itself and its goals.

Consider context.

Your evaluation of a Web site should be informed by considerations outside the site itself. Chief among these is your own knowledge. What do you already know about the site's subject and the prevailing views of it? Where does this site seem to fit into that picture? What can you learn from this site that you don't already know?

In addition, you can follow some of the site's links to see how they support, or don't support, the site's credibility. For instance, links to scholarly sources lend authority to a site—but *only* if the scholarly sources actually relate to and back up the site's claims.

Look at presentation.

Considering both the look of a site and the way it's written can illuminate its intentions and reliability. Are the site's elements all functional and well integrated, or is the site cluttered with irrelevant material and graphics? Does the site seem carefully constructed and well maintained, or is it sloppy? Does the design reflect the apparent purpose of the site, or does it undercut or conceal that purpose in some way? Is the text clearly written, or is it difficult to understand? Is it error-free, or does it contain typos and grammatical errors?

Analyze content.

With information about a site's author, purpose, and context, you're in a position to evaluate its content. Are the ideas and information current, or are they dated? (Check the publication date.) Are they slanted and, if so, in what direction? Are the views and data authoritative, or do you need to balance them—or even reject them? Are claims made on the site supported by evidence drawn from reliable sources? These questions require close reading of both the text and its sources.

4 | Evaluating other online sources

Blogs, online discussions, and online images, video, and audio require the same critical scrutiny as Web sites do. Blogs and discussion groups can be sources of reliable data and opinions, but you will also encounter wrong or misleading data and skewed opinions. One podcast may provide an interview with a recognized expert while another claims authority that it doesn't deserve. A *YouTube* search using "I have a dream" brings up videos of Martin Luther King, Jr., delivering his famous speech as well as videos of people speaking hatefully about King and the speech.

Use the following strategy for evaluating such online sources. See the next two pages for Justin Malik's use of this strategy with a blog he found while researching green consumerism.

Questions for evaluating blogs, online discussions, images, video, and audio

Supplement these questions with those on pages 580–81.

- **Who is the author or creator?** How credible is he or she?
- **What is the author's or creator's purpose?** What can you tell about why the author or creator is publishing the work?
- **What does the context reveal?** What do other responses to the work, including responses to a blog posting or the other messages in a discussion thread, indicate about the source's balance and reliability?
- **How worthwhile is the content?** Are the claims made by the author or creator supported by evidence? Is the evidence from reliable sources?
- **How does the source compare with other sources?** Do the claims made by the author or creator seem accurate and fair given what you've seen in sources you know to be reliable?

Evaluating a blog

Opposite is a screen shot from a blog that Justin Malik consulted for his paper on green consumerism. Malik evaluated the blog against the questions in the boxes on pages 580–81 and 589.

Author and sponsor

Listed author is a climate scientist. (A link provides her credentials.) Blog sponsor is the Environmental Defense Fund, a nonprofit organization operating for more than forty years.

Purpose and bias

Advocacy site and blog with self-stated purpose of drawing on "science, economics, and law to create . . . solutions to society's most urgent environmental problems." Urges site visitors to join the organization and donate money to support its work. Posting assumes readers are somewhat familiar with the science of climate change.

Context

One of many blogs advocating and enlisting readers in action against climate change.

Presentation

Clean, professionally designed site with error-free writing.

Content

Posting is current (date under the title) and clearly explains recent findings with links to government and scholarly sources.

Assessment

Probably reliable: The site sponsor has a bias toward environmental causes, but it has a strong reputation, the author of the blog posting is an expert, and the posting cites reliable sources.

Identify the author or creator.

Checking out the author or creator of a blog, online posting, video file, or podcast can help you judge its reliability. If the author or creator uses a screen name, write directly to him or her requesting full name and credentials. Do not use the source if you don't get a response. Once you know the person's name, you may be able to obtain background information from a keyword search of the Web or a biographical dictionary.

You can also get a sense of the interests and biases of an author or creator by tracking down his or her other publications. For a blog, check whether the author cites or links to other writing. For a discussion-group posting, look for an archive or other feature that allows you to find additional messages by the same author. For multimedia sources, try to gain an overview of the creator's work.

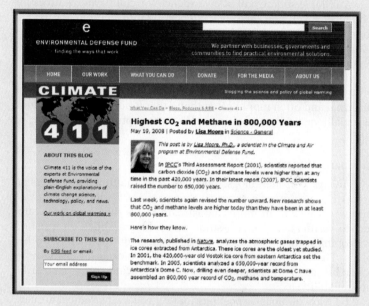

Posting on the blog *Climate 411*, sponsored by the
Environmental Defense Fund

Analyze the author's or creator's purpose.

What can you tell about *why* the author or creator is publishing
the work? Look for claims, the use (or lack) of evidence, and the
treatment of opposing views. All these convey the person's stand on
the subject and general fairness, and they will help you position the
source among your other sources.

Consider the context.

Blogs, discussion-group postings, and multimedia sources are
often difficult to evaluate in isolation. Looking beyond a particular contribution to the responses of others will give you a sense of
how the author or creator is regarded. On a blog, look at the comments others have posted. Do the same with postings, going back
to the initial posting in the discussion thread and reading forward.

Analyze content.

A reliable source will offer evidence for claims and sources for evidence. If you don't see such supporting information, ask the author or creator for it. (If he or she fails to respond, don't use the source.) Then verify the sources with your own research: are they reputable?

The tone of writing can also be a clue to its purpose and reliability. Blogs, online discussions, and some podcasts tend to be more informal and often more heated than other kinds of dialog, but look especially critically at writing that's contemptuous, dismissive, or shrill.

Compare with other sources.

Always consider blogs, postings, and multimedia sources in comparison to other sources so that you can distinguish singular, untested views from more mainstream views that have been subject to verification. Don't assume that a blog author's information and opinions are mainstream just because you see them on other blogs. The technology allows content to be picked up instantly by other blogs, so widespread distribution indicates only popularity, not reliability.

Be wary of blogs or postings that reproduce periodical articles, reports, or other publications. Try to locate the original version of the publication to be sure it has been reproduced fully and accurately, not quoted selectively or distorted. If you can't locate the original version, don't use the publication as a source.

Exercise 43.1 Evaluating a source

Imagine that you are researching a paper on the advertising techniques that are designed to persuade consumers to buy products. You have listed the following book in your working bibliography:

Vance Packard, *The Hidden Persuaders,* revised edition, 1981.

On your own or with your classmates (as your teacher wishes), obtain this book from a library and evaluate it as a source for your paper. Use the guidelines on pages 580–81.

Exercise 43.2 Evaluating Web sites

Find and evaluate two Web sites: a commercial site, such as Microsoft's or Apple's, and a site for a nonprofit organization, such as the American Medical Association or Greenpeace. What do you know or can you infer about each site's sponsor or author? What seems to be the site's purpose or purposes? What do the site's links contribute? How effective is the site's design? How reliable do you judge the site's information to be? How do the two sites differ in these respects?

Exercise 43.3 Evaluating a blog

Visit *bloglines.com* or *blogcatalog.com* to find a blog on a controversial subject such as stem-cell research or online sharing of music files. Who is responsible for the blog? What can you tell about its purpose? How reliable do you judge its ideas and information to be?

Exercise 43.4 Evaluating an online discussion

Using *groups.google.com,* locate a newsgroup on a subject that interests you. (If you already participate in an online discussion group, you can use it instead.) Pick one series of at least ten related messages on a single topic. Write a brief summary of each message (see pp. 136–37 on summarizing). Then analyze and synthesize the messages to develop a one- or two-paragraph evaluation of the discussion. Which messages seem reliable? Which don't? Why?

43b Synthesizing sources

When you begin to locate the differences and similarities among sources, you move into the most significant part of research writing: forging relationships for your own purpose. This **synthesis** is an essential step in reading sources critically, and it continues through the drafting and revision of a research paper. As you infer connections—say, between one writer's opinions and another's or between two works by the same author—you create new knowledge.

Your synthesis of sources will grow more detailed and sophisticated as you proceed through the process of working with sources described in the balance of this chapter: gathering information from sources (pp. 596–97); deciding whether to summarize, paraphrase, or quote directly from sources (pp. 597–600); and integrating sources into your sentences (pp. 601–06). Unless you are analyzing primary sources such as the works of a poet, at first read your sources quickly and selectively to obtain an overview of your subject and a sense of how the sources approach it (pp. 601–06). Don't get bogged down in gathering detailed information, but *do* record your ideas about sources in your research journal (p. 551) or your annotated bibliography (p. 557).

Respond to sources.

Write down what your sources make you think. Do you agree or disagree with the author? Do you find his or her views narrow, or do they open up new approaches for you? Is there anything in the source that you need to research further before you can understand it? Does the source prompt questions that you should keep in mind while reading other sources?

Connect sources.

When you notice a link between sources, jot it down. Do two sources differ in their theories or their interpretations of facts? Does one source illuminate another—perhaps commenting or clarifying or supplying additional data? Do two or more sources report studies that support a theory you've read about or an idea of your own?

Heed your insights.

Apart from ideas prompted by your sources, you are sure to come up with independent thoughts: a conviction, a point of confusion that suddenly becomes clear, a question you haven't seen anyone else ask. These insights may occur at unexpected times, so it's good practice to keep a notebook or computer handy to record them.

Draw your own conclusions.

As your research proceeds, the responses, connections, and insights you form through synthesis will lead you to answer your starting research question with a statement of your thesis (see p. 616). They will also lead you to the main ideas supporting your thesis—conclusions you have drawn from your synthesis of sources, forming the main divisions of your paper.

Use sources to support your conclusions.

Effective synthesis requires careful handling of evidence from sources so that it meshes smoothly into your sentences and yet is clearly distinct from your own ideas. When drafting your paper, make sure that each paragraph focuses on an idea of your own, with the support for the idea coming from your sources. Generally, open each paragraph with your idea, provide evidence from a source or sources with appropriate citations, and close with an interpretation of the evidence. (Avoid ending a paragraph with a source citation; instead, end with your own idea.) In this way, your paper will synthesize others' work into something wholly your own. For more on structuring paragraphs in academic writing, see pages 166–67.

Exercise 43.5 Synthesizing sources

The three passages below address the same issue, the legalization of drugs. What similarities do you see in the authors' ideas? What differences? Write a paragraph of your own in which you use these authors' views as a point of departure for your own view about drug legalization.

Perhaps the most unfortunate victims of drug prohibition laws have been the residents of America's ghettos. These laws have proved largely futile in deterring ghetto-dwellers from becoming drug abusers, but they do account for much of what ghetto residents identify as the drug problem. Aggressive, gun-toting drug dealers often upset law-abiding residents far more than do addicts nodding out in doorways. Meanwhile other residents perceive the drug dealers as heroes and successful role models. They're symbols of success to children who see no other options. At the same time the increasingly harsh criminal penalties imposed on adult drug dealers have led drug traffickers to recruit juveniles. Where once children started dealing drugs only after they had been using them for a few years, today the sequence is often reversed. Many children start using drugs only after working for older drug dealers for a while. Legalization of drugs, like legalization of alcohol in the 1930s, would drive the drug-dealing business off the streets and out of apartment buildings and into government-regulated, tax-paying stores. It also would force many of the gun-toting dealers out of the business and convert others into legitimate businessmen.

—Ethan A. Nadelmann, "Shooting Up"

Statistics argue against legalization. The University of Michigan conducts an annual survey of twelfth graders, asking the students about their drug consumption. In 1980, 56.4 percent of those polled said they had used marijuana in the past twelve months, whereas in 2007 only 41.7 percent had done so. Cocaine use was even more reduced in the same period (22.6 percent to 7.8 percent). At the same time, twelve-month use of legally available drugs—alcohol and nicotine-containing cigarettes—remained constant at about 72 percent and 55 percent, respectively. The numbers of illegal drug users haven't declined nearly enough: those teenaged marijuana and cocaine users are still vulnerable to addiction and even death, and they threaten to infect their impressionable peers. But clearly the prohibition of illegal drugs has helped, while the legal status of alcohol and cigarettes has not made them less popular.

—Sylvia Runkle, "The Case Against Legalization"

I have to laugh at the debate over what to do about the drug problem. Everyone is running around offering solutions—from making drug use a more serious criminal offense to legalizing it. But there isn't a real solution. I know that. I used and abused drugs, and people, and society, for two decades. Nothing worked to get me to stop all that behavior except just plain being sick and tired. Nothing. Not threats, not ten-plus years in prison, not anything that was said to me. I used until I got through. Period. And that's when you'll win the war. When all the dope fiends are done. Not a minute before.

—Michael W. Posey, "I Did Drugs Until They Wore Me Out. Then I Stopped."

Exercise 43.6 Evaluating and synthesizing sources

Look up the sources in the working bibliography you made in Exercises 42.2 and 42.3 (p. 579). Evaluate the sources for their relevance and reliability. If the sources seem unreliable or don't seem to give you what you need, expand your working bibliography and evaluate the new sources. In your research journal or annotated bibliography, write down your responses to sources, the connections you perceive among sources, and other original ideas that occur to you.

43c Gathering information from sources

You can accomplish a great deal of synthesis while gathering information from your sources. This information gathering is not a mechanical process. Rather, as you read you assess and organize the information in your sources.

Researchers vary in their methods for working with sources, but all methods share the same goals:

- **Keep accurate records of what sources say.** Accuracy helps prevent misrepresentation and plagiarism.
- **Keep accurate records of how to find sources.** These records are essential for retracing steps and for citing sources in the final paper. (See pp. 557–59 on keeping a working bibliography.)
- **Synthesize sources.** Information gathering is a critical process, leading to an understanding of sources, the relationships among them and your own ideas, and their support for your ideas.

To achieve these goals, you can take handwritten notes, type notes into your computer, annotate photocopies or printouts of sources, or annotate downloaded documents. On any given project, you may use all the methods. Each has advantages and disadvantages.

- **Handwritten notes:** Taking notes by hand is especially useful if you come across a source with no computer or photocopier handy. But handwritten notes can be risky. It's easy to introduce errors as you work from source to paper. And it's possible to copy source language and then later mistake and use it as your own, thus plagiarizing the source. Always take care to make accurate notes and to place big quotation marks around any passage you quote.
- **Notes on computer:** Taking notes on a computer can streamline the path of source to note to paper because you can import the notes into your draft as you write. However, computer notes have the same disadvantages as handwritten notes: the risk of introducing errors and the risk of plagiarizing. As with handwritten notes, be a stickler for accuracy and use quotation marks for quotations.
- **Photocopies and printouts:** Photocopying from print sources or printing out online sources each has the distinct advantages of convenience and reduction in the risks of error and plagiarism during information gathering. But each method has disadvantages, too. The busywork of copying or printing can distract you from the crucial work of synthesizing sources. And you have to make a special effort to annotate copies and printouts with the publication information for sources. If you

don't have this information for your final paper, you can't use the source.

■ **Downloads:** Researching online, you can usually download full-text articles, Web pages, discussion-group messages, and other materials onto your computer. While drafting, you can import source information from one file into another. Like photocopies and printouts, though, downloads can distract you from interacting with sources and can easily become separated from the publication information you must have in order to use the sources. Even more important, directly importing source material creates a high risk of plagiarism. You must keep clear boundaries between your own ideas and words and those of others.

43d Using summary, paraphrase, and quotation

Deciding whether to summarize, paraphrase, or quote directly from sources is an important step in synthesizing the sources' ideas and your own. You engage in synthesis when you use your own words to summarize an author's argument or paraphrase a significant example or when you select a significant passage to quote. Choosing summary, paraphrase, or quotation should depend on why you are using a source.

Note Summaries, paraphrases, and quotations all require source citations. A summary or paraphrase without a source citation or a quotation without quotation marks and a source citation is plagiarism. (See pp. 607–14 for more on plagiarism.)

1 Summarizing

When you **summarize,** you condense an extended idea or argument into a sentence or more in your own words. A full discussion of summary appears on pages 136–37, and you should read that section if you have not already done so.

Summary is most useful when you want to record the gist of an author's idea without the background or supporting evidence. Following is a passage from a scholarly essay about consumption and its impact on the environment. Then a sample computer note shows a summary of the passage.

Original quotation

Such intuition is even making its way, albeit slowly, into scholarly circles, where recognition is mounting that ever-increasing pressures on ecosystems, life-supporting environmental services, and critical natural cycles are driven not only by the sheer number of resource users and the inefficiencies of their resource use, but also by the patterns of resource use themselves. In global environmental policymaking arenas, it is becoming more and more difficult to ignore the fact that the overdeveloped North must restrain its consumption if it expects the underdeveloped South to embrace a more sustainable trajectory.

—Thomas Princen, Michael Maniates, and Ken Conca, "Confronting Consumption," p. 4

Summary of source

Environmental consequences of consumption

Princen, Maniates, and Conca 4

Overconsumption may be a more significant cause of environmental problems than increasing population is.

---

2 Paraphrasing

When you **paraphrase,** you follow much more closely the author's original presentation, but you restate it using your own words and sentence structures. Paraphrase is most useful when you want to present or examine an author's line of reasoning but you don't feel the original words merit direct quotation. Here is a paraphrase of the quotation from the essay "Confronting Consumption."

Paraphrase of source

Environmental consequences of consumption

Princen, Maniates, and Conca 4

Scholars are coming to believe that consumption is partly to blame for changes in ecosystems, reduction of essential natural resources, and changes in natural cycles. Policy makers increasingly see that wealthy nations have to start consuming less if they want developing nations to adopt practices that reduce pollution and waste. Rising population around the world does cause significant stress on the environment, but consumption is increasing even more rapidly than population.

Notice that the paraphrase follows the original but uses different words and different sentence structures. In contrast, an unsuccessful paraphrase—one that plagiarizes—copies the author's words or sentence structures or both *without quotation marks.* (See p. 611 for examples.)

Paraphrasing a source

- **Read the relevant material several times to be sure you understand it.**
- **Restate the source's ideas in your own words and sentence structures.** You need not put down in new words the whole passage or all the details. Select what is relevant to your topic, and restate only that. If complete sentences seem too detailed or cumbersome, use phrases.
- **Be careful not to distort meaning.** Don't change the source's emphasis or omit connecting words, qualifiers, and other material whose absence will confuse you later or cause you to misrepresent the source.

CULTURE LANGUAGE If English is not your native language and you have difficulty paraphrasing the ideas in sources, try this. Before attempting a paraphrase, read the original passage several times. Then, instead of "translating" line by line, try to state the gist of the passage without looking at it. Check your effort against the original to be sure you have captured the source author's meaning and emphasis without using his or her words and sentence structures. If you need a synonym for a word, look it up in a dictionary.

3 Quoting

Your notes from sources may include many quotations, especially if you rely on photocopies, printouts, or downloads. Whether to use a quotation in your draft, instead of a summary or paraphrase, depends on how important the exact words are and on whether the source is primary or secondary (p. 555):

- **Quote extensively when you are analyzing primary sources,** such as literary works and historical documents. The quotations will often be both the target of your analysis and the chief support for your ideas.
- **Quote selectively when you are drawing on secondary sources.** Favor summaries and paraphrases over quotations, and put every quotation to both tests in the box on the next page. Most papers of ten or so pages should not need more than two or three quotations that are longer than a few lines each.

When you quote a source, either in your notes or in your draft, take precautions to avoid plagiarism or misrepresentation of the source:

- **Copy the material carefully.** Take down the author's exact wording, spelling, capitalization, and punctuation.

Tests for direct quotations from secondary sources

The author's original satisfies one of these requirements:

- The language is unusually vivid, bold, or inventive.
- The quotation cannot be paraphrased without distortion or loss of meaning.
- The words themselves are at issue in your interpretation.
- The quotation represents and emphasizes a body of opinion or the view of an important expert.
- The quotation emphatically reinforces your own idea.
- The quotation is an illustration, such as a graph, diagram, or table.

The quotation is as short as possible:

- It includes only material relevant to your point.
- It is edited to eliminate examples and other unneeded material, using ellipsis marks and brackets (pp. 341–45).

- **Proofread every direct quotation at least twice.**
- **Use quotation marks around the quotation** so that later you won't confuse it with a paraphrase or summary. Be sure to transfer the quotation marks into your draft as well, unless the quotation is long and is set off from your text. For advice on handling long quotations, see pages 665–66 (MLA style) and 763 (APA style).
- **Use brackets** to add words for clarity or to change the capitalization of letters (see pp. 345 and 358).
- **Use ellipsis marks** to omit irrelevant material (see pp. 342–44).
- **Cite the source of the quotation in your draft.** See pages 614–15 on documentation.

Exercise 43.7 Summarizing and paraphrasing

Prepare two source notes, one summarizing the entire paragraph below and the other paraphrasing the first four sentences (ending with the word *autonomy*). Use the format for a note illustrated on page 598, omitting only the subject heading.

> Federal organization [of the United States] has made it possible for the different states to deal with the same problems in many different ways. One consequence of federalism, then, has been that people are treated differently, by law, from state to state. The great strength of this system is that differences from state to state in cultural preferences, moral standards, and levels of wealth can be accommodated. In contrast to a unitary system in which the central government makes all important decisions (as in France), federalism is a powerful arrangement for maximizing regional freedom and autonomy. The great weakness of our federal system, however, is that people in some states receive less than the best or the most advanced or the least expensive services and policies

that government can offer. The federal dilemma does not invite easy solution, for the costs and benefits of the arrangement have tended to balance out. —Peter K. Eisinger et al., *American Politics*, p. 44

Exercise 43.8 Combining summary, paraphrase, and direct quotation

Prepare a source note containing a combination of paraphrase or summary and direct quotation that states the main idea of the passage below. Use the format for a note illustrated on page 598, omitting only the
subject heading.

> Most speakers unconsciously duel even during seemingly casual
> conversations, as can often be observed at social gatherings where they
> show less concern for exchanging information with other guests than for
> asserting their own dominance. Their verbal dueling often employs very
> subtle weapons like mumbling, a hostile act which defeats the listener's
> desire to understand what the speaker claims he is trying to say (but is
> really not saying because he is mumbling!). Or the verbal dueler may
> keep talking after someone has passed out of hearing range—which is
> often an aggressive challenge to the listener to return and acknowledge
> the dominance of the speaker. —Peter K. Farb, *Word Play*, p. 107

Exercise 43.9 Gathering information from sources

Continuing from Exercise 43.6 (p. 595), as the next step in preparing a
research paper, gather and organize the information from your sources.
Mark every note, photocopy, printout, and download with the source's
publication information and a heading related to your paper. Annotate
relevant passages of photocopies, printouts, and downloads. For handwritten or computer notes, use direct quotation, summary, or paraphrase
as seems appropriate, being careful to avoid inaccuracy and plagiarism.
(If you need help recognizing plagiarism, see Chapter 44.)

43e | Integrating sources into your text

Integrating sources into your sentences is key to synthesizing
others' ideas and information with your own. Evidence drawn from
sources should *back up* your conclusions, not *be* your conclusions:
you don't want to let your evidence overwhelm your own point of
view. The point of research is to investigate and go beyond sources, to
interpret them and use them to support your own independent ideas.

Note The examples in this section use the MLA style of source
documentation and also present-tense verbs (such as *disagrees* and
claims). See pages 605–06 for specific variations in documentation
style and verb tense within the academic disciplines. Several other
conventions governing quotations are discussed elsewhere in this
book:

■ **Using commas to punctuate signal phrases** (pp. 315–16).

- Placing other punctuation marks with quotation marks (pp. 337–38).
- Using brackets and the ellipsis mark to indicate changes in quotations (pp. 342–44).
- Punctuating and placing parenthetical citations (pp. 626–27).
- Formatting long prose quotations and poetry quotations in MLA style (pp. 665–66) and APA style (p. 763).

1 Introducing borrowed material

Readers will be distracted from your point if borrowed material does not fit into your sentence. In the passage below, the writer has not meshed the structures of her own and her source's sentences:

| Awkward | One editor disagrees with this view and "a good reporter does not fail to separate opinions from facts" (Lyman 52). |

In the following revision the writer adds words to integrate the quotation into her sentence:

| Revised | One editor disagrees with this view, <u>maintaining that</u> "a good reporter does not fail to separate opinions from facts" (Lyman 52). |

To mesh your own and your source's words, you may sometimes need to make a substitution or addition to the quotation, signaling your change with brackets:

Words added	"The tabloids [of England] are a journalistic case study in bad reporting," claims Lyman (52).
Verb form changed	A bad reporter, Lyman implies, is one who "[fails] to separate opinions from facts" (52). [The bracketed verb replaces *fail* in the original.]
Capitalization changed	"[T]o separate opinions from facts" is the work of a good reporter (Lyman 52). [In the original, *to* is not capitalized.]
Noun supplied for pronoun	The reliability of a news organization "depends on [reporters'] trustworthiness," says Lyman (52). [The bracketed noun replaces *their* in the original.]

2 Interpreting borrowed material

You need to work borrowed material into your sentences so that readers see without effort how it contributes to the points you are making. If you merely dump source material into your paper without explaining how you intend it to be interpreted, readers will have to struggle to understand your sentences and the relationships you are trying to establish. For example, the following passage forces us to figure out for ourselves that the writer's sentence and the quotation state opposite points of view:

> Dumped   Many news editors and reporters maintain that it is impossible to keep personal opinions from influencing the selection and presentation of facts. "True, news reporters, like everyone else, form impressions of what they see and hear. However, a good reporter does not fail to separate opinions from facts" (Lyman 52).

In the revision, the underlined additions tell us how to interpret the quotation:

> Revised   Many news editors and reporters maintain that it is impossible to keep personal opinions from influencing the selection and presentation of facts. <u>Yet not all authorities agree with this view. One editor grants that</u> "news reporters, like everyone else, form impressions of what they see and hear." <u>But, he insists,</u> "a good reporter does not fail to separate opinions from facts" (Lyman 52).

Signal phrases

The words *One editor grants* and *he insists* in the revised passage above are **signal phrases:** they tell readers who the source is and what to expect in the quotations that follow. Signal phrases usually contain (1) the source author's name (or a substitute for it, such as *One editor* and *he*) and (2) a verb that indicates the source author's attitude or approach to what he or she says.

Some verbs for signal phrases appear in the following list. These verbs are in the present tense, which is typical of writing in the humanities. In the social and natural sciences, the past tense (*noted*) or present perfect tense (*has noted*) is more common. See pages 605–06.

Author is neutral	Author infers or suggests	Author argues	Author is uneasy or disparaging
comments	analyzes	claims	belittles
describes	asks	contends	bemoans
explains	assesses	defends	complains
illustrates	concludes	holds	condemns
notes	considers	insists	deplores
observes	finds	maintains	deprecates
points out	predicts		derides
records	proposes	**Author agrees**	disagrees
relates	reveals		laments
reports	shows	admits	warns
says	speculates	agrees	
sees	suggests	concedes	
thinks	supposes	concurs	
writes		grants	

Vary your signal phrases to suit your interpretation of borrowed material and also to keep readers' interest. A signal phrase may precede, interrupt, or follow the borrowed material:

Precedes	<u>Lyman insists</u> that "a good reporter does not fail to separate opinions from facts" (52).
Interrupts	"However," <u>Lyman insists</u>, "a good reporter does not fail to separate opinions from facts" (52).
Follows	"[A] good reporter does not fail to separate opinions from facts," <u>Lyman insists</u> (52).

Background information

You can add information to a quotation to integrate it into your text and to inform readers why you are using it. In most cases, provide the author's name in the text, especially if the author is an expert or if readers will recognize the name:

Author named	<u>Harold Lyman</u> grants that "news reporters, like everyone else, form impressions of what they see and hear." But, Lyman insists, "a good reporter does not fail to separate opinions from facts" (52).

If the source title contributes information about the author or the context of the quotation, you can provide it in the text:

Title given	Harold Lyman, <u>in his book *The Conscience of the Journalist*</u>, grants that "news reporters, like everyone else, form impressions of what they see and hear." But, Lyman insists, "a good reporter does not fail to separate opinions from facts" (52).

If the quoted author's background and experience reinforce or clarify the quotation, you can provide these credentials in the text:

Credentials given	Harold Lyman, <u>a newspaper editor for more than forty years</u>, grants that "news reporters, like everyone else, form impressions of what they see and hear." But, Lyman insists, "a good reporter does not fail to separate opinions from facts" (52).

You need not name the author, source, or credentials in your text when you are simply establishing facts or weaving together facts and opinions from varied sources. In the following passage, the information is more important than the source, so the name of the source is confined to a parenthetical acknowledgment:

To end the abuses of the British, many colonists were urging three actions: forming a united front, seceding from Britain, and taking control of their own international relations (Wills 325–36).

3 Following discipline styles for integrating sources

The preceding guidelines for introducing and interpreting borrowed material apply generally across academic disciplines, but there are differences in verb tenses and documentation style.

English and some other humanities

Writers in English, foreign languages, and related disciplines use MLA style for documenting sources and generally use the present tense of verbs in signal phrases. In discussing sources other than works of literature, the present perfect tense is also sometimes appropriate:

> Lyman insists . . . [present]
> Lyman has insisted . . . [present perfect]

In discussing works of literature, use only the present tense to describe both the work of the author and the action in the work:

> Kate Chopin builds irony into every turn of "The Story of an Hour." For example, Mrs. Mallard, the central character, finds joy in the death of her husband, whom she loves, because she anticipates "the long procession of years that would belong to her absolutely" (23).

Avoid shifting tenses in writing about literature. You can, for instance, shorten quotations to avoid their past-tense verbs.

| Shift | Her freedom elevates her, so that "she carried herself unwittingly like a goddess of victory" (24). |
| No shift | Her freedom elevates her, so that she walks "unwittingly like a goddess of victory" (24). |

History and other humanities

Writers in history, art history, philosophy, and related disciplines generally use the present perfect tense or present tense of verbs in signal phrases.

> Lincoln persisted, as Haworth has noted, in "feeling that events controlled him."[3]
> What Miller calls Lincoln's "severe self-doubt"[6] undermined his effectiveness on at least two occasions.

The raised numbers after the quotations are part of the Chicago documentation style, used in history and other disciplines.

Social and natural sciences

Writers in the sciences generally use a verb's present tense just for reporting the results of a study (*The data suggest* . . .). Otherwise, they use a verb's past tense or present perfect tense in a signal phrase, as when introducing an explanation, interpretation, or other commentary. (Thus when you are writing for the sciences, generally convert the list of signal-phrase verbs on page 603 from the present to the present perfect tense or past tense.)

Lin (1999) has suggested that preschooling may significantly affect children's academic performance through high school (pp. 22–23).

In an exhaustive survey of the literature published between 1990 and 2000, Walker (2001) found "no proof, merely a weak correlation, linking place of residence and rate of illness" (p. 121).

These passages conform to APA documentation style. APA style, or one quite similar to it, is also used in sociology, education, nursing, biology, and many other sciences.

Exercise 43.10   Introducing and interpreting borrowed material

Drawing on the ideas in the following paragraph and using examples from your own observations and experiences, write a paragraph about anxiety. Integrate at least one direct quotation and one paraphrase from the following paragraph into your own sentences. In your paragraph, identify the author by name and give his credentials: he is a professor of psychiatry and a practicing psychoanalyst.

There are so many ways in which human beings are different from all the lower forms of animals, and almost all of them make us uniquely susceptible to feelings of anxiousness. Our imagination and reasoning powers facilitate anxiety; the anxious feeling is precipitated not by an absolute impending threat—such as the worry about an examination, a speech, travel—but rather by the symbolic and often unconscious representations. We do not have to be experiencing a potential danger. We can experience something related to it. We can recall, through our incredible memories, the original symbolic sense of vulnerability in childhood and suffer the feeling attached to that. We can even forget the original memory and be stuck with the emotion—which is then compounded by its seemingly irrational quality at this time. It is not just the fear of death which pains us, but the anticipation of it; or the anniversary of a specific death; or a street, a hospital, a time of day, a color, a flower, a symbol associated with death.

—Willard Gaylin, "Feeling Anxious," p. 23

44

Avoiding Plagiarism and Documenting Sources

The knowledge building that is the focus of academic writing rests on the integrity of everyone who participates in using and crediting sources, including students. The work of a writer or creator is his or her intellectual property. You and others may borrow the work's ideas and even its words or an image, but you *must* acknowledge that what you borrowed came from someone else.

When you acknowledge sources in your writing, you are doing more than giving credit to the writer or creator of the work you consulted. You are also showing what your own writing is based on, which in turn gives you credibility as a researcher and writer. Acknowledging sources creates the trust among scholars, students, writers, and readers that knowledge building requires.

Plagiarism (from a Latin word for "kidnapper") is the presentation of someone else's work as your own. Whether deliberate or accidental, plagiarism is a serious offense. It breaks trust, and it undermines or even destroys your credibility as a researcher and writer.

■ *Deliberate* plagiarism:

Copying or downloading a phrase, a sentence, or a longer passage from a source and passing it off as your own by omitting quotation marks and a source citation.

Summarizing or paraphrasing someone else's ideas without acknowledging your debt in a source citation.

Handing in as your own work a paper you have bought, copied off the Web, had a friend write, or accepted from another student.

■ *Accidental* plagiarism:

Reading a wide variety of print or Web sources on a subject without taking notes on them, and then not remembering the difference between what you recently learned and what you already knew.

Checklist for avoiding plagiarism

Type of source

Are you using

- your own independent material,
- common knowledge, or
- someone else's independent material?

You must acknowledge someone else's material.

Quotations

- Do all quotations exactly match their sources? Check them.
- Have you inserted quotation marks around quotations that are run into your text?
- Have you shown omissions with ellipsis marks and additions with brackets?
- Does every quotation have a source citation?

Paraphrases and summaries

- Have you used your own words and sentence structures for every paraphrase and summary? If not, use quotation marks around the original author's words.
- Does every paraphrase and summary have a source citation?

The Web

- Have you obtained any necessary permission to use someone else's material on the Web?

Source citations

- Have you acknowledged every use of someone else's material in each place you used it?
- Does your list of works cited include entries for all the sources you have used?

Forgetting to place quotation marks around another writer's words.

Carelessly omitting a source citation for a paraphrase.

Omitting a source citation for another's idea because you are unaware of the need to acknowledge the idea.

The way to avoid plagiarism is to acknowledge your sources by documenting them. This chapter discusses plagiarism and the Internet, shows how to distinguish what doesn't require acknowledgment from what does, and provides an overview of source documentation.

 The concept of intellectual property and thus the rules governing plagiarism are not universal. In some other cultures, for instance, students may be encouraged to copy the words of scholars without acknowledgment in order to demonstrate their mastery of or respect for the scholars' work. In the United States, however, using an author's work without a source citation is considered theft. When in doubt about the guidelines in this chapter, ask your teacher for advice.

44a Committing and detecting plagiarism on the Internet

The Internet has made it easier to plagiarize than ever before, but it has also made plagiarism easier to catch.

Even honest students risk accidental plagiarism by downloading sources and importing portions into their drafts. Dishonest students may take advantage of downloading to steal others' work. They may also use the term-paper businesses on the Web, which offer both ready-made research and complete papers, usually for a fee. **Paying for research or a paper does not make it the buyer's work.** Anyone who submits someone else's work as his or her own is a plagiarist.

Students who plagiarize from the Internet both deprive themselves of an education in honest research and expose themselves to detection. Teachers can use search engines to locate specific phrases or sentences anywhere on the Web, including among scholarly publications, all kinds of Web sites, and term-paper collections. They can search the term-paper sites as easily as students can, looking for similarities with papers they've received. They can also use detection programs such as *Turnitin* that compare students' work with other work anywhere on the Internet, seeking matches as short as a few words.

Some teachers suggest that their students use plagiarism-detection programs to verify that their own work does not include accidental plagiarism from the Internet.

44b Knowing what you need not acknowledge

1 Using your independent material

Your own observations, thoughts, compilations of facts, or experimental results—expressed in your words and format—do not require acknowledgment. You should describe the basis for your conclusions so that readers can evaluate your thinking, but you need not cite sources for them.

2 Using common knowledge

Common knowledge consists of the standard information on a subject as well as folk literature and commonsense observations.

- **Standard information** includes the major facts of history, such as the dates during which Charlemagne ruled as emperor of Rome (800–14). It does *not* include interpretations of facts, such as a historian's opinion that Charlemagne was sometimes needlessly cruel in extending his power.
- **Folk literature,** such as the fairy tale "Snow White," is popularly known and cannot be traced to a particular writer. Literature traceable to a writer is *not* folk literature, even if it is very familiar.
- **Commonsense observations** are things most people know, such as that inflation is most troublesome for people with low and fixed incomes. However, a particular economist's argument about the effects of inflation on Chinese immigrants is *not* a commonsense observation.

As long as you express it in your own words and sentence structures, you may use common knowledge as your own.

If you do not know a subject well enough to determine whether a piece of information is common knowledge, make a record of the source as you would for any other quotation, paraphrase, or summary. As you read more about the subject, the information may come up repeatedly without acknowledgment, in which case it is probably common knowledge. But if you are still in doubt when you finish your research, always acknowledge the source.

44c Knowing what you *must* acknowledge

You must always acknowledge other people's independent material—that is, any facts or ideas that are not common knowledge or your own. The source may be anything, including a book, an article, a movie, an interview, a microfilmed document, a Web page, a newsgroup posting, or an opinion expressed on the radio. You must acknowledge summaries or paraphrases of ideas or facts as well as quotations of the language and format in which ideas or facts appear: wording, sentence structures, arrangement, and special graphics (such as a diagram). You must acknowledge another's material no matter how you use it, how much of it you use, or how often you use it.

1 Using copied language: Quotation marks and a source citation

The following example baldly plagiarizes the original quotation from Jessica Mitford's *Kind and Usual Punishment,* page 9. Without quotation marks or a source citation, the example matches Mitford's wording (underlined) and closely parallels her sentence structure:

Original quotation	"The character and mentality of the keepers may be of more importance in understanding prisons than the character and mentality of the kept."
Plagiarism	But <u>the character</u> of prison officials (<u>the keepers</u>) is <u>of more importance in understanding prisons than the character</u> of prisoners (<u>the kept</u>).

To avoid plagiarism, the writer can paraphrase and cite the source (see the examples on the next page) or use Mitford's actual words *in quotation marks* and *with a source citation* (here, in MLA style):

Revision (quotation)	According to one critic of the penal system, "The character and mentality of the keepers may be of more importance in understanding prisons than the character and mentality of the kept" (Mitford 9).

Even with a source citation and with a different sentence structure, the next example is still plagiarism because it uses some of Mitford's words (underlined) without quotation marks:

Plagiarism	According to one critic of the penal system, the psychology of <u>the kept</u> may say less about prisons than the psychology of <u>the keepers</u> (Mitford 9).
Revision (quotation)	According to one critic of the penal system, the psychology of "the kept" may say less about prisons than the psychology of "the keepers" (Mitford 9).

2 │ Paraphrase or summary: Your own words and sentence structure and a source citation

The example below changes the sentence structure of the original Mitford quotation at the top of this page, but it still uses Mitford's words (underlined) without quotation marks and without a source citation:

Plagiarism	<u>In understanding prisons</u>, we should know more about <u>the character and mentality of the keepers</u> than of <u>the kept</u>.

To avoid plagiarism, the writer can use quotation marks and cite the source (see above) or *use his or her own words* and still *cite the source* (because the idea is Mitford's, not the writer's):

Revision (paraphrase)	Mitford holds that we may be able to learn more about prisons from the psychology of the prison officials than from that of the prisoners (9).
Revision (paraphrase)	We may understand prisons better if we focus on the personalities and attitudes of the prison workers rather than those of the inmates (Mitford 9).

In the next example, the writer cites Mitford and does not use her words but still plagiarizes her sentence structure:

Plagiarism	One critic of the penal system maintains that <u>the psychology of prison officials may be more informative about prisons than the psychology of prisoners</u> (Mitford 9).
Revision (paraphrase)	One critic of the penal system maintains that we may be able to learn less from the psychology of prisoners than from the psychology of prison officials (Mitford 9).

Exercise 44.1 Recognizing plagiarism

The following numbered items show various attempts to quote or paraphrase the passage below. Carefully compare each attempt with the original passage. Which attempts are plagiarized, inaccurate, or both, and which are acceptable? Why?

I would agree with the sociologists that psychiatric labeling is dangerous. Society can inflict terrible wounds by discrimination, and by confusing health with disease and disease with badness.
—George E. Vaillant, *Adaptation to Life,* p. 361

1. According to George Vaillant, society often inflicts wounds by using psychiatric labeling, confusing health, disease, and badness (361).
2. According to George Vaillant, "psychiatric labeling [such as 'homosexual' or 'schizophrenic'] is dangerous. Society can inflict terrible wounds by . . . confusing health with disease and disease with badness" (361).
3. According to George Vaillant, when psychiatric labeling discriminates between health and disease or between disease and badness, it can inflict wounds on those labeled (361).
4. Psychiatric labels can badly hurt those labeled, says George Vaillant, because they fail to distinguish among health, illness, and immorality (361).
5. Labels such as "homosexual" and "schizophrenic" can be hurtful when they fail to distinguish among health, illness, and immorality.
6. "I would agree with the sociologists that society can inflict terrible wounds by discrimination, and by confusing health with disease and disease with badness" (Vaillant 361).

44d Acknowledging online sources

Online sources are so accessible and so easy to download into your own documents that it may seem they are freely available, exempting you from the obligation to acknowledge them. They are not. Acknowledging online sources is somewhat trickier than acknowledging print sources, but it is no less essential. Further, if you are publishing your work on the Web, you need to take account of sources' copyright restrictions as well.

1 Citing online sources in an unpublished project

When you use material from an online source in a print or online document to be distributed just to your class, your obligation to cite sources does not change: you must acknowledge someone else's independent material in whatever form you find it. With online sources, that obligation can present additional challenges:

- **Record complete publication information each time you consult an online source.** Online sources may change or even disappear entirely. See page 558 for the information to record, such as the electronic address and the publication date. Without the proper information, you *may not* use the source.
- **Acknowledge linked sites.** If you use a Web site and one or more of its linked sites, you must acknowledge the linked sites as well. One person's use of a second person's work does not release you from the responsibility to cite the second work.
- **Seek the author's permission before using an e-mail message, discussion-group posting, or blog contribution.** Obtaining permission advises the author that his or her ideas are about to be distributed more widely and lets the author verify that you have not misrepresented the ideas.

2 Citing print and online sources in a Web composition

When you use material from print or online sources in a composition for the Web, you must not only acknowledge your sources but also take the additional precaution of observing copyright restrictions.

A Web site is a medium of publication just as a book or magazine is and so involves the same responsibility to obtain reprint permission from copyright holders. The exception is a password-protected site (such as a course site), which many copyright holders regard as private. You can find information about copyright holders and permissions on the copyright page of a print publication (following the title page) and on a page labeled something like "Terms of Use" on a Web site. If you don't see an explicit release for student use or publication on private Web sites, assume you must seek permission.

The legal convention of fair use allows an author to reprint a small portion of copyrighted material without obtaining the copyright holder's permission, as long as the author acknowledges the source. The online standards of fair use differ for print and online sources and are not fixed in either case. The guidelines below are conservative:

- **Print sources:** Quote without permission fewer than fifty words from an article or fewer than three hundred words from a book. You'll need permission to use any longer quotation from an article or book; any quotation at all from a play, poem, or song; and any use of an entire work, such as a photograph, chart, or other illustration.

- **Online sources:** Quote without permission text that represents just a small portion of the whole—say, up to forty words out of three hundred. Follow the print guidelines above for plays, poems, songs, and illustrations, adding multimedia elements (audio or video clips) to the list of works that require reprint permission for any use.

- **Links:** You may need to seek permission to link your site to another one—for instance, if you rely on the linked site to substantiate your claims or to provide a multimedia element.

44e Documenting sources

Every time you borrow the words, facts, or ideas of others, you must **document** the source—that is, supply a reference (or document) telling readers that you borrowed the material and where you borrowed it from.

Editors and teachers in most academic disciplines require special documentation formats (or styles) in their scholarly journals and in students' papers. All the styles use a citation in the text that serves two purposes: it signals that material is borrowed, and it refers readers to detailed information about the source so that they can locate both the source and the place in the source where the borrowed material appears. The detailed source information appears either in footnotes or at the end of the paper.

Aside from these essential similarities, the disciplines' documentation styles differ markedly in citation form, arrangement of source information, and other particulars. Each discipline's style reflects the needs of its practitioners for certain kinds of information presented in certain ways. For instance, the currency of a source is important in the social sciences, where studies build on and correct each other; thus in-text citations in the social sciences include a source's date of publication. In the humanities, however, currency is less important, so in-text citations do not include date of publication.

The disciplines' documentation formats are described in style guides listed elsewhere in this book for the humanities (p. 724), the social sciences (pp. 741–42), and the natural and applied sciences (p. 773). This book discusses and illustrates four common documentation styles:

- **MLA style,** used in English, foreign languages, and some other humanities (pp. 619–63).

- Chicago style, used in history, art history, philosophy, religion, and some other humanities (pp. 724–35).
- APA style, used in psychology and some other social sciences (pp. 741–61).
- CSE style, used in the biological and some other sciences (pp. 773–79).

Always ask your teacher which documentation style you should use. If your teacher does not require a particular style, use the one in this book that's most appropriate for the discipline in which you're writing. Do follow a single system for citing sources so that you provide all the necessary information in a consistent format.

Note Bibliography software—*Zotero, Refworks, Endnote,* and others—can help you format your source citations in the style of your choice. Always ask your teachers if you may use such software for your papers. The programs prompt you for needed information (author's name, book title, and so on) and then arrange, capitalize, underline, and punctuate the information as required by the style. But no program can anticipate all the varieties of source information, nor can it substitute for your own care and attention in giving your sources complete acknowledgment using the required form.

45

Writing the Paper

This chapter complements and extends the detailed discussion of the writing situation and the writing process in Chapters 1–3 (pp. 2–73), which also include many tips for using a word processor. If you haven't already done so, you may want to read those chapters before this one.

45a Focusing and organizing the paper

Before you begin using your source notes in a draft, give some thought to your main idea and your organization.

my**comp**lab

Visit *mycomplab.com* for more resources and exercises on writing and revising a research paper.

1 | Developing a thesis statement

You began research with a question about your subject (see p. 553). Though that question may have evolved during research, you should be able to answer it once you've consulted most of your sources. Try to state that answer in a **thesis statement,** a claim that narrows your subject to a single idea. Here, for example, are the research question and thesis statement of Justin Malik, whose final paper appears on pages 668–80:

Research question
How can green consumerism help the environment?

Thesis statement
Although green consumerism can help the environment, consumerism itself is the root of some of the most pressing ecological problems we face. To make a real difference, we must consume less.

A precise thesis statement will give you a focus as you organize and draft your paper. For more on thesis statements, see pages 29–34.

2 | Creating a structure

To structure your paper, you'll need to synthesize, or forge relationships among ideas (see pp. 593–94). Here is one approach:

- **Arrange source information in categories.** Each group should correspond to a main section of your paper: a key idea of your own that supports the thesis.
- **Review your research journal** for connections between sources and other thoughts that can help you organize your paper.
- **Look objectively at your categories.** If some are skimpy, with little information, consider whether you should drop the categories or conduct more research to fill them out. If most of your information falls into one or two categories, consider whether they are too broad and should be divided. (If any of this rethinking affects your thesis statement, revise it accordingly.)
- **Within each group, distinguish between the main idea and the supporting ideas and evidence.** Only the support should come from your sources. The main idea should be your own.

See pages 35–44 for more on organizing a paper, including samples of both informal and formal outlines.

Exercise 45.1 Developing a thesis statement
Draft and revise a thesis statement for your developing research paper. Make sure the revised version specifically asserts your main idea.

Exercise 45.2 Creating a structure

Continuing from Exercise 45.1, arrange your notes into a structure. As specified by your teacher, make an informal outline or a formal sentence or topic outline to guide the drafting of your paper.

45b Drafting, revising, and formatting the paper

1 Drafting

In drafting your paper, you do not have to proceed methodically from introduction to conclusion. Instead, draft in sections, beginning with the one you feel most confident about. Each section should center on a principal idea contributing to your thesis, a conclusion you have drawn from reading and responding to sources. Start the section by stating the idea; then support it with information, summaries, paraphrases, and quotations from your notes. Remember to insert source information from your notes as well.

2 Revising and editing

For a complex project like a research paper, you'll certainly want to revise in at least two stages—first for thesis, structure, and other whole-paper issues, and then for clarity, grammar, and other sentence-level issues. Chapter 3 supports this two-stage approach with checklists for revision (p. 56) and editing (pp. 61–62). The box on the next page provides additional steps to take when revising a research paper.

3 Formatting

The final draft of your paper should conform to the document format recommended by your teacher or by the style guide of the discipline in which you are writing. This book details two common formats: Modern Language Association (pp. 664–66) and American Psychological Association (pp. 761–64).

In any discipline, you can use a word processor to present your ideas effectively and attractively with readable typefonts, headings, illustrations, and other elements. See pages 118–26 for ideas.

Before you submit your paper, proofread it carefully for typographical errors, misspellings, and other errors. (See p. 67 for tips on proofreading.) Unless the errors are very numerous (more than several on a page), you can correct them by whiting out or crossing out (neatly) and inserting the correction (neatly) in ink. Don't let the pressure of a deadline prevent you from proofreading, for even minor errors can impair clarity or annoy readers and thus negate some of the hard work you have put into your project.

Checklist for revising a research paper

Assignment
How does the draft satisfy all of the criteria stated in your teacher's assignment?

Thesis statement
How well does your thesis statement describe your subject and your perspective as they emerged during drafting?

Structure
(Outlining your draft can help you see structure at a glance. See p. 54.)

How consistently does borrowed material illuminate and support—not lead and dominate—your own ideas? How well is the importance of ideas reflected in the emphasis they receive? Will the arrangement of ideas be clear to readers?

Evidence
Where might evidence seem weak or irrelevant to readers?

Reasonableness and clarity
How reasonable will readers find your argument? (See pp. 202–06.) Where do you need to define terms or concepts that readers may not know or may dispute?

Exercise 45.3 Drafting your paper
Draft the research paper you have been developing in Chapters 41–44. Before beginning the draft, study your research journal and your source information. While drafting, follow your thesis statement and outline as closely as you need to, but stay open to new ideas, associations, and arrangements.

Exercise 45.4 Revising and editing your paper
Using the revision and editing checklists on pages 56 and 61–62 and the checklist and pointers here, revise and edit your research paper. Work to improve not only the presentation of ideas but also, if necessary, the ideas themselves. Make sure you have provided an in-text citation for every summary, paraphrase, and direct quotation of a source and that your list of sources is complete.

Exercise 45.5 Preparing and proofreading your final draft
Prepare the final draft of your research paper, following your teacher's requirements for document format. If your teacher does not specify a format, follow the MLA guidelines on pages 664–66. Proofread and correct the paper before submitting it.

46

Using MLA Documentation and Format

English, foreign languages, and some other humanities use the documentation style of the Modern Language Association, recently updated in the *MLA Handbook for Writers of Research Papers*, 7th ed., 2009.

MLA documentation style employs brief parenthetical citations within the text that direct readers to a list of works cited at the end of the text. A parenthetical citation might look like this:

Only one article mentions this discrepancy (Wolfe 62).

The name *Wolfe* directs readers to the article by Wolfe in the list of works cited, and the page number 62 specifies the page in the article on which the cited material appears.

This chapter presents the essentials of MLA style: what to include in a parenthetical citation (below), where to place citations (p. 625), when to use footnotes or endnotes in addition to parenthetical citations (p. 628), how to create the list of works cited (p. 628), and how to format the entire paper (p. 664).

46a Using MLA in-text citations

1 Writing parenthetical text citations

In-text citations of sources must include just enough information for the reader to locate both of the following:

- The *source* in your list of works cited.
- The *place* in the source where the borrowed material appears.

mycomplab

Visit *mycomplab.com* for more resources and exercises on MLA documentation and format.

619

For any kind of source, you can usually meet both these requirements by providing the author's last name and (if the source uses them) the page numbers where the material appears. The reader can find the source in your list of works cited and find the borrowed material in the source itself.

Note For most sources, you will provide the author's or authors' last names and a page reference. Do not include the title unless you are citing more than one work by exactly the same author or authors or unless the source has no listed author (models 5 and 6, p. 622). The examples below cite a book to which neither of these exceptions applies:

Incorrect One textbook discusses the "ethical dilemmas in public relations practice" (Wilcox, Ault, and Agee, *Public Relations* 125).

Incorrect One textbook discusses the "ethical dilemmas in public relations practice" (*Public Relations* 125).

Correct One textbook discusses the "ethical dilemmas in public relations practice" (Wilcox, Ault, and Agee 125).

1. Author not named in your text

When you have not already named the author in your sentence, provide the author's last name and the page number(s), with no punctuation between them, in parentheses.

One researcher concludes that "women impose a distinctive construction on moral problems, seeing moral dilemmas in terms of conflicting responsibilities" (Gilligan 105-06).

MLA parenthetical citations

See model 6 for the form to use when the source does not have an author. And see models 10 and 11 for the forms to use when the source does not provide page numbers.

2. Author named in your text

When you have already given the author's name with the material you're citing, do not repeat it in the parenthetical citation. Give just the page number(s).

> Carol Gilligan concludes that "women impose a distinctive construction on moral problems, seeing moral dilemmas in terms of conflicting responsibilities" (105-06).

See model 6 for the form to use when the source does not list an author. And see models 10 and 11 for the forms to use when the source does not provide page numbers.

3. A work with two or three authors

If the source has two or three authors, give all their last names in the text or in the citation. Separate two authors' names with and:

> As Frieden and Sagalyn observe, "The poor and the minorities were the leading victims of highway and renewal programs" (29).

> According to one study, "The poor and the minorities were the leading victims of highway and renewal programs" (Frieden and Sagalyn 29).

With three authors, add commas and also and before the final name:

> The textbook by Wilcox, Ault, and Agee discusses the "ethical dilemmas in public relations practice" (125).

> One textbook discusses the "ethical dilemmas in public relations practice" (Wilcox, Ault, and Agee 125).

4. A work with more than three authors

If the source has more than three authors, you may list all their last names or give only the first author's name followed by et al. (the abbreviation for the Latin *et alii*, "and others"). The choice depends on what you do in your list of works cited (see p. 632).

> Increased competition means that employees of public relations firms may find their loyalty stretched in more than one direction (Cameron et al. 417).

> Increased competition means that employees of public relations firms may find their loyalty stretched in more than one direction (Cameron, Wilcox, Reber, and Shin 417).

5. A work by an author of two or more cited works

If your list of works cited includes two or more works by the same author, then your citation must tell the reader which of the author's works you are referring to. Give the title either in the text or in a parenthetical citation. In a parenthetical citation, give the full title only if it is brief; otherwise, shorten the title to the first one, two, or three main words (excluding *A*, *An*, or *The*).

> At about age seven, children begin to use appropriate gestures with their stories (Gardner, *Arts* 144-45).

The full title of Gardner's book is *The Arts and Human Development* (see the works-cited entry on p. 632). This shortened title is italicized because the source is a book.

6. An anonymous work

For a work with no named author or editor (whether an individual or an organization), use a full or shortened version of the title, as explained above. In your list of works cited, you alphabetize an anonymous work by the first main word of the title (see p. 633), so the first word of a shortened title should be the same. The following citations refer to an unsigned source titled "The Right to Die." The title appears in quotation marks because the source is a periodical article.

> One article notes that a death-row inmate may demand his own execution to achieve a fleeting notoriety ("Right" 16).

> "The Right to Die" notes that a death-row inmate may demand execution to achieve a fleeting notoriety (16).

If two or more anonymous works have the same title, distinguish them with additional information in the text citation, such as the publication date.

7. A work with a corporate author

Some works list as author a government body, association, committee, company, or other group. Cite such a work by the organization's name. If the name is long, work it into the text to avoid an intrusive parenthetical citation.

> A 2008 report by the Hawaii Department of Education provides evidence of an increase in graduation rates (12).

8. A nonprint source

Cite a nonprint source such as a Web page or a DVD just as you would any other source. If your works-cited entry lists the source under the name of an author or other contributor, use that name in the text citation. The following example cites an authored source that has page numbers.

Business forecasts for the fourth quarter tended to be optimistic (White 4).

If your works-cited entry lists the work under its title, cite the work by title in your text, as explained in model 6. The next example cites an entire work (a film on DVD) and gives the title in the text, so it omits a parenthetical citation (see model 10).

Seven decades after its release, *Citizen Kane* is still remarkable for its rich black-and-white photography.

9. A multivolume work

If you consulted only one volume of a multivolume work, your list of works cited will say so (see model 30 on p. 642), and you can treat the volume as you would any book.

If you consulted more than one volume of a multivolume work, give the appropriate volume in your text citation.

After issuing the Emancipation Proclamation, Lincoln said, "What I did, I did after very full deliberations, and under a very heavy and solemn sense of responsibility" (5: 438).

The number 5 indicates the volume from which the quotation was taken; the number 438 indicates the page number in that volume. When the author's name appears in such a citation, place it before the volume number with no punctuation: (Lincoln 5: 438).

If you are referring generally to an entire volume of a multivolume work and are not citing specific page numbers, add the abbreviation vol. before the volume number, as in (vol. 5) or (Lincoln, vol. 5) (note the comma after the author's name). Then readers will not misinterpret the volume number as a page number.

10. An entire work or a work with no page or other reference numbers

When you cite an entire work rather than a part of it, you may omit any page or other reference number. If the work you cite has an author, try to work the author's name into your text. You will not need a parenthetical citation then, but the source still must appear in your list of works cited.

Boyd deals with the need to acknowledge and come to terms with our fear of nuclear technology.

Use the same format when you cite a specific passage from a work with no page, paragraph, or other reference numbers, such as a Web source.

If the author's name does not appear in your text, put it in a parenthetical citation.

Almost 20 percent of commercial banks have been audited for the practice (Friis).

11. A work with numbered paragraphs or sections instead of pages

Some electronic sources number each paragraph or section instead of each page. In citing passages in these sources, give the paragraph or section number(s) and distinguish them from page numbers: after the author's name, put a comma, a space, and par. (one paragraph), pars. (more than one paragraph), sec., or secs.

Twins reared apart report similar feelings (Palfrey, pars. 6-7).

12. An indirect source

When you want to use a quotation that is already in quotation marks—indicating that the author you are reading is quoting someone else—try to find the original source and quote directly from it. If you can't find the original source, then your citation must indicate that your quotation of it is indirect. In the following citation, qtd. in ("quoted in") says that Davino was quoted by Boyd.

George Davino maintains that "even small children have vivid ideas about nuclear energy" (qtd. in Boyd 22).

The list of works cited then includes only Boyd (the work consulted), not Davino.

13. A literary work

Novels, plays, and poems are often available in many editions, so your instructor may ask you to provide information that will help readers find the passage you cite no matter what edition they consult.

- **Novels:** The page number comes first, followed by a semicolon and then information on the appropriate part or chapter of the work.

  Toward the end of James's novel, Maggie suddenly feels "the thick breath of the definite—which was the intimate, the immediate, the familiar, as she hadn't had them for so long" (535; pt. 6, ch. 41).

- **Poems that are not divided into parts:** You may omit the page number and supply the line number(s) for the quotation. To prevent confusion with page numbers, precede the numbers with line or lines in the first citation; then use just the numbers.

In Shakespeare's Sonnet 73 the speaker identifies with the trees of late autumn, "Bare ruined choirs, where late the sweet birds sang" (line 4). "In me," Shakespeare writes, "thou seest the glowing of such fire / That on the ashes of his youth doth lie . . ." (9-10).

(See pp. 714–15 for a sample paper on a poem.)

■ **Verse plays and poems that are divided into parts:** Omit a page number and cite the appropriate part—act (and scene, if any), canto, book, and so on—plus the line number(s). Use Arabic numerals for parts, including acts and scenes (3.4), unless your instructor specifies Roman numerals (III.iv).

Later in Shakespeare's *King Lear* the disguised Edgar says, "The prince of darkness is a gentleman" (3.4.147).

(See pp. 717–18 for a sample paper on a verse play.)

■ **Prose plays:** Provide the page number followed by the act and scene, if any. See the reference to *Death of a Salesman* on page 627.

14. The Bible

When you cite passages of the Bible in parentheses, abbreviate the title of any book longer than four letters—for instance, Gen. (Genesis), 1 Sam. (1 Samuel), Ps. (Psalms), Prov. (Proverbs), Matt. (Matthew), Rom. (Romans). Then give the chapter and verse(s) in Arabic numerals.

According to the Bible, at Babel God "did . . . confound the language of all the earth" (Gen. 11.9).

15. Two or more works in the same citation

When you refer to more than one work in a single parenthetical citation, separate the references with a semicolon.

Two recent articles point out that a computer badly used can be less efficient than no computer at all (Gough and Hall 201; Richards 162).

Since long citations in the text can distract the reader, you may choose to cite several or more works in an endnote or footnote rather than in the text. See page 628.

2 Positioning and punctuating parenthetical citations

The following guidelines will help you place and punctuate text citations to distinguish between your own and your sources' ideas and to make your own text readable. See also pages 601–06 on editing quotations and using signal phrases to integrate source material into your sentences.

Where to place citations

Position text citations to accomplish two goals:

- **Make it clear exactly where your borrowing begins and ends.**
- **Keep the citation as unobtrusive as possible.**

You can accomplish both goals by placing the parenthetical citation at the end of the sentence element containing the borrowed material. This sentence element may be a phrase or a clause, and it may begin, interrupt, or conclude the sentence. Usually, as in the following examples, the element ends with a punctuation mark.

> The inflation rate might climb as high as 30 percent (Kim 164), an increase that could threaten the small nation's stability.

> The inflation rate, which might climb as high as 30 percent (Kim 164), could threaten the small nation's stability.

> The small nation's stability could be threatened by its inflation rate, which, one source predicts, might climb as high as 30 percent (Kim 164).

In the last example the addition of *one source predicts* clarifies that Kim is responsible only for the inflation-rate prediction, not for the statement about stability.

When your paraphrase or summary of a source runs longer than a sentence, clarify the boundaries by using the author's name in the first sentence and placing the parenthetical citation at the end of the last sentence.

> Juliette Kim studied the effects of acutely high inflation in several South American and African countries since World War II. She discovered that a major change in government accompanied or followed the inflationary period in 56 percent of cases (22-23).

When you cite two or more sources in the same paragraph, position authors' names and parenthetical citations so that readers can see who said what. In the following example, the beginnings and ends of sentences clearly mark the different sources.

> Schools use computers extensively for drill-and-practice exercises, in which students repeat specific skills such as spelling words, using the multiplication facts, or, at a higher level, doing chemistry problems. But many education experts criticize such exercises for boring students and failing to engage their critical thinking and creativity. Jane M. Healy, a noted educational psychologist and teacher, takes issue with "interactive" software for children as well as drill-

and-practice software, arguing that "some of the most popular 'educational' software . . . may be damaging to independent thinking, attention, and motivation" (20). Another education expert, Harold Wenglinsky of the Educational Testing Service, found in a well-regarded 1998 study that fourth and eighth graders who used computers frequently, including for drill and practice, actually did worse on tests than their peers who used computers less often (*Does It Compute?* 21). In a later article, Wenglinsky concludes that "the quantity of use matters far less than the quality of use." In schools, he says, high-quality computer work, involving critical thinking, is still rare ("In Search" 17).

How to punctuate citations

Generally place a parenthetical citation *before* any punctuation required by your sentence. If the borrowed material is a quotation, place the citation *between* the closing quotation mark and the punctuation:

> Spelling argues that during the 1970s American automobile manufacturers met consumer needs "as well as could be expected" (26), but not everyone agrees with him.

The exception is a quotation ending in a question mark or exclamation point. Then use the appropriate punctuation inside the closing quotation mark, and follow the quotation with the text citation and a period.

> "Of what use is genius," Emerson asks, "if the organ . . . cannot find a focal distance within the actual horizon of human life?" ("Experience" 60). Mad genius is no genius.

When a citation appears at the end of a quotation set off from the text, place it one space *after* the punctuation ending the quotation. Do not use additional punctuation with the citation or quotation marks around the quotation.

> In Arthur Miller's *Death of a Salesman*, the most poignant defense of Willie Loman comes from his wife, Linda:
>
> > He's not the finest character that ever lived. But he's a human being, and a terrible thing is happening to him. So attention must be paid. He's not to be allowed to fall into his grave like an old dog. Attention, attention must finally be paid to such a person. (56; act 1)

(This citation of a play includes the act number as well as the page number. See p. 625.)

See the two sample research papers starting on pages 668 and 681 for further examples of placing parenthetical references in relation to summaries, paraphrases, and quotations.

3 | Using footnotes or endnotes in special circumstances

Occasionally you may want to use footnotes or endnotes in place of parenthetical citations. If you need to refer to several sources at once, listing them in a long parenthetical citation could be intrusive. In that case, signal the citation with a numeral raised above the appropriate line of text and write a note beginning with the same numeral to cite the sources:

Text   At least five studies have confirmed these results.[1]

Note   1. Abbott and Winger 266-68; Casner 27; Hoyenga 78-79;
Marino 36; Tripp, Tripp, and Walk 179-83.

You may also use a footnote or endnote to comment on a source or to provide information that does not fit easily into your text:

Text   So far, no one has confirmed these results.[2]

Note   2. Manter tried repeatedly to replicate the experiment, but he
was never able to produce the high temperatures (616).

Indent a note one-half inch, type the numeral on the text line, and follow the numeral with a period and a space. If the note appears as a footnote, place it at the bottom of the page on which the citation appears, set it off from the text with quadruple spacing, and single-space the note itself. If the note appears as an endnote, place it in numerical order with the other endnotes on a page between the text and the list of works cited. Double-space all the endnotes.

46b | Preparing the MLA list of works cited

In MLA documentation style, your in-text parenthetical citations (discussed in 46a) refer the reader to complete information on your sources in a list you title Works Cited and place at the end of your paper. The list should include all the sources you quoted, paraphrased, or summarized in your paper. (If your teacher asks you to include sources you examined but did not cite, title the list Works Consulted.)

Follow this format for the list of works cited:

- **Arrange your sources in alphabetical order** by the last name of the author. If an author is not given in the source, alphabetize the source by the first main word of the title (excluding *A*, *An*, or *The*).
- **Type the entire list double-spaced,** both within and between entries.

MLA works-cited page

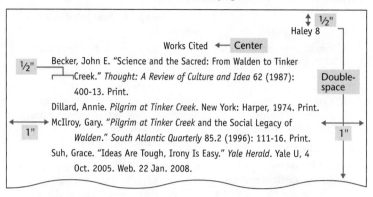

- **Indent the second and subsequent lines of each entry one-half inch from the left.** Your word processor can format this so-called hanging indent automatically.

For complete lists of works cited, see the papers by Justin Malik (pp. 679–80) and Vanessa Haley (p. 686).

The box on pages 630–31 directs you to the MLA formats for works-cited entries. Use your best judgment in adapting the models to your particular sources. If you can't find a model that exactly matches a source you used, locate and follow the closest possible match. You will certainly need to combine formats—for instance, drawing on model 2 ("Two or three authors") and model 10 ("An article in a national newspaper") for a national newspaper article with two authors.

Note MLA style now requires that you give the medium for every source you cite, such as print, Web, DVD, or television. For example, if you consulted an article in a print magazine, your works-cited entry should list the medium as Print. If you consulted a book on the Web, your works-cited entry should list the medium as Web. The models here all conform to this standard.

1 Listing authors

The following models show how to handle authors' names in citing any kind of source.

1. One author

Ehrenreich, Barbara. *Dancing in the Streets: A History of Collective Joy.* New
York: Metropolitan-Holt, 2006. Print.

Give the author's full name—last name first, a comma, first name, and any middle name or initial. Omit any title, such as *Dr.* or *PhD*.

(continued on p. 632)

MLA works-cited models

(continued from p. 629)
End the name with a period. If your source lists an editor as author, see model 22, page 640.

2. Two or three authors

Lifton, Robert Jay, and Greg Mitchell. *Who Owns Death: Capital Punishment,*
  the American Conscience, and the End of Executions. New York: Morrow,
  2000. Print.

Wilcox, Dennis L., Phillip H. Ault, and Warren K. Agee. *Public Relations: Strate-*
  gies and Tactics. 8th ed. New York: Irwin, 2006. Print.

Give the authors' names in the order provided on the title page. Reverse the first and last names of the first author *only*, not of any other authors. Separate two authors' names with a comma and and; separate three authors' names with commas and with and before the third name. If your source lists two or three editors as authors, see model 22, page 640.

3. More than three authors

Cameron, Glen T., Dennis L. Wilcox, Bryan H. Reber, and Jae-Hwa Shin. *Public*
  Relations Today: Managing Competition and Conflict. New York: Pearson,
  2007. Print.

Cameron, Glen T., et al. *Public Relations Today: Managing Competition and Con-*
  flict. New York: Pearson, 2007. Print.

You may, but need not, give all authors' names if the work has more than three authors. If you choose not to give all names, provide the name of the first author only, and follow the name with a comma and the abbreviation et al. (for the Latin *et alii*, meaning "and others"). If your source lists more than three editors as authors, see model 22, page 640.

4. The same author(s) for two or more works

Gardner, Howard. *The Arts and Human Development.* New York: Wiley, 1973. Print.

---. *Five Minds for the Future.* Boston: Harvard Business School P, 2007. Print.

Give the author's name only in the first entry. For the second and any subsequent works by the same author, substitute three hyphens for the author's name, followed by a period. Note that the three hyphens stand for *exactly* the same name or names. If the second Gardner source were by Gardner and somebody else, both names would have to be given in full.

  Place an entry or entries using three hyphens immediately after the entry that names the author. Within the set of entries by the same author, arrange the sources alphabetically by the first main word of the title, as in the Gardner examples (*Arts*, then *Five*).

If you cite two or more sources that list as author(s) exactly the same editor(s), follow the hyphens with a comma and ed. or eds. as appropriate. (See model 22, p. 640.)

5. A corporate author

Vault Technologies. *Turnkey Parking Solutions*. Salt Lake City: Mills, 2008. Print.

Corporate authors include associations, committees, institutions, government bodies, companies, and other groups. List the name of the group as author when a source gives only that name and not an individual's name.

6. Author not named (anonymous)

The Dorling Kindersley World Reference Atlas. London: Dorling, 2007. Print.

List a work that names no author—neither an individual nor a group—by its full title. If the work is a book, italicize the title. If the work is a periodical article or other short work, enclose the title in quotation marks:

"Let the Horse Race Begin." *Time* 31 Mar. 2008: 22. Print.

Alphabetize the work by the title's first main word, excluding *A, An*, or *The* (*Dorling* in the first example and Let in the second).

2 Listing periodical print sources

Print periodicals include scholarly journals, newspapers, and magazines that are published at regular intervals (quarterly, monthly, weekly, or daily). To cite more than one author, two or more articles by the same author, a corporate author, or an article with no named author, see models 1–6.

Note The treatment of volume and issue numbers and publication dates varies depending on the kind of periodical being cited, as the models indicate. For the distinction between journals and magazines, see page 565.

Articles in scholarly journals

7. An article in a journal with volume and issue numbers (print)

Bee, Robert. "The Importance of Preserving Paper-Based Artifacts in a Digital Age." *Library Quarterly* 78.2 (2008): 174-94. Print.

The next page shows the basic format for an article in a periodical (a journal) and the location of the required information in the journal. See page 636 for parallel information on a newspaper article.

Format for a print journal article

①   ②

Bee, Robert. "The Importance of Preserving Paper-Based Artifacts in a Digital Age."

     ③   ④   ⑤   ⑥   ⑦

Library Quarterly 78.2 (2008): 179-94. Print.

⑦ Medium. Give the medium of the article, Print, followed by a period.

③ Title of periodical, in italics. Omit any *A*, *An*, or *The* from the beginning of the title. Do not end with a period.

④ Volume and issue numbers, in Arabic numerals, separated by a period. Do not add a period after the issue number.

⑤ Year of publication, in parentheses and followed by a colon.

② Title of article, in quotation marks. Give the full title and any subtitle, separating them with a colon. End the title with a period inside the final quotation mark.

① Author. Give the full name—last name first, a comma, first name, and any middle name or initial. Omit *Dr., PhD,* or any other title. End the name with a period.

⑥ Inclusive page numbers of article, without "pp." Provide only as many digits in the last number as needed for clarity, usually two.

Journal cover

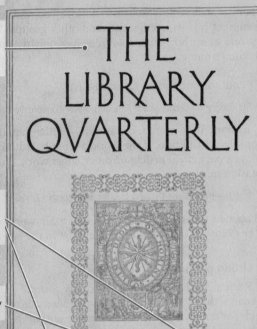

THE
LIBRARY
QVARTERLY

VOLUME 78 · APRIL 2008 · NUMBER 2

First page of article

THE IMPORTANCE OF PRESERVING PAPER-BASED ARTIFACTS IN A
DIGITAL AGE

Robert Bee[1]

reservation of paper-based artifacts is an essential issue for collection man-
nt in academic libraries. In recent years, the library science profession has

[*Library Quarterly*, vol. 78, no. 2, pp. 179–194]
© 2008 by The University of Chicago. All rights reserved.
0024-2519/2008/7802-0002$10.00

179

8. An article in a journal with only issue numbers (print)

Rymhs, Deena. "David Collier's *Surviving Saskatoon* and New Comics." *Canadian Literature* 194 (2007): 75-92. Print.

If a scholarly journal numbers only issues, not volumes, give the issue number alone after the journal title.

9. An abstract of a journal article or a dissertation (print)

Lever, Janet. "Sex Differences in the Games Children Play." *Social Problems* 23.2 (1996): 478-87. *Psychological Abstracts* 63.5 (1996): item 1431. Print.

For an abstract of a journal article, first provide the publication information for the article, following model 7. Then give the information for the abstract. If the abstract publisher lists abstracts by item rather than page number, add item before the number.

For an abstract appearing in *Dissertation Abstracts* (*DA*) or *Dissertation Abstracts International* (*DAI*), give the author's name and the title, Diss. (for "Dissertation"), the institution granting the author's degree, the date of the dissertation, and the publication information.

Steciw, Steven K. "Alterations to the Pessac Project of Le Corbusier." Diss. U of Cambridge, England, 1986. *DAI* 46.10 (1986): 565C. Print.

See also model 40 on page 645 (entire dissertation), model 63 on page 656 (abstract on the Web), and model 65 on page 658 (abstract in an online database).

Note Most teachers expect you to consult and cite full articles, not abstracts. See page 568.

Articles in newspapers

10. An article in a national newspaper (print)

Stout, David. "Blind Win Court Ruling on US Currency." *New York Times* 21 May 2008, natl. ed.: A23. Print.

See the next page for an analysis of this entry and the location of the required information in the newspaper.

11. An article in a local newspaper (print)

Arntaenius, Linda. "Merwick Rezoning Pushes Senior Housing Debate." *Town Topics* [Princeton] 21 May 2008: 1+. Print.

If the city of publication does not appear in the title of a local newspaper, follow the title with the city name, not italicized, in brackets.

Format for a print newspaper article

① ② ③ ④
Stout, David. "Blind Win Court Ruling on US Currency." *New York Times* 21 May 2008,
⑤ ⑥ ⑦
natl. ed.: A23. Print.

⑥ **Page number of article,** without "pp." Include a section designation before the number when the newspaper does the same, as here. Otherwise, give the section between the edition and the colon. Add a plus sign to the page number when the article continues on a later page.

① **Author.** Give the full name—last name first, a comma, first name, and any middle name or initial. Omit *Dr., PhD,* or any other title. End with a period.

First page of article

THE NEW YORK TIMES **NATIONAL** WEDNESDAY, MAY 21, 2008 A23

Blind Win Court Ruling on U.S. Currency

By DAVID STOUT

WASHINGTON — In a decision that could radically change the size, the color and even the feel of American money, a federal appeals court ruled on Tuesday that the United States discriminates against the blind and those with limited vision because its paper currency is all the same size regardless of a bill's value.

blind or visually impaired," said Brookly McLaughlin, deputy assistant secretary for public affairs.

Ms. McLaughlin said the Bureau of Engraving and Printing, the Treasury agency that makes paper money, had already contracted with a research firm to study ways to help those who are blind or have poor vision. The re-

in the country could cost $3.5 billion...

② **Title of article,** in quotation marks. Give the full title and any subtitle, separating them with a colon. End with a period inside the final quotation mark.

Judge Randolph said.

The suit was brought under the Rehabilitation Act of 1973, which addresses discrimination in fed...

③ **Name of newspaper,** in italics. Give the title as it appears on the first page, omitting any *A, An,* or *The* from the beginning.

First page of newspaper

"All the News That's Fit to Print"

The New York Times

National Edition
Northern California: Morning clouds in coastal areas, mostly sunny elsewhere. Cooler, with highs in low 60s at coast to low 80s in Central Valley. Weather map, Page A39.

VOL. CLVII.... No. 54,317 ©2008 The New York Times WEDNESDAY, MAY 21, 2008 Printed in California $1.25

⑦ **Medium.** Give the medium of the article, Print, followed by a period.

④ **Date of publication.** Give the day of the month first, then month, then year. Abbreviate all months except May, June, and July. End the date with a comma if listing the newspaper edition and/or the section designation. Otherwise, end with a colon.

⑤ **Edition.** If the newspaper lists an edition at the top of the first page, include it after the date. End with a comma if listing the section designation. Otherwise, end with a colon.

Articles in magazines

12. An article in a weekly or biweekly magazine (print)

Fortini, Amanda. "Pomegranate Princess." *New Yorker* 31 Mar. 2008: 92-99. Print.

Give the author, title of the article, and title of the magazine. Follow the magazine title with the day, the month, and the year of publication. (Abbreviate all months except May, June, and July.) Don't place the date in parentheses, and don't provide a volume or issue number. Give the page numbers of the article and the medium, Print.

13. An article in a monthly or bimonthly magazine (print)

Douthat, Ross. "The Return of the Paranoid Style." *Atlantic Monthly* Apr. 2008: 52-59. Print.

Follow the magazine title with the month and the year of publication. (Abbreviate all months except May, June, and July.) Don't place the date in parentheses, and don't provide a volume or issue number. Give the page numbers of the article and the medium, Print.

Reviews, editorials, letters to the editor, interviews

14. A review (print)

Glasswell, Kathryn, and George Kamberelis. "Drawing and Redrawing the Map of Writing Studies." Rev. of *Handbook of Writing Research*, by Charles A. MacArthur, Steve Graham, and Jill Fitzgerald. *Reading Research Quarterly* 42.2 (2007): 304-23. Print.

Rev. is an abbreviation for "Review." The names of the authors of the work being reviewed follow the title of the work, a comma, and by. If the review has no title of its own, then Rev. of and the title of the reviewed work immediately follow the name of the reviewer.

15. An editorial (print)

"A Global AIDS Campaign Stalled." Editorial. *New York Times* 21 June 2008, natl. ed.: A18. Print.

For an editorial with no named author, begin with the title and add the word Editorial after the title, as in the example. For an editorial with a named author, start with his or her name and then proceed as in the example.

16. A letter to the editor (print)

McBride, Thad. "Swapping the Suit and Tie." Letter. *Economist* 29 Mar. 2008: 30. Print.

Add the word Letter after the title, if there is one, or after the author's name.

17. An interview (print)

Aloni, Shulamit. Interview. *Palestine-Israel Journal of Politics, Economics, and Culture* 14.4 (2007): 63-68. Print.

Begin with the name of the person interviewed. If the interview does not have a title (as in the example), add Interview after the name. (Replace this description with the title if there is one.) You may also add the name of the interviewer if you know it—for example, Interview by Benson Wright. See model 75 (p. 660) to cite a broadcast interview or an interview you conduct yourself.

Articles in series or in special issues

18. An article in a series (print)

Kleinfeld, N. R. "Living at an Epicenter of Diabetes, Defiance, and Despair." *New York Times* 10 Jan. 2006, natl. ed.: A1+. Print. Pt. 2 of a series, Bad Blood, begun 9 Jan. 2006.

Cite an article in a series following the appropriate model on pages 633–37 for a scholarly journal, newspaper, or magazine. If you wish, end the entry with a description to indicate that the article is part of a series.

19. An article in a special issue (print)

Rubini, Monica, and Michela Menegatti. "Linguistic Bias in Personnel Selection." *Celebrating Two Decades of Linguistic Bias Research.* Ed. Robbie M. Sutton and Karen M. Douglas. Spec. issue of *Journal of Language and Social Psychology* 27.2 (2008): 168-81. Print.

Cite an article in a special issue of a periodical by starting with the author and title of the article. Follow with the title of the special issue, Ed., and the names of the issue's editor(s). Add Spec. issue of before the periodical title. Conclude with publication information, using the appropriate model on pages 633–37 for a journal or magazine.

3　Listing nonperiodical print sources

Nonperiodical print sources are works that are not published at regular intervals, such as books, government publications, and pamphlets. To cite more than one author, two or more articles by the same author, a corporate author, or a source with no named author, see models 1–6.

Books

20. Basic format for a book (print)

Lahiri, Jhumpa. *Unaccustomed Earth.* New York: Knopf, 2008. Print.

The facing page shows the basic format for a book and the location of the required information in the book. When other information is

Format for a print book

①   ②   ③   ④   ⑤   ⑥

Lahiri, Jhumpa. *Unaccustomed Earth*. New York: Knopf, 2008. Print.

Title page

Unaccustomed Earth

Jhumpa Lahiri

Alfred A. Knopf   New York • Toronto 2008

② **Title,** in italics. Give the full title and any subtitle, separating them with a colon. End the title with a period.

① **Author.** Give the full name—last name first, a comma, first name, and any middle name or initial. Omit *Dr., PhD,* or any other title. End the name with a period.

④ **Publisher's name.** Shorten most publishers' names ("UP" for University Press, "Little" for Little, Brown). Give both imprint and publisher's names when they appear on the title page: e.g., "Vintage-Random" for Vintage Books and Random House.

③ **City of publication.** Precede the publisher's name with its city, followed by a colon. Use only the first city if the title page lists more than one.

⑤ **Date of publication.** If the date doesn't appear on the title page, look for it on the next page. End the date with a period.

⑥ **Medium.** Give the medium of the book, Print, followed by a period.

required, it usually falls either between the author's name and the title or between the title and the publication information, as in the following models.

21. A second or subsequent edition (print)

Bolinger, Dwight L. *Aspects of Language*. 3rd ed. New York: Harcourt, 1981.
    Print.

For any edition after the first, place the edition number after the title. (If an editor's name follows the title, place the edition number after the name. See model 26.) Use the appropriate designation for editions that are named or dated rather than numbered—for instance, Rev. ed. for "Revised edition."

22. A book with an editor (print)

Holland, Merlin, and Rupert Hart-Davis, eds. *The Complete Letters of Oscar
    Wilde*. New York: Holt, 2000. Print.

Handle editors' names like authors' names (models 1–4), but add a comma and the abbreviation ed. (one editor) or eds. (two or more editors) after the last editor's name.

23. A book with an author and an editor (print)

Mumford, Lewis. *The City in History*. Ed. Donald L. Miller. New York: Pantheon,
    1986. Print.

When citing the work of the author, give his or her name first, and give the editor's name after the title, preceded by Ed. (singular only, meaning "Edited by"). When citing the work of the editor, use model 22 for a book with an editor, adding By and the author's name after the title:

Miller, Donald L., ed. *The City in History*. By Lewis Mumford. New York:
    Pantheon, 1986. Print.

24. A book with a translator (print)

Alighieri, Dante. *The Inferno*. Trans. John Ciardi. New York: NAL, 1971. Print.

When citing the work of the author, as in the preceding example, give his or her name first, and give the translator's name after the title, preceded by Trans. ("Translated by").

When citing the work of the translator, give his or her name first, followed by a comma and trans. Follow the title with By and the author's name:

Ciardi, John, trans. *The Inferno*. By Dante Alighieri. New York: NAL, 1971.
    Print.

When a book you cite by author has a translator *and* an editor, give the translator's and editor's names in the order used on the book's title page.

25. An anthology (print)

Kennedy, X. J., and Dana Gioia, eds. *Literature: An Introduction to Fiction,*
   Poetry, and Drama. 10th ed. New York: Longman, 2007. Print.

Cite an entire anthology only when citing the work of the editor or
editors or when your instructor permits cross-referencing like that
shown in model 27. Give the name of the editor or editors (followed
by ed. or eds.) and then the title of the anthology.

26. A selection from an anthology (print)

Mason, Bobbie Ann. "Shiloh." *Literature: An Introduction to Fiction, Poetry,*
   and Drama. Ed. X. J. Kennedy and Dana Gioia. 10th ed. New York: Longman, 2007. 604-13. Print.

This listing adds the following to the anthology entry in model 25:
author of selection, title of selection (in quotation marks), and inclusive page numbers for the selection (without the abbreviation "pp.").
If you wish, you may also supply the original date of publication for
the work you are citing, after its title. See model 32 on page 643.

If the work you cite comes from a collection of works by one
author that has no editor, use the following form:

Auden, W. H. "Family Ghosts." *The Collected Poetry of W. H. Auden*. New York:
   Random, 1945. 132-33. Print.

If the work you cite is a scholarly article that was previously
printed elsewhere, provide the complete information for the earlier
publication of the piece, followed by Rpt. in ("Reprinted in") and the
information for the source in which you found the piece:

Molloy, Francis C. "The Suburban Vision in John O'Hara's Short Stories."
   Critique: Studies in Modern Fiction 25.2 (1984): 101-13. Rpt. in *Short*
   Story Criticism: Excerpts from Criticism of the Works of Short Fiction Writ-
   ers. Ed. David Segal. Vol. 15. Detroit: Gale, 1989. 287-92. Print.

27. Two or more selections from the same anthology (print)

Erdrich, Louise. "Indian Boarding School: The Runaways." Kennedy and Gioia
   1106.

Kennedy, X. J., and Dana Gioia, eds. *Literature: An Introduction to Fiction,*
   Poetry, and Drama. 10th ed. New York: Longman, 2007. Print.

Merwin, W. S. "For the Anniversary of My Death." Kennedy and Gioia 877-78.

Stevens, Wallace. "Thirteen Ways of Looking at a Blackbird." Kennedy and
   Gioia 880-82.

When you are citing more than one selection from the same source,
your teacher may allow you to avoid repetition by giving the source

in full (the Kennedy and Gioia entry) and then simply cross-referencing it in entries for the works you used. Thus the Erdrich, Merwin, and Stevens examples replace full publication information with Kennedy and Gioia and the appropriate pages in that book. Note that each entry appears in its proper alphabetical place among other works cited. Because each entry cross-references the Kennedy anthology, the medium is not required.

28. An article in a reference work (print)

"Reckon." *Merriam-Webster's Collegiate Dictionary*. 11th ed. 2008. Print.

Wenner, Manfred W. "Arabia." *The New Encyclopaedia Britannica: Macropaedia*.

    15th ed. 2007. Print.

List an article in a reference work by its title (first example) unless the article is signed (second example). For works with entries arranged alphabetically, you need not include volume or page numbers. For works that are widely used and often revised, like those above, you may omit the editors' names and all publication information except any edition number, the publication year, and the medium. For works that are specialized—with narrow subjects and audiences—give full publication information:

"Hungarians in America." *The Ethnic Almanac*. Ed. Stephanie Bernardo Johns.

    6th ed. New York: Doubleday, 2002. 121-23. Print.

See also models 48 (p. 650) and 68 (p. 658), respectively, to cite reference works appearing on the Web or on a CD-ROM or DVD-ROM.

29. An illustrated book or graphic narrative (print)

Wilson, G. Willow. *Cairo*. Illus. M. K. Perker. New York: Vertigo-DC Comics,

    2005. Print.

When citing the work of the writer of a graphic narrative or illustrated book, follow the example above: author's name, title, Illus. ("Illustrated by"), and the illustrator's name. When citing the work of an illustrator, list his or her name first, followed by a comma and illus. ("illustrator"). After the title and By, list the author's name.

Williams, Garth, illus. *Charlotte's Web*. By E. B. White. 1952. New York: Harper,

    1999. Print.

30. A multivolume work (print)

Lincoln, Abraham. *The Collected Works of Abraham Lincoln*. Ed. Roy P. Basler.

    Vol. 5. New Brunswick: Rutgers UP, 1953. Print. 8 vols.

If you use only one volume of a multivolume work, give that volume number before the publication information (Vol. 5 in the preceding example). You may add the total number of volumes at the end of the entry (8 vols. in the example).

If you use two or more volumes of a multivolume work, give the work's total number of volumes before the publication information (8 vols. in the following example). Your text citation will indicate which volume you are citing (see p. 623).

> Lincoln, Abraham. *The Collected Works of Abraham Lincoln*. Ed. Roy P. Basler.
>
> 8 vols. New Brunswick: Rutgers UP, 1953. Print.

If you cite a multivolume work published over a period of years, give the inclusive years as the publication date: for instance, Cambridge: Harvard UP, 1978-90.

31. A series (print)

> Bergman, Ingmar. *The Seventh Seal*. New York: Simon, 1995. Print. Mod. Film
>
> Scripts Ser. 12.

Place the name of the series (not quoted or italicized) at the end of the entry, followed by a series number (if any) and a period. Abbreviate common words such as *modern* and *series*.

32. A republished book (print)

> James, Henry. *The Bostonians*. 1886. New York: Penguin, 2001. Print.

Republished books include books reissued under new titles and paperbound editions of books originally released in hard covers. Place the original publication date (but not the place of publication or the publisher's name) after the title, and then provide the full publication information for the source you are using. If the book was originally published under a different title, add this title after Rpt. of ("Reprint of") at the end of the entry (after Print) and move the original publication date after the title—for example, Rpt. of *Thomas Hardy: A Life*. 1941.

33. The Bible (print)

> The Bible. Print. King James Vers.
>
> *The Holy Bible*. Trans. Ronald Youngblood et al. Grand Rapids: Zondervan,
>
> 1984. Print. New Intl. Vers.

When citing a standard version of the Bible (first example), do not italicize the title or the name of the version at the end. You need not provide publication information. For an edition of the Bible (second example), italicize the title, provide editors' and/or translators' names, give full publication information, and add the version name at the end.

34. A book with a title in its title (print)

> Eco, Umberto. *Postscript to* The Name of the Rose. Trans. William Weaver. New
>
> York: Harcourt, 1983. Print.

When a book's title contains another book title (here *The Name of the Rose*), do not italicize the second title. When a book's title contains a quotation or the title of a work normally placed in quotation marks, keep the quotation marks and italicize both titles: *Critical Response to Henry James's "The Beast in the Jungle."*

35. Published proceedings of a conference (print)

Stimpson, Bill, ed. *2007 Annual Conference and Exhibition*. Proc. of Amer. Wind
    Energy Assn. Conf., 3-6 June 2007, New York. Red Hook: Curran, 2008.
    Print.

To cite the published proceedings of a conference, use a book model—here, an edited book (model 22). Between the title and the publication data, add information about the conference, such as its name, date, and location. You may omit any of this information that already appears in the source title. Treat a particular presentation at the conference like a selection from an anthology (model 26).

36. An introduction, preface, foreword, or afterword (print)

Donaldson, Norman. Introduction. *The Claverings*. By Anthony Trollope. New
    York: Dover, 1977. vii-xv. Print.

An introduction, foreword, or afterword is often written by someone other than the book's author. When citing such a piece, give its name without quotation marks or italics, as with Introduction above. (If the piece has a title of its own, provide it, in quotation marks, between the name of the author and the name of the book.) Follow the title of the book with By and the book author's name. Give the inclusive page numbers of the part you cite. (In the example above, the small Roman numerals refer to the front matter of the book, before page 1.)

When the author of a preface or introduction is the same as the author of the book, give only the last name after the title:

Gould, Stephen Jay. Prologue. *The Flamingo's Smile: Reflections in Natural
    History*. By Gould. New York: Norton, 1985. 13-20. Print.

37. A book lacking publication information or pagination (print)

Carle, Eric. *The Very Busy Spider*. New York: Philomel, 1984. N. pag. Print.

Some books are not paginated or do not list a publisher or a place of publication. To cite such a book, provide as much information as you can and indicate the missing information with an abbreviation: N.p. if no city of publication, n.p. if no publisher, n.d. if no publication date, and N. pag. if no page numbers.

Other nonperiodical print sources

38. A government publication (print)

United Nations. Dept. of Economic and Social Affairs. *World Youth Report 2007: Young People's Transition to Adulthood—Progress and Challenges*. New York: United Nations, 2008. Print.

United States. Cong. House. Committee on Agriculture, Nutrition, and Forestry. *Food and Energy Act of 2007*. 110th Cong., 1st sess. Washington: GPO, 2007. Print.

Wisconsin. Dept. of Public Instruction. *Bullying Prevention Program: Grades 6-8*. Madison: Wisconsin Dept. of Public Instruction, 2007. Print.

If a government publication does not list a person as author or editor, give the appropriate agency as author, as in the above examples. Provide information in the order illustrated, separating elements with periods: the name of the government, the name of the agency (which may be abbreviated), and the title and publication information. For a congressional publication (second example), give the house and committee involved before the title, and give the number and session of Congress after the title. In this example, GPO stands for the US Government Printing Office.

If a government publication lists a person as author or editor, treat the source as an authored or edited book:

Putko, Michelle. *Women in Combat Compendium*. Carlisle: US Army War Coll., Strategic Studies Inst., 2008. Print.

See model 47 (p. 650) to cite a government publication you find on the Web.

39. A pamphlet or brochure (print)

Understanding Childhood Obesity. Tampa: Obesity Action Coalition, 2008. Print.

Most pamphlets and brochures can be treated as books. In this example, the pamphlet has no listed author, so the title comes first. If your source has an author, give his or her name first, followed by the title and publication information.

40. A dissertation (print)

McFaddin, Marie Oliver. *Adaptive Reuse: An Architectural Solution for Poverty and Homelessness*. Diss. U of Maryland, 2007. Ann Arbor: UMI, 2007. Print.

Treat a published dissertation like a book, but after the title insert Diss. ("Dissertation"), the institution granting the degree, and the year.

For an unpublished dissertation, use quotation marks rather than italics for the title and omit publication information.

Wilson, Stuart M. "John Stuart Mill as a Literary Critic." Diss. U of Michigan, 1990. Print.

41. A letter (print)

Buttolph, Mrs. Laura E. Letter to Rev. and Mrs. C. C. Jones. 20 June 1857. *The Children of Pride: A True Story of Georgia and the Civil War*. Ed. Robert Manson Myers. New Haven: Yale UP, 1972. 334-35. Print.

List a published letter under the writer's name. Specify that the source is a letter and to whom it was addressed, and give the date on which it was written. Treat the remaining information like that for a selection from an anthology (model 26, p. 641). (See also model 16, p. 637, for the format of a letter to the editor of a periodical.)

For an unpublished letter in the collection of a library or archive, specify the writer, recipient, and date, as for a published letter. Then provide the medium, either MS ("manuscript") or TS ("typescript"). End with the name and location of the archive.

James, Jonathan E. Letter to his sister. 16 Apr. 1970. MS. Jonathan E. James Papers. South Dakota State Archive, Pierre.

For a letter you received, give the name of the writer, note the fact that the letter was sent to you, provide the date of the letter, and add the medium, MS or TS.

Wynne, Ava. Letter to the author. 6 Apr. 2008. MS.

To cite an e-mail message or a discussion-group posting, see models 70–71 (p. 659).

4 | Listing nonperiodical Web sources

This section shows how to cite nonperiodical sources that you find on the Web. These sources may be published only once or occasionally, or they may be updated frequently but not regularly. (Most online magazines and newspapers fall into the latter category, even if they relate to printed periodicals, because their content changes often and unpredictably. See models 45 and 46.) Some nonperiodical Web sources are available only on the Web (facing page); others are available in other media as well (pp. 653–54). See models 62–67 (pp. 655–58) to cite a scholarly journal that you find on the Web and any periodical that you find in an online database.

The MLA no longer recommends providing a URL (electronic address) in Web source citations because URLs change frequently and because users can search for documents using search engines. However, do include a URL if your source is hard to find without it, if your source could be confused with another one, or if your instructor requires you to include URLs. See model 61 (p. 655) for the form to use when citing a URL.

Note The *MLA Handbook* does not label its examples of nonperiodical Web sources as particular types. For ease of reference, the following models identify and illustrate the kinds of Web sources you are likely to encounter. If you don't see just what you need, consult the index of models on pages 630–61 for a similar source type whose format you can adapt. If your source does not include all of the information needed for a complete citation, find and list what you can.

Nonperiodical sources available only on the Web

Many nonperiodical Web sources are available only online. The following list, adapted from the *MLA Handbook*, itemizes the possible elements in a nonperiodical Web publication, in order of their appearance in a works-cited entry:

1. **Name of the author or other person responsible for the source,** such as an editor, translator, or performer. See models 1–6 (pp. 629, 632–33) for the handling of authors' names. For other kinds of contributors, see models 22–24 (editors and translators) and models 74, 76–77, and 83 (performers, directors, and so on).

2. **Title of the cited work.** Use quotation marks for titles of articles, blog entries, and other sources that are parts of larger works. Use italics for books, plays, and other sources that are published independently.

3. **Title of the Web site,** in italics.

4. **Version or edition cited,** if any, following model 21 (p. 640)— for example, *Index of History Periodicals.* 2nd ed.

5. **Publisher or sponsor of the site,** followed by a comma. If you cannot find a publisher or sponsor, use N.p. ("No publisher") instead.

6. **Date of electronic publication, latest revision, or posting.** If no date is available, use n.d. ("no date") instead.

7. **Medium of publication:** Web.

8. **Date of your access:** day, month, year.

For some Web sources, you may want to include information that is not on this list, such as the names of both the writer and the performers on a television show.

42. A short work with a title (Web)

Molella, Arthur. "Cultures of Innovation." *The Lemelson Center for the Study of Invention and Innovation.* Smithsonian Inst., Natl. Museum of Amer. Hist., Spring 2005. Web. 3 Aug. 2008.

See the next page for an analysis of this entry and the location of the required information on the Web site. If the short work you are

---

Format for a short work on the Web

① ② ③
Molella, Arthur. "Cultures of Innovation." *The Lemelson Center for the Study of Inven-*

④ ⑤
tion and Innovation. Smithsonian Inst., Natl. Museum of Amer. Hist., Spring

⑥ ⑦
2005. Web. 3 Aug. 2008.

Top of page

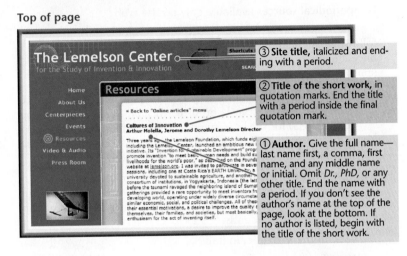

③ **Site title,** italicized and ending with a period.

② **Title of the short work,** in quotation marks. End the title with a period inside the final quotation mark.

① **Author.** Give the full name—last name first, a comma, first name, and any middle name or initial. Omit *Dr., PhD,* or any other title. End the name with a period. If you don't see the author's name at the top of the page, look at the bottom. If no author is listed, begin with the title of the short work.

Bottom of page

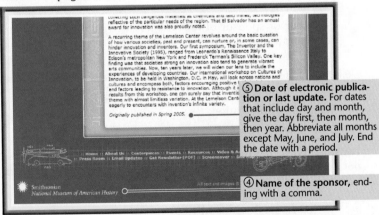

⑤ **Date of electronic publication or last update.** For dates that include day and month, give the day first, then month, then year. Abbreviate all months except May, June, and July. End the date with a period.

④ **Name of the sponsor,** ending with a comma.

⑥ **Medium.** Give the medium of the article, Web, followed by a period.

⑦ **Date of your access.** Give the day first, then month, then year. Abbreviate all months except May, June, and July. End the date with a period. (Since this date does not appear on the site, you'll need to record it separately.)

citing lacks an author, follow model 6 (p. 633) for an anonymous source, starting the entry with the title of the work:

> "Clean Energy." *Union of Concerned Scientists: Citizens and Scientists for Envi-*
> *ronmental Solutions.* Union of Concerned Scientists, 5 Feb. 2008. Web.
> 11 Mar. 2008.

To cite a short Web source that also appears in another medium (such as print), see models 56–60 (pp. 653–54). To cite an article from a Web journal or from an online database, see models 62–67 (pp. 655–58).

43. A short work without a title (Web)

> Crane, Gregory, ed. Home page. *The Perseus Digital Library.* Dept. of Classics,
> Tufts U, n.d. Web. 21 July 2008.

If you are citing an untitled short work from a Web site, such as the home page of a site or a posting to a blog, insert Home page, Online posting, or another descriptive label in place of the title. Do not use quotation marks or italics for this label.

Note that this source lacks a publication date, indicated by n.d. after the sponsor's name.

44. An entire site (Web)

> Cheit, Ross E., ed. *The Recovered Memory Project.* Taubman Center for Public
> and Amer. Insts., Brown U, July 2007. Web. 8 Oct. 2008.

When citing an entire Web site—for instance, a scholarly project or a foundation site—include the name of the editor, author, or compiler (if available); the title of the site; the sponsor; the date of publication or most recent update; the medium (Web); and your date of access.

If your source lacks a named author or editor, begin with the site title:

> *Union of Concerned Scientists: Citizens and Scientists for Environmental Solutions.*
> Union of Concerned Scientists, 5 Feb. 2008. Web. 11 Mar. 2008.

If your source lacks a sponsor, use the abbreviation N.p. ("No publisher"). If it lacks a publication date, use the abbreviation n.d. The source below lacks both a sponsor and a publication date:

> Corbett, John. *STARN: Scots Teaching and Resource Network.* N.p., n.d. Web. 26
> Nov. 2008.

45. An article in a newspaper (Web)

> Carvajal, Doreen. "High-Tech Crime Is an Online Bubble That Hasn't Burst."
> *New York Times.* New York Times, 7 Apr. 2008. Web. 8 Apr. 2008.

List the author, article title, and newspaper title, as in model 10 or 11 (pp. 635–36). Then give the publishers's name and the date. End with the medium of publication (Web) and the date of your access. (See model 66 to cite a newspaper article in an online database.)

Use the preceding format to adapt the models for print periodicals if you need to cite a Web newspaper review, editorial, letter to the editor, interview, or article in a series (models 14–18, pp. 637–38).

46. An article in a magazine (Web)

Yabroff, Jennie. "Art Aimed to Shock." *Newsweek*. Newsweek, 26 Apr. 2008.
    Web. 15 May 2008.

List the author, article title, and magazine title, as in model 12 or 13 (pp. 636–37). Then give the publisher's name and the date. End with the medium (Web) and the date of your access. (See model 67 to cite a magazine article in an online database.)

Use the preceding format to adapt the models for print periodicals if you need to cite a Web magazine review, editorial, letter to the editor, interview, article in a series, or special issue (models 14–19, pp. 637–38).

47. A government publication (Web)

United States. Dept. of Agriculture. "Inside the Pyramid." *MyPyramid.gov*.
    US Dept. of Agriculture, n.d. Web. 1 Mar. 2008.

See model 38 for examples of government publications in print. Provide the same information for online publications along with the facts of Web publication. The example above includes the names of the government and department; the title of the source, in quotation marks; the title of the Web site, in italics; n.d. (because there is no publication date); the medium (Web); and the date of access.

48. An article in a reference work (Web)

"Yi Dynasty." *Encyclopaedia Britannica Online*. Encyclopaedia Britannica, 2008.
    Web. 7 Apr. 2008.

This source does not list an author, so the entry begins with the title of the article and then proceeds as for other Web sources. If a reference article has an author, place the name before the article title, as in model 42.

For reference works that you find in print or on CD-ROM or DVD-ROM, see models 28 (p. 642) and 68 (p. 658), respectively.

49. An image (Web)

To cite images that are available only on the Web, give the name of the artist or creator, the title of the work, the date of the work (if any), a word describing the type of image (if not otherwise clear from the image or site title), the title of the Web site, the sponsor, the date of the site, the medium (Web), and your date of access. The following examples show a range of possibilities.

A work of visual art:

> Simpson, Rick. *Overload. Museum of Computer Art.* Museum of Computer Art,
> 2008. Web. 1 Apr. 2008.

A photograph:

> Touboul, Jean. *Desert 1.* 2002. Photograph. *Artmuse.net.* Jean Touboul, 2007.
> Web. 14 Nov. 2008.

An advertisement:

> United States. Dept. of Educ. Federal Student Aid. Advertisement. *Facebook.*
> Facebook, 2008. Web. 6 May 2008.

A map, chart, graph, or diagram:

> "Greenhouse Effect." Diagram. *Earthguide.* Scripps Inst. of Oceanography,
> 2008. Web. 17 July 2008.

See also model 60 (p. 654) to cite an image that appears both on the Web and in another medium. And see models 78–82 (pp. 661–62) to cite images that aren't on the Web.

50. A television or radio program (Web)

> Seabrook, Andrea, host. *All Things Considered.* Natl. Public Radio, 6 Apr. 2008.
> Web. 21 Apr. 2008.

The Web sites of television and radio networks and programs often include both content that was broadcast as part of a show and content that is unique to the site. Cite such material by its title or by the name of the person whose work you cite. Identify the role of anyone but an author (host in the example). Give the site title, the sponsor, the date, the medium (Web), and the date of your access. You may also cite other contributors (and their roles) after the title, as in model 52.

See also model 74 (p. 660) to cite a television or radio program that isn't on the Web.

51. A video recording (Web)

> Green Children Foundation, prod. *The Green Children Visit China. YouTube.*
> YouTube, 7 Jan. 2008. Web. 28 June 2008.

Cite a video on the Web either by its title or by the name of the person whose work you are citing—in this example, the foundation that produced the video. Identify the role of anyone but an author (prod. in the example). Give the video title, the site title, the sponsor, the date, the medium (Web), and the date of your access. You may also cite other contributors (and their roles) after the title, as in model 52.

See also model 53 to cite a podcast of a video recording; model 59 (p. 654) to cite a video recording or film that appears both on the Web and in another medium (such as DVD); and model 77 (p. 661) to cite a film, DVD, or video recording that isn't on the Web.

52. A sound recording (Web)

Beglarian, Eve. *Five Things.* Perf. Beglarian et al. *Kalvos and Damian.* N.p., 23
Oct. 2001. Web. 8 Mar. 2008.

Cite a musical sound recording by its title or by the name of the person whose work you are citing—in this example, the composer. (If the composer's name comes after the title, precede it with By. See the next example.) This example also gives the work title, the performers of the work, the site title, the sponsor (here unknown, so replaced with N.p.), the date, the medium (Web), and the date of access.

The same format may be used for a spoken-word recording that you find on the Web:

Wasserstein, Wendy, narr. "Afternoon of a Faun." By Wasserstein. *The Borzoi
Reader Online.* Knopf, 2001. Web. 14 Feb. 2008.

See also the next model to cite a sound podcast; model 58 to cite a sound recording that appears both on the Web and in another medium (such as CD); and model 76 (p. 661) to cite a sound recording that isn't on the Web.

53. A podcast (Web)

Simon, Bob. "Exonerated." *60 Minutes. CBS News.* CBS News, 25 May 2008.
Web. 6 June 2008.

This podcast from a news program lists the author of a story on the show, the title of the story (in quotation marks), and the program (italicized) as well as the site title, sponsor, date, medium (Web), and access date. If a podcast does not list an author or other creator, begin with the title.

54. A blog entry (Web)

Marshall, Joshua Micah. "Asking the Tough Questions." *Talking Points Memo.*
TPM Media, 15 May 2008. Web. 21 May 2008.

To cite an entry from a blog, give the author, the title of the entry, the title of the blog or site, the name of the sponsor (or N.p. if no sponsor is named), the publication date, the medium (Web), and the date of your access. See model 43 (p. 649) to cite a blog entry without a title.

55. A wiki (Web)

"Podcast." *Wikipedia*. Wikimedia, n.d. Web. 20 Nov. 2008.

To cite an entry from a wiki, follow the above example: entry title, site title, sponsor, publication date (here n.d. because the wiki entry is undated), medium (Web), and date of access. Begin with the site title if you are citing the entire wiki.

Nonperiodical Web sources also available in print

Some sources you find on the Web may be books, poems, short stories, and other works that have been scanned from print versions. To cite such a source, generally provide the information for original print publication as well as that for Web publication. Begin your entry as if you were citing the print work, consulting models 20–41 for an appropriate format. Then, instead of giving "Print" as the medium, provide the title of the Web site you used, any version or edition number, the medium you used (Web), and the date of your access.

56. A short work with print publication information (Web)

Wheatley, Phillis. "On Virtue." *Poems on Various Subjects, Religious and Moral*. London, 1773. N. pag. *American Verse Project*. Web. 21 July 2008.

The print information for this poem follows model 26 (p. 641) for a selection from an anthology, but it omits the publisher's name because the anthology was published before 1900. The print information ends with N. pag. because the original source has no page numbers.

57. A book with print publication information (Web)

James, Henry. *The Ambassadors*. 1903. New York: Scribner's, 1909. *Oxford Text Archive*. Web. 5 May 2008.

The print information for this novel follows model 32 (p. 643) for a republished book, so it includes both the original date of publication (1903) and the publication information for the scanned book.

Nonperiodical Web sources also available in other media

Some images, films, and sound recordings that you find on the Web may have been published before in other media and then scanned or digitized for the Web. To cite such a source, generally provide the information for original publication as well as that for

Web publication. Begin your entry as if you were citing the original, consulting models 74–84 (pp. 660–63) for an appropriate format. Then, instead of giving the original medium of publication, provide the title of the Web site you used, the medium you used (Web), and your date of access.

58. A sound recording with other publication information (Web)

"Rioting in Pittsburgh." CBS Radio, 1968. *Vincent Voice Library*. Web.
    7 Dec. 2008.

For Web sound recordings with original publication information, base citations on model 76 (p. 661), adding the information for Web publication.

59. A film or video recording with other publication information (Web)

Coca Cola. Advertisement. Dir. Haskell Wexler. 1971. *American Memory*. Lib. of
    Cong. Web. 8 Apr. 2008.

For Web films or videos with original publication information, base citations on model 77 (p. 661), adding the information for Web publication.

60. An image with other publication information (Web)

Pollock, Jackson. *Lavender Mist: Number 1*. 1950. Natl. Gallery of Art, Washington.
    WebMuseum. Web. 7 Apr. 2008.

Keefe, Mike. "FAA Inspector in a Quandary." Cartoon. *Denver Post* 5 Apr. 2008.
    PoliticalCartoons.com. Web. 7 Apr. 2008.

For Web images with original publication information, base citations on models 78–82 (pp. 661–62), adding the information for Web publication.

Citation of a URL

61. A source requiring citation of the URL

Joss, Rich. "Dispatches from the Ice: The Second Season Begins." *Antarctic*
    Expeditions. Smithsonian Natl. Zoo and Friends of the Natl. Zoo, 26 Oct.
    2007. Web. 26 Sept. 2008. <http://nationalzoo.si.edu/
    ConservationAndScience/AquaticEcosystems/Antarctica/Expedition/
    FieldNew/2-FieldNews.cfm>.

Because a URL does not always provide a convenient or usable route to a source, the MLA no longer recommends including URLs in works-cited entries. However, you should include URLs when your teacher requires them. You should also give a URL when readers may not be able to locate a source without one. For example, using a search engine to find "Dispatches from the Ice" (the title in the example) yields more than ten hits, one of which links to the correct site but the wrong document.

If you need to include a URL, ensure accuracy by using Copy and Paste to duplicate it in a file or an e-mail to yourself. In your list of works cited, give the URL after your date of access and a period. Put angle brackets on both ends of the URL, and end with a period. Break URLs *only* after slashes—do not hyphenate.

5 Listing journals on the Web and periodicals in online databases

This section covers two kinds of periodicals: scholarly journals that you reach directly on the Web (below) and journals, newspapers, and magazines that you reach through online databases (p. 656). Newspapers and magazines that you reach directly on the Web are typically not periodicals (because their content changes often and unpredictably), so they are covered in models 45 and 46 (pp. 649–50).

Citations for Web journals and for periodicals in online databases resemble those for print periodicals, with some changes for the different medium.

Web journals consulted directly

The journals you find directly on the Web may be published only online or may be published in print versions as well. The citation format is the same in either case: begin with an appropriate print model (pp. 633–35), but replace "Print" with Web and add your access date. Because many Web journals are unpaged, you may have to substitute n. pag. for page numbers.

62. An article in a scholarly journal (Web)

Polletta, Francesca. "Just Talk: Public Deliberation after 9/11." *Journal of Public Deliberation* 4.1 (2008): n. pag. Web. 7 Apr. 2008.

See the next page for an analysis of this entry and the location of the required information in the Web journal.

Use the same format to adapt the models for print periodicals if you need to cite a Web journal review, editorial, letter to the editor, interview, article in a series, or special issue (models 14–19, pp. 637–38). For a journal article reached in an online database, see model 64.

Format for a journal article on the Web

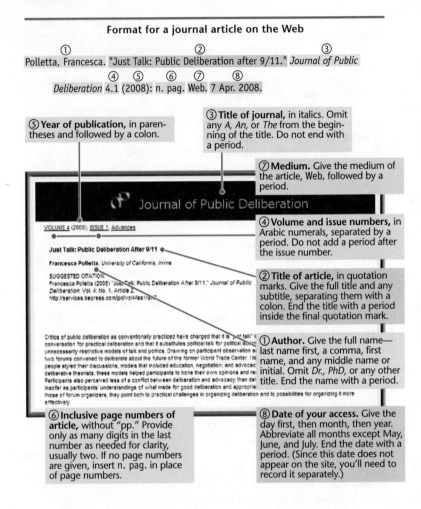

①
Polletta, Francesca. ②"Just Talk: Public Deliberation after 9/11." ③*Journal of Public*
④ ⑤ ⑥ ⑦ ⑧
Deliberation 4.1 (2008): n. pag. Web. 7 Apr. 2008.

⑤ **Year of publication,** in parentheses and followed by a colon.

③ **Title of journal,** in italics. Omit any *A, An,* or *The* from the beginning of the title. Do not end with a period.

⑦ **Medium.** Give the medium of the article, Web, followed by a period.

Journal of Public Deliberation

VOLUME 4 (2008), ISSUE 1, Advances

Just Talk: Public Deliberation After 9/11

Francesca Polletta, *University of California, Irvine*

SUGGESTED CITATION:
Francesca Polletta (2008) "Just Talk: Public Deliberation After 9/11," *Journal of Public Deliberation*: Vol. 4: No. 1, Article 2.
http://services.bepress.com/jpd/vol4/iss1/art2

Critics of public deliberation as conventionally practiced have charged that it is "just talk" in conversation for practical deliberation and that it substitutes political talk for political action. Two forums convened to deliberate about the future of the former World Trade Center. I te people styled their discussions, models that included education, negotiation, and advocac deliberative theorists, these models helped participants to hone their own opinions and re Participants also perceived less of a conflict between deliberation and advocacy than de Insofar as participants' understandings of what made for good deliberation and appropria those of forum organizers, they point both to practical challenges in organizing deliberation and to possibilities for organizing it more effectively.

④ **Volume and issue numbers,** in Arabic numerals, separated by a period. Do not add a period after the issue number.

② **Title of article,** in quotation marks. Give the full title and any subtitle, separating them with a colon. End the title with a period inside the final quotation mark.

① **Author.** Give the full name— last name first, a comma, first name, and any middle name or initial. Omit *Dr., PhD,* or any other title. End the name with a period.

⑥ **Inclusive page numbers of article,** without "pp." Provide only as many digits in the last number as needed for clarity, usually two. If no page numbers are given, insert n. pag. in place of page numbers.

⑧ **Date of your access.** Give the day first, then month, then year. Abbreviate all months except May, June, and July. End the date with a period. (Since this date does not appear on the site, you'll need to record it separately.)

63. An abstract of a journal article (Web)

Polletta, Francesca. "Just Talk: Public Deliberation after 9/11." *Journal of
Public Deliberation* 4.1 (2008): n. pag. Abstract. Web. 7 Apr. 2008.

Treat a Web abstract like a Web journal article, but add Abstract between the publication information and the medium. (You may omit this label if the journal title clearly indicates that the cited work is an abstract.) See model 65 to cite an abstract in an online database.

Web periodicals consulted in online databases

Many articles in journals, newspapers, and magazines are available in online databases that you reach through your library's Web site, such as *Academic Search Complete, ProQuest,* and *Project Muse.* Follow models 7–19 (pp. 633–38) for print periodicals, but replace "Print" with the title of the database you consulted, the medium (Web), and the date of your access.

64. An article in a scholarly journal (online database)

Gorski, Paul C. "Privilege and Repression in the Digital Era: Rethinking the

Sociopolitics of the Digital Divide." *Race, Gender and Class* 10.4 (2003):

145-76. *Ethnic NewsWatch.* Web. 23 Apr. 2008.

See below for an analysis of the preceding entry and the location of the required information in the database.

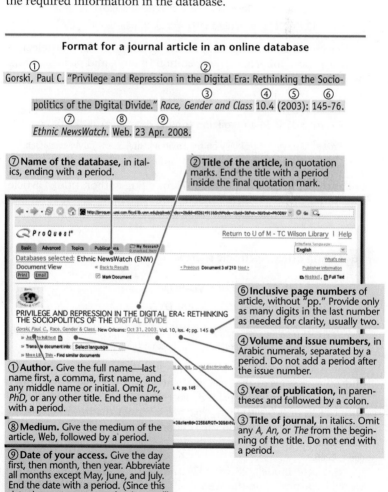

Format for a journal article in an online database

① ②
Gorski, Paul C. "Privilege and Repression in the Digital Era: Rethinking the Socio-
③ ④ ⑤ ⑥
politics of the Digital Divide." *Race, Gender and Class* 10.4 (2003): 145-76.
⑦ ⑧ ⑨
Ethnic NewsWatch. Web. 23 Apr. 2008.

⑦ **Name of the database,** in italics, ending with a period.

② **Title of the article,** in quotation marks. End the title with a period inside the final quotation mark.

⑥ **Inclusive page numbers** of article, without "pp." Provide only as many digits in the last number as needed for clarity, usually two.

④ **Volume and issue numbers,** in Arabic numerals, separated by a period. Do not add a period after the issue number.

⑤ **Year of publication,** in parentheses and followed by a colon.

① **Author.** Give the full name—last name first, a comma, first name, and any middle name or initial. Omit *Dr., PhD,* or any other title. End the name with a period.

⑧ **Medium.** Give the medium of the article, Web, followed by a period.

③ **Title of journal,** in italics. Omit any *A, An,* or *The* from the beginning of the title. Do not end with a period.

⑨ **Date of your access.** Give the day first, then month, then year. Abbreviate all months except May, June, and July. End the date with a period. (Since this date does not appear on the site, you'll need to record it separately.)

65. An abstract of a journal article (online database)

Gorski, Paul C. "Privilege and Repression in the Digital Era: Rethinking the
    Sociopolitics of the Digital Divide." *Race, Gender and Class* 10.4 (2003):
    145-76. Abstract. *Ethnic NewsWatch.* Web. 23 Apr. 2008.

Treat an abstract in an online database like a journal article in a database, but add Abstract between the publication information and the database title. (You may omit this label if the journal title clearly indicates that the cited work is an abstract.)

66. An article in a newspaper (online database)

Buckman, Rebecca. "Driver Cell Phone Bans Questioned." *Wall Street Journal*
    13 May 2008, eastern ed.: D2+. *ProQuest.* Web. 12 Oct. 2008.

Follow model 10 or 11 (p. 635) for citing author, title of article, title of newspaper, publication date, edition (if any), and page numbers. Add the title of the database, the medium (Web), and the date of your access.

67. An article in a magazine (online database)

Brown, Kathryn. "The Skinny on the Environment." *Scientific American* Jan.
    2008: 30-37. *Academic Search Premier.* Web. 3 Aug. 2008.

Follow model 12 or 13 (pp. 636–37) for citing author, title of article, title of magazine, publication date, and page numbers. Add the title of the database, the medium (Web), and the date of your access.

6 Listing other electronic sources

Publications on CD-ROM or DVD-ROM

68. A nonperiodical CD-ROM or DVD-ROM

Nunberg, Geoffrey. "Usage in the Dictionary." *The American Heritage Dictionary
    of the English Language.* 4th ed. Boston: Houghton, 2000. CD-ROM.

Single-issue CD-ROMs may be encyclopedias, dictionaries, books, and other resources that are published just once, like print books. Follow models 20–37 for print books (pp. 638–44), but replace "Print" with CD-ROM or DVD-ROM. If the disc has a vendor that differs from the publisher of the work, add the vendor's place of publication, name, and publication date after the medium—for instance, Oklahoma City: Soquest, 2006.

See also models 28 (p. 642) and 48 (p. 650) to cite reference works in print and on the Web.

69. A periodical CD-ROM or DVD-ROM

Kolata, Gina. "Gauging Body Mass Index in a Changing Body." *New York Times* 28 June 2005, natl. ed.: D1+. CD-ROM. *New York Times Ondisc.* UMI-ProQuest. Sept. 2005.

Databases on CD-ROM or DVD-ROM are issued periodically—for instance, every six months or every year. The journals, newspapers, and other publications included in such a database are generally available in print as well, so your works-cited entry should give the information for both formats. Start with information for the print version, following models 7–19 (pp. 633–38). Then replace "Print" with the medium (CD-ROM or DVD-ROM), the database title, the vendor's name (UMI-ProQuest in the example), and the database publication date.

E-mail and discussion-group postings

70. An e-mail message

Bailey, Elizabeth. "Re: London." Message to the author. 27 Mar. 2008. E-mail.

For e-mail, give the writer's name; the title, if any, from the e-mail's subject heading, in quotation marks; Message to the author (or the name of a recipient besides you); the date of the message; and the medium, E-mail. You do not need to include the date of your access.

71. A posting to a discussion group

Williams, Frederick. "Circles as Primitive." *The Math Forum @ Drexel.* Drexel U, 28 Feb. 2008. E-mail.

Cite a posting to a discussion group like a blog entry (model 54, p. 652). This example for a discussion-list posting includes author's name, title of the posting, title of the discussion list, name of the sponsor, date of the posting, and medium (E-mail). If the posting is untitled, give Online posting instead. You need not add the date of your access.

Digital files

You may want to cite a digital file that is not on the Web or on a disc, such as a PDF document, a JPEG image, or an MP3 sound recording that you downloaded onto your computer. Use the appropriate model for your kind of source (for instance, model 79 for a personal photograph), but replace the medium with the file format you're using. If you don't know the file format, use Digital file.

72. A text file (digital)

Berg, John K. "Estimates of Persons Driving While Intoxicated." *Law Enforcement Today* 17 Apr. 2008. PDF file.

Fernandez, Carlos. "Summers in Spain." 2008. *Microsoft Word* file.

73. A media file (digital)

Springsteen, Bruce. "Empty Sky." *The Rising*. Columbia, 2002. MP3 file.

Boys playing basketball. Personal photograph by Granger Goetz. 2008. JPEG file.

7 Listing other sources

The source types covered in this section are not on a computer or, generally, in printed sources. Most of them have parallel citation formats elsewhere in this chapter when you reach them through electronic and print media. See model 17 (p. 637) to cite an interview in print. See models 49–52 (pp. 650–52) to cite images, television and radio programs, video recordings, and sound recordings that are available only on the Web. See models 58–60 (p. 654) to cite such sources when they are available on the Web and in other media. And see model 73 to cite such sources in digital files.

74. A television or radio program

"Piece of My Heart." By Stacy McKee. Dir. Mark Tinker. *Grey's Anatomy*. ABC. KGO, San Francisco, 1 May 2008. Television.

Start with the title unless you are citing the work of a person or persons. The example here cites an episode title (in quotation marks) and the names of the episode's writer and director. By and Dir. identify their roles. Then the entry gives the program title (in italics), the name of the network, the call letters and city of the local station, the date, and the medium (Television). If you list individuals who worked on the entire program rather than an episode, put their names after the program title.

75. A personal or broadcast interview

Paul, William. Personal interview. 6 June 2008.

Diaz, Junot. Interview by Terry Gross. *Fresh Air*. Natl. Public Radio. WGBH, Boston, 18 Oct. 2007. Radio.

Begin with the name of the person interviewed. For an interview you conducted, specify Personal interview or the medium (such as Telephone interview or E-mail interview), and then give the date. For an interview you heard or saw, provide the title if any or Interview if there is no title. Add the name of the interviewer if he or she is identified. Then follow an appropriate model for the kind of source (here, a radio program), and end with the medium (here, Radio).

76. A sound recording

Rubenstein, Artur, perf. Piano Concerto no. 2 in B-flat. By Johannes Brahms.

> Cond. Eugene Ormandy. Philadelphia Orch. RCA, 1972. LP.

Springsteen, Bruce. "Empty Sky." *The Rising*. Columbia, 2002. CD.

Begin with the name of the individual whose work you are citing. Unless this person is the composer, identify his or her role, as with perf. ("performer") in the first example. If you're citing a work identified by form, number, and key (first example), do not use quotation marks or italics for the title. If you're citing a song or song lyrics (second example), give the title in quotation marks; then provide the title of the recording in italics. Following the title, identify the composer or author if you haven't already, after By, and name and identify other participants you want to mention. Then provide the manufacturer of the recording, the date of release, and the medium: LP in the first example, CD in the second.

77. A film, DVD, or video recording

A Beautiful Mind. Dir. Ron Howard. Universal, 2001. Film.

Start with the title of the work unless you are citing the work of a person (see the next example). Generally, identify and name the director. You may list other participants (writer, lead performers, and so on) as you judge appropriate. For a film, end with the distributor, date, and medium (Film).

For a DVD or videocassette, include the original release date (if any), the distributor's name, and the medium (DVD or Videocassette).

Balanchine, George, chor. *Serenade*. Perf. San Francisco Ballet. Dir. Hilary

> Bean. 1991. PBS Video, 2006. DVD.

78. A painting, photograph, or other work of visual art

Arnold, Leslie. *Seated Woman*. N.d. Oil on canvas. DeYoung Museum, San Francisco.

Sugimoto, Hiroshi. *Pacific Ocean, Mount Tamalpais*. 1994. Photograph.

> Private collection.

To cite an actual work of art, name the artist and give the title (in italics) and the date of creation (or N.d. if the date is unknown). Then provide the medium of the work (such as Oil on canvas or Photograph) and the name and location of the owner, if known. (Use Private collection if not.)

For a work you see only in a reproduction, provide the complete publication information for the source you used. Omit the medium of the work itself, and replace it with the medium of the reproduction (Print in the following example). Omit such information only if you examined the actual work.

Hockney, David. *Place Furstenberg, Paris*. 1985. Coll. Art Gallery, New Paltz.
David Hockney: A Retrospective. Ed. Maurice Tuchman and Stephanie
Barron. Los Angeles: Los Angeles County Museum of Art, 1988. 247. Print.

79. A personal photograph

Common milkweed on Lake Michigan shoreline. Personal photograph by the
author. 22 Aug. 2008.

For a personal photograph by you or by someone else, describe the subject (without quotation marks or italics), name the photographer, and add the date. The current edition of the *MLA Handbook* does not cover personal photographs. This format comes from the previous edition.

80. A map, chart, graph, or diagram

"The Sonoran Desert." Map. *Sonoran Desert: An American Deserts Handbook*. By
Rose Houk. Tucson: Western Natl. Parks Assn., 2000. 12. Print.

Unless the creator of an illustration is given on the source, list the illustration by its title. Put the title in quotation marks if it comes from another publication or in italics if it is published independently. Then add a description (Map, Chart, and so on), the publication information, and the medium (here, Print).

81. A cartoon or comic strip

Trudeau, Garry. "Doonesbury." Comic strip. *San Francisco Chronicle* 28 Aug.
2008: E6. Print.

Cite a cartoon or comic strip with the artist's name, the title (in quotation marks), the description Cartoon or Comic strip, the publication information, and the medium (here, Print).

82. An advertisement

Escape Hybrid by Ford. Advertisement. *New Yorker* 10 Dec. 2007: 11. Print.

Cite an advertisement with the name of the product or company advertised, the description Advertisement, the publication information, and the medium (Print, Television, Radio, and so on).

83. A performance

Levine, James, cond. Boston Symphony Orch. Symphony Hall, Boston. 2 May
2008. Performance.
The New Century. By Paul Rudnick. Dir. Nicholas Martin. Mitzi E. Newhouse
Theater, New York. 6 May 2008. Performance.

For a live performance, generally base your citation on film citations (model 77). Place the title first (second example) unless you are citing the work of an individual (first example). After the title, provide relevant information about participants as well as the theater, city, and performance date. Conclude with the medium (Performance).

84. A lecture, speech, address, or reading

Katrib, Ruba. "New Art: South Florida Exhibit." Museum of Contemporary Art.
    MOCA at Goldman Warehouse, Miami. 4 Sept. 2007. Address.

Give the speaker's name, the title if any (in quotation marks), the title of the meeting if any, the name of the sponsoring organization, the location of the presentation, and the date. End with a description of the type of presentation (Lecture, Speech, Address, Reading).

Although the MLA does not provide a specific style for citing classroom lectures in your courses, you can adapt the preceding format for this purpose.

Cavanaugh, Carol. Class lecture on teaching mentors. Lesley U. 4 Apr. 2008.
    Lecture.

Exercise 46.1 Writing works-cited entries

Prepare works-cited entries from the following information. Follow the MLA models given in this chapter unless your teacher specifies a different style. Arrange the finished entries in alphabetical order, not numbered.

1. An article titled "Use of Third Parties to Collect State and Local Taxes on Internet Sales," appearing in the print periodical *The Pacific Business Journal,* volume 5, issue 2, in 2004. The authors are Malai Zimmerman and Kent Hoover. The article appears on pages 45 through 48 of the journal.

2. A government publication you consulted on November 12, 2008, on the Web. The author is the Advisory Commission on Electronic Commerce. The commission is an agency of the United States government. The title of the publication is *Report to Congress.* It was published in April 2005.

3. A Web article with no listed author. The title and sponsor of the Web site is Center on Budget and Policy Priorities. The title of the article is "The Internet Tax Freedom Act and the Digital Divide," and the site is dated September 26, 2007. You consulted the site on November 2, 2008.

4. An article in the magazine *Forbes,* published November 28, 2007, on pages 56 through 58. The author is Janet Novack. The title is "Point, Click, Pay Tax." You accessed the source through the database *ProQuest* on November 10, 2008.

5. A print book titled *All's Fair in Internet Commerce, or Is It?* by Sally G. Osborne. The book was published in 2004 by Random House in New York.

6. An e-mail interview you conducted with Nora James on November 1, 2008.
7. An article titled "State and Local Sales/Use Tax Simplification," appearing on pages 67 through 80 of a print anthology, *The Sales Tax in the Twenty-first Century.* The anthology is edited by Matthew N. Murray and William F. Fox. The article is by Wayne G. Eggert. The anthology was published in 2004 by Praeger in Westport, Connecticut.

46c   Using MLA document format

The *MLA Handbook* provides guidelines for a fairly simple document format, with just a few elements. For guidelines on type fonts, headings, lists, illustrations, and other features that MLA style does not specify, see pages 118–26.

The samples below show the formats for the first page and a later page of a paper. For the format of the list of works cited, see pages 629–30.

First page of MLA paper

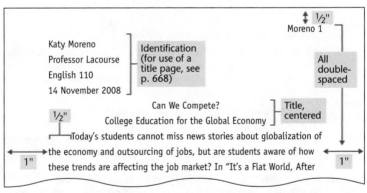

Later page of MLA paper

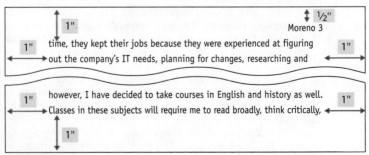

Margins Use minimum one-inch margins on all sides of every page.

Spacing and indentions Double-space throughout. Indent paragraphs one-half inch. (See below for indention of poetry and long prose quotations.)

Paging Begin numbering on the first page, and number consecutively through the end (including the list of works cited). Use Arabic numerals (1, 2, 3) positioned in the upper right, about one-half inch from the top. Place your last name before the page number in case the pages later become separated.

Identification and title MLA style does not require a title page for a paper. If your teacher asks you to supply a title page, see pages 667–68. Otherwise, follow the sample on the previous page, providing your name, the date, and other information requested by your teacher. Place this identification an inch from the top of the page, aligned with the left margin and double-spaced.

Double-space again, and center the title. Do not highlight the title with italics, underlining, boldface, larger type, or quotation marks. Capitalize the words in the title according to the guidelines on page 485. Double-space the lines of the title and between the title and the text.

Poetry and long prose quotations Treat a single line of poetry like any other quotation, running it into your text and enclosing it in quotation marks. You may run in two or three lines of poetry as well, separating the lines with a slash surrounded by space.

> An example of Robert Frost's incisiveness is in two lines from "Death of the Hired Man": "Home is the place where, when you have to go there / They have to take you in" (119-20).

Always set off from your text a poetry quotation of more than three lines. Use double spacing above and below the quotation and for the quotation itself. Indent the quotation one inch from the left margin. *Do not add quotation marks.*

> Emily Dickinson stripped ideas to their essence, as in this description of "A narrow Fellow in the Grass," a snake:
>
> > I more than once at Noon
> > Have passed, I thought, a Whip lash
> > Unbraiding in the Sun
> > When stopping to secure it
> > It wrinkled, and was gone – (12-16)

Also set off a prose quotation of more than four typed lines. (See p. 599 on when to use such long quotations.) Double-space and indent as with the preceding poetry example. *Do not add quotation marks.*

> In the influential *Talley's Corner* from 1967, Elliot Liebow observes that
> "unskilled" construction work requires more skill than is generally assumed:
>> A healthy, sturdy, active man of good intelligence requires from two
>> to four weeks to break in on a construction job. . . . It frequently
>> happens that his foreman or the craftsman he services is not willing
>> to wait that long for him to get into condition or to learn at a
>> glance the difference in size between a rough 2 x 8 and a finished
>> 2 x 10. (62)

Do not use a paragraph indention for a quotation of a single complete paragraph or a part of a paragraph. Use paragraph indentions of one-quarter inch only for a quotation of two or more complete paragraphs.

47

Two Research Papers in MLA Style

The following pages show the research papers of Justin Malik and Vanessa Haley, whose work we followed in Chapters 41–45. (Malik's paper begins on page 668, Haley's on p. 681.) Both students followed the style of the *MLA Handbook* for documenting sources and formatting their papers. Accompanying both students' papers are comments on format, source citations, and other matters.

mycomplab

Visit *mycomplab.com* for more resources as well as exercises on MLA documentation and format.

Format of a title page and outline

A title page is not required by MLA style but may be required by your teacher. If so, or if you are required to submit an outline with your paper, prepare a title page as shown on the next page. If your teacher does not require a title page, follow MLA style as shown on page 664 and in Vanessa Haley's paper on page 681: place your name, the identifying information, and the date on the first page of the paper.

Some teachers ask students to submit an outline of the final paper. For advice on constructing a formal sentence or topic outline, see pages 39–41. Justin Malik's formal sentence outline follows his title page on page 669.

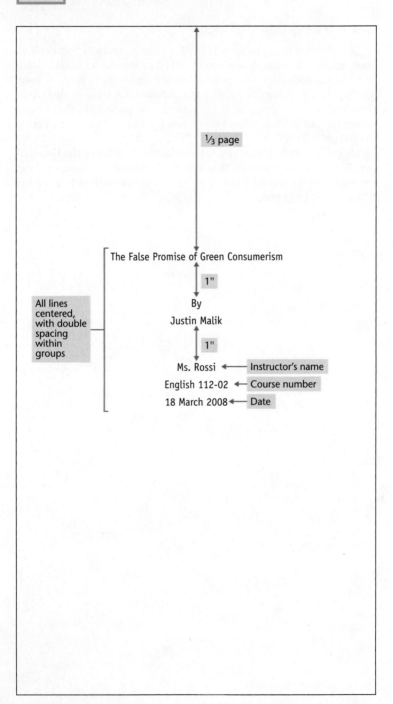

⅓ page

The False Promise of Green Consumerism

1"

By

Justin Malik

1"

All lines centered, with double spacing within groups

Ms. Rossi ← Instructor's name

English 112-02 ← Course number

18 March 2008 ← Date

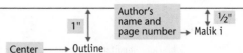

Center ──→ Outline

Thesis statement: Although green consumerism can help the environment, consumerism itself is the root of some of the most pressing ecological problems we face. To make a real difference, we must consume less.

I. Green products claiming to help the environment both appeal to and confuse consumers.

   A. The market for ecologically sound products is enormous.

   B. Determining whether or not a product is as green as advertised can be a challenge.

II. Green products don't solve the high rate of consumption that truly threatens the environment.

   A. Overconsumption is a significant cause of three of the most serious environmental problems.

      1. It depletes natural resources.

      2. It contributes to pollution, particularly from the greenhouse gases responsible for global warming.

      3. It produces a huge amount of solid waste.

   B. The availability of greener products has not reduced the environmental effects of consumption.

III. Since buying green products does not reduce consumption, other solutions must be found for environmental problems.

   A. Experts have proposed many far-reaching solutions, but they require concerted government action and could take decades to implement.

   B. For shorter-term solutions, individuals can change their own behavior as consumers.

      1. Precycling may be the greenest behavior that individuals can adopt.

         a. Precycling means avoiding purchase of products that use raw materials and excessive packaging.

b. More important, precycling means avoiding purchases of new products whenever possible.

2. For unavoidable purchases, individuals can buy green products and influence businesses to embrace ecological goals.

Malik 1

The False Promise of Green Consumerism

They line the aisles of just about any store. They seem to dominate television and print advertising. Chances are that at least a few of them belong to you. From organic jeans to household cleaners to hybrid cars, products advertised as environmentally friendly are readily available and are so popular they're trendy. It's easy to see why Americans are buying these things in record numbers. The new wave of "green" consumer goods makes an almost irresistible promise: we can save the planet by shopping.

Saving the planet does seem to be urgent. Thanks partly to former Vice President Al Gore, who sounded the alarm in 1992 with *Earth in the Balance* and again in 2006 with *An Inconvenient Truth,* the threat of global warming has become a regular feature in the news media and a recurring theme in popular culture. Unfortunately, as Gore himself points out, climate change is just one of many environmental problems competing for our attention: the rainforests are vanishing, our air and our water are dangerously polluted, alarming numbers of species are facing extinction, and landfills are overflowing (*Earth* 23-28). All the bad news can be overwhelming, and most people feel powerless to halt the damage. Thus it is reassuring that we may be able to help by making small changes in what we buy—but it is not entirely true. Although green consumerism can help the environment, consumerism itself is the root of some of the most pressing ecological problems we face. To make a real difference, we must consume less.

The market for items perceived as ecologically sound is enormous. Experts estimate that spending on green products already approaches $200 billion a year (Adler et al.). Shoppers respond well to new options, whether the purchase is as minor as a bottle of chemical-free dish soap or as major as a front-loading washing machine. Not surprisingly, businesses are responding by offering as many new eco-products as they can.

Title centered.

Double-space throughout.

Introduction: establishes the issue with examples (first paragraph) and background (second paragraph).

Citation form: no parenthetical citation because author and titles are named in the text and discussion cites entire works.

Citation form: shortened title for one of two works by the same author.

Thesis statement.

Background on green products.

Citation form: source with more than three authors; no page number because source from an online database is unnumbered.

Malik 2

Brackets signal
word added to
clarify the
quotation.

Source author
named in text, so
not named in par-
enthetical citation.

Common-
knowledge
examples of stores
and products do
not require source
citations.

Citation form:
shortened title for
anonymous
source; page
number for a one-
page source not
required.

Citation form: au-
thor not named
in the text; short-
ened title for one
of two works by
the same author.
Position of citation
clarifies which
example comes
from the source.

Environmental
effects of con-
sumption. Writer
synthesizes infor-
mation from half
a dozen sources to
develop his own
ideas.

Sandra Jones of the *Chicago Tribune* reports that "green product introductions [have] skyrocketed" lately. She cites a market research report by the Mintel International Group: in the first five years of this century, new household products labeled as green rose from zero to 153, eco-conscious health and beauty aids increased by more than a thousand percent, and organic food and beverage options nearly tripled (B1). These new products are offered for sale at stores like Wal-Mart, Target, Home Depot, Starbucks, and Pottery Barn. It seems clear that green consumerism has grown into a mainstream interest.

Determining whether or not a product is as green as advertised can be a challenge. Claims vary: a product might be labeled as organic, biodegradable, energy efficient, recycled, carbon neutral, renewable, or just about anything that sounds environmentally positive. However, none of these terms carries a universally accepted meaning, and no enforceable labeling regulations exist ("It's Not Easy"). Some of the new product options offer clear environmental benefits: for instance, compact fluorescent light bulbs last ten times as long as regular bulbs and draw about a third of the electricity (Gore, *Inconvenient* 306), and paper made from recycled fibers saves many trees. But other "green" products do little or nothing to help the environment: a disposable razor made with less plastic is still a disposable razor, destined for a landfill.

Distinguishing truly green products from those that are not so green merely scratches the surface of a much larger issue. The products aren't the problem; it's our high rate of consumption that poses the real threat to the environment. We seek what's newer and better—whether cars, clothes, phones, computers, televisions, shoes, or gadgets—and they all require resources to make, ship, and use them. Political scientists Thomas Princen, Michael Maniates, and Ken Conca maintain that overconsumption is a leading force behind several ecological crises, warning that

Malik 3

> ever-increasing pressures on ecosystems, life-
> supporting environmental services, and critical
> natural cycles are driven not only by the sheer
> number of resource users . . . but also by the pat-
> terns of resource use themselves. (4)

Those patterns of resource use are disturbing. In just the
second half of the twentieth century, gross world product
(the global output of consumer goods) grew at five times the
rate of population growth—a difference explained by a huge
rise in consumption per person. (See fig. 1.) Such growth
might be good for the economy, but it is bad for the environment. As fig. 1 shows, it is accompanied by the depletion of
natural resources, increases in the carbon emissions that
cause global warming, and increases in the amount of solid
waste disposal.

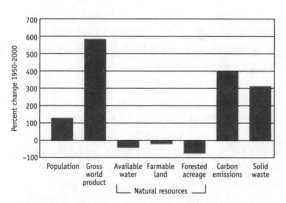

Fig. 1. Global population, consumption, and environmental impacts, 1950-2000. Data from United Nations Development Programme; *Human Development Report: Changing Today's Consumption Patterns—For Tomorrow's Human Development* (New York:
Oxford UP, 1998; 4); print; and from Earth Policy Inst.; "Eco-
Economy Indicators"; *Earth Policy Institute*; EPI, Feb. 2008; Web;
6 Mar. 2008.

Annotations (right margin):

Quotation over four lines set off without quotation marks.

Ellipsis mark signals omission.

Citation form with displayed quotation: follows sentence period. Authors named in the text, so not named in parenthetical citation.

Text refers to figure.

Figure presents numerical data visually.

Figure caption explains the chart and gives complete source information.

Malik 4

The first negative effect of overconsumption, the depletion of resources, occurs because the manufacture and distribution of any consumer product depends on the use of water,
land, and raw materials such as wood, metal, and oil. Paul
Hawken, a respected environmentalist, explains that just in
the United States "[i]ndustry moves, mines, extracts, shovels,
burns, wastes, pumps, and disposes of *4 million pounds of
material* in order to provide one average . . . family's needs
for a year" (qtd. in DeGraaf, Wann, and Naylor 85; emphasis
added). The United Nations Development Programme's 1998
Human Development Report (still the most comprehensive study
of the environmental impacts of consumerism) warns that
many regions in the world don't have enough water, productive
soil, or forests to meet the basic needs of their populations
(4). More recent data from the Earth Policy Institute show
that as manufacturing and per-person consumption continue
to rise, the supply of resources needed for survival continues
to decline. Thus heavy consumption poses a threat not only
to the environment but also to the well-being of the human
race.

In addition to using up scarce natural resources, manufacturing and distributing products harms the earth by spew-
ing pollution into the water, soil, and air. The most worrisome
aspect of that pollution may be its link to global warming. As
Al Gore explains, the energy needed to power manufacturing
and distribution comes primarily from burning fossil fuels, a
process that releases carbon dioxide and other greenhouse
gases into the air. Those gases build up and trap heat in the
earth's atmosphere. The result, most scientists now believe, is
increasing global temperatures that will raise sea levels, expand deserts, and cause more frequent floods and hurricanes
(*Inconvenient* 26-27, 81, 118-19, 184). As the preceding bar
chart shows, carbon emissions, like production of consumer
goods in general, are rising at rates out of proportion with

Brackets signal change in capitalization.

Citation form: source with three authors; "qtd. in" indicates indirect source (see p. 624); "emphasis added" indicates italics were not in original quotation.

Citation form: author named in the text, so page number only.

Citation form: no parenthetical citation because author is named in the text and online source has no page or other reference numbers.

Summary reduces six pages in the source to three sentences. Signal phrase and parenthetical citation mark boundaries of the summary.

Citation form: shortened title for one of two works by the same author.

Malik 5

population growth. The more we consume, the more we contribute to global warming.

> Writer's own conclusion from preceding data.

As harmful as they are, gradual global warming and the depletion of resources half a world away can be difficult to comprehend or appreciate. A more immediate environmental effect of our buying habits can be seen in the volumes of trash those habits create. The US Environmental Protection Agency found that in a single year (2006), US residents, corporations, and institutions produced 251 million tons of municipal solid waste, amounting to "4.6 pounds per person per day" (1-2). Nearly a third of that trash came just from the wrappers, cans, bottles, and boxes used for shipping consumer goods. Yet the mountains of trash left over from consumption are only a part of the problem. In industrial countries overall, 90 percent of waste comes not from what gets thrown out, but from the manufacturing processes of converting natural resources into consumer products (DeGraaf, Wann, and Naylor 192). Nearly everything we buy creates waste in production, comes in packaging that gets discarded immediately, and ultimately ends up in landfills that are already overflowing.

> Citation form: author (a US government body) named in text.

> Citation form: source with three authors; authors not named in text.

Unfortunately, the growing popularity of green products has not reduced the environmental effects of consumption. A study conducted by economists Jeff Rubin and Benjamin Tal for the research firm CIBC World Markets found that while eco-friendly and energy-efficient products have become more available, "consumption is growing by ever-increasing amounts." The authors give the example of automobiles: in the last generation, cars have become much more energy efficient, but the average American now drives 2500 more miles a year, for a net gain in energy use (4-5). At the same time, per-person waste production in the United States has risen by more than 20 percent (United States 1). Greener products may reduce our cost of consumption and even reduce our guilt about consumption, but they do not reduce consumption and its effects.

> Environmental effects of green consumption.

> Citation form: authors named in the text, so page numbers only.

> Citation form: US government source not named in text.

> Writer's own conclusion from data.

Malik 6

Solutions to problem of consumption.

Citation form: author's name only, because scholarly article on the Web has no page or other reference numbers.

Common-knowledge definition and writer's own examples do not require source citations.

If buying green won't solve the problems caused by overconsumption, what will? Politicians, environmentalists, and economists have proposed an array of far-reaching ideas, including creating a financial market for carbon credits and offsets, aggressively taxing consumption and pollution, offering financial incentives for environmentally positive behaviors, and even abandoning market capitalism altogether (Muldoon). However, all of these are "top-down" solutions that require concerted government action. Gaining support for any one of them, putting it into practice, and getting results could take decades. In the meantime, the environment would continue to deteriorate. Clearly, short-term solutions are also essential.

The most promising short-term solution is for individuals to change their own behavior as consumers. The greenest behavior that individuals can adopt may be precycling, the term widely used for avoiding purchases of products that involve the use of raw materials. Precycling includes choosing eco-friendly products made of recycled or nontoxic materials (such as aluminum-free deodorants and fleece made from soda bottles) and avoiding items wrapped in excessive packaging (such as kitchen tools strapped to cardboard and printer cartridges sealed in plastic clamshells). More important, though, precycling means not buying new things in the first place. Renting and borrowing, when possible, save money and resources; so do keeping possessions in good repair and not replacing them until absolutely necessary. Good-quality used items, from clothing to furniture to electronics, can be obtained for free, or very cheaply, through online communities like *Craigslist* and *Freecycle,* from thrift stores and yard sales, or by trading with friends and relatives. When consumers choose used goods over new, they can help to reduce demand for manufactured products that waste energy and resources, and they can help to keep unwanted items out of the waste stream.

Malik 7

Avoiding unnecessary purchases brings personal benefits as well. Brenda Lin, an environmental activist, explained in an e-mail interview that frugal living not only saves money but also provides pleasure:

> You'd be amazed at what people throw out or give away: perfectly good computers, oriental rugs, barely used sports equipment, designer clothes, you name it. . . . It's a game for me to find what I need in other people's trash or at Goodwill. You should see the shock on people's faces when I tell them where I got my stuff. I get almost as much enjoyment from that as from saving money and helping the environment at the same time.

Lin's experience relates to a study of the personal and social consequences of consumerism by the sociologist Juliet B. Schor. Schor found that the more people buy, the less happy they tend to feel because of the stress of working longer hours to afford their purchases (11-12). Researching the opposite effect, Schor conducted interviews with hundreds of Americans who had drastically reduced their spending so that they would be less dependent on paid work. For these people, she discovered, a deliberately lower standard of living improved quality of life by leaving more time to spend with family and pursue personal interests (136-42). Reducing consumption, it turns out, does not have to translate into sacrifice.

For unavoidable purchases like food and light bulbs, buying green can make a difference by influencing corporate decisions. Some ecologists and economists believe that as more shoppers choose earth-friendly products over their traditional counterparts—or boycott products that are clearly harmful to the environment—more manufacturers and retailers will look for ways to limit the environmental effects of their industrial practices and the goods they sell (Gore, *Earth* 193; Muldoon). Indeed, as environmental business consultant Gregory C. Unruh

Malik 8

points out in an article for *Harvard Business Review*, several major companies, among them Wal-Mart, Coca-Cola, General Electric, and Nike, have already taken up sustainability initiatives in response to market pressure. In the process, the companies have discovered that environmentally minded practices tend to raise profits and strengthen customer loyalty (111-12). By giving industry solid, bottom-line reasons to embrace ecological goals, consumer demand for earth-friendly products can magnify the effects of individual action.

Careful shopping can help the environment, but green doesn't necessarily mean "Go." All consumption depletes resources, increases the likelihood of global warming, and creates waste, so even eco-friendly products must be used in moderation. As individuals, we can each play a small role in helping the environment—and help ourselves at the same time—by not buying anything we don't really need, even if it seems environmentally sound. Reducing our personal impact on the earth is a small price to pay for preserving a livable planet for future generations.

Citation form: author is named in the text, so page numbers only.

Conclusion: summary and a call for action.

Malik 9

Works Cited

Adler, Jerry, et al. "The Greening of America." *Newsweek* 14 Aug. 2006: 46-50. *Master File Premier*. Web. 20 Feb. 2008.

DeGraaf, John, David Wann, and Thomas H. Naylor. *Affluenza: The All-Consuming Epidemic*. San Francisco: Berrett-Koehler, 2001. Print.

Earth Policy Inst. "Eco-Economy Indicators." *Earth Policy Institute*. EPI, Feb. 2008. Web. 6 Mar. 2008.

Gore, Al. *Earth in the Balance: Ecology and the Human Spirit*. Boston: Houghton, 1992. Print.

---. *An Inconvenient Truth: The Planetary Emergency of Global Warming and What We Can Do about It*. Emmaus: Rodale, 2006. Print.

"It's Not Easy Buying Green." *Consumer Reports* Sept. 2007: 9. Print.

Jones, Sandra. "Green! It's Easy Being Green When It's in Vogue." *Chicago Tribune* 27 May 2007, final ed.: B1+. Print.

Lin, Brenda. Message to the author. 7 Mar. 2008. E-mail.

Muldoon, Annie. "Where the Green Is: Examining the Paradox of Environmentally Conscious Consumption." *Electronic Green Journal* 23 (2006): n. pag. Web. 28 Feb. 2008.

Princen, Thomas, Michael Maniates, and Ken Conca. Introduction. *Confronting Consumption*. Ed. Princen, Maniates, and Conca. Cambridge: MIT P, 2002. 1-20. Print.

Rubin, Jeff, and Benjamin Tal. "Does Energy Efficiency Save Energy?" *StrategEcon*. CIBC World Markets, 27 Nov. 2007. Web. 13 Mar. 2008.

Schor, Juliet B. *The Overspent American: Upscaling, Downshifting, and the New Consumer*. New York: Basic, 1998. Print.

United Nations Development Programme. *Human Development Report 1998: Changing Today's Consumption Patterns—*

New page. Sources alphabetized by authors' last names.

An article with more than three authors, from a magazine in an online database.

A print book with three authors.

A short work on a Web site, with a corporate author.

A print book with one author.

Second source by author of two or more cited works (see p. 632).

An anonymous article in a print magazine, listed and alphabetized by title.

A print newspaper article.

A personal interview by e-mail.

An article in a Web scholarly journal that does not number pages.

An introduction to a print anthology.

A short, titled work on a Web site, by two authors.

A print book with one author.

A print book with a corporate author.

For Tomorrow's Human Development. New York: Oxford
UP, 1998. Print.

United States. Environmental Protection Agency. Solid Waste
and Emergency Response. *Municipal Solid Waste
Generation, Recycling, and Disposal in the United States:
Facts and Figures for 2006*. US Environmental Protection
Agency, Nov. 2007. Web. 4 Feb. 2008.

Unruh, Gregory C. "The Biosphere Rules." *Harvard Business Review* 86.2 (2008): 111-17. *Business Source Premier*. Web.
14 Mar. 2008.

A US government source with no named author, so government body given as author.

An article in a scholarly journal that numbers volumes and issues, consulted in an online database.

Haley 1

Vanessa Haley

Professor Moisan

English 101

6 February 2008

Format of heading and title when no title page is required (see also p. 664)

Annie Dillard's Healing Vision

It is almost a commonplace these days that human arrogance is destroying the environment. Environmentalists, naturalists, and now the man or woman on the street seem to agree: the long-held belief that human beings are separate from nature, destined to rise above its laws and conquer it, has been ruinous.

Introduction of environmental theme

Unfortunately, the defenders of nature tend to respond to this ruinous belief with harmful myths of their own: nature is pure and harmonious; humanity is corrupt and dangerous. Much writing about nature lacks a recognition that human beings and their civilization are as much a part of nature as trees and whales are, neither better nor worse. Yet without such a recognition, how can humans overcome the damaging sense of separation between themselves and the earth? How can humans develop realistic solutions to environmental problems that will work for humanity *and* the rest of nature?

Focus on issue to be resolved

One nature writer who seems to recognize the naturalness of humanity is Annie Dillard. In her best-known work, the Pulitzer Prize-winning *Pilgrim at Tinker Creek*, she is a solitary person encountering the natural world, and some critics fault her for turning her back on society. But in those encounters with nature, Dillard probes a spiritual as well as a physical identity between human beings and nature that could help to heal the rift between them.

Introduction of Dillard to resolve issue

Thesis statement

Dillard is not renowned for her sense of involvement with human society. Like Henry David Thoreau, with whom she is often compared, she retreats from rather than confronts human society. The critic Gary McIlroy points out that although

Acknowledgment of opposing critical view

Haley 2

Thoreau discusses society a great deal in *Walden*, he makes no attempt "to find a middle ground between it and his experiment in the woods" (113). Dillard has been similarly criticized. For instance, the writer Eudora Welty comments that

> Annie Dillard is the only person in her book, substantially the only one in her world; I recall no outside human speech coming to break the long soliloquy of the author. Speaking of the universe very often, she is yet self-surrounded and, beyond that, book-surrounded. Her own book might have taken in more of human life without losing a bit of the wonder she was after. (37)

It is true, as Welty says, that in *Pilgrim* Dillard seems detached from human society. However, she actually was always close to it at Tinker Creek. In a later book, *Teaching a Stone to Talk*, she says of the neighborhood, "This is, mind you, suburbia. It is a five-minute walk in three directions to rows of houses. . . . There's a 55 mph highway at one end of the pond, and a nesting pair of wood ducks at the other" (qtd. in Suh).

Rather than hiding from humanity, Dillard seems to be trying to understand it through nature. In *Pilgrim* she reports buying a goldfish, which she names Ellery Channing. She recalls once seeing through a microscope "red blood cells whip, one by one, through the capillaries" of yet another goldfish (124). Now watching Ellery Channing, she sees the blood in his body as a bond between fish and human being: "Those red blood cells are coursing in Ellery's tail now, too, in just that way, and through his mouth and eyes as well, and through mine" (125). Gary McIlroy observes that this blood, "a symbol of the sanctity of life, is a common bond between Dillard and the fish, between animal and human life in general, and between Dillard and other people" (115).

First response to opposing view

Second response to opposing view

Secondary source's analysis of Dillard

Haley 3

For Dillard, the terror and unpredictability of death unify all life. The most sinister image in *Pilgrim*—one that haunts Dillard—is that of the frog and the water bug. Dillard reports walking along an embankment scaring frogs into the water when one frog refused to budge. As Dillard leaned over to investigate, the frog "slowly crumpled and began to sag. The spirit vanished from his eyes as if snuffed. His skin emptied and dropped; his very skull seemed to collapse and settle like a kicked tent" (6). The frog was the victim of a water bug that injects poisons to "dissolve the victim's muscles and bones and organs" (6). Such events lead Dillard to wonder about a creator who would make all life "power and beauty, grace tangled in a rapture with violence" (8). Human beings no less than frogs and water bugs are implicated in this tangle.

Dillard is equally as disturbed by birth as by death. In a chapter of *Pilgrim* called "Fecundity," she focuses on the undeniable reproductive urge of entire species. Her attitude is far from sentimental:

> I don't know what it is about fecundity that so
> appalls. I suppose it is the teeming evidence that
> birth and growth, which we value, are ubiquitous
> and blind, that life itself is so astonishingly cheap,
> that nature is as careless as it is bountiful, and
> that with extravagance goes a crushing waste that
> will one day include our own cheap lives. (160)

The cheapness and brutality of life are problems Dillard wrestles with, wondering which is "amiss": the world, a "monster," or human beings, with their "excessive emotions" (177-78). No matter how hard she tries to leave human society, Dillard has no choice but to "bring human values to the creek" (179). The violent, seemingly pointless birth and death of all life are, spiritually,

---

Combination of quotation and Haley's own analysis (next four paragraphs) interprets and synthesizes Dillard's ideas

Mixture of summary and quotation provides context and keeps quotations trim

Discussion of physical identity of all creatures: death and birth

Comment on quotation advises reader what to look for

Quotations, including some long ones set off from the text, convey Dillard's voice as well as her ideas

Discussion of spiritual identity of all creatures

Haley 4

two branches of the same creek, the creek that
waters the world. . . . We could have planned
things more mercifully, perhaps, but our plan
would never get off the drawing board until we
agreed to the very compromising terms that are
the only ones that being offers. (180)

For Dillard, accepting the monstrousness as well as the beauty
of "being" is the price all living things pay for freedom.

In "The Waters of Separation," the final chapter of
Pilgrim, Dillard writes about a winged maple key, or seed. At
this point in the book, the critic Sandra Humble Johnson
notes, Dillard "has been humbled and emptied; she can no
longer apply effort to her search for meaning in a parasitic
world" (4). It is the winter solstice—the shortest day of the
year. And then Dillard spies the maple key descending to earth
and germination. "It rose, just before it would have touched a
thistle, and hovered pirouetting in one spot, then twirled on
and finally came to rest" (267). The key moved, says Dillard,
"like a creature muscled and vigorous, or a creature spread
thin to that other wind, the wind of the spirit . . ., a generous, unending breath" (268). Dillard vows to see the maple
key in all of the earth and in herself. "If I am a maple key
falling, at least I can twirl" (268).

According to the critic John Becker, "Annie Dillard does
not walk out on ordinary life in order to bear witness against
it"; instead, she uses the distance from other people "to make
meaning out of the grotesque disjointedness of man and nature" (408). Gary McIlroy says, nonetheless, that Dillard "does
not succeed in encompassing within her vision any but the
most fragmentary consequences for society at large" (116).
Possibly both are correct. In *Pilgrim at Tinker Creek*, Annie
Dillard suggests a vision of identity among all living things

Haley's interpreta-
tion of Dillard's
ideas

Resolution of
Dillard's concerns

Conclusion: ties
together diver-
gent critical views,
environmental
theme, and
Dillard's work

that could inform modern humanity's efforts to thrive in harmony with its environment, but she does not make the leap to practicalities. Life, she says, "is a faint tracing on the surface of a mystery . . . . We must somehow take a wider view, look at the whole landscape, really see it, and describe what's going on here" (9). The description, and acting on it, may take generations. As we proceed, however, we may be guided by Dillard's efforts to mend the disjointedness, to see that human beings and maple keys alike twirl equally.

Haley 6

Works Cited

Becker, John E. "Science and the Sacred: From Walden to
    Tinker Creek." *Thought: A Review of Culture and Idea* 62
    (1987): 400-13. Print.

Dillard, Annie. *Pilgrim at Tinker Creek*. New York: Harper, 1974.
    Print.

Johnson, Sandra Humble. *The Space Between: Literary
    Epiphany in the Work of Annie Dillard*. Kent: Kent State
    UP, 1992. Print.

McIlroy, Gary. "*Pilgrim at Tinker Creek* and the Social Legacy of
    Walden." *South Atlantic Quarterly* 85.2 (1996): 111-16.
    Print.

Suh, Grace. "Ideas Are Tough, Irony Is Easy." *Yale Herald*. Yale
    U, 4 Oct. 2005. Web. 22 Jan. 2008.

Welty, Eudora. Rev. of *Pilgrim at Tinker Creek*, by Annie Dillard.
    New York Times Book Review 24 Mar. 1974: 36-37.
    ProQuest Historical Newspapers. Web. 20 Jan. 2008.

PART 10

Writing in the Academic Disciplines

48

Working with the Goals and Requirements of the Disciplines

Chapter 8 outlines the general concerns of subject, purpose, and audience that figure in most academic writing situations. The disciplines have more in common as well: methods of gathering evidence, kinds of assignments, scholarly tools, language conventions, and styles for source citations and document formats. This chapter introduces these common goals and requirements. The following chapters then distinguish the disciplines along the same lines, focusing on literature (Chapter 49), other humanities (50), the social sciences (51), and the natural and applied sciences (52).

48a Using methods and evidence

The **methodology** of a discipline is the way its practitioners study their subjects—that is, how they proceed when investigating the answers to questions. Methodology relates to how practitioners analyze evidence and ideas. For instance, a literary critic and a social historian would probably approach Shakespeare's *Hamlet* quite differently: the literary critic might study the play for a theme among its poetic images; the historian might examine the play's relation to Shakespeare's context—England at the turn of the seventeenth century.

Whatever their approach, academic writers do not compose entirely out of their personal experience. Rather, they combine the evidence of their experience with that appropriate to the discipline, drawing well-supported conclusions about their subjects. The evidence of the discipline comes from research like that described in Chapters 41–43—from primary or secondary sources.

mycomplab

Visit *mycomplab.com* for more resources as well as exercises on writing in the academic disciplines.

Guidelines for academic writers

- Become familiar with the methodology and the kinds of evidence appropriate for the discipline in which you are writing.
- Analyze the special demands of each assignment. The questions you set out to answer, the assertions you wish to support, will govern how you choose your sources and evidence.
- Become familiar with the discipline's specialized tools and language.
- Use the discipline's style for source citations and document format.

- **Primary sources** are firsthand or original accounts, such as historical documents, works of art, and reports on experiments that the writer has conducted. When you use primary sources, you conduct original research and generate your own evidence. You might use your analysis of a painting as evidence for an interpretation of the painting. Or you might use data from your own survey of students to support your conclusions about students' attitudes.
- **Secondary sources** are books and articles written *about* primary sources. Much academic writing requires that you use such sources to spark, extend, or support your own ideas, as when you review the published opinions on your subject before contributing conclusions from your original research.

48b Understanding writing assignments

For most academic writing, your primary purpose will be either to explain something to your readers or to persuade them to accept your conclusions. To achieve your purpose, you will adapt your writing process to the writing situation, particularly to your readers' likely expectations for evidence and how you use it. Most assignments will contain key words that imply some of these expectations—words such as *compare, define, analyze,* and *illustrate* that express customary ways of thinking about and organizing a vast range of subjects. Pages 94–102 and 786 explore these so-called rhetorical strategies. You should be aware of such keywords and alert to them in the wording of assignments.

48c Using tools and language

When you write in an academic discipline, you use the scholarly tools of that discipline, particularly its periodical indexes. In addition, you may use the aids developed by practitioners of the discipline for efficiently and effectively approaching research, conducting it, and recording the findings. Many of these aids, such as a system for recording evidence from sources, are discussed in Chapters 41–43 and can be adapted to any discipline. Other aids are discussed in the following chapters.

Pay close attention to the texts assigned in a class and any materials given out by the teacher. These items may introduce you to valuable references and other research aids, and they will use the specialized language of the discipline. This specialized language allows practitioners to write to each other both efficiently and precisely. It also furthers certain concerns of the discipline, such as accuracy and objectivity. Scientists, for example, try to interpret their data objectively, so they avoid *undoubtedly, obviously,* and other words that slant conclusions. Some of the language conventions like this one are discussed in the following chapters. As you gain experience in a particular discipline, keep alert for such conventions and train yourself to follow them.

48d Following styles for source citations and document format

Most disciplines publish journals that require authors to use a certain style for source citations and a certain format for documents. In turn, most teachers in a discipline require the same of students writing papers for their classes.

When you cite your sources, you tell readers which ideas and information you borrowed and where they can find your sources. Thus source citations indicate how much knowledge you have and how broad and deep your research was. They also help you avoid **plagiarism,** the serious offense of presenting the words, ideas, and data of others as if they were your own. (See Chapter 44 on avoiding plagiarism.)

Document format specifies such features as margins and the placement of the title. But it also extends to special elements of the manuscript, such as tables or an abstract, that may be required by the discipline.

Chapters 50–52 direct you to the style guides published by different disciplines and outline the requirements of the ones used most often. If your teacher does not require a particular style, use that of the Modern Language Association, which is described and illustrated at length in Chapter 46.

49

Reading and Writing About Literature

By Sylvan Barnet

Why read literature? Let's approach this question indirectly by asking why people *write* literature. A thousand years ago a Japanese writer, Lady Murasaki, offered an answer. Here is one of her characters talking about what motivates a writer:

> Again and again something in one's own life or in the life around one will seem so important that one cannot bear to let it pass into oblivion. There must never come a time, the writer feels, when people do not know about this.

When we read certain works—Murasaki's *The Tale of Genji* is one of them—we share this feeling; we are caught up in the writer's world, whether it is the Denmark of Shakespeare's *Hamlet* or the America of Toni Morrison's *Beloved*. We read literature because it gives us an experience that seems important, usually an experience that is both new and familiar. A common way of putting this is to say that reading broadens us and helps us understand our own experience.

49a Using the methods and evidence of literary analysis

When we read nonliterary writings, it may be enough to get the gist of the argument; in fact, we may have to work through many words to find the heart of the matter—say, three claims on behalf of capital punishment. But when we read a story, a poem, or a play, we must pay extremely close attention to what might be called the feel of the words. For instance, the word *woods* in Robert Frost's "Stopping by Woods on a Snowy Evening" has a rural, folksy quality that *forest* doesn't have, and many such small distinctions contribute to the poem's effect.

mycomplab

Visit *mycomplab.com* for more resources as well as exercises on reading and writing about literature.

Literary authors are concerned with presenting human experience concretely, with *showing* rather than *telling*. Consider the following proverb and an unmemorable paraphrase of it:

A rolling stone gathers no moss.

If a rock is always moving around, vegetation won't have a chance to grow on it.

In the original proverb, the meaning of the concrete words *rolling, stone, gathers,* and *moss* are not literal but **figurative**—that is, the words mean something other than what they literally say. The proverb is not about stones or moss but about the way some people live their lives: rushing through, they don't take the time to reflect and develop.

The power of the proverb comes from its figurative representation of experience and also from its contrasts. Each noun (*stone, moss*) has one syllable, whereas each word of motion (*rolling, gathers*) has two syllables, with the accent on the first of the two. The six words offer a small but complete world: hard (*stone*) and soft (*moss*), inorganic and organic, rest and motion. Such relationships unify the proverb into a pleasing whole that stays in our minds.

1 Reading a work of literature

Reading literature critically involves interacting with a text. The techniques complement those for critically reading any text, so if you haven't read Chapter 7 on such reading, you should do so. Responding critically is a matter not of making negative judgments but of analyzing the parts, interpreting their meanings, seeing how the parts relate, and evaluating significance or quality.

Reading and responding

You can preview a literary text somewhat as you can preview any other text. You may gauge the length of the text and the difficulty of the language to determine whether you can read it in one sitting, and you may read a biographical note to learn about the author. In a literary text, however, you won't find aids such as section headings or summaries that can make previewing other texts especially informative. You have to dive into the words themselves.

Do write while reading. Writing your thoughts down as you read keeps you actively engaged in the text, clarifies your thoughts, and records your immediate insights for later use in writing assignments or class discussions. If you own the book you are reading, annotate the pages themselves:

- **Underline or highlight passages** as you read and during class discussions.

■ **Annotate the margins,** using the top margins to note key scenes or events and using the side margins to note passages you like, don't like, or find puzzling.

If you don't own the book, make these annotations on sticky notes, separate sheets of paper, or your computer. Whatever method you use, keep separate records of key information—moments of character development, shifts in time or setting, or recurring allusions, images, or themes.

An effective way to interact with a text is to keep a **reading journal.** A journal is not a diary in which you record your doings; instead, it is a place to develop and store your reflections on what you read, such as an answer to a question you may have posed in the margin of the text. You could make an entry in the form of a letter to the author or from one character to another. In many literature courses, students collaborate to develop their understanding of a literary work. In such a case, you may want to use your journal to reflect on what other students have said—for instance, why your opinion differs so much from someone else's.

You can keep a reading journal in a notebook or on your computer. Some readers prefer a two-column format like that illustrated on page 144, with summaries, paraphrases, and quotations from the text on the left and with their own responses to these passages on the right. Or you may prefer a less structured format like that illustrated on pages 695–96.

Reading a sample story

Here is a very short story by Kate Chopin (1851–1904). (The last name is pronounced in the French way, something like "show pan.") Following the story are a student's annotations and journal entry on the story.

Kate Chopin

The Story of an Hour

Knowing that Mrs. Mallard was afflicted with a heart trouble, great care was taken to break to her as gently as possible the news of her husband's death.

It was her sister Josephine who told her, in broken sentences, veiled hints that revealed in half concealing. Her husband's friend Richards was there, too, near her. It was he who had been in the newspaper office when intelligence of the railroad disaster was received, with Brently Mallard's name leading the list of "killed." He had only taken the time to assure himself of its truth by a second telegram, and had hastened to forestall any less careful, less tender friend in bearing the sad message.

She did not hear the story as many women have heard the same, with a paralyzed inability to accept its significance. She wept at once with sudden, wild abandonment, in her sister's arms. When the storm of grief had spent itself she went away to her room alone. She would have no one follow her.

There stood, facing the open window, a comfortable, roomy armchair. Into this she sank, pressed down by a physical exhaustion that haunted her body and seemed to reach into her soul.

She could see in the open square before her house the tops of trees that were all aquiver with the new spring life. The delicious breath of rain was in the air. In the street below a peddler was crying his wares. The notes of a distant song which some one was singing reached her faintly, and countless sparrows were twittering in the eaves.

There were patches of blue sky showing here and there through the clouds that had met and piled one above the other in the west facing her window.

She sat with her head thrown back upon the cushion of the chair quite motionless, except when a sob came up into her throat and shook her, as a child who has cried itself to sleep continues to sob in its dreams.

She was young, with a fair, calm face, whose lines bespoke repression and even a certain strength. But now there was a dull stare in her eyes, whose gaze was fixed away off yonder on one of those patches of blue sky. It was not a glance of reflection, but rather indicated a suspension of intelligent thought.

There was something coming to her and she was waiting for it, fearfully. What was it? She did not know; it was too subtle and elusive to name. But she felt it creeping out of the sky, reaching toward her through the sounds, the scents, the color that filled the air.

Now her bosom rose and fell tumultuously. She was beginning to recognize this thing that was approaching to possess her, and she was striving to beat it back with her will—as powerless as her two white slender hands would have been.

When she abandoned herself a little whispered word escaped her slightly parted lips. She said it over and over under her breath: "Free, free, free!" The vacant stare and the look of terror that had followed it went from her eyes. They stayed keen and bright. Her pulses beat fast, and the coursing blood warmed and relaxed every inch of her body.

She did not stop to ask if it were not a monstrous joy that held her. A clear and exalted perception enabled her to dismiss the suggestion as trivial.

She knew that she would weep again when she saw the kind, tender hands folded in death; the face that had never looked save with love upon her, fixed and gray and dead. But she saw beyond that bitter moment a long procession of years to come that would belong to her absolutely. And she opened and spread her arms out to them in welcome.

There would be no one to live for her during those coming years; she would live for herself. There would be no powerful will bending her in the blind persistence with which men and women believe they have a right to impose a private will upon a fellow creature. A kind intention or a cruel intention made the act seem no less a crime as she looked upon it in that brief moment of illumination.

And yet she had loved him—sometimes. Often she had not. What did it matter! What could love, the unsolved mystery, count for in face of this possession of self-assertion which she suddenly recognized as the strongest impulse of her being.

"Free! Body and soul free!" she kept whispering.

Josephine was kneeling before the closed door with her lips to the keyhole, imploring for admission. "Louise, open the door! I beg; open the door—you will make yourself ill. What are you doing, Louise? For heaven's sake open the door."

"Go away. I am not making myself ill." No; she was drinking in the very elixir of life through that open window.

Her fancy was running riot along those days ahead of her. Spring days, and summer days, and all sorts of days that would be her own. She breathed a quick prayer that life might be long. It was only yester-day she had thought with a shudder that life might be long.

She arose at length and opened the door to her sister's importunities. There was a feverish triumph in her eyes, and she carried herself unwittingly like a goddess of Victory. She clasped her sister's waist and together they descended the stairs. Richards stood waiting for them at the bottom.

Some one was opening the front door with a latchkey. It was Brently Mallard who entered, a little travel-stained, composedly carrying his grip-sack and umbrella. He had been far from the scene of accident, and did not even know there had been one. He stood amazed at Josephine's piercing cry; at Richards' quick motion to screen him from the view of his wife.

But Richards was too late.

When the doctors came they said she had died of heart disease—of joy that kills.

Following a student's work

In this chapter we'll follow the analysis and writing of a student, Janet Vong, to see one approach to Chopin's story. Vong first annotated the story while reading it. The opening five paragraphs, with her notes, appear below:

Knowing that Mrs. Mallard was afflicted with a heart trouble, great care was taken to break to her as gently as possible the news of her husband's death.

"heart disease" at end of story

no dialog— why?

It was her sister Josephine who told her, in broken sentences, veiled hints that revealed in half concealing. Her husband's friend Richards was there, too, near her. It was he who had been in the newspaper office when intelligence of the railroad disaster was received, with Brently Mallard's name leading the list of "killed." He had only taken the time to assure himself of its truth by a second telegram, and had hastened to forestall any less careful, less tender friend in bearing the sad message.

third-person narrator

Too hasty, it turns out

Would men
have heard
differently?
Is au. sexist?

She did not hear the story as many women have heard the same, with a paralyzed inability to accept its significance. She wept at once with sudden, wild abandonment, in her sister's arms. When the storm of grief had spent itself she went away to her room alone. She would have no one follow her.

←old-fashioned style

There stood, facing the open window, a comfortable, roomy armchair. Into this she sank, pressed down by a physical exhaustion that haunted her body and seemed to reach into her soul.

symbol

She could see in the open square before her house the tops of trees that were all aquiver with the new spring life. The delicious breath of rain was in the air. In the street below a peddler was crying his wares. The notes of a distant song which some one was singing reached her faintly, and countless sparrows were twittering in the eaves.

Notices spring: odd in a story of death

Writing in her journal, Vong posed questions about the story—critical points, curiosities about characters, possible implications:

Title nothing special. What might be a better title?
Could a woman who loved her husband be so heartless? Is she heartless? Did she love him?
What are (were) Louise's feelings about her husband?
Did she want too much? What did she want?
Could this story happen today? Feminist interpretation?
Sister (Josephine)—a busybody?
Tricky ending—but maybe it could be true.
"And yet she had loved him—sometimes. Often she had not." Why does one love someone "sometimes"?
Irony: plot has reversal. Are characters ironic too?

Vong's journal entry illustrates brainstorming—the discovery technique of listing ideas (or questions) however they occur, without editing (see pp. 24–25). Another productive journal technique is focused freewriting—concentrating on a single issue (such as one of Vong's questions) and writing nonstop for a set amount of time, again without editing (pp. 23–24). A double-column journal can be useful for analyzing an author's style (pp. 700–01).

2 Taking a critical approach to literature

Like any discipline, the study of literature involves particular frameworks of analysis—particular ways of seeing literary works that help determine what parts the critical reader identifies and how he or she interprets them.

■ **Historical or cultural criticism** focuses on the context in which a literary work was created and how that context affected the work. It may take the form of **biographical criticism,** which relates the author's life and ideas to a work of literature; **social or Marxist criticism,** which emphasizes issues of economics and class structure surrounding a work; or **postcolonial criticism,** focusing on works produced in former European colonies, which considers the aftereffects of European colonial rule.

- **Feminist or gender criticism** focuses on the representation of gender in literature, often in the literary canon—the body of work represented in standard anthologies, discussed in the schools, and examined in the scholarly journals. Feminist critics are especially concerned with the writings of women and with the responses of women to the depiction of both sexes in literature.

- **Archetypal criticism** uses psychological ideas about "collective memory" to explain characters and situations that appear in many literary works over time—for instance, heros and villains, star-crossed lovers, journeys, and quests.

- **Reader-response criticism** focuses on the reactions of an audience to a work of literature, asking why readers respond as they do to a text. In this view the meaning of the text lies not just on the page but in how the reader constructs the text.

- **Deconstructive criticism** regards a work of literature skeptically, resisting the obvious meanings and focusing on the ambiguities in the work, especially the internal contradictions. Perceiving that the relationship of words and their meanings is both arbitrary and forever changing—even within the same work—deconstructive critics emphasize multiple meanings and what a text does not say.

- **Formalist criticism** focuses primarily on a literary work as a constructed text, as an independent unity understood in itself rather than as an artifact of a particular context or reader response. Beginning with a personal response, the formalist critic tries to account for the response by examining the form of the work (hence *formalist*) and the relations among its elements.

This chapter emphasizes formalist criticism because it engages you immediately in the work of literature itself, without requiring extensive historical or cultural background, and because it introduces the conventional elements of literature that all critical approaches discuss, even though they view the elements differently.

3 Analyzing the elements of literature

The box on the next two pages lists the elements of literary works—plot, characters, setting, and so on—and offers questions about each one that can help you think constructively and imaginatively about what you read. After the box, we'll see how these elements both contribute to and grow out of an author's style.

Questions for a literary analysis

See also the related tips for analyzing a writer's style (p. 700). And see later boxes for specific questions on fiction (p. 711), poetry (p. 712), and drama (p. 716).

Plot

The relationships and patterns of events.

What actions happen?
What conflicts occur?
How do the events connect to each other and to the whole?

Characters

The people the author creates, including the narrator of a story or the speaker of a poem.

Who are the principal people in the work?
How do they interact?
What do their actions, words, and thoughts reveal about their personalities and the personalities of others?
Do the characters stay the same, or do they change? Why?

Point of view

The perspective or attitude of the speaker in a poem or the voice who tells a story. The point of view may be **first person** (a participant, using *I*) or **third person** (an outsider, using *he, she, it, they*). A first-person narrator may be a major or a minor character in the narrative and may be **reliable** or **unreliable** (unable to report events wholly or accurately). A third-person narrator may be **omniscient** (knows what goes on in all characters' minds), **limited** (knows what goes on in the mind of only one or two characters), or **objective** (knows only what is external to the characters).

Who is the narrator (or the speaker of a poem)?
What point of view is used in the work?
How does the narrator's point of view affect the narrative?
If there are shifts in point of view or multiple narrators, how do they affect the narrative?

Tone

The narrator's or speaker's attitude, perceived through the words (for instance, joyful, bitter, or confident).

What tone (or tones) do you hear? If there is a change, how do you account for it?
Is there an ironic contrast between the narrator's tone (for instance, confidence) and what you take to be the author's attitude (for instance, pity for human overconfidence)?

Imagery

Word pictures or details involving the senses: sight, sound, touch, smell, taste.

What images does the writer use? What senses do they draw on?
What patterns are evident in the images (for instance, religious or commercial images)?
What is the significance of the imagery?

Symbolism

Concrete images standing for larger and more abstract ideas. For instance, the American flag may symbolize freedom, a tweeting bird may symbolize happiness, or a dead flower may symbolize mortality.

What symbols does the author use? What does each one seem to signify?
How does the symbolism relate to the other elements of the work, such as character or theme?

Allusions

References to sources and events outside the work.

Does the author allude or refer to sources or events, such as a story in the Bible, a Greek myth, a war, a popular song, or an infamous crime?
What effect do these allusions have on the work?

Setting

The place and time of the action.

What does the locale contribute to the work?
Are scene shifts significant?
Does the setting have symbolic value?

Form

The shape or structure of the work.

What *is* the form? (For example, a poem might divide sharply in the middle, moving from happiness to sorrow. A story might compress some scenes and draw out others.)
What parts of the work does the form emphasize, and why?
How does each part of the work contribute to the whole?

Themes

The main ideas—conceptions of human experience suggested by the work as a whole. A theme is neither a plot (what happens) nor a subject (such as mourning or marriage). Rather it is what the author says with that plot about that subject.

Can you state each theme in a sentence? Avoid mentioning specific characters or actions; instead, write an observation applicable to humanity in general. For instance, you might state the following about Kate Chopin's "The Story of an Hour": *Happiness depends partly on freedom.*
Do certain words, passages of dialog or description, or situations seem to represent the themes most clearly?
How do the work's elements combine to develop the themes?

4 Analyzing a writer's style

The style of a literary work involves many of the elements listed in the preceding box, such as point of view, tone, imagery, and form. Through word choices, figures of speech, and sentence structures, the author tries to bring readers to share his or her view of the work's characters and plot. To analyze style, consider these questions:

- **How do the author's word choices (diction) affect the work?** Are the words simple, complex, or somewhere in between? What tone does the language create, such as humor, seriousness, anxiety, or sadness? What does any slang, dialect, or colloquial language contribute to the work? What do images, including figurative language, contribute?
- **How do sentence length and complexity affect the work?** Are sentences notably short and simple or notably long and complicated? How does their structure influence the tone?
- **Do some words, images, or symbols recur in the work?** What purpose does this repetition serve?
- **Do elements shift in the work?** What is the significance of any change in point of view, imagery, or tone?

If analyzing a writer's style seems difficult, begin by heeding your emotions as you read the work. Do you feel amused? worried? excited? sad? Where does your sympathy lie? Noting your responses is an important step to understanding what features of the work trigger those responses.

Many writers generate ideas about style with a **double-column journal**: quotations from the work or notes about it on the left and reflections on those points on the right. The following example comes from Janet Vong's analysis of Chopin's "The Story of an Hour":

Text	Responses
The husband's death is described in the first two pars.: "Brently Mallard's death leading the list of 'killed.'"	In retrospect, the quotation marks around "killed" foreshadow that the news is false.
"She did not hear the story as many women have heard the same. . . . She wept at once with sudden, <u>wild abandonment</u>. . . . When the <u>storm of grief</u> had spent itself . . ." (par. 3)	Mrs. M seems different (at first) in the face of her grief. Just a few strong words depict a raw surge of emotion.
Big shift in tone in par. 5, from "afflicted," "disaster," "paralyzed," "storm," "pressed," to spring imagery: "aquiver," "delicious," "twittering," "patches of blue sky."	More foreshadowing: Mrs. M's mood is going to change. The point of view is shifting here, too, from objective 3rd person to limited 3rd person: we're beginning to see through Mrs. M's eyes.
Pars. 9-19: "'Free, free, free!'" "coursing blood," "live for herself," "illumina-	Over and over, Mrs. M discovers and savors the new freedom she thinks she

tion," "'Free! Body and soul free!'" "elixir of life," "fancy was running riot."

has. Half the story is devoted to describing this mood.

Mrs. M's efforts to repress her joy ("striving to beat it back with her will," par. 10). Thoughts of Mr. M's kindness ("kind, tender, hands . . . never looked save with love upon her," par. 13). Source of her unhappiness (Mr. M's "powerful will bending her in . . . blind persistence," par. 14).

Mrs. M seems a bit monstrous (suggested by "monstrous joy," par. 12) but is made sympathetic by these passages that humanize and explain her.

"She arose at length. . .," "Some one was opening the door. . .," "they said she had died of heart disease—of joy that kills" (last 4 pars.).

Back to objective 3rd person: a bird's-eye view for the ironic ending.

5 | Finding meaning and evidence in literature

One significant attribute of a literary work is its *meaning,* or what we can interpret to be its meaning. Readers may well disagree over the persuasiveness of someone's argument, but they will rarely disagree over its meaning. With literature, however, disagreements over meaning occur all the time because (as we have seen) literature *shows* rather than *tells:* it gives us concrete images of imagined human experiences, but it usually does not say how we ought to understand the images.

Further, readers bring to their reading not only different critical views, as noted earlier, but also different personal experiences. A woman who has recently lost her husband may interpret "The Story of an Hour" differently from most other readers. Or a story that bores a reader at age fifteen may deeply move him at twenty-five. The words on the page remain the same, but their meaning changes.

In writing about literature, then, we can offer only our *interpretation* of meaning rather than *the* meaning. Still, most people agree that there are limits to interpretation: it must be both supported by evidence from the text and not contradicted by the text. For instance, the student who says that in "The Story of an Hour" Mrs. Mallard does not die but merely falls into a deathlike trance goes beyond the permissible limits because the story offers no evidence for such an interpretation.

The *evidence* for a literary analysis always comes from at least one primary source (the work or works being discussed) and may come from secondary sources (critical and historical works). (See p. 689 for more on primary and secondary sources.) For example, if you were writing about Chopin's "The Story of an Hour," the primary material would be the story itself, and the secondary material (if you used it) might be critical studies of Chopin.

The bulk of your evidence in writing about literature will usually be quotations from the work, although you will occasionally summarize or paraphrase as well (see pp. 597–99). When using quotations, they must support, not replace, your own insights, advancing your argument and proving your point. Keep in mind the criteria in the box on page 707.

Your teacher will probably tell you if you are expected to consult secondary sources for an assignment. They can help you understand a writer's work, but your primary concern should always be the work itself, not what critics A, B, and C say about it. In general, then, quote or summarize secondary material sparingly. And always cite your sources.

6 Seeing arguments in literature

Like nonfiction, literary texts often make arguments, sometimes overtly but more often subtly. As a reader, you can often discern the argument through its elements—the tone of the speaker or narrator, the comments of a trusted character, the workings of the plot, or the description of the setting. Following is the opening of *Hard Times* (1849), a novel by Charles Dickens. As you read, speculate about what argument the novel makes.

> "Now, what I want is, Facts. Teach these boys and girls nothing but Facts. Facts alone are wanted in life. Plant nothing else, and root out everything else. You can only form the minds of reasoning animals upon Facts; nothing else will ever be of any service to them. This is the principle on which I bring up my own children, and this is the principle on which I bring up these children. Stick to Facts, sir!"
>
> The scene was a plain, bare, monotonous vault of a schoolroom, and the speaker's square forefinger emphasized his observations by underscoring every sentence with a line on the schoolmaster's sleeve. The emphasis was helped by the speaker's square wall of a forehead, which had his eyebrows for its base, while his eyes found commodious cellarage in two dark caves, overshadowed by the wall. The emphasis was helped by the speaker's mouth, which was wide, thin, and hard set. The emphasis was helped by the speaker's voice, which was inflexible, dry, and dictatorial. The emphasis was helped by the speaker's hair, which bristled on the skirts of his bald head, a plantation of firs to keep the wind from its shining surface, all covered with knobs, like the crust of a plum pie, as if the head had scarcely warehouse-room for the hard facts stored inside. The speaker's obstinate carriage, square coat, square legs, square shoulders—nay, his very neckcloth, trained to take him by the throat with an unaccommodating grasp, like a stubborn fact, as it was—all helped the emphasis.
>
> "In this life, we want nothing but Facts, sir; nothing but Facts!"

In this passage the argument of the quoted speaker (whose name is Mr. Gradgrind) is clear: teachers should teach facts and nothing else. However, the description of Gradgrind in the second paragraph makes him so unappealing that you are unlikely to sympathize with him. For example, the repetition of *emphasis* and *square* makes Gradgrind both boringly didactic and ridiculous, a caricature of a teacher. You can expect that the narrator might advance an argument different from Gradgrind's, perhaps that education requires something besides facts.

To read Chopin's "The Story of an Hour" as an argument, you might focus on this sentence:

> There would be no powerful will bending her in the blind persistence with which men and women believe they have a right to impose a private will upon a fellow creature.

In this statement about individuality and personal freedom, the author argues for a measure of freedom and self-determination for all people.

49b Understanding writing assignments in literature

A literature teacher may ask you to write one or more of the following types of papers. The first three are the most common.

- **A literary analysis paper:** Give your ideas about a work of literature—your interpretation of its meaning, context, or representations based on specific words, characters, and events.
- **A style analysis paper:** Examine how an author uses words and constructs sentences to achieve certain effects in the work.
- **A literary research paper:** Combine analysis of a literary work with research about the work and perhaps its author. A literary research paper draws on both primary and secondary sources. For example, you might respond to what scholars have written about the symbolism in a play by Tennessee Williams, or you might research medieval England as a way to understand the context of Chaucer's *Canterbury Tales*.
- **A personal response or reaction paper:** Give your thoughts and feelings about a work of literature. For example, you might compare a novel's description of a city with your experience of the same city.
- **A book review:** Give a summary of a book and a judgment about the book's value. In a review of a novel, for example, you might discuss whether the plot is interesting, the characters are believable, and the writing style is enjoyable. You might also compare the work to other works by the author.
- **A theater review:** Give your reactions to and opinions about a theatrical performance. You might summarize the plot of the play, describe the characters, identify the prominent themes, evaluate the other elements (writing, performances, direction, stage setting), and make a recommendation to potential viewers.

49c Using the tools and language of literary analysis

1 Writing tools

The fundamental tool for writing about literature is reading critically. Asking analytical questions such as those on pages 698–99 can help you focus your ideas. In addition, keeping a reading journal can help you develop your thoughts. Keep careful, well-organized notes on any research materials. Finally, discuss the work with others who have read it. They may offer reactions and insights that will help you shape your own ideas.

2 Language considerations

Use the present tense of verbs to describe both the action in a literary work (*Brently Mallard suddenly appears*) and the writing of an author (*Chopin briefly describes the view* or *In his essay he comments that . . .*). Use the past tense to describe events that actually occurred in the past (*Chopin was born in 1851*).

Some teachers discourage students from using personal pronouns in writing about literature. *You* and *we* can seem chummy or condescending: *You can see this attitude clearly . . .* ; *We understand the character's motives to be. . . .* Both pronouns can be avoided by direct statements: *This attitude appears clearly . . .* ; *The character's motives are. . . .* The pronoun *I* can sound egotistical and can narrow the appeal of your argument. The sentence *I don't think the central irony resides in Richards's actions* focuses the attention on the writer and can be dismissed as merely one person's opinion. In contrast, *The central irony does not reside in Richards's actions* removes the writer and focuses readers on the claim.

3 Research sources

In addition to the following resources on literature, you may also want to consult some on other humanities (pp. 721–24).

Specialized encyclopedias, dictionaries, and bibliographies

Cambridge Bibliography of English Literature
Cambridge Encyclopedia of Language
Cambridge Guide to Literature in English
Dictionary of Literary Biography
Handbook to Literature
Literary Criticism Index
McGraw-Hill Encyclopedia of World Drama
New Princeton Encyclopedia of Poetry and Poetics
Oxford Companion to American Literature
Oxford Companion to the Theatre
Schomburg Center Guide to Black Literature from the Eighteenth Century to the Present

Library databases and indexes

Abstracts of Folklore Studies
Dissertation Abstracts International (doctoral dissertations)
Early English Books Online
Gale Literary Resource Center
Humanities Index
Literary Criticism Index
Literary Index
Literature Online
MLA International Bibliography of Books and Articles on the Modern Languages and Literatures
World Shakespeare Bibliography

Book reviews

Book Review Digest
Book Review Index

Sources on the open Web

Alex Catalog of Electronic Texts (*infomotions.com/alex*)
EServer (*eserver.org*)
Internet Public Library: Online Literary Criticism (*ipl.org/div/litcrit*)
Literary Resources on the Net (*andromeda.rutgers.edu/~jlynch/Lit*)
Mr. Shakespeare and the Internet (*shakespeare.palomar.edu*)
Online Books Page (*online books.library.upenn.edu*)
Voice of the Shuttle (*vos.ucsb.edu*)

49d Citing sources and formatting documents in writing about literature

Unless your teacher specifies otherwise, use the documentation style of the Modern Language Association (MLA), detailed in Chapter 46. In this style, parenthetical citations in the text of the paper refer to a list of works cited at the end. Sample papers illustrating this style appear in Chapter 47 as well as in this chapter.

Use MLA format for headings, margins, and other elements, as detailed on pages 664–66.

49e Drafting and revising a literary analysis

The process for writing a literary analysis is similar to that for any other kind of essay: once you've done the reading and thought about it, you need to focus your ideas, gather evidence, draft, and revise.

1 Conceiving a thesis

After reading, rereading, and making notes, you probably will be able to formulate a tentative thesis statement—an assertion of your main point, your argument. (For more on thesis statements, see pp. 29–34.) Clear the air by glancing over your notes and by jotting down a few especially promising ideas—brief statements of what you think your key points may be and their main support. If necessary, go back to the work to expand your notes. Here are some approaches to conceiving a thesis:

- **Seek patterns in the work.** What do recurring elements—sounds, words, images, symbols, events—contribute to the themes?
- **Study the structure of the work.** What does the author's arrangement of the parts contribute to meaning? In a novel you might consider the order of scenes and their relative emphasis. In poetry you might consider patterns of general and specific or comparison and contrast.
- **Examine a part of the work.** Does a particular character, image, symbol, event, or other element seem especially significant to overall meaning?

Considering Kate Chopin's "The Story of an Hour," Janet Vong at first explored the idea that Mrs. Mallard, the main character, was unrealistic and thus unconvincing. (See Vong's journal entry on p. 696.) But the more Vong examined the story and her notes, the more she was impressed by a pattern of ironies, or reversals, that actually helped to make Mrs. Mallard believable. In her journal Vong explored the idea that the many small reversals paved the way for Mrs. Mallard's own reversal from grief to joy:

title? "Ironies in an Hour" (?) "An Hour of Irony" (?) "Kate Chopin's Irony" (?)
thesis: irony at end is prepared for
chief irony: Mrs. M. dies just as she is beginning to enjoy life
smaller ironies:
1. "sad message" brings her joy
2. Richards is "too late" at end
3. Richards is too early at start
4. "joy that kills"
5. death brings joy and life

From these notes Vong developed her thesis statement:

The irony of the ending is believable partly because it is consistent with earlier ironies in the story.

This thesis statement asserts a specific idea that can be developed, debated, and convincingly argued with evidence from Chopin's story. A good thesis statement will neither assert a fact (*Mrs. Mallard dies soon after hearing that her husband has died*) nor overgeneralize (*The story is an insult to women*).

2 Gathering evidence

In writing about literature, you support your ideas about a work mainly with evidence gathered from the work itself: most often quotations and sometimes paraphrases. You may also draw on plot summary, and for literary research papers you will draw on secondary sources.

The box below offers guidelines for using quotations in literary analysis.

Guidelines for using quotations in literary analysis

- **Use quotations to support your assertions, not to replace them or pad the paper.** Whenever possible, embed quotations into your paragraphs to show that they are subordinate to your ideas. Quote at length only when necessary to your argument.

- **Specify how each quotation relates to your idea.** Introduce the quotation—for example, *At the outset Chopin conveys the sort of person Richards is: "..."* Sometimes, comment after the quotation. (See pages 601–06 for more on integrating quotations into your writing.)

- **Keep quotations as brief as possible.** Use only the words necessary to make your point: *She looks forward to "summer days" (13), but she will not see even the end of this spring day.*

- **Reproduce spelling, punctuation, capitalization, and all other features exactly as they appear in the source.** See page 487 for the use of brackets when you need to add something to a quotation, and see page 488 for the use of an ellipsis mark when you need to omit something from a quotation.

- **Document your sources.** See pages 614–15.

While quotations from a literary work convey the author's style and tone, paraphrases from the work can inject variety and help to establish your own writer's voice. Because a paraphrase restates the original in your own words, it can also be easier than a quotation to mesh into your idea. For more on writing paraphrases, see pages 598–99.

Summary of a work's plot also has its uses in literary analysis— to a point. Summary is *not* analysis, so it should always have a clear purpose and be as brief as possible. You may want to summarize an entire work if you think readers are unfamiliar with it, or you may want to use plot elements as evidence, the way Janet Vong uses the ironic ending of Chopin's "The Story of an Hour" in her final paper on pages 710–11.

In literary research papers, your evidence will come not only from the work itself but also from secondary sources such as scholarly works and critical appraisals. The thesis and principal ideas of the paper must still be your own, but you may supplement your reading of the work with the views of respected scholars or critics. Sometimes you may choose to build your own argument in part by disputing others' views. However you draw on secondary sources, remember that they must be clearly identified and documented, even when you use your own words.

Note You can find student essays on the Web that may lead you to other sources or may suggest ideas you hadn't considered. If you want to use another student's paper as a secondary source, you must evaluate it with special care because it will not have passed through a reviewing process, as an article in a scholarly journal does. (See pp. 584–92 on evaluating online sources.) You must also, of course, clearly identify and document the source: borrowing other students' ideas or words without credit is plagiarism. (See pp. 607–14.)

3 Writing a draft

Drafting your essay is your opportunity to develop your thesis or to discover it if you haven't already. The following draft by Janet Vong is rough: the introduction is abrupt, the thesis is not clearly stated, and the pace is rushed. But drafting did lead Vong to develop and support her ideas. The numbers in parentheses refer to the pages from which she drew the quotations. (See pp. 619–25 on this form of documentation.) Ask your teacher whether you should always give such citations, especially for a short poem or story like Chopin's.

Ironies in an Hour

After we know how the story turns out, if we reread it we find irony at the very start, as is true of many other stories. Mrs. Mallard's friends assume, mistakenly, that Mrs. Mallard was deeply in love with her husband, Brently Mallard. They take great care to tell her gently of his death. The friends mean well, and in fact they *do* well. They bring her an hour of life, an hour of freedom. They think their news is sad. Mrs. Mallard at first expresses grief when she hears the news, but soon she finds joy in it. So Richards's "sad message" (50), though sad in Richards's eyes, is in fact a happy message.

Among the ironic details is the statement that when Mallard enters the house, Richards tries to conceal him from Mrs. Mallard, but Richards is "too late" (51). This is ironic because earlier Richards has "hastened" (50) to bring his sad message; if he had been too late at the start, Brently Mallard would have arrived at home first, and Mrs. Mallard's life would not end an hour later but would simply go on as before. Yet another irony at the end of the story is the diagnosis of the doctors. The doctors say she died of "heart disease—of joy that kills" (51). In one sense the doctors are right: Mrs. Mallard has experienced a great joy. But of course the doctors totally misunderstand the joy that kills her.

The central irony resides not in the well-intentioned but ironic actions of Richards, or in the unconsciously ironic words of the doctors, but in her own life.

She "sometimes" (51) loved her husband, but in a way she has been dead. Now, his apparent death brings her new life. This new life comes to her at the season of the year when "the tops of trees . . . were all aquiver with the new spring life" (50). But, ironically, her new life will last only an hour. She looks forward to "summer days" (51), but she will not see even the end of this spring day. Her years of marriage were ironic. They brought her a sort of living death instead of joy. Her new life is ironic, too. It grows out of her moment of grief for her supposedly dead husband, and her vision of a new life is cut short.

4 Revising and editing

As in other writing, use at least two drafts to revise and edit, so that you can attend separately to the big structural issues and the smaller surface problems. See pages 56 and 61–62 for general revision and editing checklists. The additional checklist below can help you with a literary analysis.

Checklist for revising a literary analysis

- **Title:** Does the title of your essay suggest your approach to the work? Will it interest or intrigue the reader?
- **Introduction:** Does the introductory paragraph name the author and the title so that readers know exactly what work you are discussing? (Avoid opening sentences such as "In this story. . . .") Does the introduction state and develop your thesis a bit so that readers know where they will be going? Does it attempt to draw in the reader?
- **Organization:** How effective is the organization? The essay should not dwindle or become anticlimactic; rather, it should build up.
- **Quotations:** What evidence does each quotation provide? Do quotations let readers hear the author's voice? Do they support, not replace, your own ideas? Are they embedded in your paragraphs?
- **Analysis vs. summary:** Is the essay chiefly devoted to analysis, not to summary? Summarize the plot only briefly and only to further your own ideas. A summary is not an essay.
- **Verb tenses:** Have you used the present tense of verbs to describe both the author's work and the action in the work (for example, Chopin <u>shows</u> or Mrs. Mallard <u>dies</u>)?
- **Evaluation:** How well will readers understand your evaluation of the work and what it is based on? Your evaluation may be implied (as in Janet Vong's essay on "The Story of an Hour"), or it may be explicit. In either case, give the reasons why you have judged the work as you have.
- **Are all your sources documented in MLA style?**

Janet Vong's final draft appears below with annotations that highlight some of its features.

An essay on fiction (no secondary sources)

Author's name and identification in MLA format (p. 664)	Janet Vong Mr. Romano English III, period 4 20 February 2008
Paper title incorporating author and title of analyzed work	<div align="center">Ironies of Life in Kate Chopin's "The Story of an Hour"</div>
Introduction naming author/title and stating thesis	Kate Chopin's "The Story of an Hour" has an ironic ending: Mrs. Mallard dies just when she is beginning to live. On first reading, the ending seems almost too ironic for belief. On rereading the story, however, one sees that the ending is believable partly because it is consistent with other ironies in the story.
Detailing of story's ironies, using quotations and some summary to emphasize the reversals	The story's ironies appear at the very start. Because Mrs. Mallard's friends and her sister assume, mistakenly, that she was deeply in love with her husband, Brently Mallard, they take great care to tell her gently of his death. They mean well, and in fact they *do* well, bringing her an hour of life, an hour of joyous freedom, but it is ironic that they think their news is sad. True, Mrs. Mallard at first expresses grief when she hears the news, but soon (unknown to the others) she finds joy. So Richards's "sad message" (50), though sad in Richards's eyes, is in fact a happy message.
Parenthetical citations in MLA style referring to the work cited at the end of the paper (see p. 619)	Among the small but significant ironic details is the statement near the end of the story that when Mallard enters the house, Richards tries to conceal him from Mrs. Mallard, but Richards is "too late" (51). Almost at the start of the story, in the second paragraph, Richards has "hastened" (50) to bring his sad news. But if Richards had arrived too late at the start, Brently Mallard would have arrived at home first, and Mrs. Mallard's life would not end an hour later but would simply go on as before. Yet another irony at the end of the story is the diagnosis of the doctors. They say she died of "heart disease—of joy that kills" (51). In one sense they are right: Mrs. Mallard has for the last hour experienced a great joy. But of course the doctors totally misunderstand the joy that kills her. It is not joy at seeing her husband alive, but her realization that the great joy she experienced during the last hour is over.

All of these ironic details add richness to the story, but the central irony resides not in the well-intentioned but ironic actions of Richards, or in the unconsciously ironic words of the doctors, but in Mrs. Mallard's own life. She "sometimes" (51) loved her husband, but in a way she has been dead, a body subjected to her husband's will. Now, his apparent death brings her new life. Appropriately, this new life comes to her at the season of the year when "the tops of trees . . . were all aquiver with the new spring life" (50). But, ironically, her new life will last only an hour. She is "Free, free, free" (51)—but only until her husband walks through the doorway. She looks forward to "summer days" (51), but she will not see even the end of this spring day. If her years of marriage were ironic, bringing her a sort of living death instead of joy, her new life is ironic, too, not only because it grows out of her moment of grief for her supposedly dead husband, but also because her vision of "a long procession of years" (51) is cut short within an hour on a spring day.

[New page.]

Work Cited

Chopin, Kate. "The Story of an Hour." *An Introduction to Literature: Fiction, Poetry, and Drama*. Ed. Sylvan Barnet, William Burto, and William E. Cain. 15th ed. New York: Longman, 2008. 50-51. Print.

> New page for work cited in MLA style (p. 628)

49f   Writing about fiction, poetry, and drama

A work of literature falls into a category, or **genre**—such as fiction, poetry, or drama—depending on how it is structured. The different genres of literature require different approaches in writing.

1   Writing about fiction

The "Questions for a literary analysis" on pages 698–99 will help you think about any work of literature, including a story or novel, and find a topic to write on. The following questions provide additional prompts for thinking about fiction. For an example of writing about fiction, see Janet Vong's essay about Kate Chopin's short story opposite and above.

Questions for analyzing fiction

- **What happens in the story?** In your own words, summarize the plot (the gist of the happenings).
- **Is the story told in chronological order, or are there flashbacks or flashforwards?** On rereading, what foreshadowing (hints of what is to come) do you detect?

(continued)

Questions for analyzing fiction
(continued)

- **What conflicts does the work include?** How does the author use conflicts to underscore themes in the work?

- **How does the writer develop characters?** Is character revealed by explicit comment or through action? Does the author choose to develop some characters but not others? Why? Do some characters serve as **foils**, or contrasts, for other characters, thus helping to define the other characters? With which character(s) do you sympathize? Are the characters plausible? What motivates them? What do minor characters contribute to the work?

- **Who tells the story?** Is the narrator a character, or does the narrator stand entirely outside the characters' world? What does the narrator's point of view contribute to the story's theme? (On narrative points of view, see p. 698.)

- **What is the setting?** What do the time and place of the action contribute to the work? How detailed is the author's description of the setting? How important is the setting to the overall meaning of the story?

- **Are certain characters, settings, or actions symbolic?** Do they stand for something in addition to themselves?

- **Are there recurring words, phrases, or images?** Why does the author repeat them? What thematic or symbolic value do they suggest?

- **What are the themes?** That is, what does the work add up to? Are the themes familiar or unfamiliar to you? Do they reinforce or challenge your values?

- **Is the title informative?** Did its meaning change for you after you read the work?

2 Writing about poetry

Two types of essays on poetry are especially common. One is an analysis of some aspect of the poem in relation to the whole—for instance, the changes in the speaker's tone or the functions of meter and rhyme. The second is an **explication,** a line-by-line (sometimes almost word-by-word) reading that seeks to make explicit everything that is implicit in the poem. Thus an explication of the first line of Robert Frost's "Stopping by Woods on a Snowy Evening" (the line goes "Whose woods these are I think I know") might call attention to the tentativeness of the line ("I think I know") and to the fact that the words are not in the normal order ("I think I know whose woods these are"). These features might support the explanation that the poet is introducing—very quietly—a note of the *un*usual, in preparation for the experience that follows. Although one might conceivably explicate a long poem, the method is so detailed that in practice writers usually confine it to short poems or to short passages from long poems.

The "Questions for a literary analysis" on pages 698–99 will help you think about any work of literature, including a poem, and find a topic to write on. The questions below provide additional ways to think about poetry.

Questions for analyzing poetry

- **Have you read the poem more than once?** Most poems require three or more readings for thorough analysis. Look up the meanings of unfamiliar words, notice the use of punctuation, and examine figurative language and other images.

- **What parts of the poem interest or puzzle you?** The lines that grab or challenge you often have the most potential for thoughtful analysis.

- **How can you describe the poem's** *speaker* **(sometimes called the** *persona* **or the** *voice* **)?** Do not assume that the author of a poem is the speaker.

- **How can you describe the plot and setting?** What happens in the poem? Where does it take place?

- **What tone or emotion do you detect**—for instance, anger, affection, sarcasm? Does the tone change during the poem?

- **What is the structure of the poem?** Are there stanzas (groups of lines separated by space)? If so, how is the thought related to the stanzas? Do the stanzas shift in time, imagery, or theme? If there are no stanza divisions, consider why the poet chose to write without them.

- **What is the theme of the poem?** Is the theme stated or implied?

- **What images do you find?** Look for evocations of sight, sound, taste, touch, or smell. Focus closely on figurative language—metaphors, similes, personification, and so on. (See pp. 522–23.) Is there a surprising pattern of images—say, images of business in a poem about love? What does the poem suggest symbolically as well as literally? (Trust your responses. If you don't sense a symbolic overtone, move on. Don't hunt for symbols.)

An essay on poetry with secondary sources

The sample paper on the next two pages analyzes a short poem by Gwendolyn Brooks. The paper illustrates a literary analysis that draws not only on the poem itself but also on secondary sources—that is, critical works *about* the poem. In the opening paragraph, for instance, the writer uses brief quotations from two secondary sources to establish the problem, the topic that he will address. These quotations, like the two later quotations from secondary material, are used to make points, not to pad the essay.

Note In the paper, the parenthetical citations for Brooks's poem give line numbers of the poem, whereas the citations for the secondary sources give page numbers of the sources. See pages 624–25 and 619, respectively, for these two forms of citation.

Gwendolyn Brooks

The Bean Eaters

They eat beans mostly, this old yellow pair.
Dinner is a casual affair.
Plain chipware on a plain and creaking wood,
Tin flatware.

Two who are Mostly Good.   5
Two who have lived their day,
But keep on putting on their clothes
And putting things away.

And remembering . . .
Remembering, with twinklings and twinges,   10
As they lean over the beans in their rented back room that
    is full of beads and receipts and dolls and cloths,
        tobacco crumbs, vases and fringes.

Kenneth Scheff

Ms. Moran

English II, period 5

7 May 2009

Marking Time Versus Enduring in
Gwendolyn Brooks's "The Bean Eaters"

Gwendolyn Brooks's poem "The Bean Eaters" runs only eleven lines. It is written in plain language about very plain people. Yet its meaning is ambiguous. One critic, George E. Kent, says the old couple who eat beans "have had their day and exist now as time-markers" (141). However, another critic, D. H. Melhem, perceives not so much time marking as "endurance" in the old couple (123). The reader must decide whether this poem is a despairing picture of old age or a more positive portrait.

"The Bean Eaters" describes an "old yellow pair" who "eat beans mostly" (line 1) off "Plain chipware" (3) with "Tin flatware" (4) in "their rented back room" (11). Clearly, they are poor. They live alone, not with friends or relatives—children or grandchildren are not mentioned—but with memories and a few possessions (9-11). They are "Mostly Good" (5), words Brooks capitalizes at the end of a line, perhaps to stress the old people's adherence to traditional values as well as their lack of saintliness. They are unexceptional.

The isolated routine of the couple's life is something Brooks draws attention to with a separate stanza:

> Two who are Mostly Good.
>
> Two who have lived their day,
>
> But keep on putting on their clothes
>
> And putting things away. (5-8)

Brooks emphasizes how isolated the couple is by repeating "Two who." Then she emphasizes how routine their life is by repeating "putting."

A pessimistic reading of this poem seems justified. The critic Harry B. Shaw reads the lines just quoted as perhaps despairing: "they are putting things away as if winding down an operation and readying for withdrawal from activity" (80). However, Shaw observes, the word "But" also indicates that the couple resist slipping away, that they intend to hold on (80). This dual meaning is at the heart of Brooks's poem: the old people live a meager existence, yes, but their will, their self-control, and their connection with another person—their essential humanity—are unharmed.

The truly positive nature of the poem is revealed in the last stanza. In Brooks's words, the old people remember with some "twinges" perhaps, but also with "twinklings" (10), a cheerful image. As Melhem says, these people are "strong in mutual affection and shared memories" (123). And the final line, which is much longer than all the rest and which catalogs the evidence of the couple's long life together, is almost musically affirmative: "As they lean over the beans in their rented back room that is full of beads and receipts and dolls and cloths, tobacco crumbs, vases and fringes" (11).

What these people have is not much, but it is something.

[New page.]

Works Cited

Brooks, Gwendolyn. "The Bean Eaters." *An Introduction to Literature: Fiction, Poetry, and Drama*. Ed. Sylvan Barnet, William Burto, and William E. Cain. 15th ed. New York: Longman, 2008. 922. Print.

Kent, George E. *A Life of Gwendolyn Brooks*. Lexington: UP of Kentucky, 1990. Print.

Melhem, D. H. *Gwendolyn Brooks: Poetry and the Heroic Voice*. Lexington: UP of Kentucky, 1987. Print.

Shaw, Harry B. *Gwendolyn Brooks*. Boston: Twayne, 1980. Print. Twayne's United States Authors Ser. 395.

3 Writing about drama

Because plays—even some one-act plays—are relatively long, analytic essays on drama usually focus on only one aspect of the play, such as the structure of the play, the function of a single scene, or a character's responsibility for his or her fate. The essay's introduction indicates what the topic is and why it is of some importance, and the introduction may also state the thesis. The conclusion often extends the analysis, showing how a study of the apparently small topic helps to illuminate the play as a whole.

The "Questions for a literary analysis" on pages 698–99 will help you think about any work of literature, including a play, and find a topic to write on. The questions in the following box provide additional prompts for thinking about drama.

Questions for analyzing drama

■ **How does the plot (the sequence of happenings) unfold?** Does it seem plausible? If not, is the implausibility a fault? If there is more than one plot, are the plots parallel, or are they related by way of contrast? How do particular scenes advance the plot and ultimately contribute to the play's themes?

■ **Are certain happenings recurrent?** If so, how are they significant?

■ **What kinds of conflict are in the play**—for instance, between two groups, two individuals, or two aspects of a single individual? How are the conflicts resolved? Is the resolution satisfying to you?

■ **How does the author develop the characters?** How trustworthy are the characters when they describe themselves or others? What purpose does each character serve? Do some characters serve as **foils**, or contrasts, for other characters, thus helping to define the other characters? Do the characters change as the play proceeds? Are the characters' motivations convincing? How do minor characters contribute to the play's meaning?

■ **What do the author's stage directions add to your understanding of the play?** If there are few stage directions, what do the speeches imply about the characters' manner, tone, and gestures?

■ **What do you make of the setting, or location?** Does it help to reveal character or theme? Do changes in setting parallel changes in plot or character development? How do various settings contribute to the themes of the play?

■ **Do certain costumes** (dark suits, flowery shawls, stiff collars) **or properties** (books, pictures, candlesticks) **strike you as symbolic?**

■ **What is the author's relationship to the audience?** Do characters speak directly to the audience in asides or soliloquies? If so, what is their effect?

An essay on drama (no secondary sources)

The following essay on William Shakespeare's *Macbeth* focuses on the title character, examining the extent to which he is and is not a tragic hero. Although the writer bases the essay on his personal response to the play, he does not simply state a preference, as if saying he likes vanilla more than chocolate; instead, he argues a case and offers evidence from the play to support his claims.

The writer delays stating his thesis fully until the final paragraph: Macbeth is a hero even though he is a villain. But this thesis is nonetheless evident throughout the essay, from the title through the opening three paragraphs (which establish a context and the case the writer will oppose) through each of the five body paragraphs (which offer five kinds of evidence for the thesis).

Note The parenthetical citations in this essay include act, scene, and line numbers—MLA style for citations of verse plays (see p. 625).

Michael Spinter
Professor Nelson
English III, period 4
8 October 2008

Macbeth as Hero

When people imagine a tragic hero, they probably think of a fundamentally sympathetic person who is entangled in terrifying circumstances and who ultimately dies, leaving the world a diminished place. For instance, Hamlet must avenge his father's murder, and in doing so he performs certain actions that verge on the wrongful, such as behaving cruelly to his beloved Ophelia and his mother and killing Rosencrantz and Guildenstern. But in the end Hamlet seems fundamentally a decent man and Denmark seems the poorer for his death.

Macbeth, however, is different. He kills King Duncan and Duncan's grooms, kills Banquo, attempts to kill Banquo's son, and finally kills Lady Macduff and her children as well as her servants. True, the only people whom he kills with his own hands are Duncan and the grooms—the other victims are destroyed by hired murderers—but clearly Macbeth is responsible for all of the deaths. He could seem to be an utterly unscrupulous, sneaking butcher rather than a tragic hero for whom a reader can feel sympathy.

Certainly most of the other characters in the play feel no sympathy for Macbeth. Macduff calls him a "hell-kite," or a hellish bird of prey (4.3.217), a "tyrant" (5.7.14), a "hell-hound" (5.8.3), and a "coward" (5.8.23). To Malcolm he is a "tyrant" (4.3.12), "devilish Macbeth" (4.3.117), and a "butcher" (5.8.69). Readers and spectators can hardly deny the truth of these characterizations. And yet Macbeth does not seem merely villainous. It would be going too far to say that Macbeth is always sympathetic, but he is deeply interesting and not to be dismissed as an out-and-out monster. What accounts for his hold on readers' and spectators' feelings? At least five factors play their parts.

Macbeth is appealing because he is an impressive military figure. In the first extended description of Macbeth, the Captain speaks of "brave Macbeth—well he deserves that name" (1.2.16). The Captain tells how Macbeth valiantly fought on behalf of his king, and King Duncan exclaims, "O valiant cousin! Worthy gentle-man!" (1.2.2). True, Macbeth sometimes cringes, such as when he denies responsi-bility for Banquo's death: "Thou canst not say I did it" (3.4.51). But throughout most of the play, he is a bold and courageous soldier.

Of course, Macbeth's ability as a soldier is not enough by itself to explain his appeal. He is at the same time a victim—a victim of his wife's ambition and a vic-tim of the witches. Yes, he ought to see through his wife's schemes, and he ought to resist the witches, just as Banquo resists them, but surely Macbeth is partly tricked into crime. He is responsible, but others can imagine themselves falling as he does, and his status as a victim arouses sympathy.

Also contributing to a sense of Macbeth's humanity is the conscience he retains despite his terrible deeds. For instance, after he murders Duncan he cannot sleep at night. When he tells Lady Macbeth that he has heard a voice saying "Macbeth does murder sleep" (2.2.35), she ridicules him, but the voice is prophetic: he is doomed to sleepless nights. Macbeth's torment over his deed shows that he knows he has done wrong and that he still has some decent human feelings.

Macbeth eventually loses all of his allies, even his wife, and he then claims sympathy as a lonely, guilt-haunted figure. On this point, scene 2 of act 3 is especially significant. When Lady Macbeth asks Macbeth why he keeps to himself (line 8), he confides something of the mental stress that he is undergoing. But when she asks, "What's to be done?" (44), he cannot bring himself to tell her that he is plotting the deaths of Banquo and Fleance. Instead of further involving his wife, the only person with whom he might still have a human connection, Macbeth says, "Be innocent of the knowledge, dearest chuck . . ." (45). The word chuck, an affectionate form of chick, shows warmth and intimacy that are touching, but his refusal or his inability to confide in his wife and former partner in crime shows how fully isolated he is from all human contact. Readers and spectators cannot help feeling some sympathy for him.

Finally, Macbeth is appealing, rather than disgusting, because he speaks so eloquently. The greatness of his language compels rapt attention. Some speeches are very familiar, such as "My way of life / Is fall'n into the sear, the yellow leaf . . ." (5.3.23-24) and "Tomorrow and tomorrow and tomorrow / Creeps in this petty pace from day to day . . ." (5.5.19-20). But almost every speech Macbeth utters is equally memorable, from his first, "So foul and fair a day I have not seen" (1.3.38), to his last:

> Before my body
> I throw my warlike shield. Lay on, Macduff:
> And damned be him that first cries, "Hold, enough!" (5.8.32-34)

If readers and spectators judge Macbeth only by what he does, of course they will see a foul murderer. But if they give due weight to his bravery, his role as a victim, his tormented conscience, his isolation, and especially his moving language, then they will not simply judge Macbeth. Rather, they will see that this villain is not merely awful but awesome.

[New page.]

Work Cited

Shakespeare, William. *The Tragedy of Macbeth*. Ed. Sylvan Barnet. Rev. ed. New York: NAL, 1987. Print.

50

Writing in Other Humanities

The humanities include literature, the visual arts, music, film, dance, history, philosophy, and religion. The preceding chapter discusses the particular requirements of reading and writing about literature. This chapter concentrates on history. Although the arts, religion, and other humanities have their own concerns, they share many important goals and methods with literature and history.

50a Using the methods and evidence of the humanities

Writers in the humanities record and speculate about the growth, ideas, and emotions of human beings. Based on the evidence of written words, artworks, and other human traces and creations, humanities writers explain, interpret, analyze, and reconstruct the human experience.

The discipline of history focuses particularly on reconstructing the past. In Greek the word for history means "to inquire": historians inquire into the past to understand the events of the past. Then they report, explain, analyze, and evaluate those events in their context, asking such questions as what happened before or after the events or how the events were related to then existing political and social structures.

Historians' reconstructions of the past—their conclusions about what happened and why—are always supported with reference to the written record. The evidence of history is mainly primary sources, such as eyewitness accounts and contemporary documents, letters, commercial records, and the like. For history papers, you might also be asked to support your conclusions with those in secondary sources.

mycomplab

Visit *mycomplab.com* for more resources on writing in history, the visual arts, and other humanities.

In reading historical sources, you need to weigh and evaluate their evidence. If, for example, you find conflicting accounts of the same event, you need to consider the possible biases of the authors. In general, the more a historian's conclusions are supported by public records such as deeds, marriage licenses, and newspaper accounts, the more reliable the conclusions are likely to be.

50b Understanding writing assignments in the humanities

Papers in the humanities generally perform one or more of the following operations:

- **Explanation:** for instance, showing how a painter developed a particular technique or clarifying a general's role in a historical battle.
- **Analysis:** examining the elements of a philosophical argument or breaking down the causes of a historical event.
- **Interpretation:** inferring the meaning of a film from its images or the significance of a historical event from contemporary accounts of it.
- **Synthesis:** finding a pattern in a historical period or in a composer's works.
- **Evaluation:** judging the quality of an architect's design or a historian's conclusions.

Most likely, you will use these operations in combination—say, interpreting and explaining the meaning of a painting and then evaluating it. (These operations are discussed in more detail in Chapter 7.)

50c Using the tools and language of the humanities

The tools and language of the humanities vary according to the discipline. Major reference works in each field, such as those listed on the next four pages, can clarify specific tools you need and language you should use.

1 Writing tools

A useful tool for the arts is to ask a series of questions to analyze and evaluate a work. (A list of such questions for reading literature appears on pp. 698–99.) In any humanities discipline, a journal—a log of questions, reactions, and insights—can help you discover and record your thoughts. (See pp. 142 and 551.)

In history the tools are those of any thorough and efficient researcher, as discussed in Chapters 41–43: a system for finding and tracking sources; a methodical examination of sources, including evaluating and synthesizing them; a system for gathering source information; and a separate system, such as a research journal, for tracking one's own evolving thoughts.

2 Language considerations

Historians strive for precision and logic. They do not guess about what happened or speculate about "what if." They avoid trying to influence readers' opinions with words having strongly negative or positive connotations, such as *stupid* or *brilliant*. Instead, historians show the evidence and draw conclusions from that. Generally, they avoid using *I* because it tends to draw attention away from the evidence and toward the writer.

Writing about history demands some attention to the tenses of verbs to maintain consistency. Generally, historians use the past tense to refer to events that occurred in the past. They reserve the present tense only for statements about the present or statements of general truths. For example:

> Franklin Delano Roosevelt <u>died</u> in 1945. Many of Roosevelt's economic reforms <u>persist</u> in programs such as Social Security, unemployment compensation, and farm subsidies.

3 Research sources

The following lists give resources in the humanities. (Resources for literature appear on pp. 704–05.)

Specialized encyclopedias, dictionaries, and bibliographies

The arts

Architecture: From Prehistory to Post-modernity
Baker Biographical Dictionary of Music
Dictionary of Art
Encyclopedia of World Art
Film Literature Index
Film Review Index
Garland Encyclopedia of World Music
Guide to the Literature of Art History 2
Guinness Encyclopedia of Popular Music
International Encyclopedia of Dance
International Television and Video Almanac
MLA International Bibliography of Books and Articles on the Modern Languages and Literatures
New Grove Dictionary of Music and Musicians

New Grove Dictionary of Opera
Oxford Companion to Twentieth-Century Art

History
Afro-American Reference
American Decades
American Indian Studies: A Bibliographic Guide
Dictionary of American History
Dictionary of the Middle Ages
Encyclopedia of American History
Encyclopedia of Latin American History and Culture
Encyclopedia of Russian History
Encyclopedia of World History
Harvard Guide to American History
History: Illustrated Search Strategy and Sources
Middle East Abstracts and Index
New Cambridge Modern History
Oxford Classical Dictionary

Philosophy and religion
Anchor Bible Dictionary
Catholic Encyclopedia
Dictionary of the History of Ideas
Encyclopedia Judaica
Encyclopedia of Asian Philosophy
Encyclopedia of Ethics
Encyclopedia of Philosophy
Encyclopedia of Religion
Oxford Dictionary of Islam
Oxford Dictionary of the Christian Church

Library databases and indexes
America: History and Life
Art Index
Arts and Humanities Citation Index
ARTStor
ATLA Religion Database
Avery Index to Architectural Periodicals
Dissertation Abstracts International (doctoral dissertations)
Film Literature Index
Historical Abstracts
Humanities Index
Index Islamicus
JSTOR
MLA International Bibliography
Music Index
Nineteenth-Century Masterfile
Philosopher's Index

Book reviews

Book Review Digest
Book Review Index

Sources on the open Web

General

Arts and Humanities Data Service (ahds.ac.uk)
BUBL LINK (bubl.ac.uk)
EDSITEment (edsitement.neh.gov)
Internet Public Library (ipl.org/div/subject/browse/hum00.00.00)
Intute: Arts and Humanities (www.intute.ac.uk/artsandhumanities)
Librarians Internet Index: Arts and Humanities (search.lii.org/
    index.jsp?more=SubTopic)
Voice of the Shuttle Humanities (vos.ucsb.edu)

Art

Art History Resources on the Web (witcombe.sbc.edu/ARTHLinks.html)
Artnet (artnet.com)
ArtSource (www.ilpi.com/artsource/welcome.html)
BUBL LINK: The Arts (bubl.ac.uk/link/linkbrowse.cfm?menuid=9847)
World Wide Arts Resources (wwar.com/browse.html)

Dance

Artslynx International Dance Resources (www.artslynx.org/dance)
BUBL LINK: Dance (bubl.ac.uk/link/d/dance.htm)

Film

CinemaSpot (cinemaspot.com)
Film Studies on the Internet (www.library.ualberta.ca/subject/film/websites/
    index.cfm)
Internet Movie Database (imdb.com)

History

History: North America (www.libraries.rutgers.edu/rul/rr_gateway/
    research_guides/history_us/history_us.shtml)
Best of History Web Sites (besthistorysites.net)
National Women's History Project (nwhp.org)

Music

American Music Resource (amrhome.net)
MusicMoz (musicmoz.org)
Music Theory Online (societymusictheory.org/mto)
Web Resources for Research in Music (www.music.ucc.ie/wrrm)

Philosophy

Philosophy Documentation Center (pdcnet.org)
P-Search (philosophy.hku.hk/psearch/info.php)
Social Science Information Gateway: Philosophy (www.intute.ac.uk/
    artsandhumanities/philosophy)

Stanford Encyclopedia of Philosophy (plato.stanford.edu)
Voice of the Shuttle: Philosophy (vos.ucsb.edu/browse.asp?id=2724)

Religion
Academic Info: Religion Gateway (academicinfo.net/religindex.html)
Pluralism Project (pluralism.org/directory/index.php)
Religious Studies Web Guide (www.acs.ucalgary.ca/~lipton)
Religious Worlds (www.religiousworlds.com/index.html)
Virtual Religion Index (virtualreligion.net/vri)

Theater
McCoy's Brief Guide to Internet Resources in Theater and Performance Studies (www2.stetson.edu/csata/thr_guid.html)
TheatreHistory.com (*theatrehistory.com*)

50d Citing sources in Chicago style

Writers in the humanities generally rely on one of the following guides for source-citation style:

The Chicago Manual of Style, 16th ed., 2010
A Manual for Writers of Research Papers, Theses, and Dissertations, by Kate L. Turabian, 7th ed., rev. Wayne C. Booth, Gregory G. Colomb, and Joseph M. Williams, 2007
MLA Handbook for Writers of Research Papers, 7th ed., 2009

The recommendations of the *MLA Handbook* are discussed and illustrated in Chapter 46. Unless your teacher specifies otherwise, use these recommendations for papers in English and foreign languages. In history, art history, and many other disciplines, however, writers rely on *The Chicago Manual of Style* or the student reference adapted from it, *A Manual for Writers.*

Both books detail two documentation styles. One, used mainly by scientists and social scientists, closely resembles the style of the American Psychological Association, covered in Chapter 51. The other style, used more in the humanities, calls for footnotes or endnotes and an optional bibliography. This style is described below and follows the guidelines in *The Chicago Manual.* The spacing of the notes and bibliography entries is based on *A Manual for Writers,* which offers more specific advice than *The Chicago Manual.*

1 Using Chicago notes and a bibliography

In the Chicago note style, a raised numeral in the text refers the reader to source information in an endnote or a footnote. In these notes, the first citation of each source contains all the information readers need to find the source. Thus your teacher may consider a bibliography optional because it provides much the same information. Ask your teacher whether you should use footnotes or endnotes and whether you should include a bibliography in your paper.

Whether you are providing footnotes or endnotes, use single spacing for each note and double spacing between notes, as shown in the samples below. Separate footnotes from the text with a short line. Place endnotes directly after the text, beginning on a new page. For a list of sources at the end of the paper, use the format on the following page. Arrange the sources alphabetically by the authors' last names.

Chicago footnotes

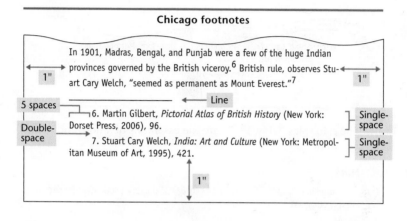

Chicago endnotes

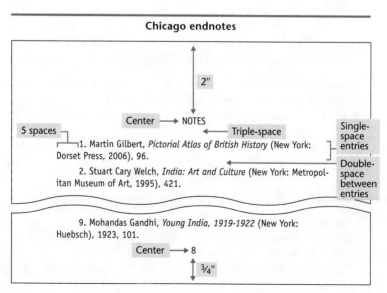

Chicago bibliography

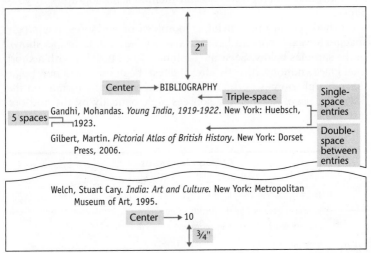

The examples below illustrate the essentials of a note and a bibliography entry.

Note

> 6. Martin Gilbert, *Pictorial Atlas of British History* (New York: Dorset Press, 2006), 96.

Bibliography entry

> Gilbert, Martin. *Pictorial Atlas of British History*. New York: Dorset Press, 2006.

Treat some features of notes and bibliography entries the same:

- Single-space each note or entry, and double-space between them.
- Italicize the titles of books and periodicals.
- Enclose in quotation marks the titles of parts of books or articles in periodicals.
- Do not abbreviate publishers' names, but omit "Inc.," "Co.," and similar abbreviations.
- Do not use "p." or "pp." before page numbers.

Treat other features of notes and bibliography entries differently:

Note	Bibliography entry
Start with the same number that is in the text.	Do not begin with a number.
Indent the first line five spaces.	Indent the second and subsequent lines five spaces.

Give the author's name in normal order.	Begin with the author's last name.
Use commas between elements such as author's name and title.	Use periods between elements.
Enclose publication information in parentheses, with no preceding punctuation	Precede the publication information with a period, and don't use parentheses.
Include the specific page number(s) you borrowed from, omitting "p." or "pp."	Omit page numbers except for parts of books or articles in periodicals.

You can instruct your computer to position footnotes at the bottoms of appropriate pages. It will also automatically number notes and renumber them if you add or delete one or more.

2 Following Chicago models

The Chicago models for common sources are indexed on the next page. The models show notes and bibliography entries together for easy reference. Be sure to use the numbered note form for notes and the unnumbered bibliography form for bibliography entries.

Listing authors

1. One, two, or three authors

1. Carol Gilligan, *In a Different Voice: Psychological Theory and Women's Development* (Cambridge: Harvard University Press, 1982), 27.

Gilligan, Carol. *In a Different Voice: Psychological Theory and Women's Development*. Cambridge: Harvard University Press, 1982.

1. Dennis L. Wilcox, Phillip H. Ault, and Warren K. Agee, *Public Relations: Strategies and Tactics,* 6th ed. (New York: Irwin, 2005), 182.

Wilcox, Dennis L., Phillip H. Ault, and Warren K. Agee. *Public Relations: Strategies and Tactics*. 6th ed. New York: Irwin, 2005.

2. More than three authors

2. Geraldo Lopez et al., *China and the West* (Boston: Little, Brown, 2004), 461.

Lopez, Geraldo, Judith P. Salt, Anne Ming, and Henry Reisen. *China and the West*. Boston: Little, Brown, 2004.

The Latin abbreviation et al. means "and others."

3. Author not named (anonymous)

3. *The Dorling Kindersley World Reference Atlas* (London: Dorling Kindersley, 2005), 150-51.

The Dorling Kindersley World Reference Atlas. London: Dorling Kindersley, 2005.

Chicago note and bibliography models

Listing print periodicals: Journals, newspapers, magazines

4. An article in a journal (print)

4. Janet Lever, "Sex Differences in the Games Children Play," *Social Problems* 23 (Spring 1996): 482.

Lever, Janet. "Sex Differences in the Games Children Play." *Social Problems* 23 (Spring 1996): 478-87.

Provide the issue number if the journal numbers issues, as shown below. Note that the issue number is required for any journal that pages each issue separately or that numbers only issues, not volumes.

4. Robert Bee, "The Importance of Preserving Paper-Based Artifacts in a Digital Age," *The Library Quarterly* 78, no. 2 (April 2008): 176.

Bee, Robert. "The Importance of Preserving Paper-Based Artifacts in a Digital Age." *The Library Quarterly* 78, no. 2 (April 2008): 174-94.

5. An article in a newspaper (print)

    5. David Stout, "Blind Win Court Ruling on US Currency," *New York Times,* May 21, 2008, national edition, A23.

Stout, David. "Blind Win Court Ruling on US Currency." *New York Times,* May 21, 2008, national edition, A23.

Chicago style does not require page numbers for newspaper articles, whether in notes or in bibliography entries. Thus A23 could be omitted from the above examples.

6. An article in a magazine (print)

    6. Amanda Fortini, "Pomegranate Princess," *New Yorker,* March 31, 2008, 94.

Fortini, Amanda. "Pomegranate Princess." *New Yorker,* March 31, 2008, 92-99.

Chicago bibliography style does not require inclusive page numbers for magazine articles, so 92-99 could be omitted from the preceding example.

7. A review (print)

    7. John Gregory Dunne, "The Secret of Danny Santiago," review of *Famous All over Town,* by Danny Santiago, *New York Review of Books,* August 16, 1994, 25.

Dunne, John Gregory. "The Secret of Danny Santiago." Review of *Famous All over Town,* by Danny Santiago. *New York Review of Books,* August 16, 1994, 17-27.

Listing print books

8. Basic format for a book (print)

    8. Barbara Ehrenreich, *Dancing in the Streets: A History of Collective Joy* (New York: Henry Holt, 2006), 97-117.

Ehrenreich, Barbara. *Dancing in the Streets: A History of Collective Joy.* New York: Henry Holt, 2006.

9. A book with an editor (print)

    9. Hendrick Ruitenbeek, ed., *Freud as We Knew Him* (Detroit: Wayne State University Press, 1973), 64.

Ruitenbeek, Hendrick, ed. *Freud as We Knew Him.* Detroit: Wayne State University Press, 1973.

10. A book with an author and an editor (print)

    10. Lewis Mumford, *The City in History,* ed. Donald L. Miller (New York: Pantheon, 1986), 216-17.

Mumford, Lewis. *The City in History.* Edited by Donald L. Miller. New York: Pantheon, 1986.

11. A translation (print)

11. Dante Alighieri, *The Inferno,* trans. John Ciardi (New York: New American Library, 1971), 51.

Alighieri, Dante. *The Inferno*. Translated by John Ciardi. New York: New American Library, 1971.

12. A later edition (print)

12. Dwight L. Bolinger, *Aspects of Language,* 3rd ed. (New York: Harcourt Brace Jovanovich, 1981), 20.

Bolinger, Dwight L. *Aspects of Language*. 3rd ed. New York: Harcourt Brace Jovanovich, 1981.

13. A work in more than one volume (print)

Citation of one volume without a title:

13. Abraham Lincoln, *The Collected Works of Abraham Lincoln,* ed. Roy P. Basler (New Brunswick: Rutgers University Press, 1953), 5:426-28.

Lincoln, Abraham. *The Collected Works of Abraham Lincoln*. Edited by Roy P. Basler. Vol. 5. New Brunswick: Rutgers University Press, 1953.

Citation of one volume with a title:

13. Linda B. Welkin, *The Age of Balanchine,* vol. 3 of *The History of Ballet* (New York: Columbia University Press, 1999), 56.

Welkin, Linda B. *The Age of Balanchine*. Vol. 3 of *The History of Ballet*. New York: Columbia University Press, 1999.

14. A selection from an anthology (print)

14. Rosetta Brooks, "Streetwise," in *The New Urban Landscape,* ed. Richard Martin (New York: Rizzoli, 2005), 38-39.

Brooks, Rosetta. "Streetwise." In *The New Urban Landscape,* ed. Richard Martin, 37-60. New York: Rizzoli, 2005.

15. A work in a series (print)

15. Ingmar Bergman, *The Seventh Seal,* Modern Film Scripts 12 (New York: Simon and Schuster, 1995), 27.

Bergman, Ingmar. *The Seventh Seal*. Modern Film Scripts 12. New York: Simon and Schuster, 1995.

16. An article in a reference work (print)

16. *Merriam-Webster's Collegiate Dictionary,* 11th ed., s.v. "reckon."

Merriam-Webster's Collegiate Dictionary. 11th ed. S.v. "reckon."

Use the abbreviation s.v. (Latin *sub verbo,* "under the word") for reference works that are alphabetically arranged. Well-known works like the one listed here do not need publication information except for edition number. Chicago style generally recommends notes only, not bibliography entries, for reference works; a bibliography model is given here in case your teacher requires such entries.

Listing Web and other electronic sources

The *Chicago Manual*'s models for documenting electronic sources mostly begin as those for print sources do. Then you add electronic publication information that will help readers locate the source, such as a URL or a Digital Object Identifier (DOI), a unique identifier that many publishers assign to articles. If an article has a DOI, include it as shown in models 17 and 20. Otherwise give the URL.

For Web pages and other electronic sources that are likely to change, *The Chicago Manual* suggests including the date of the most recent update in a statement beginning last modified (see model 22). If no date is available, give the date of your access (see model 26).

Note Chicago style allows many ways to break URLs between the end of one line and the beginning of the next: after a colon or double slash and before a single slash, period, comma, hyphen, and most other marks. *Do not* break after a hyphen or add any hyphens.

17. An article in a journal (Web)

17. Andrew Palfrey, "Choice of Mates in Identical Twins," *Modern Psychology* 4, no. 1 (Fall 2003): 28, doi:10.1080/143257962345987215.

Palfrey, Andrew. "Choice of Mates in Identical Twins." *Modern Psychology* 4, no. 1 (Fall 2003): 26-40. doi:10.1080/143257962345987215.

Give a DOI if one is available (as here) or a URL if not (next two models).

18. An article in a magazine (Web)

18. Nina Shen Rastogi, "Peacekeepers on Trial," *Slate,* May 28, 2008, http://www.slate.com/id/2192272.

Rastogi, Nina Shen. "Peacekeepers on Trial." *Slate,* May 28, 2008. http://www.slate.com/id/2192272.

19. An article in a newspaper (Web)

19. Elissa Gootman, "Gifted Programs in the City Are Less Diverse," *New York Times,* June 19, 2008, http://www.nytimes.com/2008/06/19/nyregion/19gifted.html.

Gootman, Elissa. "Gifted Programs in the City Are Less Diverse." *New York Times,* June 19, 2008. http://www.nytimes.com/2008/06/19/nyregion/19gifted.html.

20. An article in an online database (Web)

20. Jonathan Dickens, "Social Policy Approaches to Intercountry Adoption," *International Social Work* 52, no. 5 (September 2009): 600, doi:10.1177/0020872809337678.

Dickens, Jonathan. "Social Policy Approaches to Intercountry Adoption."
International Social Work 52, no. 5 (September 2009): 595-607.
doi:10.1177/0020872809337678.

If a database article has neither a DOI nor a stable URL, end with the name of the database.

21. A book (Web)

21. Jane Austen, *Emma*, ed. R. W. Chapman (1816; Oxford: Clarendon, 1926; Oxford Text Archive, 2004), chap. 1, http://ota.ahds.ac.uk/Austen /Emma.1519.

Austen, Jane. *Emma*. Edited by R. W. Chapman. 1816. Oxford: Clarendon, 1926. Oxford Text Archive, 2004. http://ota.ahds.ac.uk/Austen/Emma.1519.

Provide print publication information, if any.

22. An article in a reference work (Web)

22. *Wikipedia,* s.v. "Wuhan," last modified July 16, 2010, http://en.wikipedia.org/wiki/Wuhan.

Wikipedia. S.v. "Wuhan." Last modified July 16, 2010. http://en .wikipedia.org/wiki/Wuhan.

23. An audio or visual source (Web)

A work of art:

23. Jackson Pollock, *Shimmering Substance,* 1946, Museum of Modern Art, New York, http://moma.org/collection/conservation/pollock /shimmering_substance.html.

Pollock, Jackson. *Shimmering Substance*. 1946. Museum of Modern Art, New York. http://moma.org/collection/conservation/pollock /shimmering_substance.html.

See also model 30 to cite a work of art that you view in person.

A sound recording:

23. Ronald W. Reagan, "State of the Union Address," January 26, 1982, Vincent Voice Library, Digital and Multimedia Center, University of Michigan, http://www.lib.msu.edu/vincent/presidents/reagan.html.

Reagan, Ronald W. "State of the Union Address." January 26, 1982. Vincent Voice Library. Digital and Multimedia Center, University of Michigan. http://www .lib.msu.edu/vincent/presidents/reagan.html.

A film or film clip:

23. Leslie J. Stewart, *96 Ranch Rodeo and Barbecue* (1951); 16mm; from Library of Congress, *Buckaroos in Paradise: Ranching Culture in Northern Nevada, 1945-1982,* MPEG, http://memory.loc.gov/cgi-bin/query.

Stewart, Leslie J. 96 *Ranch Rodeo and Barbecue*. 1951; 16 mm. From Library of Congress, *Buckaroos in Paradise: Ranching Culture in Northern Nevada, 1945-1982*. MPEG, http://memory.loc.gov/cgi-bin/query.

24. A message posted to a blog or discussion group (Web)

24. Chris Horner, "EU Emissions," Cooler Heads Blog, June 18, 2008, http://www.globalwarming.org/node/2362.

Horner, Chris. "EU Emissions." Cooler Heads Blog. June 18, 2008. http://www
.globalwarming.org/node/2362.

24. Michael Tourville, "European Currency Reform," e-mail to International Finance discussion list, January 6, 2008, http://www.weg.isu
.edu/finance-dl/archive/46732.

Tourville, Michael. "European Currency Reform." E-mail to International Finance discussion list. January 6, 2008. http://www.weg.isu.edu
/finance-dl/archive/46732.

25. Electronic mail

25. Elizabeth Bailey, "Re: London," e-mail message to author, May 4, 2008.

Bailey, Elizabeth. "Re: London." E-mail message to author. May 4, 2008.

26. A Web page

26. "Toyota Safety," Toyota Motor Sales, accessed July 23, 2010, http://www.toyota.com/safety.

Toyota Motor Sales. "Toyota Safety." Accessed July 23, 2010. http://www.toyota.com/safety.

27. A work on CD-ROM or DVD-ROM

27. *The American Heritage Dictionary of the English Language,* 4th ed. (Boston: Houghton Mifflin, 2000), CD-ROM.

The American Heritage Dictionary of the English Language. 4th ed. Boston: Houghton Mifflin, 2000. CD-ROM.

Listing other sources

28. A government publication (print)

28. House Committee on Ways and Means, *Medicare Payment for Outpatient Physical and Occupational Therapy Services,* 110th Cong., 1st sess., 2007, H. Doc. 772, 18-19.

U.S. Congress. House. Committee on Ways and Means. *Medicare Payment for Outpatient Physical and Occupational Therapy Services.* 110th Cong., 1st sess., 2007. H. Doc. 772.

28. Hawaii Department of Education, *Kauai District Schools, Profile 2007-08* (Honolulu, 2008), 38.

Hawaii. Department of Education. *Kauai District Schools, Profile 2007-08.* Honolulu, 2008.

29. A published letter (print)

29. Mrs. Laura E. Buttolph to Rev. and Mrs. C. C. Jones, June 20, 1857, in *The Children of Pride: A True Story of Georgia and the Civil War,* ed. Robert Manson Myers (New Haven, CT: Yale University Press, 1972), 334.

Buttolph, Laura E. Mrs. Laura E. Buttolph to Rev. and Mrs. C. C. Jones, June 20, 1857. In *The Children of Pride: A True Story of Georgia and the Civil War,* edited by Robert Manson Myers. New Haven, CT: Yale University Press, 1972.

30. A published or broadcast interview

30. Junot Diaz, interview by Terry Gross, *Fresh Air,* NPR, October 18, 2007.

Diaz, Junot. Interview by Terry Gross. *Fresh Air*. NPR. October 18, 2007.

31. A personal letter or interview

31. Ann E. Packer, letter to author, June 15, 2008.

Packer, Ann E. Letter to author. June 15, 2008.

31. William Paul, interview by author, December 19, 2005.

Paul, William. Interview by author. December 19, 2005.

32. A work of art

32. John Singer Sargent, *In Switzerland,* 1908, Metropolitan Museum of Art, New York.

Sargent, John Singer. *In Switzerland*. 1908. Metropolitan Museum of Art, New York.

33. A film, DVD, or video recording

33. George Balanchine, *Serenade,* DVD, San Francisco Ballet (New York: PBS Video, 2006).

Balanchine, George. *Serenade*. DVD. San Francisco Ballet. New York: PBS Video, 2006.

34. A sound recording

34. Johannes Brahms, *Piano Concerto no. 2 in B-flat,* Artur Rubinstein, Philadelphia Orchestra, Eugene Ormandy, compact disc, RCA BRC4-6731.

Brahms, Johannes. *Piano Concerto no. 2 in B-flat*. Artur Rubinstein. Philadelphia Orchestra. Eugene Ormandy. Compact disc. RCA BRC4-6731.

Using shortened notes

To streamline documentation, Chicago style recommends shortened notes for sources that are fully cited elsewhere, either in a complete bibliography or in previous notes. Ask your teacher whether your paper should include a bibliography and, if so, whether you may use shortened notes for first references to sources as well as for subsequent references.

A shortened note contains the author's last name, the work's title (minus any initial *A*, *An*, or *The*), and the page number. Reduce long titles to four or fewer key words.

Complete note

4. Janet Lever, "Sex Differences in the Games Children Play," *Social Problems* 23 (Spring 1996): 482.

Complete bibliography entry

Lever, Janet. "Sex Differences in the Games Children Play." *Social Problems* 23 (Spring 1996): 478-87.

Shortened note

12. Lever, "Sex Differences," 483.

You may use the Latin abbreviation ibid. (meaning "in the same place") to refer to the same source cited in the preceding note. Give a page number if it differs from that in the preceding note.

12. Lever, "Sex Differences," 483.

13. Gilligan, *In a Different Voice,* 92.

14. Ibid., 93.

15. Lever, "Sex Differences," 483.

Chicago style allows for in-text parenthetical citations when you cite one or more works repeatedly. In the following example, the raised number 2 refers to the source information in a note; the number in parentheses is a page number in the same source.

British rule, observes Stuart Cary Welch, "seemed as permanent as Mount Everest."[2] Most Indians submitted, willingly or not, to British influence in every facet of life (42).

51

Writing in the Social Sciences

The social sciences—including anthropology, economics, education, management, political science, psychology, and sociology—focus on the study of human behavior. As the name implies, the social sciences examine the way human beings relate to themselves, to their environment, and to one another.

51a Using the methods and evidence of the social sciences

Researchers in the social sciences systematically pose a question, formulate a **hypothesis** (a generalization that can be tested), collect data, analyze those data, and draw conclusions to support, refine, or disprove their hypothesis. This is the scientific method developed in the natural sciences (see p. 768).

Social scientists gather data in several ways:

- **They make firsthand observations of human behavior,** recording the observations in writing or electronically.
- **They interview subjects about their attitudes and behavior,** recording responses in writing or electronically. (See p. 577 for guidelines on conducting an interview.)
- **They conduct broader surveys using questionnaires,** asking people about their attitudes and behavior. (See pp. 577–78 for guidelines on conducting a survey.)
- **They conduct controlled experiments,** structuring an environment in which to encourage and measure a specific behavior.

In their writing, social scientists explain their own research or analyze and evaluate others' research.

Visit *mycomplab.com* for more resources as well as exercises on writing in the social sciences.

Social science research methods generate two kinds of data:

- *Quantitative data* **are numerical,** such as statistical evidence based on surveys, polls, tests, and experiments. When public-opinion pollsters announce that 47 percent of US citizens polled approve of the President's leadership, they are offering quantitative data gained from a survey. Social science writers present quantitative data in graphs, charts, and other illustrations that accompany their text.
- *Qualitative data* **are not numerical but more subjective:** they are based on interviews, firsthand observations, and inferences, taking into account the subjective nature of human experience. Examples include an anthropologist's description of the initiation rites in a culture she is studying or a psychologist's interpretation of interviews he conducted with a group of adolescents.

51b Understanding writing assignments in the social sciences

Depending on what social science classes you take, you may be asked to complete a variety of assignments:

- **A summary or review of research** reports on the available research literature on a subject, such as infants' perception of color.
- **A case analysis** explains the components of a phenomenon, such as a factory closing.
- **A problem-solving analysis** explains the components of a problem, such as unreported child abuse, and suggests ways to solve it.
- **A research paper** interprets and sometimes analyzes and evaluates the writings of other social scientists about a subject, such as the effect of national versus local appeals in campaign advertising. An example appears in Chapter 47, pages 668–80.
- **A research report** explains the author's own original research or the author's attempt to replicate someone else's research. A research report begins on page 764.

Many social science disciplines have special requirements for the content and organization of each kind of paper. The requirements appear in the style guides of the disciplines, listed on pages 741–42. For instance, the American Psychological Association specifies the format for research reports that is illustrated on pages 764–67. Because of the differences among disciplines and even among different kinds of papers in the same discipline, you should always ask your teacher what he or she requires for an assignment.

51c ## Using the tools and language of the social sciences

The following guidelines for tools and language apply to most social sciences. However, the particular discipline you are writing in, or a teacher in a particular class, may have additional requirements. Many of the research sources listed on the next several pages can tell you more about your discipline's conventions.

1 Writing tools

Many social scientists rely on a **research journal** or **log,** in which they record their ideas throughout the research-writing process. Even if a research journal is not required in your class, you may want to use one. As you begin formulating a hypothesis, you can record preliminary questions. Then when you are in the field conducting research, you can use the journal to react to the evidence you are collecting, to record changes in your perceptions and ideas, and to assess your progress. (See pp. 142 and 551 for more on journals.)

To avoid confusing your reflections on the evidence with the evidence itself, keep records of actual data—notes from interviews, observations, surveys, and experiments—separately from the journal.

2 Language considerations

Each social science discipline has specialized terminology for concepts basic to the discipline. In sociology, for example, the words *mechanism, identity,* and *deviance* have specific meanings different from those of everyday usage. And *identity* means something different in sociology, where it applies to groups of people, than in psychology, where it applies to the individual. Social scientists also use precise terms to describe or interpret research. For instance, they say *The subject* <u>*expressed a feeling of*</u> rather than *The subject* <u>*felt*</u> because human feelings are not knowable for certain; or they say *These studies* <u>*indicate*</u> rather than *These studies* <u>*prove*</u> because conclusions are only tentative.

Just as social scientists strive for objectivity in their research, they also strive to demonstrate their objectivity through language in their writing. They avoid expressions such as *I think* in order to focus attention on what the evidence shows, not the researcher's opinions. (However, many social scientists prefer *I* to *the researcher* when they refer to their own actions, as in *I then interviewed the subjects.* Ask your teacher for his or her preferences.) Social scientists also avoid direct or indirect expression of their personal biases or emotions, either in discussions of other researchers' work or in descriptions of research subjects. Thus one social scientist does not call another's work *sloppy* or *immaculate* and does not refer to his or her own subjects as *drunks* or *innocent victims*. Instead, the writer uses neutral language and ties conclusions strictly to the data.

3 Research sources

The following lists give resources in social sciences.

Specialized encyclopedias, dictionaries, and bibliographies

General
International Bibliography of the Social Sciences
International Encyclopedia of the Social and Behavioral Sciences
Dictionary of the Social Sciences

Business and economics
Advertising Age Encyclopedia of Advertising
Blackwell Encyclopedia of Management
Dictionary of Business and Management
Encyclopedia of Banking and Finance
Encyclopedia of Business Information Sources
McGraw-Hill Encyclopedia of Economics
The MIT Dictionary of Modern Economics
The New Palgrave Dictionary of Economics and the Law

Education
Encyclopedia of American Education
Encyclopedia of Education
Encyclopedia of Educational Research
The Philosophy of Education: An Encyclopedia

Political science and law
Black's Law Dictionary
Encyclopedia of Government and Politics
Information Sources of Political Science
Oxford Companion to American Law
West's Encyclopedia of American Law

Psychology, sociology, and anthropology
APA Dictionary of Psychology
Blackwell Dictionary of Sociology
Countries and Their Culture
Encyclopedia of Anthropology
Encyclopedia of Crime and Justice
Encyclopedia of North American Indians
Encyclopedia of Psychology
Encyclopedia of Sociology
Handbook of Psychology
Macmillan Dictionary of Anthropology
Race and Ethnic Relations
Sage Handbook of Sociology

Library databases and indexes

ABI/INFORM (business)
Abstracts in Anthropology
Anthropology Plus
AnthroSource
Business Periodicals Index
Business Source Premier
Communication and Mass Media Complete
Criminal Justice Periodicals
Dissertation Abstracts International (doctoral dissertations)
EconLit
Education Index
Educational Resources Information Center (ERIC)
Hispanic American Periodicals Index
Human Resources Abstracts
Index to Legal Periodicals
International Political Science Abstracts
LexisNexis Academic Universe (legal publications and news sources)
PAIS International (government publications and political science
   journals)
PsychInfo
Social Sciences Index
Sociological Abstracts
Urban Affairs Abstracts
Wilson Business Abstracts
Worldwide Political Science Abstracts

Book reviews

Index to Book Reviews in the Social Sciences

Sources on the open Web

General

Data on the Net (*3stages.org/idata*)
Social Science Information Gateway (*sosig.ac.uk*)
WWW Virtual Library: Social and Behavorial Sciences (*vlib.org/SocialSciences*)

Anthropology

American Anthropological Association (*aaanet.org*)
American Folklife Center (*loc.gov/folklife*)
Anthro.Net (*home1.gte.net/ericjw1/index.html*)
Anthropology Review Database (*wings.buffalo.edu/anthropology/ARD*)
National Anthropological Archives (*www.nmnh.si.edu/naa/index.htm*)

Business and economics

Academic Info: Business Administration (*academicinfo.net/bus.html*)
Biz/ed (*www.bized.co.uk*)
Resources for Economists on the Internet (*rfe.org*)
Virtual International Business and Economic Sources (*library.uncc.edu/
   display/?dept=reference&format=open&page=68*)

Education

Educator's Reference Desk (*eduref.org*)
Gateway to Educational Materials (*thegateway.org*)
Learner.org (*learner.org*)
Social Science Information Gateway: Education (*sosig.ac.uk/roads/ subject-listing/World/educ.html*)
US Department of Education (*ed.gov*)

Ethnic and gender studies

Diversity and Ethnic Studies (*public.iastate.edu/~savega/divweb2.htm*)
Gender Inn (*www.uni-koeln.de/phil-fak/englisch/datenbank/e_index.htm*)
National Women's History Project Resource Center (*www.nwhp.org/ resourcecenter/index.php*)
Voice of the Shuttle: Gender Studies (*vos.ucsb.edu/browse.asp?id=2711*)

Political science and law

Legal Information Institute (*www.law.cornell.edu*)
Librarians' Index to the Internet: Law (*search.lii.org/index.jsp?more=SubTopic3*)
Oyez: US Supreme Court Multimedia (*www.oyez.org*)
Political Science Resources (*www.psr.keele.ac.uk*)
Thomas Legislative Information on the Internet (*thomas.loc.gov*)
Ultimate Political Science Links (*upslinks.net*)

Psychology

Encyclopedia of Psychology (*www.psychology.org*)
National Institute of Mental Health (*www.nimh.nih.gov*)
Psychology: Online Resource Central (*psych-central.com*)
Psych Web (*psywww.com*)

Sociology

Social Science Information Gateway: Sociology (*sosig.ac.uk/roads/ subject-listing/World/sociol.html*)
SocioSite (*www2.fmg.uva.nl/sociosite*)
SocioWeb (*socioweb.com*)
WWW Virtual Library: Sociology (*socserv2.socsci.mcmaster.ca/w3virtsoclib*)

51d Citing sources in APA style

Some of the social sciences publish style guides that advise practitioners how to organize, document, and type papers in those fields. The following is a partial list:

American Anthropological Association, *AAA Style Guide*, 2003 (*www .aaanet.org/publications/guidelines.cfm*)

American Political Science Association, *Style Manual for Political Science*, 2006

American Psychological Association, *Publication Manual of the American Psychological Association*, 6th ed., 2010

American Sociological Association, *ASA Style Guide,* 3rd ed., 2007
Linguistic Society of America, "LSA Style Sheet," published every December in *LSA Bulletin*
A Uniform System of Citation (law), 18th ed., 2005

By far the most widely used style is that of the American Psychological Association (APA), so we detail it here. The guidelines reflect the second printing of the *Publication Manual*, which corrected some errors in the first printing. (The corrections are posted on the APA's Web site: *apastyle.org.*)

1 Using APA parenthetical text citations

In APA documentation style, parenthetical citations within the text refer the reader to a list of sources at the end of the text. A parenthetical citation contains the author's last name, the date of publication, and sometimes the page number from which material is borrowed.

1. Author not named in your text

One critic of Milgram's experiments insisted that the subjects "should have been fully informed of the possible effects on them" (Baumrind, 1988, p. 34).

When you do not name the author in your text, place in parentheses the author's last name, the date of the source, and sometimes the page number as explained on the next page. Separate the elements with commas. Position the reference so that it is clear what material is being documented *and* so that the reference fits as smoothly as possible into your sentence structure. (See pp. 626–27 for guidelines.) The following would also be correct:

In the view of one critic of Milgram's experiments (Baumrind, 1988), the subjects "should have been fully informed of the possible effects on them" (p. 34).

APA parenthetical text citations

1. Author not named in your text *742*
2. Author named in your text *743*
3. A work with two authors *743*
4. A work with three to five authors *743*
5. A work with six or more authors *744*
6. A work with a group author *744*
7. A work with no author or an anonymous work *744*
8. One of two or more works by the same author(s) *744*
9. Two or more works by different authors *745*
10. An indirect source *745*
11. An electronic source *745*

Unless none is available, the APA requires a page or other identifying number for a direct quotation (as in the preceding examples) and recommends an identifying number for a paraphrase. Use an appropriate abbreviation before the number—for instance, p. for *page* and para. for *paragraph*. The identifying number may fall with the author and date (first example) or by itself in a separate pair of parentheses (second example). See also model 11, page 745.

2. Author named in your text

Baumrind (1988) insisted that the subjects in Milgram's study "should have been fully informed of the possible effects on them" (p. 34).

When you use the author's name in the text, do not repeat it in the reference. Place the source date in parentheses after the author's name. Place any page or paragraph reference either after the borrowed material (as in the example) or with the date: (1988, p. 34). If you cite the same source again in the paragraph, you need not repeat the reference as long as it is clear that you are using the same source and the page number (if any) is the same. Here is a later sentence from the same paragraph containing the example above:

Baumrind also criticized the experimenters' rationale.

3. A work with two authors

Pepinsky and DeStefano (1997) demonstrated that a teacher's language often reveals hidden biases.

One study (Pepinsky & DeStefano, 1997) demonstrated the hidden biases often revealed in a teacher's language.

When given in the text, two authors' names are connected by and. In a parenthetical citation, they are connected by an ampersand, &.

4. A work with three to five authors

Pepinsky, Dunn, Rentl, and Corson (1999) further demonstrated the biases evident in gestures.

In the first citation of a work with three to five authors, name all the authors.

In the second and subsequent references to a work with three to five authors, generally give only the first author's name, followed by et al. (Latin abbreviation for "and others"):

In the work of Pepinsky et al. (1999), the loaded gestures included head shakes and eye contact.

However, two or more sources published in the same year could shorten to the same form—for instance, two references shortening to Pepinsky et al., 1999. In that case, cite the last names of as many authors as you need to distinguish the sources, and then give et al.: for instance, (Pepinsky, Dunn, et al., 1999) and (Pepinsky, Bradley, et al., 1999).

5. A work with six or more authors

One study (Rutter et al., 2003) attempted to explain these geographical differences in adolescent experience.

For six or more authors, even in the first citation of the work, give only the first author's name, followed by et al. If two or more sources published in the same year shorten to the same form, give additional names as explained with model 4.

6. A work with a group author

The students' later work improved significantly (Lenschow Research, 2009).

For a work that lists an institution, agency, corporation, or other group as author, treat the name of the group as if it were one person's name. If the name is long and has a familiar abbreviation, you may use the abbreviation in the second and subsequent citations. For example, you might abbreviate American Psychological Association as APA.

7. A work with no author or an anonymous work

One article ("Right to Die," 1996) noted that a death-row inmate may crave notoriety.

For a work with no named author, use the first two or three words of the title in place of an author's name, excluding an initial *The, A,* or *An.* Italicize book and journal titles, place quotation marks around article titles, and capitalize the significant words in all titles cited in the text. (In the reference list, however, do not use quotation marks for article titles, and capitalize only the first word in all but periodical titles. See p. 747.)

For a work that lists "Anonymous" as the author, use that word in the citation: (Anonymous, 2007).

8. One of two or more works by the same author(s)

At about age seven, most children begin to use appropriate gestures to reinforce their stories (Gardner, 1973a).

When you cite one of two or more works by the same author(s), the date will tell readers which source you mean—as long as your reference list includes only one source published by the author(s) in that year. If your reference list includes two or more works published by the same author(s) *in the same year,* the works should be lettered in the reference list (see p. 749). Then your parenthetical citation should include the appropriate letter with the date: 1973a in the example.

9. Two or more works by different authors

Two studies (Marconi & Hamblen, 1999; Torrence, 2007) found that monthly safety meetings can dramatically reduce workplace injuries.

List the sources in alphabetical order by their authors' names. Insert a semicolon between sources.

10. An indirect source

Supporting data appeared in a study by Chang (as cited in Torrence, 2007).

The phrase as cited in indicates that the reference to Chang's study was found in Torrence. Only Torrence then appears in the list of references.

11. An electronic source

Ferguson and Hawkins (2006) did not anticipate the "evident hostility" of participants (para. 6).

Electronic sources can be cited like printed sources, usually with the author's last name and the publication date. When quoting or paraphrasing electronic sources that number paragraphs instead of pages, provide the paragraph number preceded by para. If the source does not number pages or paragraphs but does include headings, list the heading under which the quotation appears and then (counting paragraphs yourself) the number of the paragraph in which the quotation appears—for example, (Decker & Endter, 2008, Method section, para. 3). When the source does not number pages or paragraphs or provide frequent headings, omit any reference number.

2 Using an APA reference list

In APA style, the in-text parenthetical citations refer to the list of sources at the end of the text. This list, titled References, includes full publication information on every source cited in the paper. The list falls at the end of the paper, numbered in sequence with the preceding pages.

The following sample shows the format of the first page of the APA reference list:

APA reference list

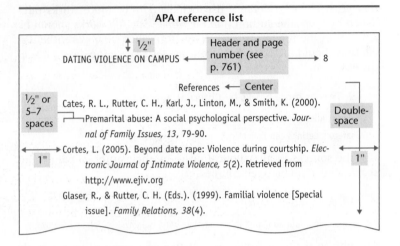

Arrangement Arrange sources alphabetically by the author's last name. If there is no author, alphabetize by the first main word of the title.

Spacing Double-space everything in the references, as shown in the sample, unless your instructor requests single spacing. (If you do single-space the entries themselves, always double-space *between* them.)

Indention As illustrated in the sample, begin each entry at the left margin, and indent the second and subsequent lines five to seven spaces or one-half inch. Your word processor can create this so-called hanging indent automatically.

Punctuation Separate the parts of the reference (author, date, title, and publication information) with a period and one space. Do not use a final period in references that conclude with a DOI or URL (see p. 753).

Authors For works with up to seven authors, list all authors with last name first, separating names and parts of names with commas. Use initials for first and middle names even when names are listed fully on the source itself. Use an ampersand (&) before the last author's name. See model 3, page 748, for the treatment of eight or more authors.

Publication date Place the publication date in parentheses after the author's or authors' names, followed by a period. Generally, this date is the year only, though for some sources (such as magazine and newspaper articles) it includes the month and sometimes the day as well.

Titles In titles of books and articles, capitalize only the first word of the title, the first word of the subtitle, and proper nouns; all other words begin with small letters. In titles of journals, capitalize all significant words (see p. 785 for guidelines). Italicize the titles of books and journals. Do not italicize or use quotation marks around the titles of articles.

City and state of publication For sources that are not periodicals (such as books or government publications), give the city of publication, a comma, the two-letter postal abbreviation of the state, and a colon. Omit the state if the publisher is a university whose name includes the state name, such as University of Arizona.

Publisher's name Also for nonperiodical sources, give the publisher's name after the place of publication and a colon. Shorten names of many publishers (such as Morrow for William Morrow), and omit *Co., Inc.,* and *Publishers.* However, give full names for associations, corporations, and university presses (such as Harvard University Press), and do not omit *Books* or *Press* from a publisher's name.

Page numbers Use the abbreviation p. or pp. before page numbers in books and in newspapers. Do *not* use the abbreviation for journals and magazines. For inclusive page numbers, include all figures: 667-668.

See the next page for an index to APA reference-list models. If you don't see a model for a kind of source you used, try to find one that comes close, and provide ample information so that readers can trace the source. Often you will have to combine models to cite a source accurately.

Listing authors

1. One author

Rodriguez, R. (1982). *A hunger of memory: The education of Richard Rodriguez.* Boston, MA: Godine.

The initial R. appears instead of the author's first name, even though the author's full first name appears on the source. In this book title, only the first words of the title and subtitle and the proper name are capitalized.

2. Two to seven authors

Nesselroade, J. R., & Baltes, P. B. (1999). *Longitudinal research in behavioral studies.* New York, NY: Academic Press.

APA reference-list models

Authors
1. One author *747*
2. Two to seven authors *747*
3. Eight or more authors *748*
4. A group author *749*
5. Author not named (anony-mous) *749*
6. Two or more works by the same author(s) published in the same year *749*

Print periodicals
7. An article in a journal *749, 751*
8. An abstract of a journal article *750*
9. An article in a newspaper *750*
10. An article in a magazine *750*
11. A review *750*

Print books
12. Basic format for a book *752*
13. A book with an editor *752*
14. A book with a translator *752*
15. A later edition *752*
16. A work in more than one volume *752*
17. An article or a chapter in an edited book *753*

Web and other electronic sources
18. A journal article with a Digital Object Identifier (DOI) *753, 754*
19. A journal article without a DOI *755*

20. A periodical article in an online database *755*
21. An abstract of a journal article *755*
22. An article in a newspaper *755*
23. An article in a magazine *756*
24. Supplemental periodical content that appears only online *756*
25. A review *756*
26. A report or other material from the Web site of an organization or government *756*
27. A book *757*
28. An article in a reference work *757*
29. An article in a wiki *757*
30. A dissertation *757*
31. A podcast *758*
32. A film or video recording *758*
33. An image *758*
34. A message posted to a blog or discussion group *758*
35. A personal communication *758*

Other sources
36. A report *758*
37. A government publication *759*
38. A dissertation *759*
39. An interview *759*
40. A motion picture *760*
41. A musical recording *760*
42. A television series or episode *760*

With two to seven authors, separate authors' names with commas and use an ampersand (&) before the last author's name.

3. Eight or more authors

Wimple, P. B., Van Eijk, M., Potts, C. A., Hayes, J., Obergau, W. R., Smith, H., . . . Zimmer, S. (2001). *Case studies in moral decision making among adolescents.* San Francisco, CA: Jossey-Bass.

For a work by eight or more authors, list the first six authors' names, insert an ellipsis mark (three spaced periods), and then give the last author's name.

4. A group author

Lenschow Research. (2008). *Trends in secondary curriculum.* Baltimore, MD: Arrow Books.

For a work with a group author—such as a research group, a committe, a government agency, or a corporation—begin the entry with the group name. In the reference list, alphabetize the work as if the first main word (excluding any *The, A,* and *An*) were an author's last name.

5. Author not named (anonymous)

Merriam-Webster's collegiate dictionary (11th ed.). (2008). Springfield, MA: Merriam-Webster.

Heroes of the environment. (2009, October 5). *Time, 174*(13), 45-54.

When no author is named, list the work under its title and alphabetize it by the first main word (excluding any *The, A, An*).

For a work whose author is actually given as "Anonymous," use that word in place of the author's name and alphabetize it as if it were a name:

Anonymous. (2006). *Teaching research, researching teaching.* New York, NY: Alpine Press.

6. Two or more works by the same author(s) published in the same year

Gardner, H. (1973a). *The arts and human development.* New York, NY: Wiley.

Gardner, H. (1973b). *The quest for mind: Piaget, Lévi-Strauss, and the structuralist movement.* New York, NY: Knopf.

When citing two or more works by exactly the same author(s), published in the same year, arrange them alphabetically by the first main word of the title and distinguish the sources by adding a letter to the date. Both the date and the letter are used in citing the source in your text (see p. 744).

When citing two or more works by exactly the same author(s) but *not* published in the same year, arrange the sources in order of their publication dates, earliest first.

Listing print periodicals: Journals, newspapers, magazines

7. An article in a journal (print)

Selwyn, N. (2005). The social processes of learning to use computers. *Social Science Computer Review, 23,* 122-135.

The facing page shows the basic format for a print journal article and the location of the required information in the journal. If the print article has a Digital Object Identifier, add it at the end of the entry. See model 18, page 753.

Note Some journals number the pages of issues consecutively throughout a year, so that each issue after the first begins numbering where the previous issue left off—say, at page 132 or 416. For this kind of journal, give the volume number after the title, as in the preceding example. The page numbers are enough to guide readers to the issue you used. Other journals and most magazines start each issue with page 1. For these journals and magazines, place the issue number (not italicized) in parentheses immediately after the volume number. See model 10 for an example of a volume and issue number.

8. An abstract of a journal article (print)

Emery, R. E. (2006). Marital turmoil: Interpersonal conflict and the children of discord and divorce. *Psychological Bulletin, 92*, 310-330. Abstract obtained from *Psychological Abstracts*, 2007, *69*, Item 1320.

When you cite the abstract of an article rather than the article itself, give full publication information for the article, followed by Abstract obtained from and the information for the collection of abstracts, including title, date, volume and issue numbers, and either page number or other reference number (Item 1320 in the example).

9. An article in a newspaper (print)

Stout, D. (2008, May 28). Blind win court ruling on U.S. currency. *The New York Times*, p. A23.

Give month *and* day along with year of publication. Use *The* in the newspaper name if the paper itself does. Precede the page number(s) with p. or pp.

10. An article in a magazine (print)

Newton-Small, J. (2009, October 5). Divided loyalties. *Time, 174*(13), 38.

Give the full date of the issue: year, followed by a comma, month, and day (if any). Give all page numbers even when the article appears on discontinuous pages, without "pp." If a magazine has volume and issue numbers, provide both because magazine issues are paginated separately. (See the note in model 7, above.)

11. A review (print)

Dinnage, R. (1987, November 29). Against the master and his men [Review of the book *A mind of her own: The life of Karen Horney*, by S. Quinn]. *The New York Times Book Review*, 10-11.

Format for a print journal article

① ② ③ ④
Selwyn, N. (2005). The social processes of learning to use computers. *Social Science*

⑤ ⑥
Computer Review, 23, 122-135.

Journal cover

SPRING 2005 VOLUME 23 NUMBER I

SOCIAL SCIENCE COMPUTER REVIEW

⑤ **Volume number,** italicized and followed by a comma. See the facing page for when to include the issue number.

② **Year of publication,** in parentheses and followed by a period.

④ **Title of periodical,** in italics. Capitalize all significant words and end with a comma.

③ **Title of article.** Give the full article title and any subtitle, separating them with a colon. Capitalize only the first words of the title and subtitle, and do not place the title in quotation marks.

First page of article

The Social Processes of Learning to Use Computers

NEIL SELWYN
Cardiff School of Social Sciences

① **Author.** Give the last name first, a comma, the initial of the first name, and any middle initial, following each initial with a period. Omit *Dr., PhD,* or any other title.

The ability to use a computer is assumed to be a cornerstone of effective ci Age, with a range of initiatives and educational provisions being introdu become competent with information technology (IT). Despite such provi and competence have been found to vary widely throughout the general population, and we know little of how different ways of learning to use computers contribute to people's eventual use of IT. Based on data from in-depth interviews with 100 adults in the United Kingdom, this article examines the range and social stratification of formal and informal learning about computers that is taking place, suggesting that formal computer instruction orientated toward the general public may inadvertently widen the digital knowledge gap. In particular, the data highlight the importance of informal learning about IT and of encouraging such learning, especially in the home.

AUTHOR'S NOTE: This article is based on a project funded by the Economic and Social Research Council (R000239518). I would like to thank the other members of the Adults Learning @ Home project (Stephen Gorard and John Furlong) as well as the individuals who took part in the in-depth interviews. Correspondence concerning this article may be addressed to Neil Selwyn, School of Social Sciences, Cardiff University, Glamorgan Building, King Edward VII Avenue, Cardiff CF10 3WT, UK; e-mail: selwynnc@cardiff.ac.uk.

122

⑥ **Inclusive page numbers of article,** without "pp." Do not omit any numerals.

If the review is not titled, use the bracketed information as the title, keeping the brackets.

Listing print books

12. Basic format for a book (print)

Ehrenreich, B. (2007). *Dancing in the streets: A history of collective joy.*
New York, NY: Holt.

Give the author's or authors' names, following models 1–4. Then give the complete title, including any subtitle. Italicize the title, and capitalize only the first words of the title and subtitle. End the entry with the city and state of publication and the publisher's name. (See p. 747 for how to treat these elements.)

13. A book with an editor (print)

Dohrenwend, B. S., & Dohrenwend, B. P. (Eds.). (1999). *Stressful life events:
Their nature and effects.* New York, NY: Wiley.

List the editors' names as if they were authors, but follow the last name with (Eds.).—or (Ed.). with only one editor. Note the periods inside and outside the final parenthesis.

14. A book with a translator (print)

Trajan, P. D. (1927). *Psychology of animals* (H. Simone, Trans.). Washington,
DC: Halperin.

The name of the translator appears in parentheses after the title, followed by a comma, Trans. and a closing parenthesis, and a final period.

15. A later edition (print)

Bolinger, D. L. (1981). *Aspects of language* (3rd ed.). New York, NY: Harcourt
Brace Jovanovich.

The edition number in parentheses follows the title and is followed by a period.

16. A work in more than one volume (print)

Lincoln, A. (1953). *The collected works of Abraham Lincoln* (R. P. Basler, Ed.).
(Vol. 5). New Brunswick, NJ: Rutgers University Press.
Lincoln, A. (1953). *The collected works of Abraham Lincoln* (R. P. Basler, Ed.).
(Vols. 1-8). New Brunswick, NJ: Rutgers University Press.

The first entry cites a single volume (5) in the eight-volume set. The second cites all eight volumes. Use the abbreviation Vol. or Vols. in parentheses and follow the closing parenthesis with a period. In the absence of an editor's name, the description of volumes would follow the title directly: *The collected works of Abraham Lincoln* (Vol. 5).

17. An article or a chapter in an edited book (print)

Paykel, E. S. (1999). Life stress and psychiatric disorder: Applications of the clinical approach. In B. S. Dohrenwend & B. P. Dohrenwend (Eds.), *Stressful life events: Their nature and effects* (pp. 239-264). New York, NY: Wiley.

Give the publication date of the collection (1999 here) as the publication date of the article or chapter. After the article or chapter title and a period, say In and then provide the editors' names (in normal order), (Eds.) and a comma, the title of the collection, and the page numbers of the article in parentheses.

Listing Web and other electronic sources

In APA style, most electronic references begin as those for print references do: author, date, title. Then you add information on how to retrieve the source, generally giving either a DOI (see model 18) or a URL (see model 19). In addition, note the following:

- APA does not require your access date if the source is unlikely to change or if it has a publication date or edition or version number. See model 29 for use of an access date.
- APA does not require a full URL if the source can be located by searching the home page of a Web site. See model 32 for an example of a complete URL.
- When you need to divide a URL or DOI from one line to the next, APA calls for breaking before punctuation such as a period or slash. (But break after the two slashes in http://.) Do not hyphenate a URL or a DOI.

If you don't see a model for your particular electronic source, consult the index of models on page 748 for a similar source type whose format you can adapt. If your source does not include all of the information needed for a complete citation, find and list what you can.

18. A journal article with a Digital Object Identifier (DOI) (Web)

Cunningham, J. A., & Selby, P. (2007). Relighting cigarettes: How common is it? *Nicotine and Tobacco Research, 9,* 621-623. doi:10.1080 /14622200701239688

The illustration below shows the basic format for a periodical article that you access either directly online or through an online database as well as the location of the required information on the source.

Format for a journal article on the Web

①   ②   ③

Cunningham, J. A., & Selby, P. (2007). Relighting cigarettes: How common is it?

    ④   ⑤ ⑥ ⑦

  Nicotine and Tobacco Research, 9, 621-623. doi:10.1080

   /14622200701239688

④ **Title of periodical,** in italics. Capitalize all significant words and end with a comma.

⑤ **Volume number,** italicized and followed by a comma. See page 750 for when to include the issue number.

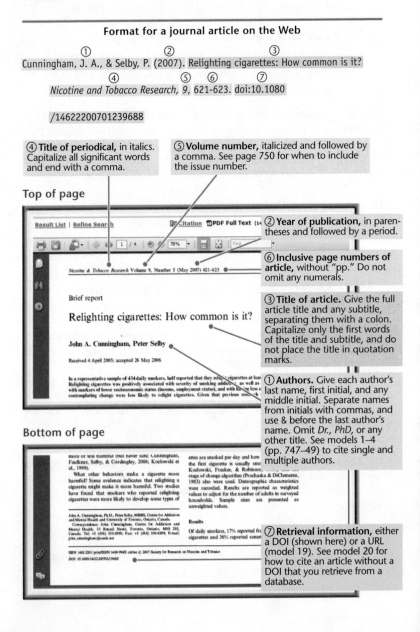

Top of page

② **Year of publication,** in parentheses and followed by a period.

⑥ **Inclusive page numbers of article,** without "pp." Do not omit any numerals.

③ **Title of article.** Give the full article title and any subtitle, separating them with a colon. Capitalize only the first words of the title and subtitle, and do not place the title in quotation marks.

① **Authors.** Give each author's last name, first initial, and any middle initial. Separate names from initials with commas, and use & before the last author's name. Omit *Dr., PhD,* or any other title. See models 1–4 (pp. 747–49) to cite single and multiple authors.

Bottom of page

⑦ **Retrieval information,** either a DOI (shown here) or a URL (model 19). See model 20 for how to cite an article without a DOI that you retrieve from a database.

Many publishers now assign a Digital Object Identifier (DOI) to journal articles and other documents. A DOI functions as a unique identifier and a link to the text. When a DOI is available, include it instead of a URL or a database name. (The DOI may be evident on the source, or it may be found by clicking on "Article" or "Cross-Ref.") Do not add a period at the end of the DOI.

19. A journal article without a DOI (Web)

Polletta, F. (2008). Just talk: Public deliberation after 9/11. *Journal of Public Deliberation, 4*(1). Retrieved from http://services.bepress.com/jpd

When a journal article does not have a DOI, give the URL of the journal's home page in a statement beginning Retrieved from. Do not add a period at the end of the URL.

20. A periodical article in an online database (Web)

Rosen, I. M., Maurer, D. M., & Darnall, C. R. (2008). Reducing tobacco use in adolescents. *American Family Physician, 77*, 483-490. Retrieved from http://www.aafp.org/online/en/home/publications/journals/afp.html

Generally, do not give the name of the database in which you found your source, because readers may not be able to find the source the same way you did. Instead, use a search engine to find the home page of the periodical and give the home page URL in your retrieval statement (preceding example).

If you don't find the home page of the periodical, then give the database name in your retrieval statement, as in this example:

Smith, E. M. (1926, March). Equal rights—internationally! *Life and Labor Bulletin, 4*, 1-2. Retrieved from Women and Social Movements in the United States, 1600-2000, database.

21. An abstract of a journal article (Web)

Polletta, F. (2008). Just talk: Public deliberation after 9/11. *Journal of Public Deliberation, 4*(1). Abstract retrieved from http://services.bepress.com/jpd

22. An article in a newspaper (Web)

Gootman, E. (2008, June 19). Gifted programs in the city are less diverse. *The New York Times.* Retrieved from http://www.nytimes.com

Give the URL of the newspaper's home page in the retrieval statement. If you found the article in an online database, see model 20.

23. An article in a magazine (Web)

Young, E. (2009, February 21). Sleep well, keep sane. *New Scientist, 201*(26), 34-37. Retrieved from http://www.newscientist.com

Give the URL of the magazine's home page in the retrieval statement. If you found the article in an online database, see model 20.

24. Supplemental periodical content that appears only online (Web)

Gawande, A. (2009, June 1). More is less [Supplemental material]. *The New Yorker*. Retrieved from http://www.newyorker.com

If you cite material from a periodical's Web site that is not included in the print version of the publication, add [Supplemental material] after the title and give the URL of the publication's home page.

25. A review (Web)

Bond, M. (2008, December 18). Does genius breed success? [Review of the book *Outliers: The story of success,* by M. Gladwell]. *Nature, 456,* 785. doi:10.1038/456874a

Cite an online review like a print review (model 11, p. 750), concluding with retrieval information (here, a DOI).

26. A report or other material from the Web site of an organization or government (Web)

Ellerman, D., & Joskow, P. L. (2008, May). *The European Union's emissions trading system in perspective.* Retrieved from the Pew Center on Global Climate Change website: http://www.pewclimate.org

Treat the title of an independent Web document like the title of a book. Provide the name of the publishing organization as part of the retrieval statement when the publisher is not listed as the author, as in the preceding example.

If the document you cite is difficult to locate from the organization's home page, give the complete URL in the retrieval statement:

Union of Concerned Scientists. (2009, April 24). *Clean vehicles.* Retrieved from http://www.ucsusa.org/clean_vehicles

If the document you cite is undated, use the abbreviation n.d. in place of the publication date and give the date of your access in the retrieval statement:

U.S. Department of Agriculture. (n.d.). *Inside the pyramid*. Retrieved April 23,
2008, from http://www.mypyramid.gov

27. A book (Web)

Hernandez, L. M., & Munthali, A. W. (Eds.). (2007). *Training physicians for
public health careers*. Retrieved from http://books.nap.edu/catalog
.php?record_id=11915

For online books, replace the publisher's city and name with a retrieval statement. See models 14–17 (pp. 752–53) to cite variations
in book entries: a translator, a later edition, a book in more than
one volume, and an article or a chapter in a book.

28. An article in a reference work (Web)

Perception. (2008). In *Encyclopaedia Britannica Online*. Retrieved from
http://www.britannica.com

29. An article in a wiki (Web)

Clinical neuropsychology. (2008, January 27). Retrieved August 3, 2009, from
Wikipedia: http://en.wikipedia.org/wiki/Clinical_neuropsychology

Give your date of retrieval for sources that are likely to change, such
as this wiki.

30. A dissertation (Web)

A dissertation in a commercial database:

McFaddin, M. O. (2007). *Adaptive reuse: An architectural solution for poverty
and homelessness* (Doctoral dissertation). Available from ProQuest
Dissertations and Theses database. (ATT 1378764)

If a dissertation is from a commercial database, give the name of
the database in the retrieval statement, followed by the accession or
order number in parentheses.

A dissertation in an institutional database:

Chang, J. K. (2003). *Therapeutic intervention in treatment of injuries to the
hand and wrist* (Doctoral dissertation). Retrieved from http://medsci
.archive.liasu.edu/61724

If a dissertation is from an institution's database, give the URL in
the retrieval statement.

See also model 38 (p. 759) for examples of print dissertations.

31. A podcast (Web)

Ferracca, J. (Producer). (2008, June 11). Who owns antiquities? [Audio podcast].
  Here on earth: Radio without borders. Retrieved from http://www.wpr
  .org/hereonearth

32. A film or video recording (Web)

Green Children Foundation (Producer). (2008, January 7). *The green children
  visit China* [Video file]. Retrieved from http://youtube.com
  /watch?v=uD4xfLTxCsY

If the film or video you cite is difficult to locate from the home page
of the Web site, give the complete URL in the retrieval statement.

33. An image (Web)

United Nations Population Fund (Cartographer). (2005). *Percent of population
  living on less than $1/day* [Demographic map]. Retrieved from
  http://www.unfpa.org

34. A message posted to a blog or discussion group (Web)

Munger, D. (2009, May 9). Does recess really improve classroom behavior?
  [Web log post]. Retrieved from http://scienceblogs.com/cognitivedaily

Include postings to blogs and discussion groups in your list of references *only* if they are retrievable by others. (The source above is
retrievable by a search of the home page URL.) Follow the message
title with [Web log post], [Electronic mailing list message], or [Online forum
comment]. Include the name of the blog or discussion group in the
retrieval statement if it isn't part of the URL.

35. A personal communication (text citation)

At least one member of the research team has expressed reservations about
the design of the study (L. Kogod, personal communication, February 6, 2006).

Personal e-mail and other online postings that are not retrievable by
others should be cited only in the text, not in the list of references.

Listing other sources

36. A report (print)

Gerald, K. (2003). *Medico-moral problems in obstetric care* (Report No. NP-71).
  St. Louis, MO: Catholic Hospital Association.

Treat a printed report like a book, but provide any report number in
parentheses after the title, with no punctuation between them.

For a report from the Educational Resources Information Center (ERIC), provide the ERIC document number in parentheses at the end of the entry:

Jolson, M. K. (2001). *Music education for preschoolers* (Report No. TC-622). New York, NY: Teachers College, Columbia University. (ERIC Document Reproduction Service No. ED264488)

37. A government publication (print)

Hawaii. Department of Education. (2008). *Kauai district schools, profile 2007-08*. Honolulu, HI: Author.

Stiller, A. (2002). *Historic preservation and tax incentives*. Washington, DC: U.S. Department of the Interior.

If no person is named as the author, list the publication under the name of the sponsoring agency. When the agency is both the author and the publisher, use Author in place of the publisher's name, as in the first example.

For legal materials such as court decisions, laws, and testimony at hearings, the APA recommends formats that correspond to conventional legal citations. The following example of a congressional hearing includes the full title, the number of the Congress, the page number where the hearing transcript starts in the official publication, and the date of the hearing.

Medicare payment for outpatient physical and occupational therapy services: Hearing before the Committee on Ways and Means, House of Representatives, 110th Cong. 3 (2007).

38. A dissertation (print)

A dissertation abstracted in DAI:

Steciw, S. K. (1986). Alterations to the Pessac project of Le Corbusier. *Dissertation Abstracts International, 46*(6), 565C.

An unpublished dissertation:

Holcomb, C. M. (2008). *Dance as therapy for reducing anxiety in elementary-age children: Case studies in grades 1 through 6*. (Unpublished doctoral dissertation). University of Washington.

39. An interview (print)

Schenker, H. (2007). No peace without third-party intervention [Interview with Shulamit Aloni]. *Palestine-Israel Journal of Politics, Economics, and Culture, 14*(4), 63-68.

List a published interview under the interviewer's name, and provide the title, if any, without italics or quotation marks. If there is no title, or if the title does not indicate the interview format or the interviewee (as in the example), add a bracketed explanation. End with the publication information for the kind of source the interview appears in (here, a journal).

An interview you conduct yourself should not be included in the list of references. Instead, use an in-text parenthetical citation, as shown in model 35 (p. 758) for a personal communication.

40. A motion picture

American Psychological Association (Producer). (2001). *Ethnocultural psychotherapy*. [DVD]. Available from http://www.apa.org/videos

Howard, R. (Director). (2001). *A beautiful mind* [Motion picture]. United States: Universal.

Depending on whose work you are citing, begin with the name or names of the creator, director, producer, or primary contributor, followed by the function in parentheses. (The second example would begin with the producer's name if you were citing the motion picture as a whole, not specifically the work of the director.) Add the medium in brackets after the title: [Motion picture] (for film), [DVD], or [Videocassette]. For a work in wide circulation (second example), give the country of origin and the studio that released the picture. For a work that is not widely circulated (first example), give the distributor's address or URL.

41. A musical recording

Springsteen, B. (2002). Empty sky. On *The rising* [CD]. New York, NY: Columbia.

Begin with the name of the writer or composer. (If you cite another artist's recording of the work, provide this information after the title of the work—for example, [Recorded by E. Davila].) Give the medium in brackets ([CD], [LP], and so on). Finish with the city, state, and name of the recording label.

42. A television series or episode

Rhimes, S. (Executive Producer). (2008). *Grey's anatomy* [Television series]. New York, NY: CBS.

McKee S. (Writer), & Tinker, M. (Director). (2008). Piece of my heart [Television series episode]. In S. Rhimes (Executive Producer), *Grey's anatomy*. New York, NY: CBS.

For a television series, begin with the producers' names and identify their function in parentheses. Add [Television series] after the series title, and give the city and name of the network. For an episode, begin with the writer and then the director, identifying the function of each in parentheses, and add [Television series episode] after the episode title. Then provide the series information, beginning with In and the producers' names and function, giving the series title, and ending with the city and name of the network.

51e Formatting documents in APA style

The following guidelines for document format reflect the second printing of the APA *Publication Manual,* 6th edition, which corrected some errors in the first printing. (The corrections are posted on the APA's Web site: *apastyle.org.*) Check with your instructor for any modifications to this format.

Note See pages 746–47 for the APA format of a reference list. And see pages 118–26 for guidelines on type fonts, lists, tables and figures, and other elements of document design.

Margins Use one-inch margins on the top, bottom, and both sides.

Spacing and indentions Double-space everywhere. (The only exception is tables and figures, where related data, labels, and other elements may be single-spaced.) Indent paragraphs and displayed quotations one-half inch or five to seven spaces.

Paging Begin numbering on the title page, and number consecutively through the end (including the reference list). Provide a header about one-half inch from the top of every page, as shown in the samples on the next page. The header consists of the page number on the far right and your full or shortened title on the far left. Type the title in all-capital letters. On the title page only, precede the title with the label Running head and a colon. Omit this label on all other pages.

Title page Include the full title, your name, the course title, the instructor's name, and the date. (See the next page.) Type the title on the top half of the page, followed by the identifying information, all centered horizontally and double-spaced.

Abstract Summarize (in a maximum of 120 words) your subject, research method, findings, and conclusions. (See the next page.) Put the abstract on a page by itself.

Body Begin with a restatement of the paper's title and then an introduction (not labeled). (See the next page.) The introduction presents the problem you researched, your method, the relevant background (such as related studies), and the purpose of your research.

APA title page

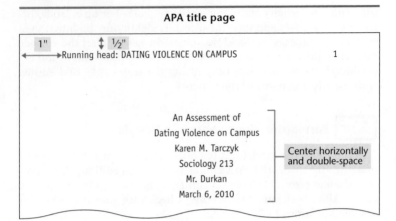

1" ↕ ½"
→Running head: DATING VIOLENCE ON CAMPUS   1

An Assessment of
Dating Violence on Campus
Karen M. Tarczyk
Sociology 213
Mr. Durkan
March 6, 2010

Center horizontally and double-space

APA abstract

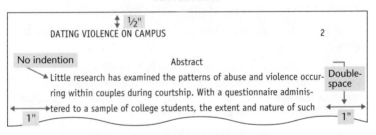

↕ ½"
DATING VIOLENCE ON CAMPUS   2

No indention

Abstract

→Little research has examined the patterns of abuse and violence occurring within couples during courtship. With a questionnaire adminis-
→tered to a sample of college students, the extent and nature of such

Double-space

1"   1"

First page of APA body

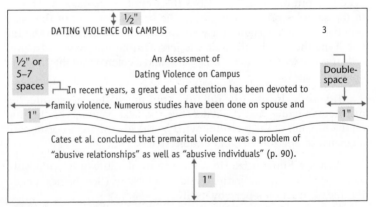

↕ ½"
DATING VIOLENCE ON CAMPUS   3

An Assessment of
Dating Violence on Campus

½" or 5–7 spaces

In recent years, a great deal of attention has been devoted to
→family violence. Numerous studies have been done on spouse and

Double-space

1"   1"

Cates et al. concluded that premarital violence was a problem of
"abusive relationships" as well as "abusive individuals" (p. 90).

1"

After the introduction, a section labeled **Method** provides a detailed discussion of how you conducted your research, including a
description of the research subjects, any materials or tools you used
(such as questionnaires), and the procedure you followed. In the

illustration below, the label **Method** is a first-level heading and the label **Sample** is a second-level heading.

Later page of APA body

DATING VIOLENCE ON CAMPUS   4

    All the studies indicate a problem that is being neglected. My objective was to gather data on the extent and nature of premarital violence and to discuss possible interpretations.

Method → Double-

Sample → space

    I conducted a survey of 200 students (134 females, 66 males) at a large state university in the northeastern United States. The sample consisted of students enrolled in an introductory sociology course.

Format headings (including a third level, if needed) as follows:

First-Level Heading

Second-Level Heading

    Third-level heading. Run this heading into the text paragraph with a standard paragraph indention.

The **Results** section (labeled with a first-level heading) summarizes the data you collected, explains how you analyzed them, and presents them in detail, often in tables, graphs, or charts.

The **Discussion** section (labeled with a first-level heading) interprets the data and presents your conclusions. (When the discussion is brief, you may combine it with the previous section under the heading **Results and Discussion**.)

The References section, beginning a new page, includes all your sources. See pages 746–47 for an explanation and sample.

Long quotations Run into your text all quotations of forty words or less, and enclose them in quotation marks. For quotations of more than forty words, set them off from your text by indenting all lines one-half inch or five spaces, double-spacing throughout.

Echoing the opinions of other Europeans at the time, Freud (1961) had a poor view of Americans:

    The Americans are really too bad. . . . Competition is much more pungent with them, not succeeding means civil death to every one, and they have no private resources apart from their profession, no hobby, games, love or other interests of a cultured person. And success means money. (p. 86)

Do not use quotation marks around a quotation displayed in this way.

Illustrations Present data in tables, graphs, or charts, as appropriate. (See the sample on p. 766 for a clear table format to follow.) Begin each illustration on a separate page. Number each kind of illustration consecutively and separately from the other (Table 1, Table 2, etc., and Figure 1, Figure 2, etc.). Refer to all illustrations in your text—for instance, (see Figure 3). Generally, place illustrations immediately after the text references to them. (See pp. 122–26 for more on illustrations.)

51f Examining a sample social science paper

Below and on the following pages are excerpts from a sociology paper. The student followed the organization described on the preceding pages both in establishing the background for her study and in explaining her own research. She also followed the APA style of source citation and document format, although page borders and running heads are omitted here and only the required page breaks are indicated.

Excerpts from a research report

[Title page.]

An Assessment of

Dating Violence on Campus

Karen M. Tarczyk

Sociology 213

Mr. Durkan

March 6, 2010

[New page.]

Abstract

Little research has examined the patterns of abuse and violence occurring within couples during courtship. With a questionnaire administered to a sample of college students, the extent and nature of such abuse and violence were investigated. The results, some interpretations, and implications for further research are discussed.

[New page.]

An Assessment of Dating

Violence on Campus

In recent years, a great deal of attention has been devoted to family violence. Numerous studies have been done on spouse and child abuse. However, violent behavior occurs in dating relationships as well, yet the problem of dating violence has been relatively ignored by sociological research. It should be examined further since the premarital relationship is one context in which individuals learn and adopt behaviors that surface later in marriage.

The sociologist James Makepeace (1989) contended that courtship violence is a "potential mediating link" between violence in one's family of orientation and violence in one's later family of procreation (p. 103). Studying dating behaviors at Bemidji State University in Minnesota, Makepeace reported that one-fifth of the respondents had had at least one encounter with dating violence. He then extended these percentages to students nationwide, suggesting the existence of a major hidden social problem.

More recent research supports Makepeace's. Cates, Rutter, Karl, Linton, and Smith (2000) found that 22.3% of respondents at Oregon State University had been either the victim or the perpetrator of premarital violence. Another study (Cortes, 2005) found that so-called date rape, while much more publicized and discussed, was reported by many fewer woman respondents (2%) than was other violence during courtship (21%).

[The introduction continues.]

All these studies indicate a problem that is being neglected. My objective was to gather data on the extent and nature of premarital violence and to discuss possible interpretations.

Method

Sample

I conducted a survey of 200 students (134 females, 66 males) at a large state university in the northeastern United States. The sample consisted of students enrolled in an introductory sociology course.

[The explanation of method continues.]

The Questionnaire

A questionnaire exploring the personal dynamics of relationships was distributed during regularly scheduled class. Questions were answered anonymously in a 30-minute time period. The survey consisted of three sections.

[The explanation of method continues.]

Section 3 required participants to provide information about their current dating relationships. Levels of stress and frustration, communication between partners, and patterns of decision making were examined. These variables were expected to influence the amount of violence in a relationship. The next part of the survey was adopted from Murray Strauss's Conflict Tactics Scales (1992). These scales contain 19 items designed to measure conflict and the means of conflict resolution, including reasoning, verbal aggression, and actual violence.

Results

The questionnaire revealed significant levels of verbal aggression and threatened and actual violence among dating couples. A high number of students, 50% (62 of 123 subjects), reported that they had been the victim of verbal abuse. In addition, almost 14% (17 of 123) of respondents admitted being threatened with some type of violence, and more than 14% (18 of 123) reported being pushed, grabbed, or shoved. (See Table 1.)

[The explanation of results continues.]

[Table on a page by itself.]

Table 1

Incidence of Courtship Violence

Type of violence	Number of students reporting	Percentage of sample
Insulted or swore	62	50.4
Threatened to hit or throw something	17	13.8
Threw something	8	6.5
Pushed, grabbed, or shoved	18	14.6
Slapped	8	6.5
Kicked, bit, or hit with fist	7	5.7
Hit or tried to hit with something	2	1.6
Threatened with a knife or gun	1	0.8
Used a knife or gun	1	0.8

Discussion

Violence within premarital relationships has been relatively ignored. The results of the present study indicate that abuse and force do occur in dating relationships. Although the percentages are small, so was the sample. Extending them to the entire campus population would mean significant numbers. For example, if the nearly 6% incidence of being kicked, bitten, or hit with a fist is typical, then 300 students of a 5,000-member student body might have experienced this type of violence.

[The discussion continues.]

If the courtship period is characterized by abuse and violence, what accounts for it? The other sections of the survey examined some variables that appear to influence the relationship. Level of stress and frustration, both within the relationship and in the respondent's life, was one such variable. The communication level between partners, both the frequency of discussion and the frequency of agreement, was another.

[The discussion continues.]

The method of analyzing the data in this study, utilizing frequency distributions, provided a clear overview. However, more tests of significance and correlation and a closer look at the social and individual variables affecting the relationship are warranted. The courtship period may set the stage for patterns of married life. It merits more attention.

[New page.]

References

Cates, R. L., Rutter, C. H., Karl, J., Linton, M., & Smith, K. (2000). Premarital abuse: A social psychological perspective. *Journal of Family Issues, 13*, 79-90.

Cortes, L. (2005). Beyond date rape: Violence during courtship. *Electronic Journal of Intimate Violence, 5*(2). Retrieved from http://www.ejiv.org

Glaser, R., & Rutter, C. H. (Eds.). (1999). Familial violence [Special issue]. *Family Relations, 38*(4).

Makepeace, J. M. (1989). Courtship violence among college students. *Family Relations, 28*(6), 97-103.

Strauss, M. L. (1992). *Conflict Tactics Scales.* New York, NY: Sociological Tests.

52

Writing in the Natural and Applied Sciences

The natural and applied sciences include biology, chemistry, physics, mathematics, engineering, computer science, and their branches. Their purpose is to understand natural and technological phenomena. (A *phenomenon* is a fact or event that can be known by the senses.) Scientists conduct experiments and write to explain the step-by-step processes in their methods of inquiry and discovery.

mycomplab

Visit *mycomplab.com* for more resources on writing in the natural and applied sciences.

52a | Using the methods and evidence of the sciences

Scientists investigate phenomena by the **scientific method,** a process of continual testing and refinement.

The scientific method

- **Observe carefully.** Accurately note all details of the phenomenon being researched.
- **Ask questions about the observations.**
- **Formulate a** *hypothesis,* or preliminary generalization, that explains the observed facts.
- **Test the hypothesis** with additional observation or controlled experiments.
- **If the hypothesis proves accurate, formulate a** *theory,* or unified model, that explains *why.*
- **If the hypothesis is disproved, revise it or start anew.**

Scientific evidence is almost always quantitative—that is, it consists of numerical data obtained from the measurement of phenomena. These data are called **empirical** (from a Greek word for "experience"); they result from observation and experience, generally in a controlled laboratory setting but also (as sometimes in astronomy or biology) in the natural world. Often the empirical evidence for scientific writing comes from library research into other people's reports of their investigations. Surveys of known data or existing literature are common in scientific writing.

52b | Understanding writing assignments in the sciences

No matter what your assignment, you will be expected to document and explain your evidence carefully so that anyone reading can check your sources and replicate your research. It is important for your reader to know the context of your research—both the previous experimentation and research on your particular subject (acknowledged in the survey of the literature) and the physical conditions and other variables surrounding your own work.

Assignments in the natural and applied sciences include the following:

- **A summary** distills a research article to its essence in brief, concise form. (Summary is discussed in detail on pp. 136–37.)
- **A critique** summarizes and critically evaluates a scientific report.

- **A laboratory report** explains the procedure and results of an experiment conducted by the writer. (See p. 780 for an example.)
- **A research report** explains the experimental research of other scientists and the writer's own methods, findings, and conclusions.
- **A research proposal** reviews the relevant literature and explains a plan for further research.

A laboratory report has four or five major sections:

1. **"Abstract":** a summary of the report.
2. **"Introduction" or "Objective":** a review of why the study was undertaken, a summary of the background of the study, and a statement of the problem being studied.
3. **"Method" or "Procedure":** a detailed explanation of how the study was conducted, including any statistical analysis.
4. **"Results":** an explanation of the major findings (including unexpected results) and a summary of the data presented in graphs and tables.
5. **"Discussion":** an interpretation of the results and an explanation of how they relate to the goals of the experiment. This section also describes new hypotheses that might be tested as a result of the experiment. If the section is brief, it may be combined with the previous section in a single section labeled "Conclusions."

In addition, laboratory or research reports may include a list of references (if other sources were consulted). They almost always include tables and figures (graphs and charts) containing the data from the research (see p. 781).

52c Using the tools and language of the sciences

Tools and language concerns vary from discipline to discipline in the sciences. Consult your teacher for specifics about the field in which you are writing. You can also discover much about a discipline's tools and language from the research sources listed on the next three pages.

1 Writing tools

In the sciences a **lab notebook** or **scientific journal** is almost indispensable for accurately recording the empirical data from observations and experiments. Use such a notebook or journal for these purposes:

- **Record observations** from reading, from class, or from the lab.
- **Ask questions and refine hypotheses.**

- Record procedures.
- Record results.
- **Keep an ongoing record of ideas and findings** and how they change as data accumulate.
- **Sequence and organize your material** as you compile your findings and write your report.

Make sure that your records of data are clearly separate from your reflections on the data so that you don't mistakenly confuse the two in drawing your conclusions.

2 Language considerations

Science writers prefer to use objective language that removes the writer as a character in the situation and events being explained, except as the impersonal agent of change, the experimenter. Although usage is changing, scientists still rarely use *I* in their reports and evaluations, and they often resort to the passive voice of verbs, as in *The mixture was then subjected to centrifugal force.* This conscious objectivity focuses attention (including the writer's) on the empirical data and what they show. It discourages the writer from, say, ascribing motives and will to animals and plants. For instance, instead of asserting that the sea tortoise *evolved* its hard shell *to protect* its body, a scientist would write only what could be observed: that the hard shell *covers and thus protects* the tortoise's body.

Science writers typically change verb tenses to distinguish between established information and their own research. For established information, such as that found in journals and other reliable sources, use the present tense: *Baroreceptors monitor blood pressure.* For your own and others' research, use the past tense: *The bacteria died within three hours. Marti reported some success.*

Each discipline in the natural and applied sciences has a specialized vocabulary that permits precise, accurate, and efficient communication. Some of these terms, such as *pressure* in physics, have different meanings in the common language and must be handled carefully in science writing. Others, such as *enthalpy* in chemistry, have no meanings in the common language and must simply be learned and used correctly.

3 Research sources

The following lists give resources in the sciences.

Specialized encyclopedias, dictionaries, and bibliographies

American Medical Association Encyclopedia of Medicine
Concise Encyclopedia of Computer Science

Concise Oxford Dictionary of Mathematics
Dorland's Illustrated Medical Dictionary
Encyclopedia of Astronomy and Astrophysics
Encyclopedia of Bioethics
Encyclopedia of Chemistry
Encyclopedia of Electronics
Encyclopedia of Environmental Science
Encyclopedia of Geology
Encyclopedia of Physics
Grzimek's Animal Life Encyclopedia
Introduction to Reference Sources in Health Sciences
McGraw-Hill Encyclopedia of Science and Technology
Science and Technology in World History
Space Almanac
Van Nostrand's Scientific Encyclopedia
Wiley Encyclopedia of Electrical and Electronics Engineering
World Resources (environment)

Library databases and indexes

ACM Digital Library
Aerospace and High Technology Database
Applied Science and Technology Index
Biological Abstracts
Biological and Agricultural Index
Chemical Abstracts
CINAHL: Cumulative Index to Nursing and Allied Health Literature
Compendex Engineering Index
Computer Abstracts
Dissertation Abstracts International
Ecology Abstracts
GeoRef
Inspec
MathSciNet: Mathematical Reviews
Medline
Pollution Abstracts
Science Citation Index
Toxline

Book reviews

Technical Book Review Index

Sources on the open Web

General

BUBL LINK: Natural Sciences and Mathematics (*bubl.ac.uk/linkbrowse
.cfm?menuid=6402*)
Google Directory: Science (*directory.google.com/Top/Science*)
Intute: Science, Engineering and Technology (*www.intute.ac.uk/sciences*)
Librarians' Internet Index: Science (*search.lii.org/index.jsp?more=SubTopic13*)

The National Academies: Science, Engineering, and Medicine (nas.edu)
The Public Library of Science (www.plos.org)
WWW Virtual Library: Natural Sciences and Mathematics (vlib.org/Science.html)

Biology
Biology.Arizona.Edu (biology.arizona.edu)
National Biological Information Infrastructure (www.nbii.gov)

Chemistry
Chemistry.org (chemistry.org/portal/a/c/s/1/home.html)
ChemSpy (www.chemspy.com)
ChemWeb (www.chemweb.com)
WWW Virtual Library: Links for Chemists (liv.ac.uk/Chemistry/Links/links.html)

Computer science
IEEE Computer Society (computer.org)
University of Texas Virtual Computer Library (utexas.edu/computer/vcl)
WWW Virtual Library: Computing and Computer Science (vlib.org/Computing)

Engineering
National Academy of Engineering (nae.edu)
TechXtra: Engineering, Mathematics, and Computing (www.techxtra.ac.uk)

Environmental science
Center for International Earth Science Information Network (ciesin.org)
EE-Link: Environmental Education on the Internet (eelink.net)
EnviroLink (envirolink.org)
Environment Directory (webdirectory.com)

Geology
American Geological Institute (www.agiweb.org)
Digital Library for Earth System Education (dlese.org)
Geosource (www.library.uu.nl/geosource)
US Geological Survey Library (library.usgs.gov)

Health sciences
American Medical Association (ama-assn.org)
Centers for Disease Control and Prevention (www.cdc.gov)
Hardin MD (www.lib.uiowa.edu/hardin/md)
PubMed (www.ncbi.nlm.nih.gov/sites/entrez)
World Health Organization (who.int/en)

Mathematics
Internet Mathematics Library (mathforum.org/library)
Mathematical Atlas (math-atlas.org)

Physics and astronomy
American Institute of Physics (aip.org)
Astronomy Links (astronomylinks.com)
PhysicsWeb (physicsweb.org)
Science@NASA (science.hq.nasa.gov/index.html)

52d Citing sources in CSE style

Within the natural and applied sciences, practitioners use one of two styles of documentation, varying slightly from discipline to discipline. Following are some of the style guides most often consulted:

American Chemical Society, *ACS Style Guide: A Manual for Authors and Editors*, 3rd ed., 2006

American Institute of Physics, *Style Manual for Guidance in the Preparation of Papers*, 4th ed., 1997

American Medical Association Manual of Style, 10th ed., 2007

Council of Science Editors, *Scientific Style and Format: The CSE Manual for Authors, Editors, and Publishers*, 7th ed., 2006

The most thorough and widely used of these guides is the last one, *Scientific Style and Format*, which details both styles of scientific documentation: one using author and date and one using numbers. Both types of text citation refer to a list of references at the end of the paper (see the next page). Ask your teacher which style you should use.

1 Using CSE name-year text citations

In the CSE name-year style, parenthetical text citations provide the last name of the author being cited and the source's year of publication. At the end of the paper, a list of references, arranged alphabetically by authors' last names, provides complete information on each source.

The CSE name-year style closely resembles the APA name-year style detailed on pages 742–61. You can follow the APA examples for in-text citations, making several notable changes for CSE:

- Do not use a comma to separate the author's name and the date: (Baumrind 1968, p. 34).
- Separate two authors' names with **and** (not "&"): (Pepinsky and DeStefano 1997).
- For sources with three or more authors, use **et al.** (Latin abbreviation for "and others") after the first author's name: (Rutter et al. 1996).

2 Using CSE numbered text citations

In the CSE number style, raised numbers in the text refer to a numbered list of references at the end of the paper.

Two standard references[1,2] use this term.

These forms of immunity have been extensively researched.[3]

Hepburn and Tatin[2] do not discuss this project.

Assignment of numbers The number for each source is based on the order in which you cite the source in the text: the first cited source is 1, the second is 2, and so on.

Reuse of numbers When you cite a source you have already cited and numbered, use the original number again (see the last example on the previous page, which reuses the number 2 from the first example).

This reuse is the key difference between the CSE numbered citations and numbered references to footnotes or endnotes. In the CSE style, each source has only one number, determined by the order in which the source is cited. With notes, in contrast, the numbering proceeds in sequence, so that each source has as many numbers as it has citations in the text.

Citation of two or more sources When you cite two or more sources at once, arrange their numbers in sequence and separate them with a comma and no space, as in the first example on the previous page.

3 | Using a CSE reference list

For both the name-year and the number styles of in-text citation, provide a list, titled References, of all sources you have cited.

The following examples show the differences and similarities between the name-year and number styles:

Name-year style

Hepburn PX, Tatin JM. 2005. Human physiology. New York (NY): Columbia University Press.

Number style

2. Hepburn PX, Tatin JM. Human physiology. New York (NY): Columbia University Press; 2005.

Spacing In both styles, single-space each entry and double-space between entries.

Arrangement In the name-year style, arrange entries alphabetically by authors' last names. In the number style, arrange entries in numerical order—that is, in order of their citation in the text.

Format In both styles, begin the first line of each entry at the left margin.

Authors In both styles, list each author's name with the last name first, followed by initials for first and middle names. Do not use a comma between an author's last name and initials, and do not use periods or spaces with the initials. Do use a comma to separate authors' names.

Placement of dates In the name-year style, the date follows the author's or authors' names. In the number style, the date follows the publication information (for a book) or the periodical title (for a journal, magazine, or newspaper).

Journal titles In both styles, do not italicize or underline journal titles. For titles of two or more words, abbreviate words of six or more letters (without periods) and omit most prepositions, articles, and conjunctions. Capitalize each word. For example, *Journal of Chemical and Biochemical Studies* becomes J Chem Biochem Stud.

Book and article titles In both styles, do not italicize, underline, or use quotation marks around a book or an article title. Capitalize only the first word and any proper nouns.

Publication information for journal articles The name-year and number styles differ in the placement of the publication date (see opposite). However, both styles end with the journal's volume number, any issue number in parentheses, a colon, and the inclusive page numbers of the article, run together without space: 28:329-30 or 62(2):26-40.

The following box indexes the CSE models. The models include examples of both a name-year reference and a number reference for each type of source.

CSE reference-list models

Listing authors

1. One author

Gould SJ. 1987. Time's arrow, time's cycle. Cambridge (MA): Harvard University Press.

1. Gould SJ. Time's arrow, time's cycle. Cambridge (MA): Harvard University Press; 1987.

2. Two to ten authors

Hepburn PX, Tatin JM, Tatin JP. 2008. Human physiology. New York (NY): Columbia University Press.

2. Hepburn PX, Tatin JM, Tatin JP. Human physiology. New York (NY): Columbia University Press; 2008.

3. More than ten authors

Evans RW, Bowditch L, Dana KL, Drumond A, Wildovitch WP, Young SL, Mills P, Mills RR, Livak SR, Lisi OL, et al. 2004. Organ transplants: ethical issues. Ann Arbor (MI): University of Michigan Press.

3. Evans RW, Bowditch L, Dana KL, Drummond A, Wildovitch WP, Young SL, Mills P, Mills RR, Livak SR, Lisi OL, et al. Organ transplants: ethical issues. Ann Arbor (MI): University of Michigan Press; 2004.

4. Author not named

Health care for children with diabetes. 2008. New York (NY): US Health Care.

4. Health care for children with diabetes. New York (NY): US Health Care; 2008.

5. Two or more cited works by the same author(s) published in the same year

Gardner H. 1973a. The arts and human development. New York (NY): Wiley.

Gardner H. 1973b. The quest for mind: Piaget, Lévi-Strauss, and the structuralist movement. New York (NY): Knopf.

(The number style does not require such forms.)

Listing print periodicals: Journals, newspapers, magazines

6. An article in a journal (print)

Kim P. 2006. Medical decision making for the dying. Milbank Quar. 64(2):26-40.

6. Kim P. Medical decision making for the dying. Milbank Quar. 2006;64(2):26-40.

If a journal article has a Digital Object Identifier (DOI), you may include the number at the end of the entry for readers' convenience. (See p. 755 for more on DOIs.)

7. An article in a newspaper (print)

Stout D. 2008 May 28. Blind win court ruling on US currency. New York Times (National Ed.). Sect. A:23 (col. 3).

7. Stout D. Blind win court ruling on US currency. New York Times (National Ed.). 2008 May 28;Sect. A:23 (col. 3).

8. An article in a magazine (print)

Wilkinson A. 2008 June 2. Crime fighting of the future. New Yorker. 26-33.

8. Wilkinson A. Crime fighting of the future. New Yorker. 2008 June 2:26-33.

Listing print books

9. Basic format for a book (print)

Wilson EO. 2004. On human nature. Cambridge (MA): Harvard University Press.

9. Wilson EO. On human nature. Cambridge (MA): Harvard University Press; 2004.

10. A book with an editor (print)

Jonson P, editor. 2008. Anatomy yearbook 2008. Los Angeles (CA): Anatco.

10. Jonson P, editor. Anatomy yearbook 2008. Los Angeles (CA): Anatco; 2008.

11. A selection from a book (print)

Kriegel R, Laubenstein L, Muggia F. 2005. Kaposi's sarcoma. In: Ebbeson P, Biggar RS, Melbye M, editors. AIDS: a basic guide for clinicians. 2nd ed. Philadelphia (PA): Saunders. p. 100–26.

11. Kriegel R, Laubenstein L, Muggia F. Kaposi's sarcoma. In: Ebbeson P, Biggar RS, Melbye M, editors. AIDS: a basic guide for clinicians. 2nd ed. Philadelphia (PA): Saunders; 2005. p. 100–26.

Listing Web and other electronic sources

Do not add a period after a URL at the end of an entry. If you must break a URL from one line to the next, do so only after a slash, and do not hyphenate.

12. An article in a journal (Web)

Grady GF. 2007. The here and now of hepatitis B immunization. Today's Med [Internet]. [cited 2007 Dec 7]; 6(2):39-41. Available from: http://www.fmrt.org/todayamedicine/Grady050293.pdf6

12. Grady GF. The here and now of hepatitis B immunization. Today's Med [Internet]. 2007 [cited 2007 Dec 7]; 6(2):39-41. Available from: http://www.fmrt.org/todaysmedicine/Grady050293.pdf6

Give the date of your access, preceded by "cited," in brackets: [cited 2007 Dec 7] in the examples. If the article has no reference numbers (pages, paragraphs, and so on), give your calculation of its length in brackets—for instance, [about 15 p.] or [20 paragraphs]. If the article has a Digital Object Identifier (DOI), you may include the number for readers' convenience. Add it to the end of the entry after a space. (See p. 755 for more on DOIs.)

13. An article in a database (Web)

McAskill MR, Anderson TJ, Jones RD. 2005. Saccadic adaptation in neurological disorders. Prog Brain Res. 140:417-431. PubMed [database on the Internet]. Bethesda (MD): National Library of Medicine; [cited 2007 Mar 6]. Available from: http://www.ncbi.nlm.nih.gov/PubMed

13. McAskill MR, Anderson TJ, Jones RD. Saccadic adaptation in neurological disorders. Prog Brain Res. 2005;140:417-431. PubMed [database on the Internet]. Bethesda (MD): National Library of Medicine; [cited 2007 Mar 6]. Available from: http://www.ncbi.nlm.nih.gov/PubMed

Provide information on the database: title, [database on the Internet], place of publication, and publisher. (If the database author is different from the publisher, give the author's name before the title.) If you see a date of publication or a copyright date for the database, give it after the publisher's name. Add the date of your access, preceded by cited, in brackets. If the article has a Digital Object Identifier (DOI), you may include the number for readers' convenience. Add it to the end of the entry after a space. (See p. 755 for more on DOIs.)

14. A book (Web)

Ruch BJ, Ruch DB. 2007. Homeopathy and medicine: resolving the conflict [Internet]. New York (NY): Albert Einstein College of Medicine [cited 2008 Jan 28]. Available from: http://www.einstein.edu/medicine/books/ruch.html

14. Ruch BJ, Ruch DB. Homeopathy and medicine: resolving the conflict [Internet]. New York (NY): Albert Einstein College of Medicine; 2007 [cited 2008 Jan 28]. Available from: http://www.einstein.edu/medicine/books/ruch.html

As with an online journal article, give the date of your access, preceded by cited, in brackets.

15. A Web site

American Medical Association [Internet]. 2008. Chicago (IL): American Medical Association; [cited 2008 Nov 26]. Available from: http://ama-assn.org

15. American Medical Association [Internet]. Chicago (IL): American Medical Association; 2008 [cited 2008 Nov 26]. Available from: http://ama-assn.org

16. A message posted to a discussion list

Stalinsky Q. 2007 Aug 16. Reconsidering the hormone-replacement study. Woman Physicians Congress [discussion list on the Internet]. Chicago (IL): American Medical Association; [cited 2008 Aug 17]. Available from: ama-wpc@ama-assn.org

16. Stalinsky Q. Reconsidering the hormone-replacement study. Woman Physicians Congress [discussion list on the Internet]. Chicago (IL): American Medical Association; 2007 Aug 16 [cited 2008 Aug 17]. Available from: ama-wpc@ama-assn.org

17. A personal online communication (text citation)

One member of the research team has expressed reservation about the study design (personal communication from L. Kogod, 2010 Feb 6; unreferenced).

A personal letter or e-mail message should be cited in your text, not in your reference list. The format is the same for both the name-year and the number styles.

18. A document on CD-ROM or DVD-ROM

Reich WT, editor. 2008. Encyclopedia of bioethics [DVD-ROM]. New York (NY): Co-Health.

18. Reich WT, editor. Encyclopedia of bioethics [DVD-ROM]. New York (NY): Co-Health; 2008.

Listing other sources

19. A report written and published by the same organization

Warnock M. 2006. Report of the Committee on Fertilization and Embryology. Waco (TX): Baylor University Department of Embryology. Report No.: BU/DE.4261.

19. Warnock M. Report of the Committee on Fertilization and Embryology. Waco (TX): Baylor University Department of Embryology; 2006. Report No.: BU/DE.4261.

20. A report written and published by different organizations

Hackney, JD (Rancho Los Amigos Hospital, Downey, CA). 2007. Effect of atmospheric pollutants on human physiologic function. Washington (DC): Environmental Protection Agency (US). Report No.: R-801396.

20. Hackney, JD (Rancho Los Amigos Hospital, Downey, CA). Effect of atmospheric pollutants on human physiologic function. Washington (DC): Environmental Protection Agency (US); 2007. Report No.: R-801396.

21. An audio or visual recording

Cell mitosis [DVD–ROM]. 2008. White Plains (NY): Teaching Media.

21. Cell mitosis [DVD-ROM]. White Plains (NY): Teaching Media; 2008.

52e Examining a sample science paper

The following biology paper illustrates the CSE number style for documenting sources. On page 782, passages from the paper and a reformatted list of references show the name-year style. Except for the citations and the references, the paper is formatted in APA style because CSE does not specify a format.

A laboratory report: CSE number style

[Title page.]

Exercise and Blood Pressure

Liz Garson

Biology 161

Ms. Traversa

December 13, 2009

[New page.]

Abstract

The transient elevation of blood pressure following exercise was demonstrated by pressure measurements of twenty human subjects before and after exercise.

[New page.]

Exercise and Blood Pressure

Introduction

The purpose of this experiment was to verify the changes in blood pressure that accompany exercise, as commonly reported. [1,2] A certain blood pressure is necessary for the blood to supply nutrients to the body tissues. Baroreceptors near the heart monitor pressure by determining the degree to which blood stretches the wall of the blood vessel.

[The introduction continues.]

During exercise, the metabolic needs of the muscles override the influence of the baroreceptors and result in an increase in blood pressure. This increase in blood pressure is observed uniformly (irrespective of sex or race), although men demonstrate a higher absolute systolic pressure than do women. [3] During strenuous exercise, blood pressure can rise to 40 percent above baseline. [1]

Method

The subjects for this experiment were twenty volunteers from laboratory classes, ten men and ten women. All pressure measurements were performed using a standard sphygmomanometer, which was tested for accuracy. To ensure consistency, the same sphygmomanometer was used to take all readings. In addition, all measurements were taken by the same person to avoid discrepancies in method or interpretation.

The first pressure reading was taken prior to exercise as the subject sat in a chair. This pressure was considered the baseline for each subject. All subsequent readings were interpreted relative to this baseline.

In the experiment, the subjects ran up and down stairs for fifteen minutes. Immediately after exercising, the subjects returned to the laboratory to have their pressure measured. Thirty minutes later, the pressure was measured for the final time.

[Table on a page by itself.]

Table 1. Blood pressure measurements for all subjects (mmHg)

Subject	Baseline[a]	Post-exercise	30-minute reading
Male			
1	110/75	135/80	115/75
2	125/80	140/90	135/85
3	125/70	125/70	125/70
4	130/85	170/100	140/90
5	120/80	125/95	120/80
6	115/70	135/80	125/75
7	125/70	150/80	130/70
8	130/80	145/85	130/80
9	140/75	180/85	155/80
10	110/85	135/95	115/80
Female			
11	110/60	140/85	115/60
12	130/75	180/85	130/75
13	125/80	140/90	130/80
14	90/60	90/60	90/60
15	115/65	145/70	125/65
16	100/50	130/65	110/50
17	120/80	140/80	130/80
18	110/70	135/80	120/75
19	120/80	140/90	130/80
20	110/80	145/90	120/80

[a]Normal blood pressure at rest: males, 110-130/60-90; females, 110-120/50-80.

Results

Table 1 contains the blood pressure measurements for the male and female subjects. With the exception of subjects 3 and 14, all subjects demonstrated the expected post-exercise increase in blood pressure, with a decline to baseline or near baseline thirty minutes after exercise. The data for subjects 3 and 14 were invalid because the subjects did not perform the experiment as directed.

Discussion

As expected, most of the subjects demonstrated an increase in blood pressure immediately after exercise and a decline to near baseline levels thirty minutes after exercise. The usual pressure increase was 20-40 mmHg for the systolic pressure and 5-10 mmHg for the diastolic pressure.

In the two cases in which blood pressure did not elevate with exercise (subjects 3 and 14), the subjects simply left the laboratory and returned fifteen minutes later without having exercised. The experimental design was flawed in not assigning someone to observe the subjects as they exercised.

[New page.]

References

1. Guyton AC. Textbook of medical physiology. Philadelphia (PA): Saunders; 2006.

2. Rowell LB. Blood pressure regulation during exercise. Ann Med. 2004;28:329-33.

3. Gleim GW, Stachenfeld NS. Gender differences in the systolic blood pressure response to exercise. Am Heart J. 2001;121:524-30.

A laboratory report: CSE name-year style

These excerpts from the preceding paper show documentation in CSE name-year style:

The purpose of this experiment was to verify the changes in blood pressure that accompany exercise, as commonly reported (Guyton 2006; Rowell 2004).

This increase in blood pressure is observed uniformly (irrespective of sex or race), although men demonstrate a higher absolute systolic pressure than do women (Gleim and Stachenfeld 2001). During strenuous exercise, blood pressure can rise to 40 percent above baseline (Guyton 2006).

References

Gleim GW, Stachenfeld NS. 2001. Gender differences in the systolic blood pressure response to exercise. Am Heart J. 121:524-30.

Guyton AC. 2006. Textbook of medical physiology. Philadelphia (PA): Saunders.

Rowell LB. 2004. Blood pressure regulation during exercise. Ann Med. 28:329-33.

PART 11

Special Writing Situations

53

Essay Examinations

In writing an essay for an examination, you summarize or analyze a topic, usually in several paragraphs or more and usually within a time limit. An essay question not only tests your knowledge of a subject (as short-answer and objective questions do) but also tests your ability to think critically about what you have learned. If you have not already done so, read pages 137–39 on preparing for exams and Chapter 7 on critical thinking and reading.

53a Preparing for an essay exam

To do well on an essay exam, you will need to understand the course content, not only the facts but also the interpretation of them and the relations between them.

- **Take careful class notes.**
- **Thoughtfully, critically read the assigned texts or articles.**
- **Review regularly.** Give the material time to sink in and stimulate your thinking.
- **Create summaries.** Recast others' ideas in your own words, and extract the meaning from notes and texts. (See pp. 136–37 for instructions on summarizing.)
- **Prepare notes or outlines to reorganize the course material around key topics or issues.** One technique is to create and answer likely essay questions. For instance, in a literature class you might locate a theme running through all the stories you have read by a certain author or from a certain period. In a psychology class you might outline various theorists' views of what causes a disorder such as schizophrenia. Working through such topics can help you anticipate questions, master the material, and estimate your time during the actual exam.

Visit *mycomplab.com* for more resources as well as
784   exercises on essay exams.

53b Planning your time and your answer

When you first receive an exam, take a few minutes to get your bearings and plan an approach. The time will not be wasted.

- **Read the exam all the way through at least once.** Don't start answering any questions until you've seen them all.
- **Weigh the questions.** Determine which questions seem most important, which ones are going to be most difficult for you, and approximately how much time you'll need for each question. (Your teacher may help by assigning a point value to each question as a guide to its importance or by suggesting an amount of time for you to spend on each question.)

Planning continues when you turn to an individual essay question. Resist the temptation to rush right into an answer without some planning, for a few minutes can save you time later and help you produce a stronger essay.

- **Read the question at least twice.** You will be more likely to stick to the question and answer it fully.
- **Examine the words in the question and consider their implications.** Look especially for words such as *describe, define, explain, summarize, analyze, evaluate,* and *interpret,* each of which requires a different kind of response. Here, for example, is an essay question whose key term is *explain:*

Question
How did literacy contribute to the abolitionist movement leading up to the Civil War? Explain, using specific examples from your reading.

See the box on the next page and consult earlier discussions of such terms on pages 27–28 and 94–102.

- **Make a brief outline of the main ideas you want to cover.** Use the back of the exam sheet or booklet for scratch paper. In the brief outline below, a student planned her answer to the history question above.

Outline
1. Literacy among slaves
   Douglass/Jacobs (examples)
   Writings & how they felt about literacy & freedom
2. White abolitionists & spreading antislavery message
3. Importance of *Uncle Tom's Cabin* in changing attitudes
   Popularity
   Lincoln's introduction of Stowe
   Emancipation Proclamation

Sample instructions for essay exams

Sample instructions	Key terms	Strategies for answers	Examples of wrong answers
Define *dyslexia* and compare and contrast it with two other learning disabilities.	Define	Specify the meaning of *dyslexia*—distinctive characteristics, ways the impairment works, etc.	Feelings of children with dyslexia. Causes of dyslexia.
	Compare and contrast	Analyze similarities and differences (severity, causes, treatments, etc.).	Similarities without differences, or vice versa.
Analyze the role of Horatio in *Hamlet*.	Analyze	Break Horatio's role into its elements (speeches, relations with other characters, etc.).	Plot summary of *Hamlet*. Description of Horatio's personality.
Explain the effects of the drug Thorazine.	Explain	Set forth the facts and theories objectively.	Argument for or against Thorazine.
	Effects	Analyze the consequences.	Reasons for prescribing Thorazine.
Discuss term limits for elected officials.	Discuss	Explain and compare the main points of view on the issue.	Analysis of one view. Argument for or against one view.
Summarize the process that resulted in the Grand Canyon.	Summarize	Distill the subject to its main points, elements, or steps.	Detailed description of the Grand Canyon.
How do you evaluate the Laffer curve as a predictor of economic growth?	Evaluate	Provide your opinion of significance or value, supported with evidence.	Explanation of the Laffer curve, without evaluation. Comparison of the Laffer curve and another predictor, without evaluation.

- Write a thesis statement for your essay that responds directly to the question and represents your view of the topic. (If you are unsure of how to write a thesis statement, see pp. 29–34.) Include key phrases that you can expand with supporting evidence for your view. The thesis statement of the student whose outline appears above concisely previews a three-part answer to the sample question:

Thesis statement

The abolitionist movement in the years leading up to the Civil War was strengthened by the growth of literacy among black and white Americans, which helped to spread the antislavery message and change public attitudes toward slavery.

53c Starting the essay

An essay exam does not require a smooth and inviting opening. Instead, begin by stating your thesis immediately and giving an overview of the rest of your essay. Such a capsule version of your answer tells your reader (and grader) generally how much command you have and also how you plan to develop your answer. It also gets you off to a good start.

The opening statement should address the question directly and exactly, as it does in the successful essay answer beginning on the next page. In contrast, the opening of the unsuccessful essay (p. 789) restates the question but does not answer it, nor does the opening provide any sense of the writer's thesis.

53d Developing the essay

Develop your essay as you would develop any piece of sound academic writing:

- **Observe the methods, terms, or other special requirements of the discipline in which you are writing.**
- **Support your thesis statement with solid generalizations,** each one perhaps the topic sentence of a paragraph.
- **Support each generalization with specific, relevant evidence.**

If you observe a few *don't*s as well, your essay will have more substance:

- **Avoid filling out the essay by repeating yourself.**
- **Avoid other kinds of wordiness that pad and confuse,** whether intentionally or not. (See pp. 525–32.)

■ **Avoid resorting to purely subjective feelings.** Keep focused on analysis, or whatever is asked of you. (It may help to abolish the word *I* from the essay.)

The following essays illustrate a successful and an unsuccessful answer to the sample essay question on page 785 about literacy and the abolitionist movement. Both answers were written in the allotted time of forty minutes. Marginal comments on each essay highlight their effective and ineffective elements.

Successful essay answer

Introduction answering question and stating thesis

The abolitionist movement in the years leading up to the Civil War was strengthened by the growth of literacy among black and white Americans, which helped to spread the antislavery message and change public attitudes toward slavery.

First main point: literacy among slaves

Although literacy among slaves was largely prohibited in the pre-Civil War South, many slaves learned to read and write. Those who wrote about literacy clearly saw it as related to freedom. For example, Frederick Douglass, author of *Narrative of the Life of Frederick Douglass*, and Harriet Ann Jacobs, author of *Incidents in the Life of a Slave Girl*, show in their writings the moments of learning to read and write as the moments when they understood the possibilities of freedom. Douglass points out that as he learned to read he began to imagine other worlds and that such imagining allowed him to see himself as an emancipated human being. Jacobs, reading in the attic where she hid until she escaped, came to understand how she might make her way North and become an advocate for those still in slavery.

Examples

Second main point: spreading antislavery message

Escaped, literate slaves who went North energized white abolitionists eager to spread the antislavery message. White abolitionists William Lloyd Garrison and Lydia Maria Child embraced Douglass and Jacobs, becoming their champions and citing their writings as examples of the "humanity" of the slave and as evidence of why white Northerners should support the cause of abolition. In the 1830s and 1840s, Garrison introduced Douglass to Northern white audiences, calling on them to listen to Douglass's eloquent speech and to read his powerful writing. Child spoke to audiences of white women in Boston, using Jacobs as an example of a literate Christian woman.

Third main point (with transition also): changing attitudes toward slavery

The literacy of white Americans also contributed to the abolitionist movement. When Harriet Beecher Stowe published the novel *Uncle Tom's Cabin* in 1852, her powerful, dramatic account of slavery fanned the abolitionist sentiment among an increasingly literate population. The novel quickly became extremely popular, so much so that once the Civil War began, soldiers were given copies to carry in their knapsacks. Recognizing the importance of *Uncle Tom's Cabin* in shaping public attitudes toward slavery, in 1862 Abraham Lincoln introduced Stowe as "the little woman who wrote

Examples

the book that started this great war." A year later, he issued the Emancipation Proclamation, giving freedom to all slaves.

It's clear that reading and writing—both the literacy of the slaves themselves and the growing literacy of the population at large—had much to do with the progression of the abolitionist movement and ultimate abolition of slavery in the United States.

Conclusion, restating thesis supported by essay

Unsuccessful essay answer

Literacy means to be able to read and write. Slaves were not allowed to read and write, but many learned in spite of rules against it. Douglass and Jacobs are two examples of this.

Introduction, not answering question

No thesis statement or sense of direction

In the South, it was illegal to teach a slave to read. Whites were fined or jailed if they were caught teaching slaves to read, and slaves were punished if they were caught with books or paper. Despite this, slaves taught themselves because they knew it was something they needed if they wanted to reach freedom, and they worked hard at figuring out ways to learn their letters and to find materials to write with.

Irrelevant information

Wheel spinning, discussing literacy but not abolition

In the North, once abolitionists knew slaves could be readers and writers, they used them to spread the antislavery message. They realized how much the North needed the slaves to join in the fight to abolish slavery. William Lloyd Garrison and Lydia Maria Child are examples of abolitionist writers and speakers who took up the slaves' cause in different ways. Harriet Beecher Stowe's novel *Uncle Tom's Cabin* provoked reactions from abolitionists and common readers in the North because of how it depicted the demeaning conditions of slavery. The popularity of the novel shows how many more people in the North were learning to read and write as well.

Name dropping without support

Discussion showing familiarity with literacy and abolition but not answering question

As mentioned earlier, Jacobs and Douglass were examples of slaves who showed how much literacy changed their lives for the better. They came to the North and became spokespersons for the cause of emancipation, something that finally came to pass when Lincoln issued the Emancipation Proclamation in 1863.

Assertion without support

Therefore, literacy was extremely important to the cause of abolition. Literacy is just as important today.

Irrelevant and empty conclusion

53e Rereading the essay

The time limit on an essay examination does not allow for the careful rethinking and revision you would give an essay or research paper. You need to write clearly and concisely the first time. But try to leave yourself a few minutes after finishing the entire exam for rereading the essay (or essays) and doing touch-ups.

- **Correct mistakes:** illegible passages, misspellings, grammatical errors, and accidental omissions.

- **Verify that your thesis is accurate**—that it is, in fact, what you ended up writing about.
- **Ensure that you have supported all your generalizations.** Cross out irrelevant ideas and details, and add any information that now seems important. (Write on another page, if necessary, keying the addition to the page on which it belongs.)

54

Writing Online

Both in and out of school, you will write extensively online. Many forms of online writing expand your options as a writer, but they also present distinctive challenges, both conceptual and technical. This chapter discusses some of the options and challenges of e-mail (below), online collaboration (p. 793), and Web composition (p. 796).

54a Writing effective e-mail

To use e-mail productively for school work, pause to weigh each element of the message. Consider especially your audience and purpose and how your tone will come across to readers. In the message shown below, the writer knows the recipients well and yet has serious information to convey to them, so he writes informally but states his points and concerns carefully. Writing to the corporation mentioned in the message, the writer would be more formal in both tone and approach. Although e-mail is typically more casual than printed correspondence, in academic settings a crafted message is more likely to achieve the intended purpose. Proofread all but the most informal messages for errors in grammar, punctuation, and spelling.

my**comp**lab

Visit *mycomplab.com* for more resources as well as exercises on e-mail, online collaboration, and Web composition.

E-mail message

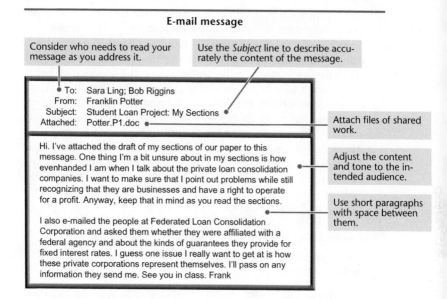

Consider who needs to read your message as you address it.

Use the *Subject* line to describe accurately the content of the message.

To: Sara Ling; Bob Riggins
From: Franklin Potter
Subject: Student Loan Project: My Sections
Attached: Potter.P1.doc

Attach files of shared work.

Hi. I've attached the draft of my sections of our paper to this message. One thing I'm a bit unsure about in my sections is how evenhanded I am when I talk about the private loan consolidation companies. I want to make sure that I point out problems while still recognizing that they are businesses and have a right to operate for a profit. Anyway, keep that in mind as you read the sections.

Adjust the content and tone to the intended audience.

Use short paragraphs with space between them.

I also e-mailed the people at Federated Loan Consolidation Corporation and asked them whether they were affiliated with a federal agency and about the kinds of guarantees they provide for fixed interest rates. I guess one issue I really want to get at is how these private corporations represent themselves. I'll pass on any information they send me. See you in class. Frank

For more on using e-mail to interact with the other students in a class, see pages 793–94. For more on using e-mail as a research tool, see page 573.

1 Addressing messages

Send a message only to the people who need to read it. As a general rule, avoid sending messages to many recipients at once—all the students in a class, say, or all the participants in a discussion group—unless what you have to say applies to all of them. Occasionally, you may indeed have a worthwhile idea or important information that everyone on the list will want to know. But spamming—flooding entire lists with irrelevant messages—is rude and irritating.

Similarly, avoid sending frivolous messages to all the members of a group. Instead of dashing off "I agree" and distributing the two-word message widely, put some time into composing a thoughtful response and send it only to those who will be interested.

2 Composing messages

The messages you send are going to people, not merely inboxes, so craft your messages with the recipients in mind.

- **Don't say or do anything you wouldn't say or do face to face.**
- **Use names.** In the body of your message, address your reader(s) by name if possible and sign off with your own name and

information on how to contact you. Your own name is especially important if your e-mail address does not spell it out.

- **Pay careful attention to tone.** Refrain from flaming, or attacking, correspondents. Don't use all capital letters, which SHOUT. And use irony or sarcasm only cautiously: in the absence of facial expressions, either one can lead to misunderstanding. To indicate irony and emotions, you can use an emoticon such as the smiley :-). These sideways faces can easily be overused, though, and they should not substitute for thoughtfully worded opinions.

- **Avoid saying anything in e-mail that you would not say in a printed document such as a letter or memo.** E-mail can usually be retrieved from the server, and in business and academic settings it may well be retrieved in disputes over contracts, grades, and other matters.

3 | Reading and responding to messages

When you read and respond to messages, again consider the people behind them.

- **Be a forgiving reader.** Avoid nitpicking over spelling or other surface errors. And because attitudes are sometimes difficult to convey, give authors an initial benefit of the doubt: a writer who at first seems hostile may simply have tried too hard to be concise; a writer who at first seems unserious may simply have failed at injecting humor into a worthwhile message.

- **Consider who will read your response.** The Reply function will automatically address the person who wrote you, whereas the

---

E-mail response

Make sure the *To* field addresses the appropriate person or people.

Use the subject of the original message unless you are changing or expanding it.

When quoting the original message, select only the parts you are responding to and delete the rest.

To: Franklin Potter
From: Bob Riggins
Subject: Re: Student Loan Project: My Sections

Franklin Potter wrote:

I also e-mailed the people at Federated Loan Consolidation Corporation and asked them whether they were affiliated with a federal agency and about the kinds of guarantees they provide for fixed interest rates. I guess one issue I really want to get at is how these private corporations represent themselves. I'll pass on any information they send me. See you in class. Frank

Hey Frank. I might be able to help with the Fed Loan Corporation. My sister just graduated and consolidated her student loans. She has a lot of information. I'll ask her if she has ever heard of them.

Bob

Reply All function will address others who may have been sent copies of the original message. Before you send the message, choose the readers who need to see the message.

- **Respect others' privacy.** Forward messages only with permission or only if you know that the author of the message won't mind. If you add more recipients to your response, make sure not to pass on previous private messages by mistake.
- **Avoid participating in flame "wars,"** overheated dialogs that contribute little or no information or understanding. If a war breaks out in a discussion, ignore it: don't rush to defend someone who is being attacked, and don't respond even if you are under attack yourself.

54b Collaborating online

Writing often involves collaborating with others as much as it does working in solitude. Indeed, many teachers and businesses expect writers to collaborate on generating ideas and producing and revising drafts. Computers have vastly expanded the options for collaboration, ranging from simple e-mail exchanges to video conferencing and virtual environments.

In this section we look at strategies for online collaboration in your classes. Your teachers or your school's technology advisers will introduce you to the system and help set you up. Here we focus on nontechnical matters of participating in discussions and working on drafts.

1 Participating in discussions

Many teachers use online conversations for discussing class readings and other topics and to help students generate ideas for writing. There are two basic types of online conversation: delayed conversation, such as that occurring by e-mail, blog, or wiki; and real-time **chat**, which occurs immediately, like a telephone conversation.

Delayed conversation

E-mail, Web discussion groups, blogs, and wikis allow detailed, thoughtful messages and responses, so they are good places to try out ideas, explore assignments, and respond to others' work. When writing in such media, observe the guidelines for composing and responding to messages on the preceding two pages.

The screen shots on the following pages show part of a discussion thread on *Blackboard* courseware and a query and responses on a course blog. The writing is casual but also thoughtful and specific.

In the *Blackboard* examples, notice that the second writer actually challenges the first writer's assumption but frames the challenge productively in the context of the issue being discussed. Disagreements are bound to occur in online conversation, but they need not be unpleasant.

Discussion on *Blackboard*

Author: Sara Ling
Subject: Internet Identity

Hi everyone. I'm hoping you can give me some advice about my topic and maybe share some of your experiences. I disagree with Kadi's argument that the Internet will lead to more fragmentation, not community. On the snowboarding forum that I sometimes participate in, I received a lot of hostile responses when I logged on as a woman. But another member of the group wrote to tell me that when she logged on as a man, she was welcomed into the group. It made me realize that the anonymity of the Internet could be used to bring people together, not split them apart.

Have any of you had similar experiences when you've been online? Do you think that anonymity can bring people together?

Sara

Author: Franklin Potter
Subject: Re: Internet Identity

I think you have a point about the names used on the Internet having a lot to do with how people relate. But I'm not sure that your experience totally challenges what Kadi is saying. When I've been online, I've found that people who are a lot alike tend to hang out and encourage each other. Even if the other woman on the snowboarding forum was able to change her identity, she still ended up confiding in you. I guess I would just be careful about claiming that anonymity will automatically bring different kinds of people together. Hope this helps.

Frank

Online chat

You may be familiar with chat conversations from using instant messaging with friends and family. In academic settings, chat will likely occur with courseware such as *WebCT* or *Blackboard*.

Collaborating via chat discussions will be more productive if you take a few tips:

■ **Use the chat space for brainstorming topics and exchanging impressions.** The pace of online chat rarely allows lengthy consideration and articulation of messages.

Discussion on a class blog

English 1201
Writing in the World

Tuesday, 9/13/08
Service-learning projects
Some of you have asked for names of groups needing help from students, especially groups that will really *use* students. I've got some ideas, but maybe other students do, too. Suggestions? 9:24 AM

Comments

Try the Neighborhood Hunger Program (326-1135). I'm going to be working with them on a project to increase food and furniture donations from the community. It'll involve a lot of writing, I think. The group also needs help organizing the warehouse and reaching out to needy families in the community.
Posted by Jessica C 9/13/08 11:03 AM

I'm talking to ReadingWorks at the Springfield VA Hospital. They teach reading and writing to veterans. They always need volunteer tutors, but I don't think I'm ready for that yet, so I hope to do some publicity for them. The director is open to my involvement, but she's very busy and worried about supervising such work. Maybe if three or four of us presented a team proposal and proved we could work independently, she'd be encouraged. Anyone want to join in?
Posted by AlexRamirez 9/13/08 5:46 PM

■ **Focus on a thread or common topic.** Online chat can be the electronic equivalent of a party, with different conversations occurring in the same space. If you have trouble tracking all the messages, concentrate on the ones that relate to your interest.

■ **Write as quickly and fluidly as possible.** Don't worry about producing perfect prose.

2 Working on drafts

In writing and other classes, you and your fellow students may be invited to exchange and respond to one another's projects by e-mail or over the Web. To guide your reading of others' work, use the revision checklist on page 56 and the collaboration tips on pages 69–72. Focus on the deep issues in others' drafts, especially early drafts: thesis, purpose, audience, organization, and support for the thesis. Hold comments on style, grammar, punctuation, and other surface matters until you're reviewing later drafts, if indeed you are expected to comment on them at all.

Exchanging drafts online generally requires a file-naming system that identifies each project's writer, title, and version. Your teacher may establish such a system, or you and your classmates can develop one.

54c Creating effective Web compositions

Creating a Web page or site is sometimes as simple as saving a document in a different format, but more often it means thinking in a new way.

The diagrams on the facing page show a key difference between traditional printed documents and Web sites. Most traditional documents are meant to be read in sequence from start to finish. In contrast, most Web sites are so-called hypertexts: they are intended to be examined in whatever order readers choose as they follow links to pages within the site and to other sites.

When you create a composition for the Web, it will likely fall into one of two categories discussed in this section: pages such as class papers that resemble printed documents in being linear and text-heavy and that call for familiar ways of writing and reading; or "native" hypertext documents that you build from scratch, which call for screen-oriented writing and reading.

These general guidelines will help you create effective Web sites:

- **Plan the site carefully.** A hypertext can disorient readers as they scroll up and down and pursue various links. Page length, links, menus, and other cues should work to keep readers oriented.
- **Anticipate what readers may see on their screens.** Each reader's screen frames and organizes the experience of a Web composition. Screen space is limited, and it varies from one computer to another. Text and visual elements should be managed for maximum clarity and effectiveness on a variety of screens.
- **Integrate visual and sound elements into the text.** Web compositions can include not only tables, charts, and photographs (which printed documents may also have) but also video (such as animation or film clips) and audio (such as music or excerpts from speeches). However, any visual or sound elements should not merely embellish the text but contribute substantially to it. In addition, you should find out whether your readers' equipment will likely be able to handle multimedia elements and whether readers themselves may have disabilities that prevent their seeing or hearing such elements (see the note on p. 798).

Traditional print document

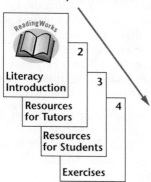

Web site

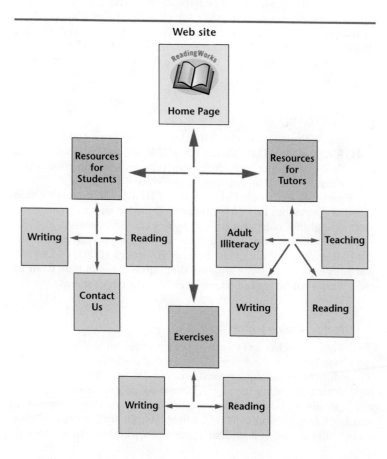

■ **Acknowledge your sources.** It's easy to incorporate material from other sources into a Web site, but you have the same obligation to cite your sources as you do in a printed document (see pp. 614–15). Further, your Web site is a form of publication, like a magazine or a book. Unless the material you are using explicitly allows copying without permission, you may need to seek the copyright holder's permission, just as print publishers do. (See pp. 612–14 for more on copyright.)

Note If you anticipate that some of your readers may have visual, hearing, or reading disabilities, you'll need to consider their needs while designing Web sites. Some of these considerations are covered under document design on page 127, and others are fundamental to any effective Web design, as discussed in this section. In addition, avoid any content that relies exclusively on images or sound, instead supplementing such elements with text descriptions. At the same time, try to provide key concepts in words as well as in images and sound. For more on Web design for readers with disabilities, visit the American Council for the Blind at *acb.org/accessible-formats.html* and the World Wide Web Consortium at *www.w3.org/WAI*.

1 Using HTML

Most Web pages are created using hypertext markup language, or HTML, and an HTML editor. The HTML editing program inserts command codes into your document that achieve the effects you want when the material appears on the Web.

From the user's point of view, most HTML editors work much as word processors do, with similar options for sizing, formatting, and highlighting copy and with a display that shows what you will see in the final version. Indeed, you can compose a Web page without bothering at all about the behind-the-scenes HTML coding. As you gain experience with Web building, however, you may want to create more sophisticated pages by editing the codes themselves.

2 Creating online papers

When a teacher asks you to post a paper to a Web site, you can compose it on your word processor and then use the Save As HTML function available on most programs to translate it into a Web page. After translating the paper, your word processor should allow you to modify some of the elements on the page, or you can open the translated document in an HTML editor. The illustration below shows the opening screen of a student's project for a composition class.

Paper submitted on the Web

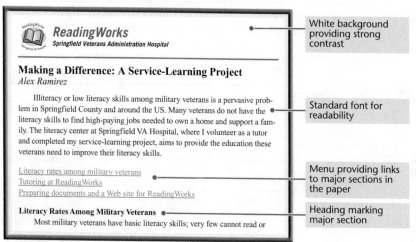

ReadingWorks
Springfield Veterans Administration Hospital

Making a Difference: A Service-Learning Project
Alex Ramirez

   Illiteracy or low literacy skills among military veterans is a pervasive problem in Springfield County and around the US. Many veterans do not have the literacy skills to find high-paying jobs needed to own a home and support a family. The literacy center at Springfield VA Hospital, where I volunteer as a tutor and completed my service-learning project, aims to provide the education these veterans need to improve their literacy skills.

Literacy rates among military veterans
Tutoring at ReadingWorks
Preparing documents and a Web site for ReadingWorks

Literacy Rates Among Military Veterans
   Most military veterans have basic literacy skills; very few cannot read or

White background providing strong contrast

Standard font for readability

Menu providing links to major sections in the paper

Heading marking major section

---

3 Creating original sites

When you create an original Web site, you need to be aware that Web readers generally alternate between skimming pages for highlights and focusing intently on sections of text. To facilitate this kind of reading, you'll want to consider the guidelines on pages 796–98 for handling text and also your site's structure and content, flow, ease of navigation, and use of images, video, and sound.

Structure and content

Organize your site so that it efficiently arranges your content and also orients readers:

- **Sketch possible site plans before getting started.** (See p. 797 for an example.) Your aim is to develop a sense of the major components of your project and to create a logical space for each component.

- **Consider how menus on the site's pages can provide overviews of the organization as well as direct access to the pages.** The Web site on the next page includes a menu on the left side of the page.

- **Treat the first few sentences of any page as a get-acquainted space for you and your readers.** In the sample on the next page, the text hooks readers with questions and orients them with general information.

■ **Distill your text so that it includes only essential information.** Concise prose is essential in any writing situation, of course. But Web readers expect to scan text quickly and, in any event, have difficulty following long text passages on a computer screen.

Original Web site

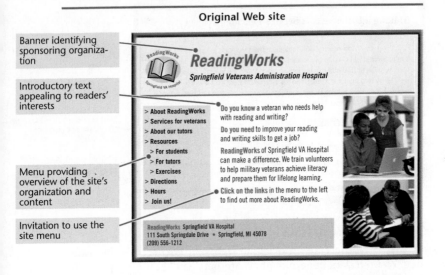

Banner identifying sponsoring organization

Introductory text appealing to readers' interests

Menu providing overview of the site's organization and content

Invitation to use the site menu

ReadingWorks
Springfield Veterans Administration Hospital

> About ReadingWorks
> Services for veterans
> About our tutors
> Resources
> For students
> For tutors
> Exercises
> Directions
> Hours
> Join us!

Do you know a veteran who needs help with reading and writing?

Do you need to improve your reading and writing skills to get a job?

ReadingWorks of Springfield VA Hospital can make a difference. We train volunteers to help military veterans achieve literacy and prepare them for lifelong learning.

Click on the links in the menu to the left to find out more about ReadingWorks.

ReadingWorks Springfield VA Hospital
111 South Springdale Drive • Springfield, MI 45078
(209) 556-1212

Flow

Beginning Web authors sometimes start at the top of the page and then add element upon element until information proceeds down the screen much as it would in a printed document. However, by thinking about how information will flow on a page, you can take better advantage of the Web's visual nature:

■ **Standardize elements of your design to create expectations in readers and to fulfill those expectations.** For instance, develop a uniform style for the main headings of pages, for headings within pages, and for menus.

■ **Make scanning easy for readers.** Focus readers on crucial text by adding space around it. Add headings to break up text and to highlight content. Use lists to reinforce the parallel importance of items. (See pp. 118–22 for more on all these design elements.)

Easy navigation

A Web site of more than a few pages requires a menu on every page so that readers can navigate the site. Like the table of contents in a book, a menu lists the features of the site, giving its plan at a glance. By clicking on any item in the list, readers can go directly to a page that interests them.

You can embed a menu at the top, side, or bottom of a page. Menus at the top or side are best on short pages because they will not scroll off the screen as readers move down the page. On longer pages, menus at the bottom prevent readers from dead-ending—that is, reaching a point where they can't easily move forward or backward. You can also use a combination of menus.

In designing a menu, keep it simple: many different type fonts and colors will overwhelm readers instead of orienting them. And make the menus look the same from one page to the next so that readers recognize them easily.

Images, video, and sound

Exploring the Web, you'll see that site designers have taken advantage of the Web's ability to handle multimedia elements—images, video, and sound. Most Web readers expect at least some enhancement of text.

Note See pages 613–14 on observing copyright restrictions with images, video, and sound.

Images

Several guidelines can help you use images effectively in your Web compositions:

- **Use visual elements for a purpose.** They should supplement or replace text, highlight important features, and direct the flow of information. Don't use them for their own sake, as mere decoration.
- **Compose descriptions of images that relate them to your text.** Don't ask the elements to convey your meaning by themselves.
- **Provide alternative descriptions of images** to give a sense of them to readers with vision loss or readers whose Web browsers can't display them.

Video and sound

Video and sound files can provide information that is simply unavailable in printed documents. For instance, as part of a film review you might place a short clip from the film on your Web page and then provide a close reading of the clip. Or as part of a project on a controversial issue you might provide links to sound files containing political speeches.

Before you incorporate video and sound into your Web compositions, make certain that they have a legitimate purpose. They should add essential information that can't be provided in any other medium, and they should be well integrated with the rest of your composition.

Sources

For the multimedia elements in a Web composition, you can use your own or obtain them from other sources:

- **Create your own graphs, diagrams, and other illustrations using a graphics program.** See pages 122–26 for tips on creating effective images.
- **Incorporate your own artwork, photographs, video clips, and sound recordings.** You may be able to find the needed equipment and software at your school's computer lab.
- **Obtain icons, photographs, video, and other multimedia elements from other electronic sources.** Be sure to acknowledge your sources and to obtain reprint permission if needed (see pp. 612–14).

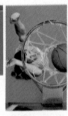

55

Public Writing

Writing outside of school, such as for business or for community work, resembles academic writing in many ways. It usually involves the same basic writing process, discussed in Part 1: assessing the writing situation, developing what you want to say, freely working out your meaning in a draft, and editing and revising so that your writing will achieve your purpose with readers. It often involves research, as discussed in Part 9. And it involves the standards of conciseness, appropriate and exact language, and correct grammar and usage discussed in Parts 3–8.

But public writing has its own conventions, too. They vary widely depending on what you're writing and why, whether it is a proposal for a school club or a flyer announcing a dinner for a community group. This chapter covers several types of public writing: business letters and memos (next page); job applications (p. 809); business

my**comp**lab

Visit *mycomplab.com* for more resources as well as exercises on job applications, business reports, and other kinds of public writing.

reports and proposals (p. 811); and flyers, newsletters, and brochures for community work (p. 814).

Note Chapter 5 discusses type fonts, headings, illustrations, and other elements of document design. In addition, a word processor's wizards or templates can help you format documents such as letters, résumés, and brochures. Before using such a tool, be sure the format is appropriate for your writing situation. And remember that a formatting tool can do nothing to help you express your ideas effectively.

CULTURE LANGUAGE Public writing in the United States, especially in business, favors efficiency. If you are accustomed to public writing in another culture, the US style may seem abrupt or impolite. A business letter elsewhere may be expected to begin with polite questions about the addressee or with compliments for the addressee's company, whereas US business letters are expected to get right to the point. (See the sample letters in this chapter for examples.)

55a Writing business letters and memos

When you write in business, you are addressing busy people who want to see quickly why you are writing and how they should respond to you. A wordy letter or a memo with grammatical errors may prevent you from getting what you want, either because the reader cannot understand your wish or because you present yourself poorly.

In all business writing, follow these general guidelines:

- **State your purpose right at the start.**
- **Be straightforward, clear, concise, objective, and courteous.**
- **Observe conventions of grammar and usage,** which make your writing clear and impress your reader with your care.

The formats of business letters and memos are fairly standardized and are thus expected by your correspondents.

1 Using a standard format for letters

Use either unlined white paper measuring $8\frac{1}{2}$" × 11" or what is called letterhead stationery with your address printed at the top of the sheet. Type the letter single-spaced, with double space between elements, on only one side of a sheet.

The two most common forms for business letters—the full block and the modified block—are illustrated on the next page and on page 809, respectively. Annotations on the samples indicate spacing, margins, and other aspects of format.

Business letter (block style)

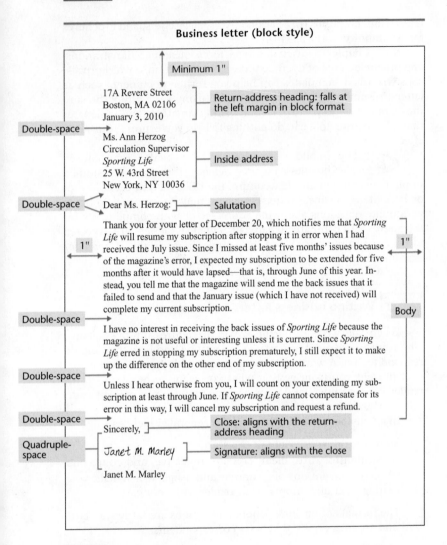

The letter

Return-address heading Unless you're using letterhead stationery, the return-address heading of the letter gives your address (but not your name) and the date. If you are using letterhead, you need add only the date.

Inside address The inside address shows the name, title, and complete address of the person you are writing to. (See p. 806 for abbreviations of state names.)

Salutation The salutation greets the addressee. Whenever possible, address your letter to a specific person. (Call the company or department to ask whom to address.) If you can't find a person's name, then use a job title (*Dear Human Resources Manager, Dear Customer Service Manager*) or use a general salutation (*Dear Smythe Shoes*). Use *Ms.* as the title for a woman when she has no other title, when you don't know how she prefers to be addressed, or when you know that she prefers to be addressed as *Ms.* If you know a woman prefers to be addressed as *Mrs.* or *Miss*, use the appropriate title.

Body The body of the letter, containing its substance, begins at the left margin in both letter styles. Instead of indenting the first line of each paragraph, place an extra line of space between paragraphs so that they are readily visible.

Close The letter's close should reflect the level of formality in the salutation. For formal letters, *Cordially, Yours truly,* and *Sincerely* are common closes. For less formal letters, you may choose to use *Regards, Best wishes,* or the like. Only the first word of the close is capitalized, and the close is followed by a comma.

Signature The signature of a business letter falls below the close and has two parts. One is your name typed on the fourth line below the close. The other is your handwritten signature, which fills the space between the close and your typed name. The signature should consist only of your name, as you sign checks and other documents.

Other information Below the signature at the left margin, you may want to include additional information such as *Enc. 3* (indicating that there are three enclosures with the letter) or *cc: Margaret Newton* (indicating that a copy is being sent to the person named).

The envelope

The envelope should accommodate the letter once it is folded horizontally in thirds. The next page shows the common Postal Service abbreviations for addresses.

Envelope for a business letter

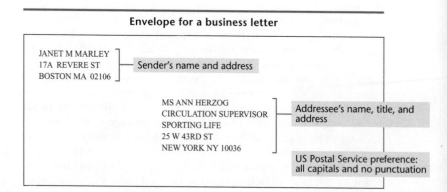

Street names

Avenue	AVE	Expressway	EXPY	Road	RD
Boulevard	BLVD	Freeway	FWY	Square	SQ
Circle	CIR	Lane	LN	Street	ST
Court	CT	Parkway	PKY	Turnpike	TPKE

Compass points

North	N	West	W	Southwest	SW
East	E	Northeast	NE	Northwest	NW

State names

Alabama	AL	Kentucky	KY	North Dakota	ND
Alaska	AK	Louisiana	LA	Ohio	OH
Arizona	AZ	Maine	ME	Oklahoma	OK
Arkansas	AR	Maryland	MD	Oregon	OR
California	CA	Massachusetts	MA	Pennsylvania	PA
Colorado	CO	Michigan	MI	Puerto Rico	PR
Connecticut	CT	Minnesota	MN	Rhode Island	RI
Delaware	DE	Mississippi	MS	South Carolina	SC
District of		Missouri	MO	South Dakota	SD
Columbia	DC	Montana	MT	Tennessee	TN
Florida	FL	Nebraska	NE	Texas	TX
Georgia	GA	Nevada	NV	Utah	UT
Hawaii	HI	New		Vermont	VT
Idaho	ID	Hampshire	NH	Virginia	VA
Illinois	IL	New Jersey	NJ	Washington	WA
Indiana	IN	New Mexico	NM	West Virginia	WV
Iowa	IA	New York	NY	Wisconsin	WI
Kansas	KS	North Carolina	NC	Wyoming	WY

2 Writing requests and complaints

Letters requesting something—for instance, a pamphlet, information about a product, a T-shirt advertised in a magazine—must be specific and accurate about the item you are requesting. The letter should describe the item completely and, if applicable, include a copy or description of the advertisement or other source that prompted your request.

Letters complaining about a product or a service (such as a wrong billing from a wireless company) should be written in a reasonable but firm tone. (See the sample letter on p. 804.) Assume that the addressee is willing to resolve the problem when he or she has the relevant information. In the first sentence of the letter, say what you are writing about. Then provide as much background as needed, including any relevant details from past correspondence (as in the sample letter). Describe exactly what you see as the problem, sticking to facts and avoiding discourse on the company's social responsibility or your low opinion of its management. In the clearest and fewest possible words and sentences, proceed directly from one point to the next without repeating yourself. Always include your opinion of how the problem can be solved. Many companies are required by law to establish a specific procedure for complaints about products and services. If you know of such a procedure, be sure to follow it.

3 | Writing business memos

Unlike business letters, which address people in other organizations, business memorandums (memos, for short) address people within the same organization. A memo can be quite long, but more often it deals briefly with a specific topic, such as an answer to a

---

Business memo

Bigelow Wax Company

TO: Aileen Rosen, Director of Sales
FROM: Patricia Phillips, Territory 12   *PP*
DATE: March 17, 2010
SUBJECT: 2009 sales of Quick Wax in Territory 12

> Heading: company's name, addressee's name, writer's name and initials, date, and subject description

Since it was introduced in January 2009, Quick Wax has been unsuccessful in Territory 12 and has not affected the sales of our Easy Shine. Discussions with customers and my own analysis of Quick Wax suggest three reasons for its failure to compete with our product.

> Body: single-spaced with double spacing between paragraphs; paragraphs not indented

1. Quick Wax has not received the promotion necessary for a new product. Advertising—primarily on radio—has been sporadic and has not developed a clear, consistent image for the product. In addition, the Quick Wax sales representative in Territory 12 is new and inexperienced; he is not known to customers, and his sales pitch (which I once overheard) is weak. As far as I can tell, his efforts are not supported by phone calls or mailings from his home office.

2. When Quick Wax does make it to the store shelves, buyers do not choose it over our product. Though priced competitively with our product, Quick Wax is poorly packaged. The container seems smaller than ours, though in fact it holds the same eight ounces. The lettering on the Quick Wax package (red on blue) is difficult to read, in contrast to the white-on-green lettering on the Easy Shine package.

3. Our special purchase offers and my increased efforts to serve existing customers have had the intended effect of keeping customers satisfied with our product and reducing their inclination to stock something new.

Copies: L. Mendes, Director of Marketing
　　　　J. MacGregor, Customer Service Manager

> People receiving copies

question, a progress report, or an evaluation. Both the content and the format of a memo aim to get to the point and dispose of it quickly. See the sample on the preceding page for the format of a memo. Use the following tips to make a memo's content effective:

- **State your reason for writing in the first sentence.** You might outline a problem, make a request, refer to a request that prompted the memo, or briefly summarize new findings. Do not, however, waste words with expressions like *The purpose of this memo is. . . .*

- **Devote the first paragraph to a succinct presentation of your solution, recommendation, answer, or evaluation.** The first paragraph should be short, and by its end your reader should know precisely what to expect from the rest of the memo: the details and reasoning that support your conclusion.

- **Deliver the support in the body of the memo.** The paragraphs may be numbered or bulleted so that the main divisions of your message are easy to see. In a long memo, you may need headings (see p. 121).

- **Suit your style and tone to your audience.** For instance, you'll want to address your boss or a large group of readers more formally than you would a coworker who is also a friend.

- **Write concisely.** Keep your sentences short and your language simple, using technical terms only when your readers will understand them. Say only what readers need to know.

4 | Communicating electronically

Electronic communication—mainly e-mail and faxes—adds a few twists to business writing. E-mail plays such a prominent role in communication of all sorts that we discuss it extensively as part of writing online (see pp. 790–93). Generally, the standards for business e-mail are the same as for other business correspondence.

Faxes follow closely the formats of print documents, but there are some unique concerns:

- **Consider legibility.** Small type, photographs, horizontal lines, and other elements that look fine on your copy may not be legible to the addressee.

- **Include a cover sheet.** Most faxes require a cover sheet with the addressee's name, company, and fax number; the date, time, and subject; your own name and fax and telephone numbers; and the total number of pages (including the cover sheet) in the fax.

- **Advise your addressee to expect a fax.** The advice is essential if the fax is confidential, because the machine is often shared.

- **Consider urgency.** Transmission by fax can imply that the correspondence is urgent. If yours isn't, you may want to use the mail instead.

55b Writing a job application

In applying for an internship or a job or requesting a job interview, send both a résumé and a cover letter. If you need to submit your application electronically, see pages 810–12.

1 Writing the cover letter

The cover letter should be formatted in block style (p. 804) or modified block style (below). In composing the letter, use the sample below and the guidelines on the next page.

Job-application letter (modified block style)

Return-address heading: falls to the right of center in modified block format —

3712 Swiss Avenue
Dallas, TX 75204
March 2, 2009

Raymond Chipault
Human Resources Manager
Dallas News
Communications Center
Dallas, TX 75222

Dear Mr. Chipault:

In response to your posting in the English Department of Southern Methodist University, I am applying for the summer job of part-time editorial assistant for the *Dallas News*.

I am now enrolled at Southern Methodist University as a sophomore, with a dual major in English literature and journalism. My courses so far have included news reporting, copy editing, and electronic publishing. I worked a summer as a copy aide for my hometown newspaper, and for two years I have edited and written sports stories and features for the university newspaper. My feature articles cover subjects as diverse as campus elections, parking regulations, visiting professors, and speech codes.

As the enclosed résumé and writing samples indicate, my education and knowledge of newspaper work prepare me for the opening you have.

I am available for an interview at your convenience and would be happy to show more samples of my writing. Please e-mail me at ianirv@mail.smu .edu or call me at 214-744-3816.

Close and signature: align with the return-address heading —

Sincerely,

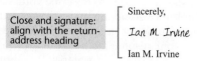

Ian M. Irvine

Enc.

- **Interpret your résumé for the particular job.** Don't detail your entire résumé, reciting your job history. Instead, highlight and reshape only the relevant parts.
- **Announce at the outset what job you seek and how you heard about it.**
- **Include any special reason you have for applying,** such as a specific career goal.
- **Summarize your qualifications for this particular job,** including relevant facts about education and employment and emphasizing notable accomplishments. Mention that additional information appears in an accompanying résumé.
- **Describe your availability.** At the end of the letter, mention that you are free for an interview at the convenience of the addressee, or specify when you will be available (for instance, when your current job or classes leave you free).

2 Writing and formatting the résumé

The résumé that accompanies your letter of application should provide information in table format that allows a potential employer to evaluate your qualifications. The résumé should include your name and address, a career objective, your education and employment history, special skills or awards, and information about how to obtain your references. All the information should fit on one uncrowded page unless your education and experience are extensive. See the sample on the next page for writing and formatting guidelines for a résumé that you submit in print.

Employers may ask for an electronic version of your résumé so that they can add it to a computerized database of applicants. The employers may scan your printed résumé to convert it to an electronic file, which they can then store in an appropriate database. Or they may ask you to provide the résumé electronically, either attaching it to or embedding it in an e-mail message. If an employer requests a scannable or electronic résumé, use the following guidelines and consult the sample on page 812.

- **Keep the design simple for accurate scanning or electronic transmittal.** Avoid images, unusual type, more than one column, vertical or horizontal lines, italics, and underlining.
- **Use concise, specific words to describe your skills and experience.** The employer's computer may use keywords (often nouns) to identify the résumés of suitable job candidates, and you want to ensure that your résumé includes the appropriate keywords. Name your specific skills—for example, the computer programs you can operate—and write concretely with words like *manager* (not *person with responsibility for*) and *reporter* (not *staff member*

Résumé (print)

Ian M. Irvine

3712 Swiss Avenue
Dallas, TX 75204
214-744-3816
ianirv@mail.smu.edu

Name and contact information

Position desired Part-time editorial assistant.

Career objective stated simply and clearly

Education *Southern Methodist University*, 2007 to present.
Current standing: sophomore.
Major: English literature and journalism.
Journalism courses: news reporting, copy editing, electronic publishing, communication arts, broadcast journalism.

Abilene (Texas) Senior High School, 2003-07.
Graduated with academic, college-preparatory degree.

Education before work experience for most high school and college students

Employment history 2007 to present. Reporter, *Daily Campus*, student newspaper of Southern Methodist University.
Write regular coverage of baseball, track, and soccer teams. Write feature stories on campus policies and events. Edit sports news, campus listings, features.

Summer 2008. Copy aide, *Abilene Reporter-News*.
Assisted reporters with copy routing and research.

Summer 2007. Painter, Longhorn Painters, Abilene.
Prepared and painted exteriors and interiors of houses.

Headings marking sections, set off with space and highlighting

Conventional use of capital letters: yes for proper nouns and after periods; no for job titles, course names, department names, and so on

Special skills Fluent in Spanish.
Proficient in Internet research and word processing.

References Available on request:

Placement Office
Southern Methodist University
Dallas, TX 75275

Standard, consistent type font

who reports). Look for likely keywords in the employer's description of the job you seek.

55c Writing business reports and proposals

Reports and proposals are text-heavy documents, sometimes lengthy, that convey information such as the results of research, a plan for action, or a recommendation for change. As with other

Résumé (scannable or electronic)

Ian M. Irvine
3712 Swiss Avenue
Dallas, TX 75204
214-744-3816
ianirv@mail.smu.edu

KEYWORDS: Editor, editorial assistant, publishing, electronic publishing.

OBJECTIVE
Part-time editorial assistant.

EDUCATION
Southern Methodist University, 2007 to present.
Major: English literature and journalism.
Journalism courses: news reporting, copy editing, electronic publishing, communication arts, broadcast journalism.

Abilene (Texas) Senior High School, 2003-07.
Academic, college preparatory degree.

EMPLOYMENT HISTORY
Reporter, Daily Campus, Southern Methodist University, 2007 to present.
Writer of articles for student newspaper on sports teams, campus policies, and local events. Editor of sports news, campus listings, and features.

Copy aide, Abilene Reporter-News, Abilene, summer 2008.
Assistant to reporters, routing copy and doing research.

Painter, Longhorn Painters, Abilene, summer 2007.
Preparation and painting of exteriors and interiors of houses.

SPECIAL SKILLS
Fluent in Spanish.
Proficient in Internet research and word processing.

REFERENCES
Available on request:
Placement Office
Southern Methodist University
Dallas, TX 75275

Margin annotations:

Accurate keywords, allowing the employer to place the résumé into an appropriate database

Simple design, avoiding unusual type, italics, multiple columns, decorative lines, and images

Standard font easily read by scanners

Every line aligning at left margin

---

business correspondence, you will prepare a report or proposal for a specific purpose, addressing interested but busy readers.

Reports and proposals usually divide into sections. The sections vary depending on purpose, but often they include a summary, which tells the reader what the document is about; a statement of the problem or need, which justifies the report or proposal; a statement of the plan or solution, which responds to the problem or need; and a recommendation or evaluation. Consider the following guidelines and the samples opposite and on page 814.

- **Do your research.** The standard formats of reports and proposals require you to be well informed, so be alert to where you have enough information or where you don't.
- **Focus on the purpose of each section.** Stick to the point of each section, saying only what you need to say, even if you have additional information. Each section should accomplish its purpose and contribute to the whole.
- **Follow an appropriate format.** In many businesses, reports and proposals have specific formatting requirements. If you are unsure about the requirements, ask your supervisor.

Report

Canada Geese at ABC Institute: An Environmental Problem

Summary
The flock of Canada geese on and around ABC Institute's grounds has grown dramatically in recent years to become a nuisance and an environmental problem. This report reviews the problem, considers possible solutions, and proposes that ABC Institute and the US Fish and Wildlife Service cooperate to reduce the flock by humane means.

The Problem
Canada geese began living at Taylor Lake next to ABC Institute when they were relocated there in 1985 by the state game department. As a nonmigratory flock, the geese are present year-round, with the highest population each year occurring in early spring. In recent years the flock has grown dramatically. The Audubon Society's annual Christmas bird census shows a thirty-fold increase from the 37 geese counted in 1986 to the 1125 counted in 2009.

The principal environmental problem caused by the geese is pollution of grass and water by defecation. Geese droppings cover the ABC Institute's grounds as well as the park's picnicking areas. The runoff from these droppings into Taylor Lake has substantially affected the quality of the lake's water, so that local authorities have twice (2007 and 2008) issued warnings against swimming.

Possible Solutions
The goose overpopulation and resulting environmental problems have several possible solutions:

- Harass the geese with dogs and audiovisual effects (light and noise) so that the geese choose to leave. This solution is inhumane to the geese and unpleasant for human neighbors.
- Feed the geese a chemical that will weaken the shells of their eggs and thus reduce growth of the flock. This solution is inhumane to the geese and also impractical, because geese are long-lived.
- Kill adult geese. This solution is, obviously, inhumane to the geese.
- Thin the goose population by trapping and removing many geese (perhaps 600) to areas less populated by humans, such as wildlife preserves.

Though costly (see figures below), the last solution is the most humane. It would be harmless to the geese, provided that sizable netted enclosures are used for traps. [Discussion of solution and "Recommendations" section follow.]

Annotations: Descriptive title conveying report's contents. Standard format: summary, statement of the problem, solutions, and (not shown) recommendations. Major sections delineated by headings. Formal tone, appropriate to a business-writing situation. Single spacing with double spacing between paragraphs and around the list. Bulleted list emphasizing alternative solutions.

Internal proposal

Memo format for internal proposal (p. 807)

Springfield Veterans Administration Hospital

To: Jefferson Green, Director, Finance and Operations
From: Kate Goodman, Director, ReadingWorks *KG*
Date: March 5, 2009
Subject: Budget proposal for ReadingWorks Awards Dinner

OVERVIEW

"Overview": statement of proposal

ReadingWorks requests funding for an awards dinner.

NEED

"Need": justification for the request

ReadingWorks, the literacy center operated by Springfield VA Hospital, has for 6 years served between 50 and 70 patients/students a year with a small paid staff and a corps of dedicated volunteers. In the past year the center's paid staff and 20 volunteers provided more than 1260 hours of literacy tutoring to 67 students, an increase of 14 students over last year. I want to recognize the efforts and accomplishments of our students and tutors by holding an awards dinner for them and their families.

Formal tone appropriate for a proposal

PLAN

"Plan": explanation of request

I propose the following event for Friday, May 22, 7:30 to 10:30 PM: dinner and nonalcoholic beverages for approximately 135 students, tutors, and their guests; entertainment; and certificates for approximately 20 students and tutors. I request the use of Suite 42 because it can accommodate as many as 200 people as well as caterers and a DJ. Hospital staff will need to have the room ready by 6:00 PM on May 22.

BUDGET

"Budget" and "Personnel": details on the proposal's requirements

Dinner and beverages for about 135 attendees	$2700
Music for two hours	200
Certificates	50
TOTAL	$2950

Bids from local businesses are attached.

PERSONNEL

Single spacing with double spacing between sections

Five hospital employees will be needed to set up, take down, and clean Suite 42 before and after the dinner.

55d Writing for community work

At some point in your life, you're likely to volunteer for a community organization such as a soup kitchen, a daycare center, a literacy program, or a tutoring center for immigrants learning English. Some high school and college classes involve service learning, in which you do such volunteer work, write about the experience for your course, and write *for* the organization you're helping.

Flyer

FIRST ANNUAL AWARDS DINNER

ReadingWorks
Springfield VA Hospital

Large type and color focusing a distant reader's attention on important information: what's happening, when, where, and who is invited

White space drawing viewers' eyes to main message and creating flow among elements

WHEN
Friday night
May 22
7:30 to 10:30

**For information
contact ReadingWorks
209-556-1212**

WHERE
Suite 42
Springfield VA Hospital

WHO
Students, tutors, and their families are invited to join us for an evening of food and music as we celebrate their efforts and accomplishments.

Color highlighting only key information

ReadingWorks of Springfield Veterans Administration Hospital
111 South Springdale Drive
Springfield, MI 45078

Less important information set in smaller type

The writing you do for a community group may range from flyers (above) to newsletters and brochures (next two pages). Two guidelines in particular will help you prepare effective projects:

- **Craft each document for its purpose and audience.** You are trying to achieve a specific aim with your readers, and the approach and tone you use will influence their responses. If, for example, you are writing letters to local businesses to raise funds for a homeless shelter, bring to mind the people who will read your letter. How can you best persuade those readers to donate money?

■ **Expect to work with others.** Much public writing is the work of more than one person. Even if you draft the document on your own, others will review the content, tone, and design. Such collaboration is rewarding, but it sometimes requires patience and goodwill. See pages 69–72 and 793–96 for advice on collaborating.

The illustrations in this section show documents prepared for ReadingWorks, a literacy program. See also pages 803–08 and 811–14 on business letters, memos, and proposals, as well as pages 823–25 on *PowerPoint* presentations.

Newsletter

Multicolumn format allowing room for headings, articles, and other elements on a single page

Two-column heading emphasizing the main article

Elements helping readers skim for highlights: spacing, varied font sizes, lines, and a bulleted list

Color focusing readers' attention on banner, headlines, and table of contents

Lively but uncluttered overall appearance

Box in the first column highlighting table of contents

 ReadingWorks

Springfield Veterans Administration Hospital   **SUMMER 2009**

From the director

Can you help? With more and more learners in the ReadingWorks program, we need more and more tutors. You may know people who would be interested in participating in the program, if only they knew about it.

Those of you who have been tutoring VA patients in reading and writing know both the great need you fulfill and the great benefits you bring to the students. New tutors need no special skills—we'll provide the training—only patience and an interest in helping others.

We've scheduled an orientation meeting for Friday, September 12, at 6:30 PM. Please come and bring a friend who is willing to contribute a couple of hours a week to our work.

Thanks,
Kate Goodman

IN THIS ISSUE

FIRST ANNUAL AWARDS DINNER

A festive night for students and tutors

The first annual ReadingWorks Awards Dinner on May 22nd was a great success. Springfield's own Golden Fork provided tasty food and Amber Allen supplied lively music. The students decorated Suite 42 on the theme of books and reading. In all, 127 people attended.

The highlight of the night was the awards ceremony. Nine students, recommended by their tutors, received certificates recognizing their efforts and special accomplishments in learning to read and write:

Ramon Berva
Edward Byar
David Dunbar
Tony Garnier
Chris Guigni
Akili Haynes
Josh Livingston
Alex Obeld
B. J. Resnansky

In addition, nine tutors received certificates commemorating five years of service to ReadingWorks:

Anita Crumpton
Felix Cruz-Rivera
Bette Elgen
Kayleah Bortoluzzi
Harriotte Henderson
Ben Obiso
Meggie Puente
Max Smith
Sara Villante

Congratulations to all!

PTSD: New Guidelines

Most of us are working with veterans who have been diagnosed with post-traumatic stress disorder. Because this disorder is often complicated by alcoholism, depression, anxiety, and other problems, the National Center for PTSD has issued some guidelines for helping PTSD patients in ways that reduce their stress.

- The hospital must know your tutoring schedule, and you need to sign in and out before and after each tutoring session.

- To protect patients' privacy, meet them only in designated visiting and tutoring areas, never in their rooms.

- Treat patients with dignity and respect, even when (as sometimes happens) they grow frustrated and angry. Seek help from a nurse or orderly if you need it.

Brochure

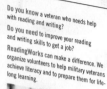

Do you know a veteran who needs help with reading and writing?

Do you need to improve your reading and writing skills to get a job?

ReadingWorks can make a difference. We organize volunteers to help military veterans achieve literacy and to prepare them for life-long learning.

For more information about our services, call Kate Goodman at 209-556-1212 or visit www.readingworks.org.

ReadingWorks
Springfield VA Hospital
111 South Springdale Drive
Springfield, MI 45078

ReadingWorks
Springfield VA Hospital

Helping
military
veterans
achieve
literacy

Panel 2: The right page when the cover is opened, the first one readers see, containing key information

Panel 6: The back, usually including the return address and space for a mailing label and postage

Panel 1: The cover, drawing readers' attention to the group's name, purpose, and affiliation

 ReadingWorks
Springfield VA Hospital

OUR MISSION
- We provide workshops and formal lessons for veterans wishing to develop their reading and writing skills
- We train volunteers to tutor veterans one on one.
- We maintain outreach programs to provide access to literacy training for all veterans.
- We create literacy resources and share them with others who promote literacy for veterans.

OUR SERVICES
One-on-one tutoring
One to three hours a week with a trained volunteer tutor.

Workshops and classes
Small-group meetings centered on reading and writing, computer skills, and English as a second language.

Library
Books and other resources for students at various literacy levels.

Computer lab
Five computers with high-speed Internet access and a full range of software.

OUR TUTORS
The goodwill and generosity of our volunteer tutors allows us to reach out to those who have served our country.

If you or someone you know can join our team, contact Kate Goodman at 209-556-1212.

Hours
12:00 to 8:00, Mon., Wed.
9:00 to 5:00, Tues., Thurs., Fri.

Eligibility
Any veteran of the US military is eligible for our services.

How to reach us
Springfield VA Hospital
Room 172, first floor
111 South Springdale Drive
Springfield, MI 45078

209-556-1212
www.readingworks.org

Panel 3: The left page when the cover is opened, reinforcing the message of panel 2

Varied type, color, and photographs, adding visual interest and focusing readers' attention

Panels 4 and 5: The inside panels, containing contact information and other details

56
Oral Presentations

At some point during your education or your work, you will probably be called on to speak to a group. Oral presentation can be anxiety producing, even for those who are experienced at it. This chapter shows you how you can apply your experiences as a writer to public speaking, and it offers some techniques that are uniquely appropriate for effective oral presentations.

56a Writing and speaking

Writing and speechmaking have much in common: both require careful consideration of your subject, purpose, and audience. Thus the mental and physical activities that go into the writing process can also help you prepare and deliver a successful oral presentation.

Despite many similarities, however, writing for readers is not the same as speaking to listeners. Whereas a reader can go back and reread a written message, a listener cannot stop a speech to re-hear a section. Several studies have reported that immediately after hearing a short talk, most listeners cannot recall half of what was said.

Effective speakers adapt to their audience's listening ability by reinforcing their ideas through repetition and restatement. They use simple words, short sentences, personal pronouns, contractions, and colloquial expressions. In formal writing, these strategies might seem redundant and too informal; but in speaking, they improve listeners' comprehension.

56b Considering purpose and audience

The most important step in developing an oral presentation is to identify your purpose: what do you want your audience to know or do as a result of your speech? Topic and purpose are *not* the same thing. Asking *What am I talking about?* is not the same as asking *Why am I speaking?*

mycomplab

Visit *mycomplab.com* for more resources as well as exercises on oral presentations and *PowerPoint*.

Checklist for an oral presentation

- **Purpose:** What do you want your audience to know or do as a result of your presentation? How can you achieve your purpose in the time and setting you've been given? (See the previous page and below.)
- **Audience:** What do you know about the characteristics and opinions of your audience? How can this information help you adapt your presentation to your audience's interests, needs, and opinions? (See below and the next page.)
- **Content:** What is the main point of your speech? Can you summarize it in one sentence? Are your supporting points relevant and interesting? Do they relate clearly to your topic and audience? (See p. 821.)
- **Organization:** How are your ideas arranged? Where might listeners have difficulty following you? What functions do your introduction and conclusion perform? (See the next page.)
- **Method of delivery:** What method of delivery do you plan: extemporaneous? reading from a text? memorized? a mixture? How does your method suit the purpose, setting, and occasion of your presentation? (See pp. 821–23.)
- **Speech delivery:** In rehearsing your presentation, what do you perceive as your strengths and weaknesses? Is your voice suitably loud for the setting? Are you speaking clearly? Are you able to move your eyes around the room so that you'll be making eye contact during the presentation? Is your posture straight but not stiff? Do your gestures reinforce your ideas? Do you use visual aids appropriately? (See pp. 823–25.)
- **Confidence and credibility:** What techniques will you use to overcome the inevitable anxiety about speaking? How will you project your confidence and competence? (See pp. 825–26.)

In school and work settings, oral presentations may include anything from a five-minute report before a few peers to an hour-long address before a hundred people. Whatever the situation, you're likely to be speaking for the same reasons that you write in school or at work: to explain something to listeners or to persuade listeners to accept your opinion or take an action. See pages 10–12 for more on these purposes.

Adapting to your audience is a critical task in public speaking as well as in writing. You'll want to consider the questions about audience on page 14. But a listening audience requires additional considerations as well:

- **Why is your audience assembled?** Listeners who attend because they want to hear you and your ideas may be easier to interest and motivate than listeners who are required to attend.

- **How large is your audience?** With a small group you can be informal. If you are speaking to a hundred or more people, you may need a public address system, a lectern, special lighting, and audiovisual equipment.
- **Where will you speak?** Your approach should match the setting—more casual for a small classroom, more formal for an auditorium.
- **How long are you scheduled to speak?** Whatever the time limit, stick to it. Audiences lose patience with someone who speaks longer than expected.

When speaking, unlike when writing, you can see and hear your audience's responses during your presentation. If you sense that an audience is bored, try to spice up your presentation. If an audience is restless, consult your watch to make sure you have not gone over your time. If you sense resistance, try to make midspeech adjustments to respond to that resistance.

56c Organizing the presentation

An effective oral presentation, like an effective essay, has a recognizable shape. The advice in Chapter 2 for organizing and outlining an essay serves the speechmaker as well as the writer (see pp. 35–45). Here are additional considerations for the introduction, conclusion, and supporting material.

1 The introduction

First impressions count. A strong beginning establishes an important relationship among three elements in an oral presentation: you, your topic, and your audience. More specifically, the beginning of an oral presentation should try to accomplish three goals:

- **Gain the audience's attention and interest.** Begin with a question, an unusual example or statistic, or a short, relevant story.
- **Put yourself in the speech.** If you demonstrate your expertise, experience, or concern, your audience will be more interested in what you say and more trusting of you.
- **Introduce and preview your topic and purpose.** By the time your introduction is over, listeners should know what your topic is and the direction in which you wish to take them as you develop your ideas.

In addition to these guidelines for beginning a speech, there are some important pitfalls to avoid:

- **Don't try to cram too much into your introduction.** Focus on engaging the audience and quickly previewing your talk.
- **Don't begin with an apology.** A statement such as *I wish I'd been given more time to get ready for this presentation* will only undermine your listeners' confidence in you.
- **Don't begin with** *My speech is about. . . .* The statement is dull, and it does little to clarify purpose.

2 Supporting material

Just as you do when writing, you can and should use facts, statistics, examples, and expert opinions to support spoken arguments (see pp. 181–83). In addition, as a speaker you can draw on other kinds of supporting material:

- **Use vivid description.** Paint a mental image of a scene, a concept, an event, or a person.
- **Use well-chosen quotations.** They can add an emotional or humorous moment to your speech.
- **Use true or fictional stories.** A memorable narrative can rivet the audience's attention and illustrate your point.
- **Use analogies.** Comparisons between essentially unlike things, such as a politician and a tightrope walker, link concepts memorably. (For more on analogy, see p. 100.)

Use a variety of supporting material in your speech. A presentation that consists of nothing but statistics can bore an audience. Nonstop storytelling may interest listeners but fail to achieve your purpose.

3 The conclusion

Last impressions count as much as first impressions. You may hope that listeners will remember every detail of your speech, but they are more likely to leave with a general impression and a few ideas about you and your message. You want your conclusion to be clear, of course, but you also want it to be memorable. Remind listeners of how your topic and main idea connect to their needs and interests.

56d Delivering the presentation

Writing and speaking differ most obviously in the form of delivery: the writer is represented in print; the speaker is represented in person. This section describes the methods and techniques of oral presentation as well as some ways of coping with stage fright.

1 Methods of delivery

An oral presentation may be delivered impromptu, extemporaneously, from a text, or from memory. No one technique is best for all speeches; indeed, a single speech may include two or more forms or even all four—perhaps a memorized introduction, an extemporaneous body in which quotations are read from a text, and impromptu responses to audience questions during or after the speech.

Speaking impromptu

Impromptu means "without preparation": an impromptu presentation is one you deliver off-the-cuff, with no planning or practice. You may be called on in a class to express your opinion or to summarize something you've written. You may speak up at a neighborhood meeting. An audience member may ask you a question at the end of an oral presentation. The only way to prepare for such incidents is to be well prepared in general—to be caught up on course reading, for instance, or to know the facts in a debate.

Speaking extemporaneously

Extemporaneous speaking—that done with some preparation, but without reading from a text—is the most common form of presentation, typical of class lectures and business briefings. With extemporaneous speaking, you have time to prepare and practice in advance. Then, instead of following a script of every word, you speak from notes that guide you through the presentation.

Speaking from a text

Delivering a presentation from a text involves writing the text out in advance and then reading aloud from it. With a text in front of you, you're unlikely to lose your way. However, a reading speaker can be dull for an audience. Try to avoid this form of delivery for an entire presentation.

If you do use a text, write it so that it sounds spoken (less formal) rather than written (more formal): for instance, the sentence *Although costs rose, profits remained steady* would sound fine in writing but stiff and awkward in speech because in conversation we rarely use such a structure. In addition, rehearse thoroughly so that you can read with expression and can look up frequently to make eye contact with listeners (see opposite).

Speaking from memory

A memorized presentation has a distinct advantage: complete freedom from notes or a text. That means you can look at your audience every minute and can move away from a lectern and even into the audience. However, you may be like most speakers in seeming less relaxed, not more relaxed, when presenting from memory: your mind is too busy retrieving the next words to attend to the responses of the audience. Further, you risk forgetting your place or a whole passage.

For these reasons, many experts discourage memorization. At least reserve the method for the introduction, perhaps, or some other part with which you want to make a strong impression. Rehearse not only to memorize the words but, beyond that, to deliver the words fresh, as if for the first time.

2 | Vocal delivery

The sound of your voice will influence how your listeners receive you. When rehearsing, consider volume, speed, and articulation.

- **Speak loudly.** In a meeting with five other people, you can speak in a normal volume. As your audience grows in size, so should your volume. Most speakers can project to as many as a hundred people, but a larger audience may require a microphone.
- **Speak slowly enough to be understandable.**
- **Speak clearly and correctly.** To avoid mumbling or slurring words, practice articulating. Sometimes it helps to open your mouth a little wider than usual.

3 | Physical delivery

You are more than your spoken words when you make an oral presentation. Your face and body also play a role in how your speech is received.

- **Make eye contact with listeners.** Move your gaze around the entire room, settle on someone, and establish direct eye contact; then move on to someone else.
- **Stand up.** Always stand for a presentation, unless it takes place in a small room where standing would be inappropriate. You can see more audience members when you stand, and they in turn can hear your voice and see your gestures more clearly.
- **Stand straight, and move around.** Turn your body toward one side of the room and then the other, step out from behind any lectern or desk, and gesture appropriately, as you would in conversation.

4 | Visual aids

You can supplement an oral presentation with visual aids such as posters, models, slides, videos, or presentation software such as *PowerPoint*. Visual aids can emphasize key points, organize related concepts, and illustrate complex procedures. They can gain the attention of listeners and improve their understanding and memory.

The following guidelines can help you create effective and appropriate visual aids:

- **Use visual aids to underscore your points.** Short lists of key ideas, illustrations such as graphs or photographs, or objects such as models can make your presentation more interesting and memorable. But use visual aids judiciously: a constant flow of illustrations or objects will bury your message.
- **Match visual aids and setting.** An audience of five people may be able to see a photograph and share a chart; an audience of a hundred will need projected images.
- **Coordinate visual aids with your message.** Time each visual aid to reinforce a point you're making. Tell listeners what they're looking at—what they should be getting from the aid. Give them enough viewing time so they don't mind turning their attention back to you.
- **Show visual aids only while they're needed.** To regain your audience's attention, remove or turn off any aid as soon as you have finished with it.

Many speakers use *PowerPoint* or other software to project visual aids. (See the sample slides on the next page.) Screens of brief points supported by data, images, or video can help listeners follow your main points. To use *PowerPoint* or other software effectively, follow the guidelines above and also the following:

- **Don't put your whole presentation on screen.** Select key points, and distill them to as few words as possible. Think of the slides as quick, easy-to-remember summaries.
- **Use a simple design.** Avoid turning your presentation into a show about the software's many capabilities.
- **Use a consistent design.** For optimal flow through the presentation, each slide should be formatted similarly.
- **Add only relevant illustrations.** Avoid loading the presentation with mere decoration.

5 Practice

Practicing an oral presentation is the equivalent of editing and proofreading a written text. You won't gain much by practicing silently in your head; instead, you need to rehearse out loud, with the notes you will be using. For your initial rehearsals, you can gauge your performance by making an audio- or videotape of yourself or by practicing in front of a mirror. A recording will let you hear mumbling, too-rapid delivery, grammatical errors, mispro-

PowerPoint slides

Making a Difference?

A Service-Learning Project at ReadingWorks

Springfield Veterans
Administration Hospital

Jessica Cho
Nathan Hall
Alex Ramirez

FALL 2009

ReadingWorks
Springfield VA Hospital

First slide, introducing the project and presentation

Simple, consistent slide design focusing viewers' attention on information, not *PowerPoint* features

Semester goals

- Tutor military veterans

- Research adult literacy

- Keep a journal

- Collaborate on documents for ReadingWorks

- Report experiences and findings

Later slide, using brief, bulleted points to be explained by the speaker

Photographs reinforcing the project's activities

nounced words, and unclear concepts. A mirror or video will reveal your stance, your gestures, and your eye contact. Any of these practice techniques will tell you if your presentation is running too long or too short.

If you plan to use visual aids, you'll need to practice with them, too, preferably in the room where you'll make the presentation and certainly with the help of anyone who will be assisting you. Your goal is to eliminate hitches (upside-down slides, missing charts) and to weave the visuals seamlessly into your presentation.

6 Stage fright

Many people report that speaking in front of an audience is their number-one fear. Even many experienced and polished speakers have some anxiety about delivering an oral presentation, but they use this nervous energy to their advantage, letting it propel them into working hard on each presentation, and rehearsing until they're satisfied with their delivery. They know that the symptoms of anxiety are usually imperceptible to listeners, who cannot see or hear a racing heart, upset stomach, cold hands, and worried thoughts.

Several techniques can help you reduce your level of anxiety:

- **Use simple relaxation exercises.** Deep breathing or tensing and relaxing your stomach muscles can ease some of the physical symptoms of speech anxiety.
- **Think positively.** Instead of worrying about the mistakes you might make, concentrate on how well you've prepared and practiced your presentation and how significant your ideas are.
- **Don't avoid opportunities to speak in public.** Practice and experience build speaking skills and offer the best insurance for success.

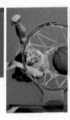

57

Applying to College

As you prepare to apply to college, you will likely take one or more standardized tests designed to assess your high school achievement and predict your success in college. College-admissions tests such as the SAT and ACT may influence your acceptance to college, while Advanced Placement (AP) exams may earn you college credit, advanced standing, or both.

Of course, the admissions staff of a college or university bases its decisions on more than just test scores. It also considers your high school courses, grades, teacher recommendations, and community activities as well as your letter of intent, or essay, on the school's application.

This chapter offers advice for taking the reading and writing sections of the SAT (opposite) and ACT (p. 837) and the AP exams in English language and composition and literature and composition (p. 839). The chapter concludes with suggestions for writing a college-application essay (p. 842).

Tips for taking timed exams

- **Be prepared.** Familiarize yourself with the format of the test you will be taking by visiting its Web site: *www.collegeboard.com* for the SAT and AP exams; *www.actstudent.org* for the ACT. Get a good night's sleep and eat breakfast before the test. Bring a snack and no. 2 pencils (with good erasers) to the test.

- **Read all directions carefully.** Under time pressure, you may be tempted to skip the instructions, but don't. Knowing exactly what the question or prompt is asking allows you to answer more quickly and accurately.

- **Answer easy questions first.** All questions count for the same number of points, so first answer the ones you know for certain. Mark questions you skip or feel unsure about so that you can return to them if you have time.

- **Use the process of elimination.** On multiple-choice questions, rule out answers you know are incorrect and choose the best answer from those remaining.

- **Know how the test is scored so that you know whether to guess.** On the SAT and AP exams, incorrect answers lower your score, so it's best not to take wild guesses. However, if you can eliminate one or two answers, you should guess from those remaining. On the ACT, only correct answers are counted, so you should answer every question even if you have to guess.

- **Budget your time.** Whether you're writing an essay or working through multiple-choice or sentence-completion questions, be aware of how much time you have for each section. Avoid lingering too long over a part of an essay or a single question.

57a Preparing for the SAT and ACT exams

The most widespread college-admissions exams are the SAT and the ACT. Since the tests are similar, this section focuses on the more common SAT. See pages 837–39 for a brief discussion of the ACT.

The general SAT exam, formally called the SAT Reasoning Test, consists of three parts: writing, critical reading, and mathematics. Here we treat the first two of these, but some of the skills we discuss—such as prediction, close attention, and analysis—apply to the math exam as well.

1 Taking the SAT writing section

The writing section of the SAT consists of two sections:

- **Multiple-choice questions,** requiring you to choose revisions of sentences and paragraphs and to identify sentence errors.

- **Short essay,** testing your ability to develop and support a main idea or thesis statement, organize ideas and express them clearly, write persuasively for an audience, and craft clear and correct sentences.

SAT multiple choice

The SAT usually tests the following topics. You can review each one at the handbook pages given in parentheses. (For an overview of areas tested by the ACT, see p. 837.)

- Pronoun case (pp. 266–74) and pronoun reference (pp. 347–53)
- Verb tense (pp. 291–94) and sequence of tenses (pp. 294–97)
- Active and passive verbs (pp. 300–02)
- Subject-verb agreement (pp. 303–11) and pronoun-antecedent agreement (pp. 311–15)
- Use of adjectives, adverbs, and comparisons (pp. 317–22)
- Sentence fragments (pp. 332–39)
- Comma splices and fused sentences (pp. 340–46)
- Consistency (avoiding shifts) in person, number, tense, and mood (pp. 354–59)
- Misplaced and dangling modifiers (pp. 361–69)
- Incomplete sentences and comparisons (pp. 375–77)
- Coordination and subordination (pp. 390–97)
- Parallelism (pp. 400–04)
- Appropriate and exact language (Chapters 37–38)
- Idioms (pp. 519–21)
- Wordiness (pp. 525–32)
- Punctuation (Chapters 27–32)

Besides the tips in the box on the previous page, the following strategies will help you answer multiple-choice writing questions:

- **Read the directions carefully.** The directions tell you what to do, often contain time-saving information, and may vary from question to question.
- **Mark errors as you read.** Underline or circle sentences that don't look right to you.
- **Read the answer options all the way through before choosing or eliminating any answers.**

Improving sentences

Some of the SAT's multiple-choice questions assess your ability to recognize correct and incorrect sentences. You are given a full sentence, part or all of which is underlined. You must analyze the underlined section, determine whether it contains an error, and, if so, identify the correction.

In the following example, notice that the directions state that option A repeats the underlined part of the original sentence. Thus you don't need to read option A unless you are sure that the original sentence is already correct.

Directions: The following sentences test correctness and effectiveness of expression. Part of each sentence or the entire sentence is underlined; beneath each sentence are five ways of phrasing the underlined material. Choice A repeats the original phrasing; the other four choices are different. If you think the original phrasing produces a better sentence than any of the alternatives, select choice A; if not, select one of the other choices.

1. Experiences in the daily lives of Chinese immigrants, which are vividly described in the works of Maxine Hong Kingston.

   (A) Experiences in the daily lives of Chinese immigrants, which are vividly described in the works of Maxine Hong Kingston.

   (B) Experiences in the daily lives of Chinese immigrants being vividly described in the works of Maxine Hong Kingston.

   (C) The works of Maxine Hong Kingston vividly describe experiences in the daily lives of Chinese immigrants.

   (D) Maxine Hong Kingston, in her vivid work, describing experiences in the daily lives of Chinese immigrants.

   (E) Maxine Hong Kingston, whose work vividly describe experiences in the daily lives of Chinese immigrants.

As you read the original sentence, listen to whether or not it sounds awkward. If it seems wrong, then you can tentatively eliminate A and move on to the other four choices. Reading the example, if you recognize immediately that the original is a sentence fragment, you can then read *for* the choice that is a complete sentence. Option B is not because *being* is not a finite verb (like *are*) that can serve alone as a sentence verb. Option C, however, *is* complete, and you can tentatively select it as the answer. First, though, read through options D and E to be sure they are wrong. (For a review of sentence fragments, see pp. 332–39.)

Identifying sentence errors

Another type of multiple-choice question provides a sentence with four parts underlined. You must identify an error in one of the underlined parts or recognize that the sentence is correct as given. Here is a sample:

Directions: The following sentences test your ability to recognize grammar and usage errors. Each sentence contains either a single error or no error at all. No sentence contains more than one error. The error, if there is one, is underlined and lettered. If the sentence contains an error, select the one underlined part that must be changed to make the sentence correct. If the sentence is correct, select choice E.

1. The other negotiators and her immediately rejected the proposal
   ‾‾‾‾‾‾‾‾   ‾‾‾ ‾‾‾‾‾‾‾‾‾‾
        A   B   C
   presented by the management. No error.
   ‾‾‾‾‾‾‾‾‾‾‾   ‾‾‾‾‾‾‾‾
        D   E

You might spot option B—the pronoun *her*—as incorrect. Before committing to an answer, test it—in this case, by starting the sentence with the pronoun alone: *Her immediately rejected.* (For a review of pronoun case, see pp. 266–74.)

Improving paragraphs

A third kind of multiple-choice question asks you to recognize problems in the unity, coherence, and development of paragraphs and to choose answers that improve the paragraphs. Reading the paragraphs carefully will help you see their problems and anticipate the test questions. The following tips can focus your attention:

- **Look for the topic sentence of each paragraph.**
- **Check that sentences are clear, smooth, and specific.** Sentences that cause you to stumble in your reading are likely to need revision.
- **Check that each sentence logically follows the one before it.** Watch for abrupt transitions or sentences that seem to change the topic.
- **Notice any repetition that makes the paragraph flabby or unwieldy.**

Here is a sample draft essay and the directions for reading it:

Directions: The following passage is an early draft of an essay. Some parts of the passage need to be rewritten. Read the passage and select the best answers for the questions that follow. Some questions are about particular sentences or parts of sentences and ask you to improve sentence structure or word choice. Other questions ask you to consider organization and development. In choosing answers, follow the requirements of standard written English.

(1) Many types of frogs hibernate, essentially sleeping through the winter. (2) They protect themselves from cold by burrowing into the dirt or camping out under piles of leaves. (3) Some frogs are even equipped with mechanisms that allow them to survive being frozen. (4) One type of frog, the wood frog, can survive even when 65% of its total body water turns to ice. (5) These frogs appear to be dead but, it seems miraculous, they are not.

(6) Frozen frogs have extensive ice formation in their body cavities and in the spaces between their cells. (7) The reason that these frogs survive, however, is that no ice forms within their cells. (8) Ice crystals form within cells, they can kill an animal by puncturing certain specialized parts of the cells. (9) These frogs are protected from the

harmful effects of freezing by a chemical reaction. (10) When the first ice crystals begin to form on the skin of a hibernating frog, an internal alarm goes off. (11) This causes the frog's cells to fill with glucose. (12) Precisely the opposite occurs in the spaces between the cells. (13) There special proteins promote the formation of ice crystals. (14) This draws water away from the cells so it does not freeze there.

If you read this essay with attention to its clarity and effectiveness, you might be able to predict the sample test questions discussed below.

1. In context, which word should be inserted at the beginning of sentence 8?

   (A) Because
   (B) Although
   (C) While
   (D) If
   (E) Since

Any of the answers will make the first clause subordinate and thus fix the comma splice in sentence 8, but the correct answer must also make sense in context. In sentence 8, the first clause describes a condition (*Ice crystals form within cells*), and the second describes a result (*they can kill an animal*). The word starting the first clause must then fit this pattern, and only option D (*If*) does so. The other options set up either a contradiction (B, *Although*; C, *While*), or a cause-and-effect relationship (A, *Because*; E, *Since*). *If* also works in the context of sentence 7, which has just stated that ice does *not* form in the frogs' cells. All of the other options seem to contradict that statement.

Here is another question on the essay:

2. Which of the following facts about glucose is most important to add to sentence 11?

   (A) Glucose acts as an antifreeze.
   (B) Glucose can be stored in the liver.
   (C) Glucose is regulated by two hormones, insulin and glucagon.
   (D) Glucose is used by the cells for energy.
   (E) Glucose is a blood sugar found in vertebrates.

The answer to this question must explain why the frogs' cells filling with glucose is *Precisely the opposite* (sentence 12) of proteins' causing ice crystals between cells (sentence 13). Only option A (*Glucose acts as an antifreeze*) provides this explanation. All the others add irrelevant information to the paragraph and disrupt its unity.

SAT short essay

The short-essay section of the SAT tests your ability to write an argument about a topic supplied in a prompt. You will have twenty-five minutes to plan, draft, and review an essay that develops a main point with evidence drawn from your reading, classwork, experience, and observations. The trained graders who score your essay will view it as a rough draft but look for clearly stated ideas, evidence for the ideas, and writing that follows the conventions of standard American English.

The following prompt and assignment are similar to those given on the SAT:

> Life's trials, not its comforts, are what shape and mold us into who we are.
>
> **Assignment:** Do you agree with the statement above, or are there times when you believe it proves false? Plan and write an essay in which you develop your point of view on this issue. Support your position with reasoning and examples taken from your reading, studies, experience, or observation.

Always read the prompt carefully to be sure you understand it. In the sample prompt, for instance, the word *trials* is key. If its meaning in this context is unfamiliar, you can infer from its position in the statement that it is the opposite of *comforts*. Once you're certain of the prompt's meaning, decide on your position—whether you agree or disagree with the statement—and begin developing the evidence for your view.

The following guidelines can help you produce an essay:

- **Use some time for planning.** Before you start writing, take a few minutes to read the prompt, determine your position, and jot down your main ideas and evidence.
- **Write about the topic given in the prompt.** Your essay must address the prompt directly. If it doesn't, you could receive zero points for your essay.
- **State your thesis early and clearly.** Assert your position succinctly in your opening paragraph, even in your opening sentence. For instance: *An easy life free of discomfort and worry may seem a worthy goal, but it is through struggle with life's trials, meeting and overcoming challenges, that we gain strength and self-knowledge.*
- **Choose evidence that supports your thesis.** For the preceding thesis, you might use evidence drawn from literature (in *Gulliver's Travels*, Gulliver often goes out to sea to challenge himself and see how far he can open his mind), the news (hurricane devastation or the war in Iraq), history (the American Revolution or the Civil Rights struggle), or personal experience.

- **Craft sentences carefully.** Although you must write quickly, take the time to demonstrate the logic of your ideas and show the relationships between them. As much as possible, choose appropriate and exact words and use correct grammar and punctuation.
- **Write legibly.** People who are not familiar with your handwriting must be able to read what you write.
- **Allow time for review.** You won't have the leisure for thorough revision, but do allow a few minutes to reread your essay and make minor changes in wording or even in the arrangement of ideas.

(For additional help with writing essay exams, see pp. 137–39.)

2 | Taking the SAT critical-reading section

The critical-reading section of the SAT contains two types of questions:

- **Sentence-completion questions,** testing your knowledge of vocabulary and your understanding of how parts of sentences fit together.
- **Passage-based reading questions,** testing your understanding of vocabulary, content, ideas, and writing strategies.

You've practiced the skills you need to answer these questions in your high school work. For more preparation, consult Chapter 7 on critical thinking and reading (pp. 139–53).

Note As a rule, work on sentence-completion questions first because they take less time than passage-based reading questions.

SAT sentence completions

The sentence-completion questions provide sentences with blanks and ask you to choose the best word or words to complete the sentences. In addition to the general test-taking tips in the box on page 827, use the following strategies to answer sentence-completion questions:

- **Use clues in sentence structure.** Often the grammar or punctuation of a sentence provides information about the type of word or words needed in the correct answer.
- **Consider root words, prefixes, suffixes, and familiar sayings or phrases.** They can help you determine the meanings of words.

We'll look at two sample sentence-completion questions. The following directions apply to both:

Directions: Each sentence below has one or two blanks, each blank indicating that something has been omitted. Beneath the sentence are five words or sets of words labeled A through E. Choose the word or set of words that, when inserted in the sentence, *best* fits the meaning of the sentence as a whole.

1. The young reporter was glad to be learning the basics at the local newspaper, but he was becoming bored with _____ news stories and was _____ to cover more exciting action.

   (A) lengthy . . . reluctant
   (B) alluring . . . enthusiastic
   (C) diverse . . . reticent
   (D) numerous . . . fearful
   (E) routine . . . eager

Often you can find the correct answer by eliminating options that definitely aren't correct because they don't work in the context of the sentence. In question 1, you can eliminate B and C because of their first words: a reporter wouldn't be bored with *alluring* or *diverse* stories. And you can eliminate options A, C, and D because of their second words: a reporter who wants to report more exciting stories wouldn't be *reluctant, reticent,* or *fearful.* That leaves E as your response. Fitting its words into the blanks verifies the answer: *The young reporter was glad to be learning the basics at the local newspaper, but he was becoming bored with* routine *news stories and was* eager *to cover more exciting action.*

The next question is more difficult:

2. Mrs. Surice felt that Ed's _____ comments during class discussion helped the other students understand the complex ideas presented in the book.

   (A) predictive
   (B) incisive
   (C) derisive
   (D) erratic
   (E) sarcastic

The correct answer will define comments that *helped the other students understand the complex ideas presented in the book.* You might know the correct word right away: *incisive* (B), which means "penetrating, clear." If you don't spot the right word, eliminate the words you know to be wrong: *sarcastic* (E), "scornful"; *derisive* (C), "mocking, ridiculing"; and *erratic* (D), "uneven." Even if you don't know *predictive* (A), you probably know *predict,* which suggests comments that say what comes next, not enlighten.

SAT passage-based reading

Passage-based reading questions test your ability to draw conclusions from reading selections of 100 to 850 words. The passages are drawn from a variety of texts—fiction, general nonfiction, and academic writing—and they include narrative, exposition, and argument. Questions test your understanding of vocabulary and content and often ask you to evaluate some aspect of the text. Sometimes passages are paired, and the questions address both the individual passages and comparisons between them.

In addition to the general test-taking tips in the box on page 827, use the following strategies to work through passage-based reading questions:

- **Read carefully.** The information you need to answer the questions is always in the passage.
- **Don't jump from passage to passage.** Answer as many questions as you can about a passage before moving on. That way, you don't have to refamiliarize yourself with the passage at a later time.
- **Determine the meanings of unfamiliar words** by considering related words, the context of the passage, familiar sayings or phrases, and root words, prefixes, and suffixes.

The following sample includes two questions about a pair of passages.

Directions: The passages below are followed by questions based on their content; questions following a pair of related passages may also be based on the relationship between the paired passages. Answer the questions on the basis of what is stated or implied in the passages and in any introductory material that may be provided.

The legend of King Arthur and the Knights of the Round Table is one of the most enduring in Western literature. Below, two authors consider the factual foundations of the myth.

Passage 1

The Arthur who has become part of the fabric of our lives today is mostly a creation of medieval times, when troubadours and chroniclers made him into a hero of romance, a noble ruler whose knights were patterns of chivalry. The myth has become so real to us that we tend to forget the existence of an actual, historical Arthur. He may not have been a king in the sense that we understand kingship. He may not have been even a particularly good or generous or idealistic man. All we know, in starting out to search for him, is that he must have been a remarkable person, because fame does not come without good reason.

Passage 2

We have no reason to think that Arthur was a territorial ruler, attached to a particular kingdom. It is more likely that he was either a freelance who offered the services of himself and a band of followers to whatever king would pay best, or an overall commander appointed collectively by the kings of the Britons. Britons were capable of taking cooperative action to appoint a commander who could fight their enemies wherever they appeared. Such a role might fit a phrase in the *Historia Britonum,** in which Arthur was said to have fought "along with the kings of the Britons," but he himself was a *dux bellorum* [warrior, or "war duke"].

* Or *History of the Britons*, probably written in the 9th century.

1. The authors of both passages assume that the legendary King Arthur was

    (A) the leader of a heroic group of knights
    (B) an actual historical figure
    (C) a military rather than a political leader
    (D) the invention of poets
    (E) hired by several different kings

Question 1 asks you to look for a similarity between the two passages. You can start by eliminating the choices that don't describe *both* passages: option A, because only passage 1 describes Arthur as a leader of a heroic group of knights; option C, because only passage 2 considers him as a military leader; option D, because neither passage makes him a fictional figure; and option E, because only passage 2 describes him as possibly hired by a group of kings. The answer has to be B: both writers assume Arthur was an actual historical figure.

The following question asks you to draw a conclusion from your reading about one of the passages:

2. In passage 1, "a king in the sense that we understand kingship" most probably refers to

    (A) one member of a group of rulers sharing power in a certain region
    (B) a warlord with a loyal band of followers
    (C) the hero of a romantic folktale
    (D) a military commander for hire
    (E) the political ruler of a specific area

To answer this question, you want to locate the common meanings of *king* and *kingship*. Again eliminate the options that definitely don't work: *member of a group of rulers sharing power* (A), *warlord* (B), and *military commander* (D). (We think of kings as ruling alone and of war making as being only sometimes one of their roles.) Option C, *hero of a romantic folktale*, may seem attractive because passage 1 refers to Arthur as such in medieval times. But the passage goes on to emphasize Arthur's actuality, and in any event we know kings to be real. That leaves option E, *the political ruler of a specific area*, which is indeed a common meaning of *king*.

3 Taking the ACT

The ACT exam is divided into four tests: English, mathematics, reading, and science. A fifth test, a short-essay exam, is optional. In this section we discuss the English, reading, and writing tests.

ACT English test

The ACT English exam includes multiple-choice in two subsections: identifying sentence errors and improving sentences and paragraphs. The following topics will likely be tested on the ACT. To review, consult the handbook chapters and pages in parentheses.

- The writing process (Chapters 1–3)
- Organization (Chapter 2; Chapter 4, pp. 82–86)
- Style, including emphasis, parallelism, variety, appropriate and exact language, idioms, and conciseness (Chapters 23–26 and 37–39)
- Case of nouns and pronouns (pp. 266–74)
- Verbs (pp. 274–303)
- Subject-verb agreement (pp. 303–11)
- Pronoun-antecedent agreement (pp. 311–15)
- Adjectives and adverbs (pp. 317–22)
- Sentence fragments (pp. 332–39)
- Comma splices and fused sentences (pp. 340–46)
- Pronoun reference (pp. 347–53)
- Misplaced and dangling modifiers (pp. 361–69)
- Shifts (pp. 354–59)
- Coordination and subordination (pp. 390–97)
- Punctuation, including the relation between punctuation and meaning (Chapters 27–32)

As you prepare for the ACT, use the test-taking strategies in the box on page 827. You can also review strategies for taking the corresponding parts of the SAT: "Improving sentences" (p. 828), "Identifying sentence errors" (p. 829), and "Improving paragraphs" (p. 830). Be aware that the ACT's question format differs from that of the SAT, so you should consult the sample test questions at *www.actstudent.org* to familiarize yourself with the ACT format.

Following is a sample sentence from an ACT English test, with a potential error underlined and numbered. The ACT presents such sentences in the context of full paragraphs, and on the actual exam this sentence falls in a six-paragraph passage with fifteen questions.

After <u>the final performance of one last</u> practice

₁

landing, the French instructor nodded to the

young African-American woman at the controls

and jumped to the ground.

1. (A) NO CHANGE
   (B) one finally
       ultimate
   (C) one final
   (D) one last final

The underlined section of the sentence is wordy and redundant. Options B and D reduce the wordiness, but they are still redundant (*finally ultimate* and *last final*). Option C is the correct choice.

ACT reading test

The ACT reading test asks you to answer questions about four passages drawn from the social sciences, natural sciences, humanities, and prose fiction. Unlike the SAT, which sometimes asks for comparison of two passages, the ACT always gives only one passage at a time. The multiple-choice questions that follow the four passages test abilities such as determining main ideas, locating and interpreting important details, understanding the sequence of events, making comparisons and generalizations, and analyzing the author's style, voice, and method. The ACT does not test vocabulary, so it contains nothing comparable to the SAT's sentence-completion questions.

To prepare for the ACT reading test, consult the discussion of the SAT passage-based reading section on pages 835–37, the sample test questions and analysis at *www.actstudent.org*, and also this book's Chapter 8 on critical thinking and reading.

ACT writing test

The ACT writing test is optional. Before you decide to take it, check to see whether it is required by the colleges you are applying to. If you choose to take the writing test, consult the advice on pages 832–33 of this chapter as well as the guidelines for taking any essay exam on pages 784–90.

ACT writing prompts, such as the one below, usually draw on general knowledge. They also provide details to help you frame your response. Here is an example:

> In some high schools, many teachers and parents have encouraged the school to adopt a dress code that sets guidelines for what students can wear in the school building. Some parents and teachers support a dress code because they think it will improve the learning environment in the school. Other teachers and parents do not support a dress code because they think it restricts the individual student's freedom of expression. In your opinion, should high schools adopt dress codes for students?

In your essay, take a position on this question. You may write about either one of the two points of view given, or you may present a different point of view on this question. Use specific reasons and examples to support your position.

As with the SAT, be sure you understand the prompt and the instructions before you begin to write. Here, you are asked to express an opinion about the dress-code debate and to support the opinion using specific reasons and examples. You should decide quickly what your opinion is and think of a few examples to use in support of your position. Your next step is to state it clearly, and argue for it with evidence drawn from your reading, observations, and experience. You may use reasons given in the prompt as long as you provide details to back them up.

57b Preparing for the AP English exams

Advanced Placement (AP) courses in high school teach the kinds of thinking, reading, and writing activities typical of an introductory college course. Some of these courses prepare students to take the two AP English exams, the literature and composition exam and the language and composition exam. Because high scores on the exams can exempt you from college courses or earn you credits toward a college degree, AP exams are more rigorous and more specific than the general SAT and ACT exams.

Both AP English exams require you to answer multiple-choice questions about passages of prose or poetry and to answer three free-response questions based on passages or prompts. The College Board, sponsor of the AP test, does not permit reproduction of its sample questions. For samples and additional test-taking strategies, visit the AP Web site at *collegeboard.com.*

1 Answering AP multiple-choice questions

The multiple-choice questions on both AP English exams test a variety of reading skills, including your ability to do the following:

- **Read closely and analyze a variety of texts,** including nonfiction prose, fiction, poetry, and drama.
- **Interpret the meaning of a text by analyzing an author's style,** including sentence structure, word choice, tone, and figurative language.
- **Analyze organization and structure,** including the writer's strategies for openings and closings, transitions among ideas, and repetition and variation in sentence structure and paragraphs.
- **Recognize rhetorical strategies,** understanding the relationships among speaker, subject, and audience.

The literature and composition exam uses literary texts from a variety of historical periods, in various genres, and on a wide range of topics. The language and composition exam frequently supplies nonfiction prose (narrative, expository, and argumentative), as well as fiction and poetry.

As with any timed test, be sure to read the text closely and completely before answering any questions. Try to infer the meanings of unfamiliar words from the context of the passage, and prepare yourself for the questions that follow by predicting as you read. Answer easy questions first, use the process of elimination to make the best choices, and mark questions you skip so that you can return to them later if you have time. In addition, use the general test-taking tips in the box on page 827.

2 Answering AP free-response questions

Both of the AP English exams require students to write three essays in two hours. Unlike the SAT and ACT essay prompts, which are fairly open-ended, most or all of the AP essay prompts ask you to read passages and respond to them directly. Even when the third essay question is more open-ended, it is still more academic than the SAT and ACT prompts.

Plan to spend forty minutes on each essay, including the time it takes to read the directions and the prompt or passage. Focus on demonstrating interpretive skill, developing ideas carefully, and writing clearly and persuasively. Use the following strategies to craft your essays:

- **Read the directions and assignment before you start reading the passage or prompt.** Be sure that you do what's required, whether analyzing style, interpreting meaning, arguing a position, explaining a writer's strategies, or something else.
- **Read the passage or prompt carefully,** marking words or phrases for ideas and quotations.
- **Develop your thesis statement.** In a sentence or two, address the assignment directly and identify your main points.
- **Choose evidence that supports your thesis and main points.** Use concrete, specific details to support your ideas, quoting or paraphrasing the passage. Allot roughly equal space to each of your main points.
- **Write legibly.** People who are not familiar with your handwriting must be able to read what you write.
- **Allow time for review.** You won't have the leisure for thorough revision, but do allow a few minutes to reread your essay and make minor changes in wording or even in the arrangement of ideas.

For additional help with answering AP free-response questions, see this book's discussion of essay exams (pp. 784–90) as well as the AP Web site at *collegeboard.com*.

AP literature and composition exam

The three free-response questions on the literature and composition exam typically include two that ask you to read and respond to a literary work, either an excerpt from a longer work or a short story or poem. The third question is often (but not always) open-ended, asking you to respond to a prompt and to support your main idea using a literary work you have read in school.

AP language and composition exam

The free-response questions on the language and composition exam often ask you to compare and contrast two passages, analyze an argument, or produce an argument in response to a prompt. In addition, the exam includes a question asking students to synthesize information from several related sources and to write an essay that supports a position, using and citing several of the sources. (Students are given an extra fifteen minutes to read the sources and plan their essays.)

To complete the assignment, you will need to read the instructions and sources quickly but carefully, choose a position and the sources that support it, and organize your points and ideas. You must formulate a clear argument and demonstrate control over it by quoting, paraphrasing, and summarizing sources to support your position. Avoid simply repeating what sources say; instead, use quotation, summary, and paraphrase to show that you understand what the sources say and how they support your argument. (See pp. 601–04 for more on integrating sources into your writing.) You must cite the sources you use in your essay, but you are not required to use a particular citation style. The exam lists the sources by letter (source A, source B, and so on), and the instructions say to refer to them by letter.

Use the following strategies to approach a synthesis question:

- **Consider your position as you read.** The directions, introduction, and assignment should start you thinking about the position you will take. The first one or two sources should help you firm up your position. The earlier you have it, the more efficiently you will read the remaining sources.
- **Eliminate sources not relevant to your argument.** You need not use all of the sources as evidence in your argument; you must use the number stated in the instructions. As you read, note similarities and differences among the sources so that you can evaluate and synthesize them.

- **Mark sources you plan to use.** Once you have decided on your position and read all the sources, mark facts, opinions, and quotations that you plan to use in your essay. Note points of agreement and disagreement among sources, and make connections between sources.
- **Open your essay by stating your position.** For example, if the claim given in the assignment is that television plays a positive role in presidential campaigns, your thesis might oppose it: *Although television is clearly a useful tool in political campaigns, its effects on the voting public are negative.* Or the thesis statement might agree with the claim: *Although television is often criticized for pulling voters' attention away from the issues in presidential campaigns, it has brought Americans into the political process in a way the Founding Fathers could not have imagined.* Or the thesis statement might qualify the claim: *Those who champion television's role in presidential campaigns and those who criticize its role are both correct: TV takes the democratic process into virtually every American home, but what it does there too often undermines the process.*
- **Support your position using opinions and examples from the sources.** Work to synthesize information from sources, forging connections to support your position. For more on synthesizing sources, see pages 593–94.

57c Writing a college-application essay

In addition to transcripts, letters of recommendation, and standardized tests, many colleges require students to submit a personal essay as part of the application process. While some colleges assign a topic, many provide open-ended prompts, such as a time you learned something new, an influential person in your life, or something interesting about yourself. Whatever topic you choose to write on, be sure the essay establishes you as someone who welcomes the opportunity for a college education.

Give yourself ample time to plan, develop, and revise your essay, using the following guidelines:

- **Understand the writing situation.** The purpose of your essay is to persuade an audience of admissions officers that you should be offered admission. Do your homework by investigating the college's admissions criteria as well as its programs and mission statement. Make your essay stand out by writing clearly, honestly, and confidently. For more on the writing situation, see pages 2–17.

- **Choose an appropriate subject.** Use the essay to tell the college something about you that isn't evident from your transcript, letters of recommendation, or test scores, such as a nonacademic achievement, a challenge you've surmounted, or why you want to attend the college you're applying to. Gather ideas by talking to others, including teachers, who have experience with writing and reading application essays. For more on choosing a subject, see pages 7–9.

- **Use your strengths as a writer.** If you're adept at storytelling, consider an essay that develops from a narrative. If argument comes easily, consider a persuasive essay about a topic you care about. If you're funny, consider a humorous essay. If you aren't sure what your strengths are, look back at writing you've done in school to see what your peers and teachers liked and didn't like.

- **Choose examples carefully.** Use experiences, reading, and other sources to make your ideas concrete and specific: a conversation you had, something you witnessed, a difficult choice, or a moment of enlightenment. For more on developing and shaping ideas, see pages 18–46.

- **Take care with the introduction and conclusion.** Your introduction should draw readers into your essay, focusing them on your subject and what you have to say. Your conclusion should not summarize your essay but instead comment on what you've said in the essay or look to the future. For more on introductions and conclusions, see pages 105–10.

- **Share your completed draft with friends, family, or teachers.** Other readers may see opportunities for developing an example or idea, catch unclear or incorrect sentence constructions, or suggest changes in wording. For more on revising an essay, see pages 52–72.

- **Edit and proofread your essay before you send it.** Readers will look for polished sentences, correct punctuation, and perfect spelling in your essay, so take the time you need to read it carefully before you send it. See the editing and proofreading checklists on pages 61–62 and 67.

The student who wrote the following application essay was responding to a general prompt suggesting that she tell of an experience that had changed her. Notice that she makes the experience specific while holding her focus on the change it caused.

As I waited for my student on my first day as a literacy tutor, I felt young and inexperienced. I was a newly certified tutor, but my eight hours of training now seemed distant and possibly useless. When my student, a Hmong woman named Mai Thao, entered the room, I summoned my courage, smiled, and greeted her, and she smiled back. We got to work, and to my relief the hour went smoothly. Today, with over a year of weekly tutoring sessions behind me, I have gained confidence in my ability as a tutor, but even more I have learned to appreciate the experiences of immigrants and have found direction for my college career.

Tutoring Mai Thao and meeting other clients of the literacy center have opened my eyes to a world far beyond my high school. Like other immigrants, Mai Thao chose to leave her home and come to the United States in the hope of economic opportunity. She works hard at her job, studies English, and educates her children, trying to maintain her cultural identity while also assimilating into US culture. She had little formal education, so as she learns to speak and understand English she is also learning to read and write in any language. Activities that most glide through—shopping for food, making a doctor's appointment, asking for directions, taking a driver's test—have been huge hurdles for her. I don't think I or most people I know could surmount such challenges.

As much as tutoring has opened my mind, so has it confirmed my ability to teach and shown me a path. I have prepared lesson plans, handouts, and props that have helped Mai Thao learn the everyday language she needs to negotiate life in the United States. I've come to love teaching and to appreciate my own education, which until a year ago I had taken for granted. I am eager to attend _____ College, where the programs in foreign languages, teaching, and public policy will prepare me for what I see as a lifetime's commitment to education.

It's often said that globalization is making the world smaller, but I see the world as growing larger: through the media and from immigrants in our communities, we are more aware of people different from ourselves and of their opportunities and challenges. The leaders of the future will have to be open to difference and willing to bridge it. I want to be one of those leaders.

Glossary of Usage

This glossary provides notes on words or phrases that often cause problems for writers. The recommendations for standard American English are based on current dictionaries and usage guides such as the ones listed on pp. 514–15. Items labeled **nonstandard** should be avoided in academic and business settings. Those labeled **colloquial** and **slang** occur in speech and in some informal writing but are best avoided in formal college and business writing. (Words and phrases labeled *colloquial* include those labeled by many dictionaries with the equivalent term *informal*.) See Chapters 37 and 38 for further discussion of word choice and for exercises in usage. See p. 514 for a description of dictionary labels. Also see pp. 534–35 for a list of commonly confused words that are pronounced the same or similarly.

The glossary is necessarily brief. Keep a dictionary handy for all your writing, and make a habit of referring to it whenever you doubt the appropriateness of a word or phrase.

a, an   Use *a* before words beginning with consonant sounds, including those spelled with an initial pronounced *h* and those spelled with vowels that are sounded as consonants: *a* historian, *a one-o'clock class, a university.* Use an before words that begin with vowel sounds, including those spelled with an initial silent *h: an organism, an L, an honor.*

The article before an abbreviation depends on how the abbreviation is read: *She was once an AEC undersecretary (AEC* is read as three separate letters); *Many Americans opposed a SALT treaty (SALT* is read as one word, *salt*).

For the use of *a/an* versus *the,* see pp. 324–27.

accept, except   *Accept* is a verb meaning "receive." *Except* is usually a preposition or conjunction meaning "but for" or "other than"; when it is used as a verb, it means "leave out." *I can accept all your suggestions except the last one. I'm sorry you excepted my last suggestion from your list.*

adverse, averse   *Adverse* and *averse* both mean "opposed" or "hostile." But *averse* describes the subject's opposition to something, whereas *adverse* describes something opposed to the subject: *The President was averse to adverse criticism.*

advice, advise   *Advice* is a noun, and *advise* is a verb: *Take my advice; do as I advise you.*

affect, effect   Usually *affect* is a verb, meaning "to influence," and *effect* is a noun, meaning "result": *The drug did not affect his driving; in fact, it seemed to have no effect at all.* But *effect* occasionally is used as a verb meaning "to bring about": *Her efforts effected a change.* And *affect* is used in psychology as a noun meaning "feeling or emotion": *One can infer much about affect from behavior.*

aggravate *Aggravate* should not be used in its colloquial meaning of "irritate" or "exasperate" (for example, *We were aggravated by her constant arguing*). *Aggravate* means "make worse": *The President was irritated by the Senate's indecision because he feared any delay might aggravate the unrest in the Middle East.*

agree to, agree with *Agree to* means "consent to," and *agree with* means "be in accord with": *How can they agree to a treaty when they don't agree with each other about the terms?*

ain't Nonstandard for *am not, isn't*, or *aren't*.

all, all of Usually *all* is sufficient to modify a noun: *all my loving, all the things you are*. Before a pronoun or proper noun, *all of* is usually appropriate: *all of me, in all of France*.

all ready, already *All ready* means "completely prepared," and *already* means "by now" or "before now": *We were all ready to go to the movie, but it had already started.*

all right *All right* is always two words. *Alright* is a common error.

all together, altogether *All together* means "in unison" or "gathered in one place." *Altogether* means "entirely." *It's not altogether true that our family never spends vacations all together.*

allusion, illusion An *allusion* is an indirect reference, and an *illusion* is a deceptive appearance: *Paul's constant allusions to Shakespeare created the illusion that he was an intellectual.*

almost, most *Almost* means "nearly"; *most* means "the greater number (or part) of." In formal writing, *most* should not be used as a substitute for *almost*: *We see each other almost* [not *most*] *every day.*

a lot *A lot* is always two words, used informally to mean "many." *Alot* is a common misspelling.

among, between Use *among* for relationships involving more than two people or things. Use *between* for relationships involving only two or for comparing one thing to a group to which it belongs. *The four of them agreed among themselves that the choice was between New York and Los Angeles.*

amongst Although common in British English, in American English *amongst* is an overrefined substitute for *among*.

amount, number Use *amount* with a singular noun that names something not countable (a noncount noun): *The amount of food varies*. Use *number* with a plural noun that names more than one of something countable (a plural count noun): *The number of calories must stay the same.*

an, and *An* is an article (see *a, an*). *And* is a coordinating conjunction.

and etc. *Et cetera (etc.)* means "and the rest"; *and etc.* therefore is redundant. See also *et al., etc.*

and/or *And/or* indicates three options: one or the other or both (*The decision is made by the mayor and/or the council*). If you mean all three options, *and/or* is appropriate. Otherwise, use *and* if you mean both, *or* if you mean either.

and which, and who   *And which* or *and who* is correct only when used to introduce a second clause beginning with the same relative pronoun: *Jill is my cousin <u>who</u> goes to school here <u>and who</u> calls me constantly.* Otherwise, *and* is not needed: *WCAS is my favorite AM radio station, <u>which</u>* [not <u>*and which*</u>] *I listen to every morning.*

ante-, anti-   The prefix *ante-* means "before" (*antedate, antebellum*); *anti-* means "against" (*antiwar, antinuclear*). Before a capital letter or *i, anti-* takes a hyphen: *anti-Freudian, anti-isolationist.*

anxious, eager   *Anxious* means "nervous" or "worried" and is usually followed by *about. Eager* means "looking forward" and is usually followed by *to. I've been <u>anxious about</u> getting blisters. I'm <u>eager</u>* [not <u>*anxious*</u>] *to get new running shoes.*

anybody, any body; anyone, any one   *Anybody* and *anyone* are indefinite pronouns; *any body* is a noun modified by *any; any one* is a pronoun or adjective modified by *any. How can <u>anybody</u> communicate with <u>any body</u> of government? Can <u>anyone</u> help Amy? She has more work than <u>any one</u> person can handle.*

any more, anymore   *Any more* means "no more"; *anymore* means "now." Both are used in negative constructions: *He doesn't want <u>any more</u>. She doesn't live here <u>anymore</u>.*

anyplace   Colloquial for *anywhere.*

anyways, anywheres   Nonstandard for *anyway* and *anywhere.*

apt, liable, likely   *Apt* and *likely* are interchangeable. Strictly speaking, though, *apt* means "having a tendency to": *Horace is <u>apt</u> to forget his lunch in the morning. Likely* means "probably going to": *Horace is leaving so early today that he's <u>likely</u> to catch the first bus.*

 Liable normally means "in danger of" and should be confined to situations with undesirable consequences: *Horace is <u>liable</u> to trip over that hose.* Strictly, *liable* means "responsible" or "exposed to": *The owner will be <u>liable</u> for Horace's injuries.*

are, is   Use *are* with a plural subject (*books <u>are</u>*), *is* with a singular subject (*book <u>is</u>*).

as   *As* may be vague or ambiguous when it substitutes for *because, since,* or *while: <u>As</u> the researchers asked more questions, their money ran out.* (Does *as* mean "while" or "because"?) *As* should never be used as a substitute for *whether* or *who. I'm not sure <u>whether</u>* [not <u>*as*</u>] *we can make it. That's the man <u>who</u>* [not <u>*as*</u>] *gave me directions.*

as, like   See *like, as.*

as, than   In comparisons, *as* and *than* precede a subjective-case pronoun when the pronoun is a subject: *I love you more <u>than he</u>* [*loves you*]. *As* and *than* precede an objective-case pronoun when the pronoun is an object: *I love you as much <u>as</u>* [*I love*] *him.* (See also p. 270.)

assure, ensure, insure   *Assure* means "to promise": *He <u>assured</u> us that we would miss the traffic. Ensure* and *insure* often are used interchangeably to mean "make certain," but some reserve *insure* for matters of legal and financial protection and use *ensure* for more general meanings: *We left early to <u>ensure</u> that we would miss the traffic. It's expensive to <u>insure</u> yourself against floods.*

as to A stuffy substitute for *about: The suspect was questioned about* [not *as to*] *her actions.*

at The use of *at* after *where* is wordy and should be avoided: *Where are you meeting him?* is preferable to *Where are you meeting him at?*

at this point in time Wordy for *now, at this point,* or *at this time.*

averse, adverse See *adverse, averse.*

awful, awfully Strictly speaking, *awful* means "awe-inspiring." As intensifiers meaning "very" or "extremely" (*He tried awfully hard*), *awful* and *awfully* should be avoided in formal speech or writing.

a while, awhile *Awhile* is an adverb; *a while* is an article and a noun. Thus *awhile* can modify a verb but cannot serve as the object of a preposition, and *a while* is just the opposite: *I will be gone awhile* [not *a while*]. *I will be gone for a while* [not *awhile*].

bad, badly In formal speech and writing, *bad* should be used only as an adjective; the adverb is *badly. He felt bad because his tooth ached badly.* In *He felt bad,* the verb *felt* is a linking verb and the adjective *bad* is a subject complement. (See also pp. 320–21.)

being as, being that Colloquial for *because,* the preferable word in formal speech or writing: *Because* [not *Being as*] *the world is round, Columbus never did fall off the edge.*

beside, besides *Beside* is a preposition meaning "next to." *Besides* is a preposition meaning "except" or "in addition to" as well as an adverb meaning "in addition." *Besides, several other people besides you want to sit beside Dr. Christensen.*

better, had better *Had better* (meaning "ought to") is a verb modified by an adverb. The verb is necessary and should not be omitted: *You had better* [not just *better*] *go.*

between, among See *among, between.*

bring, take Use *bring* only for movement from a farther place to a nearer one and *take* for any other movement. *First, take these books to the library for renewal, then take them to Mr. Daniels. Bring them back to me when he's finished.*

bunch In formal speech and writing, *bunch* (as a noun) should be used only to refer to clusters of things growing or fastened together, such as bananas and grapes. Its use to mean a group of items or people is colloquial; *crowd* or *group* is preferable.

burst, bursted; bust, busted *Burst* is a standard verb form meaning "to fly apart suddenly." Its main forms are *burst, burst, burst;* the form *bursted* is nonstandard. The verb *bust* (*busted*) is slang.

but, hardly, scarcely These words are negative in their own right; using *not* with any of them produces a double negative (see p. 322). *We have but* [not *haven't got but*] *an hour before our plane leaves. I could hardly* [not *couldn't hardly*] *make out her face.*

but, however, yet Each of these words is adequate to express contrast. Don't combine them. *He had finished, yet* [not *but yet*] *he continued.*

but that, but what These wordy substitutes for *that* and *what* should be avoided: *I don't doubt that* [not *but that*] *you are right.*

calculate, figure, reckon   As substitutes for *expect* or *imagine* (*I figure I'll go*), these words are colloquial.

can, may   Strictly, *can* indicates capacity or ability, and *may* indicates permission: *If I may talk with you a moment, I believe I can solve your problem. May* also indicates possibility: *You may like what you hear.*

can't help but   This idiom is common but redundant. Either *I can't help wishing* or the more formal *I cannot but wish* is preferable to *I can't help but wish.*

case, instance, line   Expressions such as *in the case of, in the instance of,* and *along the lines of* are usually padding and should be avoided.

censor, censure   To *censor* is to edit or remove from public view on moral or some other grounds; to *censure* is to give a formal scolding. *The lieutenant was censured by Major Taylor for censoring the letters her soldiers wrote home from boot camp.*

center around   *Center on* is more logical than, and preferable to, *center around.*

climatic, climactic   *Climatic* comes from *climate* and refers to weather: *Recent droughts may indicate a climatic change. Climactic* comes from *climax* and refers to a dramatic high point: *During the climactic duel between Hamlet and Laertes, Gertrude drinks poisoned wine.*

complement, compliment   To *complement* something is to add to, complete, or reinforce it: *Her yellow blouse complemented her black hair.* To *compliment* something is to make a flattering remark about it: *He complimented her on her hair. Compliment* also functions as a noun: *She thanked him for the compliment.* The adjective *complimentary* can also mean "free": *complimentary tickets.*

compose, comprise   *Compose* means "to make up": *The parts compose the whole. Comprise* means "to consist of": *The whole comprises the parts.* Thus, *The band comprises* [not *is comprised of*] *twelve musicians. Twelve musicians compose* [not *comprise*] *the band.*

conscience, conscious   *Conscience* is a noun meaning "a sense of right and wrong"; *conscious* is an adjective meaning "aware" or "awake." *Though I was barely conscious, my conscience nagged me.*

contact   Often used imprecisely as a verb instead of a more exact word such as *consult, talk with, telephone,* or *write to.*

continual, continuous   *Continual* means "constantly recurring": *Most movies on television are continually interrupted by commercials. Continuous* means "unceasing": *Some cable channels present movies continuously without commercials.*

convince, persuade   In the strictest sense, to *convince* someone means to change his or her opinion; to *persuade* someone means to move him or her to action. *Convince* is thus properly followed by *of* or *that,* whereas *persuade* is followed by *to: Once he had convinced Othello of Desdemona's infidelity, Iago easily persuaded him to kill her.*

could care less   The expression is *could not* [*couldn't*] *care less. Could care less* indicates some care, the opposite of what is intended.

could of   See *have, of.*

couple of Used colloquially to mean "a few" or "several."

credible, creditable, credulous *Credible* means "believable": *It's a strange story, but it seems credible to me. Creditable* means "deserving of credit" or "worthy": *Steve gave a creditable performance. Credulous* means "gullible": *The credulous Claire believed Tim's lies.* See also *incredible, incredulous.*

criteria The plural of *criterion* (meaning "standard for judgment"): *Our criteria are strict. The most important criterion is a sense of humor.*

data The plural of *datum* (meaning "fact"): *Out of all the data generated by these experiments, not one datum supports our hypothesis.* Usually, a more common term such as *fact, result,* or *figure* is preferred to *datum.* Though *data* is often used with a singular verb, many readers prefer the plural verb and it is always correct: *The data fail* [not *fails*] *to support the hypothesis.*

device, devise *Device* is the noun, and *devise* is the verb: *Can you devise some device for getting his attention?*

different from, different than *Different from* is preferred: *His purpose is different from mine.* But *different than* is widely accepted when a construction using *from* would be wordy: *I'm a different person now than I used to be* is preferable to *I'm a different person now from the person I used to be.*

differ from, differ with To *differ from* is to be unlike: *The twins differ from each other only in their hairstyles.* To *differ with* is to disagree with: *I have to differ with you on that point.*

discreet, discrete *Discreet* (noun form *discretion*) means "tactful": *What's a discreet way of telling Maud to be quiet? Discrete* (noun form *discreteness*) means "separate and distinct": *Within a computer's memory are millions of discrete bits of information.*

disinterested, uninterested *Disinterested* means "impartial": *We chose Pete, as a disinterested third party, to decide who was right. Uninterested* means "bored" or "lacking interest": *Unfortunately, Pete was completely uninterested in the question.*

don't *Don't* is the contraction for *do not,* not for *does not: I don't care, you don't care,* and *he doesn't* [not *don't*] *care.*

due to *Due* is an adjective or noun; thus *due to* is always acceptable as a subject complement: *His gray hairs were due to age.* Many object to *due to* as a preposition meaning "because of" (*Due to the holiday, class was canceled*). A rule of thumb is that *due to* is always correct after a form of the verb *be* but questionable otherwise.

due to the fact that Wordy for *because.*

each and every Wordy for *each* or *every.* Write *each one of us* or *every one of us,* not *each and every one of us.*

eager, anxious See *anxious, eager.*

effect See *affect, effect.*

elicit, illicit *Elicit* is a verb meaning "bring out" or "call forth." *Illicit* is an adjective meaning "unlawful." *The crime elicited an outcry against illicit drugs.*

emigrate, immigrate *Emigrate* means "to leave one place and move to another" (the Latin prefix *e-* means "out of": "migrate out of"): *The Chus emigrated from Korea.* *Immigrate* means "to move into a place where one was not born" (the Latin prefix *im-* means "into": "migrate into"): *They immigrated to the United States.*

ensure See *assure, ensure, insure.*

enthused Used colloquially as an adjective meaning "showing enthusiasm." The preferred adjective is *enthusiastic: The coach was enthusiastic* [not *enthused*] *about the team's victory.*

especially, specially *Especially* means "particularly" or "more than other things"; *specially* means "for a specific reason." *I especially treasure my boots. They were made specially for me.*

et al., etc. Use *et al.*, the Latin abbreviation for "and other people," only in source citations: *Jones et al.* Avoid *etc.*, the Latin abbreviation for "and other things," in formal writing, and do not use it to refer to people or to substitute for precision, as in *The government provides health care, etc.* See also *and etc.*

everybody, every body; everyone, every one *Everybody* and *everyone* are indefinite pronouns: *Everybody* [or *Everyone*] *knows Tom steals. Every one* is a pronoun modified by *every*, and *every body* is a noun modified by *every*. Both refer to each thing or person of a specific group and are typically followed by *of: The game commissioner has stocked every body of fresh water in the state with fish, and now every one of our rivers is a potential trout stream.*

everyday, every day *Everyday* is an adjective meaning "used daily" or "common"; *every day* is a noun modified by *every: Everyday problems tend to arise every day.*

everywheres Nonstandard for *everywhere.*

except See *accept, except.*

except for the fact that Wordy for *except that.*

explicit, implicit *Explicit* means "stated outright": *I left explicit instructions. He explicitly consented. Implicit* means "implied, unstated": *We had an implicit understanding. I trust Marcia implicitly.*

farther, further *Farther* refers to additional distance (*How much farther is it to the beach?*), and *further* refers to additional time, amount, or other abstract matters (*I don't want to discuss this any further*).

feel Avoid this word in place of *think* or *believe: She thinks* [not *feels*] *that the law should be changed.*

fewer, less *Fewer* refers to individual countable items (a plural count noun), *less* to general amounts (a noncount noun, always singular): *Skim milk has fewer calories than whole milk. We have less milk left than I thought.*

field The phrase *the field of* is wordy and generally unnecessary: *Margaret plans to specialize in* [not *in the field of*] *family medicine.*

figure See *calculate, figure, reckon.*

fixing to Avoid this colloquial substitute for "intend to": *The school intends* [not *is fixing*] *to build a new library.*

flaunt, flout *Flaunt* means "show off": *If you have style, flaunt it. Flout* means "scorn" or "defy": *Hester Prynne flouted convention and paid the price.*

flunk A colloquial substitute for *fail.*

former, latter *Former* refers to the first-named of two things, *latter* to the second-named: *I like both skiing and swimming, the former in the winter and the latter all year round.* To refer to the first- or last-named of three or more things, say *first* or *last: I like jogging, swimming, and hang gliding, but the last is inconvenient in the city.*

fun As an adjective, *fun* is colloquial and should be avoided in most writing: *It was a pleasurable* [not *fun*] *evening.*

further See *farther, further.*

get This common verb is used in many slang and colloquial expressions: *get lost, that really gets me, getting on. Get* is easy to overuse; watch out for it in expressions such as *it's getting better* (substitute *improving*) and *we got done* (substitute *finished*).

go As a substitute for *say* or *reply, go* is colloquial: *He says* [not *goes*], *"How do you do, madam?"*

good, well *Good* is an adjective, and *well* is nearly always an adverb: *Larry's a good dancer. He and Linda dance well together. Well* is properly used as an adjective only to refer to health: *You look well.* (*You look good,* in contrast, means "Your appearance is pleasing.")

good and Colloquial for "very": *I was very* [not *good and*] *tired.*

had better See *better, had better.*

had ought The *had* is unnecessary and should be omitted: *He ought* [not *had ought*] *to listen to his mother.*

half Either *half a* or *a half* is appropriate usage, but *a half a* is redundant: *Half a loaf* [not *A half a loaf*] *is better than none. I'd like a half-gallon* [not *a half a gallon*] *of mineral water, please.*

hanged, hung Though both are past-tense forms of *hang, hanged* is used to refer to executions and *hung* is used for all other meanings: *Tom Dooley was hanged* [not *hung*] *from a white oak tree. I hung* [not *hanged*] *the picture you gave me.*

hardly See *but, hardly, scarcely.*

have, of Use *have,* not *of,* after helping verbs such as *could, should, would, may,* and *might: You should have* [not *should of*] *told me.*

he, she; he/she Convention has allowed the use of *he* to mean "he or she": *After the infant learns to creep, he progresses to crawling.* However, many writers today consider this usage inaccurate and unfair because it seems to exclude females. The construction *he/she,* one substitute for *he,* is awkward and objectionable to most readers. The better choice is to make the pronoun plural, to rephrase, or, sparingly, to use *he or she.* For instance: *After infants learn to creep, they progress to crawling. After learning to creep, the infant progresses to crawling. After the infant learns to creep, he or she progresses to crawling.* (See also pp. 313–15 and 510–12.)

herself, himself   See *myself, herself, himself, yourself.*

hisself   Nonstandard for *himself.*

hopefully   *Hopefully* means "with hope": *Freddy waited hopefully for a glimpse of Eliza.* The use of *hopefully* to mean "it is to be hoped," "I hope," or "let's hope" is now very common; but since many readers continue to object strongly to the usage, you should avoid it. *I hope* [not *Hopefully*] *the law will pass.*

idea, ideal   An *idea* is a thought or conception. An *ideal* (noun) is a model of perfection or a goal. *Ideal* should not be used in place of *idea: The idea* [not *ideal*] *of the play is that our ideals often sustain us.*

if, whether   For clarity, use *whether* rather than *if* when you are expressing an alternative: *If I laugh hard, people can't tell whether I'm crying.*

illicit   See *elicit, illicit.*

illusion   See *allusion, illusion.*

immigrate, emigrate   See *emigrate, immigrate.*

impact   Both the noun and the verb *impact* connote forceful or even violent collision. Avoid the increasingly common diluted meanings of *impact:* "an effect" (noun) or "to have an effect on" (verb). The diluted verb (*The budget cuts impacted social science research*) is bureaucratic jargon.

implicit   See *explicit, implicit.*

imply, infer   Writers or speakers *imply,* meaning "suggest": *Jim's letter implies he's having a good time.* Readers or listeners *infer,* meaning "conclude": *From Jim's letter I infer he's having a good time.*

in, into   *In* indicates location or condition: *He was in the garage. She was in a coma. Into* indicates movement or a change in condition: *He went into the garage. She fell into a coma.* Generally avoid the slang sense of *into* meaning "interested in" or "involved in": *I am into Zen.*

in . . .   A number of phrases beginning with *in* are needlessly wordy and should be avoided: *in the event that* (for *if*); *in the neighborhood of* (for *approximately* or *about*); *in this day and age* (for *now* or *nowadays*); *in spite of the fact that* (for *although* or *even though*); and *in view of the fact that* (for *because* or *considering that*). Certain other *in* phrases are nothing but padding and can be omitted entirely: *in nature, in number, in reality,* and *in a very real sense.* (See also pp. 527–28.)

incredible, incredulous   *Incredible* means "unbelievable"; *incredulous* means "unbelieving": *When Nancy heard Dennis's incredible story, she was frankly incredulous.* See also *credible, creditable, credulous.*

individual, person, party   *Individual* should refer to a single human being in contrast to a group or should stress uniqueness: *The US Constitution places strong emphasis on the rights of the individual.* For other meanings *person* is preferable: *What person* [not *individual*] *wouldn't want the security promised in that advertisement? Party* means "group" (*Can you seat a party of four for dinner?*) and should not be used to refer to an individual except in legal documents. See also *people, persons.*

infer   See *imply, infer.*

in regards to   Nonstandard for *in regard to*, *as regards*, or *regarding*. See also *regarding*.

inside of, outside of   The *of* is unnecessary when *inside* and *outside* are used as prepositions: *Stay inside* [not *inside of*] *the house. The decision is outside* [not *outside of*] *my authority. Inside of* may refer colloquially to time, though in formal English *within* is preferred: *The law was passed within* [not *inside of*] *a year.*

instance   See *case, instance, line*.

insure   See *assure, ensure, insure*.

irregardless   Nonstandard for *regardless*.

is, are   See *are, is*.

is because   See *reason is because*.

is when, is where   These are faulty constructions in sentences that define: *Adolescence is a stage* [not *is when a person is*] *between childhood and adulthood. Socialism is a system in which* [not *is where*] *government owns the means of production.* (See also p. 373.)

its, it's   *Its* is the pronoun *it* in the possessive case: *That plant is losing its leaves. It's* is a contraction for *it is* or *it has: It's* [*It is*] *likely to die. It's* [*It has*] *got a fungus.* Many people confuse *it's* and *its* because possessives are most often formed with *-'s;* but the possessive *its*, like *his* and *hers*, never takes an apostrophe.

-ize, -wise   The suffix *-ize* changes a noun or adjective into a verb: *revolutionize, immunize.* The suffix *-wise* changes a noun or adjective into an adverb: *clockwise, otherwise, likewise.* Avoid the two suffixes except in established words: *The two nations are ready to settle on* [not *finalize*] *an agreement. I'm highly sensitive* [not *sensitized*] *to that kind of criticism. Financially* [not *Moneywise*], *it's a good time to buy land.*

kind of, sort of, type of   In formal speech and writing, avoid using *kind of* or *sort of* to mean "somewhat": *He was rather* [not *kind of*] *tall.*

   Kind, sort, and *type* are singular and take singular modifiers and verbs: *This kind of dog is easily trained.* Agreement errors often occur when these singular nouns are combined with the plural adjectives *these* and *those: These kinds* [not *kind*] *of dogs are easily trained. Kind, sort,* and *type* should be followed by *of* but not by *a: I don't know what type of* [not *type* or *type of a*] *dog that is.*

   Use *kind of, sort of,* or *type of* only when the word *kind, sort,* or *type* is important: *That was a strange* [not *strange sort of*] *statement.*

later, latter   *Later* refers to time; *latter* refers to the second-named of two items. See also *former, latter*.

lay, lie   *Lay* means "put" or "place" and takes a direct object: *We could lay the tablecloth in the sun.* Its main forms are *lay, laid, laid. Lie* means "recline" or "be situated" and does not take an object: *I lie awake at night. The town lies east of the river.* Its main forms are *lie, lay, lain.* (See also p. 280.)

leave, let   *Leave* and *let* are interchangeable only when followed by *alone; leave me alone* is the same as *let me alone.* Otherwise, *leave* means "depart" and *let* means "allow": *Julia would not let Susan leave.*

less   See *fewer, less.*

let   See *leave, let.*

liable   See *apt, liable, likely.*

lie, lay   See *lay, lie.*

like, as   In formal speech and writing, *like* should not introduce a full clause (with a subject and a verb) because it is a preposition. The preferred choice is *as* or *as if: The plan succeeded as* [not *like*] *we hoped. It seemed as if* [not *like*] *it might fail. Other plans like it have failed.*

When *as* serves as a preposition, the distinction between *as* and *like* depends on meaning. *As* suggests that the subject is equivalent or identical to the description: *She was hired as an engineer. Like* suggests resemblance but not identity: *People like her do well in such jobs.* See also *like, such as.*

like, such as   Strictly, *such as* precedes an example that represents a larger subject, whereas *like* indicates that two subjects are comparable. *Steve has recordings of many great saxophonists such as Ben Webster and Lee Konitz. Steve wants to be a great jazz saxophonist like Ben Webster and Lee Konitz.*

Many writers prefer to keep *such* and *as* together: *Steve admires saxophonists such as* . . . rather than *Steve admires such saxophonists as.* . . .

likely   See *apt, liable, likely.*

line   See *case, instance, line.*

literally   This word means "actually" or "just as the words say," and it should not be used to qualify or intensify expressions whose words are not to be taken at face value. The sentence *He was literally climbing the walls* describes a person behaving like an insect, not a person who is restless or anxious. For the latter meaning, *literally* should be omitted.

lose, loose   *Lose* means "mislay": *Did you lose a brown glove? Loose* means "unrestrained" or "not tight": *Ann's canary got loose. Loose* can also function as a verb meaning "let loose": *They loose the dogs as soon as they spot the bear.*

lots, lots of   Colloquial substitutes for *very many, a great many,* or *much.* Avoid *lots* and *lots of* in college or business writing. When you use either one informally, be careful to maintain subject-verb agreement: *There are* [not *is*] *lots of fish in the pond.*

may, can   See *can, may.*

may be, maybe   *May be* is a verb, and *maybe* is an adverb meaning "perhaps": *Tuesday may be a legal holiday. Maybe we won't have classes.*

may of   See *have, of.*

media   *Media* is the plural of *medium* and takes a plural verb: *All the news media are increasingly visual.* The singular verb is common, even in the media, but many readers prefer the plural verb and it is always correct.

might of   See *have, of.*

moral, morale   As a noun, *moral* means "ethical conclusion" or "lesson": *The moral of the story escapes me. Morale* means "spirit" or "state of mind": *Victory improved the team's morale.*

most, almost See *almost, most.*

must of See *have, of.*

myself, herself, himself, yourself The *-self* pronouns refer to or intensify another word or words: *Paul helped himself; Jill herself said so.* The *-self* pronouns are often used colloquially in place of personal pronouns, but that use should be avoided in formal speech and writing: *No one except me* [not *myself*] *saw the accident. Our delegates will be Susan and you* [not *yourself*]. See also p. 268 on the unchanging forms of the *-self* pronouns in standard American English.

nohow Nonstandard for *in no way* or *in any way.*

nothing like, nowhere near These colloquial substitutes for *not nearly* are best avoided in formal speech and writing: *That program is not nearly* [not *nowhere near*] *as expensive.*

nowheres Nonstandard for *nowhere.*

number See *amount, number.*

of, have See *have, of.*

off of *Of* is unnecessary. Use *off* or *from* rather than *off of: He jumped off* [or *from*, not *off of*] *the roof.*

OK, O.K., okay All three spellings are acceptable, but avoid this colloquial term in formal speech and writing.

on, upon In modern English, *upon* is usually just a stuffy way of saying *on.* Unless you need a formal effect, use *on: We decided on* [not *upon*] *a location for our next meeting.*

on account of Wordy for *because of.*

on the other hand This transitional expression of contrast should be preceded by its mate, *on the one hand: On the one hand, we hoped for snow. On the other hand, we feared that it would harm the animals.* However, the two combined can be unwieldy, and a simple *but, however, yet,* or *in contrast* often suffices: *We hoped for snow. Yet we feared that it would harm the animals.*

outside of See *inside of, outside of.*

owing to the fact that Wordy for *because.*

party See *individual, person, party.*

people, persons In formal usage, *people* refers to a general group: *We the people of the United States. . . . Persons* refers to a collection of individuals: *Will the person or persons who saw the accident please notify. . . .* Except when emphasizing individuals, prefer *people* to *persons.* See also *individual, person, party.*

per Except in technical writing, an English equivalent is usually preferable to the Latin *per: $10 an* [not *per*] *hour; sent by* [not *per*] *parcel post; requested in* [not *per* or *as per*] *your letter.*

percent (per cent), percentage Both of these terms refer to fractions of one hundred. *Percent* always follows a number (*40 percent of the voters*), and the word should be used instead of the symbol (%) in general writing. *Percentage* stands alone (*the percentage of votes*) or follows an adjective (*a high percentage*).

person See *individual, person, party.*

persons See *people, persons.*

persuade See *convince, persuade.*

phenomena The plural of *phenomenon* (meaning "perceivable fact" or "unusual occurrence"): *Many phenomena are not recorded. One phenomenon is attracting attention.*

plenty A colloquial substitute for *very: The reaction occurred very* [not *plenty*] *fast.*

plus *Plus* is standard as a preposition meaning *in addition to: His income plus mine is sufficient.* But *plus* is colloquial as a conjunctive adverb: *Our organization is larger than theirs; moreover* [not *plus*], *we have more money.*

practicable, practical *Practicable* means "capable of being put into practice"; *practical* means "useful" or "sensible": *We figured out a practical new design for our kitchen, but it was too expensive to be practicable.*

precede, proceed The verb *precede* means "come before": *My name precedes yours in the alphabet.* The verb *proceed* means "move on": *We were told to proceed to the waiting room.*

prejudice, prejudiced *Prejudice* is a noun; *prejudiced* is an adjective. Do not drop the *-d* from *prejudiced: I knew that my parents were prejudiced* [not *prejudice*].

pretty Overworked as an adverb meaning "rather" or "somewhat": *He was somewhat* [not *pretty*] *irked at the suggestion.*

previous to, prior to Wordy for *before.*

principal, principle *Principal* is an adjective meaning "foremost" or "major," a noun meaning "chief official," or, in finance, a noun meaning "capital sum." *Principle* is a noun only, meaning "rule" or "axiom." *Her principal reasons for confessing were her principles of right and wrong.*

proceed, precede See *precede, proceed.*

provided, providing *Provided* may serve as a subordinating conjunction meaning "on the condition (that)"; *providing* may not. *The grocer will begin providing food for the soup kitchen provided* [not *providing*] *we find a suitable space.*

question of whether, question as to whether Wordy substitutes for *whether.*

raise, rise *Raise* means "lift" or "bring up" and takes a direct object: *The Kirks raise cattle.* Its main forms are *raise, raised, raised. Rise* means "get up" and does not take an object: *They must rise at dawn.* Its main forms are *rise, rose, risen.* (See also p. 280.)

real, really In formal speech and writing, *real* should not be used as an adverb; *really* is the adverb and *real* an adjective. *Popular reaction to the announcement was really* [not *real*] *enthusiastic.*

reason is because Although colloquially common, this expression should be avoided in formal speech and writing. Use a *that* clause after *reason is: The reason he is absent is that* [not *is because*] *he is sick.* Or: *He is absent because he is sick.*

reckon   See *calculate, figure, reckon.*

regarding, in regard to, with regard to, relating to, relative to, with respect to, respecting   Stuffy substitutes for *on, about,* or *concerning: Mr. McGee spoke about* [not *with regard to*] *the plans for the merger.*

respectful, respective   *Respectful* means "full of (or showing) respect": *Be respectful of other people. Respective* means "separate": *The French and the Germans occupied their respective trenches.*

rise, raise   See *raise, rise.*

scarcely   See *but, hardly, scarcely.*

sensual, sensuous   *Sensual* suggests sexuality; *sensuous* means "pleasing to the senses." *Stirred by the sensuous scent of meadow grass and flowers, Cheryl and Paul found their thoughts growing increasingly sensual.*

set, sit   *Set* means "put" or "place" and takes a direct object: *He sets the pitcher down.* Its main forms are *set, set, set. Sit* means "be seated" and does not take an object: *She sits on the sofa.* Its main forms are *sit, sat, sat.* (See also p. 280.)

shall, will   *Will* is the future-tense helping verb for all persons: *I will go, you will go, they will go.* The main use of *shall* is for first-person questions requesting an opinion or consent: *Shall I order a pizza? Shall we dance?* (Questions that merely inquire about the future use *will: When will I see you again?*) *Shall* can also be used for the first person when a formal effect is desired (*I shall expect you around three*), and it is occasionally used with the second or third person to express the speaker's determination (*You shall do as I say*).

should, would   *Should* expresses obligation: *I should fix dinner. You should set the table. Jack should wash the dishes. Would* expresses a wish or hypothetical condition: *I would do it. Wouldn't you?* When the context is formal, however, *should* is sometimes used instead of *would* in the first person: *We should be delighted to accept.*

should of   See *have, of.*

since   *Since* mainly relates to time: *I've been waiting since noon.* But *since* is also often used to mean "because": *Since you ask, I'll tell you.* Revise sentences in which the word could have either meaning, such as *Since I studied physics, I have been planning to major in engineering.*

sit, set   See *set, sit.*

situation   Often unnecessary, as in *The situation is that we have to get some help* (revise to *We have to get some help*) or *The team was faced with a punting situation* (revise to *The team was faced with punting* or *The team had to punt*).

so   Avoid using *so* alone as a vague intensifier: *He was so late. So* needs to be followed by *that* and a clause that states a result: *He was so late that I left without him.*

some   *Some* is colloquial as an adverb meaning "somewhat" or "to some extent" and as an adjective meaning "remarkable": *We'll have to hurry somewhat* [not *some*] *to get there in time. Those are remarkable* [not *some*] *photographs.*

somebody, some body; someone, some one *Somebody* and *someone* are indefinite pronouns; *some body* is a noun modified by *some;* and *some one* is a pronoun or an adjective modified by *some*. *Somebody ought to invent a shampoo that will give hair some body. Someone told Janine she should choose some one plan and stick with it.*

someplace Informal for *somewhere*.

sometime, sometimes, some time *Sometime* means "at an indefinite time in the future": *Why don't you come up and see me sometime? Sometimes* means "now and then": *I still see my old friend Joe sometimes. Some time* means "a span of time": *I need some time to make the payments.*

somewheres Nonstandard for *somewhere*.

sort of, sort of a See *kind of, sort of, type of.*

specially See *especially, specially.*

such Avoid using *such* as a vague intensifier: *It was such a cold winter. Such* should be followed by *that* and a clause that states a result: *It was such a cold winter that Napoleon's troops had to turn back.*

such as See *like, such as.*

supposed to, used to In both of these expressions, the *-d* is essential: *I used to* [not *use to*] *think so. He's supposed to* [not *suppose to*] *meet us.*

sure Colloquial when used as an adverb meaning *surely: James Madison sure was right about the need for the Bill of Rights.* If you merely want to be emphatic, use *certainly: Madison certainly was right.* If your goal is to convince a possibly reluctant reader, use *surely: Madison surely was right. Surely Madison was right.*

sure and, sure to; try and, try to *Sure to* and *try to* are the correct forms: *Be sure to* [not *sure and*] *vote. Try to* [not *Try and*] *vote early to avoid a line.*

take, bring See *bring, take.*

than, as See *as, than.*

than, then *Than* is a conjunction used in comparisons, *then* an adverb indicating time: *Holmes knew then that Moriarty was wilier than he had thought.*

that, which *That* always introduces an essential clause: *We should use the lettuce that Susan bought* (*that Susan bought* limits *lettuce* to a particular lettuce). *Which* can introduce both essential and nonessential clauses, but many writers reserve *which* only for nonessential clauses: *The leftover lettuce, which is in the refrigerator, would make a good salad* (*which is in the refrigerator* simply provides more information about the lettuce we already know of). Essential clauses (with *that* or *which*) are not set off by commas; nonessential clauses (with *which*) are. (See also pp. 430–31.)

that, who, which Use *that* to refer to most animals and to things: *The animals that escaped included a zebra. The rocket that failed cost millions.* Use *who* to refer to people and to animals with names: *Dorothy is the girl who visits Oz. Her dog, Toto, who accompanies her, gives her courage.* Use *which* only to refer to animals and things: *The river, which runs more than a thousand miles, empties into the Indian Ocean.* (See also pp. 352–53.)

their, there, they're *Their* is the possessive form of *they: Give them their money.* *There* indicates place (*I saw her standing there*) or functions to postpone the sentence subject (*There is a hole behind you*). *They're* is a contraction for *they are: They're going fast.*

theirselves Nonstandard for *themselves.*

them In standard American English, *them* does not serve as an adjective: *Those* [not *Them*] *people want to know.*

then, than See *than, then.*

these kind, these sort, these type, those kind See *kind of, sort of, type of.*

this, these *This* is singular: *this car* or *This is the reason I left.* *These* is plural: *these cars* or *These are not valid reasons.*

this here, these here, that there, them there Nonstandard for *this, these, that,* and *those.*

thru A colloquial spelling of *through* that should be avoided in all academic and business writing.

thusly A mistaken form of *thus.*

till, until, 'til *Till* and *until* have the same meaning; either is acceptable. *'Til,* a contraction of *until,* is an old form that has been replaced by *till.*

time period Since a *period* is an interval of time, the expression is redundant: *They did not see each other for a long time* [not *time period*]. *Six accidents occurred in a three-week period* [not *time period*].

to, too, two *To* is a preposition; *too* is an adverb meaning "also" or "excessively"; and *two* is a number. *I too have been to Europe two times.*

too Avoid using *too* as a vague intensifier: *Monkeys are too mean.* When you do use *too,* explain the consequences of the excessive quality: *Monkeys are too mean to make good pets.*

toward, towards Both are acceptable, though *toward* is preferred. Use one or the other consistently.

try and, try to See *sure and, sure to; try and, try to.*

type of See *kind of, sort of, type of.* Don't use *type* without *of: It was a family type of* [not *type*] *restaurant.* Or, better: *It was a family restaurant.*

uninterested See *disinterested, uninterested.*

unique *Unique* means "the only one of its kind" and so cannot sensibly be modified with words such as *very* or *most: That was a unique* [not *a very unique* or *the most unique*] *movie.*

until See *till, until, 'til.*

upon, on See *on, upon.*

usage, use *Usage* refers to conventions, most often those of a language: *Is "hadn't ought" proper usage? Usage* is often misused in place of the noun *use: Wise use* [not *usage*] *of insulation can save fuel.*

use, utilize *Utilize* can be used to mean "make good use of": *Many teachers utilize computers for instruction.* But for all other senses of "place in service" or "employ," prefer *use.*

used to   See *supposed to, used to*.

wait for, wait on   In formal speech and writing, *wait for* means "await" (*I'm waiting for Paul*), and *wait on* means "serve" (*The owner of the store herself waited on us*).

ways   Colloquial as a substitute for way: *We have only a little way* [not *ways*] *to go*.

well   See *good, well*.

whether, if   See *if, whether*.

which, that   See *that, which*.

which, who, that   See *that, who, which*.

who, whom   *Who* is the subject of a sentence or clause (*We don't know who will come*). *Whom* is the object of a verb or preposition (*We do not know whom we invited*). (See also pp. 271–72.)

who's, whose   *Who's* is the contraction of *who is* or *who has*: *Who's* [*Who is*] *at the door? Jim is the only one who's* [*who has*] *passed*. *Whose* is the possessive form of *who*: *Whose book is that?*

will, shall   See *shall, will*.

wise   See *-ize, -wise*.

with regard to, with respect to   See *regarding*.

would   See *should, would*.

would be   Often used instead of *is* or *are* to soften statements needlessly: *One example is* [not *would be*] *gun-control laws*. *Would* can combine with other verbs for the same unassertive effect: *would ask, would seem, would suggest*, and so on.

would have   Avoid this construction in place of *had* in clauses that begin *if* and state a condition contrary to fact: *If the tree had* [not *would have*] *withstood the fire, it would have been the oldest in the state*. (See also p. 299.)

would of   See *have, of*.

you   In all but very formal writing, *you* is generally appropriate as long as it means "you, the reader." In all writing, avoid indefinite uses of *you*, such as *In one ancient tribe your first loyalty was to your parents*. (See also p. 352.)

your, you're   *Your* is the possessive form of *you*: *Your dinner is ready*. *You're* is the contraction of *you are*: *You're bound to be late*.

yourself   See *myself, herself, himself, yourself*.

Glossary of Terms

This glossary defines terms of grammar, rhetoric, literary analysis, research, and other aspects of writing. Page numbers in parentheses refer you to sections of the text where the term is explained more fully.

absolute phrase   A phrase consisting of a noun or pronoun plus the *-ing* or *-ed* form of a verb (a participle): *Our accommodations arranged, we set out on our journey. They will hire a local person, other things being equal.* An absolute phrase modifies a whole clause or sentence (rather than a single word), and it is not joined to the rest of the sentence by a connector. (See p. 251.)

abstract and concrete   Two kinds of language. **Abstract** words refer to ideas, qualities, attitudes, and conditions that can't be perceived with the senses: *beauty, guilty, victory.* **Concrete** words refer to objects, persons, places, or conditions that can be perceived with the senses: *Abilene, scratchy, toolbox.* See also *general and specific.* (See pp. 518–19.)

acronym   A pronounceable word formed from the initial letter or letters of each word in an organization's title: for example, NATO (North Atlantic Treaty Organization).

active voice   See *verb voice.*

adjectival   A term sometimes used to describe any word or word group, other than an adjective, that is used to modify a noun. Common adjectivals include nouns (*wagon train, railroad ties*), phrases (*fool on the hill*), and clauses (*the man that I used to be*).

adjective   A word used to modify a noun (*beautiful morning*) or a pronoun (*ordinary one*). (See Chapter 16.) Nouns, some verb forms, phrases, and clauses may also serve as adjectives: *book sale; a used book; sale of old books; the sale, which occurs annually.* (See *clauses, prepositional phrases,* and *verbals and verbal phrases.*)

Adjectives come in several classes:

- A **descriptive adjective** names some quality of a noun: *beautiful morning, dark horse.*
- A **limiting adjective** narrows the scope of a noun. It may be a **possessive** (*my, their*); a **demonstrative adjective** (*this train, these days*); an **interrogative adjective** (*what time? whose body?*); or a number (*two boys*).
- A **proper adjective** is derived from a proper noun: *French language, Machiavellian scheme.*

Adjectives can also be classified according to position:

- An **attributive adjective** appears next to the noun it modifies: *full moon.*
- A **predicate adjective** is connected to its noun by a linking verb: *The moon is full.* See also *complement.*

adjective clause   See *adjective.*

adjective phrase   See *adjective.*

adverb   A word used to modify a verb (*warmly greet*), an adjective (*only three people*), another adverb (*quite seriously*), or a whole sentence (*Fortunately, she is employed*). (See Chapter 16.) Some verb forms, phrases, and clauses may also serve as adverbs: *easy to stop, drove by a farm, plowed the fields when the earth thawed.* (See *clause, prepositional phrase,* and *verbals and verbal phrases.*)

adverb clause   See *adverb.*

adverbial   A term sometimes used to describe any word or word group, other than an adverb, that is used to modify a verb, an adjective, another adverb, or a whole sentence. Common adverbials include nouns (*This little piggy stayed home*), phrases (*This little piggy went to market*), and clauses (*This little piggy went wherever he wanted*).

adverbial conjunction   See *conjunctive adverb.*

adverb phrase   See *adverb.*

agreement   The correspondence of one word to another in person, number, or gender. A verb must agree with its subject (*The chef orders egg sandwiches*), a pronoun must agree with its antecedent (*The chef surveys her breakfast*), and a demonstrative adjective must agree with its noun (*She likes these kinds of sandwiches*). (See Chapter 15.)
   Logical agreement requires consistency in number between other related words, usually nouns: *The students brought their books* [not *book*]. (See p. 356.)

allegory   A kind of narrative in which a literal story has an intended and sustained symbolic meaning. Authors often use allegory to provide a moral or lesson regarding political, religious, or social principles.

alliteration   The repetition of the same consonant sound at the beginning of a series of words: *Peter Piper picked a peck of pickled peppers.* See also *assonance* and *consonance.*

allusion   A reference to a well-known source or event, such as a Greek myth, a famous person, a work of art or literature, a popular song, a war, or a crime. (See p. 699.)

ambiguity   A quality of language or ideas in which there is no precise or single meaning. In academic writing, ambiguity is usually seen as a flaw, but in literature, especially in fiction, ambiguity often serves a purpose.

analogy   A comparison between members of different classes, such as a nursery school and a barnyard or a molecule and a pair of dancers. Usually, the purpose is to explain something unfamiliar to readers through something familiar. (See p. 100.)

analysis   The separation of a subject into its elements. Sometimes called **division,** analysis is fundamental to critical thinking, reading, and writing (pp. 148–49, 158–60) and is a useful tool for developing essays (p. 27) and paragraphs (pp. 97–98).

anecdote A concise story, often personal, used to introduce the subject of an oral presentation or essay, establish a bond with the audience, or illustrate a point.

antagonist See *character.*

antecedent The word to which a pronoun refers: *Jonah, who is not yet ten, has already chosen the college he will attend* (*Jonah* is the antecedent of the pronouns *who* and *he*). (See pp. 311–15.)

APA style The style of documentation recommended by the American Psychological Association and used in many of the social sciences. (For discussion and examples, see pp. 741–64.)

apostrophe A rhetorical device in which a narrator or speaker dramatically addresses an object, person, or idea: *"Smile O voluptuous cool-breath'd earth!"*

appeals Attempts to engage and persuade readers. (See pp. 15, 208–09.)

- An **emotional appeal (pathos)** touches readers' feelings, beliefs, and values.
- An **ethical appeal (ethos)** presents the writer as competent, sincere, and fair.
- A **logical appeal (logos)** engages readers' powers of reasoning.

appositive A word or phrase appearing next to a noun or pronoun that renames or identifies it and is equivalent to it: *My brother Michael, the best horn player in town, won the state competition* (*Michael* identifies which brother is being referred to; *the best horn player in town* renames *Michael*). (See pp. 256–57.)

argument Writing whose primary purpose is to convince readers of an idea or persuade them to act. (See Chapters 9–11.)

article The word *a, an,* or *the.* Articles are sometimes called **determiners** because they always signal that a noun follows. (See pp. 324–27 for when to use *a/an* versus *the.* See p. 845 for when to use *a* versus *an.*)

assertion See *claim.*

assonance The repetition of vowel sounds in a series of words: *a right fine life.* See also *alliteration, consonance,* and *rhyme.*

assumption A stated or unstated belief or opinion. Uncovering assumptions is part of critical thinking, reading, and writing (see pp. 149–51, 162). In argument, assumptions connect claims and evidence (see p. 188).

audience The intended readers of a piece of writing. Knowledge of the audience's needs and expectations helps a writer shape writing so that it is clear, interesting, and convincing. (See pp. 12–16, 168.)

auxiliary verb See *helping verb.*

balanced sentence A sentence consisting of two clauses with parallel constructions: *Do as I say, not as I do. Befriend all animals; exploit none.* Their balance makes such sentences highly emphatic. (See p. 385.)

belief A conviction based on morality, values, or faith. Statements of belief often serve as assumptions and sometimes as evidence, but they are not arguable and so cannot serve as the thesis in an argument. (See p. 182.)

blog A Web site, often created and maintained by a person or small group of people, with regular, dated entries of commentary or descriptions of events.

body In a piece of writing, the large central part where ideas supporting the thesis are presented and developed. See also *conclusion* and *introduction*.

brainstorming A technique for generating ideas about a subject: concentrating on the subject for a fixed time (say, fifteen minutes), you list every idea and detail that comes to mind. (See pp. 24–25.)

cardinal number The type of number that shows amount: *two, sixty, ninety-seven.* Contrast *ordinal number* (such as *second, ninety-seventh*).

case The form of a noun or pronoun that indicates its function in the sentence. Most pronouns have three cases:

- The **subjective case** (*I, she*) for the subject of a verb or for a subject complement.
- The **objective case** (*me, her*) for the object of a verb, verbal, or preposition.
- The **possessive case** to indicate ownership, used either as an adjective (*my, her*) or as a noun (*mine, hers*).

(See p. 267 for a list of the forms of personal and relative pronouns.)
Nouns use the subjective form (*dog, America*) for all cases except the possessive (*dog's, America's*).

cause-and-effect analysis The determination of why something happened or what its consequences were or will be. (See pp. 27 and 100–01.)

character The people or animals in a literary work, including the narrator of a story or the speaker of a poem. Characters are often classified by their importance in a work (major or minor), by the roles they play, and by their type. See also *foil* and p. 716.

- The **protagonist** is the central character of a work. Sometimes the protagonist is a **hero**, embodying noble or courageous values.
- The **antagonist** opposes the central character, or protagonist, of a work. Sometimes the antagonist is an **antihero** or villain, representing ignoble traits.
- A **flat character** shows a single dominant trait.
- A **round character** displays a range of human traits and behaviors.

chiasmus A rhetorical scheme in which two phrases mirror each other in reverse grammatical order: *From one who knows, who comes from two. By day we live, we die by night.*

Chicago style A style of documentation recommended by *The Chicago Manual of Style* and used in history, art, and some other humanities. (For discussion and examples, see pp. 724–35.)

chronological organization The arrangement of events as they occurred in time, usually from first to last. (See pp. 42, 83.)

citation In research writing, the way of acknowledging material borrowed from sources. Most systems of citation are basically similar: a number or brief parenthetical reference in the text indicates that particular material is borrowed and directs the reader to information on the source at the end of the work. The systems do differ, however. (See pp. 619–63 for MLA style, pp. 724–35 for Chicago style, pp. 741–61 for APA style, and pp. 773–79 for CSE style.)

claim A positive statement or assertion that requires support. Claims are the backbone of any argument. (See pp. 181–83.)

classification The sorting of many elements into groups based on their similarities. (See pp. 28 and 98–99.)

clause A group of related words containing a subject and a predicate. A **main (independent) clause** can stand by itself as a sentence. A **subordinate (dependent) clause** serves as a single part of speech and so cannot stand by itself as a sentence.

Main clause   We can go to the movies.
Subordinate clause   We can go if Julie gets back on time.

A subordinate clause may function as an adjective (*The car that hit Fred was speeding*), an adverb (*The car hit Fred when it ran a red light*), or a noun (*Whoever was driving should be arrested*). (See p. 254.)

clichés See *trite expressions.*

climactic organization The arrangement of material in order of increasing drama or interest, leading to a climax. (See pp. 44, 85.)

climax The point in a play or narrative to which all action leads, followed by plot resolution and conclusion. In *Romeo and Juliet,* the climax occurs during the lovers' death scene. See also *denouement.*

clustering A technique for generating ideas about a subject: drawing and writing, you branch outward from a center point (the subject) to pursue the implications of ideas. (See pp. 25–26.)

coherence The quality of an effective essay or paragraph that helps readers see relations among ideas and move easily from one idea to the next. (See pp. 44–45, 80–91.)

collaborative learning Students working together in groups to help each other become better writers and readers. (See pp. 69–72, 793–96.)

collective noun See *noun.*

colloquial language The words and expressions of everyday speech. Colloquial language can enliven informal writing but is generally inappropriate in formal academic or business writing. See also *formal and informal.* (See p. 507.)

comma splice A sentence error in which two main clauses are separated by a comma with no coordinating conjunction. (See Chapter 18.)

Comma splice   The book was long, it contained useful data.
Revised   The book was long; it contained useful data.
Revised   The book was long, and it contained useful data.

common noun See *noun.*

comparative See *comparison.*

comparison   The form of an adverb or adjective that shows its degree of quality or amount.

- The **positive degree** is the simple, uncompared form: *gross, shyly.*
- The **comparative degree** compares the thing modified to at least one other thing: *grosser, more shyly.*
- The **superlative degree** indicates that the thing modified exceeds all other things to which it is being compared: *grossest, most shyly.*

The comparative and superlative degrees are formed either with the endings *-er/-est* or with the words *more/most, less/least.* (See pp. 320–21.)

comparison and contrast   The identification of similarities (comparison) and differences (contrast) between two or more subjects. (See pp. 28, 99–100.)

complement   A word or word group that completes the sense of a subject, an object, or a verb. (See pp. 238–41.)

- A **subject complement** follows a linking verb and renames or describes the subject. It may be an adjective, noun, or pronoun. *I am a lion tamer, but I am not yet experienced* (the noun *lion tamer* and the adjective *experienced* complement the subject *I*). Adjective complements are also called **predicate adjectives.** Noun complements are also called **predicate nouns** or **predicate nominatives.**
- An **object complement** follows and modifies or refers to a direct object. The complement may be an adjective or a noun. *If you elect me president, I'll keep the students satisfied* (the noun *president* complements the direct object *me*, and the adjective *satisfied* complements the direct object *students*).
- A **verb complement** is a direct or indirect object of a verb. It may be a noun or pronoun. *Don't give the chimp that peanut* (*chimp* is the indirect object and *peanut* is the direct object of the verb *give*; both objects are verb complements).

complete predicate   See *predicate.*

complete subject   See *subject.*

complex sentence   See *sentence.*

compound construction   Two or more words or word groups serving the same function, such as a **compound subject** (*Harriet and Peter poled their barge down the river*), **compound predicate** (*The scout watched and waited*) or parts of a predicate (*She grew tired and hungry*), and **compound sentence** (*He smiled, and I laughed*). (See p. 258.) **Compound words** include nouns (*featherbrain, strip-mining*) and adjectives (*two-year-old, downtrodden*).

compound-complex sentence   See *sentence.*

compound predicate   See *compound construction.*

compound sentence   See *sentence.*

compound subject   See *compound construction.*

conciseness   Use of the fewest and freshest words to express meaning clearly and achieve the desired effect with readers. (See Chapter 39.)

conclusion The closing of an essay, tying off the writer's thoughts and leaving readers with a sense of completion. (See pp. 108–10 for suggestions.)

A *conclusion* is also the result of deductive reasoning. See *deductive reasoning* and *syllogism*.

concrete See *abstract and concrete.*

conditional statement A statement expressing a condition contrary to fact and using the subjunctive mood of the verb: *If she were mayor, the unions would cooperate.* See also *mood.*

conjugation A list of the forms of a verb showing tense, voice, mood, person, and number. The conjugation of the verb *know* in present tense, active voice, indicative mood is *I know, you know, he/she/it knows, we know, you know, they know.* (See p. 292 for a fuller conjugation.)

conjunction A word that links and relates parts of a sentence.

- **Coordinating conjunctions** (*and, but, or, nor, for, so, yet*) connect words or word groups of equal grammatical rank: *The lights went out, but the doctors and nurses kept caring for patients.* (See p. 259.)
- **Correlative conjunctions** or correlatives (such as *either . . . or, not only . . . but also*) are two or more connecting words that work together: *He was certain that either his parents or his brother would help him.* (See p. 259.)
- **Subordinating conjunctions** (*after, although, as if, because, if, when,* and so on) begin subordinate clauses and link them to main clauses: *The seven dwarfs whistle while they work.* (See p. 253.)

conjunctive adverb (adverbial conjunction) An adverb (such as *besides, consequently, however, indeed,* or *therefore*) that relates two main clauses in a sentence: *We had hoped to own a house by now; however, housing costs have risen too fast.* (See p. 261.) The error known as a comma splice results when two main clauses related by a conjunctive adverb are separated only by a comma. (See pp. 344–45.)

connector (connective) Any word or phrase that links words, phrases, clauses, or sentences. Common connectors include coordinating, correlative, and subordinating conjunctions; conjunctive adverbs; and prepositions.

connotation An association called up by a word, beyond its dictionary definition. Contrast *denotation.* (See pp. 516–17.)

consonance The repetition of consonant sounds in a series of words. Unlike alliteration, consonance emphasizes the consonants inside (not at the beginning) of the words: *The oak shook with fractured bark.* See also *alliteration* and *assonance.*

construction Any group of grammatically related words, such as a phrase, a clause, or a sentence.

contraction A condensation of an expression, with an apostrophe replacing the missing letters: for example, *doesn't* (for *does not*), *we'll* (for *we will*). (See pp. 458–59.)

contrast See *comparison and contrast.*

coordinate adjectives Two or more adjectives that equally modify the same noun or pronoun: *The camera panned the vast, empty desert.* (See pp. 435–36.)

coordinating conjunction   See *conjunction.*

coordination   The linking of words, phrases, or clauses that are of equal importance, usually with a coordinating conjunction: *He and I laughed, but she was not amused.* Contrast *subordination.* (See pp. 390–92.)

correlative conjunction (correlative)   See *conjunction.*

count noun   See *noun.*

critical thinking, reading, and writing   Looking beneath the surface of words and images to discern meaning and relationships and to build knowledge. (See Chapter 7.)

CSE style   Either of two styles of documenting sources recommended by the Council of Science Editors and frequently used in the natural and applied sciences and in mathematics. (For discussion and examples, see pp. 773–79.)

cumulative (loose) sentence   A sentence in which modifiers follow the subject and verb: *Ducks waddled by, their tails swaying and their quacks rising to heaven.* Contrast *periodic sentence.* (See pp. 383–84.)

dangling modifier   A modifier that does not sensibly describe anything in its sentence. (See pp. 368–69.)

> Dangling   <u>Having arrived late</u>, the concert was underway.
>
> Revised   Having arrived late, <u>we found that</u> the concert was underway.

data   In argument, a term used for *evidence.* See *evidence.*

database   A collection and organization of information (data). A database may be printed, but the term is most often used for electronic sources.

declension   A list of the forms of a noun or pronoun, showing inflections for person (for pronouns), number, and case. See p. 267 for a declension of the personal and relative pronouns.

deductive reasoning   Applying a generalization to specific circumstances in order to reach a conclusion. See also *syllogism.* Contrast *inductive reasoning.* (See pp. 203–06.)

definition   Specifying the characteristics of something to establish what it is and is not. (See pp. 27, 96–97, 183.)

degree   See *comparison.*

demonstrative adjective   See *adjective.*

demonstrative pronoun   See *pronoun.*

denotation   The main or dictionary definition of a word. Contrast *connotation.* (See pp. 516–17.)

denouement   A French term ("untying") signifying the resolution of the plot following the climax. In *Romeo and Juliet,* the denouement follows the deaths of the ill-fated lovers and concludes with the survivors resolving to end their family feuds. See also *climax.*

dependent clause   See *clause.*

derivational suffix   See *suffix.*

description   Detailing the sensory qualities of a thing, person, place, or feeling. (See pp. 27 and 95.)

descriptive adjective See *adjective*.

descriptor See *keyword(s)*.

determiner A word that marks and precedes a noun: for example, *a, an, the, my, your*. See also *article*. (See pp. 324–28 for the uses of determiners before nouns.)

developing (planning) The stage of the writing process when one finds a subject, explores ideas, gathers information, focuses on a central thesis, and organizes material. Compare *drafting* and *revising*. (See Chapters 1–2.)

dialect A variety of a language used by a specific group or in a specific region. A dialect may be distinguished by its pronunciation, vocabulary, and grammar. (See pp. 170–72 and 505–06.)

diction The choice and use of words. (See Chapters 37–39.)

dictionary form See *plain form*.

direct address A construction in which a word or phrase indicates the person or group spoken to: *Have you finished, John? Farmers, unite.*

direct object See *object*.

direct question A sentence asking a question and concluding with a question mark: *Do they know we are watching?* Contrast *indirect question*.

direct quotation (direct discourse) See *quotation*.

discussion list A mailing list of subscribers who use e-mail to converse on a particular subject.

division See *analysis*.

documentation In research writing, supplying citations that legitimate the use of borrowed material and support claims about its origins. Contrast *plagiarism*. (See pp. 614–15.)

document design The control of a document's elements to achieve the flow, spacing, grouping, emphasis, and standardization that are appropriate for the writing situation. (See Chapter 5.)

domain The part of a Web address (or URL) that gives the organization sponsoring the site.

double negative A generally nonstandard form consisting of two negative words used in the same construction so that they effectively cancel each other: *I don't have no money*. Rephrase as *I have no money* or *I don't have any money*. (See p. 322.)

double possessive A possessive using both the ending -'s and the preposition *of*: *That is a favorite expression of Mark's*.

double talk (doublespeak) Language intended to confuse or to be misunderstood. (See p. 509.)

drafting The stage of the writing process when ideas are expressed in connected sentences and paragraphs. Compare *developing (planning)* and *revising*. (See pp. 48–51.)

editing A distinct step in revising a written work, focusing on clarity, tone, and correctness. Compare *revising*. (See pp. 60–63.)

ellipsis The omission of a word or words from a quotation, indicated by the three spaced periods of an **ellipsis mark**: *"that all . . . are created equal."*

elliptical clause A clause omitting a word or words whose meaning is understood from the rest of the clause: *David likes Minneapolis better than* [*he likes*] *Chicago*. (See p. 255.)

emotional appeal See *appeals*.

emphasis The manipulation of words, sentences, and paragraphs to stress important ideas. (See Chapter 23.)

epic A long narrative poem written in an elevated style and celebrating important episodes in the life of a hero and the hero's companions. See also *genre*.

essay A nonfiction composition of multiple paragraphs, focused on a single subject and with a central idea or thesis.

essential element A word or word group that is necessary to the meaning of a sentence because it limits the thing it refers to: removing it would leave the meaning unclear or too general. Also called a **restrictive element,** an essential element is not set off by punctuation: *The keys to the car are on the table. That man who called about the apartment said he'd try again tonight*. Contrast *nonessential element*. (See pp. 429–33, 443.)

ethical appeal See *appeals*.

ethos See *appeals*.

etymology The history of a word's meanings and forms.

euphemism A presumably inoffensive word that a writer or speaker substitutes for a word deemed possibly offensive or too blunt—for example, *passed away* for "died." (See pp. 508–09.)

evaluation A judgment of the quality, value, currency, bias, or other aspects of a work. (See pp. 152–53, 163, 580–92.)

evidence The facts, examples, expert opinions, and other information that support the claims in an argument. (See pp. 184–87, 207.)

expletive A sentence that postpones the subject by beginning with *there, here,* or *it* and a form of the verb *be: It is impossible to get a ticket. There should be more seats available. Here are our options*. (See p. 263.)

exposition Writing whose primary purpose is to explain something about a subject.

fallacies Errors in reasoning. Some evade the issue of the argument; others oversimplify the argument. (See pp. 192–98.)

faulty predication A sentence error in which the meanings of subject and predicate conflict, so that the subject is said to be or do something illogical: *The installation of air bags takes up space in a car's steering wheel and dashboard*. (See pp. 373–74.)

figurative language (figures of speech) Expressions that suggest meanings different from their literal meanings in order to achieve special effects. (See pp. 522–23.) See also specific figures: *hyperbole, irony, metaphor, metonymy, paradox, personification, simile, synecdoche, understatement, zeugma*.

finite verb Any verb that makes an assertion or expresses a state of being and can stand as the main verb of a sentence or clause: *The moose eats the leaves.* (See p. 247.) Contrast *verbal*, which is formed from a finite verb but is unable to stand alone as the main verb of a sentence: *I saw the moose eating the leaves.*

first person See *person.*

foil A character in a literary work who contrasts with another character and thus helps to define that other character. (See p. 716.)

form The way in which an oral, visual, or written communication is organized, structured, or presented. Form is typically differentiated from content: whereas content refers to the ideas in a work, form refers to how ideas are represented. Form operates on many levels, ranging from sentence styles to larger organizational structures, such as genre and argument.

formal and informal Levels of usage achieved through word choice and sentence structure. More informal writing, as in a letter to an acquaintance or a personal essay, resembles some speech in its colloquial language, contractions, and short, fairly simple sentences. More formal writing, as in academic papers and business reports, avoids these attributes of speech and tends to rely on longer and more complicated sentences.

format In a document such as an academic paper or a business letter, the arrangement and spacing of elements on the page. See also *document design.*

fragment See *sentence fragment.*

free verse Poetry characterized by a lack of regular rhyme scheme and meter and by varied line lengths. See also *meter.*

freewriting A technique for generating ideas: in a fixed amount of time (say, fifteen minutes), you write continuously without stopping to reread. (See pp. 23–24.)

function word A word, such as an article, conjunction, or preposition, that serves primarily to clarify the roles of and relations between other words in a sentence: *We chased the goat for an hour but finally caught it.* Contrast *lexical word.*

fused sentence (run-on sentence) A sentence error in which two main clauses are joined with no punctuation or connecting word between them. (See p. 341.)

> Fused   I heard his lecture it was dull.
> Revised   I heard his lecture; it was dull.

future perfect tense See *tense.*

future tense See *tense.*

gender The classification of nouns or pronouns as masculine (*he, boy, handyman*), feminine (*she, woman, actress*), or neuter (*it, typewriter, dog*).

general and specific Terms designating the relative number of instances or objects included in a group signified by a word. The following list moves from most **general** (including the most objects) to most **specific** (including the fewest objects): *vehicle, four-wheeled vehicle, automobile,* *sedan, Ford Taurus, blue Ford Taurus, my sister's blue Ford Taurus named Hank.* See also *abstract and concrete.* (See pp. 518–19.)

generalization A claim inferred from evidence. See also *inductive reasoning.*

generic *he* *He* used to mean *he or she.* For ways to avoid *he* when you intend either or both genders, see pp. 313–15 and 511.

generic noun A noun that refers to a typical member of a group rather than to a specific person or thing: *Any person may come. A student needs good work habits. A school with financial problems may shortchange its students.* A singular generic noun takes a singular pronoun (*he, she,* or *it*). (See pp. 313–15.)

genitive case Another term for possessive case. See *case.*

genre The classification of writing, often literary, into large groups, such as fiction, poetry, drama, and nonfiction. Each genre can be divided into smaller genres, such as short stories and novels, epic poetry and lyric poetry, tragedy and comedy, or essays and reports.

gerund A verbal that ends in *-ing* and functions as a noun: *Working is all right for killing time* (*working* is the subject of the verb *is; killing* is the object of the preposition *for*). See also *verbals and verbal phrases.* (See p. 248.)

gerund phrase A word group consisting of a gerund plus any modifiers or objects. See also *verbals and verbal phrases.*

grammar A description of how a language works.

grounds A term used for *evidence* in argument. See *evidence.*

helping verb (auxiliary verb) A verb used with another verb to convey time, obligation, and other meanings: *You should write a letter. You have written other letters.* The **modals** include *can, could, may, might, must, ought, shall, should, will, would.* The other helping verbs are forms of *be, have,* and *do.* (See pp. 276, 282–86.)

hero See *character.*

homonyms Words that are pronounced the same but have different spellings and meanings, such as *heard/herd* and *to/too/two.* (See pp. 534–35 for a list.)

HTML (hypertext markup language) A computer language used for creating Web pages. An **HTML editor** is a program for coding documents in HTML. (See p. 798.)

hyperbole A figure of speech that makes a deliberate exaggeration: *The bag weighed a ton.*

hypertext Text such as that on the Web that provides links allowing users to move easily and variously within and among documents. Contrast *linear text.*

idiom An expression that is peculiar to a language and that may not make sense if taken literally: for example, *bide your time,* and *by and large.* See pp. 519–21 for a list of idioms involving prepositions, such as *agree with them* and *agree to the contract.*

illustration or support Examples or reasons that develop an idea. (See pp. 27 and 95–96.)

image A word or phrase that draws upon the senses of sight, hearing, touch, taste, or smell to describe an object or feeling, as in these visual images by William Carlos Williams: *a red wheel barrow, glazed with rain water, beside the white chickens.* **Imagery** is the pattern of images within a work. (See also p. 698.)

imperative See *mood.*

indefinite pronoun See *pronoun.*

independent clause See *clause.*

indicative See *mood.*

indirect object See *object.*

indirect question A sentence reporting a question, usually in a subordinate clause, and ending with a period: *The student asked when the paper was due.* Contrast *direct question.*

indirect quotation (indirect discourse) See *quotation.*

inductive reasoning Inferring a generalization from specific evidence. Contrast *deductive reasoning.* (See pp. 202–03.)

inference A conclusion drawn from logical reasoning and factual evidence. See also *premise.*

infinitive A verbal formed from the plain form of the verb plus the **infinitive marker** *to: to swim, to write.* Infinitives and infinitive phrases may function as nouns, adjectives, or adverbs. See also *verbals and verbal phrases.* (See p. 249.)

infinitive marker See *infinitive.*

infinitive phrase A word group consisting of an infinitive plus any subject, objects, or modifiers. See also *verbals and verbal phrases.*

inflection The variation in the form of a word that indicates its function in a particular context. See *declension,* the inflection of nouns and pronouns; *conjugation,* the inflection of verbs; and *comparison,* the inflection of adjectives and adverbs.

inflectional suffix See *suffix.*

informal See *formal and informal.*

intensifier A modifier that adds emphasis to the word(s) it modifies: for example, *very slow, so angry.*

intensive pronoun See *pronoun.*

interjection A word standing by itself or inserted in a construction to exclaim or command attention: *Hey! Ouch! What the heck did you do that for?*

interpretation The determination of meaning or significance—for instance, in a work such as a poem or photograph or in the literature on some issue such as job discrimination. (See pp. 149–51, 162.)

interrogative Functioning as or involving a question.

interrogative adjective See *adjective.*

interrogative pronoun See *pronoun.*

intransitive verb A verb that does not take a direct object: *The woman laughed.* (See p. 238.)

introduction   The opening of an essay, a transition for readers between their world and the writer's. The introduction often contains a statement of the writer's thesis. (See pp. 105–08 for suggestions.)

invention   The discovery and exploration of ideas, usually occurring most intensively in the early stages of the writing process. (See pp. 18–28 for invention techniques.)

inversion   A reversal of the usual word order in a sentence, as when a verb precedes its subject or an object precedes its verb: *Down swooped the hawk. Our aims we stated clearly.*

irony   The use of words to suggest a meaning different from what the words say literally: *What a happy face!* (said to someone scowling miserably); *With that kind of planning, prices are sure to go down* (written with the expectation that prices will rise). Compare *paradox* and *understatement*.

irregular verb   A verb that forms its past tense and past participle in some other way than by the addition of *-d* or *-ed* to the plain form: for example, *go, went, gone; give, gave, given.* Contrast *regular verb.* (See pp. 278–79 for a list of irregular verbs.)

jargon   In one sense, jargon is the specialized language of any group, such as doctors or baseball players. In another sense, jargon is vague, pretentious, wordy, and ultimately unclear writing such as that found in some academic, business, and government publications. (See p. 508.)

journal   A personal record of observations, reactions, ideas, and other thoughts. Besides providing a private place to think in writing, a journal is useful for making notes about reading (pp. 142, 144, 157–58, 692–93,), discovering ideas for essays (pp. 21–23), and keeping track of research (pp. 551–52, 692–93, 738, 769).

journalist's questions   A set of questions useful for probing a subject to discover ideas about it. (See pp. 26–27.)

keyword(s)   A word or words that define a subject, used for searching databases such as library catalogs and periodical indexes and for searching the Web. (See pp. 561–64.)

lexical word   A word, such as a noun, verb, or modifier, that carries part of the meaning of language. Contrast *function word*.

linear text   Text such as a conventional printed document that is intended to be read in sequence. Contrast *hypertext*. (See pp. 796–97.)

linking verb   A verb that relates a subject to its complement: *Julie is a Democrat. He looks harmless. The boy became a man.* Common linking verbs are the forms of *be;* the verbs relating to the senses, such as *look* and *smell;* and the verbs *become, appear,* and *seem.* (See p. 239.)

listserv   See *discussion list*.

litotes   See *understatement*.

logical agreement   See *agreement*.

logical fallacies   See *fallacies*.

main clause   See *clause*.

main verb   The part of a verb phrase that carries the principal meaning: *had been walking, could happen, was chilled.* See also *verb phrase*.

mass noun Another term for noncount noun. See *noun.*

mechanics The use of capital letters, italics or underlining, abbreviations, numbers, and divided words. (See Chapters 33–36.)

metaphor A figure of speech that implies a comparison between two unlike things: *The wind stabbed through our clothes.* A **mixed metaphor** is a confusing or ludicrous combination of incompatible figures: *The wind stabbed through our clothes and shook our bones.* Contrast *simile.*

meter The rhythmic patterns of accented syllables in a line of poetry. The patterns are divided up into feet. (See also *prosody.*) Common metrical feet:

- **Iamb,** two syllables with the stress on the second syllable: *away, seduce.* Five iambs in a row make an iambic pentameter line: *if music be the food of love, play on.*
- **Trochee,** two syllables with the stress on the first syllable: *someone, lady.*
- **Spondee,** two syllables with equal stress on both syllables: *hotdog, cowboy, cupcake.*
- **Anapest,** three syllables with the stress on the third syllable: *on the loose, unamused.*
- **Dactyl,** three syllables with the stress on the first syllable: *nobody, tenderly.*

metonymy A figure of speech in which a name refers to a complete entity: *The school sent the students home early because of the snowstorm.* See also *synecdoche.*

misplaced modifier A modifier so far from the term it modifies or so close to another term it could modify that its relation to the rest of the sentence is unclear. (See Chapter 21.)

Misplaced	The boys played with firecrackers that they bought illegally in the field.
Revised	The boys played in the field with firecrackers that they bought illegally.

A **squinting modifier** could modify the words on either side of it: *The plan we considered seriously worries me.*

mixed construction A sentence containing two or more parts that do not fit together in grammar or in meaning. (See pp. 371–74.)

mixed metaphor See *metaphor.*

MLA style The style of documenting sources recommended by the Modern Language Association and used in many of the humanities, including English. (For explanation and examples, see Chapter 46.)

modal See *helping verb.*

modifier Any word or word group that limits or qualifies the meaning of another word or word group. Modifiers include adjectives and adverbs as well as words, phrases, and clauses that act as adjectives and adverbs.

mood The form of a verb that shows how the speaker or writer views the action. (See pp. 298–99.)

- The **indicative mood,** the most common, is used to make statements or ask questions: *The play will be performed Saturday. Did you get the tickets?*
- The **imperative mood** gives a command: *Please get good seats.*
- The **subjunctive mood** expresses a wish, a condition contrary to fact, a recommendation, or a request: *I wish George were coming with us. Did you suggest that he join us?*

narration Recounting a sequence of events, usually in the order of their occurrence. (See pp. 27 and 94–95.) Literary narration tells a story. (See Chapter 49.)

narrator The character or voice who tells a story or the speaker in a poem. (See pp. 698, 712, and 713 and also *persona* and *speaker*.)

neologism A word coined recently and not in established use. (See p. 508.)

newsgroup An Internet discussion group with a common site where all postings are recorded. (See p. 574.)

nominal A noun, a pronoun, or a word or word group used as a noun: *Joan and I talked. The rich owe a debt to the poor* (adjectives acting as subject and object). *Baby-sitting can be exhausting* (gerund acting as subject). *I like to play with children* (infinitive phrase acting as object).

nominative Another term for subjective case. See *case*.

noncount noun See *noun*.

nonessential element A word or word group that does not limit the term or construction it refers to and thus is not essential to the meaning of the sentence. Also called a **nonrestrictive element,** a nonessential element is set off by punctuation, usually commas: *The new apartment building, in shades of tan and gray, will house fifty people* (nonessential adjective phrase). *Sleep, which we all need, occupies a third of our lives* (nonessential adjective clause). *His wife, Patricia, is a chemist* (nonessential appositive). Contrast *essential element*. (See pp. 429–33.)

nonfinite verb See *verbals and verbal phrases*.

nonrestrictive element See *nonessential element*.

nonstandard Words and grammatical forms not conforming to standard American English. (See pp. 505–06.)

noun A word that names a person, place, thing, quality, or idea: *Maggie, Alabama, clarinet, satisfaction, socialism*. Nouns normally form the possessive case by adding *-'s* (*Maggie's*) and the plural by adding *-s* or *-es* (*clarinets, messes*), although there are exceptions (*men, women, children*). The forms of nouns depend partly on where they fit in certain overlapping groups:

- **Common nouns** name general classes and are not capitalized: *book, government, music*.
- **Proper nouns** name specific people, places, and things and are capitalized: *Susan, Athens, Fenway Park*.
- **Count nouns** name things considered countable in English (they form plurals): *ounce/ounces, camera/cameras, person/people*.

- **Noncount nouns** name things not considered countable in English (they don't form plurals): *chaos, fortitude, silver, earth, information.*
- **Collective nouns** are singular in form but name groups: *team, class, family.*

noun clause A word group containing a subject and a verb and functioning as a subject, object, or complement: *Everyone wondered how the door opened. Whoever opened it had left.*

number The form of a noun, pronoun, demonstrative adjective, or verb that indicates whether it is singular or plural: *woman, women; I, we; this, these; runs, run.*

object A noun, pronoun, or word group that receives the action of or is influenced by a transitive verb, a verbal, or a preposition.

- A **direct object** receives the action of a verb or verbal and frequently follows it in a sentence: *We sat watching the stars. Emily caught whatever it was you had.* (See p. 238.)
- An **indirect object** tells for or to whom something is done: *I lent Stan my car. Reiner bought us all champagne.* (See p. 240.)
- An **object of a preposition** usually follows a preposition and is linked by it to the rest of the sentence: *They are going to Rhode Island for the blues festival.* (See p. 245.)

object complement See *complement.*

objective See *case.*

onomatopoeia A word or phrase whose meaning is similar to its sound: *clunk, drip.*

opinion A conclusion based on facts; an arguable, potentially changeable claim. Claims of opinion form the backbone of any argument. (See p. 181.)

ordinal number The type of number that shows order: *first, eleventh, twenty-fifth.* Contrast *cardinal number* (such as *one, twenty-five*).

oxymoron A contradiction in terms: *jumbo shrimp, a deafening silence, pretty ugly, good grief.*

paradox A figure of speech in which seemingly contradictory ideas come together to make a true statement: *Everybody is ignorant, only on different subjects* (nobody is an expert in everything, so everybody must be ignorant of something). Compare *irony* and *understatement.*

paragraph Generally, a group of sentences set off by a beginning indention and developing a single idea. That idea is often stated in a **topic sentence.** (See Chapter 4.)

parallelism Similarity of grammatical form between two or more coordinated elements: *Rising prices and declining incomes left many people in bad debt and worse despair.* (See Chapter 25.)

paraphrase The restatement of source material in one's own words and sentence structures, useful for borrowing the original author's line of reasoning but not his or her exact words. Paraphrases must always be acknowledged in source citations. (See pp. 598–99.)

parenthetical citation In the text of a paper, a brief reference, enclosed in parentheses, indicating that material is borrowed and directing the reader to the source of the material. See also *citation.*

parenthetical expression   A word or construction that interrupts a sentence and is not part of its main structure, called *parenthetical* because it could (or does) appear in parentheses: *Childe Hassam (1859–1935) was an American painter. The book, incidentally, is terrible.* (See pp. 474–75.)

parody   The imitation of a known work, usually for humorous purposes.

participial phrase   A word group consisting of a participle plus any objects or modifiers. See also *verbals and verbal phrases*.

participle   A verbal showing continuing or completed action, used as an adjective or part of a verb phrase but never as the main verb of a sentence or clause. (See p. 248.)

- A **present participle** ends in *-ing*: *My heart is breaking* (part of verb phrase). *I like to watch the rolling waves* (adjective).
- A **past participle** most commonly ends in *-d, -ed, -n,* or *-en* (*wished, shown, given*) but sometimes changes the spelling of the verb (*sung, done, slept*): *Jeff has broken his own record* (part of verb phrase). *The closed door beckoned* (adjective).

See also *verbals and verbal phrases*.

particle   A preposition or adverb in a two-word verb: *look up, catch on.* (See pp. 288–90.)

parts of speech   The classes into which words are commonly grouped according to their form, function, and meaning: nouns, pronouns, verbs, adjectives, adverbs, conjunctions, prepositions, and interjections. See separate entries for each part of speech.

passive voice   See *verb voice*.

past participle   See *participle*.

past perfect tense   See *tense*.

past tense   See *tense*.

pathos   See *appeals*.

patterns of development   See *rhetorical strategies*.

perfect tenses   See *tense*.

periodic sentence   A suspenseful sentence in which modifiers precede the main clause, which falls at the end: *Postponing decisions about family while striving to establish themselves in careers, many young adults are falsely accused of greed.* Contrast *cumulative sentence*. (See pp. 383–84.)

person   The form of a verb or pronoun that indicates whether the subject is speaking, spoken to, or spoken about. In English only personal pronouns and verbs change form to indicate difference in person. In the **first person**, the subject is speaking: *I am* [or *We are*] *planning a party.* In the **second person**, the subject is being spoken to: *Are you coming?* In the **third person**, the subject is being spoken about: *She was* [or *They were*] *going.*

persona   A Latin word ("mask") that describes a figure an author creates to act as the narrator or speaker in a literary work. Because the author assumes a different role or personality, the persona is distinct from the author's own voice. See also *narrator* and *speaker*.

personal pronoun　See *pronoun.*

personification　A figure of speech that attributes human qualities to a thing or idea: *The water beckoned seductively.*

persuasion　The act of convincing an audience to adopt a particular belief, idea, or point of view. (See p. 199).

phrase　A group of related words that lacks a subject or a predicate or both and that acts as a single part of speech. See *absolute phrase, prepositional phrase, verbals and verbal phrases,* and *verb phrase.*

plagiarism　The presentation of someone else's ideas or words as if they were one's own. Whether accidental or deliberate, plagiarism is a serious and often punishable offense. (See pp. 607–14.)

plain case　Another term for the subjective case of nouns. See *case.*

plain form　The dictionary form of a verb: *make, run, swivel.* See also *verb forms.*

planning　See *developing (planning).*

plot　The pattern of events in a work of literature. (See p. 698.)

plural　More than one. See *number.*

point of view　The perspective or attitude of the narrator or speaker in a work of literature. See also *person* and p. 698. Common points of view in literature:

- A **first-person narrator** is a character in the story.
- A **third-person narrator** is a voice outside the story.
- A **third-person omniscient narrator** is an all-knowing voice outside the story who can explain any character's thoughts and feelings.
- A **limited omniscient narrator** has detailed knowledge of one or more characters, but not all.
- An **unreliable narrator** provides the reader with false or misleading explanations of characters or events.

positive degree　See *comparison.*

possessive　See *case.*

predicate　The part of a sentence that makes an assertion about the subject. A predicate must contain a finite verb and may contain modifiers, objects of the verb, and complements. The **simple predicate** consists of the verb and its helping verbs: *A wiser person would have made a different decision.* The **complete predicate** includes the simple predicate and any modifiers, objects, and complements: *A wiser person would have made a different decision.* See also *intransitive verb, linking verb,* and *transitive verb.* (See pp. 233–34, 238–41.)

predicate adjective　See *complement.*

predicate noun (predicate nominative)　See *complement.*

prefix　A letter or group of letters (such as *sub, in, dis, pre*) that can be added at the beginning of a root or word to create a new word: *sub + marine = submarine; dis + grace = disgrace.* Contrast *suffix.*

premise　Generally, a claim or assumption basic to an argument. In a deductive syllogism, one premise applied to another leads logically to a conclusion. See also *inference* and *syllogism.* (See pp. 203–06.)

preposition   A word that forms a noun or pronoun (plus any modifiers) into a prepositional phrase: *about love, down the steep stairs.* The common prepositions include these as well as *after, before, by, for, from, in, on, to,* and many others. (See p. 244.)

prepositional phrase   A word group consisting of a preposition and its object, plus any modifiers. A prepositional phrase usually functions as an adjective (*The boy in green stood up*) or as an adverb (*He walked to the speaker's platform*). (See pp. 244–46.)

present participle   See *participle.*

present perfect tense   See *tense.*

present tense   See *tense.*

pretentious writing   Writing that is more elaborate than the situation requires, usually full of fancy phrases and showy words. (See pp. 508–09.)

primary source   Firsthand information, such as an eyewitness account of events; a diary, speech, or other historical document; a work of literature or art; a report of a survey or experiment; and one's own interview, observation, or correspondence. Contrast *secondary source.* (See p. 555.)

principal clause   A main or independent clause. See *clause.*

principal parts   The plain form, past-tense form, and past participle of a verb. See *verb forms.* (See pp. 274–76.)

problem-solution organization   The arrangement of material to state and explain a problem and then to propose and explain a solution. (See pp. 44, 84–85.)

process analysis   The explanation of how something works or how to do something. (See pp. 28, 101–02.)

progressive tense   See *tense.*

pronoun   A word used in place of a noun. There are eight types of pronouns:

- **Personal pronouns** refer to a specific individual or to individuals: *I, you, he, she, it, we, they.* (See p. 267.)
- **Indefinite pronouns,** such as *everybody* and *some,* do not refer to specific nouns (*Everybody speaks*). (See pp. 307–08.)
- **Relative pronouns**—*who, whoever, which, that*—relate groups of words to nouns or pronouns (*The book that won is a novel*). (See pp. 253, 267.)
- **Interrogative pronouns**—*who, whom, whose, which, what*—introduce questions (*Who will contribute?*).
- **Intensive pronouns**—personal pronouns plus -*self* or -*selves*—emphasize a noun or other pronoun (*He himself asked that question*). (See pp. 268, 856.)
- **Reflexive pronouns** have the same form as intensive pronouns. They indicate that the sentence subject also receives the action of the verb (*They injured themselves*). (See p. 268.)
- **Demonstrative pronouns** such as *this, that,* and *such* identify or point to nouns (*This is the problem*).
- **Reciprocal pronouns**—*each other* and *one another*—are used as objects of verbs when the subjects are plural (*They loved each other*).

proofreading Reading and correcting a final draft for misspellings, typographical errors, and other mistakes. (See pp. 66–67.)

proper adjective See *adjective.*

proper noun See *noun.*

protagonist See *character.*

purpose For a writer, the chief reason for communicating something about a subject to a particular audience. Purposes are both general (usually explanation or persuasion) and specific (taking into account the subject and desired outcome). (See pp. 9–11.)

quotation Repetition of what someone has written or spoken. In **direct quotation (direct discourse)**, the person's words are duplicated exactly and enclosed in quotation marks: *Polonius told his son, Laertes, "Neither a borrower nor a lender be."* An **indirect quotation (indirect discourse)** reports what someone said or wrote but not in the exact words and not in quotation marks: *Polonius advised his son, Laertes, not to borrow or lend.*

rational appeal See *appeals.*

reciprocal pronoun See *pronoun.*

reflexive pronoun See *pronoun.*

refutation A part of an argument that addresses one or more opposing views. The refutation of opposing views anticipates and responds to possible objections to the thesis. (See pp. 210–11.)

regional language Expressions common to the people in a particular geographical area. (See p. 508.)

regular verb A verb that forms its past tense and past participle by adding -d or -ed to the plain form: *love, loved, loved; open, opened, opened.* Contrast *irregular verb.* (See p. 277.)

relative clause A subordinate clause beginning with a relative pronoun such as *who* or *that* and functioning as an adjective.

relative pronoun See *pronoun.*

restrictive element See *essential element.*

revising The stage of the writing process in which one considers and improves the meaning and underlying structure of a draft. Compare *developing (planning)* and *drafting.* (See pp. 52–57.)

rhetoric The principles for finding and arranging ideas and for using language in speech or writing to achieve the writer's purpose in addressing his or her audience.

rhetorical appeals. See *appeals.*

rhetorical question A question asked for effect, with no answer expected. The person asking the question either intends to provide the answer or assumes it is obvious: *If we let one factory pollute the river, what does that say to other factories that want to dump wastes there?*

rhetorical strategies Ways of thinking that can help you develop and organize ideas in essays and paragraphs. (See pp. 27–28 and 94–102.)

rhyme Words that have similar vowel and consonant sounds: *door* and *floor, sweet* and *heat, day* and *weigh.*

rhyme scheme   A regular rhyming pattern found in successive lines of poetry. Rhyme schemes are labeled with small letters: *a* for the first rhyme, *b* for the second, and so on. The rhyme scheme for the first four lines of "Twinkle, Twinkle Little Star" would be written *aabb*.

rhythm   The regular pattern of beats, accents, stresses, and pauses in lines of poetry: *Listen my children and you shall hear / Of the midnight ride of Paul Revere*. See also *meter* and *scansion*.

run-on sentence   See *fused sentence*.

sans serif   See *serifs*.

satire   A genre of writing that mocks certain social conventions and human types. Satire uses humor to point out flaws in the social order. Throughout history, it has been used to undercut various political ideas, religious beliefs, and social norms.

scansion   A system for measuring the rhythm of poetry. See also *meter* and *rhythm*. Scansion identifies the meter and marks the accented syllables:

> *To be or not to be, that is the question*

secondary source   A source reporting or analyzing information in other sources, such as a critic's view of a work of art, a historian's report on eyewitness accounts, or a sociologist's summary of others' studies. Contrast *primary source*. (See p. 555.)

second person   See *person*.

sentence   A complete unit of thought, consisting of at least a subject and a predicate that are not introduced by a subordinating word. Sentences can be classed by structure in four ways. A **simple sentence** contains one main clause: *I'm leaving*. A **compound sentence** contains at least two main clauses: *I'd like to stay, but I'm leaving*. A **complex sentence** contains one main clause and at least one subordinate clause: *If you let me go now, you'll be sorry*. A **compound-complex sentence** contains at least two main clauses and at least one subordinate clause: *I'm leaving because you want me to, but I'd rather stay*. (See pp. 264–65.)

sentence fragment   A sentence error in which a group of words is set off as a sentence even though it begins with a subordinating word or lacks a subject or a predicate or both. (See Chapter 17.)

Fragment	She lost the race. Because she was injured. [*Because*, a subordinating conjunction, makes the underlined clause subordinate.]
Revised	She lost the race because she was injured.
Fragment	He could not light a fire. Thus could not warm the room. [The underlined word group lacks a subject.]
Revised	He could not light a fire. Thus he could not warm the room.

sentence modifier   An adverb or a word or word group acting as an adverb that modifies the idea of the whole sentence in which it appears rather than any specific word: *In fact, people will always complain*.

series   A sequence of three or more items of equal importance: *The children are named John, Hallie, and Nancy*. The items in a series are separated with commas. (See p. 435.)

serifs Small lines on the characters in type fonts, such as those at the bottom of this A. **Sans serif** type, such as Arial, does not have serifs. (See p. 119.)

setting The place where the action of a literary work happens. (See p. 699.)

sexist language Language expressing narrow ideas about men's and women's roles, positions, capabilities, or value. (See pp. 509–12.)

signal phrase Words that indicate who is being quoted: *"In the future," said Andy Warhol, "everyone will be world-famous for fifteen minutes."* (For punctuating signal phrases, see pp. 438–39. For using signal phrases to integrate quotations, see pp. 603–04.)

simile A figure of speech that compares two unlike things explicitly, using *like* or *as*: *The sky glowered like an angry parent.* Contrast *metaphor.*

simple predicate See *predicate.*

simple sentence See *sentence.*

simple subject See *subject.*

simple tense See *tense.*

singular One. See *number.*

slang Expressions used by the members of a group to create bonds and sometimes exclude others. Most slang is too vague, short-lived, and narrowly understood to be used in any but very informal writing. (See pp. 506–07.)

spatial organization In a description of a person, place, or thing, the arrangement of details as they would be scanned by a viewer—for instance, from top to bottom or near to far. (See pp. 42 and 82–83.)

speaker The voice in a literary work, usually a poem. See also *narrator* and *persona.*

specific See *general and specific.*

split infinitive The often awkward interruption of an infinitive and its marker *to* by an adverb: *Management decided to immediately introduce the new product.* (See pp. 364–65.)

squinting modifier See *misplaced modifier.*

standard American English The dialect of English used and expected by educated writers and readers in colleges and universities, businesses, and professions. (See pp. 170–72, 505–06.)

stanza Two or more lines of poetry set off with extra spacing to mark a related group.

style The distinctive way an author uses language in his or her writing. Style is a culmination of a number of traits, including diction, tone, imagery, and syntax.

subject In grammar, the part of a sentence that names something and about which an assertion is made in the predicate. The **simple subject** consists of the noun alone: *The quick brown fox jumps over the lazy dog.* The **complete subject** includes the simple subject and its modifiers: *The quick brown fox jumps over the lazy dog.* (See pp. 233–34.)

subject complement   See *complement.*

subjective   See *case.*

subjunctive   See *mood.*

subordinate clause   See *clause.*

subordinating conjunction   See *conjunction.*

subordination   The use of grammatical constructions to de-emphasize one element in a sentence by making it dependent on rather than equal to another element: *Although I left six messages for him, the doctor failed to call.* Contrast *coordination.* (See pp. 393–97.)

substantive   A word or word group used as a noun.

suffix   A **derivational suffix** is a letter or group of letters that can be added to the end of a root word to make a new word, often a different part of speech: *child, childish; shrewd, shrewdly; visual, visualize.* An **inflectional suffix** adapts a word to different grammatical relations: *boy, boys; fast, faster; tack, tacked.*

summary   A condensation and restatement of source material in one's own words and sentence structures, useful in reading for comprehending the material (see pp. 136–37) and in research writing for presenting the gist of the original author's idea (pp. 597–98). Summaries appearing in a paper must always be acknowledged in source citations.

superlative   See *comparison.*

syllogism   A form of deductive reasoning in which two premises stating generalizations or assumptions together lead to a conclusion. *Premise:* Hot stoves can burn me. *Premise:* This stove is hot. *Conclusion:* This stove can burn me. See also *deductive reasoning.* (See pp. 203–05.)

symbolism   The use of a concrete thing to suggest something larger and more abstract, as a red rose may symbolize passion. (See p. 699.)

synecdoche   A figure of speech in which a part stands for the whole: *She braved the waves and swam to safety.* Contrast *metonymy.*

synonyms   Words with approximately but not exactly the same meanings, such as *snicker, giggle,* and *chortle.* (See p. 514.)

syntax   In sentences, the grammatical relations among words and the ways those relations are indicated.

synthesis   Drawing one's own conclusions about the elements within a work (such as the images in a poem) or entire works (entire poems). Synthesis is an essential skill in critical thinking and reading (pp. 151–52, 162–63), in academic writing (pp. 166–67), and in research writing (pp. 595–96).

tag question   A question attached to the end of a statement and consisting of a pronoun, a helping verb, and sometimes the word *not: It isn't raining, is it? It is sunny, isn't it?*

tense   The form of a verb that expresses the time of its action, usually indicated by the verb's inflection and by helping verbs.

- The **simple tenses** are the **present** (*I race, you go*), the **past** (*I raced, you went*), and the **future,** formed with the helping verb will (*I will race, you will go*).

- The **perfect tenses,** formed with the helping verbs *have* and *had,* indicate completed action. They are the **present perfect** (*I have raced, you have gone*), the **past perfect** (*I had raced, you had gone*), and the **future perfect** (*I will have raced, you will have gone*).
- The **progressive tenses,** formed with the helping verb *be* plus the present participle, indicate continuing action. They include the **present progressive** (*I am racing, you are going*), the **past progressive** (*I was racing, you were going*), and the **future progressive** (*I will be racing, you will be going*).

(See p. 292 for a list of tenses with examples.)

theme   The main idea of a work of literature. (See p. 699.)

thesis   The central, controlling idea of an essay, to which all assertions and details relate. (See p. 29.)

thesis statement   A sentence or more that asserts the central, controlling idea of an essay and perhaps previews the essay's organization. (See pp. 29–34.)

third person   See *person.*

tone   The sense of a writer's attitudes toward self, subject, and readers revealed by words and sentence structures as well as by content. (See pp. 14, 189, 208–09, 698.)

topic   The subject of an essay or paragraph.

topic sentence   See *paragraph.*

tragedy   A type of drama characterized by the disastrous decline of the protagonist. Tragedies typically end in death or sad misfortune, arousing fear and pity in the audience. See *genre.*

transitional expression   A word or phrase, such as *thus* or *for example,* that links sentences and shows the relations between them. (See pp. 89–90 for a list.) The error known as a comma splice occurs when two main clauses related by a transitional expression are separated only by a comma. (See pp. 344–45.)

transitive verb   A verb that requires a direct object to complete its meaning. (See pp. 238–39.)

trite expressions (clichés)   Stale expressions that dull writing and suggest that the writer is careless or lazy. (See p. 524.)

two-word verb   A verb plus a preposition or adverb that affects the meaning of the verb: *jump off, put away, help out.* (See pp. 289–90.)

understatement   A figure of speech that deliberately describes something as being less than it really is: *It's a minor catastrophe.* **Litotes** describes something by saying what it is not: *He is no tightwad* (that is, he spends money freely). Compare *irony* and *paradox.*

unity   The quality of an effective essay or paragraph in which all parts relate to the central idea and to each other. (See pp. 44–45 and 75–78.)

URL (uniform resource locator)   An address for a document on the Web.

variety Among connected sentences, changes in length, structure, and word order that help readers see the importance and complexity of ideas. (See Chapter 26.)

verb A word or group of words indicating the action or state of being of a subject. The inflection of a verb and the use of helping verbs with it indicate its tense, mood, voice, number, and sometimes person. See separate listings for each aspect and for *predicate*. (See Chapter 14.)

verbals and verbal phrases **Verbals** are verb forms used as adjectives (*swimming children*), adverbs (*designed to succeed*), or nouns (*addicted to running*). The verbals in the preceding examples are a participle, an infinitive, and a gerund, respectively. (See separate entries for each type.) Verbal phrases consist of verbals plus objects or modifiers: *Swimming fast, the children reached the raft. Willem tried to unlatch the gate. Running in the park is his only recreation.* (See pp. 247–49.)

A verbal is a **nonfinite verb:** it cannot serve as the only verb in the predicate of a sentence. For that, it requires a helping verb. (See p. 247.)

verb forms Verbs have five distinctive forms. The first three are the verb's **principal parts:**

- The **plain form** is the dictionary form: *live, swim.*
- The **past-tense form** adds *-d* or *-ed* to the plain form if the verb is regular: *live, lived.* If the verb is irregular, the plain form changes in some other way, such as *swim, swam.*
- The **past participle** is the same as the past-tense form for regular verbs. For irregular verbs, the past participle may differ (*swum*).
- The **present participle** adds *-ing* to the plain form: *living, swimming.*
- The *-s* form adds *-s* or *-es* to the plain form: *lives, swims.*

verb phrase A verb consisting of a helping verb and a main verb: *has started, will have been invited.* A verb phrase can serve as the predicate of a clause: *The movie has started.*

verb voice The form of a verb that tells whether the sentence subject performs the action or is acted upon. In the active voice the subject acts: *We made the decision.* In the passive voice the subject is acted upon: *The decision was made by us.* (See pp. 300–01.)

voice In one meaning, *voice* is a verb form that tells whether the sentence subject performs the action or is acted upon. In the active voice the subject acts: *We made the decision.* In the passive voice the subject is acted upon: *The decision was made by us.* (See pp. 306–07.) In another meaning, *voice* in writing is like voice in speech: the author's expression through style, tone, and other elements. (See pp. 16–17.)

warrant A term used for *assumption* in argument. See *assumption*.

Web forum A discussion group on the Web, open to everyone and organized around subjects.

wiki A Web site that can be contributed to or modified by anyone who registers to use the site.

word order The arrangement of the words in a sentence, which plays a large part in determining the grammatical relation among words in English.

writing process The activities involved in producing a finished piece of writing. The overlapping stages of the process—developing or planning, drafting, and revising—vary among writers and even for the same writer in different writing situations. (See Chapters 1–3.)

writing situation The unique combination of writer, subject, audience, purpose, and other elements that defines an assignment or occasion and helps direct the writer's choices. (See pp. 4–6.)

zeugma A figure of speech in which one word governs two or more other parts of a sentence: *The robber took my wallet and then the next train.*

Credits

Text and Illustrations

Allianz DE. From Allianz Knowledge, *www.knowledge.allianz.com*. Used by permission.

Bogdanovich, Peter. *Pieces in Time*. New York: Arbor House Publishing Company, 1973.

Britt, Suzanne. "That Lean and Hungry Look." *Newsweek*, October 9, 1978.

Brooks, Gwendolyn. "The Bean Eaters" from *Blacks* by Gwendolyn Brooks. Copyright © 1991 by Gwendolyn Brooks. Reproduced by consent of Brooks Permissions.

Butler, John A. *CyberSearch*. New York: Penguin Reference, 1998.

Campbell, Neil A., and Jane B. Reece. *Biology*, 7th edition. Glenview: Benjamin Cummings, 2005, p. 47.

Catton, Bruce. "Grant and Lee: A Study in Contrasts" by Bruce Catton, 1956. Copyright U.S. Capitol Historical Society. All rights reserved. Reprinted by permission.

Crawford, Allan Pell. "Go for the Green" by Allan Pell Crawford from *Vegetarian Times*, January 2006. Used by permission.

Cunningham, John A. and Selby, Peter. "Relighting Cigarettes: How Common Is It?" by John A. Cunningham and Peter Selby, *Nicotine and Tobacco Research*, 9.5, 621–623. Used by permission of Oxford University Press.

Davies, Antony. "Unemployment Rates of High School Graduates and College Graduates, 1984–2004," from *The Economics of College Tuition* by Antony Davies. Copyright © 2005. Reprinted by permission.

Devoe, Alan. "Nature's Utmost" by Alan Devoe.

Dickinson, Emily. From "A narrow fellow in the grass" by Emily Dickinson. Reprinted by permission of the publishers and Trustees of Amherst College from *The Poems of Emily Dickinson*, Thomas H. Johnson, ed., Cambridge, MA: The Belknap Press of Harvard University Press. Copyright © 1951, 1955, 1979, 1983 by the President and Fellows of Harvard College.

Dyson, Freeman J. From *Disturbing the Universe* by Freeman J. Dyson. Copyright © 1979 by Freeman J. Dyson. Reprinted by permission of Basic Books, a member of Perseus Books Group.

EBSCO Publishing, Inc. © 2009. All rights reserved. Reprinted by permission.

EBSCO Publishing, Inc. © 2009. All rights reserved. Reproduced by permission of EBSCO and Annie Muldoon.

Eisinger, Peter K. From *American Politics: The People and the Polity* by Peter K. Eisinger, et al., New York: Little, Brown and Company, 1978, p. 44. Reproduced by permission of the author.

Environmental Defense Fund. Courtesy of the Environmental Defense Fund.

Friedman, Thomas L. "It's a Flat World After All." *The New York Times*, April 3, 2005.

Gates, Henry Louis Jr. "Two Nations" by Henry Louis Gates, Jr. Copyright © 1992 by Henry Louis Gates, Jr. Originally published in *Forbes*. Reproduced with permission of the author by Janklow and Nesbit Associates.

Google. *www.google.com*.

Goreau, Angeline. From "Hers: Worthy Women Revisited" by Angeline Goreau. Copyright © 1986 by Angeline Goreau. Originally appeared in *The New York Times*, December 11, 1986. Used by permission of Georges Borchardt, Inc., for the author.

Ik, Kim Yong. Excerpt from "A Book-Writing Venture" by Kim Yong Ik. Originally published in *The Writer*, October 1965. Copyright © Kim Yong Ik. Reprinted by permission of Faith M. Leigh.

Jackson, Tim. From "Live Better by Commuting Less?" by Tim Jackson, *Journal of Industrial Ecology*, 9.1–2 (2005), 19–36. Reproduced by permission of Wiley-Blackwell Publishing, www.interscience.wiley.com.

Jeffrey, Mac. "Does Rx Spell Rip-Off?" *The New York Times*, April 7, 1978.

Kuralt, Charles. From *Dateline America* by Charles Kuralt. Text copyright © 1979 by CBS, Inc. Reprinted by permission of Harcourt Inc.

Lahiri, Jhumpa. *Unaccustomed Earth* by Jhumpa Lahiri, copyright © 2008 by Jhumpa Lahiri. Used by permission of Alfred A. Knopf, a division of Random House, Inc.

Mayer, Lawrence. "The Confounding Enemy of Sleep." *Fortune*, June 1974.

Molella, Arthur. "Cultures of Innovation" by Arthur Molella, Lemelson Center, National Museum of American History, Smithsonian Institution. Reproduced by permission.

Nadelmann, Ethan A. From "Shooting Up" by Ethan A. Nadelmann from *The New Republic*, June 13, 1988. Reproduced by permission of the author.

Ornstein, Robert. From "A Letter to the Director" by Robert Ornstein in *Human Nature*, August 1978. Used by permission of the author.

Ouchi, William G. *Theory Z.* Reading: Addison-Wesley, 1981.

Parry, Martin, Jean Palutikof, Clair Hanson, and Jason Lowe. From "Squaring Up to Reality" by Martin Parry, Jean Palutikof, Clair Hanson, and Jason Lowe, *Commentary: Nature Reports Climate Change*, May 29, 2008. Reproduced by permission from Macmillan Publishers Ltd.

Polletta, Francesca. "Just Talk: Public Deliberation after 9/11." From *Journal of Public Deliberation*, 4.1 (2008), April 7, 2008. Used by permission.

ProQuest Basic Search Interface and ProQuest Advanced Interface is produced by ProQuest LLC. Inquiries may be made to: ProQuest LLC, 789 Eisenhower Parkway, Ann Arbor, MI 48108 USA. Telephone: (734) 761-4700; E-mail: info@proquest.com; Web-page: www.proquest.com.

Reston, Jr., James. "You Cannot Refine It." *The New Yorker*, 1985.

Rose, Phyllis. "On Shopping" in *Never Say Goodbye* by Phyllis Rose. New York: Doubleday, 1986.

Rosen, Ruth. "Search for Yesterday" by Ruth Rosen, from *Watching Television*, edited by Todd Gitlin. New York: Pantheon Books, 1986.

Sale, Kirkpatrick. "The Environmental Crisis Is Not Our Fault." Reprinted with permission from the April 30, 1990 issue of *The Nation*. For subscription information, call 1-800-333-8536. Portions of each week's *Nation* magazine can be accessed at http://www.thenation.com.

Selwyn, Neil. "The Social Processes of Learning to Use Computers" by Neil Selwyn from *Social Science Computer Review*, 23.1 (2005), 122. Copyright © 2005 by Sage Publications. Used by permission of Sage Publications.

Sowell, Thomas. "Student Loans" from *Is Reality Optional? and Other Essays* by Thomas Sowell. Copyright © 1993 by Thomas Sowell. Reprinted by permission of Creators Syndicate.

Staples, Brent. Excerpt from "Black Men and Public Space" by Brent Staples, *Harper's*, December 1986. Copyright © 1986 by Brent Staples. Reprinted by permission of the author.

Stout, David. From "Blind Win Court Ruling on U.S. Currency" by David Stout, from *The New York Times*, National Edition, May 21, 2008, copyright © 2008 The New York Times. All rights reserved. Used by permission and protected by the Copyright Laws of the United States. The printing, copying, redistribution, or retransmission of the Material without express written permission is prohibited.

Tan, Amy. "Language of Discretion" by Amy Tan. Copyright © 1990 by Amy Tan. First appeared in *State of the Language*. Reprinted by permission of the author and the Sandra Dijkstra Literary Agency.

Tuchman, Barbara. From "The Decline of Quality" by Barbara Tuchman in *The New York Times Magazine* (November 2, 1980). Copyright © 1980. Used by permission of Russell & Volkening as agents for the author.

UNFPA. "AIDS Clock" from the UNFPA Web site, *www.unfpa.org*, 2008. Produced by UNFPA, the United Nations Population Fund, using data provided by UNAIDS. Design by Allysson Lucca. Reprinted by permission.

Wax, Judith. *Starting in the Middle.* New York: Holt, Rinehart, and Winston, 1979.

Woolf, Virginia. *The Waves.* New York: Harcourt, 1931.

Zinsser, William. *The Lunacy Boom.* New York: Harper & Row, 1970.

Photos

Title page, clockwise from top: David Fischer/Digital Vision/Getty Images, Inc.; Stone/Getty; Yuri Arcurs/Shutterstock.com; Trista Weibell/istockphoto.com; Image Source/Getty; 1: Image Source/Getty; 126: NASA; 129: Blend Images/Getty; 157: *Boostup.org*; 160: Steve Simon; 176: *Boostup.org*; 215: Michael Foujols/Corbis; 216: Lydia Kibiuk/Society for Neuroscience December 2001; 217: UNICEF; 225: Big Brothers Big Sisters of America; 227: Getty; 229: Michael Foujols/Corbis; 231: The Image Bank/Getty; 331: Sabah Arar/AFP/Getty; 379: Photographer's Choice/Getty; 417: Stone/Getty; 483: Neo Vision/Getty; 503: Joe Schilling/Time Life Pictures/Getty; 549: Digital Vision/Getty; 687: Stone/Getty; 783: Stockbyte/Getty.

Index

CSE style, 777–78
MLA style, 655
Dates
BC and *AD* with, 421, 495–96
BCE and *CE* with, 495–96
commas in, 437
doubtful, indicating, 422
numerals vs. words for, 499
Days of the week
abbreviations for, 497
capitalization of, 486
Deadlines, 6
Declension, 267, 869
Deconstructive literary criticism, 697
Deductive reasoning, 203–06, 869
Defined terms
in argument, 183
italics or underlining for, 492
singular verb with, 310
Definition
defined, 869
in essay development, 27
in paragraph development, 96–97
of terms, in argument, 183
Degree for adjectives and adverbs, 320–22, 867
Demonstrative adjectives, 862
Demonstrative pronouns, 881
Denotation, 516, 869
Denouement, 869
Dependent clauses. *See* Subordinate (dependent) clauses
dependent on, 520
Derivational suffix, 885
Description
defined, 869
in essay development, 27
objective vs. subjective, 95
in paragraph development, 95
Descriptive adjectives, 862
Descriptive title, 55
Descriptors. *See* Keywords
desert, dessert, 534
Design of documents. *See* Document design and format
despite, as preposition, 245, 394
Details
in argument, 184–87
in essay development, 8–9, 12–13, 15
in paragraph development, 93–94
Determiners
a, an, the, 236, 325–27
defined, 324, 870
grammar checkers for, 325

other determiners, 327–28
uses of, 324–28
Developing (planning), 18–46, 795–96, 799, 870
Development of essay topic, 18–46
audience needs and, 5, 12–17
brainstorming for, 24–25
clustering for, 25–26
critical thinking for, 27–28
freewriting for, 23–24
journalist's questions for, 26–27
keeping a journal for, 21–23
list making for, 24–25
observing surroundings for, 23
patterns for, 27–28. *See also individual patterns*
reading for, 20–21
Development of paragraphs, 93–103
combining methods for, 102
defined, 93
patterns for, 94–102. *See also individual patterns*
rhetorical strategies for, 94–102
specific information in, 93–94
device, devise, 850
Diagrams. *See* Illustrations and artworks
Dialect. *See also* Culture-language issues
defined, 505–06, 870
grammar checkers for, 504
nonstandard, 505–06
standard American English as, 170–71, 505–06
Dialog
hesitations in, 472
paragraphing for, 111, 464
quotation marks for, 464
Diction, 504–24, 700, 870. *See also specific topics under* Words
Dictionaries
documenting: Chicago style, 733; MLA style, 642, 650, 658
electronic, 515
ESL, 515
list of, 515
for meanings, 514–15
sample entry, 515
specialized, in research, 704, 721–22, 771
vs. thesaurus, 514–15
Dictionary form of verbs. *See* Plain form of verbs
differ about, from, over, with, 520
different from, different than, 850
differ from, differ with, 850

(CULTURE LANGUAGE) Guide

Throughout this handbook, the symbol (CULTURE LANGUAGE) signals topics for linguistically and culturally diverse writers, including ESL and ELL students as well as students whose first dialect is not standard American English. These topics can be tricky because they arise from rules in standard English that are quite different in other languages and dialects. Many of the topics involve significant cultural assumptions as well.

No matter what your language background, as a high school student you are learning the culture of US education and the language that is used and shaped by that culture. The process is challenging, even for native speakers of standard American English. It requires not just writing clearly and correctly but also mastering conventions of developing, presenting, and supporting ideas. The challenge is greater if, in addition, you are trying to learn standard American English and are accustomed to other conventions. Several habits can help you succeed:

- **Read.** Besides class assignments, read newspapers, magazines, and books in English. The more you read, the more fluently and accurately you'll write.
- **Write.** Keep a journal in which you practice writing in English every day.
- **Talk and listen.** Take advantage of opportunities to hear and use English.
- **Ask questions.** Your teachers and fellow students can clarify assignments and help you identify and solve writing problems.
- **Don't try for perfection.** No one writes perfectly, and the effort to do so can prevent you from expressing yourself fluently. View mistakes not as failures but as opportunities to learn.
- **Revise first; then edit.** Focus on each essay's ideas, support, and organization before attending to grammar and vocabulary. See the revision and editing checklists on pages 56 and 61–62.
- **Set editing priorities.** Concentrate first on any errors that interfere with clarity, such as problems with word order or subject-verb agreement.

The following index leads you to text discussions of writing topics that you may need help with. The pages marked with an * include exercises for self-testing.

Editing Symbols

Boldface numbers and letters refer to chapters and sections of the handbook.

ab	Faulty abbreviation, **35**	*p*	Error in punctuation, **27–32**
ad	Misused adjective or adverb, **16**	. ? !	Period, question mark, exclamation point, **27**
agr	Error in agreement, **15**		
ap	Apostrophe needed or misused, **30**	^	Comma, **28**
		;	Semicolon, **29**
appr	Inappropriate language, **37**	˅	Apostrophe, **30**
arg	Faulty argument, **9–11**	" "	Quotation marks, **31**
awk	Awkward construction	: — ( ) [ ] . . . /	Colon, dash, parentheses, brackets, ellipsis mark, slash, **32**
case	Error in case form, **13**		
cap	Use capital letter, **33**		
cit	Missing source citation or error in form of citation, **44**	*par*, ¶	Start new paragraph, **4**
		¶ *coh*	Paragraph not coherent, **4b**
coh	Coherence lacking, **2c-4, 4b**	¶ *dev*	Paragraph not developed, **4c**
con	Be more concise, **39**	¶ *un*	Paragraph not unified, **4a**
coord	Coordination needed or faulty, **24a**	*pass*	Ineffective passive voice, **14j**
		pn agr	Error in pronoun-antecedent agreement, **15b**
cs	Comma splice, **18a–b**		
d	Ineffective diction (word choice), **37–39**	*ref*	Error in pronoun reference, **19**
		rep	Unnecessary repetition, **39c**
des	Ineffective or incorrect document design, **5**	*rev*	Revise or proofread, **3**
		shift	Inconsistency, **20**
det	Error in use of determiner, **16h**	*sp*	Misspelled word, **40**
dev	Inadequate development, **2, 4c**	*sub*	Subordination needed or faulty, **24b**
div	Incorrect word division, **40d**		
dm	Dangling modifier, **21h**	*t*	Error in verb tense, **14g–h**
eff	Ineffective sentence(s), **23–26**	*t seq*	Error in tense sequence, **14h**
emph	Emphasis lacking or faulty, **23**	*trans*	Transition needed, **4b-6, 4e**
exact	Inexact language, **39**	*und*	Underline or italicize, **34**
fp	Faulty predication, **22b**	*usage*	See Glossary of Usage, p. 845
frag	Sentence fragment, **17**	*var*	Vary sentence structure, **26**
fs	Fused sentence, **18c**	*vb*	Error in verb form, **14a–f**
gram	Error in grammar, **12–16**	*vb agr*	Error in subject-verb agreement, **15a**
hyph	Error in use of hyphen, **40d**		
inc	Incomplete construction, **22c–e**	*w*	Wordy, **39**
ital	Italicize or underline, **34**	*ww*	Wrong word, **38b**
k	Awkward construction	//	Faulty parallelism, **25**
lc	Use lowercase (small) letter, **33f**	#	Separate with a space
log	Faulty logic, **9g, 10d**	⌒	Close up the space
mech	Error in mechanics, **33–36**	⟍	Delete
mixed	Mixed construction, **22a–b**	the	Capitalize, **33**
mm	Misplaced modifier, **21a–g**	The	Use a small letter, **33**
mng	Meaning unclear	teh	Transpose letters or words
no cap	Unnecessary capital letter, **33f**	X	Obvious error
no ^	Comma not needed, **28j**	^	Something missing, **22e**
no ¶	No new paragraph needed, **4**	??	Document illegible or meaning unclear
num	Error in use of numbers, **36**		

LITTLEBROWNH 0000021

Little Brown Handbook

Property of CGCSC